Third Printing, 1967

Library of Congress catalog card number: 64-12235

THE MACMILLAN COMPANY, NEW YORK

COLLIER-MACMILLAN CANADA, LTD., TORONTO, ONTARIO

Printed in the United States of America

Problems of Philosophy

A BOOK OF READINGS

John A. Mourant
E. Hans Freund

Professors of Philosophy
The Pennsylvania State University

THE MACMILLAN COMPANY, NEW YORK

COLLIER-MACMILLAN LIMITED, LONDON

Foreword

This textbook has been designed primarily to meet the needs of the beginning student in philosophy. Composing a book of readings, we have attempted to include in the material outstanding philosophers from antiquity to the present age. We sought a balance between selections from different historical periods, but the orientation of the book centers on the basic problems and issues of philosophy, and certain periods throw such problems into better perspective than do other periods. We have also endeavored as far as possible and feasible to present a variety of selections from contemporary writers. In accordance with what seems to be a major interest today, a greater number of selections touch upon the problems of epistemology and ethics than upon other philosophical pursuits. The responsibility for the various selections is fairly evenly distributed between the editors, except that the selections on ethics are largely prepared by E. Hans Freund and those on epistemology by John A. Mourant.

There is more than enough material for a single semester—in fact, the amount of material is adequate for a year's course. This will provide a wide range of selectivity to instructors who are usually limited to a one-semester course for introductory philosophy.

The order of the text divisions is somewhat arbitrary, although it was deemed pedagogically wiser to begin with selections on ethics, because these may entail fewer difficulties for the beginning student than would selections on epistemology and metaphysics.

Throughout the text, footnotes of the editors are indicated by asterisks, and notes of the authors or translators are indicated by numbers. Both the main titles or headings and the subtitles are in most instances the contributions of the editors. Ellipses indicate any omitted material, irrespective of the amount.

We are greatly indebted to our colleagues in the Department of Philosophy at the Pennsylvania State University—Professors John M. Anderson, Aaron Druckman, Henry A. Finch, Richard A. Gotshalk, Morris

Grossman, Henry W. Johnstone, Jr., Donald B. Kuspit, Robert G. Price, Stanley H. Rosen, Albert G. Tsugawa, and Duane H. Whittier—for their many valuable suggestions and criticisms.

JOHN A. MOURANT

E. HANS FREUND

Contents

IV

Metaphysics

V

Philosophy of Religion

VI

Social and Political Philosophy   381

VII

Philosophy of Art   463

VIII

Philosophy of Science   517

I

Introduction

1

Introduction

THE NATURE OF PHILOSOPHY

From its beginning, philosophy has meant many things to many people. It has represented a diversity of viewpoints, a conflict of systems, and seemingly an ever-changing set of ideas regarding man and his relation to the universe. Yet within all the differences and changes are certain common ideas about the contents, meanings, and methods of philosophy. Philosophers may disagree about what constitutes the true philosophy, but they would no doubt agree with Royce that the truths about man's relations to the universe are manifold and that it is the function of the philosopher to discover such truths.

Philosophy as Speculation. The meaning of philosophy originated with Pythagoras, who described it as a love of wisdom. Among the early Greeks, philosophy as the love of wisdom came to be identified with speculative insight—with a kind of cosmic point of view. The very meaning of "speculate"—taken from *specula*, meaning watchtower—

3

implies a breadth of vision and a perspective that rises above that of the ordinary viewer. As Spinoza so well put it, it means to "see things *sub specie aeternitatis*"—under the aspect of eternity. This vision of all things, this striving after an eternal perspective, may be one reason why Aristotle referred to the wisdom of philosophy as being divine. This speculative point of view is frequently a detached one, resulting in contemplative insights that rise above the ordinary practical concerns of man. Like Aristotle's God, the philosopher's activity may be merely "thinking his own thoughts." Philosophy as speculation, however, must not be identified with detachment. For the deeper insights and the breadth of vision that we attribute to the philosopher frequently issue from his more detailed knowledge of the world and from his participation in the world.

Philosophy as Criticism.   To criticize means to "judge," to "analyze." Philosophy in its critical aspect questions, judges, and evaluates any and all principles and premises that may be gained through speculation. It was the Greek genius again that saw the necessity of supplementing the cosmic insights of the early Greek philosophers with a more disciplined form of philosophy. There is no denying the value of imaginative insights, but uncritical insights do not constitute philosophy. Philosophy sees the necessity of subjecting all forms of thought and contemplation to a court of rational inquiry. Out of such a rational evaluation of ideas will come a clarification of knowledge and insights that are more valuable because they are tempered by reason and dialectic. Actually, philosophy as speculation and philosophy as criticism cannot be sharply separated from one another, because analysis of an idea and clarification of language and theory may lead to new insights and more significant interpretations of man and his world. Speculation contributes the insights and intuitions necessary for the development of new ideas, but such ideas must be validated, and their validation—that is, their criticism and clarification—results in new insights and adds to our speculative vision. We have but to read a dialogue of Plato to become aware of this twofold function of philosophy. For Plato, the philosopher must contemplate the eternal truths, but he must also apply the insights so gained to the activities of men. Plato is the great contemplative, but he is also the dialectician, the destructive analyst who forces individuals to question their ideas and their ways of life.

Summing up, we may say that the meaning of philosophy is best revealed in its speculative and critical functions. Since in its speculative concern it takes the broadest possible perspective, we must not look for too specific a content. Philosophy is not about atoms and electrons, plants and animals, the history of states and the structure of governments. Yet all these are the concern of philosophy insofar as they have bearing upon man and his purposes. Similarly, philosophy is not merely a criticism of this or that specific subject, but assumes to itself the right to judge of any subject and to evaluate all things that come within human knowledge. It may conduct an inquiry, as Socrates did, into the meaning of piety; or it may analyze minutely the distinctions of the words "seems," "looks," "appears," to resolve a problem of perception. As speculation, it may arrive at the insight that the world is both divine and good, as analysis and criticism it may limit itself to a prolonged consideration of the meaning of the word "good."

Both criticism and speculation, then, have an integral place in philosophy. Without criticism, philosophy would be sheer poetry; without speculation, it would be mere logic-chopping. As Aristotle declared, the philosopher above all others is possessed of that "desire to know." But with the philosopher this is no mere idle curiosity; it is a reflective curiosity, and out of this reflective curiosity comes the knowledge and the point of view that we term philosophy. The greatness of philosophy, the reason for so many men's having embraced it with virtually religious fervor and made it a way of life, lies in this twofold strength that it possesses—the balanced point of view that reflects both speculation and criticism. The need of balance is important, for an excess of speculation may bring discredit upon philosophy: uncritical insights have little value or too frequently become sophisticated obscurantism. On the other hand, an excess of analysis narrows philosophy's enterprise and subordinates it to a minor role, making it perhaps a mere handmaid of logic, science, or theology.

The Divisions of Philosophy. To the average student aspiring to some knowledge of philosophy, it will not be enough to say simply that philosophy is both critical and speculative and to speak in generalities about the functions of philosophy. Nor should we merely counsel patience and hold out the hope that after the student has studied many of the philosophers, the meaning of philosophy will become self-evident. Certain guides are needed for a more accurate understanding of the selections to follow. We have already indicated that philosophy has a content, that it is concerned with the "general" in contrast to the more specific concerns of the several sciences. Elaborating upon this notion, we can list and define very briefly several basic divisions or disciplines of our subject. These are: *Ethics, Epistemology, Metaphysics, Philosophy of Religion, Political and Social Philosophy, Philosophy of Art,* and *Philosophy of Science.**

---

* These divisions are not meant to be all-inclusive, and the ordering is more or less arbitrary. Logic has not been included, for it has traditionally been regarded as an in-

Ethics.   Ethics, or moral philosophy, is concerned with problems of human conduct. It is usually termed a normative science, because it deals with the norms or standards of right and wrong as they apply to human behavior. It is held to be prescriptive rather than descriptive, because it prescribes what individuals *ought* to do rather than describing *how* they behave. To assert that there are standards of right and wrong implies that there are ends or goals that are desirable or undesirable. The moral philosopher is interested in an analysis and evaluation of such ends and the determination of whether there is some highest or ultimate end—for example, happiness, pleasure, virtue, etc.—that may be said to be the chief good of man. Standards of right and wrong and evaluations of the ultimate ends of all human conduct imply the freedom and the responsibility of the individual in the pursuit of these ends. What constitutes an ultimate value or end for the individual depends upon his insights and those of others and upon his character and moral excellence or virtue. The determination of what constitutes the highest good for the individual will depend, for one thing, upon our conception of the nature of man. And the attainment of such an end requires not only the individual moral virtues but those higher social virtues that are based upon our social nature and our relations with others. The rights and duties of the individual and the ultimate values of the moral life have no existence outside the social order. Moral philosophy merges into social and political philosophy.

Epistemology.   The term "epistemology" is derived from the Greek *epistēmē,* meaning *knowledge.* It deals with the various problems that arise concerning knowledge and is more apt to exemplify the critical rather than the speculative function of philosophy. It may consider first whether knowledge is even possible. The answer here may be some form of scepticism or the contention that at least doubting is a necessary prerequisite to the attainment of certitude. With respect to the origin of all knowledge, it may insist that all knowledge arises from experience, or it may contend that some elements of knowledge are given by the mind or discovered by reason prior to experience. The former position is known as *empiricism,* the latter as *rationalism.* For some philosophers the primary function of epistemology is the clarifying of our ideas through linguistic analysis. Such a method they urge will cure philosophy of its ills and prevent it from falling into error. Others tend to identify epistemology with methodology; they look to the scientific

---

strument (*organon*) or a means to the acquisition of true knowledge. As a science of valid reasoning, its principles apply to all forms of knowledge and not merely to philosophy. Where logic merges with philosophy it becomes metaphysics.

method as an ideal and consider that true knowledge is that which can be verified or confirmed as are scientific hypotheses. Finally, epistemology may be concerned with a number of highly complex and specialized problems of knowledge, such as the distinction between belief and knowledge (on the religious plane the problem of faith and reason), the nature of truth, or the problems of perception, the external world, meaning, other minds, etc.

Metaphysics. Meaning literally "after the physics," this was a title given, in a later collection, to a work of Aristotle's that appeared after his *Physics* and that had been left untitled. Since the time of the early Greeks, philosophers have generally agreed that metaphysics is concerned with the nature of reality, of what it means to *be*. Some have maintained that reality or being is basically material, others that it is mental or spiritual, and still others that it is life, will, God, energy, force, etc. A materialist, for example, will contend that everything is basically material and that life, mind, energy, etc. are merely different manifestations of matter. The principal distinction in the analysis of being is that between appearance (how something actually looks or appears to us) and reality (that which something actually is "deep down under" all its external appearances). The inquiry into the nature of reality also leads the metaphysician to other distinctions about the real. He may assert that all things are determined in their causes or, alternatively, that some beings (men) are free in their actions. Again, it may be argued that the universe is in reality a great machine, mechanically ordered to all that occurs. Or that the universe is purposive in its ultimate nature and order by reason of some divine or intelligible cause. The former view is termed the mechanistic, the latter the teleological. To all such queries and many others the metaphysician brings his insights and his critical skills.

Philosophy of Religion. To philosophize about religion means to consider the nature of religion in the philosophical spirit. A philosophy of religion rejects an authoritarian approach; it relies neither on faith nor revelation for religious knowledge. Its problems are principally those that concern man in his relations to God—problems such as the existence and nature of God, the meaning of the religious experience and the various forms such an experience may take, the values of the religious life and their relation to ethical values, the meanings of good and evil from the religious point of view, the natures of religious belief and of religious language, and the validity of religious knowledge.

Social and Political Philosophy. In this area the philosopher's concern is not with the particular issues or problems of the social order, such as the structure of a government, foreign policies, civil legislation, etc., but rather with the more general problems and principles that affect the entire political society of men. The interest of the philosopher, then, lies in questions of the origin of the social order; the meaning and the ethical bases of law; the origin, uses and limitations of political power; the rights and duties of individuals in a political society; and the determination of that form of society best adapted to secure the highest end of all individuals. Many of these problems and issues may also be considered in the broader perspective of history itself, and this yields a philosophy of history—the analysis and interpretation of history and the endeavor to discover if there are any laws of historical development.

Philosophy of Art (Aesthetics). In this area, the philosopher distinguishes aesthetic values from ethical values. He may propound various theories concerning the meaning, function, and place of art. More particularly he is concerned with the aesthetic experience and the idea of the beautiful. The latter may be analyzed in terms of utility, truth, pleasure, expression, form, etc. The meaning of the aesthetic experience in terms of the emotions and sentiments of the individual may be evaluated. The nature of aesthetic judgment, standards of beauty, and the objectivity of these standards constitute additional problems in the philosophy of art.

Philosophy of Science. In recent years the progress and prestige of the sciences has turned the direction of philosophical interest increasingly to the sciences. Out of this interest has emerged what is now termed the philosophy of science. Such a discipline is primarily concerned with the nature of scientific knowledge and with the methodology of the sciences. It is interested in analysis of the basic theoretical concepts of science; it studies the meaning of induction, the nature of hypotheses, and the laws of nature. It is concerned with the meaning of scientific explanation and probability statements; it seeks to understand how scientific theories may be verified or confirmed.

Thus far we have outlined very briefly the principal characteristics of the several areas of philosophy. The selections we have chosen will supplement this outline with more detailed studies of the different areas. The selections have been chosen to represent both the problems of philosophy and their historical orientations.

The selection that immediately follows stands somewhat apart from the others in the book. It has been selected as an exemplification of the philosophical method—of *dialectic,* or the "doing" of philosophy. The term dialectic first appears in Plato's Socratic dialogue the *Meno,* and the term means essentially a conversation or discourse with the purpose of discovering the truth. Plato expresses his conception of dialectic in the form of the *dialogue,* but dialectic need not take this form. Dialectic is essentially an inquiry in the form of a *discourse* into some problem. It is neither terminal nor is it dogmatic. Dialectic clarifies, distinguishes, and defines, but it also continually opens up new vistas for philosophical inquiries. It is an interminable search after the truth—interminable because human problems and human experience are never closed to questioning.

Plato

◱◱

PHILOSOPHY AS DIALECTIC

THE INCULCATION OF VIRTUE

◱◱

Biographical Note.   PLATO (428/27–348/47 B.C.), unexcelled among ancient philosophers, influenced the thinking of the West perhaps more than anyone else. He was born into an old and distinguished Athenian family when Greek culture was at its highest. The prevailing sentiment of the age, in which statesmanship was considered the most worthy of all professions, combined with his family tradition and his own preference to influence him toward entering public life. But two circumstances intervened: the corruption of political life in Athens at the turn of the fifth century with which Plato refused to be identified; and even more his acquaintance with Socrates, the self-appointed philosophic conscience of Athens, whose guidance ultimately inspired Plato to commit his life entirely to philosophy. He joined the circle of Socrates' disciples at the age of twenty and remained with it for eight years until the end of Socrates' life. In 399 B.C., an accusation was preferred against Socrates charging him with impiety and the corruption of youth; this resulted in a jury's verdict of guilty and his condemnation to death.

Plato then traveled for about twelve years in Greece, Italy, and Sicily, but he settled again in Athens at the age of forty to found his own school, the so-called Academy, which he directed until his death.

The literary form of Plato's work was the dialogue, which he developed to

From the "Meno," in *The Dialogues of Plato,* translated by Benjamin Jowett, New York, Charles Scribner's Sons, 1889, with minor alterations.

a high degree of artistry with the person of Socrates taking the central place in it. His twenty-eight known dialogues can be roughly divided into (1) early works, reflecting largely ideas expressed by Socrates himself; and (2) later ones, in which Plato's own philosophic genius, although presented as the spoken words of his teacher, asserts itself. To the former belong the *Apology, Crito,* and *Protagoras;* to the latter *The Republic, Phaedo,* and *Symposium;* the *Meno* has a place somewhere in between.

* * *

Introductory Note.   It has been suggested that the *Meno* was written when Plato established his school, the Academy, and that it specifically intended to publicize quite concretely and in some detail the nature of the program that the school was to offer. Whether this is true or not, the dialogue clearly illustrates what Plato conceived the teaching of philosophy to consist of and circumscribes the goal toward which he believed it to be directed. Just as the dialogue may have been used to introduce ancient youth to the character and significance of the enterprise we now call philosophy, so it can perform a similar function for students today, more than 2300 years later.

The question that Meno, a young aristocrat from one of the northern provinces of Greece, asks at the beginning of the dialogue appears to be of vital interest not only to him but to his contemporaries in general:

> Can you tell me, Socrates, whether virtue is acquired by teaching or by practice; or if neither by teaching nor by practice, then whether it comes to man by nature, or in what other way?

The key word in this question is "virtue," which does not adequately convey the meaning of its Greek counterpart. This is *areté* (etymologically related to *áristos,* meaning the best), and it indeed implies virtue, but its meaning is not limited to the present meaning of virtue. A fuller translation, taking in additional shades of meaning, would be rendered by the term "excellence." But why was Meno so interested in the question of how *areté,* excellence, comes about?

The reason is almost self-evident. Meno shared with his fellow Greeks the aspiration, common to their culture, of becoming a person of excellence, a man who in the performance of his duty reached the highest possible standard of accomplishment. Yet to achieve excellence in oneself, one had to know the way leading to such a condition; therefore, to find out more about the process of gaining excellence for himself was the real purpose behind Meno's inquiry.

But his motivation was even more specific. The Greeks of the classical time, distinguishing between levels of human excellence, regarded political leadership as the highest form of excellence and man's noblest aspiration. And it appears from the dialogue that this is the young aristocrat Meno's real concern: he wanted to be a leader of men; he aspired to the excellence of statesmanship exemplified in such renowned former statesmen as Themistocles and Pericles; and he is pictured as coming to Socrates in the hope of receiving some help toward this goal.

The dialogue attempts to give an answer, however preliminary, to Meno's question, evidently a most burning problem in Plato's day. And the conclusion definitely implicates the pursuit of philosophy, of philosophic knowledge, as an indispensable prerequisite for a consistent attainment of human excellence.

Plato divides the question in three ways: (1) What is the nature of the knowledge necessary for man's attaining excellence? (2) What method is available for acquiring this knowledge? (3) How can one account for the fact that excellence has been achieved in the past without the help of such knowledge?

WHAT IS VIRTUE?

MENO.* Can you tell me, Socrates, whether virtue is acquired by teaching or by practice; or if neither by teaching nor by practice, then whether it comes to man by nature, or in what other way?

SOCRATES. O Meno, there was a time when the Thessalians were famous among the other Greeks only for their riches and their riding; but now, if I'm not mistaken, they are equally famous for their wisdom. . . . How different is our lot! my dear Meno. Here at Athens, there is a dearth of the commodity, and all wisdom seems to have emigrated from us to you. I am certain that if you were to ask any Athenian whether virtue was natural or acquired, he would laugh in your face and say: "Stranger, you have far too good an opinion of me if you think that I can answer your question. For I literally do not know what virtue is, and much less whether it is acquired by teaching or not." And I myself, Meno, living as I do in this region of poverty, am as poor as the rest of the world, and I confess with shame that I know literally nothing about virtue; and if I do not know what a thing is, how could I know what its qualities are? How, if I knew nothing at all of Meno, could I tell if he was fair or the opposite of fair, rich and noble, or the reverse of rich and noble? Do you think I could?

MEN. No, indeed. But are you in earnest, Socrates, in saying that you do not know what virtue is? And am I to carry back this report of you to Thessaly?

* Meno, the aristocratic youth from Thessaly, was to become a historic figure well known to Plato's contemporaries. At an early age he was given command over part of an army of Greek mercenaries in the service of the Persian prince, Cyrus the Younger. Through them Cyrus had planned to wrest the Persian throne from his brother Artaxerxes. The attempt failed; all the Greek generals including Meno were captured and eventually executed.

Soc. Not only that, my dear boy, but you may say further that I have never known of anyone else who did, in my judgment . . . By the gods, Meno, be generous and tell me what you say that virtue is; for I shall be truly delighted to find that I have been mistaken, and that you . . . really have this knowledge, although I have just been saying that I have never found anybody who had.

MEN. There will be no difficulty, Socrates, in answering your question. Let us take first the virtue of a man—he should know how to administer the state, and in the administration of it to benefit his friends and harm his enemies, and also to be careful not to suffer harm himself. A woman's virtue, if you wish to know about that, may also be easily described: her duty is to order the house well and preserve what is indoors, and obey her husband. Every age, every condition of life, young or old, male or female, bond or free, has a different virtue: there are virtues numberless, and no lack of definitions of them; for virtue is relative to the actions and ages of each of us in all that we do. And the same may be said of vice, Socrates.

Soc. How fortunate I am, Meno! When I ask you for one virtue, you present 'me with a swarm of them, which are in your keeping. Suppose that I carry on the figure of the swarm, and ask of you, What is the nature of the bee? and you answer that there are many different kinds of bees, and I reply: But does this difference lie in their being bees or is it not by this that they are not distinguished at all, but rather by some other quality, as, for example, beauty, size, or shape? How would you answer me?

MEN. I should answer that bees do not differ from one another as bees.

Soc. And if I went on to say: That is what I desire to know, Meno; tell me what is the quality in which they do not differ, but are all alike —would you be able to answer?

MEN. I should.

Soc. And so of the virtues, however many and different they may be, they have all a common nature which makes them virtues; and on this he who is to answer the question, "What is virtue?" would do well to have his eye fixed; do you understand?

MEN. I am beginning to understand; but I do not as yet take hold of the question as I could wish.

Soc. When you say, Meno, that there is one virtue of a man, another of a woman, another of a child, and so on, does this apply only to virtue, or would you also say it of health, and size, and strength? Or is the nature of health always the same, whether in man or woman?

MEN. I should say that health is the same, both in man and woman.

Soc. And is this not true of size and strength? If a woman is strong, she will be strong by reason of the same form and of the same strength subsisting in her which there is in the man—I mean to say that strength, as strength, whether of man or woman, is the same. Is there any difference?

Men. I think not.

Soc. And will not virtue, as virtue, be the same, whether in a child or in a grown-up person, in a woman or in a man?

Men. I cannot help feeling, Socrates, that this case is different from the others.

Soc. But why? Were you not saying that the virtue of a man was to order a state well, and the virtue of a woman was to order a house?

Men. I did say so.

Soc. And is it possible to order a state well or a house or anything at all unless you do it temperately and justly?

Men. Certainly not.

Soc. Then they who order a state or a house temperately or justly order them with temperance and justice?

Men. Certainly.

Soc. Then both men and women, if they are to be good men and women, must have temperance and justice in common?

Men. True.

Soc. And what of a child or of an old man? Can they ever be good if they are intemperate and unjust?

Men. They cannot.

Soc. They must be temperate and just?

Men. Yes.

Soc. Then all men are good in the same way; for they become good when they participate in the same?

Men. Such is the inference.

Soc. And they surely would not have been good in the same way unless their virtue had been the same?

Men. They would not.

Soc. Then now that the sameness of all virtue has been proven, try and remember what you . . . say that virtue is.

Men. If you want to have one definition of them all, I know not what to say, but that virtue is the power of governing mankind.

Soc. This is what I am seeking. But does this definition of virtue cover all cases? Does it apply to a child and a slave. Meno? Can the child govern his father, or the slave his master; and would he who governed be any longer a slave?

Men. I think not, Socrates.

Soc. No, indeed; there would be small reason in that, fair friend. Moreover, consider also the following: according to you, virtue is "the power of governing"; but do you not add "justly and not unjustly"?

Men. Yes, Socrates; I agree there; for justice is virtue.

Soc. Would you say "virtue," Meno, or "a virtue"?

Men. What do you mean?

Soc. What I might say about anything; that roundness, for example, is "a shape" and not simply "shape," and I should adopt this mode of speaking, because there are other shapes.

Men. Quite right; and that is just what I am saying about virtue— that there are other virtues as well as justice.

Soc. What are they? Tell me as I would tell you the other shapes if you asked me.

Men. Courage and temperance and wisdom and magnanimity are virtues; and there are many others.

Soc. Yes, Meno; and again we are in the same trouble: in searching after one virtue we have found many, though not in the same way as before; but we have been unable to find the common virtue which runs through them all.

Men. Indeed, Socrates, for I simply cannot follow your search and find one common notion of virtue as I did in the other cases.

[Socrates at this point explains further to Meno by the examples of shape and color how the same species differentiates into many modifications and what a definition may look like which would be all inclusive. He then resumes his interrogation of Meno about virtue.]

Soc. . . . Tell me what virtue is in general; and do not make a singular into a plural, as the facetious say of those who break something, but deliver virtue to me whole and sound and not broken into a number of pieces . . .

Men. Well then, Socrates, virtue, as I take it, is when he, who desires the honorable, is able to provide it for himself; so the poet* says, and I say, too—

> Virtue is to delight in things honorable and be capable
> of them.

Soc. And does he who desires the honorable also desire the good?

Men. Certainly.

Soc. Do you then imply that there are some who desire the evil and

---

* Perhaps Simonides, a poet of the 6th century.

others who desire the good? Do not all men, my dear sir, desire the good?

MEN. I think not.

Soc. There are some who desire the evil?

MEN. Yes.

Soc. Do you mean that they think the evil that they desire to be good; or do they know that it is evil and yet desire it?

MEN. Both, I believe.

Soc. And do you really imagine, Meno, that a man knows evil to be evil and desires it notwithstanding?

MEN. Certainly I do.

Soc. And desire is of possession?

MEN. Yes, of possession.

Soc. And does he think that the evil will benefit him who possesses it, or does he know that it will do him harm?

MEN. There are some who think that the evil will benefit them, and others who know that it will do them harm.

Soc. And, in your opinion, do those who think that the evil will benefit them know that it is evil?

MEN. I do not believe that at all.

Soc. Is it not obvious that those who are ignorant of the evil do not desire it; but they desire what they suppose to be good although it is really evil; and if they are mistaken and suppose the evil to be good, they really desire the good?

MEN. Yes, in that case.

Soc. Well, and do those who, as you say, desire the evil, and believe that the evil is harmful to the possessor of it, know that they will be harmed by it?

MEN. They must know it.

Soc. And must they not suppose that those who are harmed are miserable in proportion to the harm which is inflicted upon them?

MEN. How can it be otherwise?

Soc. But are not the miserable unhappy?

MEN. Yes, indeed.

Soc. And does anyone wish to be miserable and unhappy?

MEN. I should say not, Socrates.

Soc. But if there is no one who wishes to be miserable, there is no one, Meno, who wishes evil for himself. For what is to be miserable but to desire and possess evil?

MEN. That appears to be the truth, Socrates, and I admit that nobody wishes evil.

Soc. And yet, were you not saying just now that virtue is to wish the good and be capable of it?

MEN. Yes, I did say so.

Soc. But in this definition, "to wish the good" is common to all, and one man is no better than another in that respect?

MEN. Apparently.

Soc. And if one man is not better than another in wishing the good, he must be better in his capacity for it?

MEN. Exactly.

Soc. Then, according to your account, virtue would appear to be the capacity of providing the good?

MEN. I entirely approve, Socrates, of the manner in which you now view this matter.

Soc. Then let us see whether what you say is true from another point of view; for very likely you may be right—you affirm that virtue is to be able to provide the good?

MEN. Yes.

Soc. And good you call things such as health and wealth?

MEN. Also to procure gold and silver and honors and offices in the state.

Soc. Nothing else you call good but things of that sort?

MEN. No, but everything of that sort.

Soc. Then as Meno proclaims, who is the hereditary friend of the great king,* virtue consists in providing gold and silver. Would you add that they must be gained justly and piously, or do you deem this to be of no consequence? And is any mode of procurement, even if unjust or dishonest, equally to be deemed virtue?

MEN. Surely nct, Socrates.

Soc. Rather, vice.

MEN. Entirely so.

Soc. Then justice or temperance or holiness, or some other part of virtue, as would appear, must accompany the procurement, and without them merely providing the good will not be virtue.

MEN. Why, how can there be virtue without these?

Soc. And not to provide gold and silver when it would be unjust, neither for oneself nor for another, may not this be equally virtue?

MEN. Apparently.

Soc. Then procurement of such good is no more virtue than non-procurement; but whatever is accompanied by justice or honesty is virtue, and whatever is devoid of justice is vice.

MEN. It cannot be otherwise, in my judgment.

* The reference is to the Persian kings, famous in Greece for the luxury and splendor of their court.

SOC. And were we not saying just now that justice, temperance, and the like, were each of them a part of virtue?

MEN. Yes.

SOC. And so, Meno, this is the way in which you mock me.

MEN. Why do you say that, Socrates?

SOC. Why, because I asked you to deliver virtue into my hands whole and unbroken . . . ; and you have forgotten already and tell me that virtue is to be able to provide the good with justice; and justice you acknowledge to be a part of virtue.

MEN. Yes.

SOC. Then it follows from your own admission that to do whatever you do with a part of virtue is virtue. For justice and the like you say are parts of virtue.

MEN. What of that?

SOC. What of that! Why, did I not ask you to speak of virtue, as a whole? And you are very far from telling me this, but declare every action to be virtue which is done with a part of virtue, as though you had told me and made known to me the whole of virtue when you are really chopping it up into parts. And, therefore, my dear Meno, I fear that I must begin again and repeat the same question: What is virtue? for otherwise I can only say that every action done with a part of virtue is virtue; what else is the meaning of saying that every action done with justice is virtue? Ought I not ask the question over again; for can anyone who does not know virtue know a part of virtue?

MEN. No; I do not say that he can . . .

SOC. But then, my friend, do not suppose that we can explain to anyone the nature of virtue as a whole through some unexplained portion of virtue, or anything at all in that fashion; we should only have to ask over again the old question, What is virtue? Am I not right?

MEN. I believe that you are.

SOC. Then begin again, and answer me. What, according to you . . . is the definition of virtue?

WHAT IS LEARNING?

MEN. O Socrates, I used to be told, before I knew you, that you yourself were always doubting and making others doubt; and now you are casting your spells over me, and I am simply getting bewitched and enchanted, and am at my wits' end. And if I may venture to make a jest upon you, you seem to me both in your appearance and in your power

over others to be very like the flat electric ray,* who benumbs those who
come near him and touch him, as you now have benumbed me, I think.
For my soul and my tongue are really numb, and I do not know how to
answer you; and though I have delivered an infinite variety of speeches
about virtue before, and to many persons—and very good ones they were,
as I thought—at this moment I cannot even say what virtue is. And I
think that you are very wise in not voyaging and going away from home,
for if you did in other places as you do in Athens, you would be cast into
prison as a sorcerer.

Soc. You are a rogue, Meno, and have all but caught me.

Men. What do you mean, Socrates?

Soc. I can tell you why you made a comparison about me.

Men. Why?

Soc. In order that I might make another comparison about you. For I
know that all handsome young gentlemen like to have pretty comparisons
made about them—as well they may—but I shall not return the com-
pliment. As to my being an electric ray, if the fish itself is numb as well
as the cause of numbness in others, then indeed I am like it, but not
otherwise; for I perplex others, not because I am clear, but because I am
utterly perplexed myself. And now I know not what virtue is, and you
seem to be in the same case, although you did once perhaps know, before you touched me. Yet I am willing to join with you in the inquiry.

Men. And how will you inquire, Socrates, into that of which you do
not know at all what it is? What will you put forth as the subject of
inquiry? And if you find what you want, how will you ever know that
this is the thing which you did not know?

Soc. I understand, Meno, what you mean; but just see what a tire-
some dispute you are introducing. You argue that a man cannot inquire
either about that which he knows, or about that which he does not
know; for if he knows, he has no need to inquire; and if not, he cannot;
for he does not know the very subject about which he is to inquire.

Men. Well, Socrates, and is not the argument sound?

Soc. I think not.

Men. Why not?

Soc. I will tell you why: I have heard from certain wise men and
women who spoke of things divine that—

Men. What did they say?

Soc. They spoke of a glorious truth, as I thought.

Men. What was it and who were they?

---

* The Greek word for the fish is *nárke*, which also means "numbness." The English
words *narcosis* and *narcotic* are derived from it.

Soc. Some of them were priests and priestesses concerned to account for what they administered; there have been poets also who spoke of these things, like Pindar and many others who were inspired. And they say—mark now and see whether their words are true—they say that the soul of man is immortal, and at one time has an end which is termed dying, and at another time is born again, but is never destroyed. And because of this a man ought to live always in perfect holiness.

> For in the ninth year Persephone sends the souls of those
> from whom she has received the penalty of ancient crime
> back again from beneath into the light of the sun above,
> and these are they who become noble kings and mighty
> men and great in wisdom and are called saintly heroes in
> after-ages.*

The soul, then, as being immortal, and having been born again many times, and having seen all things that exist, whether in this world or in the world below, has knowledge of them all; and it is no wonder that she should be able to call to remembrance all that she ever knew about virtue and about everything; for as all nature is akin, and the soul has learned all things, there is no difficulty in her eliciting, or as men say "learning," out of a single recollection, all the rest, if a man is dauntless and does not faint; for all inquiry and all learning is but recollection.† And therefore we ought not to listen to this fallacy about the impossibility of inquiry; for it will make us idle, and is sweet only to the sluggard; but the other saying will make us active and inquisitive. Trusting that this is true, I will gladly inquire with you into what virtue is.

Men. Yes, Socrates; but what do you mean by saying that we do not learn, and that what we call learning is only recollection? Can you teach me how this is?

Soc. A moment ago I told you, Meno, that you were a rogue, and now you ask whether I can teach you, when I am saying that there is no teaching, but only recollection, and thus you imagine that you will involve me in a contradiction.

Men. I swear, Socrates, that I had no such intention. I only asked the question from habit; but if you can prove to me that what you say is true, I wish that you would.

Soc. It will be no easy matter, but I will do my best for your sake.

---

* Probably a quotation from Pindar.

† A doctrine of immortality and transmigration of souls, although not a common belief, was known in Greece at the time of Plato, dating back to Pythagoras and his school and the Orphic mysteries. Plato's unique contribution was the combination of the concept of immortality with the theory of recollection. Whether and how the Indian doctrine of reincarnation is connected with the Greek concept is not known.

Suppose that you call one of your many slave boys, that I may demonstrate on him.

[Socrates then poses to the slave boy a geometrical problem. He draws in the sand a square which has the size of 4 square feet, that is, whose sides are 2 feet long. And he asks how long the sides would have to be to double the size of the square from 4 to 8 square feet.

The slave boy has an immediate answer ready. He thinks that to double the size of the square simply requires doubling the length of the sides from 2 to 4 feet; whereupon Socrates shows him by means of further questioning that doubling the sides of the square quadruples and does not double its size.

In his second try the boy concludes that the side of the square such as Socrates asks for, if between 2 and 4 feet, must be 3 feet long; whereupon Socrates demonstrates to him that this makes 9 square feet and would therefore more than double the original size.

At this stage Socrates describes the condition in which the boy finds himself as that of mental shock, comparable to the "numbness" which Meno complained about after having been exposed to Socrates' questioning: he has become aware of his own ignorance whereas before he thought (wrongly) he knew the answer. He is thus now ready to discover the real solution to the problem, namely that the diagonal in the original square of 4 square feet provides the wanted length of the side of a square double in size.

Having finished his demonstration on the slave boy Socrates turns back to Meno.]

Soc. What do you say of him, Meno? Were not all these answers given out of his own head?

Men. Yes, they were all his own.

Soc. And yet, as we were just now saying, he did not know?

Men. True.

Soc. But still he had in him those opinions of his—had he not?

Men. Yes.

Soc. Then he who does not know may still have true opinions of that which he does not know?

Men. Apparently.

Soc. And at present these opinions have just been stirred up in him, as in a dream; but if he were frequently asked the same questions, in different forms, he would know as well as anyone at last?

Men. I dare say.

Soc. Without anyone teaching him he will recover his knowledge for himself, if he is only asked questions?

Men. Yes.

Soc. And this spontaneous recovery of knowledge in him is recollection?

MEN. True.

Soc. And this knowledge which he now has he must either have acquired or always possessed?

MEN. Yes.

Soc. But if he always possessed this knowledge, he would always have known; and if he had acquired the knowledge, he could not have acquired it in this life unless he has been taught geometry; for he may be made to do the same with all geometry and every other branch of knowledge. Now, has anyone ever taught him all this? You must know about him if, as you say, he was born and bred in your house.

MEN. I am certain that no one ever did teach him.

Soc. And yet he has these opinions?

MEN. The fact, Socrates, is undeniable.

Soc. But if he did not acquire them in this life, then he must have had and learned them at some other time.

MEN. Clearly he must.

Soc. Which must have been the time when he was not a human?

MEN. Yes.

Soc. And if there have always been true opinions in him, both at the time when he was and was not a human, which only need to be awakened into knowledge by putting questions to him, his soul must have always possessed this knowledge; for he always either was or was not a human?

MEN. Obviously.

Soc. And if the truth of all things always existed in the soul, then the soul is immortal. Therefore, be of good cheer and try to recollect what you do not know, or rather what you do not remember.

MEN. I feel, somehow, that I like what you are saying.

Soc. And I, Meno, like it too. Some things I have said of which I am not altogether confident. But that we shall be better and braver and less idle believing that we ought to inquire into what we do not know than we would be if we believed that what we do not know is not possible to find out, and one need not even try—that is a theme upon which I am ready to fight, in word and deed, to the utmost of my power.

MEN. There again Socrates, your words seem to me excellent.

WHY IS VIRTUE KNOWLEDGE?

Soc. Then as we are agreed that a man should inquire about that which he does not know, shall you and I make an effort to inquire together into what virtue is?

MEN. By all means, Socrates. And yet I would much rather return to my original question, Whether in seeking to acquire virtue we should regard it as a thing to be taught, or as a gift of nature, or as coming to men in some other way?

Soc. Had I command over you as well as over myself, Meno, I would not have considered whether virtue can or cannot be taught, until we had first ascertained what it is. But as you think only of controlling me and never of controlling yourself—such being your notion of freedom—I must yield to you, for what else can I do? And therefore I have now to consider the qualities of a thing of which I do not as yet know what it is. At any rate, will you condescend a little and allow the question: "Whether virtue is given by instruction, or in any other way," to be argued upon hypothesis? . . . Let the first hypothesis be that virtue is or is not knowledge—in that case will it be taught or not, or, as we were just now saying, "remembered"? For there is no use in disputing about the name. But does not everyone see that knowledge alone is taught?

MEN. I agree.

Soc. Then if virtue is a kind of knowledge, virtue will be taught?

MEN. Certainly.

Soc. Then now we have made a quick end of this question: if virtue is of such a nature, it will be taught; and if not, not?

MEN. To be sure.

Soc. The next question is whether virtue is knowledge or of another species?

MEN. Yes, that appears to be the question which comes next in order.

Soc. Do we not say that virtue is a good? Is this a hypothesis which stands?

MEN. Certainly.

Soc. Now, if there be any sort of good which is distinct from knowledge, virtue may be that good; but if knowledge embraces all good, then we shall be right in thinking that virtue is a kind of knowledge?

MEN. True.

Soc. And it is through virtue that we are good?

MEN. Yes.

Soc. And if good, beneficial; for all good things are beneficial?

MEN. Yes.

Soc. Then virtue is beneficial?

MEN. That is the only inference.

Soc. Then now let us see what are the things which severally benefit us. Health and strength, and beauty and wealth—these, and the like of these, we call beneficial?

MEN. True.

Soc. And yet these things may also sometimes do us harm, would you not think so?

Men. Yes.

Soc. And what is the guiding principle which makes them beneficial or the reverse? Do they not benefit us when they are rightly used and harm us when not?

Men. Certainly.

Soc. Next, let us consider the good of the soul: to this belong temperance, justice, courage, intelligence, memory, magnanimity, and the like?

Men. Surely.

Soc. And such of these as are not knowledge, but of another sort— do they not sometimes harm us and sometimes benefit us? Take courage when it lacks judgment and is only a kind of daring. Is not a man harmed when he is daring without sense, but benefited using his sense?

Men. True.

Soc. And the same may be said of temperance and intelligence; whatever things are learned or done with sense are beneficial, but when done without sense, they are harmful?

Men. Very true.

Soc. And in general, all that the soul attempts or endures, when under the guidance of wisdom, ends in happiness; but when she is under the guidance of folly, in the opposite?

Men. That appears to be true.

Soc. If then virtue is something that is in the soul, and is admitted to be beneficial, it must be wisdom, since none of the things of the soul are either beneficial or harmful in themselves, but they are all made beneficial or harmful by the addition of wisdom or of folly; and therefore, if virtue is beneficial, it must be a sort of wisdom?

Men. I quite agree.

Soc. And the other things, such as wealth and the like, of which we were just now saying that they are sometimes good and sometimes harmful, do they not also become beneficial or harmful, accordingly as the soul guides and uses them rightly or wrongly; just as the things of the soul herself are made beneficial when under the guidance of wisdom, and harmful by folly?

Men. True.

Soc. And the wise soul guides them rightly, and the foolish soul wrongly?

Men. Yes.

Soc. And is this not true in every case that for man all other things depend upon the soul, and the things of the soul herself depend upon wisdom, if they are to be good; and so by this account that which is beneficial would be wisdom—and virtue, as we say, is beneficial?

MEN. Certainly.

Soc. And thus we arrive at the conclusion that virtue is either wholly or partly wisdom?

MEN. I think that what you are saying, Socrates, is very true.

Soc. But if this is true, then good men are not by nature good?

MEN. I think not. . . .

Soc. But if the good are not by nature good, are they made good by instruction?

MEN. There appears to be no other alternative, Socrates. On the hypothesis that virtue is knowledge, there can be no doubt that virtue is taught.

Soc. Yes, indeed; but what if the hypothesis is erroneous?

MEN. I certainly thought just now that we were right.

Soc. Yes, Meno; but a principle which has any soundness should stand firm not only just now, but always.

MEN. Well; and what intereferes with your believing that virtue is knowledge?

WHY IS VIRTUE NOT KNOWLEDGE?

Soc. I will tell you, Meno. I do not retract the assertion that if virtue is knowledge it can be taught; but I fear that I have some reason in doubting whether virtue is knowledge; for consider now and say whether virtue, and not only virtue but anything that is to be taught, must not have teachers and disciples?

MEN. Surely.

Soc. And conversely, if there are neither teachers nor disciples of something, may it not be assumed to be incapable of being taught?

MEN. True; but do you think that there are no teachers of virtue?

Soc. I have certainly often inquired whether there were any, and taken great pains to find them, and have never succeeded; and many have assisted me in the search, and they were the persons whom I thought the most likely to know.

[In what follows Socrates endeavors to prove his point that there are no teachers of virtue by discussing and rejecting claims that have been made to this effect in the past.

He deals first with the widely held belief that citizens who are themselves in possession of virtue, the so-called "good and honorable," can transmit their own distinction to others. To test this view Socrates engages in a discussion with one of its adherents, Anytus,* a high-ranking state official in Athens and friend of Meno. He is particularly qualified for the discussion, as in his view as well as that of his fellow citizens, he has successfully acquired virtue for himself. Socrates causes him to admit under questioning that anyone who belongs to "the good and honorable" must certainly be anxious to transmit this most valuable possession to his own sons if such transmission through teaching is at all possible to him. He then reminds Anytus of the well-known fact that even those Athenians who had been models of virtue in the eyes of all other Greeks, such as Themistocles, the hero of the Persian Wars, or Pericles, the creator of Athens' "golden age," left behind only mediocre sons in no way as distinguished as their fathers had been. So Socrates concludes that if those most eminent in virtue were unable to teach their excellence to anyone, not even their own sons, the theory of "the good and honorable" as possible teachers of virtue must be given up.

A second claim to teaching virtue was made by a professional class of itinerant teachers, known as the Sophists, who made rhetoric the principal subject of their teaching. But their reputation was a controversial one among the Greeks of Socrates' time (as reflected by our own use of their name), and also their qualification for teaching virtue was by no means agreed upon among themselves. Supporting evidence for the Sophists as teachers of virtue being thus contradictory, it was proved inadequate to justify any such claim.

The elimination of both "the good and honorable" and the Sophists as possible teachers of virtue allows Socrates now to continue his argument.]

Soc. Well, if neither the sophists nor "the good and honorable" themselves are teachers, clearly there can be no other teachers?

MEN. No.

Soc. And if there are no teachers, neither are there disciples?

MEN. Agreed.

Soc. And we have admitted that a thing cannot be taught of which there are neither teachers nor disciples?

MEN. We have.

Soc. And there are no teachers of virtue to be found anywhere?

MEN. There are not.

Soc. And if there are no teachers, neither are there disciples?

MEN. That, I think, is true.

Soc. Then virtue cannot be taught?

MEN. Not if our examination has been correct. But I begin to wonder, Socrates, whether there are no good men at all; or if there are, how they came into existence?

---

* Anytus again represents a historical figure: one of the three accusers who forced Socrates' trial in 399 B.C. His refutation in the dialogue may serve the additional purpose of disclosing the cause of a personal grudge he held against Socrates.

HOW DOES VIRTUE COME ABOUT?

Soc. I am afraid, Meno, that you and I are rather careless men. . . . This I say, because I observe that in the previous discussion neither of us noticed that right and good action is possible to man under other guidance than that of knowledge—and indeed if this be denied, there is no seeing how there can be any good men at all.

Men. How do you mean, Socrates?

Soc. I mean that good men must be useful (beneficial). Were we not right in admitting this? It must be so.

Men. Yes.

Soc. And in supposing that they will be useful (beneficial) only if they guide us rightly in our actions—also in this we were correct?

Men. Yes.

Soc. But when we said that a man cannot guide rightly unless he has knowledge, in this we were wrong.

Men. What do you mean by that?

Soc. I will explain. If a man knew the way to Larissa,* or anywhere else, and went to the place and led others, would he not be a right and good guide?

Men. Certainly.

Soc. And a person who had a right opinion about the way, but had never been there and did not really know, would he not also guide rightly?

Men. Certainly.

Soc. And while he has right opinion about that which the other knows, he will in no way be a worse guide if he believes the truth, than he who knows the truth?

Men. Exactly.

Soc. Then true opinion is as a guide to right action in no way inferior to knowledge; and that was a point which we omitted in our consideration of the nature of virtue, when we said that knowledge only is a guide of right action; whereas there is also true opinion.

Men. So it seems.

Soc. Then right opinion is no less beneficial than knowledge?

Men. The difference, Socrates, is only that he who has knowledge will always be right; but he who has right opinion will sometimes be right, and sometimes not.

Soc. What do you mean? Will the latter not always be right, so long as he has right opinion?

* A town in Thessaly.

MEN. I see now that he must, and therefore, Socrates, I wonder that knowledge should be preferred to right opinion—or why they should ever differ.

Soc. And shall I explain this wonder to you?

MEN. Do tell me.

Soc. You would not wonder if you had ever observed the images of Daedalus;* but perhaps you have not got them in your country?

MEN. What have they to do with the question?

Soc. Because if they are not fastened, they play truant and run away, but if fastened, they stay where they are.

MEN. Well, what of that?

Soc. I mean to say that they are not very valuable possessions if they are at liberty, for they will walk off like runaway slaves; but when fastened, they are of great value, for they are really beautiful works of art. Now this is an illustration of the nature of true opinions: while they abide with us they are beautiful and fruitful, but they run away out of the human soul, and do not remain long, and therefore they are not of much value until they are fastened with a reckoning of their reason; and this fastening of them, friend Meno, is recollection, as you and I have agreed to call it. But when they are bound, in the first place, they have the nature of knowledge; and, in the second place, they are abiding. And this is why knowledge is preferred to right opinion because it is fastened by a chain.

MEN. What you are saying, Socrates, seems to be very much like the truth.

Soc. I, too, speak rather in ignorance; I only conjecture. And yet that knowledge differs from right opinion is no matter of conjecture with me. There are not many things which I profess to know, but this is most certainly one of them.

MEN. Yes, Socrates; and you are quite right in saying so.

Soc. And am I not also right in saying that true opinion when leading the way completes an action quite as well as knowledge?

MEN. There again, Socrates, I think you are right.

Soc. Then right opinion is not a whit inferior to knowledge or less beneficial in action; nor is the man who has right opinion inferior to him who has knowledge?

MEN. True.

Soc. Then surely the good man has been acknowledged by us to be useful (beneficial)?

* A legendary Greek sculptor of such great skill that he was said to have given his statues the power of movement.

MEN. Yes.

Soc. Seeing then that men become good and useful (beneficial) to states, not only because they have knowledge, but because they have right opinion, and that neither knowledge nor right opinion comes to man by nature but is acquired by him—(do you imagine either of them to be given by nature?

MEN. Not I.)

Soc. Then if they are not given by nature, neither are good people good by nature?

MEN. Certainly not.

Soc. And nature being excluded, then came the question whether virtue is acquired by teaching?

MEN. Yes.

Soc. If virtue was wisdom, then, as we thought, it could be taught?

MEN. Yes.

Soc. And if it could be taught, it was wisdom?

MEN. Certainly.

Soc. And if there were teachers, it could be taught; and if there were no teachers, not?

MEN. True.

Soc. But surely we acknowledged that there were no teachers of virtue?

MEN. Yes.

Soc. Then we acknowledged that it was not taught, and was not wisdom.

MEN. Certainly.

Soc. And yet we admitted that it was a good.

MEN. Yes.

Soc. And that beneficial and good is that which guides rightly?

MEN. Certainly.

Soc. And the only right guides are knowledge and true opinion— these are the guides of man; for things which happen by chance are not under the guidance of man; but the guides of man are true opinion and knowledge.

MEN. I think so, too.

Soc. But if virtue is not taught, we cannot say either any longer that it comes through knowledge.

MEN. Clearly not.

Soc. Then of two good and beneficial things, one, which is knowledge, has been eliminated and cannot be supposed to be our guide in political life.

MEN. I think not.

Soc. And therefore not by any wisdom, and not because they were wise, did Themistocles and those others of whom Anytus spoke govern states. This was the reason why they were unable to make others like themselves—because their virtue was not grounded on knowledge.

MEN. That is probably true, Socrates.

Soc. But if not by knowledge, the only alternative which remains is that statesmen must have guided states by right opinion, which is in politics what divination is in religion; for diviners and also prophets say many things truly, but they know not what they say.

MEN. So I believe.

Soc. And may we not, Meno, truly call those men "divine" who, having no understanding, yet succeed in many a grand deed and word?

MEN. Certainly.

Soc. Then we shall also be right in calling divine those whom we were just now speaking of as diviners and prophets, including the whole tribe of poets. Yes, and statesmen above all may be said to be divine and illumined, being inspired and possessed of God, in which condition they say many grand things, not knowing what they say.

MEN. Yes. . . .

Soc. . . . To sum up our inquiry—the result seems to be if our argument has been correct, that virtue comes to man neither through nature nor through teaching, but through divine providence without understanding; unless there may be supposed to be among statesmen someone who is capable of making a statesman of another. And if there be such a one, he may be said to be among the living what Homer says that Teiresias* was among the dead, "he alone has sense; but the rest are flitting shades"; and he and his virtue in like manner will be a reality among shadows.

MEN. That is excellent, Socrates.

Soc. Then, Meno, the conclusion is that virtue comes to us through divine providence (to whomever it comes). But we shall never know the certain truth until, before asking in what way virtue comes to men, we endeavor to inquire what virtue is, in and by itself.

STUDY QUESTIONS

1. What are Meno's successive definitions of virtue, and what fault does Socrates find with them?

* A legendary seer who was said to have retained his mental powers and the gift of prophecy in Hades, the shadow world of the dead of Greek mythology.

2. How does Socrates demonstrate to Meno that "all learning is but recollection"?

3. What different stages in the process of learning or "recollecting" are distinguishable in Meno's responses to Socrates' questioning and are also reflected in the episode with the slave boy?

4. How does Socrates prove that "virtue is a kind of knowledge"?

5. What reason does Socrates have to doubt his first conclusion that "virtue is either wholly or partly wisdom"?

6. What error does Socrates uncover in his own argument regarding virtue being a matter of knowledge?

7. What final conclusion does Socrates reach about the way in which virtue or excellence is acquired by man?

8. In what sense does the end of the dialogue hold out hope for the attainment of human virtue or excellence that is far superior to what has yet been reached?

II

Ethics

Aristotle

THE IDEAL OF SELF-REALIZATION

Biographical Note. ARISTOTLE (384-322 B.C.) was born at Stagira in the Chalcidic peninsula of northern Greece. He is known variously as the "Stagirite," after his birthplace, the "Peripatetic" from his habit of teaching while walking about with his students, and as "The Philosopher," as he was called by his medieval admirers because of his great wisdom. He entered Plato's Academy while still a youth of eighteen and remained a member for twenty years up to Plato's death—first as a student and later as a teacher. He then left Athens, and he subsequently accepted a call from Philip, King of Macedonia, to join his court as tutor for Prince Alexander, later known as Alexander the Great. Upon his pupil's accession to the throne, Aristotle returned to Athens and established his own school at a place called the Lyceum, located just outside the city. Here he continued his research and teaching for twelve more years. The death of Alexander in 323 B.C. caused Aristotle to leave Athens to escape an outbreak of anti-Macedonian feeling, expressed against him in a public accusation of impiety. Aristotle is said to have explained his departure on the ground that he did not wish the Athen-

From Aristotle, *The Nicomachean Ethics,* translated by R. W. Browne, London, Henry G. Bohn, 1853, with minor alterations. Selections are from Book I, Chapters 1, 2, 4, 7, and 13; Book II, Chapters 1, 2, 3, 4, 6, 7, 8, and 9; and Book X, Chapters 7 and 8. The final section is from Aristotle, *The Nicomachean Ethics,* translated by H. Rackham, Cambridge, Mass., The Loeb Classical Library and The Harvard University Press, 1926. The selection is from Book IX, Chapter 8. It is used by permission of the publishers. Omissions are not indicated in the text.

3 5

ians to sin twice against philosophy (Socrates having been the victim of their first "sin"). He died the following year.

In addition to his works in philosophy, Aristotle's studies include texts in sciences such as zoology and botany. But his main body of writings is philosophical in character, embracing such significant works as his *Metaphysics, Organon* (treatises on logic), *Nicomachean Ethics, Politics, Poetics,* and *De Anima* (about the soul).

* * *

Introductory Note. Ethics is understood by Aristotle to be the science of the ultimate ends or aims of life. There are two such ends toward which nature itself directs man and which he cannot help aiming for: happiness and goodness. Ethics thus becomes for Aristotle the science of the good and happy life, providing man with the knowledge he needs to strive effectively for the attainment of these ends.

The Greek term for goodness is *areté,* previously referred to as the key concept in Plato's *Meno.* In the following selections, the words "virtue" and "excellence" are used to translate it; neither word alone does justice to the Greek meaning, but they seem to be adequate when alternated according to suitability. The term "goodness" may be appropriate for bringing these different aspects of the Greek concept together in one word.

Aristotle's moral treatises are committed to a clarification of happiness and goodness as man's primary concerns. And it is here that Aristotle, following in the footsteps of Plato, made the great discovery for which moral philosophy is indebted to him; namely, that happiness and goodness (goodness meaning both virtue and excellence) belong together—that in a certain sense one is dependent on the other. Of course, Aristotle would readily agree that a man can be good without being happy, but he would most strenuously insist that a man cannot be happy without also being good. Goodness, in other words, has proved to be necessary although not sufficient for happiness.

The *Nicomachean Ethics* follows a threefold plan, and the selections here are representative of the three parts. First, it sets out to define happiness and to demonstrate the kind of interconnection that exists between happiness and goodness. Second, it attempts to describe the different forms and aspects of human goodness, introducing the distinction between two basic types that has dominated moral thinking ever since—that is, the distinction between moral goodness (called moral virtue or excellence in the text) and intellectual goodness (called intellectual virtue or excellence in the text). Third, it establishes a hierarchy among the different forms of goodness, showing that moral goodness is inferior and subservient to intellectual goodness, and that among the different forms of intellectual goodness, one can claim the highest rank of all: the wisdom of the philosopher.

Two major doctrines developed in the *Nicomachean Ethics* are emphasized in the selections: (1) the doctrine of the mean, which maintains that moral goodness in any of its many forms—such as temperance or courage—consists in the observance of a mean between two extremes or vices; and (2) the doctrine that the activity of contemplation, in which man makes use of the highest form of intellectual goodness—that is, philosophic wisdom, is divine in character and constitutes the most complete happiness that man can attain.

THE GOOD AS HAPPINESS

Every art and every inquiry, and in like manner every course of action and deliberate pursuit, seems to aim at some good; and consequently "the Good" has been well defined as "that which all things aim at."

Now since there are many actions, arts, and sciences, it follows that there are many ends or aims; for of medicine the end is health; of ship-building, a ship; of strategy, victory; of economics, wealth. But whatever of such arts are contained under any one faculty (as, for instance, under horsemanship is contained the art of making bridles and all other horse equipment; and this and the whole art of war is contained under strategy; and in the same manner other arts are contained under different faculties), in all these the ends or aims of the chief arts are things more to be desired than the ends of the subordinate ones; because for the sake of the former, the latter are pursued.

If, therefore, among the ends at which our actions aim there be one which we wish for on its own account, and if we wish for all other things on account of this, and do not choose everything for the sake of something else (for thus we should go on to infinity, so that all desire would be empty and vain), it is evident that this must be "the good," and the greatest good. Has not, then, the knowledge of this end a great influence on the conduct of life? and, like archers, shall we not be more likely to attain that which is right, if we have a target to aim at? If so, we ought to endeavor to give an outline at least of its nature.

What is the highest good of all things that action can achieve? As to its name, indeed, almost all men are agreed; for both the vulgar [*hoi polloi*, the many] and the educated call it *happiness*, and they suppose that to live well and to do well are synonymous with being happy. But concerning the nature of happiness they are at variance, and "the many" do not give the same definition of it as the educated; for the former imagine it to be an obvious and well-known object—such as pleasure, or wealth, or honor; some say one thing and some another; and frequently even the same person entertains different opinions regarding it at different times; for, when sick, he believes it to be health; when poor, wealth; but conscious of their own ignorance, they admire those who say that it is something great, and beyond them.

From Book I, Chapters 1, 2, and 4.

DEFINITION OF HAPPINESS

Since ends appear to be more than one, and of these we choose some for the sake of others, it is plain that they are not all final. But the chief good appears to be something final; so that if there is some one end which is alone final, that must be the very thing which we are in search of; but if there are many, it must be the most final of them. Now we say, that the object pursued for its own sake is more final than that pursued for the sake of another; and that the object which is never chosen on account of another thing is more final than those which are desirable both by themselves and for the sake of that other: we call that absolutely final which is always desirable for its own sake, and never on account of anything else.

Of such a kind does happiness seem in a peculiar manner to be; for this we always choose on its own account, and never on account of anything else. But honor, and pleasure, and intelligence, and every virtue we choose partly on their own account (for were no further advantage to result from them, we should still choose each of them), but we choose them also for the sake of happiness, because we suppose that we shall attain happiness by their means; but no one chooses happiness for the sake of these, nor in short for the sake of anything else.

The same result seems also to arise from a consideration of the self-sufficiency of happiness; for the final good appears to be self-sufficient. We define the "self-sufficient" as that which, when separated from everything else, makes life desirable, and in want of nothing. And such we suppose the nature of happiness to be; and moreover, we suppose it the most desirable of all things, even when not reckoned together with any other good. Happiness, then, appears something final and self-sufficient, being the end or aim of all human actions.

But, perhaps, to say that happiness is the greatest good, appears like stating something which is already granted; and it is desirable that we should explain still more clearly what it is. Perhaps, then, this may be done, if we ascertain what is man's peculiar work;* for as to the flute-player and sculptor and to every craftsman, and in short, to all who have any work or course of action, the good and excellence of each appears to reside in their peculiar work; so would it appear to be with man, if there is any peculiar work belonging to him. But can we suppose that there is no peculiar work of man, and he is left by nature without a work? or, as

From Book I, Chapter 7.

* *Work* translates the Greek *ergon*, from which comes our "erg" (unit of work) and which is also found in "energy." Another translation which perhaps brings out the meaning of *ergon* more fully in this context would be *job*.

there appears to be a certain work peculiarly belonging to the eye, the hand, and the foot, and in fine, to each of the members, in like manner would not one assume a certain work besides all these peculiarly belonging to man?

What, then, must this peculiar work be? Not merely to live, of course; for life man appears to share even with plants; but his *peculiar* work is the object of our inquiry: we must, therefore, exclude the life of nutrition and growth. Next comes sentient life; but this also he appears to have in common with the horse, the ox, and in fact all animals whatever.

There remains, therefore, the practical life of man insofar as he possesses reason. And we conclude that the work of man is an activity of the soul in conformity with, or at any rate involving, the exercise of reason.

We say that the work of a craftsman and that of a good craftsman is the same generically as in the case of a harpist and a good harpist (and so, in short, in all cases, superiority in each particular excellence being added to each particular work); for it is the work of a harpist to play the harp and that of a good harpist to play it well. This being so, if we assume the peculiar work of man to be a certain kind of life, *i.e.* an activity and conduct of the soul that involves reason; and if it is a peculiar work of a good man to perform such activities well and nobly; and if a work is well performed when it is performed according to its proper excellence, we may conclude that the good of man [*i.e.* happiness] is "an activity of the soul in accordance with excellence (virtue*)"; or, if the virtues are more than one, according to the best and most perfect of them; besides this, we must add, in a complete life. For as one swallow does not make a summer neither does one fine day; similarly one day or a short time does not make a man blessed and happy.

MORAL AND INTELLECTUAL EXCELLENCE

Since happiness is a certain activity of the soul in accordance with highest excellence (virtue), we must next consider the subject of excellence (virtue); for thus, perhaps, we should see more clearly regarding happiness. But, of course, the excellence we must study is human excellence; for the good which we were in search of is human good, and the happiness, human happiness; but by human excellence we mean not

---

* The corresponding Greek term is *aretē*, which is particularly difficult to translate because it denotes both *excellence* in general and *moral excellence* or *virtue* in particular. For this reason, both terms—*excellence* and *virtue*—are used to translate the same Greek word. *Virtue* also is a more convenient translation whenever the text calls for the plural form, since *excellence* can only be used in the singular.

From Book I, Chapter 13.

that of the body, but that of the soul; and happiness also we defined to be an activity of the soul.

We may adopt here certain doctrines about the soul that are currently taught in the schools: as that the soul may be distinguished into two parts, one of which is non-rational while the other possesses reason. Of the non-rational part, one division is like that which is common also to plants; that, I mean, which is the cause of nutrition and growth. Now the excellence of this part appears common to all animate beings, and not peculiar to man. We must therefore put aside the nutritive part of the soul, since it has naturally no connection with human excellence.

Now another element of the soul appears to be non-rational, but to participate in reason in some sort. For while we praise reason and the part of the soul that manifests it in the case of the continent and incontinent man alike, on the ground that it exhorts them rightly and urges them to do what is best, yet we find within these men another element different in nature from the rational element which contends with and resists reason. But this part also seems to partake of reason; at least in the continent man it obeys reason; and in the man who is at once temperate and courageous it is perhaps still more ready to listen to reason: for in him it entirely agrees with reason.

The non-rational part therefore appears to be twofold; the part which is also common to plants does not at all partake of reason; the part which contains the desires and appetites generally in some sense partakes of reason, in that it is submissive and obedient to it. But if it is necessary to say that this has reason likewise, the part which has reason will be twofold also; one part properly and in itself, the other as though listening to the suggestions of a parent.*

Excellence too is divided according to this difference; for we call some forms of excellence intellectual, others moral—wisdom, and sagacity, and prudence, we call intellectual, but liberality and temperance, moral.

---

* A diagram may clarify this twofold division of the soul. (From Hans Freund, *The Balanced Life*, New York, Philosophical Library, 1959, p. 95).

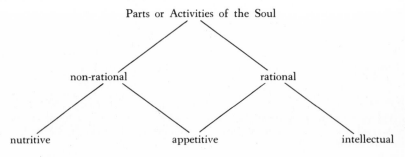

Parts or Activities of the Soul

non-rational   rational

nutritive   appetitive   intellectual

MORAL EXCELLENCE A RESULT OF PRACTICE

Excellence being twofold, one part intellectual and the other moral, intellectual excellence has its origin and growth for the most part from teaching; therefore it stands in need of experience and time; but moral excellence arises from habit, whence also it has got its name (*ethiké*), which is only in a small degree altered from *éthos* (habit).

From this it is also clear, that none of the moral virtues springs up in us from nature, for no natural property can be changed by habit; for instance, the stone which by nature goes downwards could never be trained to go upwards, even if one should attempt ten thousand times, by throwing it up, to give it this habit; nor could fire be habituated to burn downwards; nor could anything else that has one natural property get another different one from habit.

The moral virtues are acquired by first exercising them, as is the case also in all the other arts; for those things we have to learn before we can do them, we learn to do by doing them; as, for example, by building houses men become builders, and by playing on the harp, harpists; thus, also, by doing just actions we become just, by performing temperate actions, temperate, and by performing courageous actions we become courageous.

Moreover, that which happens in all states bears testimony to this; for legislators, by giving their citizens good habits, make them good; and this is the intention of every lawgiver, and all who do not do it well, fail; and it is in this that a good constitution differs from a bad one.

From the same causes and by the same means that a (moral) virtue is produced, it may also be corrupted; and in like manner every art; for from playing on the harp people become both good and bad harpists; and, analagously builders and all the rest; for from building well men will become good builders, and from building badly, bad ones; for if this were not the case, there would be no need of a person to teach, but everybody would be born a good or bad craftsman as the case may be. The same holds good in the case of the virtues also; for by taking part in transactions with other men, some of us become just and some unjust; and by acting in circumstances of danger, and being accustomed to be fearful or confident, some become courageous and others cowardly. The same thing is true in cases of desire and anger; for some become temperate and mild, and others intemperate and passionate—one class from having behaved themselves in one way, and the other class in another. Thus, in one word, states of character arise out of like activities; therefore, the

From Book II, Chapters 1 and 4.

activities in which we engage must be of a certain kind; for, with the differences of the activities the states of character correspond. It does not therefore make a slight, but an important, nay, rather the whole difference, whether we have been brought up in these habits or in others from childhood.

The question might be asked what we mean when we say that it is necessary for men to become just by performing just actions, and temperate by performing temperate ones; for if they do just and temperate actions, they are already just and temperate; exactly as, if they do what is in accordance with the laws of grammar and of music, they are grammarians and musicians.

The case of the arts, however, is not really similar to that of the virtues; for the productions of art have their goodness in themselves. It is enough, then, that they should themselves be of a certain character; but acts of virtue are done justly and temperately, not, if they have themselves a certain character, but only if the agent also is in a certain condition: first, if he does them knowingly; then if with deliberate choice, and deliberate choice on their own account; and, thirdly, if his action proceeds from a fixed and unchangeable character. Now as to the possession of all other arts, these qualifications, with the exception of knowledge, are of no account; but towards the possession of the virtues, knowledge has little or no weight, while the other qualifications are not of small, but rather of infinite importance, since they arise from the frequent practice of just and temperate actions.

Acts, then, are called just and temperate when they are such as the just or temperate man would do; but he who merely performs these acts is not a just or temperate man, but he who performs them in such a manner as just and temperate men do them. It is well said, therefore, that from performing just actions, a man becomes just; and from performing temperate ones, temperate; but without performing them no person would even be likely to become good. Yet most people do not do these things, but taking refuge in words, they think that they are philosophers, and that in this manner they will become good men; and what they do is like what sick people do, who listen attentively to their physicians, and then do not attend to the things which they prescribe. Just as the latter, then, will never be in a good state of body under such treatment, so the former will never be in a good state of mind, if this is their philosophy.

THE NATURE OF MORAL EXCELLENCE

Since our present treatise is not for the purpose of mere theoretical knowledge, as all others are, the object of our investigation not being to know what human goodness or virtue is, but to become good ourselves (since otherwise there would be no use in it), it is necessary to study the subject of actions, and how we must perform them; for these determine also the nature of the states of character that are produced, as we have said.

This, then, we must first observe that the virtues we have been discussing are naturally destroyed both by defect and excess, just as we see in the case of strength and health; for too much as well as too little exercise destroys strength. In like manner drink and food, whether there be too little or too much of them, destroy health, while due proportion causes, increases and preserves it. The same thing, then, holds good in the case of temperance, and courage, and the other virtues; for he who flees from and is afraid of everything, and stands up against nothing, becomes a coward; and he who fears nothing at all, but goes boldly at everything, becomes rash. In like manner, he who indulges in the enjoyment of every pleasure, and refrains from none, is intemperate; but he who shuns all, as boors do, becomes a kind of insensible man. For temperance and courage are destroyed both by the excess and the defect, but are preserved by the mean.

The best index of our states of character is found in the pleasure or pain that accompanies our action. For he who abstains from the bodily pleasures, and in this very thing takes pleasure, is temperate; but he who feels pain at it is intemperate; and he who meets dangers and rejoices at it, or at least feels no pain, is courageous; but he who feels pain is a coward. For moral excellence is concerned with pleasures and pains; it is by reason of pleasure that we do what is bad, and through pain we abstain from noble acts. Therefore it is necessary to be in some manner trained immediately from our childhood, as Plato says, so as to feel pleasure and pain at proper objects, for this is right education.

The following consideration will also make plain the specific nature of (moral) virtue. In everything that is continuous and divisible, it is possible to take more, less, or an equal amount, and that either with relation to the thing itself, or to ourselves; but the equal is some mean between excess and defect. And by the mean with relation to the thing itself, I understand that which is equidistant from both of the extremes, and this is one and the same in all cases; but by the mean with relation to ourselves, I understand that which is neither too much nor too little for

From Book II, Chapters 2, 3, and 6.

us. But this is not one and the same to all. For example, if ten is too many and two too few, six is taken for the absolute mean, for it exceeds two as much as it is exceeded by ten. This is the mean according to arithmetical proportion. But the relative mean is not to be taken in this manner; for it does not follow that if ten pounds are too much for any person to eat, and two pounds too little, the trainer will prescribe six pounds; for perhaps this is too much or too little for the person who is to eat it. For it is too little for Milo,* but too much for one just commencing gymnastics. Thus, an expert in any field shuns the excess and the defect, but seeks for the mean and chooses it; not the absolute mean, but the one relative to us.

If, then, every art or science accomplishes its work well by keeping the mean in view and directing its work to it (whence people are accustomed to say of perfect works of art that it is impossible to take anything away or add anything to them, implying that excess and defect destroy perfection but the being in the mean preserves it), and if good craftsmen, as we say, perform their work, keeping this in view, then human excellence, being like nature more accurate and better than any art, must aim at hitting the mean. But I speak of moral excellence; for it is concerned with passions and actions; and in these there is defect and excess, and the mean; as, for example, we may feel fear, confidence, desire, anger, pity, and, in a word, pleasure and pain, both too much and too little, and in both cases improperly. But to feel them at the right time, on the right occasion, toward the right people, for the right purpose, and in the right way, constitutes the mean and the best; and this is the mark of excellence.

Moral excellence, then, is a "state of character, concerned with choice, consisting essentially in the observance of the mean relative to us, determined by reason, as a prudent man would determine it." It is a mean state between two vices, one in excess, the other in defect; and it is so, moreover, because of the vices one division falls short of, and the other exceeds what is right, both in passions and actions, while virtue discovers the mean and chooses it. Therefore, with reference to its essence and the definition of its basic nature, moral excellence (virtue) is a mean state; but with reference to what is best and right, it is an extreme.

APPLICATION OF THE DOCTRINE OF THE MEAN

It is necessary that this should not only be stated generally but that it should also be applied to the particular cases; for in discussions on sub-

From Book II, Chapter 7.

* One of the most renowned athletes of antiquity (6th century B.C.), whose enormous strength won him innumerable victories at the Olympic Games.

jects of moral action, general statements are apt to be too vague, but particular ones are more consistent with truth; for actions are concerned with particulars, and it is necessary that the statements should agree with them.

Now, on the subject of fear and confidence, courage is the mean. Of the persons who are in excess, he who is in excess of fearlessness has no name; but there are many cases without names; and he who is in excess of confidence, is called rash; but he who is in excess of fear and deficient in confidence, is cowardly. On the subject of pleasures and pains (but not all pleasures and pains, and less in the case of pains than pleasures), temperance is the mean, and intemperance the excess. But there are, in fact, none who are deficient in the enjoyment of pleasures;* therefore these also have no name; but let them be called insensible.

On the subject of the giving and receiving of money, liberality is the mean, and the defect prodigality and stinginess. But in these, the excess and defect are mutually contrary to each other, for the prodigal man is in excess in spending money, and is in defect in receiving; while the stingy man is in excess in receiving, and in defect in giving.

On the subject of honor and dishonor, magnanimity is the mean; the excess may be called vanity; the defect, pettiness. There are also on the subject of anger an excess, a defect, and a mean state; but since they may be said to be nameless, and as we call him who is in the mean gentle, we will call the mean gentleness; but of the extremes, let him who is in excess be called irascible and his vice irascibility; him who is in defect, insensible to anger, and the defect insensibility to anger.

TO BE GOOD NO EASY TASK

To the mean in some cases the defect is more opposed, and in some cases the excess; as, for example, rashness, which is the excess is not so much opposed to courage, as cowardice, which is the defect; and insensibility, which is a defect, is less opposed to temperance than intemperance which is the excess.

But this happens for two reasons; the first from the nature of the thing itself; for because one extreme is nearer to and more like the mean than the other, it is not this but its contrary which we set down as more opposed; as, since rashness appears to be nearer and more like courage than cowardice, we oppose cowardice to courage rather than rashness, because

From Book II, Chapters 8 and 9.

* The ascetic ideal was evidently alien to Aristotle's thinking.

those things that are further from the mean appear to be more opposed to it. This, therefore, is one reason arising from the nature of the thing itself; the other originates in ourselves; for those things to which we are more naturally disposed, appear to be more contrary to the mean; as for instance, we are more naturally disposed to pleasures, and therefore we are more easily carried away to intemperance than to propriety of conduct. Those things, then, toward which there is more of an inclination, we call more opposed to the mean; and for this reason, intemperance which is the excess, is more opposed to temperance.

That moral excellence is a mean state, and how, and that it is a mean between two vices, one on the side of excess, and the other on the side of defect; and that it is so because it aims at the mean in passions and actions, has been sufficiently proved. It is therefore also no easy task to be good; for in each case it is difficult to find the mean; just as it is not in every man's power, but only in the power of him who knows how, to find the center of a circle. It is easy and in every man's power to be angry, and to give and spend money; but to do this to the right person, and to the right extent, at the right time, with the right motive, and in the right manner, is no longer in every man's power, nor is it easy; therefore excellence is rare, and praiseworthy and noble.

It is therefore needful for him who aims at the mean, first to keep away from that extreme which is more opposed to it. For of the extremes, one is more and one less erroneous. Since, then, it is difficult to hit the mean exactly, we must, as a second best, as people say, take the lesser of two evils; and this will be best done in the manner which we have stated.

The second rule is to consider to which of the vices we ourselves are most inclined; for some of us are naturally disposed to one, and some to another; and this we shall be able to discover from the pleasure and pain which arise in us. But it is necessary to drag ourselves away toward the opposite extreme; for by steering wide of our besetting error, we shall make a middle course.

Thirdly, we must be upon our guard against what is pleasant, and pleasure, for we are not unbiased judges of it. Just, then, as the Trojan elders felt respecting Helen, must we feel respecting pleasure, and in all cases pronounce sentence as they did; for thus, by "sending her* away," we shall be less likely to fall into error.

By so doing, then, to speak summarily, we shall be best able to hit the

---

* *Pleasure* is of feminine gender in Greek, and *her* means here both pleasure and Helen. The verses in Homer's *Iliad* referred to are:
> And yet, despite her beauty, let her go,
> Nor bring on us and on our sons a curse.

(*Iliad*, III, 159/60, translated by Edward Earl of Derby.)

mean. Perhaps this may be difficult, and especially in particular cases. But he who transgresses the right a little is not blamed, whether it be on the side of excess or defect, but he who does it too much; for he does not escape notice. But it is not easy to define how far and to what point a man must deviate before he becomes blameworthy.

What we have said hitherto, therefore, proves, that the mean state is in every case praiseworthy, but that we must incline sometimes towards excess, and sometimes towards deficiency; for thus we shall most easily hit the mean and what is right.

PRIMARY AND SECONDARY DEGREES OF HAPPINESS

If happiness is an activity in accordance with excellence, it is reasonable to suppose that it is in accordance with the highest type of excellence; and this must be the excellence of the best part of man. Whether, then, this best part be the intellect, or something else which is thought to be our natural ruler and guide; the activity of this part in accordance with its proper excellence must be perfect happiness; and this activity is the activity of contemplation.*

That happiness consists in contemplation, also would seem to agree with what was said before, and with the truth: for this activity is the noblest; since the intellect is the noblest thing within us, and of subjects of knowledge, those are noblest with which the intellect is concerned. It is also most continuous; for we are better able to contemplate continuously than to do anything else continuously. We think also that pleasure must be mixed with happiness. But of all the activities in accordance with excellence, that in accordance with wisdom is admittedly the most pleasant: at any rate philosophy seems to contain pleasures admirable for their purity and stability.

Again, the activity of contemplation will be found to possess in the highest degree what is called self-sufficiency; for both the wise man and the just, and all others, need the necessaries of life; but supposing them to be sufficiently supplied with such goods, the just man still requires persons toward whom and with whom he may act justly; and in like manner the temperate man and the courageous man, and so on with all the rest. But the wise man, even when by himself, is able to contemplate,

From Book X, Chapters 7 and 8. A concluding evaluation of the nature of happiness is given here and under the next heading.

* Contemplation is the practice of the philosopher's peculiar intellectual excellence, which is called "wisdom" (sophia; philosophia: love of wisdom).

and the more so the wiser he is; perhaps he will do better if he has fellow-workers, but nevertheless, he is most self-sufficient. This would also seem to be the only activity which is loved for its own sake; for it has no result beyond the act of contemplation; but from the other activities we gain more or less beyond the performance of the action.

The life of moral excellence, on the other hand, is happy only in a secondary degree. For the activities in accordance with it are purely human; for we do in our intercourse with our fellows what is just and courageous and everything else which is in accordance with the virtues when we observe what is due to each in contracts and services and in actions and passions of every kind. But all these things seem to be purely human; some of them even seem to arise from the body, and moral excellence is thought to be in many ways bound up with the passions. But then they are related to our composite nature, and the virtues of our composite nature are purely human; and therefore the life according to them, and the happiness according to them, are human, whereas the happiness that belongs to the intellect [i.e. contemplation] is a thing apart.

THE DIVINE CHARACTER OF CONTEMPLATION

Such a life as this [the contemplative one], would be superior to anything merely human; for man would live thus, not in so far as he is man, but as there is in him something divine. And so far as this divine part surpasses our composite nature, so far does its activity surpass that in accordance with all other virtues. If, then, the intellect be divine when compared with man, the life also which is in accordance with it, will be divine, when compared with human life. But a man ought not to entertain human thoughts, as some would advise, because he is human, nor mortal thoughts because he is mortal: but as far as it is possible he should make himself immortal, and do everything with a view to living in accordance with the highest principle in him; although it be small in size, yet in power and value it far surpasses all the rest. It may even be held that this is man's true self since it is the authoritative and better part of him. And it would be absurd, surely, if a man were to choose not the life of his self but the life of some other than himself.

That perfect happiness is a kind of contemplative activity, might be shown also from the following consideration. We suppose the gods to be pre-eminently blessed and happy. But what sort of actions can we

From Book X, Chapters 7 and 8.

attribute to them? Shall they be just actions? Or will it not appear ridiculous to represent them as making bargains, and restoring deposits, and so forth? Shall we, then, attribute to them courageous acts, making them endure terrors, and run risks, because it is noble to do so? Or liberal acts? But to whom will they give? And it is absurd to suppose that they have money, or anything of that sort. And if we say that they are temperate, what would that mean? Is not the praise absurd, because they have not bad desires? And if we went through every case, such moral actions would seem insignificant and unworthy of gods. Yet all suppose that they live, and therefore live actively. To him, then, who lives, if we take away moral action, and still more so production, what remains but contemplation? So that the activity of God, as it surpasses all others in blessedness, must be contemplative: and therefore, of human activities, that which is most akin to this must be the happiest.

He also who is active with his intellect and cultivates it and keeps it in the best condition is likely to be most beloved by the gods; for if any regard is paid to human affairs by the gods, as it is thought that there is, it is reasonable to suppose that they would delight in that which is best and most akin to themselves: but this must be the intellect; and that they would be kind in return to those who love and honor this most as to persons who pay attention to their friends, and who act rightly and nobly. But that all these qualities especially belong to the wise man, is quite clear; it is probable, therefore, that he is at the same time most dear to the gods, and most happy; so that even in this way the wise man must be the happiest man.

PROSPERITY AND THE HAPPY LIFE AND ITS TEST OF TRUTH

The happy man will also need external prosperity; for human nature is not self-sufficient for the purpose of contemplation, but our body also must be healthy, and it must have food and all other care and attention. We must not, however, imagine that the person that is to be happy will need many and great goods if supreme blessedness is not possible without external goods; for self-sufficiency does not depend on excessive abundance, nor does moral conduct. But it is possible to perform noble acts without being rulers of earth and sea; for a man may be able to act according to virtue with moderate means. We may see this plainly: for private individuals are thought to perform good acts no less than rulers,

From Book X, Chapter 8.

but even more so. And it is sufficient to have just so much; for the life of that man will be happy who is active in accordance with excellence.

Solon* also perhaps gave a good description of the happy man, when he said, that in his opinion those men were happy who while moderately supplied with external goods had done the noblest deeds, and lived temperately; for it is possible that men who had moderate possessions should do what they ought. Anaxagoras† also seems to have conceived the happy man to be neither rich nor powerful, when he said that he should not be surprised if he was thought absurd by the many; for they judge by externals, having a perception of such things only.

The opinions of wise men, therefore, seem to agree with what has been said; and such statements carry with them some weight. But we judge of truth in practical matters from facts and from life; for these are the decisive factor. We must therefore examine all that has been said by bringing it to the test of the facts of life: if our arguments agree with the facts, we may accept them; but if they are at variance, we must consider them as mere words.

THOU SHALT LOVE THYSELF MOST

The question is also raised whether one ought to love oneself or some-one else most. People criticize those who put themselves first, and "lover of self" is used as a term of reproach. And it is thought that a bad man considers himself in all he does, and the more so the worse he is whereas a good man acts from a sense of what is noble, and the better he is the more he so acts, and considers his friend's interest, disregarding his own.

But the facts do not accord with these theories; nor is this surprising. For we admit that one should love one's best friend most; but our best friend is he who wishes us well for our own sake, and even though no one should know of it. Now this condition is most fully realized in a man's regard for himself, as indeed are all the other attributes that make up the definition of a friend. For a man is his own best friend. Therefore he ought to love himself most.

Now perhaps the proper course where there is a conflict of opinion is to get the two views clearly distinguished, and to define how far and in

From Book IX, Chapter 8. Although this section in the original text precedes the past few selections, it was placed last because it offers what amounts to a final formulation of the principle of Aristotle's ethics.

* Athenian legislator and sage of the 6th century B.C.
† Greek philosopher of the 5th century B.C., frequently quoted by Aristotle.

what way each of them is true. So probably the matter may become clear if we ascertain what meaning each side attaches to the term "self-love."

Those who make it a term of reproach call men lovers of self when they assign to themselves the larger share of money, honors, or bodily pleasures; since these are the things which most men desire and set their hearts on as being the greatest goods, and which accordingly they compete with each other to obtain. Now those who take more than their share of these things are men who indulge their appetites, and generally their passions and the non-rational part of their souls. But most men are of this kind. Accordingly the use of the term "lover of self" as a reproach has arisen from the fact that self-love of the ordinary kind is bad. Hence self-love is rightly censured in those who are lovers of self in this sense. And that it is those who take too large a share of things of this sort whom most people usually mean when they speak of lovers of self, is clear enough.

If [on the other hand] a man were always bent on outdoing everyone else in acting justly or temperately or in displaying any other of the virtues, and in general were always trying to secure for himself moral nobility, no one would charge him with love of self nor find any fault with him. Yet as a matter of fact such a man might be held to be a lover of self in an exceptional degree. At all events he takes for himself the things that are noblest and most truly good. Also it is the most authoritative part of himself that he indulges and obeys in everything. But as in the state it is the sovereign that is held in the fullest sense to *be* the state, and in any other composite whole it is the authoritative part that is deemed especially to be that whole, so it is with man. He therefore who loves and indulges the authoritative part of himself is a lover of self in the fullest degree.

Persons, then, who are exceptionally covetous of noble actions are universally approved and commended; and if all men vied with each other in moral nobility and strove to perform the noblest deeds, the common welfare would be fully realized, while individuals also could enjoy the greatest of goods, in as much as excellence is the greatest good.

But it is also true of the good man that he is often guided by the interests of his friends and of his country, and that he will if necessary lay down his life in their behalf. For he will surrender wealth and power and all the goods that men struggle to win, if he can secure nobility for himself; since he would prefer one hour of rapture to a long period of mild enjoyment, a year of noble life to many years of ordinary existence, one great and glorious exploit to many cheap successes. It may even happen that he will surrender to his friend the performance of some achievement, and that it may be nobler for him to be the cause of his friend's performing it than to perform it himself.

Therefore in all spheres of praiseworthy conduct it is manifest that the good man takes the larger share of moral nobility for himself. In this sense, then, as we said above, it is right to be a lover of self, though self-love of the ordinary sort is wrong.

STUDY QUESTIONS

1. What are formal characteristics of happiness which distinguish it from any other good?
2. How does Aristotle arrive at his definition of happiness as "an activity of the soul in accordance with excellence"?
3. What is the basis for Aristotle's distinction between moral and intellectual virtue or excellence?
4. Why has knowledge little or no weight for the attainment of the moral virtues?
5. In what sense is moral excellence a mean or aiming at a mean?
6. What three rules are to be kept in mind so one can hit the mean, and how can they be justified?
7. What gives the life of contemplation—that is, the practice of intellectual excellence—superiority over the life of mere moral excellence?
8. How is the problem of the morality (goodness) or immorality (badness) of self-love solved?

Marcus Aurelius

═══

THE COSMIC COMMUNITY

═══

Biographical Note.　　MARCUS AURELIUS ANTONINUS (121–180 A.D.) came from a family belonging to Rome's ruling caste. His winning charm and sincerity as a boy was noted by the Emperor Hadrian, who made him a member of his circle and caused his son by adoption, the later Emperor Antoninus Pius, to adopt Marcus in turn, who thus was designated as Hadrian's second successor.

During the reign of Antoninus Pius (138–161 A.D.), Marcus remained closely attached to him while entrusted with the highest offices of state. His admiration for his adoptive father was boundless, and his written work gives moving expression of this admiration.

At the age of forty, Marcus Aurelius followed Antoninus Pius as emperor and for twenty years gave the world an example of what the ancients regarded as "the perfect rule." A contemporary historian wrote after his death that "there was no virtue (*aretē*) which he did not possess" and that he "neither intentionally nor unintentionally ever gave offense to anyone." His life was devoted to "imitating the gods in doing good as much as possible to the most people possible." Later generations cherished his memory as sacred, and his statue was almost universally given an honored place among the household gods.

From *The Thoughts of the Emperor M. Aurelius Antoninus,* translated by George Long, New York, J. B. Alden, 1891, with minor alterations.

The two numbers at the beginnings of paragraphs identify selections by book and number of meditation. Omissions are not indicated in the text.

The writing for which he is now most remembered and from which selections follow is known under the title *Meditations*. It is in the nature of a journal or diary, never meant for publication, but containing entries, jotted down from day to day when he lived in Rome, and even more while he was engaged in his many campaigns to protect the empire from the threat of barbarian invasion. They were written for his own guidance and support, to impress upon himself the high principles in which he believed and by which he endeavored to live.

*   *   *

Introductory Note.   The general context out of which Marcus Aurelius' thinking arises is the philosophy of Stoicism, one of the great philosophic movements of antiquity which from its founding by Zeno (around 300 B.C.) remained for many centuries a vital source of illumination helping to guide the ancient world on its road through history. Marcus Aurelius belongs to the later period in the development of Stoicism, marked by a religious coloring which brings out some affinity to Christian teaching and a return to the orthodoxy of its founders.

In its ethical theory, Stoicism proclaims that there is only one goal in life which provides the ruling principle for doing what is right and for keeping from doing what is wrong: always to act "in accordance with nature"; that is, to act in accordance with the harmony that permeates the whole of reality with which nature is identified. In his faculty of reason, man is said to possess within himself a "divine part," telling him what is and what is not according to nature, with nothing in the world or in man himself capable of preventing him from following the verdict of the "divinity planted in his breast" if he decides to do so.

The close relation between goodness and happiness had already been explained by Aristotle. Marcus Aurelius, following Stoic thought, goes even further than Aristotle and teaches that goodness and happiness not only belong together, but actually coincide. Goodness is now not merely necessary for happiness, it is sufficient for it. As individual man, therefore, is given control over his individual goodness, so he is also given control over his individual happiness.

But it is in another direction that Marcus Aurelius develops his most important moral insight, at least when compared with the moral thought of the classical period, and where an 'affinity' to Christian thought becomes conspicuous, although he himself was far from being aware of it. (In his reign the persecution of the Christians continued unabatedly.) For Aristotle (and Plato as well), no one and nothing was more important to the individual than the individual himself, and self-love in the sense of loving the "most authoritative part" of self became man's highest obligation. One can almost speak of a "Copernican turn" occurring in Marcus Aurelius (and in other Stoics), shifting the center of attention away from the self and onto the world of which he is merely an insignificant part. Man can only acquire significance for his own existence to the extent to which he willingly and cheerfully plays the role assigned to him as a member of the cosmic community, regardless of what this role may be.

> Whatever act of thine has no reference either immediately or re-motely to a social end, this tears asunder thy life, and does not allow it to be one, and it is of the nature of a mutiny.

COSMIC HARMONY

(4:40) Constantly regard the Universe as one living being, having one substance and one soul; and observe how all things have reference to one perception, the perception of this one living being; and how all things act with one movement; and how all existing things are joint causes of all things that come into existence; observe too the continuous spinning of the thread and the contexture of the web.

(4:45) In the series of things those which follow are always aptly fitted to those which have gone before; for this series is not like a mere enumeration of disjointed things, which has only a necessary sequence, but it is a rational connection: and as all existing things are arranged to-gether harmoniously, so the things which come into existence exhibit no mere succession, but a certain wonderful relationship.

(6:36) Asia, Europe are corners of the Universe: all the sea a drop in the Universe; Athos* a little clod of the Universe: all the present time is a point in eternity. All things are little, changeable, perishable. All things come from that one source, from that ruling Reason of the Universe, either directly proceeding or by way of sequence. And accordingly the lion's gaping jaws, and that which is poisonous, and every harmful thing as a thorn, as mud, are after-products of the grand and beautiful.

(6:37) He who has seen present things has seen all, both everything which has taken place from all eternity and everything which will be for time without end; for all things are of one kin and of one form.

(7:9) All things are implicated with one another, and the bond is holy; and there is hardly anything unconnected with any other thing. For all things have been co-ordinated, and they combine to form the same Universe. For there is one Universe made up of all things, and one God who pervades all things, and one substance, and one law, one common reason in all intelligent animals, and one truth; if indeed there is also one perfection for all animals which are of the same stock and participate in the same reason.

* A mountain on the Easternmost part of the Chalcidic peninsula in Greece.

(8:50) A cucumber is bitter.—Throw it away.—There are briars in the road.—Turn aside from them.—This is enough. Do not add, And why were such things made in the world? For thou wilt be ridiculed by a man who is acquainted with nature, as thou wouldst be ridiculed by a carpenter and shoemaker if thou didst find fault because thou seest in their workshop shavings and cuttings from the things which they make. And yet they have places into which they can throw these shavings and cuttings, and the Universal Nature has no external space; but the wondrous part of her art is that though she has circumscribed herself, everything within her which appears to decay and to grow old and to be useless she changes into herself, and again makes other new things from these very same, so that she requires neither substance from without nor wants a place into which she may cast that which decays. She is content then with her own space, and her own matter and her own art.

(10:21) "The earth loves the shower"; and "the solemn ether loves"; and the Universe loves to make whatever is about to be. I say then to the Universe, that I love as thou lovest. Is it not a way we have of speaking to say, "This or that loves to be so"?

(5:8) Just as we must understand when it is said, that Aesculapius* prescribed to this man riding exercise, or bathing in cold water or going without shoes; so we must understand it when it is said, that the nature of the Universe prescribed to this man disease or mutilation or loss or anything else of the kind. For in the first case Prescribed means something like this: he prescribed this for this man as a thing adapted to procure health; and in the second case it means: That which happens to (or, suits) every man is fixed in a manner for him suitably to his destiny. For this is what we mean when we say that things are suitable to us, as the workmen say of squared stones in walls or pyramids that they are suitable, when they fit them to one another in some kind of connection. For there is altogether one fitness, harmony. And as the Universe is made up out of all bodies to be such a body as it is, so out of all existing causes Destiny is made up to be such a cause as it is.

(6:1) The substance of the Universe is obedient and compliant; and the reason which governs it has in itself no cause for doing evil, for it has no malice, nor does it do evil to anything, nor is anything harmed by it. But all things are made and perfected according to this reason.

(8:35) As rational Nature has given to every rational being all the other powers that it has, so we have received from it this power also: that as this Nature converts and fixes in its predestined place everything which stands in the way and opposes it, and makes such things a part of

---

* Greco-Roman God of Medicine.

itself, so also the rational animal is able to make every hindrance its own material, and to use it for such purposes as it may have designed.

(12:23) Any one activity whatever it may be, when it has ceased at its proper time, suffers no evil because it has ceased; nor he who has done this act, does he suffer any evil for this reason that the act has ceased. In like manner then the sum total which consists of all the acts, which is our life, if it cease at its proper time, suffers no evil for this reason that it has ceased; nor he who has terminated this series at the proper time, has he been ill dealt with. But Nature fixes the proper time and the limit; it is sometimes, as in old age, man's individual nature, but always the Universal Nature, by the change of whose parts the whole Universe continues ever young and perfect. And everything which is useful to the Whole is always good and in season. Therefore the termination of life for every man is not only no evil—for it brings him no disgrace, if in fact it is both outside our choice and not opposed to the general interest—but a good, since it is seasonable and profitable to and congruent with the Whole. For then is he, who is borne along on the same path as God, and borne in his judgment toward the same things, indeed a man god-borne.

HUMAN PERFECTION AND HAPPINESS AS COMPLIANCE WITH COSMIC HARMONY

(2:9) This thou must always bear in mind, what is the nature of the whole, and what is my nature, and how this is related to that, and what kind of a part it is of what kind of a whole; and that there is no one who hinders thee from always doing and saying the things which are according to the nature of which thou art a part.

(4:23) Everything harmonizes with me, which is harmonious to thee, O Universe. Nothing for me is too early nor too late, which is in due time for thee. Everything is fruit to me which thy seasons bring, O Nature: from thee are all things, in thee are all things, to thee all things return.

(3:12) If thou workest at that which is before thee, following right reason seriously, vigorously, calmly, without allowing anything else to distract thee, but keeping thy divine part pure, as if thou shouldst be bound to give it back immediately; if thou holdest to this, expecting nothing, fearing nothing, but satisfied with thy present activity according to nature, and with heroic truth in every word and sound which thou utterest, thou wilt live happy. And there is no man who is able to prevent this.

(3:16) Body, soul, intelligence: to the body belong sensations, to the soul desires, to the intelligence principles. To receive impressions by way of the senses belongs even to animals; to be pulled by the strings of desire belongs both to wild beasts and men; and to have the intelligence that guides to the things which appear to be suitable belongs also to those who do not believe in the gods, and who betray their country, and do their impure deeds behind closed doors.* If then everything else is common to all that I have mentioned, there remains that which is peculiar to the good man to delight in and to welcome what befalls and what is spun for him by destiny; and not to defile the divinity which is planted in his breast, nor disturb it by a crowd of images, but to preserve it tranquil, following it obediently as a god, neither saying anything contrary to the truth, nor doing anything contrary to justice. And even if all men refuse to believe that he lives a simple, modest and cheerful life, he is neither angry with any of them, nor does he deviate from the way which leads to his life's goal, to which a man ought to come pure, tranquil, ready to depart, and needing no force to bring him into accord with his lot.

(9:1) He who acts unjustly acts impiously. For since the Nature of the Universe has made rational animals for the sake of one another to help one another according to their merits, but in no way to injure one another, he who transgresses her will, is clearly guilty of impiety towards the highest divinity. And he too who lies is guilty of impiety to the same divinity; for the Nature of the Universe is the nature of things that are; and things that are have a relation to all things that come into existence. And further, this Nature is named truth, and is the prime cause of all things that are true. He then who lies intentionally is guilty of impiety in as much as he acts unjustly by deceiving; and he also is guilty who lies unintentionally, in as much as he is at variance with the Nature of the Whole, and in as much as he disturbs the order by fighting against the nature of the world; for he fights against it, who is moved of himself to that which is contrary to truth, having received powers from nature through the neglect of which he is not able now to distinguish falsehood from truth.

And indeed he who pursues pleasure as good, and avoids pain as evil, is guilty of impiety. For of necessity such a man must often find fault with the Universal Nature, alleging that it assigns things to the bad

* This may refer to the Christians who were usually accused of these three things: atheism, disloyalty, and secret orgies.

and the good contrary to their merits, because frequently the bad are
in the enjoyment of pleasure and possess the things which procure
pleasure, but the good have pain for their share and the things which
cause pain. And further, he who is afraid of pain will sometimes also
be afraid of some of the things which will happen in the world, and
even this is impiety.

But those, who are of one mind with Nature and would walk in
her ways, must hold an attitude of indifference towards those things
towards which the Universal Nature is neutral—for she would not be
the Maker of both were she not neutral towards both. So he clearly
acts with impiety who is not himself neutral towards pain and pleasure,
death and life, honor and dishonor, things which the Nature of the
Universe treats with neutrality.

(4:49) Be like the promontory against which the waves continuously
break, but it stands firm and tames the fury of the water around it.

Unhappy am I, because this has happened to me.—Not so, but happy
am I, though this has happened to me, because I continue free from
pain, neither crushed by the present nor fearing the future. For such
a thing as this might have happened to every man; but every man would
not have continued free from pain on such an occasion. Why then is
that rather a misfortune than this a good fortune? And dost thou in
all cases call that a man's misfortune, which is not a deviation from
man's nature? And does a thing seem to thee to be a deviation from
man's nature, when it is not contrary to the will of man's nature? Well,
thou knowest the will of nature. Will then this which has happened
prevent thee from being just, high-minded, temperate, prudent, straightforward; will it prevent thee from having modesty, freedom, and everything else, by the presence of which man's nature obtains all that is its
own? Remember too on every occasion which leads thee to feel hurt,
to apply this principle: not that this is a misfortune, but that to bear
it nobly is good fortune.

(6:41) Whatever of the things which are not within thy power thou
shalt suppose to be good for thee or evil, it must of necessity be that,
if such a bad thing befall thee or the loss of such a good thing, thou
wilt blame the gods, and hate men too, those who are the cause of the
misfortune or the loss, or those who are suspected of being likely to be
the cause; and indeed we do much injustice, because we make a difference between these things. But if we judge only those things to be
good or bad which are in our power, there remains no reason either
for finding fault with God or standing in a hostile attitude to man.

(5:29) As thou intendest to live when thou art gone out, so it is in thy power to live here. But if men do not permit thee, then take your way out of life, yet not as one who suffers evil. The house is smoky and I quit it. Why dost thou think that this is a great matter? But so long as nothing of the kind drives me out, I remain, am free, and no man shall hinder me from doing what I choose; and I choose to do what is according to the nature of the rational and social animal.*

(7:68) It is in thy power to live free from all compulsion in the greatest tranquillity of mind, even if all the world cry out against thee as much as they choose, and even if wild beasts tear in pieces the members of this kneaded matter which has grown around thee.† For what hinders the mind in the midst of all this from maintaining itself in tranquillity and in a just judgment of all surrounding things and in a ready use of the objects which are presented to it, so that the judgment may say to the thing which falls under its observation: This thou are in substance (reality), though in men's opinion thou mayest appear to be of a different kind; and the use shall say to that which falls under the hand: Thou art the thing that I was seeking; for to me that which presents itself is always a material for virtue both rational and civic, and in a word for the art of a man or of God. For everything which happens has a relationship either to God or man, and is neither new nor difficult to handle, but familiar and feasible.

(4:29) He is an abscess on the Universe who withdraws and separates himself from the order of our common nature through being displeased with the things which happen; for the same nature produces this, that has produced thee too: he is a piece rent asunder from the community, who cuts off his own soul from the soul of all rational things, which is but one.

(8:55) Generally, wickedness does no harm at all to the Universe; and particularly, the wickedness of one man does no harm to another. It is only harmful to the one individual alone, and he has been given the option of being released from it, as soon as he shall choose.

(8:56) To my own free will the free will of my neighbor is just as indifferent as his poor breath and flesh. For though we are made especially for the sake of one another, yet our ruling reason is in each case master in its own house. For otherwise my neighbor's wickedness would be my harm, which God has not willed in order that my unhappiness may not depend on another.

(8:43) Different things delight different people. But it is my delight to keep my ruling reason sound without turning away either from any

---

* In Stoic moral thought, suicide is not denounced as immoral as in most other ethical theories.
† Possibly written with the persecution of the Christians in mind.

man or from any of the things which happen to men, but looking at and receiving all with welcome eyes and using everything according to its value.

(10:14) To her who gives and takes back all, to Nature, the man who is educated and modest says, Give what thou wilt; take back what thou wilt. And he says this not proudly, but obediently and well pleased with her.

(11:4) Have I done something for the general interest? Well then I have had my reward. Let this always be present to thy mind, and never stop doing such good.

(11:5) What is thy vocation? "To be a good man." And how is this accomplished well except by general principles, some about the nature of the Universe, and others about the proper constitution of man?

(12:32) How small a part of the boundless and unfathomable time is assigned to every man? For it is very soon swallowed up in the eternal. And how small a part of the Universal Substance? And how small a part of the Universal Soul? And on what a small clod of the whole earth thou creepest? Reflecting on all this consider nothing to be great, except to act as thy nature leads thee and to endure that which the Universal Nature brings.

(12:1) All those things at which thou wishest to arrive by a circuitous road, thou canst have now, if thou dost not refuse them to thyself; that is, if thou wilt take no notice of all the past, and trust the future to Providence, and direct the present only conformably to piety and justice: Conformably to piety, that thou mayest be content with the lot which is assigned to thee, for Nature designed it for thee and thee for it; conformably to justice, that thou mayest always speak the truth freely and without disguise, and do the things which are agreeable to law and according to the worth of each. If then, whatever the time may be when thou shalt be near to thy departure, neglecting everything else thou shalt respect only thy ruling reason and the divinity within thee, and if thou shalt be afraid not because thou must some time cease to live, but if thou shalt fear never to have begun to live according to Nature —then thou wilt be a man worthy of the Universe which has produced thee, and thou wilt cease to be a stranger in thy native land.

WORLD COMMUNITY AND LOVE OF NEIGHBOR

(4:4) If the intellectual capacity is common to us all, reason also in respect of which we are rational beings, is common: if this is so, common also is that reason which commands us what to do, and what not to do; if this is so, there is a common law also; if this is so, we are fellow-citizens; if this is so, we are fellow members of an organized community; if this is so, the world is in a manner a community.

(2:1) I who have seen the nature of the good that it is beautiful, and of the bad that it is ugly, and the nature of him who does wrong, that it is akin to me, not only of the same blood or seed, but that it participates in the same intelligence and the same portion of the divinity, I can neither be injured by any of them, for no one can fix on me what is ugly nor can I be angry with my kinsman, nor hate him. For we are made for cooperation, like feet, like hands, like eyelids, like the rows of the upper and lower teeth. To act against one another then is contrary to nature; and it is acting against one another to be annoyed and to turn away.

(5:6) One man, when he has done a service to another, is ready to set it down to his account as a favor conferred. Another is not ready to do this, but still in his own mind he thinks of the man as his debtor, and he knows what he has done. A third in a manner does not even know what he has done, but he is like a vine which has produced grapes, and seeks for nothing more after it has once produced its proper fruit. As a horse when he has run, a dog when he has tracked the game, a bee when it has made the honey, so a man when he has done a good act, does not call out for others to come and see, but he goes on to another act, as a vine goes on to produce again the grapes in season.

(5:20) In one respect man is the nearest thing to me, so far as I must do good to men and endure them. But so far as some men make themselves obstacles to my proper acts, man becomes to me one of the things which are indifferent, no less than the sun or wind or a wild beast. Now it is true that these may impede my action, but they are no impediments to my initiative and disposition, which have the power of conditional action and of changing: for the mind converts and changes every hindrance to its activity into an aid; and so that which is a hindrance is made a furtherance to an act, and that which is an obstacle on the road helps us on this road.

(6:42) We are all working together to one end, some with knowledge and design, and others without knowing what they do; just as Heraclitus,* I think, says that even when they sleep men are laborers and co-operators in the things which take place in the Universe. But men co-operate after different fashions: and even those co-operate abundantly who find fault with what happens and those who try to oppose it and to hinder it; for the Universe had need even of such men as these. It remains then for thee to understand among what kind of workmen

* Well known pre-Socratic philosopher around 500 B.C.

thou placest thyself; for he who rules all things will certainly make a right use of thee, and he will receive thee among some part of the co-operators and of those whose labors conduce to one end.

(7:13) Just as it is with the members of bodies which are united in one organism, so it is with rational beings which exist separate, for they have been constituted for one co-operation. And the perception of this will be more apparent to thee, if thou often sayest to thyself that I am a *member* of the system of rational beings. But if thou sayest that thou art a *part,* thou dost not yet love men from thy heart; well-doing does not yet delight thee for its own sake; thou still doest it barely as a thing of propriety, and not yet as doing good to thyself.

(7:22) It is peculiar to man to love even those who do wrong. And this happens, if when they do wrong it occurs to thee that they are kinsmen, and that they do wrong through ignorance and unintentionally, and that soon both of you will die; and above all, that the wrong-doer has done thee no harm, for he has not made thy ruling reason worse than it was before.

(7:26) When a man has done thee any wrong, immediately consider with what opinion about good or evil he has done wrong. For when thou hast seen this, thou wilt pity him, and wilt neither wonder nor be angry. For thou hast still thyself either the same notion of good and evil as he or another not unlike. It is thy duty then to forgive him. And if thou dost not think such things to be good or evil, thou wilt more readily be well disposed to him who is in error.

(9:9) All things which participate in anything which is common to them all move towards that which is of the same kind with themselves. Accordingly then everything also which participates in the common in-telligent nature moves in like manner toward that which is of the same kind with itself, or moves even more. For so much as it is superior in comparison with all other things, in the same degree also is it more ready to mingle with and to be fused with that which is akin to it. Ac-cordingly among animals devoid of reason we find swarms of bees, and herds of cattle, and the nurture of young birds, and in a manner, love-associations. But in rational animals there are political communities and friendships, and families and meetings of people; and in wars, treaties and armistices.

See, then, what now takes place. For only intelligent animals have now forgotten this mutual desire and inclination, and here alone there is no sign of like flowing to like. But still though men strive to avoid this union, they are caught and held by it, for their nature is too strong for them.

(9:23) As thou thyself art a component part of a social system, so let every act of thine be a component part of social life. Whatever act of thine then has no reference either immediately or remotely to a social end, this tears asunder thy life, and does not allow it to be one, and it is of the nature of a mutiny, just as when in a popular assembly a man acting by himself stands apart from the general agreement.

(9:42) When thou blamest a man as faithless or ungrateful, turn to thyself. For the fault is manifestly thy own, whether thou didst trust that a man who had such a disposition would keep his promise, or when conferring thy kindness thou didst not confer it absolutely, nor yet in such a way as to have received from thy very act all the profit.

(10:33) Remember that nothing harms him who is really a citizen, which does not harm the state; nor yet does anything harm the state, which does not harm law. What then does not harm law does not harm either state or citizen.

(11:8) A branch cut off from the adjacent branch must of necessity be cut off from the whole tree also. So too a man when he is separated from another man has fallen off from the whole social community. Now a branch is cut off by others, but a man by his own act separates himself from his neighbor when he hates him and turns away from him, and he does not know that he has at the same time cut himself off from the whole social system. Yet he has this privilege certainly from Zeus who framed society that it is in our power to grow again to that which is near to us, and again to become a part which helps to make up the whole. However, if it often happens, this kind of separation, it makes it difficult for that which detaches itself to be brought to unity and to be restored to its former condition.

(11:9) As those who try to stand in thy way when thou art proceeding according to right reason, will not be able to turn thee aside from thy proper action, so neither let them drive thee from thy benevolent feelings towards them, but be on thy guard equally in both matters, not only in the matter of steady judgment and action, but also in the matter of gentleness towards those who try to hinder or otherwise trouble thee. For this also is weakness, to be vexed at them, as well as to be diverted from thy course of action and to give way through fear; for both are equally deserters from their post, the man who does it through fear, and the man who is alienated from him who is by nature a kinsman and a friend.

(11:18) Consider that kindness is invincible, if it be genuine, and not an affected smile and acting a part. For what will the most violent man do to thee, if thou persist in being kindly to him, and if, as opportunity offers, thou gently admonishest him and calmly correctest his errors at the very time when he is trying to do thee harm, saying, Not so, my child: we are constituted by nature for something else: I shall certainly not be injured, but thou art injuring thyself, my child.—And show him with gentle tact and without any personal reference that this is so, and that even bees do not do as he does, nor any animals which are formed by nature to be gregarious. And thou must do this neither with any double meaning nor in the way of reproach, but affectionately and without any bitterness at heart; and not as if thou wert lecturing him, nor yet to impress the bystanders, but as if he were indeed alone even though others are present.

STUDY QUESTIONS

1. In what sense is it said that everything in Nature "is always good and in season"?
2. How is whatever happens to each man related to the Universe as a whole?
3. What does the happy life solely depend upon and why can no one and nothing prevent us from leading it?
4. Toward what things must the good man be indifferent, and why is this necessary?
5. Why is wickedness only harmful to the wicked man himself and not to anyone else?
6. Why should we not allow ourselves either to be annoyed by or to turn away from one another?
7. With what different attitudes can a man do a service to another and how are they to be evaluated?
8. How can anyone prove (at least to himself) that he truly loves his fellow-men from his heart?
9. How should an individual relate himself to social life and what are the grounds for such relationship?

St. Augustine

```
▣▣▣▣▣▣▣▣▣▣▣▣▣▣▣▣▣▣▣▣▣▣▣▣▣▣▣▣▣▣▣▣▣▣▣▣▣▣▣▣▣▣
```

HAPPINESS AND THE LOVE OF GOD

```
▣▣▣▣▣▣▣▣▣▣▣▣▣▣▣▣▣▣▣▣▣▣▣▣▣▣▣▣▣▣▣▣▣▣▣▣▣▣▣▣▣▣▣▣▣▣
```

Biographical Note.   ST. AUGUSTINE (354–430 A.D.) was born of Roman parents in Tagaste in the Roman province of North Africa, his mother, Monica, being a devoted Christian. He received a traditional education and went to Carthage at the age of seventeen to study rhetoric, which became and remained his chosen profession for fifteen more years. Having changed from a student to a teacher of rhetoric, he finally left for Rome in his twenty-ninth year for the chief and almost only reason, as he wrote, that he had heard that "students there were kept quiet under a restraint of more regular discipline; whereas at Carthage there reigns among the students a most disgraceful and unruly license." Shortly afterwards, a lectureship was offered him in Milan, which he accepted in the hope of procuring a secure professional future.

Two years later his conversion to Christianity occurred, preceded by an inordinately long time of inward intellectual and emotional struggle of almost unendurable intensity and culminating in his baptism by Ambrose, the Bishop of Milan, on Easter in 387. His is one of the most celebrated conversions in

From *Of the Morals of the Catholic Church,* translated by the Rev. Richard Stothert, in *A Select Library of the Nicene and Post-Nicene Fathers of the Christian Church,* Philip Schaff, ed., First Series, Vol. IV, Grand Rapids, Wm. B. Eerdmans Publishing Company, 1956, pp. 42–48; and from *On Christian Doctrine,* translated by the Rev. Professor J. F. Shaw, in *A Select Library of the Nicene and Post-Nicene Fathers of the Christian Church,* Philip Schaff, ed., First Series, Vol. II, Grand Rapids, Wm. B. Eerdmans Publishing Company, 1956, pp. 528–534.

recorded history, owing chiefly to the brilliant account of it that he gave in his *Confessions.*

St. Augustine now left his former career and went back to his family estate in Africa to settle with his friends for a life of study and devotion. Three years later he was ordained to the priesthood and in 395 was consecrated as Bishop of Hippo in North Africa where he remained until his death.

In the history of Western philosophy and religion, St. Augustine occupies the place of the most influential Christian thinker, equally at home in both realms and recognized by Protestant no less than by Catholic theologians as an authoritative interpreter of Christian faith. His literary output was immense. Apart from his informal writings in innumerable letters and sermons, he calculated the formal tractates and larger works he had written as more than 230. Most important of these are *Confessions, On Trinity,* and *The City of God.*

* * *

Introductory Note. In the readings that follow, St. Augustine seems not to differ from Aristotle in his point of departure when he declares happiness to be the goal of human desire and defines ethics as the inquiry into "what manner of life must be held in order to obtain happiness." Aristotle would in no way take exception to St. Augustine's further argument that happiness is the possession and enjoyment of man's chief good. It is in the understanding of what constitutes this chief good of man that the main difference lies between the ethical teaching of the Greek classical period and that of the Judaeo-Christian tradition as represented by St. Augustine.

His basic proposition is encountered in his answer to the problem discussed at the beginning of the selection, the question of where the chief good is to be found. St. Augustine presents reasons why this chief good cannot possibly reside in man, neither in his body nor in his soul; cannot possibly consist of virtue, as necessary as virtue is for man's perfection. The chief good can only reside outside of man, can be found in God alone. "God then remains, in following after whom we live well, and in reaching whom we live both well and happily."

To characterize distinctly what has happened here in the evolution of Western moral thinking, the term "Copernican turn" may again be applicable. Man, hitherto relying for his self-perfection and happiness on nobody but himself, now becomes aware of his total dependence upon something else through which alone the goal of his striving can be realized. As in Marcus Aurelius a definite shift of attention occurred, leading the individual away from himself and to the world, so now a further shift takes place, transcending even the world, and making man, the finite creature, directly bound to the Infinite, to God himself.

Virtue then, in the old Greek sense of the word, no longer suffices to circumscribe the goodness required for the happy life; it takes on an entirely new characteristic through which alone man's relationship to his chief good can be established. This is called "love of God," and it becomes man's most essential distinction in the light of which such former virtues as courage and temperance must now be reinterpreted.

The hierarchy of virtues that Aristotle developed to serve as a guide for the attainment of true goodness and happiness is supplemented by a hierarchy of forms of love, all of them necessary for happiness although not equal in rank. Hence man's major moral problem is seen as that of continuous vigilance not to allow an inferior love, which is to be used as means to an end only, to be treated as if it were the end itself, a good to rest in or to be enjoyed for its own sake.

> We are to love the things by which we are borne only for the sake of that toward which we are borne.

THE MEANING OF HAPPINESS

How, according to reason, ought man to live? We all certainly desire to live happily; and there is no human being but assents to this statement almost before it is made. But the title happy cannot, in my opinion, belong either to him who has not what he loves, whatever it may be, or to him who has what he loves if it is hurtful, or to him who does not love what he has, although it is good in perfection. For one who seeks what he cannot obtain suffers torture, and one who has got what is not desirable is cheated, and one who does not seek for what is worth seeking for is diseased. Now in all these cases the mind cannot but be unhappy, and happiness and unhappiness cannot reside at the same time in one man; so in none of these cases can the man be happy.

I find, then, a fourth case, where the happy life exists—when that which is man's chief good is both loved and possessed. For what do we call enjoyment but having at hand the objects of love? And no one can be happy who does not enjoy what is man's chief good, nor is there anyone who enjoys this who is not happy. We must then have at hand our chief good, if we think of living happily.

We must now inquire what is man's chief good, which of course cannot be anything inferior to man himself. For whoever follows after what is inferior to himself, becomes himself inferior. But every man is bound to follow what is best. Wherefore man's chief good is not inferior to man. Is it then something similar to man himself? It must be so, if there is nothing above man which he is capable of enjoying. But if we find something which is both superior to man, and can be possessed

From *Of the Morals of the Catholic Church*, Chapters 3–6.

by the man who loves it, who can doubt that in seeking for happiness man should endeavor to reach that which is more excellent than the being who makes the endeavor. For if happiness consists in the enjoyment of a good than which there is nothing better, which we call the chief good, how can a man be properly called happy who has not yet attained to his chief good? or how can that be the chief good beyond which something better remains for us to arrive at? Such, then, being the chief good, it must be something which cannot be lost against the will. For no one can feel confident regarding a good which he knows can be taken from him, although he wishes to keep and cherish it. But if a man feels no confidence regarding the good which he enjoys, how can he be happy while in such fear of losing it?

Let us then see what is better than man. This must necessarily be hard to find, unless we first ask and examine what man is. I am not now called upon to give a definition of man. The question here seems to me to be—since almost all agree, or at least, which is enough, those I have now to do with are of the same opinion with me, that we are made up of soul and body—What is man? Is he both of these? or is he the body only or the soul only? For although the things are two, soul and body, and although neither without the other could be called man (for the body would not be man without the soul, nor again would the soul be man if there were not a body animated by it), still it is possible that one of these may be held to be man, and may be called so. What then do we call man? Is he soul and body, as in a double harness, or like a centaur? Or do we mean the body only, as being in the service of the soul which rules it, as the word lamp denotes not the light and the case together, but only the case, yet it is on account of the light that it is so called? Or do we mean only the mind, and that on account of the body which it rules, as horseman means not the man and the horse, but the man only, and that as employed in ruling the horse?

This dispute is not easy to settle; or, if the proof is plain, the statement requires time. This is an expenditure of time and strength which we need not incur. For whether the name man belongs to both, or only to the soul, the chief good of man is not the chief good of the body; but what is the chief good either of both soul and body, or of the soul only, that is man's chief good.

Now if we ask what is the chief good of the body, reason obliges us to admit that it is that by means of which the body comes to be in its best state. But of all the things which invigorate the body, there is nothing better or greater than the soul. The chief good of the body, then, is not bodily pleasure, not absence of pain, not strength, not beauty, not

swiftness, or whatever else is usually reckoned among the goods of the
body, but simply the soul. For all the things mentioned the soul supplies
to the body by its presence, and, what is above them all, life. Hence
I conclude that the soul is not the chief good of man, whether we give
the name of man to soul and body together, or to the soul alone. For
as, according to reason, the chief good of the body is that which is better
than the body, and from which the body receives vigor and life, so
whether the soul itself is man, or soul and body both, we must discover
whether there is anything which goes before the soul itself, in following
which the soul comes to the perfection of good of which it is capable
in its own kind. If such a thing can be found, all uncertainty must be
at an end, and we must pronounce this to be really and truly the chief
good of man.

If, again, the body is man, it must be admitted that the soul is the
chief good of man. But clearly, when we treat of morals—when we
inquire what manner of life must be held in order to obtain happiness
—it is not the body to which the precepts are addressed, it is not bodily
discipline which we discuss. In short, the observance of good *customs*
belongs to that part of us which inquires and learns, which are the
prerogatives of the soul; so, when we speak of attaining to virtue, the
question does not regard the body. But if it follows, as it does, that
the body which is ruled over by a soul possessed of virtue is ruled both
better and more honorably, and is in its greatest perfection in consequence of the perfection of the soul which rightfully governs it, that
which gives perfection to the soul will be man's chief good, though we
call the body man. For if my coachman, in obedience to me, feeds and
drives the horses he has charge of in the most satisfactory manner,
himself enjoying the more of my bounty in proportion to his good conduct, can anyone deny that the good condition of the horses, as well
as that of the coachman, is due to me? So the question seems to me to
be not, whether soul and body is man, or the soul only, or the body only,
but what gives perfection to the soul; for when this is obtained, a man
cannot but be either perfect, or at least much better than in the absence
of this one thing.

No one will question that virtue gives perfection to the soul. But it is
a very proper subject of inquiry whether this virtue can exist by itself or
only in the soul. Here again arises a profound discussion, needing
lengthy treatment; but perhaps my summary will serve the purpose.
God will, I trust, assist me, so that, notwithstanding our feebleness, we
may give instruction on these great matters briefly as well as intelligibly.
In either case, whether virtue can exist by itself without the soul, or

can exist only in the soul, undoubtedly in the pursuit of virtue the soul follows after something, and this must be either the soul itself, or virtue, or something else. But if the soul follows after itself in the pursuit of virtue, it follows after a foolish thing; for before obtaining virtue it is foolish. Now the height of a follower's desire is to reach that which he follows after. So the soul must either not wish to reach what it follows after, which is utterly absurd and unreasonable, or, in following after itself while foolish, it reaches the folly which it flees from. But if it follows after virtue in the desire to reach it, how can it follow what does not exist? or how can it desire to reach what it already possesses? Either, therefore, virtue exists beyond the soul, or if we are not allowed to give the name of virtue except to the habit and disposition of the wise soul, which can exist only in the soul, we must allow that the soul follows after something else in order that virtue may be produced in itself; for neither by following after nothing, nor by following after folly, can the soul, according to my reasoning, attain to wisdom.

This something else, then, by following after which the soul becomes possessed of virtue and wisdom, is either a wise man or God. But we have said already that it must be something that we cannot lose against our will. No one can think it necessary to ask whether a wise man, supposing we are content to follow after him, can be taken from us in spite of our unwillingness or our persistence. God then remains, in following after whom we live well, and in reaching whom we live both well and happily. . . .

THE NATURE OF VIRTUE

As to virtue leading us to a happy life, I hold virtue to be nothing else than perfect love of God. For the fourfold division of virtue I regard as taken from four forms of love. For these four virtues (would that all felt their influence in their minds as they have their names in their mouths!), I should have no hesitation in defining them: that temperance is love giving itself entirely to that which is loved; courage is love readily bearing all things for the sake of the loved object; justice is love serving only the loved object, and therefore ruling rightly; prudence is love distinguishing with sagacity between what hinders it and what helps it. The object of this love is not anything, but only God, the chief good, the highest wisdom, the perfect harmony. So we may express the definition thus: that temperance is love keeping itself entire and

Op. cit., from Chapters 15, 19, 22, 24, and 25.

incorrupt for God; courage is love bearing everything readily for the sake of God; justice is love serving God only, and therefore ruling well all else, as subject to man; prudence is love making a right distinction between what helps it towards God and what might hinder it. . . .

First let us consider temperance, which promises us a kind of integrity and incorruption in the love by which we are united to God. The office of temperance is in restraining and quieting the passions which make us pant for those things which turn us away from the laws of God and from the enjoyment of His goodness, that is, in a word, from the happy life. For there is the abode of truth; and in enjoying its contemplation, and in cleaving closely to it, we are assuredly happy; but departing from this, men become entangled in great errors and sorrows. . . .

On courage we must be brief. The love, then, of which we speak, which ought with all sanctity to burn in desire for God, is called temperance, in not seeking for earthly things, and courage, in bearing the loss of them. But among all things which are possessed in this life, the body is, by God's most righteous laws, for the sin of old, man's heaviest bond, which is well known as a fact, but most incomprehensible in its mystery. Lest this bond should be shaken and disturbed, the soul is shaken with the fear of toil and pain; lest it should be lost and destroyed, the soul is shaken with the fear of death. For the soul loves it from the force of habit. . . .

Then there is the great struggle with pain. But there is nothing, though of iron hardness, which the fire of love cannot subdue. And when the mind is carried up to God in this love, it will soar above all torture free and glorious . . . Otherwise God must allow the lovers of gold, the lovers of praise, the lovers of women, to have more courage than the lovers of Himself, though love in those cases is rather to be called passion or lust. . . .

What of justice that pertains to God? As the Lord says, "Ye cannot serve two masters" (Mt. 6:24), and the apostle denounces those who serve the creature rather than the Creator (Rom. 1:25), was it not said before in the Old Testament, "Thou shalt worship the Lord thy God, and Him only shalt thou serve" (Deut. 6:13)? I need say no more on this, for these books are full of such passages. The lover, then, whom we are describing, will get from justice this rule of life, that he must with perfect readiness serve the God whom he loves, the highest good, the highest wisdom, the highest peace; and as regards all other things, must either rule them as subject to himself, or treat them with a view to their subjection. . . .

With equal brevity we must treat of prudence, to which it belongs to discern between what is to be desired and what to be shunned. Without this, nothing can be done of what we have already spoken. It is the part of prudence to keep watch with most anxious vigilance, lest any evil influence should stealthily creep in upon us. Thus the Lord often exclaims, "Watch" (Mt. 24:42); and He says, "Walk while we have the light, lest darkness come upon you" (John 12:35). And then it is said, "Know ye not that a little leaven leaveneth the whole lump?" (I Cor. 5:6). And no passage can be quoted from the Old Testament more expressly condemning this mental somnolence, which makes us insensible to destruction advancing on us step by step, than those words of the prophet, "He who despiseth small things shall fall by degrees" (Ecclesiasticus 19:1). . . .

Let us then, as many as have in view to reach eternal life, love God with all the heart, with all the soul, with all the mind (Deut. 6:5). For eternal life contains the whole reward in the promise of which we rejoice; nor can the reward precede desert, nor be given to a man before he is worthy of it. What can be more unjust than this, and what is more just than God? We should not then demand the reward before we deserve to get it. Here, perhaps, it is not out of place to ask what is eternal life; or rather let us hear the Bestower of it: "This," He says, "is life eternal, that they should know Thee, the true God, and Jesus Christ whom Thou hast sent" (Jn. 17:3). So eternal life is the knowledge of the truth . . . What else, then, have we to do but first to love with sincere affection Him whom we desire to know?

LOVE OF SELF AND THE COMMANDMENT OF LOVE

. . . There are four kinds of things that are to be loved—first, that which is above us; second, ourselves; third, that which is on a level with us; fourth, that which is beneath us—no precepts need be given about the second and fourth of these. For, however far a man may fall away from the truth, he still continues to love himself, and to love his own body. The soul which flies away from the unchangeable Light, the Ruler of all things, does so that it may rule over itself and over its own body; and so it cannot but love both itself and its own body.

Moreover, it thinks it has attained something very great if it is able to lord it over its companions, that is, other men. For it is inherent in the sinful soul to desire above all things, and to claim as due to itself,

From *On Christian Doctrine,* Book I, Chapters 23–26.

that which is properly due to God only. . . . Now the health of the soul is to cling steadfastly to the better part, that is, to the unchangeable God. But when it aspires to lord it even over those who are by nature its equals—that is, its fellowmen—this is a reach of arrogance utterly intolerable.

No man, then, hates himself. On this point, indeed, no question was ever raised by any sect. But neither does any man hate his own body. For the apostle says truly, "No man ever yet hated his own flesh" (Eph. 5:29). And when some people say that they would rather be without a body altogether, they entirely deceive themselves. For it is not their body, but its corruptions and its heaviness, that they hate. And so it is not no body, but an uncorrupted and very light body, that they want . . . And as to the fact that they seem in some sort to scourge their bodies by abstinence and toil, those who do this in the right spirit do it not that they may get rid of their body, but that they may have it in subjection and ready for every needful work. For they strive by a kind of toilsome exercise of the body itself to root out those lusts that are hurtful to the body, that is, those habits and affections of the soul that lead to the enjoyment of unworthy objects. They are not destroying themselves; they are taking care of their health. . . .

Man, therefore, ought to be taught the due measure of loving, that is, in what measure he may love himself so as to be of service to himself. For that he does love himself, and does desire to do good to himself, nobody but a fool would doubt. He is to be taught, too, in what measure to love his body, so as to care for it wisely and within due limits. For it is equally manifest that he loves his body also, and desires to keep it safe and sound. And yet a man may have something that he loves better than the safety and soundness of his body. For many have been found voluntarily to suffer both pains and amputations of some of their limbs that they might obtain other objects which they valued more highly. But no one is to be told not to desire the safety and health of his body because there is something he desires more. For the miser, though he loves money, buys bread for himself—that is, he gives away money that he is very fond of and desires to heap up—but it is because he values more highly the bodily health which the bread sustains. . . .

Seeing, then, that there is no need of a command that every man should love himself and his own body—seeing, that is, that we love ourselves, and what is beneath us but connected with us, through a law of nature which has never been violated, and which is common to us with the beasts (for even the beasts love themselves and their own bodies)—it only remained necessary to lay injunctions upon us in regard to God above us, and our neighbor beside us. "Thou shalt love," He says, "the Lord thy God with all thy heart, and with all thy soul, and with all thy mind; and thou shalt love thy neighbor as thyself. On these two commandments hang all the law and the prophets" (Mt. 22:37-40). Thus the end of the commandment is love, and that twofold, the love of God and the love of our neighbor.

Now, if you take yourself in your entirety—that is, soul and body together—and your neighbor in his entirety, soul and body together (for man is made up of soul and body), you will find that none of the classes of things that are to be loved is overlooked in these two commandments. For though, when the love of God comes first, and the measure of our love for Him is prescribed in such terms that it is evident all other things are to find their center in Him, nothing seems to be said about our love for ourselves; yet when it is said, "Thou shalt love thy neighbor as thyself," it at once becomes evident that our love for ourselves has not been overlooked.

MAN'S LOVE AND GOD'S LOVE

Now he is a man of just and holy life who forms an unprejudiced estimate of things, and keeps his affections also under strict control, so that he neither loves what he ought not to love, nor fails to love what he ought to love, nor loves that more which ought to be loved less, nor loves that equally which ought to be loved either less or more, nor loves that less or more which ought to be loved equally.

No sinner is to be loved as a sinner; and every man is to be loved as a man for God's sake; but God is to be loved for His own sake. And if God is to be loved more than any man, each man ought to love God more than himself. Likewise we ought to love another man better than our own body, because all things are to be loved in reference to God, and another man can have fellowship with us in the enjoyment of God, whereas our body cannot; for the body only lives through the soul, and it is by the soul that we enjoy God.

Further, all men are to be loved equally. But since you cannot do good to all, you are to pay special regard to those who, by the accidents of time, or place, or circumstance, are brought into closer connection with you. For, suppose that you had a great deal of some commodity, and felt bound to give it away to somebody who had none, and that it could not be given to more than one person; if two persons presented themselves,

Op. cit., Chapters 27, 28, 29, 33, 4, 31, 32.

neither of whom had either from need or relationship a greater claim upon you than the other, you could do nothing fairer than choose by lot to which you would give what could not be given to both. Just so among men: since you cannot consult for the good of them all, you must take the matter as decided for you by a sort of lot, according as each man happens for the time being to be more closely connected with you.

Now of all who can with us enjoy God, we love partly those to whom we render services, partly those who render services to us, partly those who both help us in our need and in turn are helped by us, partly those upon whom we confer no advantage and from whom we look for none. We ought to desire, however, that they should all join with us in loving God, and all the assistance that we either give them or accept from them should tend to that one end. For in the theatres, dens of iniquity though they be, if a man is fond of a particular actor, and enjoys his art as a great or even as the very greatest good, he is fond of all who join with him in admiration of his favorite, not for their own sakes, but for the sake of him whom they admire in common; and the more fervent he is in his admiration, the more he works in every way he can to secure new admirers for him, and the more anxious he becomes to show him to others; and if he find anyone comparatively indifferent, he does all he can to excite his interest by urging his favorite's merits: if, however, he meet with anyone who opposes him, he is exceedingly displeased by such a man's contempt of his favorite, and strives in every way he can to remove it. Now, if this be so, what can we be expected to do who live in the fellowship of the love of God, the enjoyment of whom is true happiness of life, to whom all who love Him owe both their own existence and the love they bear Him, concerning whom we have no fear that anyone who comes to know Him will be disappointed in Him, and who desires our love, not for any gain to Himself, but that those who love Him may obtain an eternal reward, even Himself whom they love?

And hence it is that we love even our enemies. For we do not fear them, seeing they cannot take away from us what we love; but we pity them rather, because the more they hate us the more are they separated from Him whom we love. For if they would turn to Him, they must of necessity love Him as the supreme good, and love us too as partakers with them in so great a blessing. . . .

When you have joy of a man in God, it is God rather than man that you enjoy. For you enjoy Him by whom you are made happy, and you rejoice to have come to Him in whose presence you place your hope of joy. And accordingly, Paul says to Philemon, "Yea, brother, let me have joy of thee in the Lord" (Philem. 20). For if he had not added "in the Lord," but had only said, "Let me have joy of thee," he would have implied that he fixed his hope of happiness upon him . . . For when the thing that we love is near us, it is a matter of course that it should bring delight with it. And if you pass beyond this delight, and make it a means to that which you are permanently to rest in, you are using it, and it is an abuse of language to say that you enjoy it. But if you cling to it, and rest in it, finding your happiness complete in it, then you may be truly and properly said to enjoy it. And this we must never do except in the case of the . . . Supreme and Unchangeable Good.

*. . . Suppose we were wanderers in a strange country, and could not live happily away from our fatherland, and that we felt wretched in our wandering, and wishing to put an end to our misery, determined to return home. We find, however, that we must make use of some mode of conveyance, either by land or water, in order to reach that fatherland where our enjoyment is to commence. But the beauty of the country through which we pass, and the very pleasure of the motion, charm our hearts, and turning these things which we ought to use into objects of enjoyment, we become unwilling to hasten the end of our journey; and becoming engrossed in a factitious delight, our thoughts are diverted from that home whose delights would make us truly happy.

Such is a picture of our condition in this life of mortality. We have wandered far from God; and if we wish to return to our Father's home, this world must be used, not enjoyed, that so the invisible things of God may be clearly seen, being understood by the things that are made (Rom. 1:20)—that is, that by means of what is material and temporary we may lay hold upon that which is spiritual and eternal. . . .

When we say that we enjoy only that which we love for its own sake, and that nothing is a true object of enjoyment except that which makes us happy, and that all other things are for use, there seems still to be something that requires explanation. For God loves us, and Holy Scripture frequently sets before us the love He has towards us. In what way then does He love us? As objects of use or as objects of enjoyment? If He enjoys us, He must be in need of good from us, and no sane man will say that; for all the good we enjoy is either Himself, or what comes from Himself. And no one can be ignorant or in doubt as to the fact that the light stands in no need of the glitter of the things it has itself lit up. The Psalmist says most plainly, "I said to the Lord, Thou art my God, for Thou needest not my goodness" (Ps. 16:2). He does not enjoy

---

* This passage is inserted from an earlier chapter (Chapter 4), since the analogy it provides seems pertinent.

us then, but makes use of us. For if He neither enjoys nor uses us, I am at a loss to discover in what way he can love us.

But neither does he use after our fashion of using. For when we use objects, we do so with a view to the full enjoyment of the goodness of God. God, however, in His use of us, has reference to His own goodness. For it is because He is good we exist; and so far as we truly exist we are good. And further, because He is also just, we cannot with impunity be evil; and so far as we are evil, so far is our existence less complete. Now He is the first and supreme existence, who is altogether unchangeable, and who could say in the fullest sense of the words, "I AM THAT I AM," and "Thou shalt say to them, I AM hath sent me unto you" (Ex. 3:14); so that all other things that exist, both owe their existence entirely to Him, and are good only so far as He has given it to them to be so. That use, then, which God is said to make of us has no reference to his own advantage, but to ours only; and, so far as He is concerned, has reference only to His goodness. When we take pity upon a man and care for him, it is for his advantage we do so; but somehow or other our own advantage follows by a sort of natural consequence, for God does not leave the mercy we show to him who needs it to go without reward. Now this is our highest reward, that we should fully enjoy Him, and that all who enjoy Him should enjoy one another in Him.

FULFILLMENT IN THIS LIFE AND THEREAFTER

Of all, then, that has been said since we entered upon the discussion about things, this is the sum: that we should clearly understand that the fulfillment and the end of the Law, and of all Holy Scripture, is the love of an object which is to be enjoyed, and the love of an object which can enjoy that other in fellowship with ourselves. For there is no need of a command that each man should love himself. The whole temporal dispensation for our salvation, therefore, was framed by the providence of God that we might know this truth and be able to act upon it; and we ought to use that dispensation, not with such love and delight as if it were a good to rest in, but with a transient feeling rather, such as we have towards the road, or carriages, or other things that are merely means. Perhaps some other comparison can be found that will more suitably express the idea that we are to love the things by which we are borne only for the sake of that towards which we are borne.

Whoever, then, thinks that he understands the Holy Scriptures, or

Op. cit., from Chapters 35, 36, 38, and 39.

any part of them, but puts such an interpretation upon them as does not tend to build up this twofold love of God and our neighbor, does not yet understand them as he ought. If, on the other hand, a man draws a meaning from them that may be used for the building up of love, even though he does not happen upon the precise meaning which the author whom he reads intended to express in that place, his error is not pernicious, and he is wholly clear from the charge of deception. . . . He goes astray in much the same way as a man who by mistake quits the high road, but yet reaches through the fields the same place to which the road leads. He is to be corrected, however, and to be shown how much better it is not to quit the straight road, lest, if he get into a habit of going astray, he may sometimes take cross roads, or even go in the wrong direction altogether. . . .

These are the three things to which all knowledge and all prophecy are subservient: faith, hope, love.

But sight shall displace faith; and hope shall be swallowed up in that perfect bliss to which we shall come: love, on the other hand, shall wax greater when these others fail. For if we love by faith that which as yet we see not, how much more shall we love it when we begin to see! And if we love by hope that which as yet we have not reached, how much more shall we love it when we reach it! For there is this great difference between things temporal and things eternal, that a temporal object is valued more before we possess it, and begins to prove worthless the moment we attain it, because it does not satisfy the soul, which has its only true and sure resting-place in eternity: an eternal object, on the other hand, is loved with greater ardor when it is in possession than while it is still an object of desire, for no one in his longing for it can set a higher value on it than really belongs to it, so as to think it comparatively worthless when he finds it of less value than he thought; on the contrary, however high the value any man may set upon it when he is on his way to possess it, he will find it, when it comes into his possession, of higher value still.

And thus a man who is resting upon faith, hope and love, and who keeps a firm hold upon these, does not need the Scriptures except for the purpose of instructing others. Accordingly, many live without copies of the Scriptures, even in solitude, on the strength of these three graces. So that in their case, I think, the saying is already fulfilled: "Whether there be prophecies, they shall fail; whether there be tongues, they shall cease; whether there be knowledge, it shall vanish away" (I Cor. 13:8). Yet by means of these instruments (as they may be called), so great an edifice of faith and love has been built up in them, that, holding to what is perfect, they do not seek for what is only in part perfect—of course, I mean, so far as is possible in this life; for, in comparison with the future life, the life of no just and holy man is perfect here. Therefore the apostle says: "Now abideth faith, hope, love, these three; but the greatest of these is love" (I Cor. 13:13); because, when a man shall have reached the eternal world, while the other two graces will fail, love will remain greater and more assured.

STUDY QUESTIONS

1. How are happiness and man's chief good connected with each other?
2. What are the characteristics of the chief good, and why can they not be found in anything human?
3. How does a fourfold division of virtue correspond to four forms of love?
4. How is justice related to the other virtues?
5. What four kinds of things are loved by man, and why are precepts given only about two of these?
6. What are the restrictions under which man's love of neighbor ought to be kept?
7. In what sense should we love our own enemies?
8. How can the love of God for man be defined?
9. How does the possession of a temporal object differ from that of an eternal object?
10. Why is love greater than faith and hope?

Immanuel Kant

🙰🙰

THE MORAL LAW

🙰🙰

Biographical Note.　　IMMANUEL KANT (1724–1804) was born in the East Prussian capital of Koenigsberg into a lower-middle-class family. He completed high school (the German Gymnasium) with distinction at the age of sixteen and entered the University of Koenigsberg to study philosophy, mathematics, and natural science. Finishing his studies after six years, he worked for a time as a tutor to sons of the landed gentry near Koenigsberg.

In 1755, a dissertation submitted to the University of Koenigsberg earned him the master's degree (corresponding to today's Ph.D.); this was followed by his appointment as instructor. In this position he remained for fifteen years, lecturing an average of sixteen hours a week until he finally received a full professorship in logic and metaphysics.

The book through which he was to make his greatest contribution to philosophy, and which more than any other work of his century has influenced subsequent philosophic thought, was the *Critique of Pure Reason,* an essay on the foundations of metaphysics, published in 1781. Four years later his *Foundations of the Metaphysics of Morals* came out, from which a selection follows. Two other principal works are the *Critique of Practical Reason,* an essay on the foundations of ethics, and the *Critique of Judgment,* dealing with the foundations of aesthetics.

One event in his life stands out dramatically: the government's interference

From Immanuel Kant, *Fundamental Principles of the Metaphysic of Morals,* translated by Thomas Kingsmill Abbott, Fifth Edition, First Section, New York, Longmans, Green, and Co., 1895, with minor alterations.

with his academic freedom. In 1794 he received a written reprimand by order of the king, accusing him of misrepresentation of the Christian faith in his latest work on religion and warning him "to use his authority and talent only to further the sovereign's intentions." Kant promised to abstain in future from writing and lecturing on this subject. Justifying in a private paper the stand he took, he wrote: "Retraction and denial of one's inner conviction is despicable. But to keep quiet in a case like this is the duty of a subject, and if everything which one says must be true, this does not also make it a duty to say every truth in public." Three years later the king died, and Kant was no longer held to his promise. But by then he was seventy-three years old and had given up lecturing.

* * *

Introductory Note.   There is a presupposition underlying the moral philosophy of Kant that constitutes its self-evident foundation and from which the stern, rigid character of his moral demands can alone be understood. Goodness for him is an objective quality inherent in rationality—that is, a rational order of things, governed by universally valid laws. Man's goodness then is derivative in nature; it can only be defined in terms of its reflecting the objective goodness of rationality.

Many qualities that man may possess or acquire are praiseworthy; they contribute to and are even necessary for his goodness. But only one of them, Kant argues, can ever be considered absolutely good, good without qualification: that is the act of commitment to rationality. Such a commitment, indicating "not a mere wish, but the summoning of all means in our power," is called a *good will.*

Kant's concept of *duty* includes that of a good will. Duty is an injunction placed upon man by his aspiration for goodness, the injunction to accept the dictate of the good will as the primary motivating power in all his actions. But why is this so difficult an undertaking, perhaps the greatest challenge that man encounters in his life? As a creature of sense and sensation, man is not only committed to goodness by way of the good will, he is committed to happiness as well. And happiness has to do with the fulfillment of one's desires or inclinations; it is defined as "the concept of satisfaction of all inclinations." These two commitments may be but need not be in harmony, they are frequently opposed to each other. For to honor one of them fully can never be done except at the expense of the other.

It is then the sole aim of man's moral strivings to prove his highest allegiance to the dictates of duty in preference to those of happiness whenever conflict occurs. This highest allegiance Kant calls *respect for the law;* not any particular law, but law in general. Just as everything else in nature is subject to universal laws by which it is controlled, so also man as a moral being in his respect for the law feels called upon freely to subordinate his own will to the same principle of being governed by universally applicable laws, regardless of the price he has to pay in terms of happiness forfeited in the process. The Kantian moral law or, as he also calls it, "the categorical imperative" then demands: Always act in such a way that you do not contradict by your action the rational order of things—that is, an order governed by universally applicable laws.

Kant's principle of morality, of moral goodness, is as stern as it is uncompromising. He does not denounce happiness. On the contrary, to secure it conditionally he even considers a duty. But he also leaves no doubt that the fulfillment of one's inclinations in the pursuit of happiness must give way to the lead of the good will, even if this should result in "the thwarting of all inclinations."

THE GOOD WILL

Nothing can possibly be conceived in the world, or even out of it, which can be called good without qualification, except a GOOD WILL. Intelligence, wit, judgment, and the other *talents* of the mind, however they may be named, or courage, resolution, perseverance, as qualities of *temperament,* are undoubtedly good and desirable in many respects; but these gifts of nature may also become extremely bad and harmful if the will which is to make use of them, and which, therefore, constitutes what is called *character,* is not good. It is the same with the *gifts of fortune.* Power, riches, honor, even health, and the general well-being and contentment with one's condition which is called *happiness,* inspire pride, and often presumption, if there is not a good will to correct the influence of these on the mind, and with this also to rectify the whole principle of acting, and adapt it to its end; without mentioning that the sight of a being who is not adorned with a single feature of a pure and good will, yet enjoys unbroken prosperity, can never give pleasure to an impartial rational observer. Thus a good will appears to constitute the indispensable condition even of being worthy of happiness.

There are even some qualities which are of service to this good will itself, and may facilitate its action, yet which have no intrinsic unconditional worth, but always presuppose a good will, and this qualifies the esteem that we justly have for them, and does not permit us to regard them as absolutely good. Moderation in the affections and passions, self-control and calm deliberation are not only good in many respects, but even seem to constitute part of the *inner* worth of the person; but they are far from deserving to be called good without qualification, although they have been so unconditionally praised by the ancients. For without the principles of a good will, they may become extremely bad, and the coolness of a villain not only makes him far more dangerous, but also directly makes him more abominable in our eyes than he would have been without it.

A good will is good not because of what it performs or effects, not by its aptness for the attainment of some proposed end, but simply by virtue of its willing, that is, it is good in itself. And considered by itself it is to be esteemed much higher than all that can be brought about by it in favor of any inclination, nay, even of the sum total of all inclinations. Even if it should happen that, owing to special disfavor of fortune, or the niggardly provision of a step-motherly nature, this will should wholly lack power to accomplish its purpose, if with its greatest efforts it should yet achieve nothing, and there should remain only the good will (not, to be sure, a mere wish, but the summoning of all means in our power), then like a jewel, it would still sparkle in its own right, as a thing which has its whole worth in itself. Its usefulness or fruitlessness can neither add nor take away anything from this worth. It would be, as it were, only the setting to enable us to handle it the more conveniently in common commerce, or to attract to it the attention of those who are not yet connoisseurs, but not to recommend it to true connoisseurs, or to determine its worth.

There is, however, something so strange in this idea of the absolute worth of the mere will, in which no account is taken of its utility, that notwithstanding the thorough assent of even common reason to the idea, yet a suspicion must arise that it may perhaps really be the product of mere high-flown fancy, and that we may have misunderstood the purpose of nature in assigning reason as the governor of our will. Therefore we will examine this idea from this point of view.

THE FUNCTION OF REASON

In the natural constitution of an organized being, that is a being adapted suitably to the purposes of life, we assume it as a fundamental principle that no organ for any purpose will be found but what is also the fittest and best adapted for that purpose. Now in a being which has reason and a will, if the proper object of nature were its *preservation*, its *welfare*, in a word, its *happiness*, then nature would have hit upon a very bad arrangement in selecting the reason of the creature to carry out this purpose. For all the actions which the creature has to perform with a view to this purpose, and the whole rule of its conduct, would be far more surely prescribed to it by instinct, and that end would have been attained thereby much more certainly than it ever can be by reason. Should reason have been granted to this favored creature over and above, it would have served only to contemplate the happy constitution of its nature, to admire it, to congratulate itself thereon, and to feel thankful for it to the benificent cause, but not that it should subject its desires to that weak and delusive guidance, and meddle bunglingly with the purpose of nature. In a word, nature would have taken care that reason should not break forth into *practical use,* nor have the presumption, with its weak insight, to think out for itself the plan of happiness, and of the means of attaining it. Nature would have taken over not only the choice of ends, but also of the means, and with wise foresight would have entrusted both to instinct.

And, in fact, we find that the more a cultivated reason applies itself with deliberate purpose to the enjoyment of life and happiness, so much the more does the man fail of true contentment. And from this circumstance there arises in many, if they are candid enough to confess it, a certain degree of *misology,* that is, hatred of reason, especially in the case of those who are most experienced in the use of it. After calculating all the advantages they derive, I do not say from the invention of all the arts of common luxury, but even from the sciences (which seem to them to be after all only a luxury of the understanding), they nevertheless find that they have, in fact, only brought more trouble on their shoulders, rather than gained in happiness; and they end by envying, rather than despising, the more common stamp of men who keep closer to the guidance of mere instinct, and do not allow their reason much influence on their conduct. And this we must admit, that the judgment of those who would very much lower the lofty eulogies of the advantages which reason gives us in regard to the happiness and contentment of life, or who would even reduce them below zero, is by no means morose or ungrateful to the goodness with which the world is governed. Rather there lies at the root of these judgments the idea that our existence has a different and far nobler end, for which, and not for happiness, reason is properly intended, and which must, therefore, be regarded as the supreme condition to which the private ends of men must, for the most part, defer.

For as reason is not competent to guide the will with certainty in regard to its objects and the satisfaction of all our wants (which it to some extent even multiplies), this being an end to which an implanted instinct would have led with much greater certainty; and since, nevertheless, reason is imparted to us as a practical faculty, *i.e.* as one which is to have influence on the *will,* therefore reason's proper function must be to produce a *will*, not merely good as a *means* to something else, but *good in itself*, for which reason was absolutely necessary if nature has everywhere distributed capacities suitable to the functions they are to perform. This will then, though not indeed the sole and complete good, must be the supreme good and the condition of every other, even of the desire for happiness. Under these circumstances, there is nothing inconsistent with the wisdom of nature in the fact that the cultivation of reason, which is requisite for the first and unconditional purpose, does in many ways interfere, at least in this life, with the attainment of the second, which is always conditional, namely, happiness. Nay, it may even reduce it to nothing, without nature thereby failing of her purpose. For reason recognizes the establishment of a good will as its highest practical function, and in attaining this purpose is capable only of a contentment of its own proper kind, namely, that [contentment] from the attainment of an end, which end again is determined by reason only, notwithstanding that this may involve many a disappointment to the ends of inclination.

We have then to develop the concept of a will which is to be esteemed as good of itself without regard to anything else, a concept which exists already in common sense, requiring rather to be cleared up than to be taught, and which in estimating the total worth of our actions always takes the first place, and constitutes the condition of all the rest. In order to do this we will take the concept of DUTY, which includes that of a good will, although implying certain subjective restrictions and hindrances. These, however, far from concealing it, or rendering it unrecognizable, rather bring it out by contrast and make it shine forth so much the brighter.

DUTY AND MORAL WORTH

I omit here all actions which are already recognized as inconsistent with duty, although they may be useful for this or that purpose, for with these the question whether they are done *from duty* cannot arise at all, since they even conflict with it. I also set aside those actions which really conform to duty, but to which men have *no* direct *inclination*, performing them because they are impelled thereto by some other inclination. For in this case we can readily distinguish whether the action which agrees with duty is done *from duty*, or for some selfish purpose. It is much harder to make this distinction when the action accords with duty, and the subject has besides a *direct* inclination to it. For example, it is always a matter of duty that a dealer should not overcharge an inexperienced customer, and wherever there is much commerce the prudent merchant does not overcharge, but keeps a fixed price for everyone, so that a child buys of him as well as any other [customer]. Men are thus *honestly* served; but this is not enough to make us believe that the merchant has so acted from duty and from principles of honesty: his own advantage required it; it is out of the question in this case to suppose that he might besides have a direct inclination in favor of the purchasers, so that, as it were, from love he should give no advantage to one over another. Accordingly the action was done neither from duty nor from direct inclination, but merely for a selfish purpose.

On the other hand, it is a duty to preserve one's life; and in addition, every one has also a direct inclination to do so. But on this account the often anxious care which most men take for it has no intrinsic worth, and the maxim of doing so has no moral import. They preserve their lives *according to duty*, but not *from duty*. On the other hand, if adversity and hopeless sorrow have completely taken away the relish for life; if the unfortunate man, strong in mind, indignant at his fate rather than despondent or dejected, wishes for death, and yet preserves his life without loving it—not from inclination or fear, but from duty—then his maxim has a moral import.

To be charitable when we can is a duty; and besides this, there are many minds so sympathetically constituted that, without any other motive of vanity or self-interest, they find a pleasure in spreading joy around them, and can take delight in the contentment of others so far as it is their own work. But I maintain that in such a case an action of this kind, however dutiful, however amiable it may be, has nevertheless no true moral worth, but is on a level with other inclinations, *e.g.* the inclination to honor, which, if it is happily directed to that which is in fact of public utility and accordant with duty, and consequently honorable, deserves praise and encouragement, but not esteem. For the maxim lacks the moral import, namely, that such actions be done *from duty*, not from inclination. But assume that the mind of that philanthropist were clouded by sorrow of his own, extinguishing all sympathy with the lot of others, and that while he still has the power to benefit others in distress, he is not touched by their trouble because he is absorbed with his own; and now suppose that he tears himself out of this dead insensibility, and performs the action without any inclination to it, but simply from duty: only then has his action its genuine moral worth. Further still; if nature has put little sympathy in the heart of this or that man; if he, supposed to be an upright man, is by temperament cold and indifferent to the sufferings of others, perhaps because in respect of his own he is provided with the special gift of patience and fortitude, and supposes, or even requires, that others should have the same—and such a man would certainly not be the meanest product of nature—but if nature had not specially framed him for a philanthropist, would he not still find in himself a source from whence to give himself a far higher worth than that of a good natured temperament could be? Unquestionably. It is just in this that the moral worth of the character is brought out which is incomparably the highest of all, namely, that he is charitable, not from inclination, but from duty.

To secure one's own happiness is a duty, at least indirectly; for discontent with one's condition, under a pressure of many anxieties and amidst unsatisfied wants, might easily become a great *temptation to transgression of duty*. But here again, without looking to duty, all men have already the strongest and most intimate inclination to happiness, because it is just in this idea that all inclinations are combined in one total. But the precept of happiness is often of such a sort that it greatly interferes wih some inclinations, and yet a man cannot form any definite and certain conception of the sum of satisfaction of all of them which is called happiness. It is not then to be wondered at that a single inclination, definite both as to what it promises and as to the time within which it can be gratified, is often able to overcome such a fluctuating idea, and that a gouty patient, for instance, can choose to enjoy what he likes, and to suffer what he may, since, according to his calculation, on this occasion at least, he has not sacrificed the enjoyment of the present moment to a possibly mistaken expectation of a happiness which is supposed to be found in health. But even in this case, if general desire for happiness did not influence his will, and supposing that in his particular case health was not a necessary element in this calculation, there yet remains in this, as in all other cases, this law, namely, that he should promote his happiness not from inclination, but from duty, and by this would his conduct first acquire true moral worth.

It is in this way, undoubtedly, that we are to understand those passages of Scripture also in which we are commanded to love our neighbor, even our enemy. For love, as an affection, cannot be commanded, but benevolence for duty's sake may; even though we are not impelled to it by any inclination—nay, are even repelled by a natural and unconquerable aversion. This is love *in practice*, and not *in feeling*—a love which is seated in the will, and not in the propensities of sense—in principles of action and not in tender sympathy; and it is this love alone which can be commanded.

[Thus the first proposition of morality is that to have moral worth an action must be done from duty.]

The second proposition is: That an action done from duty derives its moral worth, *not from the purpose* which is to be attained by it, but from the maxim by which it is determined, and therefore does not depend on the realization of the object of the action, but merely on the *principle of volition* by which the action has taken place, without regard to any object of desire. It is clear from what precedes that the purposes which we may have in view in our actions, or their effects regarded as ends and incentives of the will, cannot give to actions any unconditional and moral worth. In what, then, can their worth lie, if it is not to consist in the will in relation to its hoped-for effect? It cannot lie anywhere but in the *principle of the will* without regard to the ends which can be attained by the action. For the will stands between its *a priori* principle, which is formal, and its *a posteriori* incentive, which is material, as between two roads, and as it must be determined by something, it follows that it must be determined by the formal principle of volition when an action is done from duty, in which case every material principle has been withdrawn from it.

The third proposition, which is the consequence of the two preceding, I would express thus: *Duty is the necessity of acting from respect for the law.* I may have *inclination* for an object as the effect of my proposed action, but I cannot have *respect* for it, just for this reason, that it is an effect and not an activity of the will. Similarly, I cannot have respect for inclination, whether my own or another's; I can at most, if my own, approve it; if another's, sometimes even love it; *i.e.* look on it as favorable to my own interest. It is only what is connected with my will as ground, by no means as an effect—what does not serve my inclination, but over-powers it, or at least in case of choice excludes it from its calculation—in other words, law itself, which can be an object of respect, and hence a command. Now an action done from duty must wholly exclude the influence of inclination, and with it every object of the will, so that nothing remains which can determine the will except objectively the *law,* and subjectively *pure respect* for this practical law, and conse-quently the maxim that I should follow this law even to the thwarting of all my inclinations.

Thus the moral worth of an action does not lie in the effect expected from it, nor in any principle of action which requires to borrow its motive from this expected effect. For all these effects—agreeableness of one's condition, and even the promotion of the happiness of others—could have been also brought about by other causes, so that for this there would have been no need of the will of a rational being; whereas it is in this will alone that the supreme and unconditional good can be found. The preeminent good which we call moral can therefore consist in nothing else than *the conception of the law* in itself, *which indeed can take place only in a rational being*, in so far as this conception and not the hoped-for effect, determines the will. This is a good which is already present in the person who acts accordingly, and we do not have to wait for it to appear first in the result.[1]

THE MORAL LAW

But what sort of law can that be, the conception of which must determine the will, even without paying any regard to the effect expected from it, in order that this will may be called good absolutely and without qualification? As I have deprived the will of every impulse which could arise to it from obedience to any particular law, there remains nothing but the universal conformity of its actions to law in general, which alone is to serve the will as a principle, *i.e.* I am never to act otherwise than so *that I could also will that my maxim should become a universal law*. Here now, it is the simple conformity to law in general, without assuming any particular law applicable to certain actions, that serves the will as its principle, and must so serve it, if duty is not to be a vain delusion and a chimerical notion. The common reason of men in its practical judgments perfectly coincides with this, and always holds in view the principle here suggested.

[1] It might be objected to me that I take refuge behind the word respect in an obscure feeling, instead of giving a clear solution of the question by a concept of reason. But although respect is a feeling, it is not a feeling *received* through influence from outside, but is *self-wrought* by a rational concept, and, therefore, is specifically distinct from all feelings of the former kind which may be referred either to inclination or fear. What I recognize directly as a law for myself, I recognize with respect. This merely signifies the consciousness that my will is *subordinate* to a law, without the intervention of other influences on my mind. The direct determination of the will by the law, and the consciousness of this is called *respect*, so that this is regarded as an *effect* of the law on the subject, and not as the *cause* of it. Respect is properly the conception of a worth which thwarts my self-love. Accordingly it is something which is considered neither as an object of inclination nor of fear, although it has something analogous to both. The *object* of respect is the *law* only, and that is the law which we impose *on ourselves*, and yet recognize as necessary in itself. As a law, we are subject to it without consulting self-love; as imposed by us on ourselves it is a result of our will. In the former regard it has an analogy to fear, in the latter to inclination. All respect for a person is really only respect for the law (of honesty, etc.) of which he gives us an example. Since we also look on the improvement of our talents as a duty, we imagine that we see in a person of talents, as it were, the *example of a law* (viz. to become like him in this by exercise), and this constitutes our respect. All so-called moral *interest* consists simply in *respect* for the law.

Let the question be, for example: May I when in distress make a promise with the intention not to keep it? I readily distinguish here between the two meanings which the question may have: Whether it is prudent, or whether it conforms to my duty to make a false promise. The former may undoubtedly often be the case. I see clearly indeed that it is not enough to extricate myself from a present difficulty by means of this subterfuge, but it must be well considered whether there may not hereafter spring from this lie much greater inconvenience than that from which I now free myself; for as, with all my supposed *cunning,* the consequences cannot be so easily foreseen but that credit once lost may be much more injurious to me than all the evil which I seek to avoid at present, it must be asked whether it would not be *more prudent* to act herein according to a universal maxim, and to make it a habit to promise nothing except with the intention of keeping it. But it is soon clear to me that such a maxim will still only be based on the fear of consequences. Now it is a wholly different thing to be truthful from duty, than to be so from apprehension of injurious consequences. In the first case, the very notion of the action implies a law for me; in the second case, I must first look about elsewhere to see what results may be combined with it which would affect myself. For to deviate from the principle of duty is beyond all doubt evil; but to be unfaithful to my maxim of prudence may often be very advantageous to me, although to abide by it is certainly safer. The shortest way, however, and an unerring one, to discover the answer to this question whether a lying promise is consistent with duty, is, to ask myself, Should I be content that my maxim (to extricate myself from difficulty by a false promise) should hold good as a universal law, for myself as well as for others? and should I be able to say to myself, "Everyone may make a deceitful promise when he finds himself in a difficulty from which he cannot otherwise extricate himself"? Then I presently become aware that while I can will the lie, I can by no means will that lying should be a universal law. For with such a law there would be no promises at all, since it would be in vain to allege my intention in regard to my future actions to those who would not believe this allegation, or if they overhastily did so would pay me back in my own coin. Hence my maxim, as soon as it should be made a universal law, would necessarily destroy itself.

I do not, therefore, need any far-reaching penetration to discern what I have to do in order that my will may be morally good. Inexperienced in the course of the world, incapable of being prepared for all its contingencies, I only ask myself: Canst thou also will that thy maxim should be a universal law? If not, then it must be rejected, and that not because of a disadvantage accruing from it to myself or even to others, but because it cannot enter as a principle into a possible universal legislation, and reason extorts from me immediate respect for such legislation. . . . To duty every other motive must give place, because it is the condition of a will being good *in itself,* and the worth of such a will is above everything.

Thus moral knowledge of common human reason has been traced to its principle. And although, no doubt, common human reason does not conceive it in such an abstract and universal form, but it always has it really before its eyes and uses it as the standard of its judgments. Here it would be easy to show how, with this compass in hand, men are well able to distinguish, in every case that occurs, what is good, what is bad, what is consistent or inconsistent with duty, if, without in the least teaching them anything new, we only, like Socrates, direct their attention to the principle they themselves employ; and that therefore we do not need science and philosophy to know what we should do to be honest and good, yea, even wise and virtuous.

STUDY QUESTIONS

1. Why is nothing unconditionally good except a good will?
2. What was and what was not the purpose of nature in providing man with reason as a practical faculty?
3. How does nature's unconditional purpose compare with its second purpose, the attainment of happiness?
4. What would be examples of acts done from duty as against those done according to duty?
5. In what sense could it happen that even happiness is promoted not from inclination, but from duty?
6. What does and what does not establish the moral worth of an action?
7. How can duty be defined and what is the "pre-eminent good"?
8. How can a law determining the will as absolutely good be formulated?
9. Why is a lying promise incompatible with the moral law?

John Stuart Mill

PLEASURE AS THE GOOD

Biographical Note.   JOHN STUART MILL (1806–1873), along with his father James, is best known as one of the moving spirits in the intellectual history of British liberalism. Educated exclusively by his father, John Stuart at the age of seventeen entered the services of the East-India Company, a trading monopoly with political authority over India. He rose from a junior clerk, working under his father, to have charge of the company's relations with the native Indian states, and on the dissolution of the company in 1858 he was head of the examiner's office. Subsequently he served a term as a Member of Parliament.

Mill wrote prodigiously in the areas of economics and philosophy, with major concentration on political and social thought. Most widely read are his essays *On Liberty* (1854) and *Utilitarianism* (1863); he also wrote a two-volume work, *A System of Logic* (1843), formulating the method of scientific investigation, and his *Autobiography,* published posthumously, which besides giving the story of his unique education brilliantly presents a picture of his age.

* * *

Introductory Note.   John Stuart Mill's moral philosophy, which he designated as "utilitarianism," is so closely connected with his social and

From John Stuart Mill, *Utilitarianism,* 14th impression. London, New York and Bombay, Longmans, Green & Co., 1907, most of Chapter II, "What Utilitarianism Is."

political philosophy that it may be considered an outgrowth of it. More than anything else he was dedicated to social reform—to a radical change from the existing conditions of "wretched education and wretched social arrangements" which plagued the society of early 19th century England. But to impress the general public with the urgency for social action and to bring such action about required a moral philosophy that would define necessary legislation as society's moral duty, clearly and irrefutably establishing the need for reform on moral grounds. Mill found a recent system of ethics that had been developed for precisely this reason: it was a work by Jeremy Bentham, eminent British legal philosopher and friend of Mill's father, *An Introduction to the Principles of Morals and Legislation,* published in 1789. Here Bentham formulated his so-called "principle of utility," which made the greatest happiness of the greatest number the standard for moral judgment. To present this principle in its most favorable light while deviating from Bentham in some aspects of its interpretation was Mill's main objective in his *Utilitarianism.*

Basically he agrees with Kant that it is the business of ethics to sharpen man's awareness of a possible conflict between the requirements of his own happiness and his dedication to duty or virtue. Also, his definition of happiness in terms of pleasure combined with the absence of pain does not differ much from Kant's understanding of it as the sum total of satisfaction of all inclinations. Mill's concept of duty, however, would hardly be acceptable to Kant, nor would Kant agree with his presentation of the conflict as essentially soluble.

Duty to Mill implies a demand for man's dedication to the happiness of others, even the general happiness of mankind, which a person's concern for his own private happiness cannot be allowed to affect adversely. To be morally good, then, an action, be it an act of an individual or an act of legislation, must be directed toward increasing the sum total of the happiness of those who are affected by it. This does not mean that all people "should fix their minds upon so wide a generality as the world, or society at large." In the great majority of cases it would suffice for the most virtuous man to promote the interests of a few, provided of course that this does not violate the legitimate rights of others. But accepting Mill's principle for moral discrimination does mean that moral progress is conceived exclusively in terms of a decrease of mankind's overall suffering and an increase of its overall enjoyment of life.

In the text that follows, Mill's major effort is devoted to a clarification of what a happy existence really consists of and why to strive for it as a universal goal and highest good constitutes man's most worthwhile endeavor, from which "every mind sufficiently intelligent and generous to bear a part, however small and inconspicuous, will draw a noble enjoyment which he would not for any bribe in the form of selfish indulgence consent to be without."

THE PRINCIPLE OF UTILITY DEFINED

The creed which accepts as the foundation of morals *utility,* or the *greatest happiness principle,* holds that actions are right in in proportion as they tend to promote happiness, wrong as they tend to produce the reverse of happiness. By 'happiness' is intended pleasure, and the absence of pain; by 'unhappiness,' pain, and the privation of pleasure. To give a clear view of the moral standard set up by the theory, much more requires to be said; in particular, what things it includes in the ideas of pain and pleasure; and to what extent this is left an open question. But these supplementary explanations do not affect the theory of life on which this theory of morality is grounded—namely, that pleasure, and freedom from pain, are the only things desirable as ends; and that all desirable things (which are as numerous in the utilitarian as in any other scheme) are desirable either for the pleasure inherent in themselves, or as means to the promotion of pleasure and the prevention of pain.

INFERIOR AND SUPERIOR PLEASURES

Now such a theory of life excites in many minds, and among them in some of the most estimable in feeling and purpose, inveterate dislike. To suppose that life has (as they express it) no higher end than pleasure —no better and nobler object of desire and pursuit—they designate as utterly mean and groveling; as a doctrine worthy only of swine, to whom the followers of Epicurus were, at a very early period, contemptuously likened; and modern holders of the doctrine are occasionally made the subject of equally polite comparisons by its German, French, and English assailants.

When thus attacked, the Epicureans have always answered that it is not they, but their accusers, who represent human nature in a degrading light; since the accusation supposes human beings to be capable of no pleasures except those of which swine are capable. If this supposition were true, the charge could not be gainsaid, but would then be no longer an imputation; for if the sources of pleasure were precisely the same to human beings and to swine, the rule of life which is good enough for the one would be good enough for the other. The comparison of the Epicurean life to that of beasts is felt as degrading, precisely because a beast's pleasures do not satisfy a human being's conceptions of happiness. Human beings have faculties more elevated than the animal appetites, and when once made conscious of them, do not regard anything as happiness which does not include their gratification.

I do not, indeed, consider the Epicureans to have been by any means faultless in drawing out their scheme of consequences from the utilitarian principle. To do this in any sufficient manner, many Stoic, as well as Christian elements require to be included. But there is no known Epicurean theory of life which does not assign to the pleasures of the intellect, of the feelings and imagination, and of the moral sentiments, a much higher value as pleasures than to those of mere sensation. It must be admitted, however, that utilitarian writers in general have placed the superiority of mental over bodily pleasures chiefly in the greater permanency, safety, uncostliness, etc., of the former—that is, in their circumstantial advantages rather than in their intrinsic nature. And on all these points utilitarians have fully proved their case; but they might have taken the other, and, as it may be called, higher ground, with entire consistency. It is quite compatible with the principle of utility to recognize the fact, that some *kinds* of pleasure are more desirable and more valuable than others. It would be absurd that while, in estimating all other things, quality is considered as well as quantity, the estimation of pleasures should be supposed to depend on quantity alone.

If I am asked what I mean by difference of quality in pleasures, or what makes one pleasure more valuable than another, merely as a pleasure, except its being greater in amount, there is but one possible answer. Of two pleasures, if there be one to which all or almost all who have experience of both give a decided preference, irrespective of any feeling of moral obligation to prefer it, that is the more desirable pleasure. If one of the two is, by those who are competently acquainted with both, placed so far above the other that they prefer it, even though knowing it to be attended with a greater amount of discontent, and would not resign it for any quantity of the other pleasure which their nature is capable of, we are justified in ascribing to the preferred enjoyment a superiority in quality, so far outweighing quantity as to render it, in comparison, of small account.

Now it is an unquestionable fact that those who are equally acquainted with, and equally capable of appreciating and enjoying both, do give a most marked preference to the manner of existence which employs their higher faculties. Few human creatures would consent to be changed into any of the lower animals, for a promise of the fullest allowance of a beast's pleasures; no intelligent human being would consent to be a fool, no instructed person would be an ignoramus, no person of feeling and conscience would be selfish and base, even though they should be persuaded that the fool, the dunce, or the rascal is better satisfied with his lot than they are with theirs. They would not resign what they possess more than he, for the most complete satisfaction of all the desires which they have in common with him. If they ever fancy they would, it is only in cases of unhappiness so extreme, that to escape from it they would exchange their lot for almost any other, however undesirable in their own eyes.

A being of higher faculties requires more to make him happy, is capable probably of more acute suffering, and is certainly accessible to it at more points, than one of an inferior type; but in spite of these liabilities, he can never really wish to sink into what he feels to be a lower grade of existence. We may give what explanation we please of this unwillingness; we may attribute it to pride, a name which is given indiscriminately to some of the most and to some of the least estimable feelings of which mankind are capable; we may refer it to the love of liberty and personal independence, an appeal to which was to the Stoics one of the most effective means for the inculcation of it; to the love of power, or to the love of excitement, both of which do really enter into and contribute to it: but its most appropriate appellation is a sense of dignity, which all human beings possess in one form or another, and in some, though by no means in exact, proportion to their higher faculties, and which is so essential a part of the happiness of those in whom it is strong, that nothing which conflicts with it could be, otherwise than momentarily, an object of desire to them.

Whoever supposes that this preference takes place at a sacrifice of happiness—that the superior being, in anything like equal circumstances, is not happier than the inferior—confounds the two very different ideas of happiness and content. It is indisputable that the being whose capacities of enjoyment are low, has the greatest chance of having them fully satisfied; and a highly endowed being will always feel that any happiness which he can look for, as the world is constituted, is imperfect. But he can learn to bear its imperfections, if they are at all bearable; and they will not make him envy the being who is indeed unconscious of the imperfections, but only because he feels not at all the good which those imperfections qualify. It is better to be a human being dissatisfied than a pig satisfied; better to be Socrates dissatisfied than a fool satisfied. And if the fool, or the pig, are of different opinion, it is because they only know their own side of the question. The other party to the comparison knows both sides.

It may be objected that many who are capable of the higher pleasures, occasionally, under the influence of temptation, postpone them to the lower. But this is quite compatible with a full appreciation of the intrinsic superiority of the higher. Men often, from infirmity of character, make their election for the nearer good, though they know it to be the less valuable; and this no less when the choice is between two bodily pleasures, than when it is between bodily and mental. They pursue sensual indulgences to the injury of health, though perfectly aware that health is the greater good.

It may be further objected that many who begin with youthful enthusiasm for everything noble, as they advance in years sink into indolence and selfishness. But I do not believe that those who undergo this very common change, voluntarily choose the lower description of pleasures in preference to the higher. I believe that before they devote themselves exclusively to the one, they have already become incapable of the other. Capacity for the nobler feelings is in most natures a very tender plant, easily killed, not only by hostile influences, but by mere want of sustenance; and in the majority of young persons it speedily dies away if the occupations to which their position in life has devoted them, and the society into which it has thrown them, are not favorable to keeping that higher capacity in exercise. Men lose their high aspirations as they lose their intellectual tastes, because they have not time or opportunity for indulging them; and they addict themselves to inferior pleasures not because they deliberately prefer them, but because they are either the only ones to which they have access, or the only ones which they are any longer capable of enjoying. It may be questioned whether anyone who has remained equally susceptible to both classes of pleasures, ever knowingly and calmly preferred the lower; though many, in all ages, have broken down in an ineffectual attempt to combine both. . . .

THE PRINCIPLE OF UTILITY REFORMULATED

According to the *greatest happiness principle,* as above explained, the ultimate end, with reference to and for the sake of which all other things are desirable (whether we are considering our own good or that of other people), is an existence exempt as far as possible from pain, and as rich as possible in enjoyments, both in point of quantity and quality; the test of quality, and the rule for measuring it against quantity, being the preference felt by those who in their opportunities of experience, to which must be added their habits of self-consciousness and self-observation, are best furnished with the means of comparison. This, being, according to the utilitarian opinion, the end of human action, is necessarily also the standard of morality; which may accordingly be defined as the rules and precepts for human conduct, by the observation of which an existence such as has been described might be, to the greatest extent possible, secured to all mankind; and not to them only, but, so far as the nature of things admits, to the whole sentient creation.

ELEMENTS OF HAPPINESS

Against this doctrine, however, rises another class of objectors, who say that happiness, in any form, cannot be the rational purpose of human life and action; because, in the first place, it is unattainable: and they contemptuously ask, What right hast thou to be happy? . . . Next, they say that men can do *without* happiness; that all noble human beings have felt this, and could not have become noble but by learning the lesson of *Entsagen,* or renunciation; which lesson, thoroughly learned and submitted to, they affirm to be the beginning and necessary condition of all virtue.

The first of these objections would go to the root of the matter were it well founded; for if no happiness is to be had at all by human beings, the attainment of it cannot be the end of morality, or of any rational conduct. . . . When, however, it is thus positively asserted to be impossible that human life should be happy, the assertion, if not something like a verbal quibble, is at least an exaggeration. If by happiness be meant a continuity of highly pleasurable excitement, it is evident enough that this is impossible. A state of exalted pleasure lasts only moments, or in some cases, and with some intermissions, hours and days, and is the occasional brilliant flash of enjoyment, not its permanent and steady flame. Of this the philosophers who have taught that happiness is the end of life were as fully aware as those who taunt them. The happiness which they meant was not a life of rapture; but moments of such, in an existence made up of few and transitory pains, many and various pleasures, with a decided predominance of the active over the passive, and having as the foundation of the whole, not to expect more from life than it is capable of bestowing. A life thus composed, to those who have been fortunate enough to obtain it, has always appeared worthy of the name of happiness. And such an existence is even now the lot of many, during some considerable portion of their lives. The present wretched education, and wretched social arrangements, are the only real hindrance to its being attainable by almost all.

The objectors perhaps may doubt whether human beings, if taught to consider happiness as the end of life, would be satisfied with such a moderate share of it. But great numbers of mankind have been satisfied with much less. The main constituents of a satisfied life appear to be two, either of which by itself is often found sufficient for the purpose: tranquillity and excitement. With much tranquillity, many find that they can be content with very little pleasure; with much excitement many can reconcile themselves to a considerable quantity of pain. There is assuredly no inherent impossibility in enabling even the mass of mankind to unite both; since the two are so far from being incompatible that they are in natural alliance, the prolongation of either being a preparation for, and exciting a wish for, the other. It is only those in whom indolence amounts to a vice, that do not desire excitement after an interval of repose; it is only those in whom the need of excitement is a disease, that feel the tranquillity which follows excitement dull and insipid, instead of pleasurable in direct proportion to the excitement which preceded it.

When people who are tolerably fortunate in their outward lot do not find in life sufficient enjoyment to make it valuable to them, the cause generally is, caring for nobody but themselves. To those who have neither public nor private affections, the excitements of life are much curtailed, and in any case dwindle in value as the time approaches when all selfish interests must be terminated by death; while those who leave after them objects of personal affection, and especially those who have also cultivated a fellow-feeling with the collective interests of mankind, retain as lively an interest in life on the eve of death as in the vigor of youth and health.

Next to selfishness, the principal cause which makes life unsatisfactory, is want of mental cultivation. A cultivated mind—I do not mean that of a philosopher, but any mind to which the fountains of knowledge have been opened, and which has been taught, in any tolerable degree, to exercise its faculties—finds sources of inexhaustible interest in all that surrounds it; in the objects of nature, the achievements of art, the imaginations of poetry, the incidents of history, the ways of mankind past and present, and their prospects in the future. It is possible, indeed, to become indifferent to all this, and that too without having exhausted a thousandth part of it; but only when one has had from the beginning no moral or human interest in these things, and has sought in them only the gratification of curiosity.

OBSTRUCTIONS TO HAPPINESS

There is absolutely no reason in the nature of things why an amount of mental culture sufficient to give an intelligent interest in these objects of contemplation, should not be the inheritance of everyone born in a civilized country. As little is there an inherent necessity that any human being should be a selfish egotist, devoid of every feeling or care but those which center in his own miserable individuality. Something far superior to this is sufficiently common even now, to give ample earnest of what the human species may be made. Genuine private affections, and a sincere interest in the public good, are possible, though in unequal degrees, to every rightly brought up human being. In a world in which there is so much to interest, so much to enjoy, and so much also to correct and improve, everyone who has this moderate amount of moral and intellectual requisites is capable of an existence which may be called enviable; and unless such a person, through bad laws, or subjection to the will of others, is denied the liberty to use the sources of happiness within his reach, he will not fail to find this enviable existence, if he escape the positive evils of life, the great sources of physical and mental suffering—such as indigence, disease, and the unkindness, worthlessness, or premature loss of objects of affection.

The main stress of the problem lies, therefore, in the contest with these calamities, from which it is a rare good fortune entirely to escape; which, as things now are, cannot be obviated, and often cannot be in any material degree mitigated. Yet no one whose opinion deserves a moment's consideration can doubt that most of the great positive evils of the world are in themselves removable, and will, if human affairs continue to improve, be in the end reduced within narrow limits.

Poverty, in any sense implying suffering, may be completely extinguished by the wisdom of society, combined with the good sense and providence of individuals. Even that most intractable of enemies, disease, may be indefinitely reduced in dimensions by good physical and moral education, and proper control of noxious influences; while the progress of science holds out a promise for the future of still more direct conquests over this detestable foe. And every advance in that direction relieves us from some, not only of the chances which cut short our own lives, but, what concerns us still more, which deprive us of those in whom our happiness is wrapped up. As for vicissitudes of fortune, and other disappointments connected with worldly circumstances, these are principally the effect either of gross imprudence, of ill-regulated desires, or of bad or imperfect social institutions. All the grand sources, in short, of human suffering are in a great degree, many of them almost entirely, conquerable by human care and effort; and though their removal is grievously slow—though a long succession of generations will perish in the breach before the conquest is completed, and this world becomes all that, if will and knowledge were not wanting, it might easily be made— yet every mind sufficiently intelligent and generous to bear a part, however small and inconspicuous, in the endeavor, will draw a noble enjoyment from the contest itself, which he would not for any bribe in the form of selfish indulgence consent to be without.

"UNIVERSAL" HAPPINESS AS MORAL STANDARD

And this leads to the true estimation of what is said by the objectors concerning the possibility, and the obligation, of learning to do without happiness. Unquestionably it is possible to do without happiness; it is done involuntarily by nineteen-twentieths of mankind, even in those parts of our present world which are least deep in barbarism; and it often has to be done voluntarily by the hero or the martyr, for the sake of something which he prizes more than his individual happiness. But this something, what is it, unless the happiness of others, or some of the requisites of happiness? It is noble to be capable of resigning entirely one's own portion of happiness or chances of it: but, after all, this self-sacrifice must be for some end; it is not its own end; and if we are told that its end is not happiness, but virtue, which is better than happiness, I ask, would the sacrifice be made if the hero or martyr did not believe that it would earn for others immunity from similar sacrifices? Would it be made if he thought that his renunciation of happiness for himself would produce no fruit for any of his fellow creatures, but to make their lot like his, and place them also in the condition of persons who have renounced happiness? All honor to those who can abnegate for themselves the personal enjoyment of life, when by such renunciation they contribute worthily to increase the amount of happiness in the world; but he who does it, or professes to do it for any other purpose, is no more deserving of admiration than the ascetic mounted on his pillar. He may be an inspiriting proof of what men *can* do, but assuredly not an example of what they *should*.

Though it is only in a very imperfect state of the world's arrangements that anyone can best serve the happiness of others by the absolute sacrifice of his own, yet so long as the world is in that imperfect state, I fully acknowledge that the readiness to make such a sacrifice is the highest virtue which can be found in man. I will add that in this condition of the world, paradoxical as the assertion may be, the conscious ability to do without happiness gives the best prospect of realizing such happiness as is attainable. For nothing except that consciousness can raise a person above the chances of life, by making him feel that, let fate and fortune do their worst, they have not power to subdue him; which, once felt, frees him from excess of anxiety concerning the evils of life, and enables him, like many a Stoic in the worst times of the Roman Empire, to cultivate in tranquillity the sources of satisfaction accessible to him, without concerning himself about the uncertainty of their duration any more than about their inevitable end. . . .

I must again repeat, what the assailants of utilitarianism seldom have the justice to acknowledge, that the happiness which forms the utilitarian standard of what is right in conduct, is not the agent's own happiness, but that of all concerned. As between his own happiness and that of others, utilitarianism requires him to be as strictly impartial as a disinterested and benevolent spectator. In the golden rule of Jesus of Nazareth, we read the complete spirit of the ethics of utility. To do as one would be done by, and to love one's neighbor as oneself, constitute the ideal perfection of utilitarian morality.

As the means of making the nearest approach to this ideal, utility would enjoin, first, that laws and social arrangements should place the happiness, or (as speaking practically it may be called) the interest, of every individual, as nearly as possible in harmony with the interest of the whole; and secondly, that education and opinion, which have so vast a power over human character, should so use that power as to establish in the mind of every individual an indissoluble association between his own happiness and the good of the whole; especially between his own happiness and the practice of such modes of conduct, negative and positive, as regard for the universal happiness prescribes; so that not only he may be unable to conceive the possibility of happiness to himself, consistently with conduct opposed to the general good, but also that a direct impulse to promote the general good may be in every individual one of the habitual motives of action, and the sentiments connected therewith may fill a large and prominent place in every human being's sentient existence. . . .

TWO MOTIVES FOR MORAL ACTIONS

The objectors to utilitarianism cannot always be charged with representing it in a discreditable light. On the contrary, those among them who entertain anything like a just idea of its disinterested character sometimes find fault with its standard as being too high for humanity. They say it is exacting too much to require that people shall always act from the inducement of promoting the general interests of society. But this is to mistake the very meaning of a standard of morals, and to confound the rule of action with the motive of it. It is the business of ethics to tell us what are our duties, or by what test we may know them; but no system of ethics requires that the sole motive of all we do shall be a feeling of duty; on the contrary, ninety-nine hundredths of all our actions are done from other motives, and rightly so done, if the rule of duty does not condemn them. . . .

He who saves a fellow creature from drowning does what is morally right, whether his motive be duty, or the hope of being paid for his trouble; he who betrays the friend that trusts him, is guilty of a crime even if his object be to serve another friend to whom he is under greater obligation. But to speak only of actions done from the motive of duty, and in direct obedience to principle: it is a misapprehension of the utilitarian mode of thought, to conceive it as implying that people should fix their minds upon so wide a generality as the world, or society at large. The great majority of good actions are intended not for the benefit of the world, but for that of individuals, of which the good of the world is made up; and the thoughts of the most virtuous man need not on these occasions travel beyond the particular persons concerned, except so far as is necessary to assure himself that in benefiting them he is not violating the rights—that is, the legitimate and authorized expectations—of anyone else.

The multiplication of happiness is, according to the utilitarian ethics, the object of virtue: the occasions on which any person (except one in a thousand) has it in his power to do this on an extended scale, in other words to be a public benefactor, are but exceptional; and on these occasions alone is he called on to consider public utility; in every other case, private utility, the interest or happiness of some few persons, is all he has to attend to. Those alone, the influence of whose actions extends to society in general, need concern themselves habitually about so large an object.

In the case of abstinences indeed—of things which people forbear to do from moral considerations, though the consequences in the particular case might be beneficial—it would be unworthy of an intelligent agent not to be consciously aware that the action is of a class which, if practiced generally, would be generally injurious, and that this is the ground of the obligation to abstain from it. The amount of regard for the public interest implied in this recognition is no greater than is demanded by every system of morals; for they all enjoin to abstain from whatever is manifestly pernicious to society.

STUDY QUESTIONS

1. How does the principle of utility discriminate between right and wrong?
2. How is superiority of one pleasure over another defined?
3. In what way can the distinction between superior and inferior pleasures be applied to human life and happiness?
4. Why is it better to be a human being dissatisfied than a pig satisfied?
5. In what sense is and in what sense is not happiness attainable by almost all?
6. What is the role of tranquillity and excitement within the happy life?
7. How can some of the principal causes for an unsatisfactory life be traced to the individual himself?
8. Why may the great positive evils of the world which are beyond individual control be reducible within narrow limits?
9. How is the pursuit of one's own happiness connected with that of the happiness of others?
10. Why is "private utility" rather than "public utility" sufficient as the legitimate concern of most people?

William James

🮑🮑🮑🮑🮑🮑🮑🮑🮑🮑🮑🮑🮑🮑🮑🮑🮑🮑🮑🮑🮑🮑🮑🮑🮑🮑🮑🮑🮑🮑🮑🮑🮑🮑🮑🮑🮑

THE ENERGIES OF MEN

🮑🮑🮑🮑🮑🮑🮑🮑🮑🮑🮑🮑🮑🮑🮑🮑🮑🮑🮑🮑🮑🮑🮑🮑🮑🮑🮑🮑🮑🮑🮑🮑🮑🮑🮑🮑🮑

Biographical Note.　　WILLIAM JAMES (1842–1910), renowned American psychologist and philosopher, was born in New York City, the first son of the Reverend Henry James, friend of Emerson and Thoreau and well known in his lifetime as both author and theologian. William received his early schooling in New York and in Europe, the latter where his family spent a number of years. At the age of nineteen he entered Harvard, and after some interruptions through research trips abroad, completed his studies at Harvard with a doctorate in medicine eight years later. He began his academic career—also at Harvard—in 1872, as instructor in physiology, but soon changed over to psychology in which field he published his first great work, *Principles of Psychology* (1890). A second transition occurred when he moved to the field of philosophy, as manifest in his next major publication, *The Will to Believe and Other Essays* (1897), and in his classic treatise in the philosophy and psychology of religion, *The Varieties of Religious Experience* (1902). Probably his best known work is his book on *Pragmatism* (1907), identifying the type of philosophy with which he associated himself and of which he is now counted a prominent exponent.

* * *

Introductory Note. Ever since St. Paul's desperate complaint, "I do not do the good I want, but the evil I do not want is what I do" (Romans 7:19), Western moral thought has been most keenly aware that the problem of human goodness is also the problem of man's power to carry out the demands of goodness. Knowledge of the good alone was recognized as insufficient (though necessary) for attaining the good as long as such knowledge was not matched by a power strong enough to implement it. And St. Paul's observation was echoed again and again that what was wrong with the world of man was connected less with the lack of moral vision than with the feebleness of man's power to comply with this vision.

William James in his epoch-making investigation into the nature of religious experience came upon the discovery that what is called religious conversion invariably expresses itself, if it is genuine, in a new unification of all of man's energies, opening up a pattern of regenerated activities undreamed of by the person involved. Further research convinced him that such reactivating or reenergizing of man's available powers can happen equally under other quasi-emergency conditions and led him to the hypothesis, formulated in the following selection, that there are at the disposal of man, every man, latent physical and mental powers which apart from rare exceptions he habitually fails to use.

Throughout the history of our civilization, so James would claim, we have developed a "habit of inferiority to our full self," which must take the blame for many of the past shortcomings and deficiencies of human kind. Instead of being a nation of weaklings, therefore, of people who continuously live far below their optimum in powers used for the good of all, we might attain to heroic proportions if we only learned to unravel two apparent secrets of human life, to solve two problems of farthest reaching importance: 1. What are the limits of latent power—muscular, emotional, moral, spiritual—inherent in every individual? 2. Through what kind of educational devices might such powers be made available on a national scale?

In the essay that follows, James does no more than raise the question, trying to find sufficient support in common experience to demonstrate it as a genuine problem, worthy of further inquiry. Unfortunately, what we may call his "philosophy of heroism" remained a wholly unfinished project with him; some readers will feel it well deserves to be taken out of the "cold storage" in which it has now been held for more than half a century.

ENERGY RESERVES

Everyone knows what it is to start a piece of work, either intellectual or muscular. . . . And everybody knows what it is to "warm up" to his job. The process of warming up gets particularly striking in the phenomenon known as "second wind." On usual occasions we make a practice of stopping an occupation as soon as we meet the first effective layer (so to call it) of fatigue. We have then walked, played, or worked "enough," so we desist. That amount of fatigue is an efficacious obstruction on this side of which our usual life is cast. But if an unusual necessity forces us to press onward, a surprising thing occurs. The fatigue gets worse up to a certain critical point, when gradually or suddenly it passes away, and we are fresher than before. We have evidently tapped a level of new energy, masked until then by the fatigue-obstacle usually obeyed. There may be layer after layer of this experience. A third and a fourth "wind" may supervene. Mental activity shows the phenomenon as well as physical, and in exceptional cases we may find, beyond the very extremity of fatigue-distress, amounts of ease and power that we never dreamed ourselves to own—sources of strength habitually not taxed at all, because habitually we never push through the obstruction, never pass those early critical points.

For many years I have mused on the phenomenon of second wind, trying to find a physiological theory. It is evident that our organism has stored-up reserves of energy that are ordinarily not called upon, but that may be called upon: deeper and deeper strata of combustible or explosible material, discontinuously arranged, but ready for use by anyone who probes so deep, and repairing themselves by rest as well as do the superficial strata. Most of us continue living unnecessarily near our surface. Our energy-budget is like our nutritive budget. Physiologists say that a man is in "nutritive equilibrium" when day after day he neither gains nor loses weight. But the odd thing is that this condition may obtain on astonishingly different amounts of food. Take a man in nutritive equilibrium, and systematically increase or lessen his rations. In the first case he will begin to gain weight, in the second case to lose it. The change will be greatest on the first day, less on the second, less still on the third; and so on, till he has gained all that he will gain, or lost all that he will lose, on that altered diet. He is now in nutritive equilibrium again, but with a new weight; and this neither lessens nor increases because his various combustion-processes have adjusted themselves to the changed dietary. He gets rid, in one way or another, of just as much N, C, H, etc., as he takes in *per diem*.

Just so one can be in what I might call "efficiency-equilibrium" (neither gaining nor losing power when once the equilibrium is reached) on astonishingly different quantities of work, no matter in what direction the work may be measured. It may be physical work, intellectual work, moral work, or spiritual work.

Of course there are limits: the trees don't grow into the sky. But the plain fact remains that men the world over possess amounts of resource which only very exceptional individuals push to their extremes of use. But the very same individual, pushing his energies to their extreme, may in a vast number of cases keep the pace up day after day, and find no "reaction" of a bad sort, so long as decent hygienic conditions are preserved. His more active rate of energizing does not wreck him; for the organism adapts itself, and as the rate of waste augments, augments correspondingly the rate of repair. . . .

THE PROBLEM OF MAXIMUM USE

If my reader will put together these two conceptions, first, that few men live at their maximum of energy, and second, that anyone may be in vital equilibrium at very different rates of energizing, he will find, I think, that a very pretty practical problem of national economy, as well as of individual ethics, opens upon his view. In rough terms, we may say that a man who energizes below his normal maximum fails by just so much to profit by his chance at life; and that a nation filled with such men is inferior to a nation run at higher pressure. The problem is, then, how can men be trained up to their most useful pitch of energy? And how can nations make such training most accessible to all their sons and daughters. This, after all, is only the general problem of education, formulated in slightly different terms.

"Rough" terms, I said just now, because the words "energy" and "maximum" may easily suggest only *quantity* to the reader's mind, whereas in measuring the human energies of which I speak, qualities as well as quantities have to be taken into account. Everyone feels that his total *power* rises when he passes to a higher qualitative level of life.

Writing is higher than walking, thinking is higher than writing, deciding higher than thinking, deciding "no" higher than deciding "yes" —at least the man who passes from one of these activities to another will usually say that each later one involves a greater element of *inner work* than the earlier ones, even though the total heat given out or the footpounds expended by the organism, may be less. Just how to conceive this inner work physiologically is as yet impossible, but psychologically we all know what the word means. We need a particular spur or effort to start us upon inner work; it tires us to sustain it; and when long sustained, we know how easily we lapse. When I speak of "energizing," and its rates and levels and sources, I mean therefore our inner as well as our outer work.

Let no one think, then, that our problem of individual and national economy is solely that of the maximum of pounds raisable against gravity, the maximum of locomotion, or of agitation of any sort, that human beings can accomplish. That might signify little more than hurrying and jumping about in inco-ordinated ways; whereas inner work, though it so often reinforces outer work, quite as often means its arrest. To relax, to say to ourselves "Peace! be still!" is sometimes a great achievement of inner work. When I speak of human energizing in general, the reader must therefore understand that sum-total of activities, some outer and some inner, some muscular, some emotional, some moral, some spiritual, of whose waxing and waning in himself he is at all times so well aware. How to keep it at an appreciable maximum? How not to let the level lapse? That is the great problem. But the work of men and women is of innumerable kinds, each kind being, as we say, carried on by a particular faculty; so the great problem splits into two sub-problems thus:

(1) What are the limits of human faculty in various directions?

(2) By what diversity of means, in the differing types of human beings, may the faculties be stimulated to their best results?

Read in one way, these two questions sound both trivial and familiar: there is a sense in which we have all asked them ever since we were born. Yet *as a methodical program of scientific inquiry,* I doubt whether they have ever been seriously taken up. If answered fully, almost the whole of mental science and of the science of conduct would find a place under them. I propose, in what follows, to press them on the reader's attention in an informal way.

A POINT OF FACT

The first point to agree upon in this enterprise is that *as a rule men habitually use only a small part of the powers which they actually possess and which they might use under appropriate conditions.*

Everyone is familiar with the phenomenon of feeling more or less alive on different days. Everyone knows on any given day that there are energies slumbering in him which the incitements of that day do not call forth, but which he might display if these were greater. Most of us feel as if a sort of cloud weighed upon us, keeping us below our highest notch of clearness in discernment, sureness in reasoning, or firmness in deciding. Compared with what we ought to be, we are only half awake. Our fires are damped, our drafts are checked. We are making use of only a small part of our possible mental and physical resources. . . .

Stating the thing broadly, the human individual thus lives usually far within his limits; he possesses powers of various sorts which he habitually fails to use. He energizes below his *maximum,* and he behaves below his *optimum.* In elementary faculty, in co-ordination, in power of *inhibition* and control, in every conceivable way, his life is contracted like the field of vision of an hysteric subject—but with less excuse, for the poor hysteric is diseased, while in the rest of us it is only an inveterate *habit*—the habit of inferiority to our full self—that is bad.

Admit so much, then, and admit also that the charge of being inferior to their full self is far truer of some men than of others; then the practical question ensues: *to what do the better men owe their escape? and, in the fluctuations which all men feel in their own degree of energizing, to what are the improvements due, when they occur?*

STIMULI FOR POWER RELEASE

In general terms the answer is plain:

Either some unusual stimulus fills them with emotional excitement, or some unusual idea of necessity induces them to make an extra effort of will. *Excitements, ideas, and efforts,* in a word, are what carry us over the dam. . . .

There seems no doubt that *we are each and all of us to some extent victims of habit-neurosis.* We have to admit the wider potential range and the habitually narrow actual use. We live subject to arrest by degrees of fatigue which we have come only from habit to obey. Most of us may learn to push the barrier farther off, and to live in perfect comfort on much higher levels of power.

Country people and city people, as a class, illustrate this difference. The rapid rate of life, the number of decisions in an hour, the many things to keep account of, in a busy city man's or woman's life, seem monstrous to a country brother. He doesn't see how we live at all. A day in New York or Chicago fills him with terror. The danger and noise make it appear like a permanent earthquake. But *settle* him there, and in a year or two he will have caught the pulse-beat. He will vibrate to the city's rhythms; and if he only succeeds in his avocation, whatever that may be, he will find a joy in all the hurry and the tension, he will keep the pace as well as any of us, and get as much out of himself in any week as he ever did in ten weeks in the country.

The stimuli of those who successfully respond and undergo the transformation here, are duty, the example of others, and crowd-pressure and contagion. The transformation, moreover, is a chronic one: the new level of energy becomes permanent. The duties of new offices of trust are constantly producing this effect on the human beings appointed to them. . . .

John Stuart Mill somewhere says that women excel men in the power of keeping up sustained moral excitement. Every case of illness nursed by wife or mother is a proof of this; and where can one find greater examples of sustained endurance than in those thousands of poor homes, where the woman successfully holds the family together and keeps it going by taking all the thought and doing all the work. . . .

Turning from more chronic to acuter proofs of human nature's reserves of power, we find that the stimuli that carry us over the usually effective dam are most often the classic emotional ones, love, anger, crowd-contagion or despair. Despair lames most people, but it wakes others fully up. Every siege or shipwreck or polar expedition brings out some hero who keeps the whole company in heart. . . .

But when the normal tasks and stimulations of life don't put a man's deeper levels of energy on tap, and he requires distinctly deleterious excitements, his constitution verges on the abnormal. The normal opener of deeper and deeper levels of energy is the will. The difficulty is to use it, to make the effort which the word volition implies. . . .

The emotions and excitements due to usual situations are the usual inciters of the will. But these act discontinuously; and in the intervals the shallower levels of life tend to close in and shut us off. Accordingly the best practical knowers of the human soul have invented the thing known as methodical ascetic discipline to keep the deeper levels constantly in reach. Beginning with easy tasks, passing to harder ones, and exercising day by day, it is, I believe, admitted that disciples of asceticism can reach very high levels of freedom and power of the will.

Ignatius Loyola's spiritual exercises must have produced this result in innumerable devotees. But the most venerable ascetic system, and the one whose results have the most voluminous experimental corroberation is undoubtedly the Yoga system in Hindustan. From time immemorial, by Hatha Yoga, Raja Yoga, Karma Yoga, or whatever code of practice it might be, Hindu aspirants to perfection have trained themselves, month in and out, for years. The result claimed, and certainly in many cases accorded by impartial judges, is strength of character, personal power, unshakability of soul. . . .

Few of us would have the will to start upon the Yoga training, which, once started, seemed to conjure the further will power needed out of itself. And not all of those who could launch themselves would have reached the same results. . . .

IDEAS AS STIMULI

Certain men can be influenced, while others cannot be influenced, by certain sorts of *ideas*. This leads me to say a word about ideas considered as stimuli for unlocking what would otherwise be unused reservoirs of individual power.

One thing that ideas do is to contradict other ideas and keep us from believing them. An idea that thus negates a first idea may itself in turn be negated by a third idea, and the first idea may thus regain its natural influence over our belief and determine our behavior. Our philosophic and religious development proceeds thus by credulities, negations, and the negating of negations.

But whether for arousing or for stopping belief, ideas may fail to be efficacious, just as a wire at one time alive with electricity, may at another time be dead. Here our insight into causes fails us, and we can only note results in general terms. In general, whether a given idea shall be a live idea depends more on the person into whose mind it is injected than on the idea itself. Which is the suggestive idea for this person, and which for that one? . . .

But apart from individually varying susceptibilities, there are common lines along which men simply as men tend to be inflammable by ideas. As certain objects naturally awaken love, anger, or cupidity, so certain ideas naturally awaken the energies of loyalty, courage, endurance, or devotion. When these ideas are effective in an individual's life, their effect is often very great indeed. They may transfigure it, unlocking innumerable powers which, but for the idea, would never have come into play. "Fatherland," "the Flag," "the Union," "Holy Church," "the Monroe Doctrine," "Truth," "Science," "Liberty," Garibaldi's phrase, "Rome or Death," etc., are so many examples of energy-releasing ideas. The social nature of such phrases is an essential factor of their dynamic power. They are forces of detent in situations in which no other force produces equivalent effects, and each is a force of detent only in a specific group of men.

The memory that an oath or vow has been made will nerve one to abstinences and efforts otherwise impossible; witness the "pledge" in the history of the temperance movement. A mere promise to his sweetheart will clean up a youth's life all over—at any rate for a time. For such effects an educated susceptibility is required. The idea of one's "honor," for example, unlocks energy only in those of us who have had the education of a "gentleman," so called.

That delightful being, Prince Pueckler-Muskau,* writes to his wife from England that he has invented "a sort of artificial resolution respecting things that are difficult of performance. My device," he continues, "is this: *I give my word of honor most solemnly to myself* to do or to leave undone this or that. I am of course extremely cautious in the use of this expedient, but when once the word is given, even though I afterwards think I have been precipitate or mistaken, I hold it to be perfectly irrevocable, whatever inconveniences I foresee likely to result. If I were capable of breaking my word after such mature consideration, I should lose all respect for myself,—and what man of sense would not prefer death to such an alternative? . . . I find something very satisfactory in the thought that man has the power of framing such props and weapons out of the most trivial materials, indeed out of nothing, merely by the force of his will, which thereby truly deserves the name of omnipotent."

Conversions, whether they be political, scientific, philosophic, or religious, form another way in which bound energies are let loose. They unify us, and put a stop to ancient mental interferences. The result is freedom, and often a great enlargement of power. A belief that thus settles upon an individual always acts as a challenge to his will. But, for the particular challenge to operate, he must be the right challeng*ee*. In religious conversions we have so fine an adjustment that the idea may be in the mind of the challengee for years before it exerts effects; and why it should do so then is often so far from obvious that the event is taken for a miracle of grace, and not a natural occurrence. Whatever it is, it may be a highwater mark of energy, in which "noes," once impossible, are easy, and in which a new range of "yeses" gains the right of way. . . .

The most genuinely saintly person I have ever known is a friend of mine now suffering from cancer of the breast—I hope that she may pardon my citing her here as an example of what ideas can do. Her ideas have kept her a practically well woman for months after she should have given up and gone to bed. They have annulled all pain and weakness and given her a cheerful active life, unusually beneficent to others to whom she has afforded help. Her doctors, acquiescing in results they could not understand, have had the good sense to let her go her own way. . . .

---

* German nobleman (1785–1871) famous in his time as landscape-architect, world traveler, and author of travel books.

POWER BARRIERS AND THE PROBLEM OF EDUCATION

But in few of us are functions not tied up by the exercise of other functions. Relatively few medical men and scientific men, I fancy, can pray. Few can carry on any living commerce with "God." Yet many of us are well aware of how much freer and abler our lives would be, were such important forms of energizing not sealed up by the critical atmosphere in which we have been reared. There are in every one potential forms of activity that actually are shunted out from use. Part of the imperfect vitality under which we labor can thus be easily explained. One part of our mind dams up—even *damns* up!—the other parts.

Conscience makes cowards of us all. Social conventions prevent us from telling the truth after the fashion of the heroes and heroines of Bernard Shaw. We all know persons who are models of excellence, but who belong to the extreme philistine type of mind. So deadly is their intellectual respectability that we can't converse about certain subjects at all, can't let our minds play over them, can't even mention them in their presence. An intellect thus tied down by literality and decorum makes on one the same sort of an impression that an able-bodied man would who should habituate himself to do his work with only one of his fingers, locking up the rest of his organism and leaving it unused.

I trust that by this time I have said enough to convince the reader both of the truth and of the importance of my thesis. The two questions, first, that of the possible extent of our powers; and, second, that of the various avenues of approach to them, the various keys for unlocking them in diverse individuals, dominate the whole problem of individual and national education. We need a topography of the limits of human power, similar to the chart which oculists use of the field of human vision. We need also a study of the various types of human being with reference to the different ways in which their energy-reserves may be appealed to and set loose. . . . So here is a program of concrete individual psychology. . . . It is replete with interesting facts, and points to practical issues superior in importance to anything we know.

STUDY QUESTIONS

1. In what sense is the individual's "efficiency-equilibrium" subject to change?
2. What does the problem of "human energizing" consist in and why can it be spoken of as "the general problem of education"?

3. What is the incontestable fact from which any approach to the problem of human energizing must start?

4. Explain and illustrate how transformations of individuals to a wider use of energy reserves may be brought about.

5. How can ideas serve as stimuli opening up new ranges of individual power?

6. How are religious conversions connected with the problem of enlarging a person's available power?

7. What conditions may act as power barriers accounting for the "philistine type of mind"?

8. Why would you, or would you not agree that the problem raised by James "points to practical issues superior in importance to anything we know"?

G. E. Moore

FREE WILL

Biographical Note. GEORGE EDWARD MOORE (1873–1958) was born in London, and he was educated at Cambridge, where he also had his professional career, starting as university lecturer in moral science in 1911 and retiring in 1939 as professor of philosophy. Subsequently he taught for a number of years as a visiting professor at various American colleges and universities.

Moore published mainly in the fields of ethics and epistemology, exercising an immense influence on English philosophic thought. His major works are *Principia Ethica* (1903), *Ethics* (1912), from which a selection follows, *Philosophical Studies* (1922), and *Some Main Problems of Philosophy* (1953).

* * *

Introductory Note. There are few philosophers in modern time who have not expressed extreme puzzlement about the fact that with regard to the most fundamental questions "absolutely every answer which has ever been given by any one philosopher will be denied to be true by many others." Immanuel Kant, for instance, speaking about metaphysics in his *Prolegomena To Any Future Metaphysics,* considered it "almost ridiculous, while every other science is continually advancing, that in this, which pretends to be Wisdom incarnate, we should constantly move around the same spot, with-

From G. E. Moore, *Ethics,* Home University Library of Modern Knowledge, Vol. No. 52, 1912, pp. 7–9, 202–221. Used by permission of Oxford University Press.

out gaining a single step." And even as does Kant, so also Moore emphasizes the contrast to the progress of the sciences, complaining that "there is no such consensus of opinion among experts about fundamental ethical questions, as there is about many fundamental propositions in Mathematics and the Natural Sciences."

Throughout the history of modern philosophy, recognition of such a critical deficiency in some of its branches has quite often proved an important incentive toward trying to overcome this glaring defect and to bring philosophy up to and in line with the other sciences. This certainly holds true for Kant, but no less for G. E. Moore, who in his first great work on ethics, the *Principia Ethica,* testified to his endeavor "to write 'Prolegomena to any future Ethics that can possibly pretend to be scientific.'"

In the preface to the same work, Moore further explains the cause of the obvious shortcomings by which ethics has so far been plagued: it lies in "the attempt to answer questions, without first discovering precisely *what* question it is which you desire to answer." It should surprise no one, therefore, that answers to questions, ill-defined to begin with, could not be agreed upon by the philosophers "owing to the fact that what they have before their minds is not one question but several, to some of which the true answer is 'No,' to others, 'Yes.'"

To remedy this situation, a "resolute attempt" must be made to see exactly what the question is to which one wants an answer. And this Moore sets out to do in his ethical treatises.

The selection that follows can serve as an illustration of the new method of analysis that he employs. The problem under consideration is that of "free will," traditionally one of the most controversial issues in philosophy. Indeed, so controversial was it that any treatment of it that would bring about a "consensus of opinion among experts" appeared to be out of reach. It is here that Moore's work of analysis and distinction yields definite results that—although somewhat narrow in scope in this particular case—may help to substantiate his prediction that if his lead were followed "many of the most glaring difficulties and disagreements in philosophy would disappear."

DIVERSITY OF OPINION IN ETHICS

Ethics is a subject about which there has been and still is an immense amount of difference of opinion, in spite of all the time and labor which have been devoted to the study of it. There are indeed certain matters about which there is not much disagreement. Almost everybody is agreed that certain kinds of actions ought, as a general rule, to be avoided; and that under certain circumstances, which constantly recur, it is, as a general rule, better to act in certain specified ways rather than in others. There is, moreover, a pretty general agreement, with regard to certain things which happen in the world, that it would be better if they never happened, or, at least, did not happen so often as they do; and with regard to others, that it would be better if they happened more often than they do. But on many questions, even of this kind, there is great diversity of opinion. Actions which some philosophers hold to be generally wrong, others hold to be generally right, and occurrences which some hold to be evils, others hold to be goods.

And when we come to more fundamental questions the difference of opinion is even more marked. Ethical philosophers have, in fact, been largely concerned, not with laying down rules to the effect that certain ways of acting are generally or always right, and others generally or always wrong, nor yet with giving lists of things which are good and others which are evil, but with trying to answer more general and fundamental questions such as the following. What, after all, is it that we mean to say of an action when we say that it is right or ought to be done? And what is it that we mean to say of a state of things when we say that it is good or bad? . . . I think it is true that absolutely every answer which has ever been given by any one philosopher would be denied to be true by many others. There is, at any rate, no such consensus of opinion among experts about these fundamental ethical questions, as there is about many fundamental propositions in Mathematics and the Natural Sciences.

Now, it is precisely questions of this sort, about every one of which there are serious differences of opinion, that I wish to discuss. . . . I shall try to state and distinguish clearly from one another what seem to me to be the most important of the different views which may be held upon a few of the most fundamental ethical questions. Some of these views seem to me to be much nearer the truth than others, and I shall try to indicate which these are. But even where it seems pretty certain that some one view is erroneous, and that another comes, at least, rather nearer to the truth, it is very difficult to be sure that the latter is strictly and absolutely true. . . .

THE PROBLEM STATED

Let us begin with the question: Is it ever true that a man *could* have done anything else, except what he actually did do? And, first of all, I think I had better explain exactly how this question seems to me to be related to the question of Free Will. For it is a fact, that, in many discussions about Free Will, this precise question is never mentioned at all; so that it might be thought that the two have really nothing whatever to do with one another. And indeed some philosophers do, I think, definitely imply that they *have* nothing to do with one another: they seem to hold that our wills can properly be said to be free even if we *never* can, in any sense at all, do anything else except what, in the end, we actually do do. But this view, if it is held, seems to me to be plainly a mere abuse of language. The statement that we have Free Will is certainly ordinarily understood to imply that we really sometimes have the power of acting differently from the way in which we actually do act; and hence, if anybody tells us that we have Free Will, while at the same time he means to deny that we ever have such a power, he is simply misleading us. We certainly have *not* got Free Will, in the ordinary sense of the word, if we never really *could*, in any sense at all, have done anything else than what we did do; so that, in this respect, the two questions certainly are connected. But, on the other hand, the mere fact (if it is a fact) that we sometimes *can*, in *some* sense, do what we don't do, does not necessarily entitle us to say that we *have* Free Will. We certainly *haven't* got it, *unless* we can; but it doesn't follow that we *have* got it, even if we *can*. Whether we have or not will depend upon the precise sense in which it is true that we can. So that even if we do decide that we really *can* often, in *some* sense, do what we don't do, this decision by itself does not entitle us to say that we have Free Will.

FIRST CLARIFICATION

And the first point about which we can and should be quite clear is, I think, this: namely, that we certainly often *can*, in *some* sense, do what we don't do. It is, I think, quite clear that this is so; and also very important that we should realize that it is so. For many people are inclined to assert, quite without qualification: No man ever *could*, on any occasion, have done anything else than what he actually did do on that occasion. By asserting this quite simply, without qualification, they imply, of course (even if they do not mean to imply), that there is *no* proper sense of the word "could," in which it is true that a man *could* have acted differently. And it is this implication which is, I think, quite certainly absolutely false. For this reason, anybody who asserts, without qualification, "Nothing ever *could* have happened, except what actually did happen," is making an assertion which is quite unjustifiable, and which he himself cannot help constantly contradicting. And it is important to insist on this, because many people do make this unqualified assertion, without seeing how violently it contradicts what they themselves, and all of us, believe, and rightly believe, at other times. If, indeed, they insert a qualification—if they merely say, "In *one* sense of the word '*could*' nothing ever *could* have happened, except what did happen," then, they may perhaps be perfectly right: we are not disputing that they may. All that we are maintaining is that, in *one* perfectly proper and legitimate sense of the word "could," and that one of the very commonest senses in which it is used, it is quite certain that some things which didn't happen *could* have happened. And the proof that this is so, is simply as follows.

It is impossible to exaggerate the frequency of the occasions on which we *all* of us make a distinction between two things, neither of which *did* happen,—a distinction which we express by saying, that whereas the one *could* have happened, the other could *not*. No distinction is commoner than this. And no one, I think, who fairly examines the instances in which we make it, can doubt about three things: namely (1) that very often there really is *some* distinction between the two things, corresponding to the language which we use; (2) that this distinction, which really *does* subsist between the things, is *the* one which we mean to express by saying that the one was possible and the other impossible; and (3) that this way of expressing it is a perfectly proper and legitimate way. But if so, it absolutely follows that one of the commonest and most legitimate usages of the phrases "could" and "could not" is to express a difference, which often really does hold between two things *neither* of which did actually happen.

Only a few instances need be given. I could have walked a mile in twenty minutes this morning, but I certainly could *not* have run two miles in five minutes. I did not, *in fact,* do either of these two things; but it is pure nonsense to say that the mere fact that I *did* not, does away with the distinction between them, which I express by saying that the one *was* within my powers, whereas the other was *not*. *Although* I did neither, yet the one was certainly *possible* to me in a sense in which the other was totally *impossible*. Or, to take another instance: It is true, as a rule, that cats *can* climb trees, whereas dogs *can't*. Suppose that on a particular afternoon neither A's cat nor B's dog *do* climb a tree. It is quite absurd to say that this mere fact proves that we must be wrong if we say (as we certainly often should say) that the cat *could* have climbed a tree, though she didn't, whereas the dog *couldn't*. Or, to take an instance which concerns an inanimate object. Some ships *can* steam 20 knots, whereas others *can't* steam more than 15.

And the mere fact that, on a particular occasion, a 20-knot steamer *did* not *actually* run at this speed certainly does not entitle us to say that she *could* not have done so, in the sense in which a 15-knot one *could* not. On the contrary, we all can and should distinguish between cases in which (as, for instance, owing to an accident to her propeller) she did not, *because* she could not, and cases in which she did not, *although* she *could*.

Instances of this sort might be multiplied quite indefinitely; and it is surely quite plain that we all of us do *continually* use such language: we continually, when considering two events, neither of which *did* happen, distinguish between them by saying that whereas the one *was* possible, though it didn't happen, the other was *im*possible. And it is surely quite plain that what we mean by this (whatever it may be) is something which is often perfectly true. But, if so, then anybody who asserts, without qualification, "Nothing ever *could* have happened, except what did happen," is simply asserting what is false.

It is, therefore, quite certain that we often *could* (in *some* sense) have done what we did not do. And now let us see how this fact is related to the argument by which people try to persuade us that it is *not* a fact. :

SECOND CLARIFICATION

The argument is well known: it is simply this. It is assumed (for reasons which I need not discuss) that absolutely everything that happens has a *cause* in what precedes it. But to say this is to say that it follows *necessarily* from something that preceded it; or, in other words, that, once the preceding events which are its cause had happened, it was absolutely *bound* to happen. But to say that it was *bound* to happen, is to say that nothing else *could* have happened instead; so that, ·if *everything* has a cause, *nothing* ever could have happened except what did happen. :

And now let us assume that the premise of this argument is correct: that everything really *has* a cause. What really follows from it? Obviously all that follows is that, in *one* sense of the word "could," nothing ever *could* have happened, except what did happen. This really *does* follow. But, *if* the word ·"could" is ambiguous:—if, that is to say, it is used in different senses on different occasions—it is obviously quite possible that though, in *one* sense, nothing ever could have happened except what did happen, yet in *another* sense, it may at the same time be perfectly true that some things which did not happen *could* have happened. And can anybody undertake to assert with certainty that the word "could" is *not* ambiguous? that it may not have more than one legitimate sense? *Possibly* it is not ambiguous; and, *if* it is not, then the fact that some things, which did not happen, could have happened, really would contradict the principle that everything has a cause; and, in that case, we should, I think, have to give up this principle, because the fact that we often *could* have done what we did not do, is so certain.

But the assumption that the word "could" is *not* ambiguous is an assumption which certainly should not be made without the clearest proof. And yet I think it often is made, without any proof at all; simply because it does not occur to people that words often are ambiguous. It is, for instance, often assumed, in the Free Will controversy, that the question at issue is solely as to whether everything is caused, or whether acts of will are sometimes uncaused. Those who hold that we *have* Free Will, think themselves bound to maintain that acts of will sometimes have *no* cause; and those who hold that everything is caused think that this proves completely that we have not Free Will. But, in fact, it is extremely doubtful whether Free Will is at all inconsistent with the principle that everything is caused. Whether it is or not, all depends on a very difficult question as to the meaning of the word "could." All that is certain about the matter is (1) that, if we have free will, it must be true, in *some* sense, that we sometimes *could* have done, what we did not do; and (2) that, if everything is caused, it must be true, in *some* sense, that we *never could* have done, what we did not do. What is very *un*certain, and what certainly needs to be investigated, is whether these two meanings of the word "could" are the same.

THIRD CLARIFICATION

Let us begin by asking: What is the sense of the word "could," in which it is so certain that we often *could* have done, what we did not do? What, for instance, is the sense in which I *could* have walked a mile in twenty minutes this morning, though I did not? There is one suggestion, which is very obvious: namely, that what I mean is simply after all that I could, *if* I had chosen; or (to avoid a possible complication) perhaps we had better say "that I *should, if* I had chosen." In other words, the suggestion is that we often use the phrase *"I could"* simply and solely as a short way of saying "I *should, if* I had chosen."

And in all cases, where it is certainly true that we *could* have done, what we did not do, it is, I think, very difficult to be quite sure that this (or something similar) is *not* what we mean by the word "could." The case of the ship may seem to be an exception, because it is certainly not true that she would have steamed twenty knots if *she* had chosen; but even here it seems possbile that what we mean is simply that she *would,* if *the men on board of her* had chosen. There are certainly good reasons for thinking that·we *very often* mean by "could" merely "would, *if* so and so had chosen." And if so, then we have a sense of the word "could" in which the fact that we often *could* have done what we did not do, is perfectly compatible with the principle that everything has a cause: ·for to say that, *if* I had performed a certain act of will, I should have done something which I did not do, in no way contradicts this principle.

And an additional reason for supposing that this *is* what we often mean by "could," and one which is also a reason why it is important to insist on the obvious fact that we very often really *should* have acted differently, *if* we had willed differently, is that·those who deny that we ever *could* have done anything, which we did not do, often speak and think as if this really did involve the conclusion that we never should have acted differently, even ·*if* we had willed differently. This occurs, I think, in two chief instances—one in reference to the future, the other in reference to the past. The first occurs when, because they hold that nothing *can* happen, except what *will* happen, people are led to adopt the view called Fatalism—the view that *whatever we will,* the result will always be the same; that it is, therefore, *never* any use to make one choice rather than another. And this conclusion will really follow if by "can" we mean *"would* happen, even *if* we were to will it." But it is certainly untrue, and it certainly does not follow from the principle of causality. On the contrary, reasons of exactly the same sort and exactly as strong as those which lead us to suppose that everything has a cause, lead to the conclusion that if we choose one course, the result will *always* be different in *some* respect from what it would have been, if we had chosen another; and we know also that the difference would *sometimes* consist in the fact that *what* we chose would come to pass.·It is certainly often true of the future, therefore, that whichever of two actions we *were* to choose, *would* actually be done, although it is quite certain that only one of the two *will* be done.:

And the second instance, in which people are apt to speak and think, as if, *because* no man ever *could* have done anything but what he did do, it follows that he would not, even *if* he had chosen, is as follows. Many people seem, in fact, to conclude directly from the first of these two propositions, that we can never be justified in praising or blaming a man for anything that he does, or indeed for making any distinction between what is right or wrong, on the one hand, and what is lucky or unfortunate on the other. They conclude, for instance, that there is never any reason to treat or to regard the voluntary commission of a crime in any different way from that in which we treat, or regard the involuntary catching of a disease. The man who committed the crime *could* not, they say, have helped committing it any more than the other man could have helped catching the disease; both events were equally inevitable; and though both may of course be great *misfortunes,* though both may have very bad consequences and equally bad ones—there is no justification whatever, they say, for the distinction we make between them when we say that the commission of the crime was *wrong,* or that the man was morally to blame for it, whereas the catching of the disease was *not* wrong and the man was not to blame for it. And this conclusion, again, will really follow if by "could not," we mean "*would* not, even if we had willed to avoid it."

But the point I want to make is, that it follows *only* if we make this assumption. That is to say, the mere fact that the man *would* have succeeded in avoiding the crime, *if* he had chosen (which is certainly often true), whereas the other man would *not* have succeeded in avoiding the disease, even *if* he had chosen (which is certainly also often true) gives an ample justification for regarding and treating the two cases differently. It gives such a justification, because, where the occurrence of an event *did* depend upon the will, there, by acting on the will (as we may do by blame or punishment) we have often a reasonable chance of preventing similar events from recurring in the future; whereas, where it did *not* depend upon the will, we have no such chance. We may, therefore, fairly say that those who speak and think, as if a man who brings about a misfortune *voluntarily* ought to be treated and regarded in exactly the same way as one who brings about an equally great misfortune *involuntarily,* are speaking and thinking *as if* it were not true that we ever should have acted differently, even *if* we had willed to do so. And that is why it is extremely important to insist on the absolute certainty of the fact that we often really *should* have acted differently, *if* we had willed differently.

FIRST CONCLUSION

There is, therefore, much reason to think that when we say that we *could* have done a thing which we did not do, we *often* mean merely that we *should* have done it, *if* we had chosen. And if so, then it is quite certain that, in *this* sense, we often really could have done what we did not do, and that this fact is in no way inconsistent with the principle that everything has a cause. And for my part I must confess that I cannot feel certain that this may not be *all* that we usually mean and understand by the assertion that we have Free Will; so that those who deny that we have it are really denying (though, no doubt, often unconsciously) that we ever *should* have acted differently, even if we had willed differently. It has been sometimes held that this *is* what we mean; and I cannot find any conclusive argument to the contrary. And if it is what we mean, then it absolutely follows that we really *have* Free Will, and also that this fact is quite consistent with the principle that everything has a cause. . . .

FOURTH CLARIFICATION

But, no doubt, there are many people who will say that this is *not* sufficient to entitle us to say that we have Free Will; and they will say this for a reason, which certainly has some plausibility, though I cannot satisfy myself that it is conclusive. They will say, namely: Granted that we often *should* have acted differently, *if* we had chosen differently, yet it is not true that we have Free Will, unless it is *also* often true in such cases that we *could* have *chosen* differently. The question of Free Will has been thus represented as being merely the question whether we ever *could* have chosen, what we did not choose, or ever *can* choose, what, in fact, we shall not choose. And since there is some plausibility in this contention, it is, I think, worth while to point out that here again it is absolutely certain that, in two different senses, at least, we often *could* have chosen, what, in fact, we did not choose; and that in neither sense does this fact contradict the principle of causality.

The first is simply the old sense over again. If by saying that we *could* have done, what we did not do, we often mean merely that we *should* have done it, *if* we had chosen to do it, then obviously, by saying that we *could* have *chosen* to do it, we may mean merely that we *should* have so chosen, *if* we had chosen *to make the choice*. And I think there is no doubt it is often true that we should have chosen to do a particular thing *if* we had chosen to make the choice; and that this is a very important sense in which it is often in our power to make a choice. There certainly is such a thing as making an effort to induce ourselves to *choose* a particular course; and I think there is no doubt that often if we *had* made such an effort, we *should* have made a choice, which we did not in fact make.

And besides this, there is another sense in which, whenever we have several different courses of action in view, it is *possible* for us to choose any one of them; and a sense which is certainly of some practical importance, even if it goes no way to justify us in saying that we have Free Will. This sense arises from the fact that in such cases we can hardly ever *know for certain* beforehand, *which* choice we actually *shall* make; and one of the commonest senses of the word "possible" is that in which we call an event "possible" when no man can *know for certain* that it will *not* happen. It follows that almost, if not quite always, when we make a choice, after considering alternatives, it *was* possible that we should have chosen one of these alternatives, which we did not actually choose; and often, of course, it was not only possible, but highly probable, that we should have done so. And this fact is certainly of practical importance, because many people are apt much too easily to assume that it is quite certain that they *will not* make a given choice, which they know they ought to make, if it were possible; and their belief that they *will* not make it tends, of course, to prevent them from making it. For this reason it is important to insist that they can hardly ever know for certain with regard to any given choice that they will *not* make it. :

SECOND CONCLUSION

It is, therefore, quite certain (1) that we often *should* have *acted* differently, if we had chosen to; (2) that similarly we often should have *chosen* differently, *if* we had chosen so to choose; and (3) that it was almost always *possible* that we should have chosen differently, in the sense that no man could know for certain that we should *not* so choose. All these three things are facts, and all of them are quite consistent with the principle of causality. Can anybody undertake to say for certain that none of these three facts and *no* combination of them will justify us in saying that we have Free Will? Or, suppose it granted that we have not Free Will, unless it is often true that we *could* have chosen, what we did not choose:—Can any defender of Free Will, or any opponent of it, show conclusively that what he means by "*could* have chosen" in this proposition, is anything different from the two certain facts, which I have numbered (2) and (3), or some combination of the two? Many people, no doubt, will still insist that these two facts alone are by no means sufficient to entitle us to say that we have Free Will: that it must be true that we were *able* to choose, in some quite other sense. But nobody, so far as I know, has ever been able to tell us exactly what that sense is. For my part, I can find no conclusive argument to show either that some such other sense of "can" is necessary, or that it is not.

STUDY QUESTIONS

1. What is a serious deficiency of ethical philosophers as compared with experts in mathematics and the natural sciences and what does Moore propose to do about it?
2. What is Moore's first question and how is it related to the question of free will?
3. Explain and illustrate in what sense we often *can* do what we don't do?
4. How is it shown that the view called fatalism is certainly untrue?
5. Why would we draw a wrong conclusion in claiming that there is no real distinction between what is right or wrong on the one hand and what is lucky or unfortunate on the other?
6. In what sense is it absolutely certain that we often *should* have acted differently if we had willed differently?
7. In what sense is it absolutely certain that we often should have chosen differently if we had chosen so to choose?
8. What is Moore's conclusion regarding man's having or not having free will?

III

Epistemology

Plato*

⌸⌸

KNOWLEDGE AND THE ETERNAL IDEAS

⌸⌸

Introductory Note. The Platonic epistemology is based upon the theory of Ideas and arises out of the distinction that Plato draws between knowledge and opinion. Opinion is limited to sense experience, to the world of change. Knowledge transcends sense experience and is concerned with the intelligible world of *Eternal Ideas* or *Forms.* Since we have a knowledge of these Ideas or Forms—we understand, for example, the meanings of beauty, justice, equality, etc.—and since these Ideas are eternal and immutable in their truth, they cannot have been derived from sense experience and the world of change. For Plato, the only adequate explanation for our knowledge of such Ideas is the doctrine of recollection. We must have acquired a knowledge of such Ideas in a previous existence and all present knowledge of the Ideas is a recollection based upon occasions of sense experience of particular instances of such Ideas. Thus we do not perceive equality as such, but rather things that are more or less equal, that participate in the Idea of equality. But we could not know that particular things are more or less equal without some previous knowledge of equality in itself and apart from all particular manifestations.

For Plato, the world of Ideas is hierarchical. Above the world of sense and lowest on the scale of intelligible reality are the Forms or Ideas of science. From a knowledge of such Forms, the mind can ascend to the sphere of mathematics; still further—above the abstract realm of mathematics—is the

* For a biographical note on Plato, see the selection from the *Meno,* page 10.

sphere of dialectic. By means of dialectic we can clarify and analyze our basic principles and definitions, and this activity gives us a more precise knowledge of the Forms and ultimately an insight into the Form of the Good.

The material from the *Phaedo* illustrates Plato's conception of knowledge as recollection, and it may be read in conjunction with the selection from the *Meno* that stresses a similar point. The material from the *Republic* affords a brief exposition of Plato's attempt to explain the meaning of the Good in terms of a metaphor with the sun; the implication is drawn that not only is the Good the highest form of knowledge, but also that the Idea of the Good is the author of all being. The metaphor of the divided line represents in some detail Plato's account of the distinction between knowledge and opinion and the respective realms of each. Note especially here the distinction drawn between mathematics and dialectic, in which it is maintained that the former takes its principles for granted, but that dialectic considers such principles as hypotheses and uses mathematics to attain a higher knowledge of the Forms. Finally, *The Allegory of the Cave* affords a vivid illustration of the theory of knowledge in highly persuasive language. Plato remarks that "every feature in this parable is meant to fit our earlier analysis," with the added implication that knowledge is a long and difficult process and not appreciated by those who do not undergo it.

KNOWLEDGE AS RECOLLECTION

. . . Cebes added: Your favorite doctrine, Socrates, that knowledge is simply recollection, if true also necessarily implies a previous time in which we have learned that which we now recollect. But this would be impossible unless our soul had been in some place before existing in the form of man; here then is another proof of the soul's immortality.

But tell me Cebes, said Simmias, interposing, what arguments are urged in favor of this doctrine of recollection. I am not very sure at the moment that I remember them.

One excellent proof, said Cebes, is afforded by questions. If you put a question to a person in a right way, he will give a true answer of himself, but how could he do this unless there were knowledge and right reason already in him? And this is most clearly shown when he is taken to a diagram or to anything of that sort.[1]

But if, said Socrates, you are still incredulous, Simmias, I would ask you whether you may not agree with me when you look at the matter in another way;—I mean, if you are still incredulous as to whether knowledge is recollection?

From the "Phaedo," *The Dialogues of Plato*, translated by Benjamin Jowett, London, The Macmillan Company, 1892, 73–77.

[1] Cp. *Meno* 83 ff.

Incredulous I am not, said Simmias; but I want to have this doctrine of recollection brought to my own recollection, and, from what Cebes has said, I am beginning to recollect and be convinced: but I should still like to hear what you were going to say.

This is what I would say, he replied:—We should agree, if I am not mistaken, that what a man recollects he must have known at some previous time.

Very true.

And what is the nature of this knowledge or recollection? I mean to ask, whether a person who, having seen or heard or in any way perceived anything, knows not only that, but has a conception of something else which is the subject, not of the same but of some other kind of knowledge, may not be fairly said to recollect that of which he has the conception?

What do you mean?

I mean what I may illustrate by the following instance:—The knowledge of a lyre is not the same as the knowledge of a man?

True.

And yet what is the feeling of lovers when they recognize a lyre, or a garment, or anything else which the beloved has been in the habit of using? Do not they, from knowing the lyre, form in the mind's eye an image of the youth to whom the lyre belongs? And this is recollection. In like manner anyone who sees Simmias may remember Cebes; and there are endless examples of the same thing.

Endless, indeed, replied Simmias.

And recollection is most commonly a process of recovering that which has been already forgotten through time and inattention.

Very true, he said.

Well; and may you not also from seeing the picture of a house or a lyre remember a man? and from the picture of Simmias, you may be led to remember Cebes.

True.

Or you may also be led to the recollection of Simmias himself?

Quite so.

And in all these cases the recollection may be derived from things either like or unlike.

It may be.

And when the recollection is derived from like things, then another consideration is sure to arise, which is—whether the likeness in any degree falls short or not of that which is recollected?

Very true, he said.

And shall we proceed a step further, and affirm that there is such a thing as equality, not of one piece of wood or stone with another, but that, over and above this, there is absolute equality?

By all means, replied Simmias.

And do we know the nature of this absolute essence?

To be sure, he said.

And whence did we obtain our knowledge? Did we not see equalities of material things, such as pieces of wood and stones, and gather from them the idea of an equality which is different from them? For you will acknowledge that there is a difference. Or look at the matter in another way. Do not the same pieces of wood or stone appear at one time equal, and at another time unequal?

That is certain.

But are real equals ever equal? or is the idea of equality the same as of inequality?

Impossible, Socrates.

Then these (so-called) equals are not the same with the idea of equality.

I should say, clearly not, Socrates.

And yet from these equals, although differing from the idea of equality, you conceived and attained that idea?

Very true, he said.

Which might be like, or might be unlike them?

Yes.

But that makes no difference: whenever from seeing one thing you conceived another, whether like or unlike, there must surely have been an act of recollection?

Very true.

But what would you say of equal portions of wood and stone, or other material equals? and what is the impression produced by them? Are they equals in the same sense in which absolute equality is equal? or do they fall short of this perfect equality in a measure?

Yes, he said, in a very great measure too.

And must we not allow, that when I or anyone, looking at any object, observes that the thing which he sees aims at being some other thing, but falls short of, and cannot be, that other thing, but is inferior, he who makes this observation must have had a previous knowledge of that to which the other, although similar, was inferior.

Certainly.

And has not this been our own case in the matter of equals and of absolute equality?

Precisely.

Then we must have known equality previously to the time when we first saw the material equals, and reflected that all these apparent equals strive to attain absolute equality, but fall short of it?

Very true.

And we recognize also that this absolute equality has only been known, and can only be known, through the medium of sight or touch, or of some other of the senses which are all alike in this respect.

Yes, Socrates, as far as the argument is concerned, one of them is the same as the other.

From the senses then is derived the knowledge that all sensible things aim at an absolute equality of which they fall short?

Yes.

Then before we began to see or hear or perceive in any way, we must have had a knowledge of absolute equality, or we could not have referred to that standard the equals which are derived from the senses?—for to that they all aspire, and of that they fall short.

No other inference can be drawn from the previous statements.

And did we now see and hear and have the use of our other senses as soon as we were born?

Certainly.

Then we must have acquired the knowledge of equality at some previous time?

Yes.

That is to say, before we were born, I suppose?

True.

And if we acquired this knowledge before we were born, and were born having the use of it, then we also knew before we were born and at the instant of birth not only the equal or the greater or the less, but all other ideas; for we are not speaking only of equality, but of beauty, goodness, justice, holiness, and of all which we stamp with the name of essence in the dialectical process, both when we ask and when we answer questions. Of all this we may certainly affirm that we acquired the knowledge before birth?

We may.

But if, after having acquired, we have not forgotten what in each case we acquired, then we must always have come into life having knowledge, and shall always continue to know as long as life lasts— for knowing is the acquiring and retaining knowledge and not forgetting. Is not forgetting, Simmias, just the losing of knowledge?

Quite true, Socrates.

But if the knowledge which we acquired before birth was lost by us at birth, and if afterwards by the use of the senses we recovered what we previously knew, will not the process which we call learning be a recovering of the knowledge which is natural to us, and may not this be rightly termed recollection?

Very true.

So much is clear—that when we perceive something, either by the help of sight, or hearing, or some other sense, from that perception we are able to obtain a notion of some other thing like or unlike which is associated with it but has been forgotten. Whence, as I was saying, one of two alternatives follows: either we had this knowledge at birth, and continued to know through life; or, after birth, those who are said to learn only remember, and learning is simply recollection.

Yes, that is quite true, Socrates.

And which alternative, Simmias, do you prefer? Had we the knowledge at our birth, or did we recollect the things which we knew previously to our birth?

I cannot decide at the moment.

At any rate you can decide whether he who has knowledge will or will not be able to render an account of his knowledge? What do you say?

Certainly, he will.

But do you think that every man is able to give an account of these very matters about which we are speaking?

Would that they could, Socrates, but I rather fear that tomorrow at this time, there will no longer be any one alive who is able to give an account of them such as ought to be given.

Then you are not of opinion, Simmias, that all men know these things?

Certainly not.

They are in process of recollecting that which they learned before?

Certainly.

But when did our souls acquire this knowledge?—not since we were born as men?

Certainly not.

And therefore, previously?

Yes.

Then Simmias, our souls must also have existed without bodies before they were in the form of man, and must have had intelligence.

Unless indeed you suppose, Socrates, that these notions are given to us at the very moment of birth; for this is the only time which remains.

Yes, my friend, but if so, when do we lose them? for they are not in us when we are born—that is admitted. Do we lose them at the moment of receiving them, or if not at what other time?

No, Socrates, I perceive that I was unconsciously talking nonsense.

Then may we not say, Simmias, that if, as we are always repeating, there is an absolute beauty, and goodness, and an absolute essence of all things; and if to this, which is now discovered to have existed in our former state, we refer all our sensations, and with this compare them, finding these ideas to be pre-existent and our inborn possession—then our souls must have had a prior existence, but if not, there would be no force in the argument. There is the same proof that these ideas must have existed before we were born, as that our souls existed before we were born; and if not the ideas, then not the souls.

Yes, Socrates; I am convinced that there is precisely the same necessity for the one as for the other; and the argument retreats success-fully to the position that the existence of the soul before birth cannot be separated from the existence of the essence of which you speak. For there is nothing which to my mind is so patent as that beauty, goodness, and the other notions of which you were just now speaking, have a most real and absolute existence; and I am satisfied with the proof.

KNOWLEDGE AND THE GOOD

First we must come to an understanding. Let me remind you of the distinction we drew earlier and have often drawn on other occasions, between the multiplicity of things that we call good or beautiful or whatever it may be and, on the other hand, Goodness itself or Beauty itself and so on. Corresponding to each of these sets of many things, we postulate a single Form or real essence, as we call it.

Yes, that is so.

Further, the many things, we say, can be seen, but are not objects of rational thought; whereas the Forms are objects of thought, but invisible.

Yes, certainly.

And we see things with our eyesight, just as we hear sounds with our ears and, to speak generally, perceive any sensible thing with our sense-faculties.

Of course. Have you noticed, then, that the artificer who designed

From *The Republic,* translated with introduction and notes by Francis Mac-Donald Cornford, Oxford, The Clarendon Press, 1941, 507A–509C. Used by permission of the Clarendon Press.

the senses has been exceptionally lavish of his materials in making the eyes able to see and their objects visible?

That never occurred to me.

Well, look at it in this way. Hearing and sound do not stand in need of any third thing, without which the ear will not hear nor sound be heard; and I think the same is true of most, not to say all, of the other senses. Can you think of one that does require anything of the sort?

No, I cannot.

But there is this need in the case of sight and its objects. You may have the power of vision in your eyes and try to use it, and color may be there in the objects; but sight will see nothing and the colors will remain invisible in the absence of a third thing peculiarly constituted to serve this very purpose.

By which you mean—?

Naturally I mean what you call light; and if light is a thing of value, the sense of sight and the power of being visible are linked together by a very precious bond, such as unites no other sense with its object.

No one could say that light is not a precious thing.

And of all the divinities in the skies[2] is there one whose light, above all the rest, is responsible for making our eyes see perfectly and making objects perfectly visible?

There can be no two opinions: of course you mean the Sun.

And how is sight related to this deity? Neither sight nor the eye which contains it is the Sun, but of all the sense-organs it is the most sun-like; and further, the power it possesses is dispensed by the Sun, like a stream flooding the eye. And again, the Sun is not vision, but it is the cause of vision and also is seen by the vision it causes.

Yes.

It was the Sun, then, that I meant when I spoke of that offspring which the Good has created in the visible world, to stand there in the same relation to vision and visible things as that which the Good itself bears in the intelligible world to intelligence and to intelligible objects.

How is that? You must explain further.

You know what happens when the colors of things are no longer irradiated by the daylight, but only by the fainter luminaries of the night: when you look at them, the eyes are dim and seem almost blind, as if there were no unclouded vision in them. But when you look at things on which the Sun is shining, the same eyes see distinctly and it becomes evident that they do contain the power of vision.

Certainly.

[2] Plato held that the heavenly bodies are immortal living creatures, i. e. gods.

Apply this comparison, then, to the soul. When its gaze is fixed upon an object irradiated by truth and reality, the soul gains understanding and knowledge and is manifestly in possession of intelligence. But when it looks towards that twilight world of things that come into existence and pass away, its sight is dim and it has only opinions and beliefs which shift to and fro, and now it seems like a thing that has no intelligence.

That is true.

This, then, which gives to the objects of knowledge their truth and to him who knows them his power of knowing is the Form or essential nature of Goodness. It is the cause of knowledge and truth; and so, while you may think of it as an object of knowledge, you will do well to regard it as something beyond truth and knowledge and, precious as these both are, of still higher worth. And, just as in our analogy light and vision were to be thought of as like the Sun, but not identical with it, so here both knowledge and truth are to be regarded as like the Good, but to identify either with the Good is wrong. The Good must hold a yet higher place of honor.

You are giving it a position of extraordinary splendor, if it is the source of knowledge and truth and itself surpasses them in worth. You surely cannot mean that it is pleasure.

Heaven forbid, I exclaimed. But I want to follow up our analogy still further. You will agree that the Sun not only makes the things we see visible, but also brings them into existence and gives them growth and nourishment; yet he is not the same thing as existence. And so with the objects of knowledge: these derive from the Good not only their power of being known, but their very being and reality; and Goodness is not the same thing as being, but even beyond being, surpassing it in dignity and power.

Glaucon exclaimed with some amusement at my exalting Goodness in such extravagant terms.

It is your fault, I replied; you forced me to say what I think.

Yes, and you must not stop there. At any rate complete your comparison with the Sun, if there is any more to be said.

There is a great deal more, I answered.

Let us hear it, then; don't leave anything out.

I am afraid much must be left unspoken. However, I will not, if I can help it, leave out anything that can be said on this occasion.

Please do not.

FOUR STAGES OF COGNITION. THE LINE

OBJECTS	STATES OF MIND	
The Good	Intelligence (*noesis*) or	
Forms	D Knowledge (*episteme*)	Intelligible World
Mathematical objects	C Thinking (*dianoia*)	
Visible things	B Belief (*pistis*)	World of Appearances
Images	A Imagining (*eikasia*)	

Conceive, then, that there are these two powers I speak of, the Good reigning over the domain of all that is intelligible, the Sun over the visible world—or the heaven as I might call it; only you would think I was showing off my skill in etymology. At any rate you have these two orders of things clearly before your mind: the visible and the intelligible?

I have.

Now take a line divided into two unequal parts, one to represent the visible order, the other the intelligible; and divide each part again in the same proportion, symbolizing degrees of comparative clearness or obscurity. Then (A) one of the two sections in the visible world will stand for images. By images I mean first shadows, and then reflections in water or in close-grained, polished surfaces, and everything of that kind, if you understand.

Yes, I understand.

Let the second section (B) stand for the actual things of which the first are likenesses, the living creatures about us and all the works of nature or of human hands.

So be it.

Will you also take the proportion in which the visible world has been divided as corresponding to degrees of reality and truth, so that the likeness shall stand to the original in the same ratio as the sphere of appearances and belief to the sphere of knowledge?

Certainly.

Now consider how we are to divide the part which stands for the

Ibid., 509D–511E.

intelligible world. There are two sections. In the first (C) the mind uses
as images those actual things which themselves had images in the visible
world; and it is compelled to pursue its inquiry by starting from assumptions and travelling, not up to a principle, but down to a conclusion.
In the second (D) the mind moves in the other direction, from an assumption up towards a principle which is not hypothetical; and it makes
no use of the images employed in the other section, but only of Forms,
and conducts its inquiry solely by their means.

I don't quite understand what you mean.

Then we will try again; what I have just said will help you to understand. (C) You know, of course, how students of subjects like geometry
and arithmetic begin by postulating odd and even numbers, or the various figures and the three kinds of angle, and other such data in each
subject. These data they take as known; and, having adopted them as
assumptions, they do not feel called upon to give any account of them
to themselves or to anyone else, but treat them as self-evident. Then,
starting from these assumptions, they go on until they arrive, by a series
of consistent steps, at all the conclusions they set out to investigate.

Yes, I know that.

You also know how they make use of visible figures and discourse
about them, though what they really have in mind is the originals of
which these figures are images: they are not reasoning, for instance,
about this particular square and diagonal which they have drawn, but
about *the* Square and *the* Diagonal; and so in all cases. The diagrams
they draw and the models they make are actual things, which may have
their shadows or images in water; but now they serve in their turn as
images, while the student is seeking to behold those realities which only
thought can apprehend.[3]

True.

This, then, is the class of things that I spoke of as intelligible, but
with two qualifications: first, that the mind, in studying them, is compelled to employ assumptions, and, because it cannot rise above these,
does not travel upwards to a first principle; and second, that it uses as
images those actual things which have images of their own in the section
below them and which, in comparison with those shadows and reflections, are reputed to be more palpable and valued accordingly.

I understand: you mean the subject matter of geometry and of the
kindred arts.

[3] Conversely, the fact that the mathematician can use visible objects as illustrations
indicates that the realities and truths of mathematics are embodied, though imperfectly,
in the world of visible and tangible things; whereas the counterparts of the moral
Forms can only be beheld by thought.

(D) Then by the second section of the intelligible world you may understand me to mean all that unaided reasoning apprehends by the power of dialectic, when it treats its assumptions, not as first principles, but as *hypotheses* in the literal sense, things 'laid down' like a flight of steps up which it may mount all the way to something that is not hypothetical, the first principle of all; and having grasped this, may turn back and, holding on to the consequences which depend upon it, descend at last to a conclusion, never making use of any sensible object, but only of Forms, moving through Forms from one to another, and ending with Forms.

I understand, he said, though not perfectly; for the procedure you describe sounds like an enormous undertaking. But I see that you mean to distinguish the field of intelligible reality studied by dialectic as having a greater certainty and truth than the subject matter of the 'arts', as they are called, which treat their assumptions as first principles. The students of these arts are, it is true, compelled to exercise thought in contemplating objects which the senses cannot perceive; but because they start from assumptions without going back to a first principle, you do not regard them as gaining true understanding about those objects, although the objects themselves, when connected with a first principle, are intelligible. And I think you would call the state of mind of the students of geometry and other such arts, not intelligence, but thinking, as being something between intelligence and mere acceptance of appearances.

You have understood me quite well enough, I replied. And now you may take, as corresponding to the four sections, these four states of mind: *intelligence* for the highest, *thinking* for the second, *belief* for the third, and for the last *imagining*. These you may arrange as the terms in a proportion, assigning to each a degree of clearness and certainty corresponding to the measure in which their objects possess truth and reality.

I understand and agree with you. I will arrange them as you say.

THE ALLEGORY OF THE CAVE

Next, said I, here is a parable to illustrate the degrees in which our nature may be enlightened or unenlightened. Imagine the condition of men living in a sort of cavernous chamber underground, with an en-

Ibid., 514A–517B.

trance open to the light and a long passage all down the cave.[4] Here
they have been from childhood, chained by the leg and also by the neck,
so that they cannot move and can see only what is in front of them,
because the chains will not let them turn their heads. At some distance
higher up is the light of a fire burning behind them; and between the
prisoners and the fire is a track[5] with a parapet built along it, like the
screen at a puppetshow, which hides the performers while they show
their puppets over the top.

I see, said he.

Now behind this parapet imagine persons carrying along various artificial objects, including figures of men and animals in wood or stone
or other materials, which project above the parapet. Naturally, some of
these persons will be talking, others silent.[6]

It is a strange picture, he said, and a strange sort of prisoners.

Like ourselves, I replied; for in the first place prisoners so confined
would have seen nothing of themselves or of one another, except the
shadows thrown by the fire-light on the wall of the Cave facing them,
would they?

Not if all their lives they had been prevented from moving their heads.

And they would have seen as little of the objects carried past.

Of course.

Now, if they could talk to one another, would they not suppose that
their words referred only to those passing shadows which they saw?

Necessarily.

And suppose their prison had an echo from the wall facing them?
When one of the people crossing behind them spoke, they could only
suppose that the sound came from the shadow passing before their eyes.

No doubt.

In every way, then, such prisoners would recognize as reality nothing
but the shadows of those artificial objects.

Inevitably.

Now consider what would happen if their release from the chains and

---

[4] The *length* of the 'way in' (*eisodos*) to the chamber where the prisoners sit is an
essential feature, explaining why no daylight reaches them.

[5] The track crosses the passage into the cave at right angles, and is *above* the parapet
built along it.

[6] A modern Plato would compare his Cave to an underground cinema, where the
audience watch the play of shadows thrown by the film passing before a light at their
backs. The film itself is only an image of 'real' things and events in the world
outside the cinema. For the film Plato has to substitute the clumsier apparatus of a
procession of artificial objects carried on their heads by persons who are merely part
of the machinery, providing for the movement of the objects and the sounds whose
echo the prisoners hear. The parapet prevents these persons' shadow from being cast on
the wall of the Cave.

the healing of their unwisdom should come about in this way. Suppose one of them set free and forced suddenly to stand up, turn his head, and walk with eyes lifted to the light; all these movements would be painful, and he would be too dazzled to make out the objects whose shadows he had been used to see. What do you think he would say, if someone told him that what he had formerly seen was meaningless illusion, but now, being somewhat nearer to reality and turned towards more real objects, he was getting a truer view? Suppose further that he were shown the various objects being carried by and were made to say, in reply to questions, what each of them was. Would he not be perplexed and believe the objects now shown him to be not so real as what he formerly saw?

Yes, not nearly so real.

And if he were forced to look at the fire-light itself, would not his eyes ache, so that he would try to escape and turn back to the things which he could see distinctly, convinced that they really were clearer than these other objects now being shown to him?

Yes.

And suppose someone were to drag him away forcibly up the steep and rugged ascent and not let him go until he had hauled him out into the sunlight, would he not suffer pain and vexation at such treatment, and, when he had come out into the light, find his eyes so full of its radiance that he could not see a single one of the things that he was now told were real?

Certainly he would not see them all at once.

He would need, then, to grow accustomed before he could see things in that upper world. At first it would be easiest to make out shadows, and then the images of men and things reflected in water, and later on the things themselves. After that, it would be easier to watch the heavenly bodies and the sky itself by night, looking at the light of the moon and stars rather than the Sun and the Sun's light in the day time.

Yes, surely.

Last of all, he would be able to look at the Sun and contemplate its nature, not as it appears when reflected in water or any alien medium, but as it is in itself in its own domain.

No doubt.

And now he would begin to draw the conclusion that it is the Sun that produces the seasons and the course of the year and controls everything in the visible world, and moreover is in a way the cause of all that he and his companions used to see.

Clearly he would come at last to that conclusion.

Then if he called to mind his fellow prisoners and what passed for wisdom in his former dwelling-place, he would surely think himself happy in the change and be sorry for them. They may have had a practice of honoring and commending one another, with prizes for the man who had the keenest eye for the passing shadows and the best memory for the order in which they followed or accompanied one another, so that he could make a good guess as to which was going to come next. Would our released prisoner be likely to covet those prizes or to envy the men exalted to honor and power in the Cave? Would he not feel like Homer's Achilles, that he would far sooner 'be on earth as a hired servant in the house of a landless man' or endure anything rather than go back to his old beliefs and live in the old way?

Yes, he would prefer any fate to such a life.

Now imagine what would happen if he went down again to take his former seat in the Cave. Coming suddenly out of the sunlight, his eyes would be filled with darkness. He might be required once more to deliver his opinion on those shadows, in competition with the prisoners who had never been released, while his eyesight was still dim and unsteady; and it might take some time to become used to that darkness. They would laugh at him and say that he had gone up only to come back with his sight ruined; it was worth no one's while even to attempt the ascent. If they could lay hands on the man who was trying to set them free and lead them up, they would kill him.

Yes, they would.

Every feature in this parable, my dear Glaucon, is meant to fit our earlier analysis. The prison dwelling corresponds to the region revealed to us through the sense of sight, and the firelight within it to the power of the Sun. The ascent to see the things in the upper world you may take as standing for the upward journey of the soul into the region of the intelligible; then you will be in possession of what I surmise, since that is what you wish to be told. Heaven knows whether it is true; but this, at any rate, is how it appears to me. In the world of knowledge, the last thing to be perceived and only with great difficulty is the essential Form of Goodness. Once it is perceived, the conclusion must follow that, for all things, this is the cause of whatever is right and good; in the visible world it gives birth to light and to the lord of light, while it is itself sovereign in the intelligible world and the parent of intelligence and truth. Without having had a vision of this Form no one can act with wisdom, either in his own life or in matters of state.

So far as I can understand, I share your belief.

STUDY QUESTIONS

1. Supposing the Platonic theory of recollection to be true, would such a theory constitute in your opinion a good argument for the immortality of the soul?

2. Evaluate and criticize Plato's theory of recollection as an adequate explanation of our knowledge of the eternal ideas.

3. Apart from the Platonic theory of recollection and the doctrine of the eternal ideas, how would you account for the origin and nature of such ideas as equality, beauty, number, etc.

4. What function do the senses play in the Platonic theory of knowledge? How does the soul's vision of the eternal ideas differ from sense knowledge?

5. Would you identify Plato's Idea of the Good with the notion of God? Why or why not?

6. Is the Idea of the Good a cause of being as well as a cause of knowledge and truth? Discuss and relate to the metaphor of the sun.

7. Describe in detail the Platonic theory of knowledge in terms of the divided line. What problems of significance do you find here?

8. Distinguish between the world of appearances and the intelligible world. What is the function of dialectic in the intelligible world? How do we attain a knowledge of the Idea of the Good?

9. Discuss the implications of the Allegory of the Cave for the Platonic theory of knowledge and for his theory of education.

René Descartes

᠁᠁᠁᠁᠁᠁᠁᠁᠁᠁᠁᠁᠁᠁᠁᠁᠁᠁᠁᠁᠁᠁᠁᠁

THE QUEST FOR CERTAINTY

᠁᠁᠁᠁᠁᠁᠁᠁᠁᠁᠁᠁᠁᠁᠁᠁᠁᠁᠁᠁᠁᠁᠁᠁

Biographical Note.   RENÉ DESCARTES (1596–1650), was born at Touraine in France. He attended the Jesuit college of La Flèche from 1604 to 1612. The last few years at college were given over entirely to a study of logic, philosophy, and mathematics. After leaving college he decided that it was time for him to "learn from the book of the world." To accomplish this he accepted military service and he combined this profession with his mathematical studies. In 1623 he returned to Paris, but found the city too distracting and several years later moved to Holland. Here he published in 1637 his *Discourse on Method* and in 1641 the first edition of the *Meditations.* These were followed by the *Principles of Philosophy* in 1644. In addition to his philosophical contributions he was equally famous for his mathematical studies, which included his development of the basic principles of analytic geometry. In 1649, Descartes left Holland upon the invitation of Queen Christina of Sweden, who wished to be instructed in philosophy. However, the Swedish winter and his having to arise at seven each morning were too much for him. He contracted a fever in January of 1650 and died in the following month.

* * *

Introductory Note.   For a variety of reasons, Descartes has usually been characterized as the "Father of Modern Philosophy." In the first place, his

The first two of the six *Meditations on the First Philosophy* (1641), translated from the Latin by John Veitch (1853).

philosophy represents a break with the medieval tradition. Second, Descartes' principal concern is with the problem of knowledge and the necessity as he saw it of establishing man's knowledge on a firm basis. Third, his contributions to science and mathematics established his intellectual leadership and strengthened his own conviction that the true method in philosophy and the way to knowledge is the mathematical method. In effect, all of these reasons were to merge into one, and it is no exaggeration to say that it was Descartes who gave philosophy a new orientation by his analysis of knowledge. Unlike the medievals whose philosophy was God-centered, Descartes centers his philosophy on man. The Cartesian revolution was the affirmation that all philosophy begins, not with nature nor with God, but with man, with the self—a view summed up in his famous formula of the *Cogito*, the "I think."

Descartes may also be described as the first of the great rationalists in modern philosophy. As a rationalist he accepted the existence of certain self-evident and virtually innate ideas. From these as premises it was his conviction that all knowledge might be deduced with the same certitude as mathematical truths. The method of mathematics could unify all knowledge and lead man to certitude—this was his dream. To realize such a dream, Descartes felt it was necessary to combat the revival of scepticism, which was a feature of his age, and to achieve some basic and indubitable premise upon which all philosophy and all knowledge might be erected. Such a truth he believed was the *Cogito*, the "I think," a truth based upon his famous method of doubt.

The first of the *Meditations* illustrates this "method of doubt" or Methodological scepticism. Descartes shows how we may doubt the evidence of the senses, how we are often deceived by our dreams and find it difficult to distinguish them from the waking state, and how, on the supposition that the world might be controlled by some evil demon, even the truths of mathematics as well as all other knowledge may be called into question. In the second of the *Meditations*, Descartes shows that such a methodological scepticism can have but one outcome, namely, the assertion of the existence of the doubting self. For to doubt means to think and in all doubting one truth stands out, namely, that I am doubting. There can be no scepticism without the existence of a sceptic. Once the existence of the doubting self is affirmed, Descartes proceeds to elaborate upon the nature of the self as a thinking being. Upon the basis of mind as a being that thinks, he erects his entire metaphysical system.

OF THE THINGS OF WHICH WE MAY DOUBT

Several years have now elapsed since I first became aware that I had accepted, even from my youth, many false opinions for true, and that consequently what I afterwards based on such principles was highly doubtful; and from that time I was convinced of the necessity of undertaking once in my life to rid myself of all the opinions I had adopted, and of commencing anew the work of building from the foundation, if I desired to establish a firm and abiding superstructure in the sciences. But as this enterprise appeared to me to be one of great magnitude, I waited until I had attained an age so mature as to leave me no hope that at any stage of life more advanced I should be better able to execute my design. On this account, I have so long delayed that I should henceforth consider I was doing wrong were I still to consume in deliberation any of the time that now remains for action. Today, then, since I have opportunely freed my mind from all cares, and am happily disturbed by no passions, and since I am in the secure possession of leisure in a peaceable retirement, I will at length apply myself earnestly and freely to the general overthrow of all my former opinions. But, to this end, it will not be necessary for me to show that the whole of these are false—a point, perhaps, which I shall never reach; but as even now my reason convinces me that I ought not the less carefully to withhold belief from what is not entirely certain and indubitable, than from what is manifestly false, it will be sufficient to justify the rejection of the whole if I shall find in each some ground for doubt. Nor for this purpose will it be necessary even to deal with each belief individually, which would be truly an endless labor; but, as the removal from below of the foundation necessarily involves the downfall of the whole edifice, I will at once approach the criticism of the principles on which all my former beliefs rested.

All that I have, up to this moment, accepted as possessed of the highest truth and certainty, I received either from or through the senses. I observed, however, that these sometimes misled us, and it is the part of prudence not to place absolute confidence in that by which we have even once been deceived.

But it may be said, perhaps, that, although the senses occasionally mislead us respecting minute objects, and such as are so far removed from us as to be beyond the reach of close observations, there are yet many other of their informations (presentations), of the truth of which it is manifestly impossible to doubt; as for example, that I am in this place, seated by the fire clothed in a winter dressing-gown, that I hold in my hands this piece of paper, with other intimations of the same nature. But how could I deny that I possess these hands and this body, and withal escape being classed with persons in a state of insanity, whose brains are so disordered . . . as to cause them pertinaciously to assert that they are monarchs when they are in the greatest poverty; or clothed in gold and purple when destitute of any covering; or that their head is made of clay, their body of glass, or that they are gourds? I should certainly be not less insane than they, were I to regulate my procedure according to examples so extravagant.

Though this be true, I must nevertheless here consider that I am a man, and that, consequently, I am in the habit of sleeping, and representing to myself in dreams those same things, or even sometimes others less probable, which the insane think are presented to them in their waking moments. How often have I dreamt that I was in these familiar circumstances,—that I was dressed, and occupied this place by the fire, when I was lying undressed in bed? At the present moment, however, I certainly look upon this paper with eyes wide awake; the head which I now move is not asleep; I extend this hand consciously and with express purpose, and I perceive it; the occurrences in sleep are not so distinct as all this. But I cannot forget that, at other times, I have been deceived in sleep by similar illusions; and, attentively considering those cases, I perceive so clearly that there exist no certain marks by which the state of waking can ever be distinguished from sleep, that I feel greatly astonished; and in amazement I almost persuade myself that I am now dreaming.

Let us suppose, then, that we are dreaming, and that all these particulars—namely, the opening of the eyes, the motion of the head, the forth-putting of the hands—are merely illusions; and even that we really possess neither an entire body nor hands such as we see. Nevertheless, it must be admitted at least that the objects which appear to us in sleep are, as it were, representations which could not have been formed unless in the likeness of realities; and, therefore, that those general objects, at all events,—namely, eyes, a head, hands, and an entire body —are not simply imaginary, but really existent. For, in truth, painters themselves, even when they study to represent sirens and satyrs by forms the most fantastic and extraordinary, cannot bestow upon them natures absolutely new, but can only make a certain medley of the members of different animals; or if they chance to imagine something so novel that nothing at all similar has ever been seen before, and such as is, therefore, purely fictitious and absolutely false, it is at least certain that the colors of which this is composed are real.

And on the same principle, although these general objects, viz. a body, eyes, a head, hands, and the like, be imaginary, we are nevertheless absolutely necessitated to admit the reality at least of some other objects still more simple and universal than these, of which, just as of certain

real colors, all those images of things, whether true and real, or false
and fantastic, that are found in our consciousness, are formed.

To this class of objects seem to belong corporeal nature in general
and its extension; the figure of extended things, their quantity or magnitude, and their number, as also the place in, and the time during, which
they exist, and other things of the same sort. We will not, therefore,
perhaps reason illegitimately if we conclude from this that Physics,
Astronomy, Medicine, and all the other sciences that have for their end
the consideration of composite objects, are indeed of a doubtful character; but that Arithmetic, Geometry, and the other sciences of the same
class, which regard merely the simplest and most general objects, and
scarcely inquire whether or not these are really existent, contain something that is certain and indubitable; for whether I am awake or dreaming, it remains true that two and three makes five, and that a square
has but four sides; nor does it seem possible that truths so apparent can
ever fall under a suspicion of falsity or incertitude.

Nevertheless, the belief that there is a God who is all-powerful, and
who created me, such as I am, has, for a long time, obtained steady
possession of my mind. How, then, do I know that he has not arranged
that there should be neither earth, nor sky, nor any extended thing,
nor figure, nor magnitude, nor place, providing at the same time, however, for the rise in me of the perceptions of all these objects, and the
persuasion that these do not exist otherwise than as I perceive them?
And further, as I sometimes think that others are in error respecting
matters of which they believe themselves to possess a perfect knowledge,
how do I know that I am not also deceived each time I add together
two and three, or number the sides of a square, or form some judgment
still more simple, if more simple indeed can be imagined? But perhaps
Deity has not been willing that I should be thus deceived, for He is said
to be supremely good. If, however, it were repugnant to the goodness of
Deity to have created me subject to constant deception, it would seem
likewise to be contrary to his goodness to allow me to be occasionally
deceived; and yet it is clear that this is permitted. Some, indeed, might
perhaps be found who would be disposed rather to deny the existence
of a Being so powerful than to believe that there is nothing certain.
But let us for the present refrain from opposing this opinion, and grant
that all which is here said of a Diety is fabulous; nevertheless in whatever way it be supposed that I reached the state in which I exist, whether
by fate, or chance, or by an endless series of antecedents and conse-
quents, or by any other means, it is clear (since to be deceived and to
err is a certain defect) that the probability of my being so imperfect as

to be the constant victim of deception, will be increased exactly in proportion as the power possessed by the cause, to which they assign my origin, is lessened. To these reasonings I have assuredly nothing to reply, but am constrained at last to avow that there is nothing of all that I formerly believed to be true of which it is impossible to doubt, and that not through thoughtlessness or levity, but from cogent and maturely considered reasons; so that henceforward, if I desire to discover anything certain, I ought not the less carefully to refrain from assenting to those same opinions than to what might be shown to be manifestly false.

But it is not sufficient to have made these observations; care must be taken likewise to keep them in remembrance. For those old and customary opinions perpetually recur—long and familiar usage giving them the right of occupying my mind, even almost against my will, and subduing my belief; nor will I lose the habit of deferring to them and confiding in them so long as I shall consider them to be what in truth they are, viz., opinions to some extent doubtful, as I have already shown, but still highly probable, and such as it is much more reasonable to believe than deny. It is for this reason I am persuaded that I shall not be doing wrong, if, taking an opposite judgment of deliberate design, I become my own deceiver, by supposing, for a time, that all those opinions are entirely false and imaginary, until at length, having thus balanced my old by my new prejudices, my judgment shall no longer be turned aside by perverted usage from the path that may conduct to the perception of truth. For I am assured that, meanwhile, there will arise neither peril nor error from this course, and that I cannot for the present yield too much to distrust, since the end I now seek is not action but knowledge.

I will suppose, then, not that Deity, who is sovereignly good and the fountain of truth, but that some malignant demon, who is at once exceedingly potent and deceitful, has employed all his artifice to deceive me; I will suppose that the sky, the air, the earth, colors, figures, sounds, and all external things, are nothing better than the illusions of dreams, by means of which this being has laid snares for my credulity; I will consider myself as without hands, eyes, flesh, blood, or any of the senses, and as falsely believing that I am possessed of these; I will continue resolutely fixed in this belief, and if indeed by this means it be not in my power to arrive at the knowledge of truth, I shall at least do what is in my power, viz., suspend my judgment, and guard with settled purpose against giving my assent to what is false, and being imposed upon by this deceiver, whatever be his power and artifice.

But this undertaking is arduous, and a certain indolence insensibly leads me back to my ordinary course of life; and just as the captive, who, perchance, was enjoying in his dreams an imaginary liberty, when he begins to suspect that it is but a vision, dreads awakening, and conspires with the agreeable illusions that the deception may be prolonged; so I, of my own accord, fall back into the train of my former beliefs, and fear to arouse myself from my slumber, lest the time of laborious wakefulness that would succeed this quiet rest, in place of bringing any light of day, should prove inadequate to dispel the darkness that will arise from the difficulties that have now been raised.

OF THE NATURE OF THE HUMAN MIND; AND THAT IT IS MORE EASILY KNOWN THAN THE BODY

The Meditation of yesterday has filled my mind with so many doubts, that it is no longer in my power to forget them. Nor do I see, meanwhile, any principle on which they can be resolved; and, just as if I had fallen all of a sudden into very deep water, I am so greatly disconcerted as to be unable either to plant my feet firmly on the bottom or sustain myself by swimming on the surface. I will, nevertheless, make an effort, and try anew the same path on which I had entered yesterday, that is, proceed by casting aside all that admits of the slightest doubt, not less than if I had discovered it to be absolutely false; and I will continue always in this track until I shall find something that is certain, or at least, if I can do nothing more, until I shall know with certainty that there is nothing certain. Archimedes, that he might transport the entire globe from the place it occupied to another, demanded only a point that was firm and immoveable; so also, I shall be entitled to entertain the highest expectations, if I am fortunate enough to discover only one thing that is certain and indubitable.

I suppose, accordingly, that all the things which I see are false; I believe that none of those objects which my fallacious memory represents ever existed. I suppose that I possess no senses; I believe that body, figure, extension, motion, and place are merely fictions of my mind. What is there, then, that can be esteemed true? Perhaps this only, that there is absolutely nothing certain.

But how do I know that there is not something different altogether from the objects I have now enumerated, of which it is impossible to entertain the slightest doubt? Is there not a God, or some being, by whatever name I may designate him, who causes these thoughts to arise in my mind? But why suppose such a being, for it may be I myself am capable of producing them? Am I, then, at least not something. But I before denied that I possessed senses or a body; I hesitate, however, for what follows from that? Am I so dependent on the body and the senses that without these I cannot exist? But I had the persuasion that there was absolutely nothing in the world, that there was no sky and no earth, neither minds nor bodies; was I not, therefore, at the same time, persuaded that I did not exist? Far from it; I assuredly existed, since I was persuaded. But there is I know not what being, who is possessed at once of the highest power and the deepest cunning, who is constantly employing all his ingenuity in deceiving me. Doubtless, then, I exist, since I am deceived; and, let him deceive me as he may, he can never bring it about that I am nothing, so long as I shall be conscious that I am something. So that it must, in fine, be maintained, all things being maturely and carefully considered, that this proposition, I am, I exist, is necessarily true each time it is expressed by me, or conceived in my mind.

But I do not yet know with sufficient clearness what I am, though assured that I am; and hence, in the next place, I must take care, lest perchance I inconsiderately substitute some other object in place of what is properly myself, and thus wander from truth, even in that knowledge which I hold to be of all others the most certain and evident. For this reason, I will now consider anew what I formerly believed myself to be, before I entered on the present train of thought; and of my previous opinion I will retrench all that can in the least be invalidated by the grounds of doubt I have adduced, in order that there may at length remain nothing but what is certain and indubitable. What then did I formerly think I was? Undoubtedly I judged that I was a man. But what is a man? Shall I say a rational animal? Assuredly not; for it would be necessary forthwith to inquire into what is meant by animal, and what by rational, and thus, from a single question, I should insensibly glide into others, and these more difficult than the first; nor do I now possess enough of leisure to warrant me in wasting my time amid subtleties of this sort. I prefer here to attend to the thoughts that sprung up of themselves in my mind, and were inspired by my own nature alone, when I applied myself to the consideration of what I was. In the first place, then, I thought that I possessed a face, hands, arms, and all the fabric of members that appears in a corpse, and which I called by the name of body. It further occurred to me that I was nourished, that I walked, perceived, and thought, and all those actions I referred to the soul; but what the soul itself was I either did not stay to consider, or, if I did, I imagined that it was something extremely rare and subtile, like wind, or flame, or ether, spread through my grosser parts. As to the body, I did not even doubt of its nature, but thought I distinctly knew it, and if I had wished to describe it according to the notions I then entertained, I should have explained myself in this manner: By body I understand all that can be terminated by a certain figure, that can be comprised in a certain place, and so fill a certain space as therefrom to exclude every other body; that can be perceived either by touch, sight, hearing, taste, or smell; that can be moved in different ways, not indeed of itself, but by something foreign to it by which it is touched and from which it receives the impression; for the power of self-motion, as likewise that of perceiving and thinking, I held as by no means pertaining to the nature of body; on the contrary, I was somewhat astonished to find such faculties existing in some bodies.

But as to myself, what can I now say that I am, since I suppose there exists an extremely powerful, and, if I may so speak, malignant being, whose whole endeavors are directed towards deceiving me? Can I affirm that I possess any one of all those attributes of which I have lately spoken as belonging to the nature of body? After attentively considering them in my own mind, I find none of them that can properly be said to belong to myself. . . . Let us pass, then, to the attributes of the soul. The first mentioned were the powers of nutrition and walking; but, if it be true that I have no body, it is true likewise that I am capable neither of walking nor of being nourished. Perception is another attribute of the soul; but perception too is impossible without the body: besides, I have frequently during sleep, believed that I perceived objects which I afterwards observed I did not in reality perceive. Thinking is another attribute of the soul; and here I discover what properly belongs to myself. This alone is inseparable from me. I am—I exist: this is certain; but how often? As often as I think; for perhaps it would even happen, if I should wholly cease to think, that I should at the same time altogether cease to be. I now admit nothing that is not necessarily true: I am therefore, precisely speaking, only a thinking thing, that is, a mind, understanding, or reason—terms whose signification was before unknown to me. I am, however, a real thing, and really existent; but what thing? The answer was, a thinking thing. The question now arises, am I aught besides? I will stimulate my imagination with a view to discover whether I am not still something more than a thinking being. Now it is plain I am not the assemblage of members called the human body; I am not a thin and pentrating air diffused through all these members, or wind, or flame, or vapour, or breath, or any of all the things I can imagine; for I supposed that all these were not, and, without changing the supposition, I find that I still feel assured of my existence.

But it is true, perhaps, that those very things which I suppose to be non-existent, because they are unknown to me, are not in truth different from myself whom I know. This is a point I cannot determine, and do not now enter into any dispute regarding it. I can only judge of things that are known to me: I am conscious that I exist, and I who know that I exist inquire into what I am. It is, however, perfectly certain that the knowledge of my existence, thus precisely taken, is not dependent on things, the existence of which is as yet unknown to me: and consequently it is not dependent on any of the things I can feign in imagination. Moreover, the phrase itself, I frame an image, reminds me of my error; for I should in truth frame one if I were to imagine myself to be anything, since to imagine is nothing more than to contemplate the figure or image of a corporeal thing; but I already know that I exist, and that it is possible at the same time that all those images, and in general all that relates to the nature of body, are merely dreams or chimeras. From this I discover that it is not more reasonable to say, I will excite my imagination that I may know more distinctly what I am, than to express myself as follows: I am now awake, and perceive something real; but because my perception is not sufficiently clear, I will of express purpose go to sleep that my dreams may represent to me the object of my perception with more truth and clearness. And, therefore, I know that nothing of all that I can embrace in imagination belongs to the knowledge which I have of myself, and that there is need to recall with the utmost care the mind from this mode of thinking, that it may be able to know its own nature with perfect distinctness.

But what, then, am I? A thinking thing, it has been said. But what is a thinking thing? It is a thing that doubts, understands, conceives, affirms, denies, wills, refuses, that imagines also, and perceives. Assuredly it is not little, if all these properties belong to my nature. But why should they not belong to it? Am I not that very being who now doubts of almost everything; who, for all that, understands and conceives certain things, who affirms one alone as true, and denies the others; who desires to know more of them, and does not wish to be deceived; who imagines many things, sometimes even despite his will; and is likewise percipient of many, as if through the medium of the senses. Is there nothing of all this as true as that I am, even although I should be always dreaming, and although he who gave me being employed all his ingenuity to deceive me? Is there also any one of these attributes that can be properly distinguished from my thought, or that can be said to be separate from myself. For it is of itself so evident that it is I who doubt, I who understand, and I who desire, that it is here unnecessary to add anything by way of rendering it more clear. And I am as certainly the same being who imagines; for, although it may be that nothing I imagine is true, still the power of imagination does not cease really to exist in me and to form part of my thought. In fine, I am the same being who perceives, that is, who apprehends certain objects by the organs of sense, since, in truth, I see light, hear a noise, and feel heat. But it will be said that these presentations are false, and that I am dreaming. Let it be so. At all events it is certain that I seem to see light, hear a noise, and feel heat; this cannot be false, and this is what in me is properly called perceiving, which is nothing else than thinking. From this I begin to know what I am with somewhat greater clearness and distinctness than heretofore.

But, nevertheless, it still seems to me, and I cannot help believing, that corporeal things, whose images are formed by thought, which fall under the senses, and are examined by the same, are known with much greater distinctness than that I know not what part of myself which is not imaginable; although, in truth, it may seem strange to say that I know and comprehend with greater distinctness things whose existence appears to me doubtful, that are unknown, and do not belong to me, than others of whose reality I am persuaded, that are known to me, and appertain to my proper nature, in a word, than myself. But I see clearly what is the state of the case. My mind is apt to wander, and will not yet submit to be restrained within the limits of truth. Let us therefore leave the mind to itself once more, and, according to it every kind of liberty, permit it to consider the objects that appear to it from without, in order that, having afterwards withdrawn it from these gently and opportunely, and fixed on the consideration of its being and the properties it finds in itself, it may then be the more easily controlled.

Let us now accordingly consider the objects that are commonly thought to be the most easily, and likewise the most distinctly known, viz., the bodies we touch and see; not, indeed, bodies in general, for these general notions are usually somewhat more confused, but one body in particular. Take, for example, this piece of wax; it is quite fresh, having been but recently taken from the bee-hive; it has not yet lost the sweetness of the honey it contained; it still retains somewhat of the odor of the flowers from which it was gathered; its color, figure, size, are apparent to the sight, it is hard, cold, easily handled; and sounds when struck upon with the finger. In fine, all that contributes to make a body as distinctly known as possible, is found in the one before us. But, while I am speaking, let it be placed near the fire—what remained of the taste exhales, the smell evaporates, the color changes, its figure is destroyed, its size increases, it becomes liquid, it grows hot, it can hardly be handled, and, although struck upon, it emits no sound. Does the same wax still remain after this change? It must be admitted that it does remain; no one doubts it, or judges otherwise. What, then, was it I knew with so much distinctness in the piece of wax? Assuredly, it could be nothing of all that I observed by means of the senses, since all the things that fell under taste, smell, sight, touch, and hearing are changed, and yet the same wax remains. It was perhaps what I now think, viz. that this wax was neither the sweetness of honey, the pleasant odor of flowers, the whiteness, the figure, nor the sound, but only a body that a little before appeared to me conspicuous under these forms, and which is now perceived under others. But, to speak precisely, what is it that I imagine when I think of it in this way? Let it be attentively considered, and, retrenching all that does not belong to the wax, let us see what remains. There certainly remains nothing, except something extended, flexible, and movable. But what is meant by flexible and movable? Is it not that I imagine that the piece of wax, being round, is capable of becoming square, or of passing from a square into a triangular figure? Assuredly such is not the case, because I conceive that it admits of an infinity of similar changes; and I am, moreover, unable to compass this infinity by imagination, and consequently this conception which I have of the wax is not the product of the faculty of imagination. But what now is this extension? Is it not also unknown? For it becomes greater when the wax is melted, greater when it is boiled, and greater still when the heat increases; and I should not conceive clearly and according to truth, the wax as it is, if I did not suppose that the piece we are considering admitted even of a wider variety of extension than I ever imagined. I must, therefore, admit that I cannot even comprehend by imagination what the piece of wax is, and that it is the mind alone which perceives it. I speak of one piece in particular; for, as to wax in general, this is still more evident. But what is the piece of wax that can be perceived only by the understanding or mind? It is certainly the same which I see, touch, imagine; and, in fine, it is the same which, from the beginning, I believed it to be. But the perception of it is neither an act of sight, of touch, nor of imagination, and never was either of these, though it might formerly seem so, but is simply an intuition of the mind, which may be imperfect and confused, as it formerly was, or very clear and distinct, as it is at present, according as the attention is more or less direct to the elements which it contains, and of which it is composed.

But, meanwhile, I feel greatly astonished when I observe the weakness of my mind, and its proneness to error. For although, without at all giving expression to what I think, I consider all this in my own mind, words yet occasionally impede my progress, and I am almost led into error by the terms of ordinary language. We say, for example, that we see the same wax when it is before us, and not that we judge it to be the same from its retaining the same color and figure: whence I should forthwith be disposed to conclude that the wax is known by the act of sight, and not by the intuition of the mind alone, were it not for the analogous instance of human beings passing on in the street below, as observed from a window. In this case I do not fail to say that I see the men themselves, just as I say that I see the wax; and yet what do I see from the window beyond hats and cloaks that might cover artificial machines, whose motions might be determined by springs? But I judge that there are human beings from these appearances, and thus I comprehend, by the faculty of judgment alone which is in the mind, what I believed I saw with my eyes.

The man who makes it his aim to rise to knowledge superior to the common, ought to be ashamed to seek occasions of doubting from the vulgar forms of speech: instead, therefore, of doing this, I shall proceed with the matter in hand, and inquire whether I had a clearer and more perfect perception of the piece of wax when I first saw it, and when I thought I knew it by means of the external sense itself, or, at all events, by the common sense, as it is called, that is, by the imaginative faculty; or whether I rather apprehend it more clearly at present, after having examined with greater care, both what it is, and in what way it can be known. It would certainly be ridiculous to entertain any doubt on this point. For what, in that first perception, was there distinct? What did I perceive which any animal might not have perceived? But when I distinguish the wax from its exterior forms, and when, as if I had stripped it of its vestments, I consider it quite naked, it is certain, although some error may still be found in my judgment, that I cannot, nevertheless, thus apprehend it without possessing a human mind.

But, finally, what shall I say of the mind itself, that is, of myself? For as yet I do not admit that I am anything but mind. What, then! I who seem to possess so distinct an apprehension of the piece of wax, —do I not know myself with greater truth and certitude, and also much more distinctly and clearly? For if I judge that the wax exists because I see it, it assuredly follows, much more evidently, that I myself am or exist, for the same reason; for it is possible that what I see may not in truth be wax, and that I do not even possess eyes with which to see anything; but it cannot be that when I see, or, which comes to the same thing, when I think I see, I myself who think am nothing. So likewise, if I judge that the wax exists because I touch it, it will still also follow that I am; and if I determine that my imagination, or any other cause, whatever it be, persuades me of the existence of the wax, I will still draw the same conclusion. And what is here remarked of the piece of wax, is applicable to all the other things that are external to me. And further, if the notion or perception of wax appeared to me more precise and distinct, after that not only sight and touch, but many other causes besides, rendered it manifest to my apprehension, with how much greater distinctness must I now know myself, since all the reasons that contribute to the knowledge of the nature of wax, or of any body whatever, manifest still better the nature of my mind? And there are besides so many other things in the mind itself that contribute to the illustration of its nature, that those dependent on the body, to which I have here referred, scarcely merit to be taken into account.

But, in conclusion, I find I have insensibly reverted to the point I desired; for, since it is now manifest to me that bodies themselves are not properly perceived by the senses nor by the faculty of imagination, but by the intellect alone; and since they are not perceived because they are seen and touched, but only because they are understood or rightly comprehended by thought, I readily discover that there is nothing more easily or clearly apprehended than my own mind. But because it is difficult to rid one's self so promptly of an opinion to which one has been long accustomed, it will be desirable to tarry for some time at this stage, that, by long continued meditation, I may more deeply impress upon my memory this new knowledge.

STUDY QUESTIONS

1. To what extent does Descartes intend to push his sceptical doubts? To what purpose?
2. Do you believe that the senses deceive us? Discuss fully and evaluate Descartes' conclusions on this point.
3. How do you know that you are not presently dreaming? What criteria would you suggest for distinguishing between the dreaming and waking states?
4. What certitude would you attach to mathematical truths? What would you consider to be the basis of such certitude? What are Descartes' views on such issues.
5. Why does Descartes find it necessary to propose the 'malignant demon'

hypothesis. How successful is such an hypothesis for his methodological scepticism.

6. Do you think it is possible to doubt everything? Do you think the procedure of Descartes is valid, that is, do you think it is possible to construct a sound system of knowledge upon scepticism.

7. What conclusions regarding the nature of a physical object does Descartes reach with his analysis of a piece of wax? Would you agree with the analysis and the conclusions?

8. Show why, for Descartes, there is greater certitude in the knowledge of the mind than in the knowledge of any physical object, e. g. the piece of wax.

9. How do you suppose Descartes would establish the existence of an external world of physical, material objects. Discuss.

David Hume

𝕮𝕮𝕮𝕮𝕮𝕮𝕮𝕮𝕮𝕮𝕮𝕮𝕮𝕮𝕮𝕮𝕮𝕮𝕮𝕮𝕮𝕮𝕮𝕮𝕮𝕮𝕮𝕮𝕮𝕮𝕮𝕮𝕮𝕮𝕮𝕮𝕮𝕮𝕮

KNOWLEDGE AND EXPERIENCE

𝕮𝕮𝕮𝕮𝕮𝕮𝕮𝕮𝕮𝕮𝕮𝕮𝕮𝕮𝕮𝕮𝕮𝕮𝕮𝕮𝕮𝕮𝕮𝕮𝕮𝕮𝕮𝕮𝕮𝕮𝕮𝕮𝕮𝕮𝕮𝕮𝕮𝕮𝕮

Biographical Note. DAVID HUME (1721–1776) was born in Edinburgh, Scotland. He was destined by his family for a career in law, but declared that "he was seized very early with a passion for literature" and "found an insurmountable aversion to everything but the pursuits of philosophy and general learning." Following his education at the University of Edinburgh, he tried to please his family by pursuing a business career. Failing in this he went to France to study. It was there that he wrote his *Treatise of Human Nature* between the ages of 23 and 26. In 1748 he published the *Enquiry Concerning Human Understanding*. Three years later this was followed by the *Enquiry Concerning the Principles of Morals*, which he regarded as "incomparably the best" of all his works. In 1752 he accepted a post as librarian at Edinburgh and turned his attention to history, writing during the next decade several volumes on the *History of England*. These works sold well and were better received than the philosophical works. Hume had now become a leading figure in the literary world of Adam Smith, Dr. Johnson, J. J. Rousseau, and Edward Gibbon. In 1763 he was appointed secretary to the British Embassy in Paris. He enjoyed considerable success in Paris and remained there for the next several years. In 1769 he

The material that follows is taken from Sections II and IV of the *Enquiry Concerning Human Understanding*. Taken from *Enquiries concerning the Human Understanding & concerning the Principles of Morals*. Edited by L. A. Selby-Bigges, Oxford, 1897.

returned to Edinburgh and continued his writings until stricken with cancer in 1775.

* * *

Introductory Note. The development of British empiricism, begun by Locke and continued by Berkeley, attains its climax in the more radical theory of knowledge that Hume preferred to call a "mitigated scepticism." Like his immediate predecessors, Hume accepted the principle that all our knowledge originates in sense experience and he carries this principle to what logical empiricists would call its logical conclusion with the assertion that no idea or set of ideas for which there is no sense impression has any validity. With Berkeley, he rejects Locke's notion of a material substance and abstract ideas, but pushing the empirical principle further he disputes Berkeley's belief in a spiritual substance as wholly unwarranted on the basis of experience. With the rejection of spiritual substance goes the rejection of any demonstration of the existence of God. Hence experience yields only a congeries of ideas—matter, God, the self, and the external world are unknowable. But the most devastating aspect of Hume's scepticism was his denial of any demonstrable or necessary character to the law of causality. His analysis of the causal relation at one stroke undermined the necessary truths of science and aroused Kant from his dogmatic slumber.

Yet Hume's scepticism remained speculative rather than practical. As he tells us, he continued to believe in an external world and in the laws of nature. Nor did he doubt the ability of human reason provided its inquiries were properly limited. Mathematical reasoning yields necessary truths, reasoning concerning matters of fact yields only probable truths, but metaphysics has neither rational nor experiential justification.

In Hume's account of the origin of ideas two basic points may be noted: (1) the manner in which he accounts for the origin of our ideas and the distinction he draws between impressions (perceptions) and ideas (copies of impressions); and (2) that all ideas must be derived from an impression in order to justify their validity. In developing his account of causal relations, Hume emphasizes the division of knowledge into relations of ideas and matters of fact. Mathematics exemplifies the former, our knowledge of causal relations the latter, and it becomes Hume's great concern to determine the validity of such knowledge. Causal relations, he holds, are discoverable only by experience; they elude all rational demonstration. Every effect is distinct from its cause and nothing in an effect can lead us by inference to the cause. Hence all our reasoning concerning matters of fact which are based on causal relations is at best probable. Such reasoning depends upon the fact that from causes that are similar we come to expect similar effects. Our arguments regarding causal relations rest upon the principle that the future will resemble the past. But there is no demonstration of such a principle and no empirical verification for it. We may, of course, continue to believe in causality, but Hume would say our belief is a matter of custom or habit. We come to expect the same effects from the same causes, but no demonstrable inference of such a relationship is possible.

OF THE ORIGIN OF IDEAS

Everyone will readily allow that there is a considerable difference between the perceptions of the mind, when a man feels that pain of excessive heat, or the pleasure of moderate warmth, and when he afterwards recalls to his memory this sensation, or anticipates it by his imagination. These faculties may mimic or copy the perceptions of the senses; but they never can entirely reach the force and vivacity of the original sentiment. The utmost we say of them, even when they operate with the greatest vigor, is, that they represent their object in so lively a manner, that we could *almost* say we feel or see it: But, except the mind be disordered by disease or madness, they never can arrive at such a pitch of vivacity, as to render these perceptions altogether undistinguishable. All the colors of poetry, however splendid, can never paint natural objects in such a manner as to make the description be taken for a real landscape. The most lively thought is still inferior to the dullest sensation.

We may observe a like distinction to run through all the other perceptions of the mind. A man in a fit of anger is actuated in a very different manner from one who only thinks of that emotion. If you tell me, that any person is in love, I easily understand your meaning, and form a just conception of his situation; but never can mistake that conception for the real disorders and agitations of the passion. When we reflect on our past sentiments and affections, our thought is a faithful mirror, and copies its objects truly; but the colors which it employs are faint and dull, in comparison of those in which our original perceptions were clothed. It requires no nice discernment or metaphysical head to mark the distinction between them.

Here therefore we may divide all the perceptions of the mind into two classes or species, which are distinguished by their different degrees of force and vivacity. The less forcible and lively are commonly denominated *thoughts* or *ideas*. The other species want a name in our language, and in most others; I suppose, because it was not requisite for any, but philosophical purposes, to rank them under a general term or appellation. Let us, therefore, use a little freedom, and call them *impressions;* employing that word in a sense somewhat different from the usual. By the term *impression,* then, I mean all our more lively perceptions, when we hear, or see, or feel, or love, or hate, or desire, or will. And impressions are distinguished from ideas, which are the less lively perceptions, of which we are conscious, when we reflect on any of those sensations or movements above mentioned.

Nothing, at first view, may seem more unbounded than the thought of man, which not only escapes all human power and authority, but is not even restrained within the limits of nature and reality. To form monsters, and join incongruous shapes and appearances, costs the imagination no more trouble than to conceive the most natural and familiar objects. And while the body is confined to one planet, along which it creeps with pain and difficulty; the thought can in an instant transport us into the most distant regions of the universe, or even beyond the universe, into the unbounded chaos, where nature is supposed to lie in total confusion. What never was seen, or heard of, may yet be conceived; nor is anything beyond the power of thought, except what implies an absolute contradiction.

But though our thought seems to possess this unbounded liberty, we shall find, upon a nearer examination, that it is really confined within very narrow limits, and that all this creative power of the mind amounts to no more than the faculty of compounding, transposing, augmenting, or diminishing the materials afforded us by the senses and experience. When we think of a golden mountain, we can only join two consistent ideas, *gold,* and *mountain,* with which we were formerly acquainted. A virtuous horse we can conceive; because, from our own feeling, we can conceive virtue; and this we may unite to the figure and shape of a horse, which is an animal familiar to us. In short, all the materials of thinking are derived either from our outward or inward sentiment: the mixture and composition of these belongs alone to the mind and will. Or, to express myself in philosophical language, all our ideas or more feeble perceptions are copies of our impressions or more lively ones.

To prove this, the two following arguments will, I hope, be sufficient. First, when we analyze our thoughts or ideas, however compounded or sublime, we always find that they resolve themselves into such simple ideas as were copied from a precedent feeling or sentiment. Even those ideas, which, at first view, seem the most wide of this origin, are found, upon a nearer scrutiny, to be derived from it. The idea of God, as meaning an infinitely intelligent, wise, and good Being, arises from reflecting on the operations of our own mind, and augmenting, without limit, those qualities of goodness and wisdom. We may prosecute this inquiry to what length we please; where we shall always find, that every idea which we examine is copied from a similar impression. Those who would assert that this position is not universally true nor without exception, have only one, and that an easy method of refuting it; by producing that idea, which, in their opinion, is not derived from this source. It will then be incumbent on us, if we would maintain our doctrine, to produce the impression, or lively perception which corresponds to it.

Secondly. If it happen, from a defect of the organ, that a man is not susceptible of any species of sensation, we always find that he is as little susceptible of the correspondent ideas. A blind man can form no notion of colors; a deaf man of sounds. . . .

There is, however, one contradictory phenomenon, which may prove that it is not absolutely impossible for ideas to arise, independent of their correspondent impressions. I believe it will readily be allowed, that the several distinct ideas of color, which enter by the eye, or those of sound, which are conveyed by the ear, are really different from each other; though, at the same time, resembling. Now if this be true of different colors, it must no less be true of the different shades of the same color; and each shade produces a distinct idea, independent of the rest. For if this should be denied, it is possible, by the continual gradation of shades, to run a color insensibly into what is most remote from it; and if you will not allow any of the means to be different, you cannot, without absurdity, deny the extremes to be the same. Suppose, therefore, a person to have enjoyed his sight for thirty years, and to have become perfectly acquainted with colors of all kinds except one particular shade of blue, for instance, which it never has been his fortune to meet with. Let all the different shades of that color, except that single one, be placed before him, descending gradually from the deepest to the lightest; it is plain that he will perceive a blank, where that shade is wanting, and will be sensible that there is a greater distance in that place between the contiguous colors than in any other. Now I ask, whether it be possible for him, from his own imagination, to supply this deficiency, and raise up to himself the idea of that particular shade, though it had never been conveyed to him by his senses? I believe there are few but will be of opinion that he can: and this may serve as a proof that the simple ideas are not always, in every instance, derived from the correspondent impressions; though this instance is so singular, that it is scarcely worth our observing, and does not merit that for it alone we should alter our general maxim.

Here, therefore, is a proposition, which not only seems, in itself, simple and intelligible; but, if a proper use were made of it, might render every dispute equally intelligible, and banish all that jargon, which has so long taken possession of metaphysical reasonings, and drawn disgrace upon them. All ideas, especially abstract ones, are naturally faint and obscure: the mind has but a slender hold of them: they are apt to be confounded with other resembling ideas; and when we have often employed any term, though without a distinct meaning, we are apt to imagine it has a determinate idea annexed to it. On the contrary, all impressions, that is, all sensations, either outward or inward, are strong and vivid: the limits between them are more exactly determined: nor is it easy to fall into any error or mistake with regard to them. When we entertain, therefore, any suspicion that a philosophical term is employed without any meaning or idea (as is but too frequent), we need but inquire, *from what impression is that supposed idea derived?* And if it be impossible to assign any, this will serve to confirm our suspicion. By bringing ideas into so clear a light we may reasonably hope to remove all dispute, which may arise, concerning their nature and reality.

SCEPTICAL DOUBTS CONCERNING THE OPERATIONS OF THE UNDERSTANDING

Our Knowledge of Causal Relations

All the objects of human reason or inquiry may naturally be divided into two kinds, to wit, *relations of ideas*, and *matters of fact*. Of the first kind are the sciences of geometry, algebra, and arithmetic; and in short, every affirmation which is either intuitively or demonstratively certain. *That the square of the hypotenuse is equal to the squares of the other two sides*, is a proposition which expresses a relation between these figures. *That three times five is equal to the half of thirty*, expresses a relation between these numbers. Propositions of this kind are discoverable by the mere operation of thought, without dependence on what is anywhere existent in the universe. Though there never was a circle or triangle in nature, the truths demonstrated by Euclid would forever retain their certainty and evidence.

Matters of fact, which are the second objects of human reason, are not ascertained in the same manner; nor is our evidence of their truth, however great, of a like nature with the foregoing. The contrary of every matter of fact is still possible; because it can never imply a contradiction, and is conceived by the mind with the same facility and distinctness, as if ever so conformable to reality. *That the sun will not rise tomorrow* is no less intelligible a proposition, and implies no more contradiction than the affirmation, *that it will rise.* We should in vain, therefore, attempt to demonstrate its falsehood. Were it demonstratively false, it would imply a contradiction, and could never be distinctly conceived by the mind.

It may, therefore, be a subject worthy of curiosity, to inquire what is the nature of that evidence which assures us of any real existence and matter of fact, beyond the present testimony of our senses, or the records of our memory. This part of philosophy, it is observable, has been little cultivated, either by the ancients or moderns; and therefore our doubts and errors, in the prosecution of so important an inquiry, may be the more excusable, while we march through such difficult paths without any guide or direction. They may even prove useful, by exciting curiosity, and destroying that implicit faith and security, which is the bane of all reasoning and free inquiry. The discovery of defects in the common philosophy, if any such there be, will not, I presume, be a discouragement, but rather an incitement, as is usual, to attempt something more full and satisfactory than has yet been proposed to the public.

All reasonings concerning matter of fact seem to be founded on the relation of *cause and effect.* By means of that relation alone we can go beyond the evidence of our memory and senses. If you were to ask a man, why he believes any matter of fact, which is absent; for instance, that his friend is in the country, or in France; he would give you a reason; and this reason would be some other fact; as a letter received from him, or the knowledge of his former resolutions and promises. A man finding a watch or any other machine in a desert island, would conclude that there had once been men in that island. All our reasonings concerning fact are of the same nature. And here it is constantly supposed that there is a connection between the present fact and that which is inferred from it. Were there nothing to bind them together, the inference would be entirely precarious. The hearing of an articulate voice and rational discourse in the dark assures us of the presence of some person. Why? because these are the effects of the human make and fabric, and closely connected with it. If we anatomize all the other reasonings of this nature, we shall find that they are founded on the relation of cause and effect, and that this relation is either near or remote, direct or collateral. Heat and light are collateral effects of fire, and the one effect may justly be inferred from the other.

If we would satisfy ourselves, therefore, concerning the nature of that evidence, which assures us of matters of fact, we must inquire how we arrive at the knowledge of cause and effect.

I shall venture to affirm, as a general proposition, which admits of no exception, that the knowledge of this relation is not, in any instance, attained by reasonings *a priori*; but arises entirely from experience, when we find that any particular objects are constantly conjoined with each other. Let an object be presented to a man of ever so strong natural reason and abilities; if that object be entirely new to him, he will not be able, by the most accurate examination of its sensible qualities, to discover any of its causes or effects. Adam, though his rational faculties be supposed, at the very first, entirely perfect, could not have inferred from the fluidity and transparency of water that it would suffocate him, or from the light and warmth of fire that it would consume him. No object ever discovers, by the qualities which appear to the senses, either the causes which produced it, or the effects which will arise from it; nor can our reason, unassisted by experience, ever draw any inference concerning real existence and matter of fact.

This proposition, *that causes and effects are discoverable, not by reason but by experience*, will readily be admitted with regard to such objects, as we remember to have once been altogether unknown to us; since we must be conscious of the utter inability, which we then lay under, of foretelling what would arise from them. Present two smooth pieces of marble to a man who has no tincture of natural philosophy; he will never discover that they will adhere together in such a manner as to require great force to separate them in a direct line, while they make so small a resistance to a lateral pressure. Such events, as bear little analogy to the common course of nature, are also readily confessed to be known only by experience; nor does any man imagine that the explosion of gunpowder, or the attraction of a loadstone, could ever be discovered by arguments *a priori*. In like manner, when an effect is supposed to depend upon an intricate machinery or secret structure of parts, we make no difficulty in attributing all our knowledge of it to experience. Who will assert that he can give the ultimate reason, why milk or bread is proper nourishment for a man, not for a lion or a tiger?

But the same truth may not appear, at first sight, to have the same evidence with regard to events, which have become familiar to us from our first appearance in the world, which bear a close analogy to the whole course of nature, and which are supposed to depend on the simple qualities of objects, without any secret structure of parts. We are apt to imagine that we could discover these effects by the mere operation of our reason, without experience. We fancy, that were we brought on a sudden into this world, we could at first have inferred that one billiard ball would communicate motion to another upon impulse; and that we needed not to have waited for the event, in order to pronounce with certainty concerning it. Such is the influence of custom, that, where it is strongest, it not only covers our natural ignorance, but even conceals itself, and seems not to take place, merely because it is found in the highest degree.

But to convince us that all the laws of nature, and all the operations of bodies without exception, are known only by experience, the following reflections may, perhaps, suffice. Were any object presented to us, and were we required to pronounce concerning the effect, which will result from it, without consulting past observation; after what manner, I beseech you, must the mind proceed in this operation? It must invent or imagine some event, which it ascribes to the object as its effect; and it is plain that this invention must be entirely arbitrary. The mind can never possibly find the effect in the supposed cause, by the most accurate scrutiny and examination. For the effect is totally different from the cause, and consequently can never be discovered in it. Motion in the second billiard ball is a quite distinct event from motion in the first: nor is there anything in the one to suggest the smallest hint of the other. A stone or piece of metal raised into the air, and left without any support, immediately falls: but to consider the matter *a priori*, is there anything we discover in this situation which can beget the idea of a downward, rather than an upward, or any other motion, in the stone or metal?

And as the first imagination or invention of a particular effect, in all natural operations, is arbitrary, where we consult not experience; so must we also esteem the supposed tie or connection between the cause and effect, which binds them together, and renders it impossible that any other effect could result from the operation of that cause. When I see, for instance, a billiard ball moving in a straight line towards another; even suppose motion in the second ball should by accident be suggested to me, as the result of their contact or impulse; may I not conceive, that a hundred different events might as well follow from that cause? May not both these balls remain at absolute rest? May not the first ball return in a straight line, or leap off from the second in any line or direction? All these suppositions are consistent and conceivable. Why then should we give the preference to one, which is no more consistent or conceivable than the rest? All our reasonings *a priori* will never be able to show us any foundation for this preference.

In a word, then, every effect is a distinct event from its cause. It could not, therefore, be discovered in the cause, and the first invention or conception of it, *a priori*, must be entirely arbitrary. And even after it is suggested, the conjunction of it with the cause must appear equally arbitrary; since there are always many other effects, which, to reason, must seem fully as consistent and natural. In vain, therefore, should we pretend to determine any single event, or infer any cause or effect, without the assistance of observation and experience.

Hence we may discover the reason why no philosopher, who is rational and modest, has ever pretended to assign the ultimate cause of any natural operation, or to show distinctly the action of that power, which produces any single effect in the universe. It is confessed, that the utmost effort of human reason is to reduce the principles, productive of natural phenomena, to a greater simplicity, and to resolve the many particular effects into a few general causes, by means of reasonings from analogy, experience, and observation. But as to the causes of these general causes, we should in vain attempt their discovery; nor shall we ever be able to satisfy ourselves, by any particular explication of them. These ultimate springs and principles are totally shut up from human curiosity and inquiry. Elasticity, gravity, cohesion of parts, communication of motion by impulse; these are probably the ultimate causes and principles which we ever discover in nature; and we may esteem ourselves sufficiently happy, if, by accurate inquiry and reasoning, we can trace up the particular phenomena to, or near to, these general principles. The most perfect philosophy of the natural kind only staves off our ignorance a little longer, as perhaps the most perfect philosophy of the moral or metaphysical kind serves only to discover larger portions of it. Thus the observation of human blindness and weakness is the result of all philosophy, and meets us at every turn, in spite of our endeavors to elude or avoid it.

ARGUMENTS FROM EXPERIENCE

But we have not yet attained any tolerable satisfaction with regard to the question first proposed. Each solution still gives rise to a new question as difficult as the foregoing, and leads us on to further inquiries. When it is asked, *What is the nature of all our reasonings concerning matter of fact?* the proper answer seems to be, that they are founded on the relation of cause and effect. When again it is asked, *What is the foundation of all our reasonings and conclusions concerning that relation?* it may be replied in one word, *experience*. But if we still carry on our sifting humor, and ask, *What is the foundation of all conclusions from experience?* this implies a new question, which may be of more difficult solution and explication. . . .

I shall content myself, in this section with an easy task, and shall pretend only to give a negative answer to the question here proposed. I say then, that, even after we have experience of the operations of cause and effect, our conclusions from that experience are *not* founded on reasoning, or any process of the understanding. This answer we must endeavor both to explain and to defend.

It must certainly be allowed, that nature has kept us at a great distance from all her secrets, and has afforded us only the knowledge of a few superficial qualities of objects; while she conceals from us those powers and principles on which the influence of those objects entirely depends. Our senses inform us of the color, weight, and consistence of bread; but neither sense nor reason can ever inform us of those qualities which fit it for the nourishment and support of a human body. Sight or feeling conveys an idea of the actual motion of bodies; but as to that wonderful force or power, which would carry on a moving body for ever in a continued change of place, and which bodies never lose but by communicating it to others; of this we cannot form the most distant conception. But notwithstanding this ignorance of natural powers and principles, we always presume, when we see like sensible qualities, that they have like secret powers, and expect that effects, similar to those which we have experienced, will follow from them. If a body of like color and consistence with that bread, which we have formerly eat, be presented to us, we make no scruple of repeating the experiment, and foresee, with certainty, like nourishment and support. Now this is a process of the mind or thought, of which I would willingly know the foundation. It is allowed on all hands that there is no known connection between the sensible qualities and the secret powers; and consequently, that the mind is not led to form such a conclusion concerning their constant and regular conjunction, by anything which it knows of their nature. As to past *experience*, it can be allowed to give direct and certain information of those precise objects only, and that precise period of time, which fell under its cognizance: but why this experience should be extended to future times, and to other objects, which, for aught we know, may be only in appearance similar; this is the main question on which I would insist. The bread, which I formerly eat, nourished me; that is, a body of such sensible qualities was, at that time, endued with such secret powers: but does it follow, that other bread must also nourish me at another time, and that like sensible qualities must always be attended with like secret powers? The consequence seems no wise necessary. At least, it must be acknowledged that there is here a consequence drawn by the mind; that there is a certain step taken; a process of thought, and an inference, which wants to be explained. These two propositions are far from being the same, *I have found that such an object has always been attended with such an effect, and I foresee, that other objects, which are, in appearence, similar, will be attended with similar effects.* I shall allow, if you please, that the one proposition may justly be inferred from other; I know, in fact, that it always is inferred. But if you insist that the inference is made by a chain of reasoning, I desire you to produce that reasoning. The connection between these propositions is not intuitive. There is required a medium, which may enable the mind to draw such an inference, if indeed it be drawn by reasoning and argument. What that medium is, I must confess, passes my comprehension; and it is incumbent on those to produce it, who assert that it really exists, and is the origin of all our conclusions concerning matter of fact.

This negative argument must certainly, in process of time, become altogether convincing, if many penetrating and able philosophers shall turn their inquiries this way and no one be ever able to discover any connection proposition or intermediate step, which supports the understanding in this conclusion. But as the question is yet new, every reader may not trust so far to his own penetration, as to conclude, because an argument escapes his inquiry, that therefore it does not really exist. For this reason it may be requisite to venture upon a more difficult task; and enumerating all the branches of human knowledge, endeavor to show that none of them can afford such an argument.

All reasonings may be divided into two kinds, namely demonstrative reasoning, or that concerning relations of ideas, and moral reasoning, or that concerning matter of fact and existence. That there are no demonstrative arguments in the case seems evident; since it implies no contradiction that the course of nature may change, and that an object, seemingly like those which we have experienced, may be attended with different or contrary effects. May I not clearly and distinctly conceive that a body, falling from the clouds, and which, in all other respects, resembles snow, has yet the taste of salt or feeling of fire? Is there any more intelligible proposition than to affirm, that all the trees will flourish in December and January, and decay in May and June? Now whatever is intelligible, and can be distinctly conceived, implies no contradiction, and can never be proved false by any demonstrative argument or abstract reasoning *a priori.*

If we be, therefore, engaged by arguments to put trust in past experience, and make it the standard of our future judgment, these arguments must be probable only, or such as regard matter of fact and real existence, according to the division above mentioned. But that there is no argument of this kind, must appear, if our explication of that species of reasoning be admitted as solid and satisfactory. We have said that all arguments concerning existence are founded on the relation of cause and effect; that our knowledge of that relation is derived entirely from experience; and that all our experimental conclusions proceed upon the supposition that the future will be conformable to the past. To endeavor, therefore, the proof of this last supposition by probable arguments, or arguments regarding existence, must evidently be going in a circle, and taking that for granted, which is the very point in question.

In reality, all arguments from experience are founded on the similarity which we discover among natural objects, and by which we are induced to expect effects similar to those which we have found to follow from such objects. And though none but a fool or madman will ever pretend to dispute the authority of experience, or to reject that great guide of human life, it may surely be allowed a philosopher to have so much curiosity at least as to examine the principle of human nature, which gives this mighty authority to experience, and makes us draw advantage from that similarity which nature has placed among different objects. From causes which appear *similar* we expect similar effects. This is the sum of all our experimental conclusions. Now it seems evident that, if this conclusion were formed by reason, it would be as perfect at first, and upon one instance, as after ever so long a course of experience. But the case is far otherwise. Nothing so like as eggs; yet no one, on account of this appearing similarity, expects the same taste and relish in all of them. It is only after a long course of uniform experiments in any kind, that we attain a firm reliance and security with regard to a particular event. Now where is that process of reasoning which, from one instance, draws a conclusion, so different from that which it infers from a hundred instances that are nowise different from that single one? This question I propose as much for the sake of information, as with an intention of raising difficulties. I cannot find, I cannot imagine any such reasoning. But I keep my mind still open to instruction, if anyone will vouchsafe to bestow it on me.

Should it be said that, from a number of uniform experiences, we *infer* a connection between the sensible qualities and the secret powers; this, I must confess, seems the same difficulty, couched in different terms. The question still recurs, on what process of argument this *inference* is founded? Where is the medium, the interposing ideas, which join propositions so very wide of each other? It is confessed that the color, consistence, and other sensible qualities of bread appear not, of themselves, to have any connection with the secret powers of nourishment and support. For otherwise we could infer these secret powers from the first appearance of these sensible qualities, without the aid of experience; contrary to the sentiment of all philosophers, and contrary to plain matter of fact. Here, then, is our natural state of ignorance with regard to the powers and influence of all objects. How is this remedied by experience? It only shows us a number of uniform effects, resulting from certain objects, and teaches us that those particular objects, at that particular time, were endowed with such powers and forces. When a new object, endowed with similar sensible qualities, is produced, we expect similar powers and forces, and look for a like effect. From a body of like color and consistence with bread we expect like nourishment and support. But this surely is a step or progress of the mind, which wants to be explained. When a man says, *I have found, in all past instances, such sensible qualities conjoined with such secret powers*: And when he says, *Similar sensible qualities will always be conjoined with similar secret powers,* he is not guilty of a tautology, nor are these propositions in any respect the same. You say that the one proposition is an inference from the other. But you must confess that the inference is not intuitive; neither is it demonstrative: Of what nature is it, then? To say it is experimental, is begging the question. For all inferences from experience suppose, as their foundation, that the future will resemble the past, and that similar powers will be conjoined with similar sensible qualities. If there be any suspicion that the course of nature may change, and that the past may be no rule for the future, all experience becomes useless, and can give rise to no inference or conclusion. It is impossible, therefore, that any arguments from experience can prove this resemblance of the past to the future; since all these arguments are founded on the supposition of that resemblance. Let the course of things be allowed hitherto ever so regular; that alone, without some new argument or inference, proves not that, for the future, it will continue so. In vain do you pretend to have learned the nature of bodies from your past experience. Their secret nature, and consequently all their effects and influence, may change, without any change in their sensible qualities. This happens sometimes, and with regard to some objects: Why may it not happen always, and with regard to all objects? What logic, what process of argument secures you against this supposition? My practice, you say, refutes my doubts. But you mistake the purport of my question. As an agent, I am quite satisfied in the point; but as a philosopher, who has some share of curiosity, I will not say scepticism, I want to learn the foundation of this inference. No reading, no inquiry has yet been able to remove my difficulty, or give me satisfaction in a matter of such importance. Can I do better than propose the difficulty to the public, even though, perhaps, I have small hopes of obtaining a solution? We shall, at least by this means, be sensible of our ignorance, if we do not augment our knowledge. . . .

STUDY QUESTIONS

1. What are the two classes of the "perceptions of the mind?" Distinguish carefully between each and give some original examples.
2. What would Hume think of the doctrine of innate ideas? How does he account for the origin of knowledge? What arguments does he use in tracing the origins of our knowledge?
3. Discuss Hume's point on page 166 that in the perception of varying shades of a color we would perceive a blank where a certain shade was lacking. Would we?
4. Would you agree with Hume's conclusion at the end of the section on the origin of ideas that metaphysical disputes might be avoided if we simply asked "from what impression is that supposed idea derived"?
5. State and give examples of the two classes of knowledge. To what class does Hume confine our knowledge of causal relations?
6. What importance does Hume attach to the causal relation? Can the knowledge of such a relation ever be *a priori*? Why or why not?
7. Do you believe that we ever have a perception of the causal relation? Of causal power? For example, when striking a ball with a bat? Discuss these questions in the light of Hume's analysis of the causal relation.
8. Why does Hume say that all our reasonings based on the causal relation are probable at best? Would you agree? Give reasons.
9. Do you believe that the future will resemble the past? Can you prove it? Do you believe in the causal relation? Why?
10. On the basis of your reading of this selection, why do you think Hume preferred to call his philosophy a "mitigated scepticism"?

Bertrand Russell

KNOWLEDGE BY ACQUAINTANCE
AND KNOWLEDGE BY DESCRIPTION

Biographical Note. BERTRAND RUSSELL (3rd Earl) (1872–) was born in England and educated at Trinity College, Cambridge. After Cambridge he served briefly with the British Embassy in Paris and then went to Germany to study political theory. He has traveled extensively and has lectured at many universities in the United States and elsewhere. During the first World War he was jailed for six months for his pacifist views and activities. In 1950 he received the Nobel Prize for Literature. He has been an extremely prolific writer and is recognized as one of the world's great philosophers and mathematicians. Of his many publications the following may be cited: *The Philosophy of Leibniz* (1900); *Principles of Mathematics* (1903); with Whitehead, the *Principia Mathematica* (1910); *Mysticism and Logic* (1918); *Introduction to Mathematical Philosophy* (1919); *Analysis of Mind* (1921); *Analysis of Matter* (1927); *Conquest of Happiness* (1930); *Marriage and Morals* (1929); *Freedom and the Social Order* (1932); *History of Western Philosophy* (1946); *Satan in the Suburbs* (short stories, 1953); *Why I am not a Christian* (1957); *Has Man a Future* (1961).

* * *

From *The Problems of Philosophy,* London, Oxford University Press, 1912, Chapter V. Used by permission of the Oxford University Press.

Introductory Note.   There is a certain ambivalence and diversity of interests that make it difficult to categorize the philosophy of Bertrand Russell. There are marked differences between his earlier attitudes in philosophy and his more recent reflections. His early philosophy is more optimistic about the aims of philosophy, more imbued with confidence in science, and the possibilities of man attaining certain knowledge. His later philosophy is more markedly empirical than the earlier, closer to Hume and inclined to the view that "all human knowledge is uncertain, inexact or partial."

Although the heir of the earlier empiricists, and markedly influenced by both Berkeley and Hume, Russell is never the complete empiricist. Perhaps this is because of his conviction that philosophy must begin with the analysis of propositions, that a sound philosophy must be logical in character, that logic is the very essence of philosophy. Furthermore, his account of mathematical knowledge and the principle of induction led him to the consideration that here were types of knowledge that escaped the empirical net. On the other hand there is his enthusiasm for political and moral philosophy, his faith in science, and his delight in the problems of linguistic analysis. It is just this diversity of interest and approaches to the problems of philosophy that characterize the true genius of Russell and accounts for his considerable influence upon so many of the diverging trends in contemporary philosophy.

The essay on "Knowledge by Acquaintance and Description" is one of Russell's earliest attempts to characterize the nature of our knowledge. It is closely related to his explanation of the nature of physical objects and the whole problem of the external world—a problem he inherited from Berkeley. Like Berkeley he adopts the notion that what we know immediately are sense data rather than physical objects. The distinction between the two is then elaborated in the epistemological consideration that all our knowledge may be characterized as knowledge by acquaintance, which means a direct awareness, or knowledge by description, which will be inferential. In the first category Russell places: (1) sense data, (2) mental states, (3) universals, and (4) the awareness of the self, of the "I" that experiences mental states. In the second category are found: (1) physical objects, and (2) other minds. Russell is concerned to show that any analysis of descriptive knowledge must yield knowledge by acquaintance, that descriptive knowledge is reducible to knowledge by acquaintance. This raises some difficulties and Russell discusses in particular the problem of how our propositions about Julius Caesar (or any past historical personage) can be rendered intelligible in terms of a knowledge by description when the form of the proposition would seem to indicate a knowledge by acquaintance. The problem is in trying to account for the use of a term like Julius Caesar, apparently a proper name referring to a unique person, by means of descriptive phrases. His later accounts argued that such proper names were merely descriptive phrases in disguise. The whole theory has been much debated and frequently criticized by other philosophers.

KNOWLEDGE BY ACQUAINTANCE

In the preceding chapter we saw that there are two sorts of knowledge: knowledge of things, and knowledge of truths. In this chapter we shall be concerned exclusively with knowledge of things, of which in turn we shall have to distinguish two kinds. Knowledge of things, when it is of the kind we call knowledge by *acquaintance*, is essentially simpler than any knowledge of truths, and logically independent of knowledge of truths, though it would be rash to assume that human beings ever, in fact, have acquaintance with things without at the same time knowing some truth about them. Knowledge of things by *description*, on the contrary, always involves, as we shall find in the course of the present chapter, some knowledge of truths as its source and ground. But first of all we must make clear what we mean by 'acquaintance' and what we mean by 'description'.

We shall say that we have *acquaintance* with anything of which we are directly aware, without the intermediary of any process of inference or any knowledge of truths. Thus in the presence of my table I am acquainted with the sense-data that make up the appearance of my table—its colour, shape, hardness, smoothness, etc.; all these are things of which I am immediately conscious when I am seeing and touching my table. The particular shade of colour that I am seeing may have many things said about it—I may say that it is brown, that it is rather dark, and so on. But such statements, though they make me know truths *about* the colour, do not make me know the colour itself any better than I did before: so far as concerns knowledge of the colour itself, as opposed to knowledge of truths about it, I know the colour perfectly and completely when I see it, and no further knowledge of it itself is even theoretically possible. Thus the sense-data which make up the appearance of my table are things with which I have acquaintance, things immediately known to me just as they are.

My knowledge of the table as a physical object, on the contrary, is not direct knowledge. Such as it is, it is obtained through acquaintance with the sense-data that make up the appearance of the table. We have seen that it is possible, without absurdity, to doubt whether there is a table at all, whereas it is not possible to doubt the sense-data. My knowledge of the table is of the kind which we shall call 'knowledge by description'. The table is 'the physical object which causes such-and-such sense-data'. This *describes* the table by means of the sense-data. In order to know anything at all about the table, we must know truths connecting it with things with which we have acquaintance: we must know that 'such-and-such sense-data are caused by a physical object'. There is no state of mind in which we are directly aware of the table; all our knowledge of the table is really knowledge of *truths,* and the actual thing which is the table is not, strictly speaking, known to us at all. We know a description, and we know that there is just one object to which this description applies, though the object iself is not directly known to us. In such a case, we say that our knowledge of the object is knowledge by description.

All our knowledge, both knowledge of things and knowledge of truths, rests upon acquaintance as its foundation. It is therefore important to consider what kinds of things there are with which we have acquaintance.

Sense-data, as we have already seen, are among the things with which we are acquainted; in fact, they supply the most obvious and striking example of knowledge by acquaintance. But if they were the sole example, our knowledge would be very much more restricted than it is. We should only know what is now present to our senses: we could not know anything about the past—not even that there was a past—nor could we know any truths about our sense-data, for all knowledge of truths, as we shall show, demands acquaintance with things which are of an essentially different character from sense-data, the things which are sometimes called 'abstract ideas', but which we shall call 'universals'. We have therefore to consider acquaintance with other things besides sense-data if we are to obtain any tolerably adequate analysis of our knowledge.

The first extension beyond sense-data to be considered is acquaintance by *memory.* It is obvious that we often remember what we have seen or heard or had otherwise present to our senses, and that in such cases we are still immediately aware of what we remember, in spite of the fact that it appears as past and not as present. This immediate knowledge by memory is the source of all our knowledge concerning the past: without it, there could be no knowledge of the past by inference, since we should never know that there was anything past to be inferred.

The next extension to be considered is acquaintance by *introspection.* We are not only aware of things, but we are often aware of being aware of them. When I see the sun, I am often aware of my seeing the sun; thus 'my seeing the sun' is an object with which I have acquaintance. When I desire food, I may be aware of my desire for food; thus 'my desiring food' is an object with which I am acquainted. Similarly we may be aware of our feeling pleasure or pain, and generally of the events which happen in our minds. This kind of acquaintance, which may be called self-consciousness, is the source of all our knowledge of mental things. It is obvious that it is only what goes on in our own minds that can be thus known immediately. What goes on in the minds of others is known to us through our perception of their bodies, that is, through the sense-data in us which are associated with their bodies. But for our acquaintance with the contents of our own minds, we should be unable to imagine the minds of others, and therefore we could never arrive at the knowledge that they have minds. It seems natural to suppose that self-consciousness is one of the things that distinguish men from animals: animals, we may suppose, though they have acquaintance with sense-data, never become aware of this acquaintance. I do not mean that they *doubt* whether they exist, but that they have never become conscious of the fact that they have sensations and feelings, nor therefore of the fact that they, the subjects of their sensations and feelings, exist.

We have spoken of acquaintance with the contents of our minds as *self*-consciousness, but it is not, of course, consciousness of our *self*: it is consciousness of particular thoughts and feelings. The question whether we are also acquainted with our bare selves, as opposed to particular thoughts and feelings, is a very difficult one, upon which it would be rash to speak positively. When we try to look into ourselves we always seem to come upon some particular thought or feeling, and not upon the 'I' which has the thought or feeling. Nevertheless there are some reasons for thinking that we are acquainted with the 'I', though the acquaintance is hard to disentangle from other things. To make clear what sort of reason there is, let us consider for a moment what our acquaintance with particular thoughts really involves.

When I am acquainted with 'my seeing the sun', it seems plain that I am acquainted with two different things in relation to each other. On the one hand there is the sense-datum which represents the sun to me, on the other hand there is that which sees this sense-datum. All acquaintance, such as my acquaintance with the sense-datum which represents the sun, seems obviously a relation between the person acquainted and the object with which the person is acquainted. When a case of acquaintance is one with which I can be acquainted (as I am acquainted with my acquaintance with the sense-datum representing the sun), it is plain that the person acquainted is myself. Thus, when I am acquainted with my seeing the sun, the whole fact with which I am acquainted is 'Self-acquainted-with-sense-datum'.

Further, we know the truth 'I am acquainted with this sense-datum'. It is hard to see how we could know this truth, or even understand what is meant by it, unless we were acquainted with something which we call 'I'. It does not seem necessary to suppose that we are acquainted with a more or less permanent person, the same to-day as yesterday, but it does seem as though we must be acquainted with that thing, whatever its nature, which sees the sun and has an acquaintance with sense-data. Thus, in some sense it would seem we must be acquainted with our Selves as opposed to our particular experiences. But the question is difficult and complicated arguments can be adduced on either side. Hence, although acquaintance with ourselves seems *probably* to occur, it is not wise to assert that it undoubtedly does occur.

We may therefore sum up as follows what has been said concerning acquaintance with things that exist. We have acquaintance in sensation with the data of the outer senses, and in introspection with the data of what may be called the inner sense—thoughts, feelings, desires, etc.; we have acquaintance in memory with things which have been data either of the outer senses or of the inner sense. Further, it is probable, though not certain, that we have acquaintance with Self, as that which is aware of things or has desires towards things.

In addition to our acquaintance with particular existing things, we also have acquaintance with what we shall call *universals*, that is to say, general ideas, such as *whiteness, diversity, brotherhood*, and so on. Every complete sentence must contain at least one word which stands for a universal, since all verbs have a meaning which is universal. We shall return to universals later on, in Chapter IX; for the present it is only necessary to guard against the supposition that whatever we can be acquainted with must be something particular and existent. Awareness of universals is called *conceiving*, and a universal of which we are aware is called a *concept*.

It will be seen that among the objects with which we are acquainted are not included physical objects (as opposed to sense-data), nor other people's minds. These things are known to us by what I call 'knowledge by description', which we must now consider.

KNOWLEDGE BY DESCRIPTION

By a 'description' I mean any phrase of the form 'a so-and-so' or 'the so-and-so'. A phrase of the form 'a so-and-so' I shall call an 'ambiguous' description; a phrase of the form 'the so-and-so' (in the singular) I shall call a 'definite' description. Thus 'a man' is an ambiguous description, and 'the man with the iron mask' is a definite description. There are various problems connected with ambiguous descriptions, but I pass them by, since they do not directly concern the matter we are discussing, which is the nature of our knowledge concerning objects in cases where we know that there is an object answering to a definite description, though we are not *acquainted* with any such object. This is a matter which is concerned exclusively with *definite* descriptions. I shall therefore, in the sequel, speak simply of 'descriptions' when I mean 'definite descriptions'. Thus a description will mean any phrase of the form 'the so-and-so' in the singular.

We shall say that an object is 'known by description' when we know that it is 'the so-and-so', i. e. when we know that there is one object, and no more, having a certain property; and it will generally be implied that we do not have knowledge of the same object by acquaintance. We know that the man with the iron mask existed, and many propositions are known about him; but we do not know who he was. We know that the candidate who gets the most votes will be elected, and in this case we are very likely also acquainted (in the only sense in which one can be acquainted with some one else) with the man who is, in fact, the candidate who will get most votes; but we do not know which of the candidates he is, i. e. we do not know any proposition of the form 'A is the candidate who will get most votes' where A is one of the candidates by name. We shall say that we have 'merely descriptive knowledge' of the so-and-so when, although we know that the so-and-so exists, and although we may possibly be acquainted with the object which is, in fact, the so-and-so, yet we do not know any proposition '*a* is the so-and-so', where *a* is something with which we are acquainted.

When we say 'the so-and-so exists', we mean that there is just one object which is the so-and-so. The proposition '*a* is the so-and-so' means that *a* has the property so-and-so, and nothing else has. 'Mr. A. is the Unionist candidate for this constituency' means 'Mr. A. is a Unionist candidate for this constituency, and no one else is'. 'The Unionist candidate for this constituency exists' means 'some one is a Unionist candidate for this constituency, and no one else is'. Thus, when we are acquainted with an object which is the so-and-so, we know that the so-and-so exists; but we may know that the so-and-so exists when we are not acquainted with any object which we know to be the so-and-so, and even when we are not acquainted with any object which, in fact, is the so-and-so.

Common words, even proper names, are usually really descriptions. That is to say, the thought in the mind of a person using a proper name correctly can generally only be expressed explicitly if we replace the proper name by a description. Moreover, the description required to express the thought will vary for different people, or for the same person at different times. The only thing constant (so long as the name is rightly used) is the object to which the name applies. But so long as this remains constant, the particular description involved usually makes no difference to the truth or falsehood of the proposition in which the name appears.

Let us take some illustrations. Suppose some statement made about Bismarck. Assuming that there is such a thing as direct acquaintance with oneself, Bismarck himself might have used his name directly to designate the particular person with whom he was acquainted. In this case, if he made a judgement about himself, he himself might be a constituent of the judgement. Here the proper name has the direct use which it always wishes to have, as simply standing for a certain object, and not for a description of the object. But if a person who knew Bismarck made a judgement about him, the case is different. What this person was acquainted with were certain sense-data which he connected (rightly, we will suppose) with Bismarck's body. His body, as a physical object, and still more his mind, were only known as the body and the mind connected with these sense-data. That is, they were known by description. It is, of course, very much a matter of chance which characteristics of a man's appearance will come into a friend's mind when he thinks of him; thus the description actually in the friend's mind is accidental. The essential point is that he knows that the various descriptions all apply to the same entity, in spite of not being acquainted with the entity in question.

When we, who did not know Bismarck, make a judgement about him, the description in our minds will probably be some more or less vague mass of historical knowledge—far more, in most cases, than is required to identify him. But, for the sake of illustration, let us assume that we think of him as 'the first Chancellor of the German Empire'. Here all the words are abstract except 'German'. The word 'German' will, again, have different meanings for different people. To some it will recall travels in Germany, to some the look of Germany on the map, and so on. But if we are to obtain a description which we know to be applicable, we shall be compelled, at some point, to bring in a reference to a particular with which we are acquainted. Such reference is involved in any mention of past, present, and future (as opposed to definite dates), or of here and there, or of what others have told us. Thus it would seem that, in some way or other, a description known to be applicable to a particular must involve some reference to a particular with which we are acquainted, if our knowledge about the thing described is not to be merely what follows *logically* from the description. For example, 'the most long-lived of men' is a description involving only universals, which must apply to some man, but we can make no judgements concerning this man which involve knowledge about him beyond what the description gives. If, however, we say, 'The first Chancellor of the German Empire was an astute diplomatist', we can only be assured of the truth of our judgement in virtue of something with which we are acquainted —usually a testimony heard or read. Apart from the information we convey to others, apart from the fact about the actual Bismarck, which gives importance to our judgement, the thought we really have contains the one or more particulars involved, and otherwise consists wholly of concepts.

All names of places—London, England, Europe, the Earth, the Solar System—similarly involve, when used, descriptions which start from some one or more particulars with which we are acquainted. I suspect that even the Universe, as considered by metaphysics, involves such a connexion with particulars. In logic, on the contrary, where we are concerned not merely with what does exist, but with whatever might or could exist or be, no reference to actual particulars is involved.

It would seem that, when we make a statement about something only known by description, we often *intend* to make our statement, not in the form involving the description, but about the actual thing described. That is to say, when we say anything about Bismarck, we should like, if we could, to make the judgement which Bismarck alone can make, namely, the judgement of which he himself is a constituent. In this we are necessarily defeated, since the actual Bismarck is unknown to us. But we know that there is an object B, called Bismarck, and that B was an astute diplomatist. We can thus *describe* the proposition we should like to affirm, namely, 'B was an astute diplomatist', where B is the object which was Bismarck. If we are describing Bismarck as 'the first Chancellor of the German Empire', the proposition we should like to affirm may be described as 'the proposition asserting, concerning the actual object which was the first Chancellor of the German Empire, that this object was an astute diplomatist'. What enables us to communicate in spite of the varying descriptions we employ is that we know there is a true proposition concerning the actual Bismarck, and that however we may vary the description (so long as the description is correct) the proposition described is still the same. This proposition, which is described and is known to be true, is what interests us; but we are not acquainted with the proposition itself, and do not know *it*, though we know it is true.

It will be seen that there are various stages in the removal from acquaintance with particulars: there is Bismarck to people who knew him;

Bismarck to those who only know of him through history; the man with the iron mask; the longest-lived of men. These are progressively further removed from acquaintance with particulars; the first comes as near to acquaintance as is possible in regard to another person; in the second, we shall still be said to know 'who Bismarck was'; in the third, we do not know who was the man with the iron mask, though we can know many propositions about him which are not logically deducible from the fact that he wore an iron mask; in the fourth, finally, we know nothing beyond what is logically deducible from the definition of the man. There is a similar hierarchy in the region of universals. Many universals, like many particulars, are only known to us by description. But here, as in the case of particulars, knowledge concerning what is known by description is ultimately reducible to knowledge concerning what is known by acquaintance.

The fundamental principle in the analysis of propositions containing descriptions is this: *Every proposition which we can understand must be composed wholly of constituents with which we are acquainted.*

We shall not at this stage attempt to answer all the objections which may be urged against this fundamental principle. For the present, we shall merely point out that, in some way or other, it must be possible to meet these objections, for it is scarcely conceivable that we can make a judgement or entertain a supposition without knowing what it is that we are judging or supposing about. We must attach *some* meaning to the words we use, if we are to speak significantly and not utter mere noise; and the meaning we attach to our words must be something with which we are acquainted. Thus when, for example, we make a statement about Julius Caesar, it is plain that Julius Caesar himself is not before our minds, since we are not acquainted with him. We have in mind some *description* of Julius Caesar: 'the man who was assassinated on the Ides of March', 'the founder of the Roman Empire', or, perhaps, merely 'the man whose name was *Julius Caesar*' (In this last description, *Julius Caesar* is a noise or shape with which we are acquainted.) Thus our statement does not mean quite what it seems to mean, but means something involving, instead of Julius Caesar, some description of him which is composed wholly of particulars and universals with which we are acquainted.

The chief importance of knowledge by description is that it enables us to pass beyond the limits of our private experience. In spite of the fact that we can only know truths which are wholly composed of terms which we have experienced in acquaintance, we can yet have knowledge by description of things which we have never experienced. In view of the very narrow range of our immediate experience, this result is vital, and until it is understood, much of our knowledge must remain mysterious and therefore doubtful.

STUDY QUESTIONS

1. What does Russell mean by knowledge by acquaintance? What classes of such knowledge does he distinguish?
2. How would Russell account for our knowledge of physical objects? Of other minds? Do you find any difficulty with such forms of knowledge?
3. What does Russell mean by descriptive knowledge? What are the two kinds of descriptions and by what phrases are they identified? Give some original examples of each.
4. What kind of knowledge do we have of our own mind? How does Russell describe the nature of the self? Is it identical with particular thoughts and feelings? Does Russell have any difficulty with the notion of the 'I' or the self? What solution would you offer to this problem.
5. What are universals? How are they distinguished from concepts? Why does Russell say that every complete sentence must contain at least one word which stands for a universal?
6. Would you agree with Russell that we are not acquainted with physical objects but only with sense-data? Why or why not?
7. Using original examples show how our knowledge by description is reducible to knowledge by acquaintance.
8. What objections would you make to Russell's principle that *Every proposition which we can understand must be composed wholly of constituents with which we are acquainted.*

John Dewey

▨▨▨▨▨▨▨▨▨▨▨▨▨▨▨▨▨▨▨▨▨▨▨▨▨▨▨▨▨▨▨▨▨▨▨▨▨▨

REFLECTIVE THINKING

▨▨▨▨▨▨▨▨▨▨▨▨▨▨▨▨▨▨▨▨▨▨▨▨▨▨▨▨▨▨▨▨▨▨▨▨▨▨

Biographical Note.   JOHN DEWEY (1859–1952) was born in Burlington, Vermont. He was graduated from the University of Vermont and in 1882 was admitted to the graduate school at Johns Hopkins University. Three years later he was appointed to the philosophy department at the University of Michigan and later became the head of the department. While at Michigan he formed a close association with George Herbert Meade and James Tufts, both of whom were to become fairly eminent American philosophers. In 1894 Dewey accepted a position at the University of Chicago, where he divided his duties between philosophy and education. It was at Chicago that he established his famous "Laboratory School" and first achieved fame as an educator. By the 1920's, his educational views dominated American educational circles and this domination is still felt today. In the meantime, he accepted an appointment at Columbia University and soon became the leading American philosopher. In 1932 he retired from Columbia but continued to write and lecture. His principal publications include *Essays in Experimental Logic; Human Nature and Conduct; Reconstruction in Philosophy; Experience and Nature; The Quest for Certainty; The Public and Its Problems; Art as Experience;* and *Logic, The Theory of Inquiry.*

* * *

Introductory Note.   In its main outlines the philosophy of John Dewey owes much to various strains of 19th century philosophical thought. First an

From *How We Think*, New York, D. C. Heath and Company, 1933, Chapters six and seven. Reprinted by permission of the publishers.

Hegelian, in his metaphysics especially he expressed a somewhat naturalistic form of Hegelianism. The empirical movement is reflected in his thought largely through the influence of J. S. Mill. And the scientific thought of the 19th century, especially that of Huxley and Darwin, was to mould his conception of thought as instrumental in the evolutionary process. Above all else, perhaps, Dewey had an abiding interest in rendering philosophy practical. Thinking, he urged, must always be to some purpose, mind is an instrument for the adjustment of the individual to his environment, and ideas are instruments for the solution of problems. Speculative philosophy, the contemplative ideal, must give way before a reconstruction of philosophy in terms of practice, of philosophy as "this worldly" and not "other worldly." In all of these contentions lie the roots and the essence of Dewey's version of Pragmatism.

Dewey's theory of knowledge is pragmatic and empirical; it is directed to the development of logic as concrete rather than formal—as a method of inquiry to be applied to the problems of man.

Dewey's first exposition of this aspect of logic and epistemology was developed in the little book *How We Think,* originally written for students of education and later to be elaborated in more technical fashion as *Logic, The Theory of Inquiry.* Knowledge is the end result of all reflection and inquiry, it represents a continual interchange with experience and its problems rather than the contemplation of some supernatural reality that has little significance for every life and the problems of men. The latter form of knowledge is rejected by Dewey as the spectator theory of knowledge. True knowledge, he insists, must be an activity directed to practical ends.

The chapters from *How We Think* present simply and illustratively the cardinal points in Dewey's conception of logic as inquiry. All reflective activity, he holds, begins with a felt difficulty or some practical need. Out of this reflective activity follows a course of some five different phases: (1) suggestions or ideas for action (2) the intellectualization of the difficulty, the recognition of the problem (3) the use of suggestions or ideas as hypotheses (4) the role of reason in elaborating upon the hypotheses, and (5) the testing of the hypotheses, their experimental corroboration or verification. All these aspects of reflective thinking—and they need not follow rigorously this set pattern—represent for Dewey an activity. Thinking, then, is not for the sake of action; thinking is rather action itself. Reflective thinking—logic—is this activity of inquiring, suggesting, observing, hypothesizing, reasoning, experimenting, and verifying. Reason, observe, is only one aspect of reflective thinking. Logic is practical rather than formal.

ILLUSTRATIONS OF REFLECTIVE ACTIVITY

We have had repeated occasion to notice that there are both external and internal circumstances that call out and that guide, to some extent, thought of the reflective kind. Practical needs in connection with existing conditions, natural and social, evoke and direct thought. We begin with an instance of that sort. We have noted also that curiosity is a strong drive from within, and accordingly our second example is drawn from that field. Finally, a mind that is already exercised in scientific subjects will have inquiry aroused by intellectual problems, and our third instance is of that type.

A Case of Practical Deliberation

The other day, when I was downtown on 16th Street, a clock caught my eye. I saw that the hands pointed to 12:20. This suggested that I had an engagement at 124th Street, at one o'clock. I reasoned that as it had taken me an hour to come down on a surface car, I should probably be twenty minutes late if I returned the same way. I might save twenty minutes by a subway express. But was there a station near? If not, I might lose more than twenty minutes in looking for one. Then I thought of the elevated, and I saw there was such a line within two blocks. But where was the station? If it were several blocks above or below the street I was on, I should lose time instead of gaining it. My mind went back to the subway express as quicker than the elevated; furthermore, I remembered that it went nearer than the elevated to the part of 124th Street I wished to reach, so that time would be saved at the end of the journey. I concluded in favor of the subway, and reached my destination by one o'clock.

A Case of Reflection upon an Observation

Projecting nearly horizontally from the upper deck of the ferryboat on which I daily cross the river is a long white pole, bearing a gilded ball at its tip. It suggested a flagpole when I first saw it; its color, shape, and gilded ball agreed with this idea, and these reasons seemed to justify me in this belief. But soon difficulties presented themselves. The pole was nearly horizontal, an unusual position for a flagpole; in the next place, there was no pulley, ring, or cord by which to attach a flag; finally, there were elsewhere two vertical staffs from which flags were occasionally flown. It seemed probable that the pole was not there for flag-flying.

I then tried to imagine all possible purposes of such a pole, and to consider for which of these it was best suited: (a) Possibly it was an ornament. But as all the ferryboats and even the tug-boats carried poles this hypothesis was rejected. (b) Possibly it was the terminal of a wireless telegraph. But the same considerations made this improbable. Besides, the more natural place for such a terminal would be the highest part of the boat, on top of the pilot house. (c) Its purpose might be to point out the direction in which the boat is moving.

In support of this conclusion, I discovered that the pole was lower than the pilot house, so that the steersman could easily see it. Moreover, the tip was enough higher than the base, so that, from the pilot's position, it must appear to project far out in front of the boat. Moreover, the pilot being near the front of the boat, he would need some such guide as to its direction. Tug-boats would also need poles for such a purpose. This hypothesis was so much more probable than the others that I accepted it. I formed the conclusion that the pole was set up for the purpose of showing the pilot the direction in which the boat pointed, to enable him to steer correctly.

A Case of Reflection Involving Experiment

In washing tumblers in hot soapsuds and placing them mouth downward on a plate, I noticed that bubbles appeared on the outside of the mouth of the tumblers, and then went inside. Why? The presence of bubbles suggests air, which I note must come from inside the tumbler. I see that the soapy water on the plate prevents escape of the air save as it may be caught in bubbles. But why should air leave the tumbler? There was no substance entering to force it out. It must have expanded. It expands by increase of heat or by increase of pressure, or by both. Could the air have become heated after the tumbler was taken from the hot suds? Clearly not the air that was already entangled in the water. If heated air was the cause, cold air must have entered in transferring the tumblers from the suds to the plate. I test to see whether this supposition is true by taking several more tumblers out. Some I shake so as to make sure of entrapping cold air in them. Some I take out, holding them mouth downward in order to prevent cold air from entering. Bubbles appear on the outside of every one of the former and on one of the latter. I must be right in my inference. Air from the outside must have been expanded by the heat of the tumbler, which explains the appearance of the bubbles on the outside.

But why do they then go inside? Cold contracts. The tumbler cooled and also the air inside it. Tension was removed, and hence bubbles appeared inside. To be sure of this, I test by placing a cap of ice on the tumbler while the bubbles are still forming outside. They soon reverse.

These Three Cases Form a Series

These three cases have been purposely selected so as to form a series from the more rudimentary to more complicated cases of reflection. The first illustrates the kind of thinking done by everyone during the day's business, in which neither the data nor the ways of dealing with them lie outside the limits of everyday experience. The last furnishes a case in which neither problem nor mode of solution would have occurred except to one with some prior scientific training. The second case forms a natural transition; its materials lie well within the bounds of everyday, unspecialized experience; but the problem, instead of being directly involved in the person's business, arises indirectly in connection with what he happened to be doing and appeals to a somewhat theoretic and impartial interest.

INFERENCE TO THE UNKNOWN

No Thought Without Inference

In every case of reflective activity, a person finds himself confronted with a given, present situation from which he has to arrive at, or to conclude to, something else that is not present. This process of arriving at an idea of what is absent on the basis of what is at hand is *inference*. What is present *carries* or *bears* the mind over to the idea and ultimately the acceptance of something else. From the consideration of established facts of location and time of day, the person in the first case cited made an inference as to the best way to travel in order to keep an appointment, which is a future and, at first, uncertain event. From observed and remembered facts, the second person inferred the probable use of a long pole. From the presence under certain conditions of bubbles and from a knowledge of securely established physical facts and principles, the third person inferred the explanation or cause of a particular event, previously unknown; namely, the movement of water in the form of bubbles from the outside to the inside of a tumbler.

Inference Involves a Leap

Every inference, just because it goes beyond ascertained and known facts, which are given either by observation or by recollection of prior knowledge, involves *a jump from the known into the unknown*. It involves a leap beyond what is given and already established. . . . the inference occurs via or through the suggestion that is aroused by what is seen and remembered. Now, while the suggestion pops into the mind, just *what* suggestion occurs depends first upon the experience of the person. This in turn is dependent upon the general state of culture of the time; suggestions, for example, that occur readily now could not possibly spring up in the mind of a savage. Second, suggestions depend upon the person's own preferences, desires, interests, or even his immediate state of passion. The inevitableness of suggestion, the lively force with which it springs before the mind, the natural tendency to accept it if it is plausible or not obviously contradicted by facts, indicate the necessity of controlling the suggestion which is made the basis of an inference that is to be believed.

Proving Is Testing

This control of inference prior to, and on behalf of, belief constitutes *proof*. To prove a thing means primarily to *test* it. The guest bidden to the wedding feast excused himself because he had to *prove* his oxen. Exceptions are said to prove a rule; *i.e.*, they furnish instances so extreme that they try in the severest fashion its applicability; if the rule will stand such a test, there is no good reason for further doubting it. Not until a thing has been tried—"tried out," in colloquial language—do we know its true worth. Till then it may be pretense, a bluff. But the thing that has come out victorious in a test or trial of strength carries its credentials with it; it is approved, because it has been proved. Its value is clearly evinced, shown; *i.e.*, demonstrated. So it is with inferences. The mere fact that inference in general is an invaluable function does not guarantee, nor does it even help out, the correctness of any particular inference. Any inference may go astray; as we have seen, there are standing influences ever ready to instigate it to go wrong. *What is important is that every inference be a tested inference; or* (since this is often not possible) *that we discriminate between beliefs that rest upon tested evidence and those that do not, and be accordingly on our guard as to the kind and degree of assent or belief that is justified.*

Two Kinds of Testing

All three instances manifest the presence of testing operations that transform what would otherwise have been loose thinking into reflective activity. Examination reveals that the testing is of two kinds. Suggested inferences are tested in *thought* to see whether different elements in the suggestion are coherent with one another. They are also tested, after one has been adopted, by *action* to see whether the consequences that are anticipated in *thought* occur in *fact*. A good example of this second kind of proving is found in the first case cited, where reasoning had led to the conclusion that the use of the subway would bring the person to the place of his appointment in time. He tried or tested the idea by acting upon it, and the result confirmed the idea by bringing what was inferred actually to pass.

In the second case, the test by action could occur only as the person *imagined* himself in the place of the pilot who was using the pole to steer by. The test of coherence or consistency is markedly in evidence. Suggestions of flagpole, ornament, wireless, were rejected because, as soon as they were reflected upon, it was seen that they did not fit into some elements of the observed facts; they were dropped because they failed to agree with these elements. The idea that the pole was used to show the direction of movement of the boat, on the contrary, was found to agree with a number of important elements, such as (a) the need of the pilot, (b) the height of the pole, (c) the relative locations of its base and tip.

In the third instance, both kinds of testing are employed. After the conclusion was reached, it was acted upon by a further experiment, undertaken not only in imagination but also in fact. A cap of ice was placed upon the tumbler, and the bubbles behaved as they should behave if the inference was the correct one. Hence it was borne out, corroborated, verified. . . .

THINKING MOVES FROM A DOUBTFUL TO A SETTLED SITUATION

It Arises from a Directly Experienced Situation

Examination of the instances will show that in each case thinking arises out of a directly experienced situation. Persons do not just think at large, nor do ideas arise out of nothing. In one case a student is busy in a certain part of a city and is reminded of an engagement at another place. In the second case a person is engaged in riding on a ferryboat and begins to wonder about something in the construction of the boat. In the third case a student with prior scientific training is busy washing dishes. In each case the nature of the situation as it is actually experienced arouses inquiry and calls out reflection.

It Moves toward a Settled Situation

Examination of the three cases also shows that each situation is in some fashion uncertain, perplexed, troublesome, if only in offering to the mind an unresolved difficulty, an unsettled question. It shows in each case that the function of reflection is to bring about a new situation in which the difficulty is resolved, the confusion cleared away, the trouble smoothed out, the question it puts answered. Any particular process of thinking naturally comes to its close when the situation before the mind is settled, decided orderly, clear, for then there is nothing to call out reflection until a new bothersome or doubtful situation arises.

The function of reflective thought is, therefore, to transform a situation in which there is experienced obscurity, doubt, conflict, disturbance of some sort, into a situation that is clear, coherent, settled, harmonious.

ANALYSIS OF REFLECTIVE THINKING

FACTS AND IDEAS

Suppose you are walking where there is no regular path. As long as everything goes smoothly, you do not have to think about your walking; your already formed habit takes care of it. Suddenly you find a ditch in your way. You think you will jump it (supposition, plan); but to make sure, you survey it with your eyes (observation), and you find that it is pretty wide and that the bank on the other side is slippery (facts, data). You then wonder if the ditch may not be narrower somewhere else (idea), and you look up and down the stream (observation) to see how matters stand (test of idea by observation). You do not find any good place and so are thrown back upon forming a new plan. As you are casting about, you discover a log (fact again). You ask yourself whether you could not haul that to the ditch and get it across the ditch to use as a bridge (idea again). You judge that idea is worth trying, and so you get the log and manage to put it in place and walk across (test and confirmation by overt action).

If the situation were more complicated, thinking of course would be more elaborate. You can imagine a case in which making a raft, constructing a pontoon bridge, or making a dugout would be the ideas that would finally come to mind and have to be checked by reference to conditions of action (facts). Simple or complicated, relating to what to do in a practical predicament or what to infer in a scientific or philosophic problem, there will always be the two sides: the conditions to be accounted for, dealt with, and the ideas that are plans for dealing with them or are suppositions for interpreting and explaining the phenomena.

In predicting an eclipse, for example, a multitude of observed facts regarding position and movements of earth, sun, and moon, comes in on one side, while on the other side the ideas employed to predict and explain involve extensive mathematical calculations. In a philosophical problem, the facts or data may be remote and not susceptible of direct observation by the senses. But still there will be data, perhaps of science, or of morals, art, or the conclusions of past thinkers, that supply the subject matter to be dealt with and by which theories are checked. On the other side, there are the speculations that come to mind and that lead to search for additional subject matter which will both develop the proposed theories as ideas and test their value. Mere facts or data are dead, as far as mind is concerned, unless they are used to suggest and test some idea, some way out of a difficulty. Ideas, on the other hand, are *mere* ideas, idle speculations, fantasies, dreams, unless they are used to guide new observations of, and reflections upon, actual situations, past, present, or future. Finally, they must be brought to some sort of check by actual given material or else remain ideas. Many ideas are of great value as material of poetry, fiction, or the drama, but not as the stuff of knowledge. However, ideas may be of intellectual use to a penetrating mind even when they do not find any immediate reference to actuality, provided they stay in the mind for use when new facts come to light.

THE ESSENTIAL FUNCTIONS OF REFLECTIVE ACTIVITY

We now have before us the material for the analysis of a complete act of reflective activity. In the preceding chapter we saw that the two limits of every unit of thinking are a perplexed, troubled, or confused situation at the beginning and a cleared-up, unified, resolved situation at the close. The first of these situations may be called *pre*-reflective. It sets the problem to be solved; out of it grows the question that reflection has to answer. In the final situation the doubt has been dispelled; the situation is *post*-reflective; there results a direct experience of mastery, satisfaction, enjoyment. Here, then, are the limits within which reflection falls.

FIVE PHASES, OR ASPECTS, OF REFLECTIVE THOUGHT

In between, as states of thinking, are (1) *suggestions,* in which the mind leaps forward to a possible solution; (2) an intellectualization of the difficulty or perplexity that has been *felt* (directly experienced) into a *problem* to be solved, a question for which the answer must be sought; (3) the use of one suggestion after another as a leading idea, or *hypothesis,* to initiate and guide observation and other operations in collection of factual material; (4) the mental elaboration of the idea or supposition as an idea or supposition (*reasoning,* in the sense in which reasoning is a part, not the whole, of inference); and (5) testing the hypothesis by overt or imaginative action. . . .

THE FIRST PHASE, SUGGESTION

The most "natural" thing for anyone to do is to go ahead; that is to say, to *act* overtly. The disturbed and perplexed situation arrests such direct activity temporarily. The tendency to continue *acting* nevertheless persists. It is diverted and takes the form of an idea or a suggestion. The *idea* of what to do when we find ourselves "in a hole" is a substitute for direct action. It is a vicarious, anticipatory way of acting, a kind of dramatic rehearsal. Were there only one suggestion popping up, we should undoubtedly adopt it at once. But where there are two or more, they collide with one another, maintain the state of suspense, and produce further inquiry. The first suggestion recently cited was to jump the ditch, but the perception of conditions inhibited that suggestion and led to the occurrence of other ideas.

Some inhibition of direct action is necessary to the condition of hesitation and delay that is essential to thinking. Thought is, as it were, conduct turned in upon itself and examining its purposes and its conditions, its resources, aids, and difficulties and obstacles.

THE SECOND PHASE, INTELLECTUALIZATION

We have already noted that it is artificial, so far as thinking is concerned, to start with a ready-made problem, a problem made out of whole cloth or arising out of a vacuum. In reality such a "problem" is simply an assigned *task*. There is not at first a situation *and* a problem, much less just a problem and no situation. . . . Problem and solution stand out *completely* at the same time. Up to that point, our grasp of the problem has been more or less vague and tentative.

A blocked suggestion leads us to reinspect the conditions that confront us. Then our uneasiness, the shock of disturbed activity, gets stated in some degree on the basis of observed conditions, of objects. The width of the ditch, the slipperiness of the banks, not the mere presence of a ditch, is the trouble. The difficulty is getting located and defined; it is becoming a true problem, something intellectual, not just an annoyance at being held up in what we are doing. . . .

The word "problem" often seems too elaborate and dignified to denote what happens in minor cases of reflection. But in every case where reflective activity ensues, there is a process of *intellectualizing* what at first is merely an *emotional* quality of the whole situation. This con-

version is effected by noting more definitely the conditions that constitute the trouble and cause the stoppage of action.

The Third Phase, the Guiding Idea, Hypothesis

The first suggestion occurs spontaneously; it comes to mind auto-
matically; it *springs* up; it "pops", as we have said, "into the mind"; it
flashes upon us. There is no direct control of its occurrence; the idea just
comes or it does not come; that is all that can be said. There is nothing
intellectual about its occurrence. The intellectual element consists in
what we do with it, how we use it, *after* its sudden occurrence as an idea.
A controlled use of it is made possible by the state of affairs just described. In the degree in which we define the difficulty (which is effected by stating it in terms of objects), we get a better idea of the kind
of solution that is needed. The facts or data set the problem before us,
and insight into the problem corrects, modifies, expands the suggestion
that originally occurred. In this fashion the suggestion becomes a definite
supposition or, stated more technically, a hypothesis.

Take the case of a physician examining a patient or a mechanic in-
specting a piece of complicated machinery that does not behave properly.
There is something wrong, so much is sure. But how to remedy it cannot be told until it is known *what* is wrong. An untrained person is
likely to make a wild guess—the suggestion—and then proceed to act
upon it in a random way, hoping that by good luck the right thing will
be hit upon. So some medicine that appears to have worked before or
that a neighbor has recommended is tried. Or the person fusses, monkeys,
with the machine, poking here and hammering there on the chance of
making the right move. The trained person proceeds in a very different
fashion. He *observes* with unusual care, using the methods, the tech-
niques, that the experience of physicians and expert mechanics in general, those familiar with the structure of the organism or the machine,
have shown to be helpful in detecting trouble.

The idea of the solution is thus controlled by the diagnosis that has
been made. But if the case is at all complicated, the physician or mechanic does not foreclose further thought by assuming that the suggested
method of remedy is certainly right. He proceeds to act upon it tentatively rather than decisively. That is, he treats it as a guiding idea, a
working hypothesis, and is led by it to make more observations, to collect more facts, so as to see if the *new* material is what the hypothesis
calls for. He reasons that *if* the disease is typhoid, *then* certain phenomena will be found; and he looks particularly to see if *just* these conditions are present. Thus both the first and second operations are
brought under control; the sense of the problem becomes more adequate

and refined and the suggestion ceases to be a *mere* possibility, becoming a *tested* and, if possible, a *measured* probability.

The Fourth Phase, Reasoning (in the Narrower Sense)

Observations pertain to what exists in nature. They constitute the facts, and these facts both regulate the formation of suggestions, ideas, hypotheses and test their probable value as indications of solutions. The ideas, on the other hand, occur, as we say, in our heads, in our minds. They not only occur there, but are capable, as well, of great development there. . . .

For example, the idea of heat in the third instance in the earlier chapter was linked up with what the person already knew about heat—in his case, its expansive force—and this in turn with the contractive tendency of cold, so that the idea of expansion could be used as an explanatory idea, though the mere idea of heat would not have been of any avail. Heat was quite directly suggested by the observed conditions; water was felt to be hot. But only a mind with some prior information about heat would have reasoned that heat meant expansion, and then used the idea of expansion as a working hypothesis. In more complex cases, there are long trains of reasoning in which one idea leads up to another idea known by previous test to be related to it. The stretch of links brought to light by reasoning depends, of course, upon the store of knowledge that the mind is already in possession of. And this depends not only upon the prior experience and special education of the individual who is carrying on the inquiry, but also upon the state of culture and science of the age and place. Reasoning helps extend knowledge, while at the same time it depends upon what is already known and upon the facilities that exist for communicating knowledge and making it a public, open resource. . . .

Reasoning has the same effect upon a suggested solution that more intimate and extensive observation has upon the original trouble. Acceptance of a suggestion in its first form is prevented by looking into it more thoroughly. Conjectures that seem plausible at first sight are often found unfit or even absurd when their full consequences are traced out. . . . Suggestions at first seemingly remote and wild are frequently so transformed by being elaborated into what follows from them as to become apt and fruitful. The development of an idea through reasoning helps supply intervening or intermediate terms which link together into a consistent whole elements that at first seemingly conflict with each other, some leading the mind to one inference and others to an opposed one.

Mathematics as Typical Reasoning. Mathematics affords the

typical example of how far can be carried the operation of relating ideas to one another, without having to depend upon the observation of the senses. In geometry we start with a few simple conceptions, line, angle, parallel, surfaces formed by lines meeting, etc., and a few principles defining equalities. Knowing something about the equality of angles made by parallel lines when they intersect a straight line, and knowing, by definition, that a perpendicular to a straight line forms two right angles, by means of a combination of these ideas we readily determine that the sum of the interior angles of a triangle is equal to two right angles. By continuing to trace the implications of theorems already demonstrated, the whole subject of plane figures is finally elaborated. The manipulation of algebraic symbols so as to establish a series of equations and other mathematical functions affords an even more striking example of what can be accomplished by developing the relation of ideas to one another.

When the hypothesis indicated by a series of scientific observations and experiments can be stated in mathematical form, that idea can be transformed to almost any extent, until it assumes a form in which a problem can be dealt with most expeditiously and effectively. Much of the accomplishment of physical science depends upon an intervening mathematical elaboration of ideas. It is not the mere presence of measurements in quantitative form that yields scientific knowledge, but that particular kind of mathematical statement which can be developed by reasoning into other and more fruitful forms—a consideration which is fatal to the claim to scientific standings of many educational measurements merely because they have a quantitative form.

The Fifth Phase, Testing the Hypothesis by Action

The concluding phase is some kind of testing by overt action to give *experimental corroboration,* or *verification,* of the conjectural idea. Reasoning shows that if the *idea* be adopted, certain consequences follow. So far the conclusion is hypothetical or conditional. If when we look, we find present all the conditions demanded by the theory, and if we find the characteristic traits called for by rival alternatives to be lacking, the tendency to believe, to accept, is almost irresistible. Sometimes direct observation furnishes corroboration, as in the case of the pole on the boat. In other cases, as in that of the bubbles, experiment is required; that is, *conditions are deliberately arranged in accord with the requirements of an idea or hypothesis to see whether the results theoretically indicated by the idea actually occur.* If it is found that the experimental results agree with the theoretical, or rationally deduced, results, and if there is reason to believe that *only* the conditions in question would yield such results, the confirmation is so strong as to induce a conclusion—at least until contrary facts shall indicate the advisability of its revison.

THE SEQUENCE OF THE FIVE PHASES IS NOT FIXED

The five phases, terminals, or functions of thought, that we have noted do not follow one another in a set order. On the contrary, each step in genuine thinking does something to perfect the formation of a suggestion and promote its change into a leading idea or directive hypothesis. It does something to promote the location and definition of the problem. Each improvement in the idea leads to new observations that yield new facts or data and help the mind judge more accurately the relevancy of facts already at hand. The elaboration of the hypothesis does not wait until the problem has been defined and adequate hypothesis has been arrived at; it may come in at any intermediate time. . . .

In conclusion, we may point out that the five phases of reflection that have been described represent only in outline the indispensable traits of reflective thinking. In practice, two of them may telescope, some of them may be passed over hurriedly, and the burden of reaching a conclusion may fall mainly on a single phase, which will then require a seemingly disproportionate development. No set rules can be laid down on such matters. The way they are managed depends upon the intellectual tact and sensitiveness of the individual. When things have come out wrong, it is, however, a wise practice to review the methods by which the unwise decision was reached, and see where the misstep was made.

STUDY QUESTIONS

1. Construct an original example of a "Case of Practical Deliberation." Note and elaborate to some extent upon the reflective activity involved.
2. What does Dewey mean by inference? What does he mean that inference involves a "leap"? How is inference to be controlled?
3. What does Dewey mean by proof? What are the two kinds of testing? What kind would you use in your example in question 1?
4. Explain and comment more fully on Dewey's statement on the function of reflective thought.
5. Explain and give examples of each of the five phases or aspects of reflective thought.
6. Contrive an example of your own and show how the five phases of reflective thought could be applied to it. Indicate whether there is any overlapping or set order in the sequence of the five phases.

Ludwig Wittgenstein

⌐⌐

LANGUAGE AND MEANING

⌐⌐

Biographical Note. LUDWIG WITTGENSTEIN (1889–1951) was born in Vienna, Austria. He was of Jewish descent but was baptized a Roman Catholic. His father was an engineer, and Wittgenstein's earliest interests lay in that area. He studied first at the Technische Hochschule in Berlin and then engaged in engineering research at the University of Manchester. From research in engineering and aeronautics his interests shifted to mathematics. He was greatly influenced by Russell's work in this field, and by 1911 he was at Cambridge University as a student of Russell. His first work was the *Tractatus Logico-Philosophicus* (1922). He noted that some of the ideas on language expressed in this work occurred to him while he was reading a magazine in a trench on the Eastern front during the first World War. (He was an Austrian army volunteer in 1914.) The *Tractatus* was dispatched to Bertrand Russell in the last years of the war while Wittgenstein was in captivity. His other writings were not published until after his death, and they consist principally of *Philosophical Investigations* and the *Blue* and *Brown Books*. These latter consisted largely of notes dictated to students and colleagues. Wittgenstein was an unconventional person—for example, he disdained hats and neckties. He lived a very simple life, enjoyed the cinema—particularly American westerns, and avoided all publicity. He is said to have

From *Philosophical Investigations,* translated by G. E. M. Anscombe, New York, The Macmillan Company, 1953. Reprinted with the permission of the publishers.

been a gloomy individual who spoke of the modern age as the "dark age." He died of cancer.

* * *

Introductory Note. It is easier to show the impact and influence of Wittgenstein's philosophy than it is to trace the origins of his thought. For Wittgenstein's genius lay in his originality rather than in any scholarship or a breadth of learning. He knew few of the great figures in philosophy. He admired Plato, he had read Schopenhauer as a youth, he liked St. Augustine's way of doing philosophy in the *Confessions,* but he knew neither Hume nor Kant. He was greatly influenced by Russell's *Principles of Mathematics,* and it was probably the influence of Russell that turned him to philosophy. The influence of Wittgenstein appears predominantly in the movements known as *Logical Positivism* and *Analysis.* Through them and by his personal relationships and teaching he has come to dominate much of the thought of the Anglo-Saxon philosophical world within the last few decades.

The basic ideas of Wittgenstein's philosophy are to be found in the *Tractatus* and the *Investigations.* In the former, Wittgenstein is concerned with the logic of language and the function of philosophy. The problems of philosophy he insists arise out of a misunderstanding of language. "What can be said at all can be said clearly: and whereof one cannot speak, thereof one must remain silent." Philosophy he describes as thereapeutic, since it "cures" philosophical difficulties by showing how they arise. In particular he shows how we overlook the limits of language and attempt to render propositions that are meaningless meaningful. The *Investigations* represents a considerable revision of Wittgenstein's earlier philosophy. The more general treatment of language in the *Tractatus* as a picture of reality is replaced with the notion of "language games" in the *Investigations,* and with the important idea that the meaning of a term lies in its use, not only in philosophical language but also in ordinary language. The Russellian notion that philosophy must correct ordinary language is rejected. Also rejected is the notion of a logical atomism and an analytic theory of meaning. Meaning must be equated with *use.*

The numbered paragraphs that follow present some of the more salient features of Wittgenstein's philosophy. The earlier numbered paragraphs develop the notion of a language game and attempt to show in some detail just how words derive their meanings within given contexts or sets of language rules. The emphasis throughout is upon the derivation of the meaning of words from their use. The later paragraphs are concerned more specifically with certain aspects of linguistic behaviorism—for example, how we ought to apply language to our sensations, particularly the experience of pain. The possibility of a private language is then discussed and rejected.

LANGUAGE AND MEANING

1. "When they (my elders) named some object, and accordingly moved towards something, I saw this and I grasped that the thing was called by the sound they uttered when they meant to point it out. Their intention was shown by their bodily movements, as it were the natural language of all peoples: the expression of the face, the play of the eyes, the movement of other parts of the body, and the tone of voice, which expresses our state of mind in seeking, having, rejecting, or avoiding something. Thus, as I heard words repeatedly used in their proper places in various sentences, I gradually learnt to understand what objects they signified; and after I had trained my mouth to form these signs, I used them to express my own desires." (Augustine, *Confessions*, I. i.)

These words, it seems to me, give us a particular picture of the essence of human language. It is this: the individual words in language name objects—sentences are combinations of such names.—In this picture of language we find the roots of the following idea: Every word has a meaning. This meaning is correlated with the word. It is the object for which the word stands.

Augustine does not speak of there being any difference between kinds of word. If you describe the learning of language in this way you are, I believe, thinking primarily of nouns like "table", "chair", "bread", and of people's names, and only secondarily of the names of certain actions and properties; and of the remaining kinds of word as something that will take care of itself.

Now thinking of the following use of language: I send someone shopping. I give him a slip marked "five red apples". He takes the slip to the shopkeeper, who opens the drawer marked "apples"; then he looks up the word "red" in a table and finds a color sample opposite it; then he says the series of cardinal numbers—I assume that he knows them by heart up to the word "five" and for each number he takes an apple of the same color as the sample out of the drawer.—It is in this and similar ways that one operates with words.—"But how does he know where and how he is to look up the word 'red' and what he is to do with the word 'five'?"—Well, I assume that he *acts* as I have described. Explanations come to an end somewhere.—But what is the meaning of the word "five"?—No such thing was in question here, only how the word "five" is used.

2. That philosophical concept of meaning has its place in a primitive idea of the way language functions. But one can also say that it is the idea of a language more primitive than ours.

Let us imagine a language for which the description given by Augustine is right. The language is meant to serve for communication between a builder A and an assistant B. A is building with building-stones: there are blocks, pillars, slabs and beams. B has to pass the stones, and that in the order in which A needs them. For this purpose they use a language consisting of the words "block", "pillar", "slab", "beam". A calls them out;—B brings the stone which he has learnt to bring at such-and-such a call.—Conceive this as a complete primitive language.

3. Augustine, we might say, does describe a system of communication; only not everything that we call language is this system. And one has to say this in many cases where the question arises "Is this an appropriate description or not?" The answer is: "Yes, it is appropriate, but only for this narrowly circumscribed region, not for the whole of what you were claiming to describe.

It is as if someone were to say: "A game consists in moving objects about on a surface according to certain rules . . ." and we replied: You seem to be thinking of board games, but there are others. You can make your definition correct by expressly restricting it to those games.

4. Imagine a script in which the letters were used to stand for sounds, and also as signs of emphasis and punctuation. (A script can be conceived as a language for describing sound-patterns.) Now imagine someone interpreting that script as if there were simply a correspondence of letters to sounds and as if the letters had not also completely different functions. Augustine's conception of language is like such an oversimple conception of the script.

5. If we look at the example in #1, we may perhaps get an inkling how much this general notion of the meaning of a word surrounds the working of language with a haze which makes clear vision impossible. It disperses the fog to study the phenomena of language in primitive kinds of application in which one can command a clear view of the aim and functioning of the words.

A child uses such primitive forms of language when it learns to talk. Here the teaching of language is not explanation, but training.

6. We could imagine that the language of #2 was the *whole* language of A and B; even the whole language of a tribe. The children are brought up to perform *these* actions, to use *these* words as they do so, and to react in *this* way to the words of others.

An important part of the training will consist in the teacher's pointing to the objects, directing the child's attention to them, and at the same time uttering a word; for instance, the word "slab" as he points to that shape. (I do not want to call this "ostensive definition", because the child cannot as yet *ask* what the name is. I will call it "ostensive teaching of words". . . .) This ostensive teaching of words can be said to establish an association between the word and the thing. But what does this mean? Well, it can mean various things; but one very likely thinks first of all that a picture of the object comes before the child's mind when it hears the word. But now, if this does happen—is it the purpose of the word? Yes, it *can* be the purpose. I can imagine such a use of words (of series of sounds). (Uttering a word is like striking a note on the keyboard of the imagination.) But in the language of #2 it is *not* the purpose of the words to evoke images. (It may, of course, be discovered that that helps to attain the actual purpose.)

But if the ostensive teaching has this effect, am I to say that it effects an understanding of the word? Don't you understand the call "Slab!" if you act upon it in such-and-such a way? Doubtless the ostensive teaching helped to bring this about; but only together with a particular training. With different training the same ostensive teaching of these words would have effected a quite different understanding. . . .

7. In the practice of the use of language (2) one party calls out the words, the other acts on them. In instruction in the language the following process will occur: the learner *names* the objects; that is, he utters the word when the teacher points to the stone. And there will be this still simpler exercise: the pupil repeats the words after the teacher— both of these being processes resembling language.

We can also think of the whole process of using words in (2) as one of those games by means of which children learn their native language. I will call these games "language games" and will sometimes speak of a primitive language as a language-game.

And the process of naming the stones and of repeating words after someone might also be called language-games. Think of much of the use of words in games like ring-a-ring-a-roses.

I shall also call the whole, consisting of language and the actions into which it is woven, the "language-game".

8. Let us now look at an expansion of language (2). Besides the four words "block", "pillar", etc., let it contain a series of words used as the shopkeeper in (1) used the numerals (it can be the series of letters of the alphabet); further, let there be two words, which may as well be "there" and "this" (because this roughly indicates their purpose), that are used in connexion with a pointing gesture; and finally a number of color samples. A gives an order like: "d—slab—there". At the same time he shows the assistant a color sample, and when he says "there" he points to a place on the building site. From the stock of

slabs B takes one for each letter of the alphabet up to "d", of the same color as the sample, and brings them to the place indicated by A. On other occasions A gives the order "this—there". At "this" he points to a building stone. And so on.

9. When a child learns this language, it has to learn the series of 'numerals' a, b, c, . . . by heart. And it has to learn their use. Will this training include ostensive teaching of the words? Well, people will, for example, point to slabs and count: "a, b, c slabs". Something more like the ostensive teaching of the words "block", "pillar", etc. would be the ostensive teaching of numerals that serve not to count but to refer to groups of objects that can be taken in at a glance. Children do learn the use of the first five or six cardinal numerals in this way.

Are "there" and "this" also taught ostensively? Imagine how one might perhaps teach their use. One will point to places and things— but in this case the pointing occurs in the *use* of the words too and not merely in learning the use.

10. Now what do the words of this language *signify*? What is supposed to show what they signify, if not the kind of use they have? And we have already described that. So we are asking for the expression "This word signifies *this*" to be made a part of the description. In other words the description ought to take the form: "The word. . . . signifies. . . .".

Of course, one can reduce the description of the use of the word "slab" to the statement that this word signifies this object. This will be done when, for example, it is merely a matter of removing the mistaken idea that the word "slab" refers to the shape of building-stone that we in fact call a "block"—but the kind of 'referring' this is, that is to say the use of these words for the rest, is already known.

Equally one can say that the signs "a", "b", etc. signify numbers; when for example this removes the mistaken idea that "a", "b", "c", play the part actually played in language by "block", "slab", "pillar". And one can also say that "c" means this number and not that one; when for example this serves to explain that the letters are to be used in the order a, b, c, d, etc. and not in the order a, b, d, c.

But assimilating the descriptions of the uses of words in this way cannot make the uses themselves any more like one another. For, as we see, they are absolutely unlike.

11. Think of the tools in a tool-box: there is a hammer, pliers, a saw, a screw-driver, a rule, a glue-pot, glue, nails and screws. The functions of words are as diverse as the functions of these objects. (And in both cases there are similarities.)

Of course, what confuses us is the uniform appearance of words when we hear them spoken or meet them in script and print. For their *application* is not presented to us so clearly. Especially not, when we are doing philosophy!

12. It is like looking into the cabin of a locomotive. We see handles all looking more or less alike. (Naturally, since they are all supposed to be handled.) But one is the handle of a crank which can be moved continuously (if it regulates the opening of a valve); another is the handle of a switch, which has only two effective positions, it is either off or on; a third is the handle of a brake-lever, the harder one pulls on it, the harder it brakes; a fourth, the handle of a pump: it has an effect only so long as is moved to and fro.

13. When we say: "Every word in language signifies something" we have so far said *nothing whatever;* unless we have explained exactly what distinction we wish to make. . . .

14. Imagine someone's saying: *"All* tools serve to modify something. Thus the hammer modifies the position of the nail, the saw the shape of the board, and so on." And what is modified by the rule, the glue-pot, the nails? "Our knowledge of a thing's length, the temperature of the glue, and the solidity of the box." Would anything be gained by this assimilation of expressions?

15. The word "to signify" is perhaps used in the most straightforward way when the object signified is marked with the sign. Suppose that the tools A uses in building bear certain marks. When A shows his assistant such a mark, he brings the tool that has that mark on it.

It is in this and more or less similar ways that a name means and is given to a thing. It will often prove useful in philosophy to say to ourselves: naming something is like attaching a label to a thing.

23. But how many kinds of sentence are there? Say assertion, question, and command? There are *countless* kinds: countless different kinds of use of what we call "symbols", "words", "sentences". And this multiplicity is not something fixed, given once for all; but new types of language, new language-games, as we may say, come into existence, and others become obsolete and get forgotten. . . .

Here the term "language-*game*" is meant to bring into prominence the fact that the speaking of language is part of an activity, or of a form of life.

Review the multiplicity of language-games in the following examples, and in others:

Giving orders, and obeying them—

Describing the appearance of an object, . . .

Constructing an object from a description (a drawing)—
Reporting an event—
Speculating about an event—
Forming and testing a hypothesis—

. . . . .

25. It is sometimes said that animals do not talk because they lack the mental capacity. And this means: "they do not think, and that is why they do not talk." But—they simply do not talk. Or to put it better: they do not use language—if we except the most primitive forms of language. Commanding, questioning, recounting, chatting, are as much a part of our natural history as walking, eating, drinking, playing.

37. What is the relation between name and thing named? Well, what *is* it? Look at language-game (2) or at another one: there you can see the sort of thing this relation consists in. This relation may also consist, among many other things, in the fact that hearing the name calls before our mind the picture of what is named; and it also consists, among other things, in the name's being written on the thing named or being pronounced when that thing is pointed at.

38. But what, for example, is the word "this" the name of in language-game (8) or the word "that" in the ostensive definition "that is called . . . "? If you do not want to produce confusion you will do best not to call these words names at all. Yet, strange to say, the word "this" has been called the only *genuine* name; so that anything else we call a name was one only in an inexact, approximate way.

This queer conception springs from a tendency to sublime the logic of our language—as one might put it. The proper answer to it is: we call very different things "names"; the word "name" is used to characterize many different kinds of use of a word, related to one another in many different ways; but the kind of use that "this" has is not among them.

It is quite true that, in giving an ostensive definition for instance, we often point to the object named and say the name. And similarly, in giving an ostensive definition for instance, we say the word "this" while pointing to a thing. And also the word "this" and a name often occupy the same position in a sentence. But it is precisely characteristic of a name that it is defined by means of the demonstration expression "That is N" (or "That is called 'N' "). But do we also give the definitions: "That is called 'this' ", or "This is called 'this' "?

This is connected with the conception of naming as, so to speak, an occult process. Naming appears as a *queer* connexion of a word with an object. And you really get such a *queer* connexion when the philosopher tries to bring out *the* relation between name and thing by staring at an object in front of him and repeating a name or even the word "this" innumerable times. For philosophical problems arise when *language goes on holiday*. And *here* we may indeed fancy naming to be some remarkable act of mind, as it were a baptism of an object. And we can also say the word "this" *to* the object, as it were *address* the object as "this" —a queer use of this word, which doubtless only occurs in doing philosophy.

43. For a *large* class of cases—though not for all—in which we employ the word "meaning" it can be defined thus: the meaning of a word is its use in the language. And the *meaning* of a name is sometimes explained by pointing to its *bearer*.

65. Here we come up against the great question that lies behind all these considerations. For someone might object: "You take the easy way out! You talk about all sorts of language-games, but have nowhere said what the essence of a language-game, and hence of language, is: what is common to all these activities, and what makes them into language or parts of language. So you let yourself off the very part of the investigation that once gave you yourself most headache, the part about the *general form of propositions* and of language."

And this is true. Instead of producing something common to all that we call language, I am saying that these phenomena have no one thing in common which makes us use the same word for all,—but that they are related to one another in many different ways. And it is because of this relationship, or these relationships, that we call them all "language". I will try to explain this.

66. Consider for example the proceedings that we call "games". I mean board-games, card-games, ball-games, Olympic games, and so on. What is common to them all? Don't say: "There *must* be something common or they would not be called 'games'"—but *look and see* whether there is anything common to all. For if you look at them you will not see something that is common to *all*, but similarities, relationships, and a whole series of them at that. To repeat: don't think, but look! Look for example at board-games, with their multifarious relationships. Now pass to card-games; here you find many correspondences with the first group, but many common features drop out, and others appear. When we pass next to ball-games, much that is common is retained, but much is lost. Are they all 'amusing'? . . . In ball games there is winning and losing; but when a child throws his ball at the wall and catches it again, this feature has disappeared. Look at the parts played by skill and luck; and at the difference between skill in chess and skill in tennis. Think now of games like ring-a-ring-a-roses; here is the ele-

ment of amusement, but how many other characteristic features have disappeared! And we can go through the many, many other groups of games in the same way; can see how similarities crop up and disappear.

And the result of this examination is: we see a complicated network of similarities overlapping and criss-crossing: sometimes overall similarities, sometimes similarities of detail.

67. I can think of no better expression to characterize these similarities than "family resemblances"; for the various resemblances between members of a family: build, features, color of eyes, gait, temperament, etc. etc. overlap and criss-cross in the same way. And I shall say: 'games' form a family.

And for instance the kinds of number form a family in the same way. Why do we call something a "number"? Well, perhaps because it has a direct relationship with several things that have hitherto been called number; and this can be said to give it an indirect relationship to other things we call the same name. And we extend our concept of number as in spinning a thread we twist fibre on fibre. And the strength of the thread does not reside in the fact that some one fibre runs through its whole length, but in the overlapping of many fibres.

. . . . . .

116. When philosophers use a word—"knowledge", "being", "object", "I", "proposition", "name"—and try to grasp the *essence* of the thing, one must always ask oneself: is the word ever actually used in this way in the language-game which is its original home?

What *we* do is to bring words back from their metaphysical to their everyday use.

117. You say to me: "You understand this expression, don't you? Well then—I am using it in the sense you are familiar with."—As if the sense were an atmosphere accompanying the word, which it carried with it into every kind of application.

If, for example, someone says that the sentence "This is here" (saying which he points to an object in front of him) makes sense to him, then he should ask himself in what special circumstances this sentence is actually used. There it does make sense.

118. Where does our investigation get its importance from, since it seems only to destroy everything interesting, that is, all that is great and important? (As it were all the buildings, leaving behind only bits of stone and rubble.) What we are destroying is nothing but houses of cards and we are clearing up the ground of language on which they stand.

119. The results of philosophy are the uncovering of one or another

piece of plain nonsense and of bumps that the understanding has got by running its head up against the limits of language. These bumps make us see the value of the discovery.

120. When I talk about language (words, sentences, etc.) I must speak the language of every day. Is this language somehow too coarse and material for what we want to say? *Then how is another one to be constructed?* . . .

Your questions refer to words; so I have to talk about words.

You say: the point isn't the word, but its meaning, and you think of the meaning as a thing of the same kind as the word, though also different from the word. Here the word, there the meaning. The money, and the cow that you can buy with it. (But contrast: money, and its use.)

123. A philosophical problem has the form: "I don't know my way about."

244. How do words *refer* to sensations? There doesn't seem to be any problem here; don't we talk about sensations every day, and give them names? But how is the connexion between the name and the thing named set up? This question is the same as: how does a human being learn the meaning of the names of sensations?—of the word "pain" for example. Here is one possibility: words are connected with the primitive, the natural, expressions of the sensation and used in their place. A child has hurt himself and he cries; and then adults talk to him and teach him exclamations and, later, sentences. They teach the child new pain-behavior.

"So you are saying that the word 'pain' really means crying?"—On the contrary: the verbal expression of pain replaces crying and does not describe it.

245. For how can I go so far as to try to use language to get between pain and its expression?

246. In what sense are my sensations *private?*—Well, only I can know whether I am really in pain; another person can only surmise it.—In one way this is false, and in another nonsense. If we are using the word "to know" as it is normally used (and how else are we to use it?), then other people very often know when I am in pain.—Yes, but all the same not with the certainty with which I know it myself!—It can't be said of me at all (except perhaps as a joke) that I *know* I am in pain. What it is supposed to mean—except perhaps that I *am* in pain?

Other people cannot be said to learn of my sensations *only* from my behavior,—for I cannot be said to learn of them. I *have* them.

The truth is: it makes sense to say about other people that they doubt whether I am in pain; but not to say it about myself.

247. "Only you can know if you had that intention." One might tell someone this when one was explaining the meaning of the word "intention" to him. For then it means: *that* is how we use it.

(And here "know" means that the expression of uncertainty is senseless.)

248. The proposition "Sensations are private" is comparable to: "One plays patience by oneself".

249. Are we perhaps over-hasty in our assumption that the smile of an unweaned infant is not a pretence?—And on what experience is our assumption based?

(Lying is a language-game that needs to be learned like any other one.)

250. Why can't a dog simulate pain? Is he too honest? Could one teach a dog to simulate pain? Perhaps it is possible to teach him to howl on particular occasions as if he were in pain, even when he is not. But the surroundings which are necessary for this behavior to be real simulation are missing.

253. "Another person can't have my pains."—Which are *my* pains? What counts as a criterion of identity here? Consider what makes it possible in the case of physical objects to speak of "two exactly the same", for example, to say "This chair is not the one you saw here yesterday, but is exactly the same as it".

In so far as it makes *sense* to say that my pain is the same as his, it is also possible for us both to have the same pain. (And it would also be imaginable for two people to feel pain in the same—not just the corresponding—place. That might be the case with Siamese twins, for instance.)

I have seen a person in a discussion on this subject strike himself on the breast and say: "But surely another person can't have THIS pain!" —The answer to this is that one does not define a criterion of identity by emphatic stressing of the word "this". Rather, what the emphasis does is to suggest the case in which we are conversant with such a criterion of identity, but have to be reminded of it.

254. The substitution of "identical" for "the same" (for instance) is another typical expedient in philosophy. As if we were talking about shades of meaning and all that were in question were to find words to hit on the correct nuance. That is in question in philosophy only where we have to give a psychologically exact account of the temptation to use a particular kind of expression. What we 'are tempted to say' in such a case is, of course, not philosophy; but it is its raw material. Thus, for example, what a mathematician is inclined to say about the

objectivity and reality of mathematical facts, is not a philosophy of mathematics, but something for philosophical *treatment*.

255. The philosopher's treatment of a question is like the treatment of an illness.

256. Now, what about the language which describes my inner experiences and which only I myself can understand? *How* do I use words to stand for my sensations?—As we ordinarily do? Then are my words for sensations tied up with my natural expressions of sensations? In that case my language is not a 'private' one. Someone else might understand it as well as I. —But suppose I didn't have my natural expression of sensation, but only had the sensation? And now I simply *associate* names with sensations and use these names in descriptions.

257. "What would it be like if human beings showed no outward signs of pain (did not groan, grimace, etc.)? Then it would be impossible to teach a child the use of the word 'tooth-ache'." —Well, let's assume the child is a genius and itself invents a name for the sensation!—But then, of course, he couldn't make himself understood when he used the word.—So does he understand the name, without being able to explain its meaning to anyone?—But what does it mean to say that he has 'named his pain'?—How has he done this naming of pain?! And whatever he did, what was its purpose?—When one says "He gave a name to his sensation" one forgets that a great deal of stage-setting in the language is presupposed if the mere act of naming is to make sense. And when we speak of someone's having given a name to pain, what is presupposed is the existence of the grammar of the word "pain"; it shows the post where the new word is stationed.

258. Let us imagine the following case. I want to keep a diary about the recurrence of a certain sensation. To this end I associate it with the sign "E" and write this sign in a calendar for every day on which I have the sensation.—I will remark first of all that a definition of the sign cannot be formulated.—But still I can give myself a kind of ostensive definition.—How? Can I point to the sensation? Not in the ordinary sense. But I speak, or write the sign down, and at the same time I concentrate my attention on the sensation—and so, as it were, point to it inwardly. But what is this ceremony for? for that is all it seems to be! A definition surely serves to establish the meaning of a sign. Well, that is done precisely by the concentrating of my attention; for in this way I impress on myself the connexion between the sign and the sensation. But "I impress it on myself" can only mean: this process brings it about that I remember the connexion *right* in the future. But in the present case I have no criterion of correctness. One would like to say: whatever

is going to seem right to me is right. And that only means that here we can't talk about 'right'.

259. Are the rules of the private language *impressions* of rules? The balance on which impressions are weighed is not the *impression* of a balance.

260. "Well, I *believe* that this is the sensation E again." —Perhaps you *believe* that you believe it!

Then did the man who made the entry in the calendar make a note of *nothing whatever?*—Don't consider it a matter of course that a person is making a note of something when he makes a mark—say in a calendar. For a note has a function, and this "E" so far has none.

(One can talk to oneself. If a person talks when no one else is present, does that mean he is talking to himself?)

STUDY QUESTIONS

1. According to Wittgenstein, what is the Augustinian description of language? What evaluation does Wittgenstein make of this description?
2. Precisely what does Wittgenstein mean by "the language-game"? Give an example.
3. What is meant by "naming"? By the "ostensive teaching of words"? Is the word "this" a name? Comment. Can the word "this" be taught ostensively?
4. Comment on Wittgenstein's statement that "philosophical problems arise when *language goes on a holiday.*"
5. What does Wittgenstein mean by the expression "family resemblances"? How does he arrive at such an expression, and what application does it have to his analysis of language?
6. What meaning do you attach to Wittgenstein's statement: 'A philosophical problem has the form: "I don't know my way about" '?
7. Discuss Wittgenstein's statement that the meaning of a word is its use in the language. Indicate the extent of your agreement or disagreement.
8. What is the problem of private language? How does it arise for Wittgenstein and how does his manner of treating it reflect his philosophy?
9. What do you suppose is meant by the statement: "The philosopher's treatment of a question is like the treatment of an illness"?

Alfred J. Ayer

🄿🄿

THE ELIMINATION OF METAPHYSICS

🄿🄿

Biographical Note.   ALFRED J. AYER (1910–) was born in England and educated at Eton and Oxford. After a brief period of study at the University of Vienna, he became Lecturer in Philosophy at Christ Church in 1933. He became a Research Student at Oxford in 1935 and received his M. A. degree in 1936. At Oxford he continued as Research Student and Fellow of Wadham College until 1946. During the war he was a captain in the Welsh Guards and was also employed in military intelligence. From 1946 to 1959 he served as Grote Professor of Philosophy of Mind and Logic at the University of London. He has also served as Visiting Professor of Philosophy at New York University (1948-49) and Visiting Professor of Philosophy at City College, New York (1961-62). His principal publications are *Language, Truth and Logic; The Problem of Knowledge; The Foundations of Empirical Knowledge;* and *Philosophical Essays.* Since 1959 he has been Wykeham Professor of Logic at the University of Oxford.

* * *

Introductory Note.   The philosophy of logical positivism (logical empiricism as its proponents prefer to call it) has probably been most effectively represented and presented by the English philosopher Ayer. The term "logical positivism" is indicative of its origins and interests. Although it has no strict relationship with the positivism of the 19th century, it has strong roots in the

From *Language, Truth and Logic,* London, Victor Gollancz, Ltd., 1936; New York, Dover Publications, no date. Reprinted with the permission of the publishers.

theory and methodology of contemporary science. It originated in what became known as the "Vienna Circle," a group of philosophers, mathematicians, and scientists including the well-known figures M. Schlick, R. Carnap, F. Waismann, O. Neurath, K. Gödel, and others. Ayer was particularly influenced by Schlick and Carnap, and by the British philosophers Russell and Wittgenstein.

The central principle of Ayer's theory of logical positivism is the verification principle, which holds that the meaning of a proposition consists in its verification. This, however, would exclude mathematical and logical propositions, so it was argued that although such propositions are not empirical, they are true and meaningful because they consist of analytic propositions and hence are meaningful by definition. Thus Ayer will declare "A sentence has literal meaning if and only if the proposition is either analytic or empirically verifiable." The consequences of such a principle of verification are: (1) the elimination of metaphysics (2) an emotive theory of ethics which would reduce ethical judgments to the expression of feelings or attitudes (3) a conception of the function of philosophy as wholly critical and analytic (4) the elimination of theology.

The selection that follows is taken from the first chapter of *Language, Truth and Logic,* and its objective is to disclose the meaninglessness of all metaphysical propositions. The position of Ayer goes further than that of Kant, who merely questioned the validity of any metaphysics that transcended experience. To show that metaphysical propositions are meaningless, Ayer develops and elaborates the Verification Principle, indicating the "strong" and "weak" sense of such a principle and the necessity of distinguishing between verifiable in principle and verifiable in practice. He declares that only experiential propositions can pass the test of verification, and he illustrates the kind of propositions that are ruled out by this principle—for example, propositions dealing with the ideas of "substance," "being," etc. Even the defense of metaphysics as poetry is rejected on the ground that most poetic sentences have literal meanings, whereas metaphysical sentences, he contends, do not.

METAPHYSICS AND TRANSCENDENT REALITY

The traditional disputes of philosophers are, for the most part, as unwarranted as they are unfruitful. The surest way to end them is to establish beyond question what should be the purpose and method of a philosophical enquiry. And this is by no means so difficult a task as the history of philosophy would lead one to suppose. For if there are any questions which science leaves it to philosophy to answer, a straightforward process of elimination must lead to their discovery.

We may begin by criticizing the metaphysical thesis that philosophy affords us knowledge of a reality transcending the world of science and common sense. Later on, when we come to define metaphysics and account for its existence, we shall find that it is possible to be a metaphysician without believing in a transcendent reality; for we shall see that many metaphysical utterances are due to the commission of logical errors, rather than to a conscious desire on the part of their authors to go beyond the limits of experience. But it is convenient for us to take the case of those who believe that it is possible to have knowledge of a transcendent reality as a starting-point for our discussion. The arguments which we use to refute them will subsequently be found to apply to the whole of metaphysics.

One way of attacking a metaphysician who claimed to have knowledge of a reality which transcended the phenomenal world would be to enquire from what premises his propositions were deduced. Must he not begin, as other men do, with the evidence of his senses? And if so, what valid process of reasoning can possibly lead him to the conception of a transcendent reality? Surely from empirical premises nothing whatsoever concerning the properties, or even the existence, of anything super-empirical can legitimately be inferred. But this objection would be met by a denial on the part of the metaphysician that his assertions were ultimately based on the evidence of his senses. He would say that he was endowed with a faculty of intellectual intuition which enabled him to know facts that could not be known through sense-experience. And even if it could be shown that he was relying on empirical premises, and that his venture into a non-empirical world was therefore logically unjustified, it would not follow that the assertions which he made concerning this non-empirical world could not be true. For the fact that a conclusion does not follow from its putative premise is not sufficient to show that it is false. Consequently one cannot overthrow a system of transcendent metaphysics merely by criticizing the way in which it comes into being. What is required is rather a criticism of the nature of the actual statements which comprise it. And this is the line of argument which we shall, in fact, pursue. For we shall maintain that no statement which refers to a "reality" transcending the limits of all possible sense experience can possibly have any literal significance; from which it must follow that the labors of those who have striven to describe such a reality have all been devoted to the production of nonsense.

It may be suggested that this is a proposition which has already been proved by Kant. But although Kant also condemned transcendent metaphysics, he did so on different grounds. For he said that the human understanding was so constituted that it lost itself in contradictions when it ventured out beyond the limits of possible experience and attempted to deal with things in themselves. And thus he made the impossibility of a transcendent metaphysic not, as we do, a matter of logic, but a matter of fact. He asserted, not that our minds could not conceivably have had the power penetrating beyond the phenomenal world, but merely that they were in fact devoid of it. And this leads the critic to ask how, if it is possible to know only what lies within the bounds of sense experience, the author can be justified in asserting that real things do exist beyond, and how he can tell what are the boundaries beyond which the human understanding may not venture, unless he succeeds in passing them himself. As Wittgenstein says, "in order to draw a limit to thinking, we should have to think both sides of this limit,"[1] a truth to which Bradley gives a special twist in maintaining that the man who is ready to prove that metaphysics is impossible is a brother metaphysician with a rival theory of his own.[2]

Whatever force these objections may have against the Kantian doctrine, they have none whatsoever against the thesis that I am about to set forth. It cannot here be said that the author is himself overstepping the barrier he maintains to be impassable. For the fruitlessness of attempting to transcend the limits of possible sense-experience will be deduced, not from a psychological hypothesis concerning the actual constitution of the human mind, but from the rule which determines the literal significance of language. Our charge against the metaphysician is not that he attempts to employ the understanding in a field where it cannot profitably venture, but that he produces sentences which fail to conform to the conditions under which alone a sentence can be literally significant. Nor are we ourselves obliged to talk nonsense in order to show that all sentences of a certain type are necessarily devoid of literal significance. We need only formulate the criterion which enables us to test whether a sentence expresses a genuine proposition about a matter of fact, and then point out that the sentences under consideration fail to satisfy it. And this we shall now proceed to do. We shall first of all formulate the criterion in somewhat vague terms, and then give the explanations which are necessary to render it precise.

CRITERION OF VERIFIABILITY

The criterion which we use to test the genuineness of apparent statements of fact is the criterion of verifiability. We say that a sentence is factually significant to any given person, if, and only if, he knows how

---

[1] *Tractatus Logico-Philosophicus,* Preface.
[2] Bradley, *Appearance and Reality,* 2nd ed., p. 1.

to verify the proposition which it purports to express—that is, if he knows what observations would lead him, under certain conditions, to accept the proposition as being true, or reject it as being false. If, on the other hand, the putative propostion is of such a character that the assumption of its truth, or falsehood, is consistent with any assumption whatsoever concerning the nature of his future experience, then, as far as he is concerned, it is, if not a tautology, a mere pseudo-proposition. The sentence expressing it may be emotionally significant to him; but it is not literally significant. And with regard to questions the procedure is the same. We enquire in every case what observations would lead us to answer the question, one way or the other; and, if none can be discovered, we must conclude that the sentence under consideration does not, as far as we are concerned, express a genuine question, however strongly its grammatical appearance may suggest that it does.

As the adoption of this procedure is an essential factor in the argument of this book, it needs to be examined in detail.

Verifiability in Principle and Practise.   In the first place it is necessary to draw a distinction between practical verifiability, and verifiability in principle. Plainly we all understand, in many cases believe, propositions which we have not in fact taken steps to verify. Many of these are propositions which we could verify if we took enough trouble. But there remain a number of significant propositions, concerning matters of fact, which we could not verify even if we chose; simply because we lack the practical means of placing ourselves in the situation where the relevant observations could be made. A simple and familiar example of such a proposition is the proposition that there are mountains on the farther side of the moon. No rocket has yet been invented which would enable me to go and look at the farther side of the moon, so that I am unable to decide the matter by actual observation. But I do know what observations would decide it for me, if, as is theoretically conceivable, I were once in a position to make them. And therefore I say that the proposition is verifiable in principle, if not in practice, and is accordingly significant. On the other hand, such a metaphysical pseudo-proposition as "the Absolute enters into, but is itself incapable of, evolution and progress,"[3] is not even in principle verifiable. For one cannot conceive of an observation which would enable one to determine whether the Absolute did, or did not, enter into evolution and progress. Of course it is possible that the author of such a remark is using English words in a way in which they are not commonly used by English-speaking people, and that he does, in fact, intend to assert something which could be em-

[3] A remark taken at random from *Appearance and Reality,* by F. H. Bradley.

pirifically verified. But until he makes us understand how the proposition that he wishes to express would be verified, he fails to communicate anything to us. And if he admits, as I think the author of the remark in question would have admitted, that his words were not intended to express either a tautology or a proposition which was capable, at least in principle, of being verified, then it follows that he has made an utterance which has no literal significance even for himself.

Strong and Weak Verifiability.   A further distinction which we must make is the distinction between the "strong" and the "weak" sense of the term "verifiable." A proposition is said to be verifiable, in the strong sense of the term, if, and only if, its truth could be conclusively established in experience. But it is verifiable, in the weak sense, if it is possible for experience to render it probable. In which sense are we using the term when we say that a putative proposition is genuine only if it is verifiable?

It seems to me that if we adopt conclusive verifiability as our criterion of significance, as some positivists have proposed,[4] our argument will prove too much. Consider, for example, the case of general propositions of law—such propositions, namely, as "arsenic is poisonous"; "all men are mortal"; "a body tends to expand when it is heated." It is of the very nature of these propositions that their truth cannot be established with certainty by any finite series of observations. But if it is recognized that such general propositions of law are designed to cover an infinite number of cases, then it must be admitted that they cannot, even in principle, be verified conclusively. And then, if we adopt conclusive verifiability as our criterion of significance, we are logically obliged to treat these general propositions of law in the same fashion as we treat the statements of the metaphysician.

In the face of this difficulty, some positivists[5] have adopted the heroic course of saying that these general propositions are indeed pieces of nonsense, albeit an essentially important type of nonsense. But here the introduction of the term "important" is simply an attempt to hedge. It serves only to mark the author's recognition that their view is somewhat too paradoxical, without in any way removing the paradox. Besides, the difficulty is not confined to the case of general propositions of law, though it is there revealed most plainly. It is hardly less obvious in the case of propositions about the remote past. For it must surely be admitted that, however strong the evidence in favor of historical state-

[4] e. g. M. Schlick, "Positivismus und Realismus," *Erkenntnis*, Vol. I, 1930. F. Waismann, "Logische Analyse des Warscheinlichkeitsbegriffs," *Erkenntnis*, Vol. I, 1930.
[5] e. g. M. Schlick

ments may be, their truth can never become more than highly probable. And to maintain that they also constituted an important, or unimportant, type of nonsense would be unplausible, to say the very least. Indeed, it will be our contention that no proposition, other than a tautology, can possibly be anything more than a probable hypothesis. And if this is correct, the principle that a sentence can be factually significant only if it expresses what is conclusively verifiable is self-stultifying as a criterion of significance. For it leads to the conclusion that it is impossible to make a significant statement of fact at all. . . .

To make our position clearer, we may formulate it in another way. Let us call a proposition which records an actual or possible observation an experiential proposition. Then we may say that it is the mark of a genuine factual proposition, not that it should be equivalent to an experiential proposition, or any finite number of experiential propositions, but simply that some experiential propositions can be deduced from it in conjunction with certain other premises without being deducible from those other premises alone.[6]

This criterion seems liberal enough. In contrast to the principle of conclusive verifiability, it clearly does not deny significance to general propositions or to propositions about the past. Let us see what kinds of assertion it rules out.

Applications of the Verifiability Principle. A good example of the kind of utterance that is condemned by our criterion as being not even false but nonsensical would be the assertion that the world of sense-experience was altogether unreal. It must, of course, be admitted that our senses do sometimes deceive us. We may, as the result of having certain sensations, expect certain other sensations to be obtainable which are, in fact, not obtainable. But, in all such cases, it is further sense-experience that informs us of the mistakes that arise out of sense-experience. We say that the senses sometimes deceive us, just because the expectations to which our sense-experiences give rise do not always ac-

---

[6] This is an over-simplified statement, which is not literally correct. I give what I believe to be the correct formulation in the Introduction, p. 13.

[The correct formulation is stated:]

. . . I propose to say that a statement is directly verifiable if it is either itself an observation-statement, or is such that in conjunction with one or more observation-statements it entails at least one observation-statement which is not deducible from these other premises alone; and I propose to say that a statement is indirectly verifiable if it satisfies the following conditions: first, that in conjunction with certain other premises it entails one or more directly verifiable statements which are not deducible from these other premises alone; and secondly, that these other premises do not include any statement that is not either analytic, or directly verifiable, or capable of being independently established as indirectly verifiable. And I can now reformulate the principle of verification as requiring of a literally meaningful statement, which is not analytic, that it should be either directly or indirectly verifiable, in the foregoing sense.

cord with what we subsequently experience. That is, we rely on our senses to substantiate or confute the judgements which are based on our sensations. And therefore the fact that our perceptual judgments are sometimes found to be erroneous has not the slightest tendency to show that the world of sense-experience is unreal. And, indeed, it is plain that no conceivable observation, or series of observations, could have any tendency to show that the world revealed to us by sense-experience was unreal. Consequently, anyone who condemns the sensible world as a world of mere appearance, as opposed to reality, is saying something which, according to our criterion of significance, is literally nonsensical.

An example of a controversy which the application of our criterion obliges us to condemn as fictitious is provided by those who dispute concerning the number of substances that there are in the world. For it is admitted both by monists, who maintain that reality is one substance, and by pluralists, who maintain that reality is many, that it is impossible to imagine any empirical situation which would be relevant to the solution of their dispute. But if we are told that no possible observation could give any probability either to the assertion that reality was one substance or to the assertion that it was many, then we must conclude that neither assertion is significant. . . .

A similar treatment must be accorded to the controversy between realists and idealists, in its metaphysical aspect. . . . Let us suppose that a picture is discovered and the suggestion made that it was painted by Goya. There is a definite procedure for dealing with such a question. The experts examine the picture to see in what way it resembles the accredited works of Goya, and to see if it bears any marks which are characteristic of a forgery; they look up contemporary records for evidence of the existence of such a picture, and so on. In the end, they may still disagree, but each one knows what empirical evidence would go to confirm or discredit his opinion. Suppose, now, that these men have studied philosophy, and some of them proceed to maintain that this picture is a set of ideas in the perceiver's mind, or in God's mind, others that it is objectively real. What possible experience could any of them have which would be relevant to the solution of this dispute one way or the other? In the ordinary sense of the term "real," in which it is opposed to "illusory," the reality of the picture is not in doubt. The disputants have satisfied themselves that the picture is real, in this sense, by obtaining a correlated series of sensations of sight and sensations of touch. Is there any similar process by which they could discover whether the picture was real, in the sense in which the term "real" is opposed to "ideal"? Clearly there is none. But, if that is so, the problem is fictitious according to our criterion. . . . What we have just shown is that the question at issue between idealists and realists becomes fictitious when, as is often the case, it is given a metaphysical interpretation.

There is no need for us to give further examples of the operation of our criterion of significance. For our object is merely to show that philosophy, as a genuine branch of knowledge, must be distinguished from metaphysics. . . .

METAPHYSICS AS NONSENSE

It should be mentioned here that the fact that the utterances of the metaphysician are nonsensical does not follow simply from the fact that they are devoid of factual content. It follows from that fact, together with the fact that they are not *a priori* propositions. And in assuming that they are not *a priori* propositions, we are once again anticipating the conclusions of a later chapter in this book. For it will be shown there that *a priori* propositions, which have always been attractive to philosophers on account of their certainty, owe this certainty to the fact that they are tautologies. We may accordingly define a metaphysical sentence as a sentence which purports to express a genuine proposition, but does, in fact, express neither a tautology nor an empirical hypothesis. And as tautologies and empirical hypotheses form the entire class of significant propositions, we are justified in concluding that all metaphysical assertions are nonsensical. Our next task is to show how they come to be made.

The use of the term "substance," to which we have already referred, provides us with a good example of the way in which metaphysics mostly comes to be written. It happens to be the case that we cannot, in our language, refer to the sensible properties of a thing without introducing a word or phrase which appears to stand for the thing itself as opposed to anything which may be said about it. And, as a result of this, those who are infected by the primitive superstition that to every name a single real entity must correspond assume that it is necessary to distinguish logically between the thing itself and any, or all, of its sensible properties. And so they employ the term "substance" to refer to the thing itself. But from the fact that we happen to employ a single word to refer to a thing, and make that word the grammatical subject of the sentences in which we refer to the sensible appearances of the thing, it does not by any means follow that the thing itself is a "simple entity," or that it cannot be defined in terms of the totality of its appearances. It is true that in talking of "its" appearances we appear to distinguish the thing from the appearances, but that is simply an accident of linguistic usage. Logical analysis shows that what makes these "appearances" the "appearances of" the same thing is not their relationship to an entity other than themselves, but their relationship to one another. The metaphysician fails to see this because he is misled by a superficial grammatical feature of his language.

A simpler and clearer instance of the way in which a consideration of grammar leads to metaphysics is the case of the metaphysical concept of Being. The origin of our temptation to raise questions about Being, which no conceivable experience would enable us to answer, lies in the fact that, in our language, sentences which express existential propositions and sentences which express attributive propositions may be of the same grammatical form. For instance, the sentences "Martyrs exist" and "Martyrs suffer" both consist of a noun followed by an intransitive verb, and the fact that they have grammatically the same appearance leads one to assume that they are of the same logical type. It is seen that in the proposition "Martyrs suffer," the members of a certain species are credited with a certain attribute, and it is sometimes assumed that the same thing is true of such a proposition as "Martyrs exist." If this were actually the case, it would, indeed, be as legitimate to speculate about the Being of martyrs as it is to speculate about their suffering. But, as Kant pointed out, existence is not an attribute.[7] For, when we ascribe an attribute to a thing, we covertly assert that it exists: so that if existence were itself an attribute, it would follow that all positive existential propositions were tautologies, and all negative existential propositions self-contradictory; and this is not the case. So that those who raise questions about Being which are based on the assumption that existence is an attribute are guilty of following grammar beyond the boundaries of sense.

A similar mistake has been made in connection with such propositions as "Unicorns are fictitious." Here again the fact that there is a superficial grammatical resemblance between the English sentences "Dogs are faithful" and "Unicorns are fictitious," and between the corresponding sentences in other languages, creates the assumption that they are of the same logical type. Dogs must exist in order to have the property of being faithful, and so it is held that unless unicorns in some way existed they could not have the property of being fictitious. But, as it plainly self-contradictory to say that fictitious objects exist, the device is adopted of

[7] Vide *The Critique of Pure Reason*, "Transcendental Dialectic," Book II, chapter iii, section 4.

saying that they are real in some non-empirical sense—that they have a mode of real being which is different from the mode of being of existent things. But since there is no way of testing whether an object is real in this sense, as there is for testing whether it is real in the ordinary sense, the assertion that fictitious objects have a special non-empirical mode of real being is devoid of all literal significance. It comes to be made as a result of the assumption that being fictitious is an attribute. And this is a fallacy of the same order as the fallacy of supposing that existence is an attribute, and it can be exposed in the same way.

In general, the postulation of real non-existent entities results from the superstition, just now referred to, that, to every word or phrase that can be the grammatical subject of a sentence, there must somewhere be a real entity corresponding. For as there is no place in the empirical world for many of these "entities," a special non-empirical world is invoked to house them. To this error must be attributed, not only the utterances of a Heidegger, who bases his metaphysics on the assumption that "Nothing" is a name which is used to denote something peculiarly mysterious, but also the prevalence of such problems as those concerning the reality of propositions and universals whose senselessness, though less obvious, is no less complete.

These few examples afford a sufficient indication of the way in which most metaphysical assertions come to be formulated. They show how easy it is to write sentences which are literally nonsensical without seeing that they are nonsensical. And thus we see that the view that a number of the traditional "problems of philosophy" are metaphysical, and consequently fictitious, does not involve any incredible assumptions about the psychology of philosophers.

METAPHYSICS AND POETRY

Among those who recognize that if philosophy is to be accounted a genuine branch of knowledge it must be defined in such a way as to distinguish it from metaphysics, it is fashionable to speak of the metaphysician as a kind of misplaced poet. As his statements have no literal meaning, they are not subject to any criteria of truth or falsehood: but they may still serve to express, or arouse, emotion, and thus be subject to ethical or aesthetic standards. And it is suggested that they may have considerable value, as means of moral inspiration, or even as works of art. In this way, an attempt is made to compensate the metaphysician for his extrusion from philosophy.

I am afraid that this compensation is hardly in accordance with his deserts. The view that the metaphysician is to be reckoned among the poets appears to rest on the assumption that both talk nonsense. But this assumption is false. In the vast majority of cases the sentences which are produced by poets do have literal meaning. The difference between the man who uses language scientifically and the man who uses it emotively is not that the one produces sentences which are incapable of arousing emotion and the other sentences which have no sense, but that the one is primarily concerned with the expression of true propositions, the other with the creation of a work of art. Thus, if a work of science contains true and important propositions, its value as a work of science will hardly be diminished by the fact that they are inelegantly expressed. And similarly, a work of art is not necessarily the worse for the fact that all the propositions comprising it are literally false. But to say that many literary works are largely composed of falsehoods, is not to say that they are composed of pseudo-propositions. It is, in fact, very rare for a literary artist to produce sentences which have no literal meaning. And where this does occur, the sentences are carefully chosen for their rhythm and balance. If the author writes nonsense, it is because he considers it most suitable for bringing about the effects for which his writing is designed.

The metaphysician, on the other hand, does not intend to write nonsense. He lapses into it through being deceived by grammar, or through committing errors of reasoning, such as that which leads to the view that the sensible world is unreal. But it is not the mark of a poet simply to make mistakes of this sort. There are some, indeed, who would see in the fact that the metaphysician's utterances are senseless a reason against the view that they have aesthetic value. And, without going so far as this, we may safely say that it does not constitute a reason for it.

It is true, however, that although the greater part of metaphysics is merely the embodiment of humdrum errors, there remain a number of metaphysical passages which are the work of genuine mystical feeling; and they may more plausibly be held to have moral or aesthetic value. But, as far as we are concerned, the distinction between the kind of metaphysics that is produced by a philosopher who has been duped by grammar, and the kind that is produced by a mystic who is trying to express the inexpressible, is of no great importance: what is important to us is to realise that even the utterances of the metaphysician who is attempting to expound a vision are literally senseless; so that henceforth we may pursue our philosophical researches with as little regard for them as for the more inglorious kind of metaphysics which comes from a failure to understand the workings of our language.

STUDY QUESTIONS

1. What is Ayer's conception of metaphysics? How does his position on metaphysics differ from that of Kant?
2. Upon what grounds does Ayer attack metaphysics? What criterion does he formulate which will lead to the rejection of metaphysics?
3. Discuss Ayer's criterion of Verifiability. How and why does he distinguish between Verifiable in principle and in practice?
4. Can the proposition of Verifiability be verified? Discuss the various difficulties such a question might provoke for Ayer.
5. How does Ayer distinguish between Strong and Weak Verifiability? Would a historical proposition (for example, Caesar was assassinated) be an instance of strong or weak verifiability? What of such propositions as "God exists," or "Two and two make four"?
6. What are the grounds for Ayer's contention that the propositions of metaphysics are nonsensical? Would you agree or disagree? Discuss.
7. Is existence a predicate? State Ayer's position and indicate why he raises this issue.
8. Why does Ayer reject the notion that the metaphysician may be considered a kind of "misplaced poet"?

J. L. Austin

⌨⌨

PERFORMATIVE UTTERANCES

⌨⌨

Biographical Note. J. L. AUSTIN (1911–1960), late professor of moral philosophy at Oxford University, received his early education in classics at the Shrewsbury School and then went to Baliol College, Oxford. He became a fellow at All Souls College, Oxford, and later a tutor in philosophy at Magdalen College. During the second World War he was a member of the British Intelligence Corps. Except for brief periods in which he served as William James Lecturer at Harvard University and as Visiting Professor at the University of California at Berkeley, his academic career was confined to Oxford University. As an undergraduate at Oxford he was largely influenced by Cook Wilson and by Prichard. Like them he was strongly influenced by his classical studies, and through such studies he developed his own peculiar conception of philosophy as linguistic analysis. At Oxford he was noted for his dialectical ability—his "verbal sparring" as one of his friends put it. In discussions, he habitually challenged all technical terms and resorted to the Oxford English Dictionary for clarification of terms. His interest in linguistic analysis may have deterred him from more expansive efforts in philosophy. At any rate, his writings consist largely of articles in British journals. Of his books, *Philosophical Papers* consists of a collection of articles from journals, *How to Do Things with Words* is his William James Lectures,

From *Philosophical Papers,* London, Oxford University Press, 1961, pp. 220-239. Reprinted by permission of the publishers.

and *Sense and Sensibilia* is a commentary on Ayer's *Foundations of Empirical Knowledge,* Price's *Perception,* and Warnock's *Berkeley.*

* * *

Introductory Note.   The philosophy of J. L. Austin may be said to reveal linguistic philosophy at its best and also at its most extreme development. It owes much to the classical training of Austin and to the influence of such men as Cook Wilson, Prichard, Wittgenstein, Moore, and Russell. It is a difficult philosophy to characterize—other than as "linguistic"—because Austin was not concerned with any speculative or systematic development of the broader issues of philosophy. His interest was always with specific problems of philosophy and how linguistic analysis might clarify and resolve these problems. This is the burden of some of his more famous essays, such as "Other Minds" and his lengthy controversy with Peter Strawson on "The Meaning of a Fact." His interest in the problem of perception led to one of his longest commentaries, *Sense and Sensibilia,* in which he endeavors to refute the positions of such men as Ayer, Price, and Warnock, not only by questioning their "two entities" doctrine (that there are physical objects and sense data) but by a remarkably sharp analysis of such words as "look," "seem," and "appear."

From the early essay "Other Minds" down to his most recent work—*How to Do Things with Words,* Austin has been concerned with what he has termed "performatory utterances." In "Other Minds" he draws attention to such utterances as a special form of speech-acts and points out that language is not purely descriptive. To assert, he says, that "I know," is similar to the assertion "I promise"—it makes a commitment to the effect that I give others my word. The essay "Performative Utterances" contains a brief account of some of the essential points in this doctrine. It develops further what in many cases was merely implicit in earlier essays and lately has been modified and brought to more mature fruition in *How to Do Things with Words.* After defining performative utterances he proceeds to distinguish them from the form of speech-act that includes the making of statements, the giving of reports, and the describing of things. Rather, he says, they are the speech-acts explicit in other forms or types of verbs such as "promise," "congratulate," "swear," etc. The criterion of performative utterances is not that of truth or falsity but of convention, sincerity, etc. We may speak of the infelicities of such utterances but not of their falsity. He notes the difficulty of characterizing or classifying the great diversity of explicit verb forms—a difficulty that he more ambitiously set out to overcome in his later work. He then shows how the distinction between statements and performatives can be narrowed and in effect broken down. Finally, he observes that there is not merely the question of what an utterance means, but the question of the "force" of the utterance. The development of linguistic analysis, he concludes, points to the need not merely for an expansion of explicit performative verbs, but for an expansion of terms of appraisal for the various possible forces of utterances.

MEANING OF PERFORMATIVE UTTERANCES

You are more than entitled not to know what the word 'performative' means. It is a new word and an ugly word, and perhaps it does not mean anything very much. But at any rate there is one thing in its favor, it is not a profound word. I remember once when I had been talking on this subject that somebody afterwards said: 'You know, I haven't the least idea what he means, unless it could be that he simply means what he says'. Well, that is what I should like to mean.

Let us consider first how this affair arises. We have not got to go very far back in the history of philosophy to find philosophers assuming more or less as a matter of course that the sole business, the sole interesting business, of any utterance—that is, of anything we say—is to be true or at least false. Of course they had always known that there are other kinds of things which we say—things like imperatives, the expressions of wishes, and exclamations—some of which had even been classified by grammarians, though it wasn't perhaps too easy to tell always which was which. But still philosophers have assumed that the only things that they are interested in are utterances which report facts or which describe situations truly or falsely. In recent times this kind of approach has been questioned—in two stages, I think. First of all people began to say: 'Well, if these things are true or false it ought to be possible to decide which they are, and if we can't decide which they are they aren't any good but are, in short, nonsense'. And this new approach did a great deal of good; a great many things which probably are nonsense were found to be such. It is not the case, I think that all kinds of nonsense have been adequately classified yet, and perhaps some things have been dismissed as nonsense which really are not; but still this movement, the verification movement, was, in its way, excellent.

However, we then come to the second stage. After all, we set some limits to the amount of nonsense that we talk, or at least the amount of nonsense that we are prepared to admit we talk; and so people began to ask whether after all some of those things which, treated as statements, were in danger of being dismissed as nonsense did after all really set out to be statements at all. Mightn't they perhaps be intended not to report facts but to influence people in this way or that, or to let off steam in this way or that? Or perhaps at any rate some elements in these utterances performed such functions, or, for example, drew attention in some way (without actually reporting it) to some important feature of the circumstances in which the utterance was being made. On these lines people have now adopted a new slogan, the slogan of the 'different uses of language'. The old approach, the old statemental approach, is sometimes called even a fallacy, the descriptive fallacy.

Certainly there are a great many uses of language. It's rather a pity that people are apt to invoke a new use of language whenever they feel so inclined, to help them out of this, that, or the other well-known philosophical tangle; we need more of a framework in which to discuss these uses of language; and also I think we should not despair too easily and talk, as people are apt to do, about the *infinite* uses of language. Philosophers will do this when they have listed as many, let us say, as seventeen; but even if there were something like ten thousand uses of language, surely we could list them all in time. This, after all, is no larger than the number of species of beetle that entomologists have taken the pains to list. But whatever the defects of either of these movements —the 'verification' movement or the 'use of language' movement—at any rate they have effected, nobody could deny, a great revolution in philosophy and, many would say, the most salutary in its history. (Not, if you come to think of it, a very immodest claim.)

Now it is one such sort of use of language that I want to examine here. I want to discuss a kind of utterance which looks like a statement and grammatically, I suppose, would be classed as a statement, which is not nonsensical, and yet is not true or false. These are not going to be utterances which contain curious verbs like 'could' or 'might', or curious words like 'good', which many philosophers regard nowadays simply as danger signals. They will be perfectly straightforward utterances, with ordinary verbs in the first person singular present indicative active, and yet we shall see at once that they couldn't possibly be true or false. Furthermore, if a person makes an utterance of this sort we should say that he is *doing* something rather than merely *saying* something. This may sound a little odd, but the examples I shall give will in fact not be odd at all, and may even seem decidedly dull. Here are three or four. Suppose, for example, that in the course of a marriage ceremony I say, as people will, 'I do' (sc. take this woman to be my lawful wedded wife). Or again, suppose that I tread on your toe and say 'I apologize'. Or again, suppose that I have the bottle of champagne in my hand and say 'I name this ship the *Queen Elizabeth*'. Or suppose I say 'I bet you sixpence it will rain tomorrow'. In all these cases it would be absurd to regard the thing that I say as a report of the performance of the action which is undoubtedly done—the action of betting, or christening, or apologizing. We should say rather that, in saying what I do, I actually perform that action. When I say 'I name this ship the *Queen Elizabeth*' I do not describe the christening ceremony, I actually perform the christening; and when I say 'I do' (sc. take this woman to be my lawful wedded wife), I am not reporting on a marriage, I am indulging in it.

Now these kinds of utterance are the ones that we call *performative* utterances. This is rather an ugly word, and a new word, but there seems to be no word already in existence to do the job. The nearest approach that I can think of is the word 'operative', as used by lawyers. . . . However, the word 'operative' has other uses, and it seems preferable to have a word specially designed for the use we want.

Now at this point one might protest, perhaps even with some alarm, that I seem to be suggesting that marrying is simply saying a few words, that just saying a few words *is* marrying. Well, that certainly is not the case. The words have to be said in the appropriate circumstances, and this is a matter that will come up again later. But the one thing we must not suppose is that what is needed in addition to the saying of the words in such cases is the performance of some internal spiritual act, of which the words then are to be the report. It's very easy to slip into this view at least in difficult, portentous cases, though perhaps not so easy in simple cases like apologizing. In the case of promising —for example, 'I promise to be there tomorrow'—it's very easy to think that the utterance is simply the outward and visible (that is, verbal) sign of the performance of some inward spiritual act of promising, and this view has certainly been expressed in many classic places. There is the case of Euripides' Hippolytus, who said 'My tongue swore to, but my heart did not'—perhaps it should be 'mind' or 'spirit' rather than 'heart', but at any rate some kind of backstage artiste. Now it is clear from this sort of example that, if we slip into thinking that such utterances are reports, true or false, of the performance of inward and spiritual acts, we open a loop-hole to perjurers and welshers and bigamists and so on, so that there are disadvantages in being excessively solemn in this way. It is better, perhaps, to stick to the old saying that our word is our bond.

However, although these utterances do not themselves report facts and are not themselves true or false, saying these things does very often *imply* that certain things are true and not false, in some sense at least of that rather woolly word 'imply'. For example, when I say 'I do take this woman to be my lawful wedded wife', or some other formula in the marriage ceremony, I do imply that I'm not already married, with wife living, sane, undivorced, and the rest of it. But still it is very important to realize that to imply that something or other is true, is not at all the same as saying something which is true itself.

INFELICITIES OF PERFORMATIVE UTTERANCES

These performative utterances are not true or false, then. But they do suffer from certain disabilities of their own. They can fail to come off in special ways, and that is what I want to consider next. The various ways in which a performative utterance may be unsatisfactory we call, for the sake of a name, the infelicities; and an infelicity arises—that is to say, the utterance is unhappy—if certain rules, transparently simple rules are broken. I will mention some of these rules and then give examples of some infringements.

First of all, it is obvious that the conventional procedure which by our utterance we are purporting to use must actually exist. In the examples given here this procedure will be a verbal one, a verbal procedure for marrying or giving or whatever it may be; but it should be borne in mind that there are many non-verbal procedures by which we can perform exactly the same acts as we perform by these verbal means. It's worth remembering too that a great many of the things we do are at least in part of this conventional kind. Philosophers at least are too apt to assume that an action is always in the last resort the making of a physical movement, whereas it's usually, at least in part, a matter of convention.

The first rule is, then, that the convention invoked must exist and be accepted. And the second rule, also a very obvious one, is that the circumstances in which we purport to invoke this procedure must be appropriate for its invocation. If this is not observed, then the act that we purport to perform would not come off—it will be, one might say, a misfire. This will also be the case if, for example, we do not carry through the procedure—whatever it may be—correctly and completely, without a flaw and without a hitch. . . .

Here are some examples of this kind of misfire. Suppose that, living in a country like our own, we wish to divorce our wife. We may try standing her in front of us squarely in the room and saying, in a voice loud enough for all to hear, 'I divorce you'. Now this procedure is not accepted. We shall not thereby have succeeded in divorcing our wife, at least in this country and others like it. This is a case where the convention, we should say, does not exist or is not accepted. Again, suppose that, picking sides at a children's party, I say 'I pick George'. But George turns red in the face and says 'Not playing'. In that case I plainly, for some reason or another, have not picked George—whether because there is no convention that you can pick people who aren't playing, or because George in the circumstances is an inappropriate object for the procedure of picking. . . . Examples of flaws and hitches are perhaps scarcely necessary—one party in the marriage ceremony says 'I will', the other says 'I won't'; I say 'I bet sixpence', but nobody says 'Done', nobody takes up the offer. In all these and other such cases, the act which we purport to perform, or set out to perform, is not achieved.

But there is another and a rather different way in which this kind of utterance may go wrong. A good many of these verbal procedures are designed for use by people who hold certain beliefs or have certain feelings or intentions. And if you use one of these formulae when you do not have the requisite thoughts or feelings or intentions then there is an abuse of the procedure, there is insincerity. Take, for example, the expression, 'I congratulate you'. This is designed for use by people who are glad that the person addressed has achieved a certain feat, believe that he was personally responsible for the success, and so on. If I say 'I congratulate you' when I'm not pleased or when I don't believe that the credit was yours, then there is insincerity. Likewise if I say I promise to do something, without having the least intention of doing it or without believing it feasible. In these cases there is something wrong certainly, but it is not like a misfire. We should not say that I didn't in fact promise, but rather that I did promise but promised insincerely; I did congratulate you but the congratulations were hollow. And there may be an infelicity of a somewhat similar kind when the performative utterance commits the speaker to future conduct of a certain description and then in the future he does not in fact behave in the expected way. This is very obvious of course, if I promise to do something and then break my promise, but there are many kinds of commitment of a rather less tangible form than that in the case of promising. For instance, I may say 'I welcome you', bidding you welcome to my home or wherever it may be, but then I proceed to treat you as though you were exceedingly unwelcome. In this case the procedure of saying 'I welcome you' has been abused in a way rather different from that of simple insincerity. . . .

That, then, is perhaps enough to be going on with. We have discussed the performative utterance and its infelicities. That equips us, we may suppose, with two shining new tools to crack the crib of reality maybe. It also equips us—it always does—with two shining new skids under our metaphysical feet. The question is how we use them.

CRITERIA OF PERFORMATIVE UTTERANCES

. . . First of all let us ask a rather simple question. How can we be sure, how can we tell, whether any utterance is to be classed as a performative or not? Surely, we feel, we ought to be able to do that. And we should obviously very much like to be able to say that there is a grammatical criterion for this, some grammatical means of deciding whether an utterance is performative. All the examples I have given hitherto do in fact have the same grammatical form; they all of them begin with the verb in the first person singular present indicative active —not just any kind of verb of course, but still they all are in fact of that form. Furthermore, with these verbs that I have used there is a typical asymmetry between the use of this person and tense of the verb and the use of the same verb in other persons and other tenses, and this asymmetry is rather an important clue.

For example, when we say 'I promise that . . .', the case is very different from when we say 'He promises that . . .', or in the past tense 'I promised that . . .'. For when we say 'I promise that . . .', we do perform an act of promising—we give a promise. What we do *not* do is to report on somebody's performing an act of promising—in particular, we do not report on somebody's use of the expression 'I promise'. We actually do use it and do the promising. But if I say 'He promises', or in the past tense 'I promised', I precisely do report on an act of promising, that is to say an act of using this formula 'I promise'—I report on a present act of promising by him, or on a past act of my own. There is thus a clear difference between our first person singular present indicative active and other persons and tenses. This is brought out by the typical incident of little Willie whose uncle says he'll give him half-a-crown if he promises never to smoke till he's 55. Little Willie's anxious parent will say 'Of course he promises, don't you, Willie?' giving him a nudge, and little Willie just doesn't vouchsafe. The point here is that he must do the promising himself by saying I promise, and his parent is going too fast in saying he promises.

That, then, is a bit of a test for whether an utterance is performative or not, but it would not do to suppose that every performative utterance has to take this standard form. There is at least one other standard form, every bit as common as this one, where the verb is in the passive voice and in the second or third person, not in the first. The sort of case I mean is that of a notice inscribed 'Passengers are warned to cross the line by the bridge only', or of a document reading 'You are hereby authorized' to do so-and-so. These are undoubtedly performative, and in fact a signature is often required in order to show who it is that is doing the act of warning, or authorizing, or whatever it may be. Very typical of this kind of performative—especially liable to occur in written documents of course—is that the little word 'hereby' either actually occurs or might naturally be inserted.

Unfortunately, however, we still can't possibly suggest that every utterance which is to be classed as a performative has to take one or another of these two, as we might call them, standard forms. After all it would be a very typical performative utterance to say 'I order you to shut the door'. This satisfies all the criteria. . . . But in the appropriate circumstances surely we could perform exactly the same act by simply saying 'Shut the door', in the imperative. Or again, suppose that some-body sticks up a notice 'This bull is dangerous', or simply 'Dangerous bull', or simply 'Bull'. Does this necessarily differ from sticking up a notice, appropriately signed, saying 'You are hereby warned that this bull is dangerous'? It seems that the simple notice 'Bull' can do just the same job as the more elaborate formula. Of course the difference is that if we just stick up 'Bull' it would not be quite clear that it is a warning; it might be there just for interest or information, like 'Wallaby' on the cage at the zoo, or 'Ancient Monument'. No doubt we should know from the nature of the case that it was a warning, but it would not be explicit.

Well, in view of this break-down of grammatical criteria, what we should like to suppose—and there is a good deal in this—is that any utterance which is performative could be reduced or expanded or an-alysed into one of these two standard forms beginning 'I . . .' so and so or beginning 'You (or he) hereby . . .' so and so. If there was any justi-fication for this hope, as to some extent there is, then we might hope to make a list of all the verbs which can appear in these standard forms, and then we might classify the kinds of acts that can be performed by performative utterances. . . . Now if we make such a list of verbs we do in fact find that they fall into certain fairly well-marked classes. There is the class of cases where we deliver verdicts and make estimates and appraisals of various kinds. There is the class where we give under-takings, commit ourselves in various ways by saying something. There is the class where by saying something we exercise various rights and powers, such as appointing and voting and so on. And there are one or two other fairly well-marked classes.

Suppose this task accomplished. Then we could call these verbs in our list explicit performative verbs, and any utterance that was reduced to one or the other of our standard forms we could call an explicit per-formative utterance. 'I order you to shut the door' would be an explicit performative utterance, whereas 'Shut the door' would not—that is simply a 'primary' performative utterance or whatever we like to call it. In using the imperative we may be ordering you to shut the door, but it just isn't made clear whether we are ordering you or entreating you or imploring you or beseeching you or inciting you or tempting you, or one or another of many other subtly different acts which, in an unsophisticated primitive language, are very likely not yet discriminated. But we need not overestimate the unsophistication of primitive languages. There are a great many devices that can be used for making clear, even at the primitive level, what act it is we are performing when we say something—the tone of voice, cadence, gesture—and above all we can rely upon the nature of the circumstances, the context in which the utterance is issued. This very often makes it quite unmistakable whether it is an order that is being given or whether, say, I am simply urging you or entreating you. We may, for instance, say something like this: 'Coming from him I was bound to take it as an order'. Still, in spite of all these devices, there is an unfortunate amount of ambiguity and lack of discrimination in default of our explicit performative verbs. If I say something like 'I shall be there', it may not be certain whether it is a promise, or an expression of intention, or perhaps even a forecast of my future behavior, of what is going to happen to me; and it may matter a good deal, at least in developed societies, precisely which of these things it is. And that is why the explicit performative verb is evolved—to make clear exactly which it is, how far it commits me and in what way, and so forth.

This is just one way in which language develops in tune with the society of which it is the language. The social habits of the society may considerably affect the question of which performative verbs are evolved and which, sometimes for rather irrelevant reasons, are not. For example, if I say 'You are a poltroon', it might be that I am censuring you or it might be that I am insulting you. Now since apparently society approves of censuring or reprimanding, we have here evolved a formula 'I reprimand you', or 'I censure you', which enables us expeditiously to get this desirable business over. But on the other hand, since apparently we don't approve of insulting, we have not evolved a simple formula 'I insult you', which might have done just as well. . . .

STATEMENTS AND PERFORMATIVE UTTERANCES

So far we have been going along as though there was a quite clear difference between our performative utterances and what we have contrasted them with, statements or reports or descriptions. But now we begin to find that this distinction is not as clear as it might be. . . . In the first place, of course, we may feel doubts as to how widely our performatives extend. If we think up some odd kinds of expression we use in odd cases, we might very well wonder whether or not they satisfy our rather vague criteria for being performative utterances. Suppose, for example, somebody says 'Hurrah'. Well, not true or false; he is performing the act of cheering. Does that make it a performative utterance in our sense or not? Or suppose he says 'Damn'; he is performing the act of swearing, and it is not true or false. Does that make it performative? We feel that in a way it does and yet it's rather different. . . . Or sometimes, if somebody says 'I am sorry', we wonder whether this is just the same as 'I apologize'—in which case of course we have said it's a performative utterance—or whether perhaps it's to be taken as a description, true or false, of the state of his feelings. . . .

Considerations of this sort, then, may well make us feel pretty unhappy. If we look back for a moment at our contrast between statements and performative utterances, we realize that we were taking statements very much on trust from, as we said, the traditional treatment. Statements, we had it, were to be true or false; performative utterances on the other hand were to be felicitous or infelicitous. They were the doing of something, whereas for all we said making statements was not doing something. Now this contrast surely, if we look back at it, is unsatisfactory. Of course statements are liable to be assessed in this matter of their correspondence or failure to correspond with the facts, that is, being true or false. But they are also liable to infelicity every bit as much as are performative utterances. In fact some troubles that have arisen in the study of statements recently can be shown to be simply troubles of infelicity. For example, it has been pointed out that there is something very odd about saying something like this: 'The cat is on the mat but I don't believe it is'. Now this is an outrageous thing to say, but it is not self-contradictory. There is no reason why the cat shouldn't be on the mat without my believing that it is. So how are we to classify what's wrong with this peculiar statement? If we remember now the doctrine of infelicity we shall see that the person who makes this remark about the cat is in much the same position as somebody who says something like this: 'I promise that I shall be there, but I haven't the least intention of being there'. Once again you can of course perfectly well promise to be there without having the least intention of being there, but there is something outrageous about saying it, about actually avowing the insincerity of the promise you give. In the same way there is insincerity in the case of the person who says 'The cat is on the mat but I don't believe it is', and he is actually avowing that insincerity—which makes a peculiar kind of nonsense.

A second case that has come to light is the one about John's children—the case where somebody is supposed to say 'All John's children are bald but John hasn't got any children'. Or perhaps somebody says 'All John's children are bald', when as a matter of fact—he doesn't say so—John has no children. Now those who study statements have worried about this; ought they to say that the statement 'All John's children are bald' is meaningless in this case? Well, if it is, it is not a bit like a great many other more standard kinds of meaninglessness; and we see, if we look back at our list of infelicities, that what is going wrong here is much the same as what goes wrong in, say, the case of a contract for the sale of a piece of land when the piece of land referred to does not exist. Now what we say in the case of this sale of land, which of course would be effected by a performative utterance, is that the sale is void—void for lack of reference or ambiguity of reference; and so we can see that the statement about all John's children is likewise void for lack of reference. And if the man actually says that John has no children in the same breath as saying they're all bald, he is making the same kind of outrageous utterance as the man who says 'The cat is on the mat and I don't believe it is', or the man who says 'I promise to but I don't intend to'.

In this way, then, ills that have been found to afflict statements can be precisely paralleled with ills that are characteristic of performative utterances. And after all when we state something or describe something or report something, we do perform an act which is every bit as much an act as an act of ordering or warning. There seems no good reason why stating should be given a specially unique position. Of course philosophers have been wont to talk as though you or I or anybody could just go round stating anything about anything and that would be perfectly in order, only there's just a little question: is it true or false? But besides the little question, is it true or false, there is surely the question: *is* it in order? Can you go round just making statements about anything? Suppose for example you say to me 'I'm feeling pretty mouldy this morning'. Well, I say to you 'You're not'; and you say 'What the devil do you mean, I'm not?' I say 'Oh nothing—I'm just stating you're not, is it true or false?' And you say 'Wait a bit about whether it's true or false, the question is what did you mean by making statements about somebody else's feelings? I told you I'm feeling pretty mouldy. You're just not in a position to say, to state that I'm not'. This brings out that you can't just make statements about other people's feelings (though you can make guesses if you like); and there are very many things which, having no knowledge of, not being in a position to pronounce about, you just can't state. What we need to do for the case of stating, and by the same token describing and reporting, is to take them a bit off their pedestal, to realize that they were speech-acts no less than all those other speech-acts that we have been mentioning and talking about as performative.

Then let us look for a moment at our original contrast between the performative and the statement from the other side. In handling performatives we have been putting it all the time as though the only thing that a performative utterance had to do was to be felicitous, to come off, not to be a misfire, not to be an abuse. Yes, but that's not the end of the matter. At least in the case of many utterances which, on what we have said, we should have to class as performative—cases where we say 'I warn you to . . .', 'I advise you to . . .', and so on—there will be other questions besides simply: was it in order, was it all right, as a piece of advice or a warning, did it come off? After that surely there will be the question: was it good or sound advice? Was it a justified warning? Or in the case, let us say, of a verdict or an estimate: was it a good estimate, or a sound verdict? And these are questions that can only be decided by considering how the content of the verdict or estimate is related in some way to fact, or to evidence available about the facts. This is to say that we do require to assess at least a great many performative utterances in a general dimension of correspondence with fact. It may still be said, of course, that this does not make them *very* like statements because still they are not true or false, and that's a little black and white specialty that distinguishes statements as a class apart. But actually—though it would take too long to go on about this—the more you think about truth and falsity the more you find that very few statements that we ever utter are just true or just false. Usually there is the question are they fair or are they not fair, are they adequate or not adequate, are they exaggerated or not exaggerated. Are they too rough, or are they perfectly precise, accurate, and so on? 'True' and 'false' are just general labels for a whole dimension of different appraisals which have something or other to do with the relation between what we say and the facts. If, then, we loosen up our ideas of truth and falsity we shall see that statements, when assessed in relation to the facts, are not so very different after all from pieces of advice, warnings, verdicts, and so on.

We see then that stating something is performing an act just as much as is giving an order or giving a warning; and we see, on the other hand, that, when we give an order or a warning or a piece of advice, there is a question about how this is related to fact which is not perhaps so very different from the kind of question that arises when we discuss how a statement is related to fact. Well, this seems to mean that in its original form our distinction between the performative and the statement is considerably weakened, and indeed breaks down. I will just make a suggestion as to how to handle this matter. We need to go very much farther back, to consider all the ways and senses in which saying anything at all is doing this or that—because of course it is always doing a good many different things. And one thing that emerges when we do do this is that, besides the question that has been very much studied in the past as to what a certain utterance *means,* there is a further question distinct from this as to what was the *force,* as we may call it, of the utterance. We may be quite clear what 'Shut the door' means, but not yet at all clear on the further point as to whether as uttered at a certain time it was an order, an entreaty or what not. What we need besides the old doctrine about meanings is a new doctrine about all the possible forces of utterances, towards the discovery of which our proposed list of explicit performative verbs would be a very great help; and then, going on from there, an investigation of the various terms of appraisal that we use in discussing speech-acts of this, that, or the other precise kind—orders, warnings and the like.

The notions that we have considered then, are the performative, the infelicity, the explicit performative, and lastly, rather hurriedly, the notion of the forces of utterances. I dare say that all this seems a little unremunerative, a little complicated. Well, I suppose in some ways it is unremunerative, and I suppose it ought to be remunerative. At least, though, I think that if we pay attention to these matters we can clear up some mistakes in philosophy; and after all philosophy is used as a scapegoat, it parades mistakes which are really the mistakes of everybody. We might even clear up some mistakes in grammar, which perhaps is a little more respectable.

And is it complicated? Well, it is complicated a bit; but life and truth and things do tend to be complicated. It's not things, it's philosophers that are simple. You will have heard it said, I expect, that over-simplification is the occupational disease of philosophers, and in a way one might agree with that. But for a sneaking suspicion that it's their occupation.

STUDY QUESTIONS

1. What does Austin mean by the "verification" movement and the "use of language" movement? What is the descriptive fallacy with respect to the nature of utterances?

2. What specific use of language does Austin discuss. Give some original examples and indicate why they are not nonsensical and neither true nor false.

3. Are performative utterances in any way reports on facts? Are they true or false? May they imply that which is true or false? Give an example. Would you classify the utterance "You have been warned" as a performative?

4. What does Austin mean by the infelicities of performative utterances? Indicate how infelicities arise. Give some examples and state the rule or rules violated.

5. State two grammatical means or criteria for deciding when an utterance is performative. Do all performative utterances have to take these forms? If not, give some examples of those that do not.

6. What distinctions does Austin draw between explicit and primary performative utterances? Give examples. Why do explicit performatives evolve in language?

7. Explain the basic distinction between statements and performative utterances. Why may statements as well as performative utterances be subject to infelicities? Explain this in detail and with reference to one of Austin's examples.

8. Are the following sentences performative utterances or statements?
   "I argue (urge) that there is no backside to the moon."
   "I prophesy (or predict) that there is no backside to the moon."

9. Comment on Austin's statement that "the more you think about truth and falsity the more you find that very few statements that we ever utter are just true or false."

10. In what respects does the distinction between performative utterances and statements break down? What is the difference between what an utterance *means* and its *force*? Do you think there is any significance to this distinction?

IV

Metaphysics

IV

Metaphysics

Aristotle[*]

BEING AND SUBSTANCE

Introductory Note.   Although he did not give it a name, Aristotle created the discipline known as *Metaphysics*. For Aristotle, metaphysics was a science, and to him a science was a body of knowledge consisting of truths that are necessary, that cannot be other than they are. We may ask the meaning of the subject matter of any particular science; we may ask, for example, what it means to *be* a man, an animal, a star, a poem, etc. Our answers here, declares Aristotle, may be twofold: we may state *what* it is to be something and this leads to the definition of something, or, we may state that in the world of nature or art, to be something involves a coming into being and a passing away. Each of the sciences endeavors to set forth these answers in terms of its own science. But there is one science that treats of being as being, that is, it abstracts from all individual or particular determinations, and seeks the more general nature of being as such. In doing this it is the most abstract of the sciences. Physics, for example, is abstract to the extent that it deals with being merely as sensible. Mathematics is more abstract, for it is concerned with being merely as quantitative. But metaphysics possesses an even higher degree of abstraction, for it transcends even these determinations

The material that follows is from the *Metaphysics*, edited and translated by John Warrington, Everyman's Library, London, J. M. Dent and Sons Ltd.; New York, E. P. Dutton and Co., 1956, pp. 4–5, 115–116, 171–172, 205–207. Reprinted with the permission of the publishers.

[*] For a biographical note see the selection on Ethics, p. 35.

of the beings of physics and mathematics and strives to know *being qua being*. It was for this reason that Aristotle considered metaphysics as the highest of all the sciences.

Aristotle's answer to the metaphysical quest for the nature of being was *Substance:* to be is to be a substantial being. The Aristotelian world is a world of substances, but not of static substances, for to be involves a coming into being and a passing away. The substances of the Aristotelian universe are uncreated; they exemplify the union of form and matter.

The selection that follows is limited to certain aspects of Aristotle's study of the nature of being. Aristotle begins by distinguishing the science of being from the other sciences and develops the notion that substance is the subject matter of metaphysics. Since to know anything is to know its causes, Aristotle is concerned in the *Metaphysics* with an explanation of four kinds of cause or factor that explain the ultimate nature of anything or of reality itself. He notes two possible meanings of substance: as ultimate substratum and as form. He then proceeds to consider arguments for substance as subtratum. Rejecting this position, Aristotle concludes his analysis by stating the reasons why "form" is the primary cause of the being of things. But not, he insists, a separated form in the Platonic sense—rather a form that is inherent in things and that constitutes what might be termed a "substantial form."

THE OBJECT OF METAPHYSICS: BEING *QUA* BEING

There is a science which investigates being *qua* being and its essential attributes. This science differs from all the so-called special sciences in that none of the latter deals generally with being as such. They isolate one part of it and study the essential attributes of that one part, as do, for example, the mathematical sciences.

Now (1) since it is the first principles or ultimate causes of things for which we are looking, these must be essential attributes of something.[1] It follows (2) that the elements of existing things sought by our predecessors must be these very principles towards which our search is directed. Therefore (3) the elements must be elements of being not incidentally, but *qua* being. Hence we may infer that it is of being as such that we too must grasp the first causes.

ASPECTS OF BEING *QUA* BEING

Although 'being' has a variety of meanings, they are all related to one central point, one definite kind of thing, and have not merely the epithet 'being' in common. Consider, for example, the word 'healthy':

[1] Sc. of being *qua* being.

it always relates to health, either as safeguarding, producing, indicating, or receptive of it. Or, again, take the word 'medical': it always relates to the art of medicine, either as possessing or naturally adapted to it, or as being a function of the medical art. In just the same way, 'being' is used in several senses, but always with reference to one central point. Some things are said to 'be' because they are (a) substance; others because they are (b) modifications of substance; others because they are (c) a process towards substance, or (d) destructions or privations or qualities of substance, or (e) productive or generative of substance or of terms relating to substance, or (f) negations of some of these terms or of substance itself.[2]

So, as all healthy things are the object of one science, in whatever sense the word 'healthy' be used, the same is true of every other class of things. For it is not only those which have a common definition whose study is the province of one science, but also those which are related to one central point; and in fact even these may be said to have a common definition. Clearly, then, it is the work of one science to study being *qua* being.

Now (1) Knowledge is mainly concerned with what is primary, i.e. upon which all the rest depend and after which they are called; and because substance is the primary thing, it is of substance that a philosopher must grasp the first principles and causes.

CAUSE*

'Cause' denotes:

(1) That from which (as immanent material) a thing comes into being; e. g. the bronze of a statue, the silver of a drinking-bowl, and the classes (metal, mineral, etc.) to which bronze and silver belong.

(2) The form or pattern of a thing (i. e. the formula of its essence), the classes to which it belongs (Thus the ratio 2:1 and number in general is the cause of the octave) and its own parts.

(3) The starting-point of change or rest. Thus an adviser is the cause of an action, and a father of his child. In general, the maker is the cause of the thing made, and that which changes of that which suffers change.

(4) The end, i. e. that for the sake of which a thing is. For example, health is the cause of walking: in answer to the question, Why does one

[2] Hence we even say non-being *is* non-being.—(A.)

* A more precise term than "cause" would be "explanatory factor." The Greek term *aitia* is much broader in its connotation than the English term "cause," which is usually restricted to the notion of an efficient cause.

walk? we reply 'In order to be healthy'; and in saying so we believe we have assigned the cause. The same is true of all the means which lead from an independent source of motion to its end. Thus, slimming, purging, medicines, surgical appliances, all lead to health; all of them exist for the sake of the end, though they differ one from another in that some of them are instruments and others acts.

There you have practically all the meanings of 'cause'; and because the word has a variety of meanings, it follows that a single thing has several causes, and in no accidental sense. Sculptor and bronze are both causes of a statue considered not under two different aspects, but *qua* statue. The two, however, are not causes *in the same way*: bronze is the material, the sculptor the efficient cause.

What *causes* a thing in one sense may be its *effect* in another. Thus exercise is the cause of physical fitness, and the latter again of exercise; but *not in the same way*, for in the first case the cause is final and in the second efficient.

Again, a single cause may have opposite effects. That which when present causes one thing is sometimes, when absent, denounced as the cause of the opposite. For instance, we assign the pilot's absence as the cause of a shipwreck, whereas his presence is admitted as the cause of the vessel's safety; so that in either case, whether present or absent, he is the (efficient) cause.

The causes just described fall under four very obvious headings. Letters are the causes of syllables; the material is the cause of artifical products; fire, earth, etc., are the causes of bodies; the parts are the causes of a whole; and premises are the causes of logical demonstration. Now these are causes in the material sense, i. e. as 'that out of which' these things respectively are made;[3] but (1) some of them (e. g. the parts of a whole) are causes as substratum, (2) others as essence (i. e. the wholeness supervening on the parts, the synthesis, and the form). The semen, the physician, the adviser, and in general the agent are all forms of change or rest. The Good (or apparent good) is the end or goal of the others; for the final cause is naturally the greatest good and end of the rest.

SUBSTANCE

'Substance' (*ousia*) means: (1) The simple bodies (earth, fire, water, and all such things), and bodies generally and the things

---

[3] Note that Aristotle here includes the material and formal causes together as 'that from which'.

composed of them—living creatures as well as the stars and their parts. All these are called 'substances' because they are not predicated of a subject while everything else is predicated of them. (2) The immanent cause of being in the foregoing class of things, as the soul is of the being of animals. (3) The parts immanent in such things, defining them and marking them out as individuals, and by the destruction of which the whole is destroyed.[4] (4) The essence, whose formula is a definition.

Hence 'substance' has two senses: (a) The ultimate substratum which cannot be further predicated of anything else, and (b) that which is individual and separable, i. e. the shape or form.

SUBSTANCE AS SUBSTRATUM

Four things at the very least have a special claim to be described as substance: (A) Substratum, (B) Essence, (C) the Universal, and (D) Genus.

(A) The substratum is that of which everything else is predicated, but itself is never predicated of anything. And so we must first determine its nature; for the primary substratum is considered to be in the truest sense substance. The *matter*, the *sensible form*, and the *compound* of these two are each in its appropriate sense described as the substratum.[5] Thus, if the sensible form is prior to and more real than the matter, it is also prior to their compound. Such, in brief, is the nature of substance; but to describe it merely as 'that which is always subject and never predicate' is quite inadequate. Apart from the statement itself being vague, it seems inevitably to imply that matter is substance, i. e. that which persists when all attributes are removed. For (1) the secondary qualities of a sensible thing are merely its actions, products, and potencies; (2) length, breadth, and depth are quantities and therefore not substances;[6] when length, breadth, and depth are removed, nothing is left except what is bounded by them—i. e. matter,[7] which (4) must

---

[4] Thus it is said [by the Pythagoreans] that the plane is essential to the solid, and the line to the plane. Some [i. e. the Platonists] hold that the same applies to number generally: if it be destroyed, they say, there is nothing left, for number determines everything.—(A.)

[5] Take a statue, for example. By 'matter' I mean the bronze of which it is made; by 'sensible form' the plan of its essence; and by their 'compound' the concrete thing, i. e. the statue itself.—(A.)

[6] A quantity is not a substance, which is rather that to which length, breadth, and depth belong.—(A.)

[7] By matter I mean that which is in itself neither a particular thing, nor a quantity, and is not, in fact, designated by any of the categories. (Every category except substance is predicated of a substance, while substance is predicated of matter.) Therefore the

accordingly, on this view, be substance. But this is impossible; for it is agreed that separability and individuality belong especially to substance, so that the sensible form, and the compound of this and matter, are more truly substance than is matter itself. The compound may be dismissed as posterior in nature and familiar to sense; matter also is not very difficult to understand. We must therefore consider essence, which is the most perplexing of all three. . . .

[In the several chapters that follow Aristotle is concerned with various logical aspects of definition and its relation to substance as essence, with the analysis of physical change and its implications for the conception of substance, and with the rejection of universals and Platonic Forms as substances. In the concluding chapter, given below, Aristotle arrives at a notion of substance that might be more precisely rendered as 'substantial form'.]

THE TRUE VIEW OF SUBSTANCE

We must now resume our inquiry into the nature of substance; for it may be that we shall thereby learn something about the substance which exists apart from sensibles. We start with the fact that substance is an originative source and cause. The interrogative 'why' is always used in the sense of 'why does A belong to B?' The question 'Why is the musical man a musical man?' is either (1) of the type just mentioned, i. e. 'why is the man musical?' or (2) it is different therefrom. In this second case it is of the type 'Why is a thing itself?' Now to ask why a thing is itself is no question at all; for when we ask *why* a thing is so, we must already know *that* it is so, e. g. that the moon is eclipsed. 'Because a thing is itself' is the single answer to all such questions as 'why the man is man' or 'why the musical is musical,' unless one prefers to put it in the form 'because each thing is indivisible from itself, and this is what "being one" means.' This is an answer which meets all such cases and is a 'short and easy way' with them. However, the question 'why is man such and such a kind of animal?' *is* one which may fairly be asked. It is not equivalent to asking why he who is a man is a man; it must therefore mean 'why does A which is predicated of

---

ultimate substratum is in itself neither a particular thing, nor a particular quantity, nor otherwise positively characterized; nor yet negatively, for negations too will only apply to it accidentally.—(A.)

B belong to B?'[8] e. g. 'Why does it thunder (=why is a noise produced in the clouds?)';[9] 'why are these things, viz. bricks and stones, a house?'

Evidently, then, we are looking for the formal cause, i. e. (speaking abstractly) for the *essence*. This is in some cases (e. g. in that of a bed or a house) identical with the *final* cause, and in others with the prime mover or *efficient* cause. We look for the second only in cases of generation and destruction, but for the first in that also of being. The object of our search is particularly elusive when one term is not expressly predicated of another, e. g. in the question 'what is man?'[10] The interrogation is a simple one, not analysed into subject and attributes; we do not ask expressly 'why do these parts form this whole?' We must first make our question articulate, otherwise it shares the character both of a genuine and of a meaningless inquiry. Now since one must know *that* a thing is before one asks *why* it is, the question must always be 'why is the *matter* so-and-so?' Q. Why do these materials form a house? A. Because what-it-is-to-be-a-house, i. e. the *essence* of house, is present in them. Likewise certain matter, or rather certain matter having a certain form, is a man. Therefore what we are seeking is the cause, i. e. the *form*, whereby the matter is some definite thing; and this is the *substance* of the thing. Clearly, then, in the case of pure forms, which contain no matter, question and answer are impossible; there must be another method of inquiry[11] than that described above.

Now as regards those compounds which form a unity, not in the sense of an aggregate but as a syllable is one.[12] A syllable is not merely the sum total of its letters: BA is not just $B + A$; nor is flesh just fire + earth. For after dissolution, the compounds—flesh or the syllable—no longer exist; but the letters do, and so do fire and earth. The syllable, then, is something on its own—not merely the letters (vowel and consonant), but something else besides. Similarly, flesh is not merely fire and earth, hot and cold, but something else besides. Let us suppose that the principle of union must be either an element or a complex of elements. If (1) it is an element, this leads to an infinite regress; because flesh will then consist of fire and earth, and this element + something else, and so on *ad infinitum*. If (2) it is a complex, it must have more than one element (otherwise it will itself be that element), and the

[8] The question naturally assumes that A *does* belong to B, otherwise it would be pointless.—(A.)
[9] The correct form of the question is this predication of one thing of another.—(A.)
[10] i. e. why are these bones, flesh, etc., man?
[11] Sc. intuition.
[12] Aristotle never completed this main sentence. . . .

same difficulty will arise as in the case of flesh or in syllable. It would seem, however, that this 'something else' is something which is not an element, and that it is the cause which makes one thing flesh, another a syllable, and so on. This is the substance of things, for it is the primary cause of their being. Some things (artifacts) of course are not substances at all, but only such as are held together according to nature and by nature. Therefore this 'nature', which is not a material element but a principle, would appear to be substance. The elements, on the other hand, are the material constituents of things, into which the latter may be resolved; e. g. *A* and *B* are the elements of a syllable.

STUDY QUESTIONS

1. Would you consider metaphysics to be a science? What do you think Aristotle means by "science"? Would you also regard mathematics as a science? In what respects would it differ from metaphysics?
2. What are the several senses of "being"? Why is substance regarded by Aristotle as primary?
3. Explain and provide original examples of each of the four kinds of cause. Which kind would you say is the most familiar to us?
4. What are the various meanings that can be attached to "substance"? Why does Aristotle say it is inadequate to define it as "that which is always subject and never predicate."
5. What does Aristotle mean by matter? By quantity? By sensible form? If bronze is the "matter" of the statue, what is the "matter" of the bronze?
6. What does Aristotle mean by formal cause or essence? In what respect would the formal cause be identical with the final cause? What is the final cause of a horse? Of a snake?
7. Can the essence (nature) of anything, e. g. man, be expressed in terms of the matter? Of the elements? Of the parts? Of the aggregate? If these are to be rejected in favor of the form as substance, comment on the meaning of "substantial form."

Lucretius

MATERIALISTIC ATOMISM

Biographical Note.   TITUS LUCRETIUS CARUS (c. 99 B.C.–c. 55
B.C.) was a Roman poet and philosopher. Very little is known concerning
his personal life and career. His *De rerum natura* (*On the Nature of Things*)
is an imaginative and highly moving poem written in hexameter verse. It
is an epitome of much of the Epicurean doctrine, and Lucretius seems to
have been not only a leader of the Roman Epicureans but also a very zealous
disciple of Epicurus. According to a story reported by St. Jerome, Lucretius
was poisoned by a love philter.

* * *

Introductory Note.   Modern man is apt to be particularly impressed
with one of the oldest traditions in Greek philosophical thought—the materialistic atomism of Democritus, Epicurus, and Lucretius. The appeal of
their metaphysics lies not only in the simplicity and persuasiveness of its
materialistic point of view, but also in its association with the speculative
origins of the modern and much more scientific concept of the atom.

The first systematic attempt to set up a materialistic atomism was the work
of Democritus. Only a few fragments of the writings of Democritus are ex-
tant, and although we have substantial material from Epicurus, the most complete and at the same time faithful rendition of the atomism of antiquity is
to be found in the celebrated poem of Lucretius, *De Rerum Natura*. There

From *On the Nature of Things,* translated by the Rev. John Selby Watson, London, Bell & Daldy, 1870, (with some revisions by the editors).

is little that is original in the work of Lucretius; he was a disciple of Epicurus and owes much to him, but what Lucretius says he says extraordinarily well. To the persuasiveness of materialism he adds the charm and beauty of poetry.

The materialistic metaphysics of Lucretius can be summarized by the following points: (1) Reality is uncreated and indestructible, for nothing can come from nothing and there is no divine will to create a universe from nothing. (2) There exists an infinite void or space. (3) Matter alone is real and is composed of an infinite number of very small but indivisible particles or atoms (*atom* meaning indivisible). (4) There is a qualitative difference between atoms—some are more perfectly shaped than others, some quicker in movement than others, etc. (5) All atoms are constantly in motion. (6) Composite things come into being as a result of the fall of atoms through the void. (7) There is no determinate movement to the atoms, and allowance must be made for them to *swerve* and thus collide with one another to effect different groupings of the atoms. (8) Mind and thought are nothing more than the motions of certain types of atoms. (9) Death is something final and complete; the gods have little effect on men's lives and need not be feared.

MATTER AND SPACE

. . . lend me, O Memmius, thy unprejudiced ears, and apply thyself, released from cares, to the investigation of truth, and leave not, as things despised, my offerings arranged for thee with faithful zeal, before they are understood. For I shall proceed to discourse to thee of the whole system of heaven and the gods, and unfold to thee the first principles of all things, from which nature produces, develops, and sustains all, and into which she again resolves them at their dissolution. These, in explaining our subject, we are accustomed to call matter, and the generative bodies of things, and to designate as the seeds of all things, and to term them primary bodies, because from them as primary all things are derived. . . .

Attend, now, further: since I have shown that things cannot be produced from nothing, and also that, when produced, they cannot return to nothing; yet, lest perhaps thou shouldst begin to distrust my words, because the primary particles of things cannot be discerned by the eye, hear, in addition, what substances thou thyself must necessarily confess to exist, although they cannot be seen.

In the first place, the force of the wind, when excited, lashes the sea, agitates the tall ships, and scatters the clouds; at times, sweeping over the earth with an impetuous hurricane, it strews the plains with huge trees, and harasses the mountain-tops with forest-rending blasts; so violently does the deep chafe with fierce roar and rage with menacing murmur. The winds, then, are invisible bodies, which sweep the sea, the land, the clouds of heaven, and, agitating them, carry them along with a sudden tornado. Not otherwise do they rush forth, and spread destruction, than as when a body of liquid water is borne along in an overwhelming stream, which a vast torrent from the lofty mountains swells with large rain-floods, dashing together fragments of woods and entire groves of trees . . . Thus, therefore, must the blasts of the wind also be borne along; which (when, like a mighty flood, they have bent their force in any direction) drive all things before them, and overthrow them with repeated assaults, and sometimes catch them up in a writhing vortex and rapidly bear them off in a whirling hurricane. Wherefore, I repeat, the winds are substances, though invisible, since in their effects, and modes of operation, they are found to rival mighty rivers, which are of manifest bodily substance.

. Moreover we perceive various odors of objects, and yet never see them approaching our nostrils. Nor do we behold violent heat, or distinguish cold with our eyes; nor are we in the habit of viewing sounds; all which things, however, must of necessity consist of a corporeal nature, since they have the power of striking the senses: For nothing, except bodily substance, can touch or be touched. . . .

Besides, in the course of many revolutions of the sun, a ring upon the finger is made somewhat thinner by wearing it; the fall of the drop from the eaves hollows a stone . . . even the stone pavements of the streets we see worn by the feet of the multitude; and the bronze statues, which stand near the city gates, show their right hands made smaller by the touch of people frequently saluting them, and passing by. These objects, therefore, after they have been worn, we observe to become diminished; but what particles take their departure on each particular occasion, jealous nature has withheld from us the faculty of seeing.

Lastly, whatever substances time and nature add little by little to objects, obliging them to increase gradually, those substances no acuteness of vision, however earnestly exerted, can perceive; nor, moreover, whatever substances waste away through age and decay; nor can you discern what the rocks, which overhang the sea, and are eaten by the corroding salt of the ocean, lose every time that they are washed by the waves. Nature, therefore, carries on her operations by imperceptible particles.

Nor, however, are all things held enclosed by corporeal substance; for there is a *void* in things; a truth which it will be useful for you to know; and which will prevent you from wandering in doubt, and from perpetually inquiring about the entirety of things, and from being distrustful of my words. Wherefore, I say, there is space *intangible, empty,* and *vacant.* If this were not the case, things could by no means be moved; for that which is the quality of body, namely, to obstruct and to oppose, would be present at all times, and would be exerted against all bodies; nothing, therefore, would be able to move forward, since nothing would begin to give way. But now, throughout the sea and land and heights of heaven, we see many things moved before our eyes in various ways and by various means, which, if there were no void would have been deprived of their active motion and properly speaking could never by any means have been produced at all; since matter, crowded together on all sides, would have remained at rest, and have been unable to act.

Besides, although some things may be regarded as solid, yet you may, for the following reasons, perceive them to be of a porous consistence. In rocks and caves, the liquid moisture of the waters penetrates their substance, and all parts weep, as it were, with abundant drops; food distributes itself through the whole of the body in animals; the groves increase, and yield their fruits in their season, because nourishment is diffused through the whole of the trees, even from the lowest roots, over all the trunks and branches; voices pass through the walls, and fly across the closed apartments of houses; keen frost penetrates to the very marrow of our bones; which kind of effects, unless there were void spaces in bodies, where the several particles might pass, you would never by any means observe to take place. . . .

Material bodies are partly original elements of things, and partly those which are formed of a combination of those elements. But those which are elements of things, no force can break; for they successfully resist all force by solidity of substance; although, perhaps, it seems difficult to believe that anything of so solid a substance can be found in nature; for the lightning of heaven passes through the walls of houses, as do noises and voices; iron glows, being penetrated by heat, in the fire; rocks often burst with fervent heat; the hardness of gold, losing its firmness, is melted by heat; the icy coldness of brass, overcome by flame, melts; heat and penetrating cold, enter into the substance of silver, for we have felt both with the hand, when, as we held silver cups after our fashion, water was poured into them from above; so that, as far as these instances go, there seems to be nothing solid in nature. But because, however, right reason, and the nature of things, compel me to hold a contrary opinion, grant me your attention a while, until I make it plain, in a few verses, that there really exist such bodies as are of a solid and eternal corporeal substance; which bodies we prove to be seeds and primary particles of things, of which the whole generated universe now consists.

In the first place, since a twofold nature of two things exremely dissimilar, has been found to exist, namely, matter, and space in which everything is done, it must necessarily be that each exists by itself, for itself independently of the other, and pure from admixture; for wheresoever there is empty space, which we call a vacuum, there there is no matter, and, likewise wheresoever matter maintains itself, there by no means exists empty space. Original substances are therefore solid and without vacuity. . . .

Furthermore, if there were no empty space, all space would be solid. On the other hand, unless there were certain bodies to fill up completely the places which they occupy, all space, which anywhere exists, would be an empty void. Body, therefore, is evidently distinct from empty space, though each has its place alternately; since all space neither exists entirely full, nor again, entirely empty. There exist, therefore, certain bodies which can fill completely the places which they occupy, and distinguish empty space from full.

Again, unless there had been eternal matter, all things, before this time, would have been utterly reduced to nothing; and whatsoever objects we behold would have been reproduced from nothing. But since I have shown above, that nothing can be produced from nothing, and that that which has been produced cannot be resolved into nothing, the primary elements must be of an imperishable substance, into which primary elements every body may be dissolved, so that matter may be supplied for the reproduction of things. The primordial elements, therefore, are of pure solidity, nor could they otherwise, preserved, as they have been, for ages, repair things as they have done, through that infinite space of time which has elapsed since the commencement of this material system. . . .

To this is added, that though the primary particles of matter are perfectly solid, yet that all things, which are formed of them, may be rendered soft and yielding, as air, water, earth, fire (in whatever way they may be produced, and by whatever influence they may be directed); but this happens because there is vacant space intermingled with the substance of things compounded. But, on the other hand, if the primordial elements of things were soft, how strong flints and iron could be produced, no explanation could be given, for, by this supposition, nature will be deprived of all possibility of commencing a foundation.

The primordial elements, therefore, are endowed with pure solidity; by the dense combination of which all compound bodies may be closely compacted, and exhibit powerful strength.

But if you will not allow there is a limit to dissolution, you must then allow that there are dissoluble bodies which have not yet been assailed by any power sufficient to destroy them; but to conceive that such bodies exist, and that they have not been attacked, among all the changes in things since the beginning of time, by any force sufficient to take effect on them, is to suppose that which is scarcely credible. . . .

But since I have taught that atoms of matter, entirely solid, fly about perpetually, unwasted through all time; come now, and let us unravel whether there be any limit to their number or not; also, let us look into that which has been found to be void, or the room and space in which things happen, and learn whether the whole is entirely limited, or extends unbounded and unfathomably profound.

All that exists, therefore, I affirm, is bounded in no direction; for, if it were bounded, it must have some extremity; but it appears that there cannot be an extremity of any thing, unless there be something beyond, which may limit it; so that there may appear to be some line farther than which our vision cannot extend. Now, since it must be confessed that there is nothing beyond the whole, the whole has no extremity; nor does it matter at what part of it you stand . . . ; inasmuch as, whatever place any one occupies, he leaves the universe just as infinite as before in all directions.

Besides, if you suppose that there is a boundary to the universe, fix on the place where you think it lies, and try to throw a dart beyond it; the dart will either pass beyond it, or will be stopped by some opposing body: if it passes beyond it, you will not have fixed the boundary of the universe; if it is stopped by any body, there is something beyond your supposed boundary. For one of the two alternatives you must of necessity admit and adopt; either of the alternatives cuts off escape from you, and compels you to grant that the universe extends without limit. Since whether there is any thing to stop the dart, and to cause that it may not go on in the direction in which it was aimed . . . or whether it is borne on beyond the supposed limit, it evidently did not begin its flight from the boundary. In this manner I will go on with you, and wherever you shall fix the extreme limit of space, I will ask you what then would be the case with the dart. The conclusion must be that a limit can no where exist and that room for the flight of the dart will still extend its flight.

Further, if all the space of the universe were shut in and bounded on all sides by certain limits, the quantity of matter in the universe would before this time have flowed together to the bottom by reason of its solid weight; nor could any thing be carried on beneath the canopy of heaven; nor indeed, would there be a heaven at all, or light of the sun; for all matter, from sinking down for an infinite space of time, would be accumulated at the bottom of the universe. . . . no rest is given to the atoms . . . because no part of the universe is completely and fundamentally the lowest where the atoms might flow together and take up their position; and therefore all things are always carried on in all parts in perpetual motion, and the lowest atoms of matter, or those which we may conceive to be the lowest, stirred up from the infinite of space, are supplied for the generation of things.

Moreover, in things before our eyes, object seems to bound object, the air sets a boundary to the hills, and the hills to the air; the land limits the sea, and the sea limits the entire land; but as to the universe, there is nothing beyond it that can bound it. . . .

Besides, Nature herself prevents the universe from being able to provide bounds for itself, inasmuch as she compels body to be bounded by that which is vacuum, and that which is vacuum to be bounded by body; that so, by this alternate bounding of one by the other, she may render all things infinite. Otherwise, if one or other of these did not bound the other by its simple nature, so that one of them, the vacuum for instance, should extend unlimited, neither the sea, nor the land, nor the bright temples of heaven, nor the race of mortals, nor the sacred persons of the gods, could subsist for the small space of an hour. For the body of matter driven abroad from its union, would be borne dispersed through the mighty void, or rather, in such a case, never having been united, would never have produced any thing, since, when originally scattered it could not have been brought together.

For certainly neither the primary elements of things disposed themselves severally in their own order, by their own counsel or sagacious understanding; nor, assuredly, did they agree among themselves what motions each should produce; but because, being many, and, changed in many ways, they are for an infinite space of time agitated, being acted upon by forces throughout the universe. At length by experiencing movements and combinations of every kind, they settle into that order by which this world of ours has been produced. And this world, when it was once thrown into suitable motions, being also maintained in that state through many long years, causes the rivers to replenish the greedy sea with large floods of water, and that the earth, cherished by the heat of the sun, renews its productions; also that the race of living creatures flourishes undecayed, and that the gliding fires of heaven live. Which effects atoms could by no means produce, unless an abundant supply of matter could arise out of infinite space, whence every thing that is produced is accustomed to replace in time the parts lost. For as the nature of animals, when deprived of food, wastes and decays, losing its substance, so must all things fall away, as soon as matter, turned by any means from its course, has failed to supply itself. . . .

MOTIONS AND SHAPES OF ATOMS

For, assuredly, matter does not constantly cohere . . . since we see every object diminished, and perceive that all things flow away, as it were, through length of time, and that age withdraws them from our eyes; while, nevertheless, the sum of things seems to remain undiminished. And this happens because the particles of matter which depart from each object, lessen the object from which they depart, and endow with increase the object or objects to which they have transferred themselves; and oblige the former to decay, but the latter, on the contrary, to flourish. . . . and thus the sum of things is perpetually renewed, and the races of mortal men subsist by change and transference from one to the other. Some nations increase, others are diminished, and, in a short space of time, the tribes of living creatures are changed by successive generations, and, like the racers, deliver the torch of life from hand to hand.

If you think that the atoms can remain at rest and by remaining at rest, generate fresh motions of things, you stray widely from true reason. For since the atoms wander through the void, they must necessarily be carried forwards by their own gravity, or, as it may chance, by the force of another atom. For when on meeting, they have struck against one another, it happens that they suddenly start asunder in different directions, since . . . they are of the utmost hardness and solidity and there is nothing behind to oppose their motion. . . .

Also, we wish you to understand this: that when the atoms move downwards straight through the void of space, by their own weights, though at no fixed and determinate times and places, they deviate slightly from the straight course.

But unless the atoms deviated from the straight course, they would fall straight down, through the void profound, like drops of rain through the air; nor would there have been any contact produced, or any collision generated among the atoms; and thus nature would never have produced any thing.

But if anyone believes that the heavier atoms, moving more swiftly straight through the void of space, might fall from above on the lighter ones, and thus produce impacts which might give rise to generative movements, he departs from just reasoning. For whatsoever bodies fall downwards through the water and the air, of necessity they must quicken their motions according to their weights, inasmuch as the density of water and the subtle substance of the air, cannot equally retard every body, but yield sooner to the heavier bodies. On the contrary, a pure vacuum can afford no resistance to anything, in any place, or at any time, but must constantly allow it the free passage which its nature requires. For which reason all bodies, when put into motion, must be equally borne onwards, though not of equal weights, through the unresisting void. The heavier atoms will, therefore, never be able to fall from above on the lighter, nor, of themselves produce impacts which may vary the motions by which nature performs her operations.

For which cause, it must again and again be acknowledged that atoms decline a little but only a little from the straight course, lest we should seem to imagine oblique motions, and truth should refute that supposition. For this we see to be obvious and manifest, that heavy bodies, as far as depends on themselves, cannot, when they fall from above, advance obliquely; a fact which you may yourself see. But who is there that can see that atoms do not at all turn themselves aside, even in the least, from the straight direction of their course? . . .

Attend now, O Memmius, and learn next of what nature the atoms of things are, and how very different they are in their forms; how they are varied by manifold shapes. Not that a few only are endowed with like form, for those alike are innumerable, but because, throughout the whole, all are not similar to all, but are varied with great differences. Nor is this wonderful; for since the abundance of them is such, that, as I have shown, there is neither any limit nor sum of them, they must not, and cannot assuredly, be all universally endowed with a like figure and like shape to all others. . . .

It is very easy for us, then, by the clear guidance of reason to explain why the flame of lightning passes through the air with much more penetration than our fire, which arises from the fuel of the earth. For you may justly argue that the celestial fire of lightning, as being more subtle, consists of smaller atoms, and therefore flies through diminutive passages, which this fire of ours, taking its rise from wood, and produced by torches cannot enter. Besides, light passes through horn, but water is repelled by it. Why? unless that the atoms of light are less than those of which the genial liquid of water consists.

Wine also we observe to flow as quickly as possible through a strainer, but thick oil, on the contrary moves through it slowly; because, as it appears, the latter either consists of larger atoms, or of such as are more hooked and involved with one another. And thus it happens, that the individual atoms, not being so quickly detached from one another, cannot so easily pass through the individual pores of any body.

To this is added, that the liquids of honey and milk are moved about in the mouth with a pleasant sensation to the tongue; but, on the contrary, the bitter substance of wormwood torments the palate with a disagreeable taste; so that you may easily infer that those things which can affect the senses with pleasure, consist of smooth and round particles; but that, on the other hand, whatever things seem rough and bitter, are held united together of particles more hooked; and that, on this account, they are accustomed, as it were, to tear a way to our feelings, and to wound the skin of our body at their entrance. . . .

To the foregoing demonstration, I shall join another proposition, which depending on this, derives its credit from it: that the atoms vary in figure, but only with a limited number of shapes. If this were not so, some atoms would necessarily be of an infinite bulk of body. For within the same minute structure of any one particle, the forms of its parts cannot vary much among themselves. Suppose that the atoms consist of three or a few more small parts. When after arranging all those parts, and altering the place of the highest and lowest, and changing the right for the left, you shall have tried in every way what representation of forms each arrangement of the whole of that body offers, and if you wish still further to vary its forms, you will have to add other parts. Thence it will follow, if you wish to vary its forms still further, that a third arrangement in a similar manner will be required. An increase of bulk, therefore, follows upon the variation of shapes; for which reason you cannot believe that the atoms differ from one another by an infinite variety of shapes; otherwise you should make some to be of immense bulk; which I have already shown that it is not possible to prove. . . .

Since I have proved this, I shall proceed to join with it another observation, which depending on this derives its credit from it: that the primordial atoms of things, which are formed of a like figure one to the other, are infinite in number; for since the diversity of their forms is finite, it necessarily follows that those which are alike are infinite; otherwise all matter must be finite, which I have proved to be impossible. . . .

Which points if, being well understood, the system of nature immediately appears as a free agent, released from tyrant masters, to do every thing by itself spontaneously without the help of the gods. For (O ye sacred bosoms of the deities, that pass in tranquil peace a calm and most serene existence!) who is able to rule the whole of this immense universe? Who can hold in his hand, with power to guide them, the strong reins of this vast combination of things? What god can, at the same time, turn round all the heavens, and warm all the earth with ethereal fires? Or what god can be present at the same moment in all places, to produce darkness with clouds, and shake the calm regions of heaven with thunder, and then to hurl bolts that may often overturn his own temples; or afterwards, retiring to the desert to rage there, exercising that weapon with which he often misses the guilty and kills the innocent and undeserving? . . .

LIFE AND MIND

I now affirm that the mind and soul are held united with one another, and form of themselves one nature or substance; but that that which is as it were the head, and which rules in the whole body, is that which we call mind and understanding and this remains seated in the middle portion of the breast. For here dread and terror throb; around these parts joys soothe; here therefore is the understanding and mind. The other part of the soul, or vital power, distributed through the whole body, obeys, and is moved according to the will and impulse of the mind. And the mind thinks of itself alone, and rejoices for itself when nothing of the kind moves either the rest of the soul or the body. And when the head or the eye suffers pain and we are not afflicted throughout the whole body, so the mind is sometimes grieved itself alone, and is sometimes excited with joy, when the other part of the soul, diffused through the limbs and joints, is stimulated by no new sensation. But when the mind is more than ordinarily shaken by violent terror, we see the whole soul, throughout the several members, sympathize with it, and perspirations and paleness, in consequence, arise over the whole body, and the tongue rendered powerless and the voice die away; while we find the eyes darkened, the ears ringing, and the limbs sinking underneath.

Futhermore, we often see men faint from terror of mind; so that any one may easily understand from this, that with the mind is united the soul, which, when it has been acted upon by the power of the mind, then influences and affects the body.

This same reasoning teaches us that the nature of the mind and soul is corporeal; for when it is seen to impel the limbs, to rouse the body from sleep, and to change the countenance, and to guide and turn about the whole man;—of which effects we see that none can be produced without touch, and that touch, moreover, cannot take place without body;—must we not admit that the mind and soul are of a corporeal nature?

Besides, you see that the mind suffers with the body, and sympathizes for us with the body. If the violent force of a dart, driven into the body, the bones and nerves being divided, does not hurt the life itself, yet there follows a languor, and a kind of agreeable inclination to sink to the ground, and when we are on the ground, a perturbation and giddiness which is produced in the mind, and sometimes, as it were, an irresolute desire to rise. It therefore necessarily follows that the nature of the mind is corporeal, since it is made to suffer by corporeal weapons and violence.

I shall now proceed to give you a demonstration of what substance this mind is, and of what it consists.

In the first place, I say that it is extremely subtle, and is formed of very minute atoms. In order that you may understand clearly that this is so, consider the following arguments: Nothing is seen to be done so swiftly, as when the mind proposes it to be done and itself undertakes it. The mind, therefore, impels itself more speedily than anything whose nature is visible before our eyes. But that which is so exceedingly active, must consist of atoms exquisitely round and exquisitely minute; that they may be moved, when acted on, by a slight impulse. For water is moved, and flows with so trifling a force, inasmuch as it is composed of voluble and small particles. But the substance of honey, on the other hand, is more dense, and its fluid sluggish, and its movement more dilatory; for its whole mass of material particles clings more closely together; because, as is evident, it consists of atoms neither so small and round.   Objects have a facility of motion in proportion to their smoothness and roundness, but where they have a greater weight and roughness so much the more stable are they.

Since, therefore, the nature of the mind has been found preeminently active, it must of necessity consist of particles exceedingly small, and smooth, and round. . . .

And the mind is more efficient in holding the bars of life and preserving vitality than the power of the soul. For without the understanding and mind no part of the soul can reside in the body even for a small portion of time; but when the mind takes its departure, the soul readily follows as its companion, and leaves the chilled limbs in the cold of death. But he to whom understanding and mind have remained, continues in life, although he be mutilated, with his limbs cut off on all sides. . . .

And now attend. That thou mayest understand that living creatures have minds, and subtle souls, born and perishable, . . . take care to include both of them under one name; for example, when I proceed to speak of the soul, teaching that it is mortal, suppose that I also speak of the mind, inasmuch as they are one by mutual combination and constitute a single substance.

In the first place, since I have shown that the soul, being subtle, consists of minute particles, and is composed of much smaller atoms than the clear fluid of water, or mist, or smoke; . . . now, therefore, I say, since, when vessels are broken to pieces, you see water flow about, and any other liquid run away; and since, also, mist and smoke disperse into the air; you must conclude that the soul is likewise scattered abroad, and is dissipated much sooner than mist and smoke, and more easily resolved into its original elements, when it has once been withdrawn from the body of a man, and has taken its departure. For how can you believe that this soul can be held together by air, when the body itself (which is, as it were, its vessel) cannot contain it, if it be convulsed by any violence, or rendered thin and weak by loss of blood? How can that air which is more rare than our body confine it?

Besides, we observe that the mind is produced together with the body, and grows up together with it, and waxes old with it. For as children wander about with a weak and tender body, so the subtler sense of the mind follows and corresponds to the weakness of their frame. Then, with the robust vigor of years, their understanding is also greater and their strength of mind more enlarged. Afterwards, when the body is shaken by the power of time, the strength being depressed, the limbs sunk into infirmity, then the understanding falters, the tongue and the mind lose their sense, and all faculties fail and fade away at once. It is therefore natural that the whole substance of the soul should be dissolved, as smoke, into the sublime air of heaven; since we see that it is produced together with the body, and grows up with it, and both, as I have shown, overcome by age, decay in concert. . . .

And since we see that the mind may be healed, like a sick body, and changed by means of medicine, this also signifies that the mind is mortal. For whoever attempts to change the mind, or to alter any other nature or substance whatever, it is requisite either that he add new parts or transpose the parts in a new order, or take away at least some small portion from the whole. But any substance which is immortal, neither allows its parts to be transposed nor to be increased by addition, nor permits an atom to pass away from them. For whatever being changed, goes beyond its own limits, this change is death or the termination of that which it was before. The mind, therefore, whether it be diseased, or whether it be changed by medicine, displays mortal symptoms: so far is the force of true reason seen to oppose the false, and to cut off escape from him who shrinks from its conclusions, and to overthrow what is wrong by a double refutation. . . .

Besides, if the nature of the soul is immortal, and is infused into men at their birth, why are we unable to remember an earlier existence, nor retain any traces of past events. For if the power of the mind is so exceedingly changed, that all remembrance of past things has departed from it, that change, as I think, is not far removed from death itself. For which reason you must of necessity acknowledge, that whatever soul previously existed has perished, and that that which exists for the present has been produced for the present.

But if perchance the soul is to be accounted immortal because it is kept fortified by things perservative of life; or because objects adverse to its safety do not all approach it; or because those that do approach, being by some means diverted, retreat before we can perceive what injury they inflict—the notion of those who think thus is evidently far removed from just reasoning. For besides that it sickens in sympathy with the maladies of the body, there often happens something to trouble it concerning future events, and keep it disquieted in fear, and harass it with cares; while remorse for faults, from past acts wickedly and foolishly committed, torments and distresses it. Join to these afflictions the insanity peculiar to the mind, and the oblivion of all things; and add, besides, that it is often sunk into the black waves of lethargy. Death, therefore, is nothing, nor at all concerns us, since the nature of the soul is proved to be mortal. . . .

Nor, by protracting life, do we deduct a single moment from the duration of death; we cannot diminish aught from its reign, or cause that we may be for a less period sunk in non-existence. How many generations soever, therefore, we may pass in life, nevertheless that same eternal death will still await us. Nor will he be less long out of being, who ended his life under this day's sun, than he who died many months and years ago.

STUDY QUESTIONS

1. Does Lucretius provide any explanation for the origin of the ultimate particles of all things? Does he accept any doctrine of creation or annihilation? Is matter eternal?

2. How can Lucretius account for our knowledge of the ultimate particles (atoms) of all things? Are they a matter of sense knowledge? If not how do we know their existence? What evidence would Lucretius have for saying they are corporeal or material in nature?

3. What does Lucretius mean by the void? What function does it serve in his account of the nature of the universe?

4. What is Lucretius' conception of the nature of the atoms of material things? How does he explain the process of generation and dissolution of things? How can atoms be extended, solid, and yet indivisible?

5. Are there any limits to the spatial extent of the universe? Is the universe infinite in extent? How does Lucretius argue for infiniteness and what illustration does he use? Would you agree?

6. How does Lucretius account for the motion of the atoms? Why does he say that they deviate in their course through the void. Does he have any justification or evidence for this?

7. What shapes and forms do the atoms take? How does this enable Lucretius to account for the differences in objects and their effects upon us.

8. Are the atoms finite or infinite in number? In the diversity of their forms? Are they determined or controlled in their course of action or is nature free?

9. Show in some detail how Lucretius extends his theory of a materialistic atomism to the nature of mind or soul. Does this analysis have any religious implications? Discuss.

G. W. Leibniz

THE PRE-ESTABLISHED HARMONY

Biographical Note. GOTTFRIED WILHELM LEIBNIZ (1646–1716) was born at Leipzig in Germany. His father was Professor of Moral Philosophy at the University of Leipzig but died when Leibniz was a boy of six. At fifteen, Leibniz entered the University of Leipzig, where he studied Greek and Scholastic Philosophy and read widely on his own in modern philosophy and science. Upon graduation he pursued the study of law for three years, but the University of Leipzig refused him a doctorate in law on the grounds of his youth. In 1667 he entered the service of the Archbishop Elector of Mainz. During his years of service with the archbishop he labored without success to effect a reunion of Christendom through theological discussions. In 1673 he returned to Germany and became librarian for the Duke of Brunswick, at Hanover. In the next few years he devoted himself to historical studies, correspondence on philosophical and scientific problems, and the dream of a universal language that would enlarge the scope of the deductive method and lead to a universal science. He anticipated in a general way the later development of symbolic logic, and with Newton he was the co-discoverer of the infinitesimal calculus. The last years of his life found him out of favor with the court of Hanover, and little notice was taken of his death in 1716. His principal writings are *Monadology; De arte combinatoria; Theodicy; Discourse on Metaphysics; New Essays Concerning the Human*

From the *Principles of Nature and of Grace, Based on Reason,* translated by Robert Latta, London, Oxford, 1898 (with revisions).

Understanding; Principles of Nature and of Grace, Based on Reason; and considerable correspondence devoted largely to an elaboration of his philosophical and scientific ideas.

* * *

Introductory Note. The metaphysics of Leibniz falls within the rationalist tradition of early modern philosophy. Like Spinoza and Descartes before him, Leibniz believed in the ultimate rationality of the world. He held that there are two kinds of truths, those of reasoning and those of fact. Truths of reasoning are necessary and their opposite is impossible. Such truths must conform to the Principle of Contradiction (that a proposition cannot be both true and false at the same time). Truths of fact are contingent and their opposite is possible. These truths are based upon the Principle of Sufficient Reason (that "nothing happens without a reason why it should be so rather than otherwise"). On the basis of these two principles of reasoning and his conception of the ultimate nature of reality, Leibniz proceeded to the deduction of a complete system of metaphysics.

Central to such a system was his conception of the *monad.* For the infinite number of material atoms of Lucretius, he substituted an innumerable number of spiritual atoms or monads. As spiritual entities, monads are subject only to creation and annihilation and not to dissolution or destruction. They lack extension, they occupy no space, and are analogous to mathematical points. They are qualitatively distinct from one another and are characterized by varying degrees of the activities of perception ("the internal state of the monad representing external things") and appetition ("the action of the internal principle which causes the change or passage from one perception to another"). Some monads are mere *entelechies* or substantial forms with confused and obscure perceptions. Others are souls capable of memory and feeling. Still others are rational souls or spirits capable of reflection and apperception (perception accompanied by consciousness). Bodies are simply compounds of monads or organized collections of monads dominated by a higher monad, such as a soul or spirit.

Monads have no relations with one another and cannot act upon one another. As Leibniz expresses it, each monad "possesses no windows by which something might enter or leave." Hence each monad must mirror the universe from a different point of view. God, as the supreme monad and creator of all other monads, is the perfect mirror and contains within Himself all possible points of view of all possible monads. To account for the correspondence or agreement of the internal states of the various monads, Leibniz introduces his famous principle of pre-established harmony. Since monads cannot act upon one another, it must be supposed that the activities of each monad have been pre-established and determined by God in terms of His purposes. The principle is well illustrated in Leibniz's account of the relationship between soul and body. God may be compared to a clockmaker who has constructed two clocks to keep perfect time together, so one may be assured of their agreement at all future times. In a similar manner, soul and body may be said to agree in all their activities. The principle of the pre-established harmony and the concept of the monad may be said to represent Leibniz's attempt to resolve the problem of the one and the many and to effect the reconciliation of mechanical and final causality. His metaphysical speculations conclude with a highly optimistic outlook. Arguing for the wisdom, the goodness and the power of God, Leibniz declares that it follows that everything happens for the best in this best of all possible worlds. For man there remains the higher possibility of entering into society with God, of achieving through the grace of God the perfection of his nature and a membership in the City of God.

PHYSICS

Substance is a being capable of action. It is simple or compound. *Simple substance* is that which has no parts. *Compound substance* is the combination of simple substances or *Monads. Monas* is a Greek word, which means unity, or that which is one. Compounds or bodies are pluralities [*multitudes*]; and simple substances, lives, souls, spirits, are unities. And everywhere there must be simple substance, for without simple substances there would not be compounds; and consequently all nature is full of life.

The Monads, having no parts, can neither be made nor unmade. They can neither come into being nor come to an end by natural means, and consequently they last as long as the universe, which will be changed, but which will not be destroyed. They can have no shape [figure], otherwise they would have parts. Consequently any one Monad in itself and at a particular moment can be distinguished from any other only by internal qualities and activities [*actions*], which cannot be other than its *perceptions* (that is to say, the representations of the compound, or of that which is outside, in the simple) and its *appetitions* (that is to say, its tendencies to pass from one perception to another), which are the principles of change. For the simplicity of substance is by no means inconsistent with the multiplicity of the modifications which are to be found together in that same simple substance, and these modifications must consist in the variety of relations to the things which are external. Just as in a *centre* or point, which, although it is perfectly simple, there is an infinite number of angles formed by the lines which meet in that centre.

All nature is a *plenum*. There are simple substances everywhere, which are actually separated from one another by activities of their own, and which continually change their relations; and each specially important [*distinguée*] simple substance or Monad, which forms the centre of a compound substance (e. g. of an animal) and the principle of its unity, is surrounded by a *mass* composed of an infinity of other Monads, which constitute the particular body of this central Monad, and according to the affections of its body, the Monad represents, as in a kind of *centre,* the things which are outside of itself. This *body* is *organic,* though it forms a kind of automation or natural machine, which is a machine not only as a whole but also in the smallest perceptible parts. Since the world is a *plenum* all things are connected together and each body acts upon every other, more or less, according to their distance, and each, through reaction, is affected by every other. Hence it follows that each Monad is a living mirror, or a mirror endowed with inner activity, representative of the universe, according to its point of view, and as subject to rule as is the universe itself. And the perceptions in the Monad are produced one from another according to the laws of desires [*appétits*] or of the *final causes of good and evil,* which consist in observable perceptions, regular or irregular. On the other hand, the changes of bodies and external phenomena are produced from one another according to the laws of *efficient causes,* that is to say, of motions. Thus there is a perfect harmony between the perceptions of the Monad and the motions of bodies, a harmony pre-established from the beginning between the system of efficient causes and that of final causes. And it is in this way that soul and body are in agreement and are physically united, while it is not possible for the one to change the laws of the other.

Each Monad, with a particular body, forms a living substance. Thus not only is there everywhere life, accompanied with members or organs, but there is also an infinity of degrees in the Monads, one dominating more or less over another. But when the Monad has organs so arranged that they give prominence and distinctness to the impressions they receive, and consequently to the perceptions which represent these (as when by means of the form of the eye's humours, the rays of light are concentrated and act with more force), this may lead to feeling [*sentiment*], that is to say, to a perception accompanied by *memory,* in other words, a perception of which a certain echo long remains, so as to make itself heard on occasion. Such a living being is called an *animal,* as its Monad is called a soul. And when this soul is raised to *reason,* it is something more sublime and is reckoned among spirits [*esprits*], as will presently be explained. It is true that animals are sometimes in the condition of mere living beings and their souls in the condition of mere

Monads, namely when their perceptions are not sufficiently distinct to be remembered, as happens in a deep dreamless sleep or in a swoon. But perceptions which have become completely confused are sure to be developed again in animals, for reason which I shall presently mention. Thus it is well to make distinction between *perception*, which is the inner state of the Monad representing outer things, and *apperception*, which is *consciousness* or the reflective knowledge of this inner state, and which is not given to all souls nor to the same soul at all times. It is for lack of this distinction that the Cartesians have made the mistake of ignoring perceptions of which we are not conscious, as people ignore imperceptible bodies. It is this also that has led these same Cartesians to believe that only spirits are Monads, that the lower animals have no soul, and that still less are there other *principles of life*. And as they came into too great conflict with the common opinion of men in denying feeling to the lower animals, so on the other hand they conformed too much to the prejudices of the crowd in confounding a *prolonged unconsciousness*, which comes from a great confusion of perceptions, with *absolute death,* in which all perception would cease. This has confirmed the ill-founded opinion that some souls are destroyed, and the bad ideas of some who call themselves free-thinkers and who have disputed the immortality of our soul.

There is a connexion among the perceptions of animals which has some likeness to reason; but it is based only on the memory of *facts* or effect, and not at all on the knowledge of *causes.* Thus a dog avoids the stick with which it has been beaten, because memory represents to it the pain which this stick has caused it. And men, in so far as they are empirics, that is to say in three-fourths of their actions, do not act otherwise than the lower animals. For instance, we expect that there will be daylight tomorrow because our experience has always been so: it is only the astronomer who rationally foresees it, and even his prediction will ultimately fail when the cause of daylight, which is not eternal, ceases. But *genuine reasoning* depends upon necessary or eternal truths, such as those of logic, of number, of geometry, which produce an indubitable connexion of ideas and infallible inferences. The animals in which these inferences do not appear are called the lower animals [*bêtes*]; but those which know these necessary truths are properly those which are called *rational animals,* and their souls are called *spirits.* These souls have the power to perform acts of reflexion and to observe that which is called ego, substance, soul, mind, in a word, immaterial things and truths. And this it is which makes science or demonstrative knowledge possible to us.

Modern research has taught us, and reason confirms it, that the living beings whose organs are known to us, that is to say, plants and animals, do not come from putrefaction or chaos, as the ancients thought, but from *preformed* seeds, and consequently from the transformation of pre-existing living beings. In the seed of large animals there are animalcules which by means of conception obtain a new outward form, which they make their own and which enables them to grow and become larger so as to pass to a greater theatre and to propagate the large animal. It is true that the souls of human spermatic animals are not rational, and that they become so only when conception gives to these animals human nature. And as in general animals are not entirely born in conception or *generation*, no more do they entirely perish in what we call *death*; for it is reasonable that what does not come into being by natural means should not any more come to an end in the course of nature. Thus, throwing off their mask or their tattered covering, they merely return to a more minute theatre, where they may nevertheless be as sensitive and as well ordered as in the larger theatre. And what has just been said about the large animals applies also to the generation and death of spermatic animals themselves, that is to say, they are growths of other smaller spermatic animals, in comparison with which they in turn may be counted large, for everything in nature proceeds *ad infinitum*.[1] Thus not only souls but also animals are ingenerable and imperishable: they are only developed, enveloped, clothed, unclothed, transformed. Souls never put off the whole of their body, and do not pass from one body into another body which is entirely new to them. Accordingly there is no *metempsychosis*, but there is *metamorphosis*. Animals change, take on and put off, parts only. In nutrition this takes place gradually and by small imperceptible particles, but continually; and on the other hand, in conception or in death, when much is gained or lost all at once, it takes place suddenly and in a way that can be noticed but rarely.

METAPHYSICS

Thus far we have spoken merely as pure *physicists*: now we must rise to *metaphysics*, making use of the *great principle*, usually little employed, which affirms that *nothing takes place without sufficient reason*, that is to say, that nothing happens without its being possible for one

---

[1] 'So, naturalists observe, a flea
Has smaller fleas that on him prey;
And these have smaller still to bite 'em
And so proceed *ad infinitum*.'—Swift, *On Poetry*.

who should know things sufficiently, to give a reason which is sufficient to determine why things are so and not otherwise. This principle being laid down, the first question we are entitled to put will be—*Why does something exist rather than nothing?* For 'nothing' is simpler and easier than 'something.' Further, granting that things must exist, we must be able to give a reason *why they should exist thus* and not otherwise.

Now this sufficient reason of the existence of the universe cannot be found in the sequence of contingent things, that is to say, of bodies and their representations in souls: because, matter being in itself indifferent to motion and to rest and to one or another particular motion, we cannot find in it the reason of motion and still less the reason of one particular motion. And although the motion which is at present in matter comes from the preceding motion, we are no farther forward, however far we go; for the same question always remains. Thus the sufficient reason, which has no need of any other reason, must needs be outside of this sequence of contingent things and must be in a substance which is the cause of this sequence, or which is a necessary being, bearing in itself the reason of its own existence, otherwise we should not yet have a sufficient reason with which we could stop. And this ultimate reason of things is called *God*.

This primary simple substance must include eminently the perfections contained in the derivative substances which are its effects. Thus it will have power, knowledge and will in perfection, that is to say, it will have supreme omnipotence, omniscience and goodness. And as *justice,* taken very generally, is nothing but goodness in conformity with wisdom, there must also be in God supreme justice. The reason which has led to the existence of things through Him makes them also depend upon Him for their continued existence and working; and they continually receive from Him that which makes them have any perfection; but any imperfection that remains in them comes from the essential and original limitation of the created thing

It follows from the supreme perfection of God that in producing the universe He has chosen the best possible plan, in which there is the greatest variety along with the greatest order; ground, place, time being as well arranged as possible; the greatest effect produced by the simplest ways; the most power, knowledge, happiness and goodness in created things that the universe allowed. For as all possible things in the understanding of God claim existence in proportion to their perfections, the result of all these claims must be the most perfect actual world that is possible. And apart from this it would not be possible to give a reason why things have gone thus rather than otherwise.

The supreme wisdom of God led Him to choose specially the *laws of motion* which are most fitting and which are most in conformity with abstract or metaphysical reasons. There is conserved the same quantity of total and absolute force, or of activity, also the same quantity of relative force or of reaction, and finally the same quantity of force of direction. Further, action is always equal to reaction, and the whole effect is always equivalent to its full cause. And it is remarkable that by the sole consideration of *efficient causes* or of matter it was impossible to explain these laws of motion which have been discovered in our time and of which a part has been discovered by myself. For I have found that we must have recourse to *final causes*, and that these laws are dependent not upon the *principle of necessity*, like the truths of logic, arithmetic, and geometry, but upon the *principle of fitness*, that is, upon the choice of wisdom. And this is one of the most effective and remarkable proofs of the existence of God for those who can go deeply into these things.

Again, it follows from the perfection of the Supreme Author not only that the order of the whole universe is the most perfect that can be, but also that each living mirror representing the universe according to its point of view, that is, each *Monad*, each substantial centre, must have its perceptions and its desires as thoroughly well ordered as is compatible with all the rest. Whence it also follows that *souls*, that is to say, the most dominant Monads, or rather animals themselves cannot fail to awake again from the condition of stupor into which death or some other accident may put them.

For all is regulated in things, once for all, with as much order and mutual connexion as possible, since supreme wisdom and goodness can act only with perfect harmony. The present is big with the future, the future might be read in the past, the distant is expressed in the near. We might get to know the beauty of the universe in each soul, if we could unfold all that is enfolded in it and that is perceptibly developed only through time. But as each distinct perception of the soul includes an infinite number of confused perceptions, which involve the whole universe, the soul itself knows the things of which it has perception, only in so far as it has distinct and clear perceptions of them; and it has perfection in proportion to its distinct perceptions. Each soul knows the infinite, knows all, but confusedly; as when I walk on the seashore and hear the great noise the sea makes, I hear the particular sounds which come from the particular waves and which make up the total sound, but I do not discriminate them from one another. Our confused perceptions are the result of the impressions which the whole universe makes upon us. It is the same with each Monad. God alone has a distinct knowledge of all, for He is the source of all. It has been very well said that as a centre He is everywhere, but His circumference is nowhere, for everything is immediately present to Him without any distance from this centre.

As regards the rational soul, or *spirit,* there is in it something more than in the Monads or even in simple souls. It is not only a mirror of the universe of created beings, but also an image of the Deity. The spirit has not merely a perception of the works of God, but it is even capable of producing something which resembles them, although in miniature. For, to say nothing of the wonders of dreams, in which we invent without trouble (but also involuntarily) things which, in our waking hours, we should have to think long in order to hit upon, our soul is architectonic also in its voluntary activities and, discovering the scientific principles in accordance with which God has ordered things (*pondere, mensura, numero,* etc.) it imitates, in its own province and in the little world in which it is allowed to act, what God does in the great world.

It is for this reason that all spirits, whether of men or of angels, entering in virtue of reason and of eternal truths into a kind of fellowship with God, are members of the City of God, that is to say, of the most perfect state, formed and governed by the greatest and best of monarchs: in which there is no crime without punishment, no good action without a proportionate reward, and in short as much virtue and happiness as is possible; and this, not by any interference with the course of nature, as if what God prepares for souls were to disturb the laws of bodies, but by the very order of natural things, in virtue of the harmony pre-established from all time between the realms of nature and of grace, between God as Architect and God as Monarch, so that nature itself leads to grace, and grace, by the use it makes of nature, brings it to perfection.

Thus although reason cannot make known to us the details of the great future (which are reserved for revelation), we can be assured by this same reason that things are made in a way which exceeds our desires. Further, as God is the most perfect and most happy and consequently the most lovable of substances, and as *genuine pure* love consists in the state in which we find pleasure in the perfections and the felicity of the beloved, this love is sure to give us the greatest pleasure of which we are capable, when God is its object.

And it is easy to love God as we ought, if we know Him as I have just said. For although God cannot be perceived by our external senses, He is none the less very lovable and He gives very great pleasure. We see how much pleasure honors give to men, although they do not consist in anything that appeals to the external senses. Martyrs and fanatics (though the emotion of the latter is ill governed) show how much influence spiritual pleasure can have: and what is more, even sensuous pleasures are really intellectual pleasures confusedly known. Music charms us, although its beauty consists only in the harmonies of numbers and in the counting of the beats or vibrations of sounding bodies, which meet at certain intervals, countings of which we are not conscious and which the soul nevertheless does make. The pleasure which sight finds in good proportions is of the same nature; and the pleasures caused by the other senses will be found to amount to much the same thing, although we may not be able to explain it so distinctly.

It may even be said that from this time forth the love of God enables us to enjoy a foretaste of future felicity. And although this love is disinterested, it constitutes by itself our greatest good and interest, even though we may not seek these in it and though we may consider only the pleasure it gives without regard to the advantage it brings; for it gives us perfect confidence in the goodness of our Author and Master, which produces real tranquility of mind, not as in the case of the Stoics, who forcibly school themselves to patience, but through a present content which also assures to us a future happiness. And besides the present pleasure it affords, nothing can be of more advantage for the future than this love of God, for it fulfils our expectations also and leads us in the way of supreme happiness, because in virtue of the perfect order that is established in the universe, everything is done as well as possible both for the general good and also for the greatest individual good of those who believe in it and who are satisfied with the Divine government. And this belief and satisfaction must inevitably be the characteristic of those who have learned to love the Source of all good. It is true that supreme felicity (by whatever *beatific vision,* or knowledge of God, it may be accompanied) can never be complete, because God, being infinite, cannot be entirely known. Thus our happiness will never consist (and it is right that it should not consist) in complete enjoyment, which would leave nothing more to be desired and would make our mind stupid; but it must consist in a perpetual progress to new pleasures and new perfections.

STUDY QUESTIONS

1. Describe in some detail the principal characteristics of the monad. How do you suppose Leibniz arrived at such a notion?

2. Comment at some length on the relation of monads to one another. What does it mean to say that each monad mirrors the universe from its own point of view? That monads have no windows? That God as a centre is everywhere but His circumference is nowhere?

3. For what reasons would you say that Leibniz is a rationalist? What is the principle of sufficient reason and what significance does it have for Leibniz's metaphysics.

4. Show why it was necessary for Leibniz to postulate his principle of the pre-established harmony; illustrate with reference to the relation of soul and body.

5. Show how Leibniz distinguishes among the different classes of monads. How are living and nonliving creatures formed? What is the difference between perception and appetition? Perception and apperception?

6. How does Leibniz account for the existence of God and what attributes does he ascribe to such a being?

7. What is the basis for Leibniz's contention that this is the best of all possible worlds? How would you criticize such a contention?

8. What is the relation between nature and grace? What is the City of God? Comment on Leibniz's notion of man's supreme happiness.

George Berkeley

TO BE IS TO BE PERCEIVED

Biographical Note. GEORGE BERKELEY (1685–1753) was born near Kilkenny, Ireland, to a family of English descent. At 15, he entered Trinity College, Dublin, where he specialized in the study of philosophy, mathematics, and language. In 1707, three years after receiving his degree, he was appointed a Fellow (officer) of the College. Two years later, at 24, he published his first significant philosophical contribution—*An Essay Toward a New Theory of Vision.* This was followed in 1710 by his *A Treatise Concerning the Principles of Human Knowledge,* and in 1713 by his *Three Dialogues Between Hylas and Philonous.* Thus before he was thirty he had brought to completion his major philosophical contributions. In the meantime his interests turned to a religious career and he was ordained a priest in the Church of England. His success in this work was marked by his appointment, in 1724, as Dean of Derry. Soon afterward he went to live in the colony of Rhode Island, at Newport, where he strove to establish a university. Defeated by the failure of Parliament to support his project, he returned to Ireland in 1731. He was appointed Bishop of Cloyne in 1734, and until 1752, when he retired to Oxford, he devoted himself to his diocesan duties, to his enthusiastic belief in the virtues of tar-water as a universal panacea for illness, and to his phosophical studies.

* * *

From the *Principles of Human Knowledge,* Ed. by A. C. Fraser, London, Oxford, 1901.

Introductory Note.　　In the development of modern philosophy, Berkeley falls within the tradition known as British Empiricism, the cardinal principle of which was that all knowledge is derived from sense experience. In contrast to his fellow empiricists, Locke and Hume, Berkeley developed a metaphysical theory that shows a considerable independence and originality of thought. His metaphysics is derived from a rigorous and radical empiricism and may be described as a form of Idealism. It owes much to Berkeley's being a devout Christian, determined to refute effectively the materialistic point of view of his own time. Berkeley's principal contributions to philosophy are to be found in his analysis of abstract ideas, his theory of vision, his analysis of perception and the rejection of the distinction between primary and secondary qualities, his exposition of language and the development of the metaphor of nature as the language of God, and finally the whole armory of arguments he enlisted in the refutation of the idea of material substance.

In the selection that follows, Berkeley endeavors to establish (1) the central thesis of his philosophy—namely, that *to be is to be perceived,* that being is dependent upon being known; (2) that the conception of material substance is subject to many difficulties and contradictions—that material substance as independent of mind or perception is both untenable and meaningless; (3) that in addition to the world of ideas, which is made up of things under their more proper names, there exist individual finite souls or selves. Of these we know our own self intuitively, others inferentially; (4) that ideas are passive and incapable of causal action, but souls or spirits are active in nature; (5) finally, there exists in addition to ideas and finite spirits, that Infinite Spirit we know as God. For Berkeley, God is the author of all being, He is the perceptual perceiver who sustains all beings in existence. In this manner Berkeley avoids the charge of solipsism (the belief that only the self and its perceptions exist), and establishes the objectivity of the world of ideas. As Fr. Ronald Knox so well put it in his famous limerick:

> "There was a young man who said, God
> Must think it exceedingly odd
> If he finds that this tree continues to be
> When there's no one about in the Quad.

Reply.

Dear Sir:
> Your astonishment's odd
> I am always about in the Quad.
> And that's why the tree
> Will continue to be,
> Since observed by
> 　　　Yours faithfully, *God.*"

TO BE IS TO BE PERCEIVED

1. It is evident to anyone who takes a survey of the objects of human knowledge, that they are either ideas (1) actually imprinted on the senses, or else such as are (2) perceived by attending to the passions and operations of the mind, or lastly (3) ideas formed by help of memory and imagination, either compounding, dividing, or barely representing those originally perceived in the aforesaid ways. By sight I have the ideas of lights and colors, with their several degrees and variations. By touch I perceive hard and soft, heat and cold, motion and resistance, and of all these more and less either as to quantity or degree. Smelling furnishes me with odors, the palate with tastes, and hearing conveys sounds to the mind in all their variety of tone and composition. And as several of these are observed to accompany each other, they come to be marked by one name, and so to be reputed as one thing. Thus, for example, a certain color, taste, smell, figure, and consistence, having been observed to go together, are accounted one distinct thing, signified by the name 'apple.' Other collections of ideas constitute a stone, a tree, a book, and the like sensible things; which, as they are pleasing or disagreeable, excite the passions of love, hatred, joy, grief, and so forth.

2. But besides all that endless variety of ideas or objects of knowledge, there is likewise something which knows or perceives them, and exercises divers operations, as willing, imagining, remembering, about them. This perceiving, active being is what I call *mind, spirit, soul,* or *myself.* By which words I do not denote any one of my ideas, but a thing entirely distinct from them wherein they exist, or, which is the same thing, whereby they are perceived; for the existence of an idea consists in being perceived.

3. That neither our thoughts, nor passions, nor ideas formed by the imagination, exist without the mind, is what everybody will allow. And it seems no less evident that the various sensations or ideas imprinted on the sense, however, blended or combined together (that is, whatever objects they compose), cannot exist otherwise than in a mind perceiving them. I think an intuitive knowledge may be obtained of this by anyone that shall attend to what is meant by the term 'exist' when applied to sensible things. The table I write on I say exists—that is, I see and feel it; and if I were out of my study I should say it existed—meaning thereby that if I was in my study I might perceive it, or that some other spirit actually does perceive it. There was an odor, that is, it was smelt; there was a sound, that is, it was heard; a color or figure, and it was perceived by sight or touch. This is all that I can understand by these

and the like expressions. For as to what is said of the absolute existence of unthinking things without any relation to their being perceived, that seems perfectly unintelligible. Their *esse* is *percipi*, nor is it possible they should have any existence out of the minds or thinking things which perceive them.

4. It is indeed an opinion strangely prevailing amongst men, that houses, mountains, rivers, and in a word all sensible objects, have an existence, natural or real, distinct from their being perceived by the understanding. But with how great an assurance and acquiescence soever this principle may be entertained in the world, yet whoever shall find in his heart to call it in question may, if I mistake not, perceive it to involve a manifest contradiction. For what are the forementioned objects but the things we perceive by sense? and what do we perceive *besides our own ideas or sensations?* and is it not plainly repugnant that any one of these, or any combination of them, should exist unperceived?

5. If we thoroughly examine this tenet it will perhaps be found at bottom to depend on the doctrine of *abstract ideas*. For can there be a nicer strain of abstraction than to distinguish the existence of sensible objects from their being perceived, so as to conceive them existing unperceived? Light and colors, heat and cold, extension and figures—in a word the things we see and feel—what are they but so many sensations, notions, ideas, or impressions on the sense? And is it possible to separate, even in thought, any of these from perception? For my part, I might as easily divide a thing from itself. I may, indeed, divide in my thoughts, or conceive apart from each other, those things which perhaps I never perceived by sense so divided. Thus I imagine the trunk of a human body without the limbs, or conceive the smell of a rose without thinking on the rose itself. So far, I will not deny, I can abstract, if that may properly be called abstraction which extends only to the conceiving separately such objects as it is possible may really exist or be actually perceived asunder. But my conceiving or imagining power does not extend beyond the possibility of real existence or perception. Hence, as it is impossible for me to see or feel anything without an actual sensation of that thing, so it is impossible for me to conceive in my thoughts any sensible thing or object distinct from the sensation or perception of it.

6. Some truths there are so near and obvious to the mind that a man need only open his eyes to see them. Such I take this important one to be, to wit, that all the choir of heaven and furniture of the earth, in a word all those bodies which compose the mighty frame of the world, have not any subsistence without a mind, that their *being* is to be perceived or known; that consequently so long as they are not actually

perceived by me, or do not exist in my mind or that of any other created spirit, they must either have no existence at all, or else subsist in the mind of some Eternal Spirit; it being perfectly unintelligible, and involving all the absurdity of abstraction, to attribute to any single part of them an existence independent of a spirit. To be convinced of which, the reader need only reflect and try to separate in his own thoughts the *being* of a sensible thing from its *being perceived.*

7. From what has been said it follows there is not any other substance than *spirit,* or that which perceives. But for the fuller proof of this point, let it be considered the sensible qualities are color, figure, motion, smell, taste, etc.—that is, the ideas perceived by sense. Now, for an idea to exist in an unperceiving thing is a manifest contradiction, for to have an idea is all one as to perceive; that therefore wherein color, figure, and the like qualities exist must perceive them; hence it is clear there can be no unthinking substance or *substratum* of those ideas.

8. But, say you, though the ideas themselves do not exist without the mind, yet there may be things *like* them, whereof they are copies or resemblances, which things exist without the mind in an unthinking substance. I answer, an idea can be like nothing but an idea; a color or figure can be like nothing but another color or figure. If we look but never so little into our thoughts, we shall find it impossible for us to conceive a likeness except only between our ideas. Again, I ask whether those supposed originals or external things, of which our ideas are the pictures or representations, be themselves perceivable or no? If they are, then they are ideas and we have gained our point; but if you say they are not, I appeal to anyone whether it be sense to assert a color is like something which is invisible; hard or soft, like something which is intangible; and so of the rest.

9. Some there are who make a distinction betwixt *primary* and *secondary* qualities. By the former they mean extension, figure, motion, rest, solidity, or impenetrability, and number; by the latter they denote all other sensible qualities, as colors, sounds, tastes, and so forth. The ideas we have of these they acknowledge not to be the resemblances of anything existing without the mind or unperceived, but they will have our ideas of the primary qualities to be patterns or images of things which exist without the mind, in an unthinking substance which they call *matter.* By *matter,* therefore, we are to understand an inert, senseless substance, in which extension, figure, and motion do actually subsist. But it is evident from what we have already shown, that extension, figure, and motion are only ideas existing in the mind, and that an idea can be like nothing but another idea, and that consequently neither they

nor their archetypes can exist in an unperceiving substance. Hence, it is plain that the very notion of what is called *matter,* or *corporeal substance,* involves a contradiction in it.

10. They who assert that figure, motion, and the rest of the primary or original qualities do exist without the mind in unthinking substances, do at the same time acknowledge that color, sounds, heat, cold, and suchlike secondary qualities, do not; which they tell us are sensations existing in the mind alone, that depend on and are occasioned by the different size, texture, and motion of the minute particles of matter. This they take for an undoubted truth, which they can demonstrate beyond all exception. Now, if it be certain that those original qualities are inseparably united with the other sensible qualities, and not, even in thought, capable of being abstracted from them, it plainly follows that they exist only in the mind. But I desire anyone to reflect and try whether he can, by any abstraction of thought, conceive the extension and motion of a body without all other sensible qualities. For my own part, I see evidently that it is not in my power to frame an idea of a body extended and moving, but I must withal give it some color or other sensible quality which is acknowledged to exist only in the mind. In short, extension, figure, and motion, abstracted from all other qualities, are inconceivable. Where therefore the other sensible qualities are, there must these be also, to wit, in the mind and nowhere else.

THE DENIAL OF MATERIALISM

17. If we inquire into what the most accurate philosophers declare themselves to mean by *material substance,* we shall find them acknowledge they have no other meaning annexed to those sounds but the idea of *Being in general,* together with the relative notion of its supporting accidents. The general idea of Being appeareth to me the most abstract and incomprehensible of all other; and as for its supporting accidents, this, as we have just now observed, cannot be understood in the common sense of those words; it must therefore be taken in some other sense, but what that is they do not explain. So that when I consider the two parts or branches which make the signification of the words *material substance,* I am convinced there is no distinct meaning annexed to them. But why should we trouble ourselves any farther, in discussing this material *substratum* or support of figure and motion, and other sensible qualities? Does it not suppose they have an existence without the mind? And is not this a direct repugnancy, and altogether inconceivable?

18. But though it were possible that solid, figured, movable substances may exist without the mind, corresponding to the idea we have of bodies, yet how is it possible for us to know this? Either we must know it by sense or by reason. As for our senses, by them we have the knowledge only of our sensations, ideas, or those things that are immediately perceived by sense, call them what you will; but they do not inform us that things exist without the mind, or unperceived, like to those which are perceived. This the materialists themselves acknowledge. It remains therefore that if we have any knowledge at all of external things, it must be by reason, inferring their existence from what is immediately perceived by sense. But what reason can induce us to believe the existence of bodies without the mind, from what we perceive, since the very patrons of matter themselves do not pretend there is any necessary connection betwixt them and our ideas? I say it is granted on all hands (and what happens in dreams, frenzies, and the like, puts it beyond dispute) that *it is possible we might be affected with all the ideas we have now, though there were no bodies existing without, resembling them.* Hence, it is evident the supposition of external bodies is not necessary for the producing our ideas; since it is granted they are produced sometimes, and might possibly be produced always in the same order we see them in at present, without their concurrence.

19. But, though we might possibly have all our sensations without them, yet perhaps it may be thought easier to conceive and explain the manner of their production by supposing external bodies in their likeness rather than otherwise; and so it might be at least probable there are such things as bodies that excite their ideas in our minds. But neither can this be said; for though we give the materialists their external bodies, they by their own confession are never the nearer knowing how our ideas are produced, since they own themselves unable to comprehend in what manner body can act upon spirit, or how it is possible it should imprint any idea in the mind. Hence it is evident the production of ideas or sensations in our minds can be no reason why we should suppose matter or corporeal substances, since that is acknowledged to remain equally inexplicable with or without this supposition. If therefore it were possible for bodies to exist without the mind, yet to hold they do so, must needs be a very precarious opinion; since it is to suppose, without any reason at all, that God has created innumerable beings that are entirely useless, and serve to no manner of purpose.

20. In short, if there were external bodies, it is impossible we should ever come to know it; and if there were not, we might have the very same reasons to think there were that we have now. . . .

23. But, say you, surely there is nothing easier than for me to imagine trees, for instance, in a park, or books existing in a closet, and nobody by to perceive them. I answer, you may so, there is no difficulty in it; but what is all this, I beseech you, more than framing in your mind certain ideas which you call books and trees, and the same time omitting to frame the idea of anyone that may perceive them? But do not you yourself perceive or think of them all the while? This therefore is nothing to the purpose; it only shows you have the power of imagining or forming ideas in your mind: but it doth not show that you can conceive it possible the objects of your thought may exist without the mind. To make out this, it is necessary that you conceive them existing unconceived or unthought of, which is a manifest repugnancy. When we do our utmost to conceive the existence of external bodies, we are all the while only contemplating our own ideas. But the mind taking no notice of itself, is deluded to think it can and doth conceive bodies existing unthought of or without the mind, though at the same time they are apprehended by or exist in itself. A little attention will discover to anyone the truth and evidence of what is here said, and make it unnecessary to insist on any other proofs against the existence of *material substance*.

IDEAS AND SPIRIT

25. All our ideas, sensations, notions, or the things which we perceive, by whatsoever names they may be distinguished, are visibly inactive; there is nothing of power or agency included in them. So that one idea or object of thought cannot produce or make any alteration in another. To be satisfied of the truth of this, there is nothing else requisite but a bare observation of our ideas. For, since they and every part of them exist only in the mind, it follows that there is nothing in them but what is perceived; but whoever shall attend to his ideas, whether of sense or reflection, will not perceive in them any power of activity; there is, therefore, no such thing contained in them. A little attention will discover to us that the very being of an idea implies passiveness and inertness in it, insomuch that it is impossible for an idea to do anything, or, strictly speaking, to be the cause of anything: neither can it be the resemblance or pattern of any active being, as is evident from Sec. 8. Whence it plainly follows that extension, figure, and motion cannot be the cause of our sensations. To say, therefore, that these are the effects of powers resulting from the configuration, number, motion, and size of corpuscles, must certainly be false.

26. We perceive a continual succession of ideas, some are anew excited, others are changed or totally disappear. There is therefore some cause of these ideas, whereon they depend, and which produces and changes them. That this cause cannot be any quality or idea or combination of ideas, is clear from the preceding section. It must therefore be a substance; but it has been shown that there is no corporeal or material substance: it remains therefore that the cause of ideas is an incorporeal active substance or Spirit.

27. A spirit is one simple, undivided, active being: as it perceives ideas it is called the *understanding*, and as it produces or otherwise operates about them it is called the *will*. Hence there can be no *idea* formed of a soul or spirit; for all ideas whatever, being passive and inert (*vide* Sec. 25), they cannot represent unto us, by way of image or likeness, that which acts. A little attention will make it plain to anyone, that to have an idea which shall be like that active principle of motion and change of ideas is absolutely impossible. Such is the nature of *spirit*, or that which acts, that it cannot be of itself perceived, but only by the effects which it produceth. If any man shall doubt of the truth of what is here delivered, let him but reflect and try if he can frame the idea of any power or active being, and whether he hath ideas of two principal powers, marked by the names *will* and *understanding*, distinct from each other as well as from a third idea of substance or being in general, with a relative notion of its supporting or being the subject of the aforesaid powers—which is signified by the name *soul* or *spirit*. This is what some hold; but, so far as I can see, the words *will, soul, spirit*, do not stand for different ideas, or, in truth, for any idea at all, but for something which is very different from ideas, and which, being an agent, cannot be like unto, or represented by, any idea whatsoever. Though it must be owned at the same time that we have some *notion* of soul, spirit, and the operations of the mind such as willing, loving, hating; inasmuch as we know or understand the meaning of these words.

28. I find I can excite ideas in my mind at pleasure, and vary and shift the scene as oft as I think fit. It is no more than willing, and straightway this or that idea arises in my fancy; and by the same power it is obliterated and makes way for another. This making and unmaking of ideas doth very properly denominate the mind active. Thus much is certain and grounded on experience; but when we think of unthinking agents or of exciting ideas exclusive of volition, we only amuse ourselves with words.

29. But, whatever power I may have over my own thoughts, I find the ideas actually perceived by sense have not a like dependence on my will. When in broad daylight I open my eyes, it is not in my power to

choose whether I shall see or no, or to determine what particular objects shall present themselves to my view; and so likewise as to the hearing and other senses, the ideas imprinted on them are not creatures of my will. There is therefore some other will or spirit that produces them.

30. The ideas of sense are more strong, lively, and distinct than those of the imagination; they have likewise a steadiness, order, and coherence, and are not excited at random, as those which are the effects of human wills often are, but in a regular train or series, the admirable connection whereof sufficiently testifies the wisdom and benevolence of its Author. Now the set rules or established methods wherein the mind we depend on excites in us the ideas of sense, are called the *laws of nature;* and these we learn by experience, which teaches us that such and such ideas are attended with such and such other ideas, in the ordinary course of things.

31. This gives us a sort of foresight which enables us to regulate our actions for the benefit of life. And without this we should be eternally at a loss: we could not know how to act anything that might procure us the least pleasure, or remove the least pain of sense. That food nourishes, sleep refreshes, and fire warms us; that to sow in the seed-time is the way to reap in the harvest; and, in general, that to obtain such or such ends, such or such means are conducive—all this we know, not by discovering any necessary connection between our ideas, but only by the observation of the settled laws of nature, without which we should be all in uncertainty and confusion, and a grown man no more know how to manage himself in the affairs of life than an infant just born.

32. And yet this insistent uniform working, which so evidently displays the goodness and wisdom of that governing Spirit whose will constitutes the laws of nature, is so far from leading our thought to Him, that it rather sends them wandering after second causes. For, when we perceive certain ideas of sense constantly followed by other ideas and we know this is not of our own doing, we forthwith attribute power and agency to the ideas themselves, and make one the cause of another, than which nothing can be more absurd and unintelligible. Thus, for example, having observed that when we perceive by sight a certain round luminous figure we at the same time perceive by touch the idea or sensation called heat, we do from thence conclude the sun to be the cause of heat. And in like manner perceiving the motion and collision of bodies to be attended with sound, we are inclined to think the latter the effect of the former.

33. The ideas imprinted on the senses by the Author of nature are called *real things;* and those excited in the imagination, being less regular, vivid, and constant, are more properly termed *ideas,* or *images* of

things, which they copy and represent. But then our sensations, be they never so vivid and distinct, are nevertheless ideas, that is, they exist in the mind, or are perceived by it, as truly as the ideas of its own framing. The ideas of sense are allowed to have more reality in them, that is, to be more strong, orderly, and coherent than the creatures of the mind; but this is no argument that they exist without the mind. They are also less dependent on the spirit, or thinking substance which perceives them, in that they are excited by the will of another and more powerful spirit; yet still they are *ideas,* and certainly no idea, whether faint or strong, can exist otherwise than in a mind perceiving it.

142. After what hath been said, it is, I suppose, plain that our souls are not to be known in the same manner as senseless, inactive objects, or by the way of *idea. Spirits* and *ideas* are things so wholly different, that when we say 'they exist,' 'they are known,' or the like, these words must not be thought to signify anything common to both natures. There is nothing alike or common in them: and to expect that by any multiplication or enlargement of our faculties we may be enabled to know a spirit as we do a triangle, seems as absurd as if we should hope to see a sound. . . . We may not, I think, strictly be said to have an *idea* of an active being, or of an action, although we may be said to have a *notion* of them. I have some knowledge or notion of my mind, and its acts about ideas, inasmuch as I know or understand what is meant by these words. What I know, that I have some notion of. I will not say that the terms 'idea' and 'notion' may not be used convertibly, if the world will have it so; but yet it conduceth to clearness and propriety that we distinguish things very different by different names. . . .

145. From what hath been said, it is plain that we cannot know the existence of other spirits otherwise than by their operations, or the ideas by them excited in us. I perceive several motions, changes, and combinations of ideas, that inform me there are certain particular agents, like myself, which accompany them and concur in their production. Hence, the knowledge I have of other spirits is not immediate, as is the knowledge of my ideas; but depending on the intervention of ideas, by me referred to agents or spirits distinct from myself, as effects or concomitant signs.

146. But though there be some things which convince us human agents are concerned in producing them; yet it is evident to everyone that those things which are called the works of nature, that is, the far greater part of the ideas or sensations perceived by us, are not produced by, or dependent on, the wills of men. There is therefore some other Spirit that causes them; since it is repugnant that they should subsist by

themselves. (See Sec. 29.) But if we attentively consider the constant regularity, order, and concatenation of natural things, the surprising magnificence, beauty, and perfection of the larger, and the exquisite contrivance of the smaller parts of creation, together with the exact harmony and correspondence of the whole, but above all the never enough admired laws of pain and pleasure, and the instincts or natural inclinations, appetites, and passions of animals; I say if we consider all these things, and at the same time attend to the meaning and import of the attributes One, Eternal, Infinitely Wise, Good, and Perfect, we shall clearly perceive that they belong to the aforesaid Spirit, "who works all in all," and "by whom all things consist."

147. Hence, it is evident that God is known as certainly and immediately as any other mind or spirit whatsoever distinct from ourselves. We may even assert that the existence of God is far more evidently perceived than the existence of men; because the effects of nature are infinitely more numerous and considerable than those ascribed to human agents. There is not any one mark that denotes a man, or effect produced by him, which does not more strongly evince the being of that Spirit who is the Author of Nature. For it is evident that in affecting other persons the will of man hath no other object than barely the motion of the limbs of his body; but that such a motion should be attended by, or excite any idea in the mind of another, depends wholly on the will of the Creator. He alone it is who, "upholding all things by the word of His power," maintains that intercourse between spirits whereby they are able to perceive the existence of each other. And yet this pure and clear light which enlightens everyone is itself invisible.

149. It is therefore plain that nothing can be more evident to anyone that is capable of the least reflection than the existence of God, or a Spirit, who is intimately present to our minds, producing in them all that variety of ideas or sensations which continually affect us, on whom we have an absolute and entire dependence, in short "in whom we live, and move, and have our being." . . .

STUDY QUESTIONS

1. According to Berkeley, what are the different classes of ideas? Would you consider Berkeley to be an *empiricist?* State the reasons for your answer.
2. What is the meaning of existence as applied to sensible things? Can things have a real or natural existence apart from any mind?
3. What is the significance of Berkeley's treatment of abstract ideas for his

principle that "to be is to be perceived"? Can you separate in thought "the being of a sensible thing from its being perceived"? Discuss.

4. What objection does Berkeley have to the notion of a material substratum? Why does he say that the notion of matter or corporeal substance is contradictory?

5. Explain the nature of primary and secondary qualities, show how Berkeley distinguishes between them, and indicate the relevance of his analysis to his own position.

6. State in detail Berkeley's arguments against the existence of a material substance. What might be the motivation for his denial of materialism?

7. What is Berkeley's conception or notion of spirit or soul? Can we have an *idea* of soul or spirit? Why or why not? What is the basic difference between spirit and idea? What knowledge can I have of other spirits?

8. Is Berkeley a *solipsist*? Does he deny the real and continued existence of things independent of his own mind? What is his conception of the world of nature?

9. What is the purpose and the place of God in the metaphysics of Berkeley? Does he argue in any way for God's existence? To what extent does his system depend upon God?

Immanuel Kant

REVOLUTION IN METAPHYSICS

Introductory Note.   In his chief work, *Critique of Pure Reason* (which perhaps more than any other book of modern philosophy has influenced subsequent philosophic thought), Kant attempts to determine the limits as well as the general contours of a science of metaphysics. In the following selections from the Preface and Introduction, he characterizes his endeavor as a veritable revolution of thought, comparable to the Copernican revolution in astronomy.

Metaphysics, Kant states, is known as the oldest of the sciences and might also last the longest, not likely to be given up even if all the other sciences "were swallowed up in the abyss of an all-destroying barbarism." For metaphysics arises out of an ever-active concern of human reason to discover the principles that govern all our experience and to provide an insight into the internal structure of our world and of reality as a whole.

In connection with the effective pursuit of this function of metaphysics, Kant points out, there immediately arises a question of the utmost importance, the answer to which means "life or death to metaphysics." For the knowledge

From Immanuel Kant, *Critique of Pure Reason,* translated by F. Max Müller, London and New York, The Macmillan Company, 1896, from the Preface to the First Edition, Preface to the Second Edition, and Introduction; with minor alterations. Also from Immanuel Kant, *Prolegomena,* translated by Dr. Paul Carus, Chicago, The Open Court Publishing Co., 1902, pp. 141, 142.

For biographical information see the note included with the selection on Ethics (pages 81-82).

that metaphysics seeks cannot be derived from human experience, since the inner principles that govern all our experience are not themselves a matter of experience. And this would mean that metaphysics necessarily aims at establishing what Kant calls "*a priori* knowledge"—that is, "knowledge which is absolutely independent of all experience" as contrasted with *a posteriori* or empirical knowledge such as we use in the natural sciences. But then we are faced with the question: is such a knowledge—for instance, whether or not the world had a beginning in time—attainable at all? Perhaps it is a delusion of the mind? And is it not a fact that metaphysics in the past has been nothing more than "an arena for those who wish to exercise themselves in mock fights, and where no combatant has, as yet, succeeded in gaining an inch of ground"? Will this not necessarily "fill everyone with doubts as to its possibility"?

Kant reminds us here of David Hume, his great contemporary, who came to this very conclusion from his own studies—namely, that an *a priori* knowledge that would add to the understanding of our world of experience is entirely impossible. For he argued that such knowledge, having no ground in experience, would be incapable of being submitted to empirical tests, and thus a demonstration of its truth would be impossible.

It is at this point that Kant makes his famous proposal for a "Copernican turn" in metaphysics as a working hypothesis. In striving for metaphysical knowledge, Kant declares, it has always been supposed that this knowledge (as all other knowledge) "must conform to the objects" into which it inquires. But while adhering to this supposition, all attempts to establish *a priori* knowledge about our world of experience "have come to nothing," for no tests to demonstrate the truth of such a knowledge were available. Why then not experiment with a hypothesis which assumes the exact reverse of it; namely, not that our perception must conform to the constitution of the object, but on the contrary that "the object (as an object of the senses) conforms to the constitution of our faculty of perception"? *A priori* metaphysical knowledge would then appear at least possible. For it would be concerned with discovering the rules that the "constitution of our faculty of perception" imposes upon the perception of its objects. And such rules or principles of perception would not be a matter of experience themselves, although objects of experience would be subject to them.

His experiment with this hypothesis, Kant believes, has proved successful, and the pursuit of metaphysical knowledge has been demonstrated to be a rightful one, narrow as are the limits of the pursuit. For it is no longer the constitution of the world and its objects in and by themselves that metaphysics seeks to unravel, but rather the inner workings of the human mind, which prescribes a structural form to the world in such a manner that objects appear in it. In other words, a science of metaphysics can be established, but it cannot accomplish what so far has been its most essential purpose: to go "beyond the frontier of possible experience." For beyond this frontier lies the world of things unperceived and unperceivable by the human mind. Kant calls them things-in-themselves—indicating a realm that, precisely because of its independence of the mind, must always remain unknown to us.

THE PREDICAMENT OF METAPHYSICS

Human reason has this peculiar fate that, with reference to one class of its knowledge, it is always troubled with questions which cannot be ignored, because they spring from the very nature of reason, and which cannot be answered, because they transcend the powers of human reason.

Nor is human reason to be blamed for this. It begins with principles which, in the course of experience, it must follow, and which are sufficiently confirmed by experience. With these again, according to the necessities of its nature, it rises higher and higher to more remote conditions. But when it perceives that in this way its work remains forever incomplete, because the questions never cease, it finds itself constrained to take refuge in principles which exceed every possible empirical application, and nevertheless seem so unobjectionable that even ordinary common sense agrees with them. Thus, however, reason becomes involved in darkness and contradictions, from which, no doubt, it may conclude that errors must be lurking somewhere, but without being able to discover them, because the principles which it follows transcend all the limits of experience and therefore withdraw themselves from all empirical tests. It is the battlefield of these endless controversies which is called *metaphysics*.

There was a time when metaphysics was called the *Queen* of all the sciences, and, if the will were taken for the deed, the exceeding importance of her subject might well have secured to her that place of honor. At present it is the fashion to despise metaphysics, and the poor matron, forlorn and forsaken, complains like Hecuba: "A short while ago in the highest position . . . I am now led away, expelled and helpless." (Ovid, *Metam.*)

At first the rule of metaphysics, under the dominion of the *dogmatists,* was *despotic.* But as the laws still bore the traces of an old barbarism, internal wars and complete *anarchy* broke out, and the *sceptics,* a kind of nomads, despising all settled culture of the land, broke up from time to time all civil society. Fortunately their number was small, and they could not prevent the old settlers from returning to cultivate the ground afresh, though without any fixed plan or agreement. . . . At present, after every-

Critique of Pure Reason, from the Preface to the First Edition.

thing has been tried, so they say, and tried in vain, the prevailing mood is that of weariness and complete *indifferentism,* the mother of chaos and night in all sciences but, at the same time, the spring or, at least, the prelude of their near reform and of a new light, after an ill-applied study has rendered them dark, confused, and useless. . . .

This indifferentism, showing itself in the very midst of the most flourishing state of all sciences, and affecting the very science the teaching of which, if it could be had, would be the last to be surrendered, is a phenomenon well worthy of our attention and consideration. It is clearly the result, not of the carelessness, but of the matured *judgment* of our age, which refuses to be any longer put off with illusory knowledge. It is, at the same time, a powerful appeal to reason to undertake anew the most difficult of its duties, namely, self-knowledge, and to institute a tribunal which should protect the just rights of reason, but dismiss all groundless claims, and should do this not by means of irresponsible decrees, but according to the eternal and unalterable laws of reason. This tribunal is no other than *the Critique of Pure Reason.* . . .

PURE AND EMPIRICAL KNOWLEDGE

That all our knowledge begins with experience there can be no doubt. For how should the faculty of knowledge be called into activity, if not by objects which affect our senses, and which partly of themselves represent something to us, partly rouse the activity of our understanding to compare, to connect, or to separate it; and thus to convert the raw material of our sensuous impressions into a knowledge of objects, which we call experience? *In respect of time,* therefore, no knowledge within us is antecedent to experience, but all knowledge begins with it.

But although all our knowledge begins *with* experience, it does not follow that it arises *from* experience. For it is quite possible that even our empirical knowledge is a compound of that which we receive through impressions, and of that which our own faculty of knowledge (incited only by sensuous impressions), supplies from itself, a supplement which we do not distinguish from that raw material, until long practice has roused our attention and rendered us capable of separating one from the other.

It is therefore a question which deserves at least closer investigation, and cannot be disposed of at first sight, whether there exists a knowledge independent of experience, and even of all impressions of the senses?

Op. cit., from the Introduction, I.

Such *knowledge* is called *a priori,* and distinguished from *empirical* knowledge, which has its sources *a posteriori,* that is, in experience.

This term *a priori,* however, is not yet definite enough to indicate the full meaning of our question. For people are wont to say, even with regard to knowledge derived from experience, that we have it, or might have it, *a priori,* because we derive it from experience, not *immediately,* but from a general rule, which, however, has itself been derived from experience. Thus one would say of a person who undermines the foundations of his house, that he might have known *a priori* that it would tumble down, that is, that he need not wait for the experience of its really tumbling down. But still he could not know this entirely *a priori,* because he had first to learn from experience that bodies are heavy, and will fall when their supports are taken away.

We shall therefore, in what follows, understand by knowledge *a priori* knowledge which is *absolutely* independent of all experience, and not of this or that experience only. Opposed to this is empirical knowledge, or such as is possible *a posteriori* only, that is, by experience. Knowledge *a priori,* if mixed up with nothing empirical, is called *pure.* Thus the proposition, for example, that every change has its cause, is a proposition *a priori,* but not pure: because change is a concept which can only be derived from experience. . . .

ANALYTIC AND SYNTHETIC JUDGMENTS

In all judgments in which there is a relation between subject and predicate (I speak of affirmative judgments only, the application to negative ones being easy), that relation can be of two kinds. Either the predicate B belongs to the subject A as something contained (though covertly) in the concept A; or B lies outside the sphere of the concept A, though somehow connected with it. In the former case I call the judgment *analytic,* in the latter *synthetic.* Analytic judgments (affirmative) are therefore those in which the connection of the predicate with the subject is conceived through identity, while others in which that connection is conceived without identity, may be called synthetic. The former might be called *explicative,* the latter *expanding judgments,* because in the former nothing is added by the predicate to the concept of the subject, but the concept is only divided into its constituent concepts which were always conceived as existing within it, though confusedly; while the latter add to the concept of the subject a predicate not conceived as

Op. cit., from the Introduction, IV.

existing within it, and not to be extracted from it by any process of mere analysis. If I say, for instance, All bodies are extended, this is an analytic judgment. I need not go beyond the concept connected with the name of body, in order to find that extension is connected with it. I have only to analyze this concept and become conscious of the manifold elements always contained in it, in order to find that predicate. This is therefore an analytic judgment. But if I say, All bodies are heavy, the predicate is something quite different from what I think as the mere concept of body. The addition of such a predicate gives us a synthetic judgment.

Empirical judgments, as such, are all synthetic; for it would be absurd to found an analytic judgment on experience, because, in order to form such a judgment, I need not at all step out of my concept, or appeal to the testimony of experience. That a body is extended, is a proposition perfectly certain *a priori,* and not an empirical judgment. For, before I call in experience, I am already in possession of all the conditions of my judgment in the concept of body itself. I have only to draw out from it, according to the principle of contradiction, the required predicate, and I thus become conscious, at the same time, of the necessity of the judgment, which experience could never teach me. But, though I do not include the predicate of gravity in the general concept of body, that concept, nevertheless, indicates an object of experience through one of its parts: so that I may add other parts also of the same experience, besides those which belonged to the former concept. I may, first, by an *analytic* process, realize the concept of body, through the predicates of extension, impermeability, form, etc., all of which are contained in it. Afterwards I expand my knowledge, and looking back to the experience from which my concept of body was abstracted, I find gravity always connected with the before-mentioned predicates, and therefore I add it *synthetically* to that concept as a predicate. It is, therefore, experience on which the possibility of the synthesis of the predicate of gravity with the concept of body is founded: because both concepts, though neither of them is contained in the other, belong to each other, though accidentally only, as parts of a whole, namely, of experience, which is itself a synthetic connection of (sense) perceptions.

In synthetic judgments *a priori,* however, that help is entirely wanting. If I want to go beyond the concept A in order to find another concept B connected with it, where is there anything on which I may rest and through which a synthesis might become possible, considering that I cannot have the advantage of looking about in the field of experience? Take the proposition that all which happens has its cause. In the concept of something that happens I no doubt conceive of an existence which is preceded by a time, etc., and from this certain analytic judgments may be deduced. But the concept of cause is entirely outside that concept, and indicates something different from that which happens, and is by no means contained in that notion. How can I venture then to predicate of that which happens something totally different from it, and to apprehend the concept of cause, though not contained in it, as belonging to it, and belonging to it by necessity? What is here the unknown x, on which the understanding may rest in order to find beyond the concept A a foreign predicate B, which nevertheless is believed to be connected with it? It cannot be experience, because the proposition that all that happens has its cause represents this second predicate as added to the subject not only with greater generality than experience can ever supply, but also with a character of necessity, and therefore purely *a priori,* and based on concepts. All our speculative knowledge *a priori* aims at and rests on such synthetic, *i.e.* expanding propositions, for the analytic judgments are no doubt very important and necessary, yet only in order to arrive at that clearness of concepts which is requisite for such a safe and wide synthesis, as will lead to a really new addition to what we possess already.

APPLICATION TO THE THEORETICAL SCIENCES OF REASON

All mathematical judgments are synthetic. This proposition, though incontestably certain, seems to have hitherto escaped the observation of those who are engaged in the anatomy of human reason: nay, to be directly opposed to all their conjectures. For as it was found that all mathematical conclusions proceed according to the principle of contradiction (which is required by the nature of all apodictic certainty), it was supposed that the fundamental principles of mathematics also rested on the authority of the same principle of contradiction. This, however, was a mistake: for though a synthetic proposition may be understood according to the principle of contradiction, this can only be if another synthetic proposition is presupposed, from which the latter is deduced, but never by itself.

First of all, we ought to observe, that mathematical propositions, properly so called, are always judgments *a priori,* and not empirical, because they carry along with them necessity, which can never be deduced from experience. If people should object to this, I am quite willing to confine my statement to *pure mathematics,* the very concept of which

Op. cit., from the Introduction, V.

implies that it does not contain empirical, but only pure knowledge *a priori*.

At first sight one might suppose indeed that the proposition $7+5=12$ is merely analytic, following, according to the principle of contradiction, from the concept of a sum of 7 and 5. But, if we look more closely, we shall find that the concept of the sum of 7 and 5 contains nothing beyond the union of both sums into one, whereby nothing is told us as to what this single number may be which combines both. We by no means arrive at a concept of Twelve, by thinking that union of Seven and Five; and we may analyze our concept of such a possible sum as long as we will, still we shall never discover in it the concept of Twelve. We must go beyond these concepts, and call in the assistance of the perception* corresponding to one of the two, for instance our five fingers, or five points, and so by degrees add the units of the Five, given in perception, to the concept of the Seven. For I first take the number 7, and using the perception of the fingers of my hand, in order to form with it the concept of the 5, I gradually add the units, which I before took together to make up the number 5, by means of the image of my hand, to the number 7, and I thus see the number 12 arising before me. That 5 *should* be added to 7 was no doubt implied in my concept of a sum $7+5$, but not that this sum should be equal to 12. An arithmetical proposition is, therefore, always synthetic, which is seen more easily still by taking larger numbers, where we clearly perceive that, turn and twist our conceptions as we may, we could never, by means of the mere analysis of our concepts and without the help of perception, arrive at the sum that is wanted.

Nor is any proposition of pure geometry analytic. That the straight line between two points is the shortest, is a synthetic proposition. For my concept of *straight* contains nothing of quantity, but a quality only. The concept of the shortest is, therefore, wholly an addition, and cannot be deduced from the concept of the straight line by any analysis whatsoever. The aid of perception, therefore, must be called in, by which alone the synthesis is possible. . . .

Natural science contains synthetic judgments a priori as principles. I shall adduce, as examples, a few propositions only, such as, that in all changes of the material world the quantity of matter always remains unchanged; or that in all communication of motion, action and reaction must always equal each other. It is clear not only that both convey necessity, and that, therefore, their origin is *a priori*, but also that they

---

* Translated here and further below from the German *Anschauung*, generally rendered as *intuition*.

are synthetic propositions. For in the concept of matter I do not conceive its permanency, but only its presence in the space which it fills. I therefore go beyond the concept of matter in order to add on to it something *a priori*, which I did not before think *in it*. The proposition is, therefore, not analytic, but synthetic, and yet *a priori*, and the same applies to the other propositions of the pure part of natural science.

Metaphysics, even if we look upon it as hitherto a tentative science only, which, however, is indispensable to us, owing to the very nature of human reason, is meant to *contain synthetic knowledge a priori*. Its object is not at all merely to analyze such concepts as we make to ourselves of things *a priori*, and thus to explain them analytically, but to expand our knowledge *a priori*. This we can only do by means of principles which add something to a given concept that was not contained in it; nay, we even attempt, by means of synthetic judgments *a priori*, to go so far beyond a given concept that experience itself cannot follow us: as, for instance, in the proposition that the world must have a first beginning. Thus, at least *according to its intentions*, metaphysics consists merely of synthetic propositions *a priori*.

THE PROBLEM OF METAPHYSICS

Much is gained if we are able to bring a number of investigations under the formula of one single problem. For we thus not only facilitate our own work by defining it accurately, but enable also everybody else who likes to examine it to form a judgment, whether we have really done justice to our purpose or not. Now the real problem of pure reason is contained in the question, HOW ARE SYNTHETIC JUDGMENTS A PRIORI POSSIBLE?

That metaphysics has hitherto remained in so vacillating a state of ignorance and contradiction is entirely due to people not having thought sooner of this problem, or perhaps even of a distinction between *analytic* and *synthetic* judgments. The solution of this problem, or sufficient proof that a possibility [for synthetic judgments *a priori*] which is to be explained does in reality not exist at all, is the question of life or death to metaphysics. *David Hume*, who among all philosophers approached nearest to that problem, though he was far from conceiving it with sufficient definiteness and universality, confining his attention only to the synthetic proposition of the connection of an effect with its causes, arrived at the conclusion that such a proposition *a priori* is entirely

Op. cit., from the Introduction, VI.

impossible. According to his conclusions, everything which we call metaphysics would turn out to be a mere delusion of reason, fancying that it knows by itself what in reality is only borrowed from experience, and has assumed by mere habit the appearance of necessity. If he had grasped our problem in all its universality, he would never have thought of an assertion which destroys all pure philosophy, because he would have perceived that, according to his argument, no pure mathematical science was possible either, on account of its certainly containing synthetic propositions *a priori;* and from such an assertion his good sense would probably have saved him.

On the solution of our problem depends, at the same time, the possibility of the pure employment of reason, in establishing and developing all those sciences which contain a theoretical *a priori* knowledge of objects. . . .

As to *metaphysics,* the bad progress which it has hitherto made, and the impossibility of asserting of any of the metaphysical systems yet brought forward that it really exists, so far as its essential aim is concerned, must fill every one with doubts as to its possibility. . . .

REVOLUTIONS IN MATHEMATICS AND THE NATURAL SCIENCES

Whether the treatment of that class of knowledge with which reason is occupied follows the secure method of a science or not, can easily be determined by the result. If, after repeated preparations, it comes to a standstill, as soon as its real goal is approached, or is obliged, in order to reach it, to retrace its steps again and again, and strike into fresh paths; again, if it is impossible to produce unanimity among those who are engaged in the same work, as to the manner in which their common object should be obtained, we may be convinced that such a study is far from having attained to the secure method of a science, but is groping only in the dark. In that case we are conferring a great benefit on reason, if we only find out the right path, though many things should have to be surrendered as useless, which were comprehended in the original aim that had been chosen without sufficient reflection. . . .

Mathematics and *physics* are the two theoretical sciences of reason, which have to determine their *objects a priori;* the former quite purely, the latter partially so, and partially from other sources of knowledge besides reason.

Op. cit., from the Preface to the Second Edition.

Mathematics, from the earliest time to which the history of human reason can reach, has followed, among that wonderful people of the Greeks, the safe way of a science. But it must not be supposed that it was as easy for mathematics as for logic, in which reason is concerned with itself alone, to find, or rather to make for itself that royal road. I believe, on the contrary, that there was a long period of tentative work (chiefly still among the Egyptians), and that the change is to be ascribed to a *revolution,* produced by the happy thought of a single man, whose experiment pointed unmistakably to the path that had to be followed, and opened and traced out for the most distant times the safe way of a science. . . .

A new light flashed on the first man who demonstrated the properties of the *isosceles triangle* (whether his name was *Thales* or any other name), for he found that he had not to investigate what he saw in the figure, or the mere concept of that figure, and thus to learn its properties; but that he had to produce (by construction) what he had himself, according to concepts *a priori,* placed into that figure and represented in it, so that, in order to know anything with certainty *a priori,* he must not attribute to that figure anything beyond what necessarily follows from what he has himself placed into it, in accordance with the concept.

It took a much longer time before natural science entered on the highway of science: for no more than a century and a half has elapsed since *Bacon's* ingenious proposal partly initiated that discovery, partly, as others were already on the right track, gave a new impetus to it—a discovery which, like the former, can only be explained by a rapid intellectual revolution. In what I have to say, I shall confine myself to natural science, so far as it is founded on *empirical* principles.

When *Galileo* let balls of a particular weight, which he had determined himself, roll down an inclined plane, or *Torricelli* made the air carry a weight, which he had previously determined to be equal to that of a definite volume of water, a new light flashed on all students of nature. They comprehended that reason has insight into that only, which she herself produces on her own plan, and that she must move forward with the principles of her judgments, according to fixed law, and compel nature to answer her questions, but not allow herself to be kept by nature, as it were in leading-strings, because otherwise accidental observations, made on no previously fixed plan, will never converge toward a necessary law, which is the only thing that reason seeks and requires. Reason, holding in one hand its principles, according to which concordant appearances alone can be admitted as laws of nature, and in the other hand the experiment, which it has devised according to those principles, must approach nature, in order to be taught by it: but not in the character of a pupil, who agrees to everything the master likes, but as an appointed judge, who compels the witnesses to answer the questions which he himself proposes. Therefore even the science of physics entirely owes the beneficial revolution in its way of thinking to the happy notion, that we ought to seek in nature (and not import into it by means of fiction) whatever reason must learn from nature, and could not know by itself, and that we must do this in accordance with what reason itself has originally placed into nature. Thus only has the study of nature entered on the secure path of a science, after having for many centuries done nothing but grope in the dark.

METAPHYSICS AND THE NEED
FOR A COPERNICAN REVOLUTION

Metaphysics, a completely isolated and speculative science of reason, which rises far above all teachings of experience, and does so by means of concepts only (not, like mathematics, through their application to perception), in which reason therefore is meant to be her own pupil, has hitherto not been so fortunate as to enter on the secure path of a science, although it is older than all other sciences, and would remain, even if all the rest were swallowed up in the abyss of an all-destroying barbarism. In metaphysics, reason, even if it tries only to understand *a priori* (as it pretends to do) those laws which are confirmed by the commonest experience, is constantly brought to a standstill, and we are obliged again and again to retrace our steps because they do not lead us where we want to go; while as to any unanimity among those who are engaged in the same work, there is so little of it in metaphysics, that it has rather become an arena, specially destined, it would seem, for those who wish to exercise themselves in mock fights, and where no combatant has, as yet, succeeded in gaining an inch of ground that he could call permanently his own. It cannot be denied, therefore, that the method of metaphysics has hitherto consisted in groping only, and, what is the worst, in groping among mere concepts.

What then can be the cause that hitherto no secure method of science has been discovered? Shall we say that it is impossible? Then why should nature have visited our reason with restless aspiration to look for it, as if it were its most important concern? Nay more, how little

Op. cit., from the Preface to the Second Edition.

should we be justified in trusting our reason if, with regard to one of the most important objects we wish to know, it not only abandons us, but lures us on by vain hopes, and in the end betrays us! Or, if hitherto we have only failed to meet with the right path, what indications are there to make us hope that, if we renew our researches, we shall be more successful than others before us?

The examples of mathematics and natural science, which by one revolution have become what they now are, seem to me sufficiently remarkable to induce us to consider, what may have been the essential element in that intellectual revolution which has proved so beneficial, and to make the experiment of imitating them, at least so far as their analogy as sciences of reason with metaphysics allows.

Hitherto it has been supposed that all our knowledge must conform to the objects: but, under that supposition, all attempts to establish anything about them *a priori*, by means of concepts, and thus to enlarge our knowledge, have come to nothing. The experiment therefore ought to be made, whether we should not succeed better with the problems of metaphysics, by assuming that the objects must conform to our knowledge, for this would better agree with the demanded possibility of an *a priori* knowledge of them, which is to determine something about objects, before they are given us. We have here the same case as with the first thought of *Copernicus,* who, not being able to get on in the explanation of the movements of the heavenly bodies, as long as he assumed that all the stars turned round the spectator, tried, whether he could not succeed better, by assuming the spectator to be turning round, and the stars to be at rest. A similar experiment may be tried in metaphysics, so far as the *perception* of objects is concerned. If the perception had to conform to the constitution of objects, I do not see how we could know anything of it *a priori*; but if the object (as an object of the senses) conforms to the constitution of our faculty of perception, I can very well conceive such a possibility. As, however, I can not rest in these perceptions, if they are to become knowledge, but have to refer them, as representing something, to an object, and must determine that object by them, I have the choice of admitting, either that the *concepts,* through which I do this determining, conform to the object, being then again in the same perplexity on account of the manner how I can know anything about it *a priori*; or that the objects, or what is the same, the *experience* within which alone they are known (as given objects), must conform to those concepts. In the latter case, the solution becomes more easy, because experience, as a kind of knowledge, requires understanding, and I must therefore, even before objects are given to me, presuppose the rules of the understanding as existing within me *a priori*, these rules being expressed in concepts *a priori*, to which all objects of experience must necessarily conform, and with which they must agree. . . .

METAPHYSICS AS A CRITIQUE OF PURE REASON

This experiment . . . promises to metaphysics . . . the secure method of a science. For by thus changing our way of thinking, the possibility of knowledge *a priori* can well be explained, and, what is still more, the laws which lie *a priori* at the foundation of nature, as the sum total of the objects of experience, may be supplied with satisfactory proofs, neither of which was possible with the procedure hitherto adopted.

But there arises . . . a somewhat startling result, apparently most detrimental to the objects of metaphysics . . . namely, the impossibility of going with it beyond the frontier of possible experience, which is precisely the most essential purpose of metaphysical science. But here we have exactly the experiment which, by disproving the opposite, establishes the truth of that first estimate of our *a priori* knowledge of reason, namely, that it can refer to appearances only, but must leave the thing in itself though existing as unknown to us. For that which impels us by necessity to go beyond the limits of experience and of all appearances, is the *unconditioned,* which reason postulates in all things in themselves, and does so by necessity and by right with regard to everything conditioned. . . . If then we find that, under the supposition of our empirical knowledge conforming to the objects as things in themselves, the unconditioned *cannot be thought without contradiction,* while the contradiction vanishes when we suppose that our experience of things, as they are given to us, does not conform to them as they are in themselves, but, on the contrary, that these objects as appearances conform to our mode of representing them; and if, therefore, we thus find that the unconditioned is not to be met with in things, so far as we know them (that is, so far as they are given to us), but only so far as we do not know them, that is, so far as they are things in themselves, we clearly perceive that, what we at first assumed tentatively only, is fully confirmed.[1] . . .

Op. cit., from the Preface to the Second Edition.

[1] In the same manner the laws of gravity, determining the movements of the heavenly bodies, imparted the character of established certainty to what *Copernicus* had assumed at first as an hypothesis only, and proved at the same time the invisible force

This attempt to introduce a complete revolution in the procedure of metaphysics, after the *example* of the geometricians and natural scientists, constitutes the aim of the *Critique of Pure Speculative Reason.*

[This] Critique* stands in the same relation to the common metaphysics of the schools, as *chemistry* does to *alchemy,* or as *astronomy* to the *astrology* of the fortune-teller. I pledge myself that nobody who has read through and through, and grasped the principles of, the Critique . . . will ever return to that old and sophistical pseudo-science; but will rather with a certain delight look forward to metaphysics which is now indeed in his power. . . .

All false art, all vain wisdom, lasts its time, but finally destroys itself, and its highest culture is also the epoch of its decay. That this time is come for metaphysics appears from the state into which it has fallen among all learned nations, despite of all the zeal with which other sciences of every kind are prosecuted. . . .

That the human mind will ever give up metaphysical researches is as little to be expected as that we should prefer to give up breathing altogether, to avoid inhaling impure air. There will therefore always be metaphysics in the world; nay, everyone, especially every man of reflection, will have it, and for want of a recognized standard, will shape it for himself after his own pattern. What has hitherto been called metaphysics, cannot satisfy any critical mind, but to forego it entirely is impossible; therefore a *Critique of Pure Reason* itself must now be *attempted* or, if one exists, *investigated,* and brought to the full test, because there is no other means of supplying this pressing want.

STUDY QUESTIONS

1. What accounts for and justifies the disrepute in which metaphysics (as Kant sees it) has been held?
2. How do we distinguish between knowledge *a priori* and *a posteriori?*
3. Explain and illustrate the distinction between analytic and synthetic judgments.

(the *Newtonian* attraction) which holds the universe together, which would have remained forever undiscovered, if Copernicus had not dared, by an hypothesis, which, though contradicting the senses, was yet true, to seek the observed movements, not in the heavenly bodies, but in the spectator. I also propose my own view of metaphysics, which has so many analogies with the Copernican hypothesis, as an hypothesis only, though, in the Critique itself, it is proved by means of our perceptions of space and time, and the elementary concepts of the understanding, not hypothetically, but apodictically; for I wish that people should observe the first attempts at such a change, which must always be hypothetical.

* This and the following two paragraphs are from the *Prolegomena.*

4. What is the difference between empirical judgments and synthetic judgments *a priori?*

5. How does Kant demonstrate that all mathematical judgments are synthetic?

6. In what sense do natural science and metaphysics contain synthetic knowledge *a priori?*

7. What does the possibility of metaphysics hinge upon and what was David Hume's position regarding it?

8. Through what thought–revolutions did mathematics and physics enter "the highway of science"?

9. What "Copernican revolution" may procure for metaphysics the secure method of a science?

10. What limitation of metaphysics results from this thought–revolution?

Martin Heidegger

EXISTENCE AND POETRY

Biographical Note. MARTIN HEIDEGGER (1889–   ) was born in a rural community of southwest Germany. His father was a craftsman. An early interest in theology—he spent three high-school years at a Jesuit school —soon shifted to philosophy, on which he concentrated while attending the University of Freiburg. There he became an instructor in philosophy at the age of twenty-six, received a professorship at the University of Marburg seven years later, and finally returned to Freiburg as successor to his teacher and friend, Edmund Husserl, the founder of phenomenological philosophy, upon the latter's retirement in 1928. Accepting at first the ideology of National Socialism, he was installed as Rector of the University at the beginning of the Hitler regime, but resigned from this post a year later. Twice he declined a call to the University of Berlin, and he continued in Freiburg until 1945, when the French Army of Occupation suspended his lecturing because of sympathies shown in the past for the Nazi regime. He was officially retired in 1949, but has lectured at the University since that time.

Heidegger is generally known as a representative of the existentialist movement in philosophy, although he himself objected to this designation. The work that won him the reputation as the foremost German philosopher was *Sein und Zeit* (1927), translated in English as *Being and Time* (1962).

From Martin Heidegger, "Hölderlin and the Essence of Poetry," translated by Douglas Scott, in *Existence and Being*, Chicago, Henry Regnery Company, 1949, pp. 293–315. Used by permission of the Henry Regnery Company and Vision Press, Ltd.

Other important books of which translations appeared are *What is Philosophy?* (1958), *Introduction to Metaphysics* (1959), and a collection of essays, published under the title *Existence and Being* (1949), to which this selection belongs.

* * *

Introductory Note.   At the end of his essay "What is Metaphysics?", Heidegger formulates the problem that looms behind his philosophy as the fundamental question: "Why is there Being at all rather than—Nothing?" In other words: how does it happen that there is Being and that we are now faced with it, challenged by it, immersed in it? This is a fundamental question since it is only in and through Being that a "life-world" appears: this world in which we live, which is one "of decision and production, of action and responsibility," in which we are held "in the bonds of supreme obligation," where "responsibility of a destiny" is encountered. How is it possible to meet such supreme obligation, such ultimate responsibility without truly understanding it? How can we truly understand it unless we are also aware of how it comes about, to what "the appearance of the world" is due?

Heidegger raises, but never answers this fundamental question in philosophical terms, for he believes philosophy as conceived of today is wholly unprepared to deal with it. On several occasions, however, he indicates the direction in which an answer must be sought. The clearest account is found in his essay "Hölderlin and the Essence of Poetry," which makes up the following selection. Seemingly concerned in it with the nature of poetry, he actually probes the ultimate problem of metaphysics itself in the area of poetry. He pursues the question, not of what poetry is, but why there is poetry at all. He asks to what the appearance of poetry, so intricately a part of our life-world, is due.

Two major steps are taken in the essay, both of far reaching implications. First Heidegger clarifies the intimate relationship that exists, as he sees it, between the essence of poetry and the pattern of human life. Poetry is revealed as "the inaugural naming of being and of the essence of all things," as "the establishing of being by means of the word," or as "the naming of the gods." Whatever we discuss and deal with in everyday language is made possible because poetry has been created first as "the primitive language of a historical people." Human living, which is based on "conversation," the actual use of language, is revealed as "fundamentally poetic," grounded in poetry. We thus arrive at a surprising result: poetry by its very nature contributes to world-making, world-creating; the appearance of our life-world is "contemporaneous with it."

The second step taken by Heidegger in the essay can be put in the form of another question. If the role that the poet (the word comes from the Greek *poiein,* meaning to make, to create) plays is that of a creator of our life–world, of "this earth," how does poetry itself come about, how does it happen that there are poets at all, and how does a poet create?

Heidegger courageously faces this difficult question; but just as Plato did in the *Meno* under similar circumstances, he takes refuge in his discussion in metaphorical language shrouding the answer. A verse from Hölderlin serves as a starting point:

> Full of merit, and yet poetically, dwells
> Man on this earth.

There are many things, so Heidegger interprets these words, which are due to man's creative efforts and for which credit is rightfully earned. Yet his life-world in its fundamental, its poetical aspect, "is not recompense, but a gift." From whom is the gift received? "The gods themselves bring us to language," they are found "addressing and, as it were, claiming us." They speak to the poet through "signs" and his speech "is the intercepting of these signs in order to pass them on to his own people." The poet presents "what he has glimpsed" and this is why there are poets and poetry. Yet he does not stand entirely alone. There is also the "voice of the people," which speaks of the same truth as the poet, although in general it is "not capable of saying of itself what is true" and needs to be helped and clarified. The poet thus occupies a realm of his own, the "realm of Between," which is between two poles that exercise control over him—that of "the gods" and that of "the people."

This is a realm of surpassing insight. In our age, no one but the poet makes the dreadful discovery that ours is indeed "a new time": that "of the gods that have fled *and* of the god that is coming." It is a time of extreme poverty and need "because it lies under a double lack and a double Not: the No-more of the gods that have fled and the Not-yet of the god that is coming."

INTRODUCTION: HÖLDERLIN—POET OF THE POETS

Why has Hölderlin's* work been chosen for the purpose of showing the essence of poetry? Why not Homer or Sophocles, why not Virgil or Dante, why not Shakespeare or Goethe? The essence of poetry is realized in the works of these poets too, and more richly even, than in the creative work of Hölderlin, which breaks off so early and abruptly.

This may be so. And yet Hölderlin has been chosen, and he alone. But generally speaking is it possible for the universal essence of poetry to be read off from the work of one single poet? Whatever is universal, that is to say, what is valid for many, can only be reached through a process of comparison. For this, one requires a sample containing the greatest possible diversity of poems and kinds of poetry. From this point of view Hölderlin's poetry is only one among many others. By itself it

---

* Friedrich Hölderlin (1770–1843), one of the greatest German poets, friend of Hegel and Schelling, who understood his vocation as that of "a poet in a time of need" and in visionary lyricism pronounced "the Holy as the work of gods and men." He succumbed to insanity in the later part of his life.

can in no way suffice as a criterion for determining the essence of poetry. Hence we fail in our purpose at the very outset. Certainly—so long as we take "essence of poetry" to mean what is gathered together into a universal concept, which is then valid in the same way for every poem. But this universal which thus applies equally to every particular, is always the indifferent, that essence which can never become essential.

Yet it is precisely this essential element of the essence that we are searching for—that which compels us to decide whether we are going to take poetry seriously and if so how, whether and to what extent we can bring with us the presuppositions necessary if we are to come under the sway of poetry.

Hölderlin has not been chosen because his work, one among many, realizes the universal essence of poetry, but solely because Hölderlin's poetry was borne on by the poetic vocation to write expressly of the essence of poetry. For us Hölderlin is in a pre-eminent sense *the poet of the poet*. That is why he compels a decision. . . .

We cannot here, as would have to be done, expound separately each of Hölderlin's poems one after the other. Instead let us take only five pointers which the poet gave on the subject of poetry. The necessary order in these sayings and their inner connectedness ought to bring before our eyes the essential essence of poetry.

POETRY AS INNOCENT

In a letter to his mother in January 1799, Hölderlin calls the writing of poetry "that most innocent of all occupations." To what extent is it the "most innocent"? Writing poetry appears in the modest guise of *play*. Unfettered, it invents its world of images and remains immersed in the realm of the imagined. This play thus avoids the seriousness of decisions, which always in one way or another create guilt. Hence writing poetry is completely harmless. And at the same time it is ineffectual; since it remains mere saying and speaking. It has nothing about it of action, which grasps hold directly of the real and alters it. Poetry is like a dream, and not reality; a playing with words, and not the seriousness of action. Poetry is harmless and ineffectual. For what can be less dangerous than mere speech? But in taking poetry to be the "most innocent of all occupations," we have not yet comprehended its essence. At any rate this gives us an indication of where we must look for it. Poetry creates its works in the realm and out of the "material" of language. What does Hölderlin say about language? Let us hear a second saying of the poet.

LANGUAGE, MOST DANGEROUS OF POSSESSIONS

In a framentary sketch, dating from the same period (1800) as the letter just quoted, the poet says:

> But man dwells in huts and wraps himself in the bashful garment, since he is more fervent and more attentive too in watching over the spirit, as the priestess the divine flame; this is his understanding. And therefore he has been given arbitrariness, and to him, godlike, has been given higher power to command and to accomplish, and therefore has language, most dangerous of possessions, been given to man, so that creating, destroying, and perishing and returning to the ever-living, to the mistress and mother, he may affirm what he is—that he has inherited, learned from thee, thy most divine possession, all-preserving love.

Language, the field of the "most innocent of all occupations," is the "most dangerous of possessions." How can these two be reconciled? Let us put this question aside for the moment and consider the three preliminary questions: 1. Whose possession is language? 2. To what extent is it the most dangerous of possessions? 3. In what sense is it really a possession?

First of all we notice where this saying about language occurs: in the sketch for a poem which is to describe who man is, in contrast to the other beings of nature; mention is made of the rose, the swans, the stag in the forest. So, distinguishing plants from animals, the fragment begins: "But man dwells in huts."

And who then is man? He who must affirm what he is. To affirm means to declare; but at the same time it means: to give in the declaration a guarantee of what is declared. Man is *he* who *is*, precisely in the affirmation of his own existence. This affirmation does not mean here an additional and supplementary expression of human existence, but it does in the process make plain the existence of man. But what must man affirm? That he belongs to the earth. This relation of belonging to consists in the fact that man is heir and learner in all things. But all these things are in conflict. That which keeps things apart in opposition and thus at the same time binds them together, is called by Hölderlin "intimacy." The affirmation of belonging to this intimacy occurs through the creation of a world and its ascent, and likewise through the destruction of a world and its decline. The affirmation of human existence and hence its essential consummation occurs through freedom of decision. This freedom lays hold of the necessary and places itself in the bonds of a supreme obligation. This bearing witness of belonging to all that is existent, becomes actual as history. In order that history may be possible, language has been given to man. It is one of man's possessions.

But to what extent is language the "most dangerous of possessions"? It is the danger of all dangers, because it creates initially the possibility of a danger. Danger is the threat to existence from what is existent. But now it is only by virtue of language at all that man is exposed to something manifest, which, *as* what is existent, afflicts and enflames man in his existence, and as what is non-existent deceives and disappoints. It is language which first creates the manifest conditions for menace and confusion to existence, and thus the possibility of the loss of existence, that is to say—danger. . . .

In what sense however is this most dangerous thing one of man's possessions? Language is his own property. It is at his disposal for the purpose of communicating his experiences, resolutions and moods. Language serves to give information. As a fit instrument for this, it is a "possession."[1] But the essence of language does not consist entirely in being a means of giving information. This definition does not touch its essential essence, but merely indicates an effect of its essence. Language is not a mere tool, one of the many which man possesses; on the contrary, it is only language that affords the very possibility of standing in the openness of the existent. Only where there is language, is there world, i.e. the perpetually altering circuit of decision and production, of action and responsibility, but also of commotion and arbitrariness, of decay and confusion. Only where world predominates, is there history. Language is a possession in a more fundamental sense. It is good for the fact that (i.e. it affords a guarantee that) man can *exist* historically. Language is not a tool at his disposal, rather it is that event which disposes of the supreme possibility of human existence. We must first of all be certain of this essence of language, in order to comprehend truly the sphere of action of poetry and with it poetry itself. How does language become actual? In order to find the answer to this question, let us consider a third saying of Hölderlin's.

[1] The German word *Gut,* which has been translated throughout as "possession," also has the meaning of "a good thing"; it is thus related to the English word "goods" as in "goods and chattels."

CONVERSATION AND THE BEING OF MEN

We come across this saying in a long and involved sketch for the unfinished poem which begins "Reconciler, you who never-believed . . .":

> Much has man learnt.
> Many of the heavenly ones has he named,
> Since we have been a conversation
> And have been able to hear from one another.

Let us first pick out from these lines the part which has a direct bearing on what we have said so far: "Since we have been a conversation . . ." We—mankind—are a conversation. The being of men is founded in language. But this only becomes actual in *conversation*. Nevertheless the latter is not merely a manner in which language is put into effect, rather it is only as conversation that language is essential. What we usually mean by language, namely, a stock of words and syntactical rules, is only a threshold of language. But now what is meant by "a conversation"? Plainly, the act of speaking with others about something. Then speaking also brings about the process of coming together. But Hölderlin says: "Since we have been a conversation and have been able to hear from one another." Being able to hear is not a mere consequence of speaking with one another, on the contrary it is rather pre-supposed in the latter process. But even the ability to hear is itself also adapted to the possibility of the word and makes use of it. The ability to speak and the ability to hear are equally fundamental. We are a conversation—and that means: we can hear from one another. We are a conversation, that always means at the same time: we are a *single* conversation. But the unity of a conversation consists in the fact that in the essential word there is always manifest that one and the same thing on which we agree, and on the basis of which we are united and so are essentially ourselves. Conversation and its unity support our existence.

But Hölderlin does not say simply: we are a conversation—but: "Since we have been a conversation . . ." Where the human faculty of speech is present and is exercised, that is not by itself sufficient for the essential actualization of language—conversation. Since when have we been a conversation? Where there is to be a *single* conversation, the essential word must be constantly related to the one and the same. Without this relation an argument too is absolutely impossible. But the one and the same can only be manifest in the light of something perpetual and permanent. Yet permanence and perpetuity only appear when what persists and is present begins to shine. But that happens in the moment when time opens out and extends. After man has placed himself in the presence of something perpetual, then only can he expose himself to the changeable, to that which comes and goes; for only the persistent is changeable. Only after "ravenous time" has been riven into present, past and future, does the possibility arise of agreeing on something permanent. We have been a single conversation since the time when it "is time." Ever since time arose, we have *existed* historically. Both—existence as a *single* conversation and historical existence—are alike ancient, they belong together and are the same thing.

Since we have been a conversation—man has learned much and named many of the heavenly ones. Since language really became actual as conversation, the gods have acquired names and a world has appeared. But again it should be noticed: the presence of the gods and the appearance of the world are not merely a consequence of the actualization of language, they are contemporaneous with it. And this to the extent that it is precisely in the naming of the gods, and in the transmutation of the world into word, that the real conversation, which we ourselves are, consists.

But the gods can acquire a name only by addressing and, as it were, claiming us. The word which names the gods is always a response to such a claim. This response always springs from the responsibility of a destiny. It is in the process by which the gods bring our existence to language, that we enter the sphere of the decision as to whether we are to yield ourselves to the gods or withhold ourselves from them.

Only now can we appreciate in its entirety what is meant by: "Since we have been a conversation . . ." Since the gods have led us into conversation, since time has been time, ever since then the basis of our existence has been a conversation. The proposition that language is the supreme event of human existence, has through it acquired its meaning and foundation.

But the question at once arises: how does this conversation, which we are, begin? Who accomplishes this naming of the gods? Who lays hold of something permanent in ravenous time and fixes it in the word? Hölderlin tells us with the sure simplicity of the poet. Let us hear a fourth saying.

THE ESSENCE OF POETRY

This saying forms the conclusion of the poem "Remembrance" and runs:

But that which remains, is established by the poets.

This saying throws light on our question about the essence of poetry. Poetry is the act of establishing by the word and in the word. What is established in this manner? The permanent. But can the permanent be established then? Is it not that which has always been present? No! Even the permanent must be fixed so that it will not be carried away, the simple must be wrested from confusion, proportion must be set before what lacks proportion. That which supports and dominates the existent in its entirety, must become manifest. Being must be opened out, so that the existent may appear. But this very permanent is the transitory. "Thus, swiftly passing is everything heavenly; but not in vain." But that this should remain, is "Entrusted to the poets as a care and a service." The poet names the gods and names all things in that which they are. This naming does not consist merely in something already known being supplied with a name; it is rather that when the poet speaks the essential word, the existent is by this naming nominated as what it is. So it becomes known *as* existent. Poetry is the establishing of being by means of the word. Hence that which remains is never taken from the transitory. The simple can never be picked out immediately from the intricate. Proportion does not lie in what lacks proportion. We never find the foundation in what is bottomless. Being is never an existent. But, because being and essence of things can never be calculated and derived from what is present, they must be freely created, laid down and given. Such a free act of giving is establishment.

But when the gods are named originally and the essence of things receives a name, so that things for the first time shine out, human existence is brought into a firm relation and given a basis. The speech of the poet is establishment not only in the sense of the free act of giving, but at the same time in the sense of the firm basing of human existence on its foundation.

If we conceive this essence of poetry as the establishing of being by means of the word, then we can have some inkling of the truth of that saying which Hölderlin spoke long after he had been received into the protection of the night of lunacy.

EXISTENCE AS FUNDAMENTALLY POETIC

We find this fifth pointer in the long and at the same time monstrous poem which begins:

> In the lovely azure there flowers with its
> Metallic roof the church-tower.

Here Hölderlin says:

> Full of merit, and yet poetically, dwells
> Man on this earth.

What man works at and pursues, is through his own endeavors earned and deserved. "Yet"—says Hölderlin in sharp antithesis, all this does not touch the essence of his sojourn on this earth, all this does not reach the foundation of human existence. The latter is fundamentally "poetic." But we now understand poetry as the inaugural naming of the gods and of the essence of things. To "dwell poetically" means: to stand in the presence of the gods and to be involved in the proximity of the essence of things. Existence is "poetical" in its fundamental aspect—which means at the same time: in so far as it is established (founded), it is not a recompense, but a gift.

Poetry is not merely an ornament accompanying existence, not merely a temporary enthusiasm or nothing but an interest and amusement. Poetry is the foundation which supports history, and therefore it is not a mere appearance of culture, and absolutely not the mere "expression" of a "culture-soul."

That our existence is fundamentally poetic, this cannot in the last resort mean, that it is really only a harmless game. But does not Hölderlin himself, in the first pointer which we quoted, call poetry "That most innocent of all occupations"? How can this be reconciled with the essence of poetry as we are now revealing it? This brings us back to the question which we laid aside in the first instance. In now proceeding to answer this question, we will try at the same time to summarize and bring before the inner eye the essence of poetry and of the poet.

First of all it appeared that the field of action of poetry is language. Hence the essence of poetry must be understood through the essence of language. Afterwards it became clear that poetry is the inaugural naming of being and of the essence of all things—not just any speech, but that particular kind which for the first time brings into the open all that which we then discuss and deal with in everyday language. Hence poetry never takes language as a raw material ready to hand, rather it is poetry which first makes language possible. Poetry is the primitive language of a historical people. Therefore, in just the reverse manner, the essence of language must be understood through the essence of poetry.

The foundation of human existence is conversation, in which language does truly become actual. But primitive language is poetry, in which being is established. Yet language is the "most dangerous of possessions." Thus poetry is the most dangerous work—and at the same time the "most innocent of all occupations."

In fact—it is only if we combine these two definitions and conceive them as one, that we fully comprehend the essence of poetry.

But is poetry then truly the most dangerous work? In a letter to a friend, immediately before leaving on his last journey to France, Hölderlin writes: "O Friend! The world lies before me brighter than it was, and more serious. I feel pleasure at how it moves onward, I feel pleasure when in summer 'the ancient holy father with calm hand shakes lightnings of benediction out of the rosy clouds.' For amongst all that I can perceive of God, this sign has become for me the chosen one. I used to be able to exult over a new truth, a better insight into that which is above us and around us, now I am frightened lest in the end it should happen with me as with Tantalus of old, who received more from the gods than he was able to digest."

The poet is exposed to the divine lightnings. This is spoken of in the poem which we must recognize as the purest poetry about the essence of poetry, and which begins:

> When on festive days a countryman goes
> To gaze on his field, in the morning . . .

There, the last stanza says:

> Yet it behooves us, under the storms of God,
> Ye poets! with uncovered head to stand,
> With our hand to grasp the very lightning-flash
> Paternal, and to pass, wrapped in song,
> The divine gift to the people.

And a year later, when he had returned to his mother's house, struck down with madness, Hölderlin wrote to the same friend, recalling his stay in France:

"The mighty element, the fire of heaven and the stillness of men, their life amid nature, and their limitation and contentment, have constantly seized me, and, as it is told of the heroes, I can truly say that I have been struck by Apollo." The excessive brightness has driven the poet into the dark. Is any further evidence necessary as to the extreme danger of his "occupation"? The very destiny itself of the poet tells everything. The passage in Hölderlin's "Empedocles" rings like a premonition:

He, through whom the spirit speaks, must leave betimes.

And nevertheless: poetry is the "most innocent of all occupations,"
Hölderlin writes to this effect in his letter, not only in order to spare
his mother, but because he knows that this innocent fringe belongs to
the essence of poetry, just as the valley does to the mountain; for how
could this most dangerous work be carried on and preserved, if the poet
were not "cast out" from everyday life and protected *against* it by the
apparent harmlessness of his occupation.

Poetry looks like a game and yet it is not. A game does indeed bring
men together, but in such a way that each forgets himself in the process.
In poetry on the other hand, man is reunited on the foundation of his
existence. There he comes to rest; not indeed to the seeming rest of
inactivity and emptiness of thought, but to that infinite state of rest in
which all powers and relations are active. . . .

CONCLUSION: THE TWO-FOLD CONTROL OF POETRY
AND THE REALM OF BETWEEN

Poetry, as the act of establishing being, is subject to a *two-fold* control. In considering these integral laws we first grasp the essence entire.

The writing of poetry is the fundamental naming of the gods. But
the poetic word only acquires its power of naming, when the gods themselves bring us to language. How do the gods speak?

> . . . And signs to us from antiquity are the language
> of the gods.

The speech of the poet is the intercepting of these signs, in order
to pass them on to his own people. This intercepting is an act of receiving and yet at the same time a fresh act of giving; for "in the first signs"
the poet catches sight already of the completed message and in his word
boldly presents what he has glimpsed, so as to tell in advance of the
not-yet fulfilled. So:

> . . . the bold spirit, like an eagle
> Before the tempests, flies prophesying
> In the path of his advancing gods.

The establishment of being is bound to the signs of the gods. And
at the same time the poetic word is only the interpretation of the "voice
of the people." This is how Hölderlin names the sayings in which a
people remembers that it belongs to the totality of all that exists. But

often this voice grows dumb and weary. In general even it is not capable of saying of itself what is true, but has need of those who explain it. . . .

In this way the essence of poetry is joined on to the laws of the signs of the gods and of the voice of the people, laws which tend towards and away from each other. The poet himself stands between the former—the gods, and the latter—the people. He is one who has been cast out—out into that *Between*, between gods and men. But only and for the first time in this Between is it decided, who man is and where he is settling his existence. "Poetically, dwells man on this earth."

Unceasingly and ever more securely, out of the fullness of the images pressing about him and always more simply, did Hölderlin devote his poetic word to this realm of Between. And this compels us to say that he is the poet of the poet. . . .

Hölderlin writes poetry about the essence of poetry—but not in the sense of a timelessly valid concept. This essence of poetry belongs to a determined time. But not in such a way that it merely conforms to this time, as to one which is already in existence. It is that Hölderlin, in the act of establishing the essence of poetry, first determines a new time. It is the time of the gods that have fled *and* of the god that is coming. It is the time of *need*, because it lies under a double lack and a double Not: the No-more of the gods that have fled and the Not-yet of the god that is coming.

The essence of poetry, which Hölderlin establishes, is in the highest degree historical, because it anticipates a historical time; but as a historical essence it is the sole essential essence.

The time is needy and therefore its poet is extremely rich—so rich that he would often like to relax in thoughts of those that have been and in eager waiting for that which is coming and would like only to sleep in this apparent emptiness. But he holds his ground in the Nothing of this night. Whilst the poet remains thus by himself in the supreme isolation of his mission, he fashions truth, vicariously and therefore truly, for his people. The seventh stanza of the elegy "Bread and Wine" tells of this. What it has only been possible to analyze here intellectually, is expressed there poetically.

> But Friend! we come too late. The gods are alive, it is
>   true,
> But up there above one's head in another world.
> Eternally they work there and seem to pay little heed
> To whether we live, so attentive are the Heavenly Ones.
> For a weak vessel cannot always receive them,

Only now and then does man endure divine abundance.
Life is a dream of them. But madness
Helps, like slumber and strengthens need and night,
Until heroes enough have grown in the iron cradle,
Hearts like, as before, to the Heavenly in power.
Thundering they come. Meanwhile it often seems
Better to sleep than to be thus without companions,
To wait thus, and in the meantime what to do and say
I know not, and what use are poets in a time of need?
But, thou sayest, they are like the wine-god's holy priests,
Who go from land to land in the holy night.

STUDY QUESTIONS

1. Why was Hölderlin chosen to exemplify poetry?
2. What does it mean to speak of poetry as the "most innocent of all occupations"?
3. In what sense can language be called the "most dangerous of possessions"?
4. Why is language "the supreme event of human existence"?
5. In what way is poetry the act of establishing being "by the word and in the word"?
6. Why is human existence "fundamentally poetic"?
7. What two-fold control is poetry subject to?
8. How does the poet "fashion truth" in his realm of "Between"?

V

Philosophy
of Religion

St. Anselm

THE ONTOLOGICAL ARGUMENT

Biographical Note.   ST. ANSELM (ca. 1033–1109), was born at Aosta in the region of Piedmont, Italy. He began his schooling at Avranches in Burgundy, and took his vows as a Benedictine at the Norman abbey of Bec. His higher education was directed by Lanfranc. In 1092 he visited England, and in the following year was nominated by King William II to succeed Lanfranc to the archbishopric of Canterbury. Over the next four years, differences arose between Anselm and the king. In 1097, while Anselm was on a visit to Rome, the king seized the revenues of the see, which he held until his death. In the meantime Anselm was in exile. It was during this exile that he wrote his celebrated *Cur Deus Homo.* In 1100, King William II was killed and succeeded by Henry I, who recalled Anselm to Canterbury. Despite some differences with the king over investiture, the remainder of his life passed peacefully. In addition to the *Cur Deus Homo,* his principal works are the *Monologium,* the *Proslogion,* and the *De Veritate.*

* * *

Introductory Note.   The philosophy and theology of Anselm falls within the Augustinian tradition. Like Augustine, he draws no marked distinction between theology and philosophy. In the Augustinian spirit, he is intent on an explication of the truths of faith by reason. This approach is summed up in his famous dictum *Credo ut intelligam,* "I believe in order that I may understand."

From the *Proslogion,* translated by Sidney Norton Deane, Chicago, Open Court, 1903, pp. 1–2, 6–9.

Although he wrote considerably on the subject of theology, his fame rests more upon his explication of those religious truths that are open to human reason. Two of his works in particular are devoted to this enterprise: The *Monologium*, written at the request of the monks of the Abbey at Bec, who desired demonstrative arguments on the existence and nature of God; and the *Proslogion*, in which he developed his celebrated ontological argument.

The ontological argument may be said to stem in part from the desire of Anselm to create a simple and direct proof based upon man's experience of God and in part from the dialectical spirit of the age of Anselm. It is questionable whether the source of the argument is to be found in Augustine. Beyond question, however, is the tremendous interest the argument has aroused among philosophers in all ages. It is probably as warmly disputed by philosophers today as it was during the medieval period. Among its supporters in the history of philosophy are to be found Duns Scotus, Descartes, Spinoza, Leibniz, and Hegel. Its opponents include such equally illustrious figures as Thomas Aquinas, Locke, Hume, and Kant.

The selection that follows contains the whole text of the argument. Since it is stated so succinctly by Anselm, to recapitulate it would be to repeat it, and to paraphrase it would destroy its effectiveness. However, the reader should note the basic premises in the argument—namely, that the idea of God exists in the mind and that it is greater for an idea to exist in reality and in the mind than merely in the mind. How the inference is then drawn to God's actual existence should be carefully studied, and in particular it should be observed that the demonstration is stated both affirmatively and negatively. Actually there are two demonstrations, the negative one which argues that the denial of the necessary existence of God involves a contradiction, and the affirmative one proceeding from the perfection of God to His existence.

THE ONTOLOGICAL ARGUMENT

. . . I began to ask myself whether there might be found a single argument which would require no other for its proof than itself alone; and alone would suffice to demonstrate that God truly exists, and that there is a supreme good requiring nothing else, which all other things require for their existence and well-being; and whatever we believe regarding the divine Being.

Although I often and earnestly directed my thought to this end, and at some times that which I sought seemed to be just within my reach, while again it wholly evaded my mental vision, at last in despair I was about to cease, as if from the search for a thing which could not be found. But when I wished to exclude this thought altogether, lest, by busying my mind to no purpose, it should keep me from other thoughts, in which I might be successful; then more and more, though I was unwilling and shunned it, it began to force itself upon me, with a kind of importunity. So, one day, when I was exceedingly wearied with resisting its importunity, in the very conflict of my thoughts, the proof of which I had despaired offered itself, so that I eagerly embraced the thoughts which I was strenuously repelling. . . .

I do not endeavor, O Lord, to penetrate thy sublimity, for in no wise do I compare my understanding with that; but I long to understand in some degree thy truth, which my heart believes and loves. For I do not seek to understand that I may believe, but I believe in order to understand. For this also I believe,—that unless I believed, I should not understand. . . .

And so Lord, do thou, who dost give understanding to faith, give me, so far as thou knowest it to be profitable, to understand that thou art as we believe; and that thou art that which we believe. And, indeed, we believe that thou art a being than which nothing greater can be conceived. Or is there no such nature, since the fool hath said in his heart, there is no God? But, at any rate, this very fool, when he hears of this being of which I speak—a being than which nothing greater can be conceived—understands what he hears, and what he understands is in his understanding; although he does not understand it to exist.

For, it is one thing for an object to be in the understanding, and another to understand that the object exists. When a painter first conceives of what he will afterwards perform, he has it in his understanding, but he does not yet understand it to be, because he has not yet performed it. But after he has made the painting, he both has it in his understanding, and he understands that it exists, because he has made it.

Hence, even the fool is convinced that something exists in the understanding, at least, than which nothing greater can be conceived. For, when he hears of this, he understands it. And whatever is understood, exists in the understanding. And assuredly that, than which nothing greater can be conceived, cannot exist in the understanding alone. For, suppose it exists in the understanding alone: then it can be conceived to exist in reality; which is greater.

And it assuredly exists so truly, that it cannot be conceived not to exist. For, it is possible to conceive of a being which cannot be conceived not to exist, and this is greater than one which can be conceived not to exist. Hence, if that, than which nothing greater can be conceived, can be conceived not to exist, it is not that, than which nothing greater can be conceived. But this is an irreconcilable contradiction.

There is, then, so truly a being than which nothing greater can be conceived to exist, that it cannot even be conceived not to exist; and this being thou art, O Lord, our God.

So truly, therefore, dost thou exist, O Lord, my God, that thou canst not be conceived not to exist; and rightly. For if a mind could conceive of a being better than thee, the creature would rise above the Creator; and this is most absurd. And, indeed, whatever else there is, except thee alone, can be conceived not to exist. To thee alone, therefore, it belongs to exist more truly than all other beings, and hence in a higher degree than all others. For, whatever else exists does not exist so truly, and hence in a less degree it belongs to it to exist. Why, then, has the fool said in his heart, there is no God, since it is so evident to a rational mind, that thou dost exist in the highest degree of all? Why, except that he is dull and a fool?

STUDY QUESTIONS

1. Discuss the meaning and the implications of Anselm's statement that "I believe in order to understand . . ."
2. Why does Anselm insist that it is not possible for the fool to deny that he has an idea of God?
3. State in detail each of the two versions of the ontological argument.
4. The German philosopher Kant declared of the ontological argument that by similar reasoning one could argue from the *idea* of one hundred dollars in my purse to the actual existence of one hundred dollars in my purse. Show that the Kantian criticism is mistaken and irrelevant.
5. How would you criticize the argument of Anselm? Ask a fellow student to refute your refutation.

St. Thomas Aquinas

THE FIVE WAYS

Biographical Note.   ST. THOMAS AQUINAS (1225–1274) was born
at Roccasecca near Aquino, Italy. In 1231 he entered the Benedictine Monastery at Monte Cassino as an oblate, and he pursued his early academic
studies there until 1239. In that year he entered the University of Naples,
and for the next four or five years he studied the liberal arts. In 1244 he
decided to become a Dominican, and in the following year he went to Paris
for his studies in theology. In 1248 he went to Cologne with Albertus
Magnus and studied with him until 1252. In 1256 he became a professor of
theology at the University of Paris. He returned to Italy in 1259 and taught
at Rome and other cities for the next several years. In 1268, St. Thomas
returned once more to Paris and assumed the leadership in the philosophical
struggle against the Latin Averroists. In 1272 he was commissioned by
his Order to establish a new house of studies at the University of Naples.
Two years later he was summoned to the Council of Lyons by Pope Gregory
X, but on the way to the council he died—at the Cistercian monastery of
Fossanuova on March 7, 1274. He was canonized on July 18, 1323, and in
1567 he was named the Angelic Doctor by Pope Pius V. His most celebrated
works are *Summa Theologica*, *Summa Contra Gentiles*, and *Disputed Questions on Truth.*

* * *

From St. Thomas Aquinas, *Summa Theologica*, New York: Random House, 1945,
Question 2, Articles 2 and 3. Reprinted with permission of the publisher and
Burns & Oates Ltd., London.

Introductory Note.   The philosophy of Aquinas is a synthesis of Aristotelianism and Christianity. From Aristotle, Aquinas adapted (1) the hylomorphic view of reality, (2) a conception of science and methodology, (3) the principal results of Aristotelian scientific research, and (4) with certain significant modifications, the basic principles of a metaphysics, a psychology, and an ethics. Although he accepted much from Aristotle, and in particular a conviction of the autonomy of human reason, he never hesitated to sacrifice any Aristotelian doctrine or principle when it appeared that it would conflict with Christian faith. Nowhere is this tendency more pronounced than in the Thomistic conception of God and His existence.

For Aquinas, God is not merely the ultimate cause of the physcial universe nor merely a necessary adjunct to a metaphysical system; He is the God of Christianity with all the attributes of such a God and all the relations of such a God to the universe. For Aristotle, God is not a creator; He is merely an Unmoved Mover, a Being whose sole activity is to "think his own thoughts." For Aquinas, God is much more than this. God is not merely a final cause, the Unmoved Mover who attracts all things to Him, but He is an efficient cause as well, for He is the creator of the universe. Furthermore, He is a necessary being in a world of contingency, the source of all that is good and of all that is intelligible and orderly in the universe. For Aristotle there has always been a world of substances. For Aquinas, "In the beginning God created heaven and earth."

For these reasons, the selection on God embodies much more than will be found in any Aristotelian account of God. Particularly to be noted in the selection that follows is the nature of the Thomistic demonstration, the contention that the demonstration of God's existence must proceed from the effects of God and not from the idea of God. All five ways emphasize the importance of beginning the demonstration with certain evident facts in experience—change or motion, causes and effects, contingencies, grades of perfection, and design or order. All five ways also employ the principle of causality. Aside from these common characteristics of the five ways, it may be noted that in the first way Aquinas is assuming the eternity of the universe, the equivalence of motion with change, and the analysis of change in terms of the Aristotelian concepts of potentiality and actuality. Of the second way, it may be observed that an infinite regress is denied of a hierarchical series of beings, but not of a series of beings limited to one class. This point is also more or less implicit in the other ways. In the third way, it may be noted that an infinite time is assumed for the realization of all possibilities taken as an entire class. Finally, each of the arguments says no more of the nature of God than that he is that being "to which everyone gives the name of God."

WHETHER IT CAN BE DEMONSTRATED THAT GOD EXISTS

Objection 1. It seems that the existence of God cannot be demonstrated. For it is an article of faith that God exists. But what is of faith cannot be demonstrated, because a demonstration produces scientific knowledge, whereas faith is of the unseen, as is clear from the Apostle (*Heb.* xi. 1). Therefore it cannot be demontrated that God exists.

Obj. 2. Further, essence is the middle term of demonstration. But we cannot know in what God's essence consists, but solely in what it does not consist, as Damascene says. Therefore we cannot demonstrate that God exists.

Obj. 3. Further, if the existence of God were demonstrated, this could only be from His effects. But His effects are not proportioned to Him, since He is infinite and His effects are finite, and between the finite and infinite there is no proportion. Therefore, since a cause cannot be demonstrated by an effect not proportioned to it, it seems that the existence of God cannot be demonstrated.

On the contrary, the Apostle says: *The invisible things of Him are clearly seen, being understood by the things that are made* (*Rom.* i. 20). But this would not be unless the existence of God could be demonstrated through the things that are made; for the first thing we must know of anything is, whether it exists.

I answer that, Demonstration can be made in two ways: One is through the cause, and is called *propter quid,* and this is to argue from what is prior absolutely. The other is through the effect, and is called a demonstration *quia;* this is to argue from what is prior relatively only to us. When an effect is better known to us than its cause, from the effect we proceed to the knowledge of the cause. And from every effect the existence of its proper cause can be demonstrated, so long as its effects are better known to us; because, since every effect depends upon its cause, if the effect exists, the cause must pre-exist. Hence the existence of God, in so far as it is not self-evident to us, can be demonstrated from those of His effects which are known to us.

Reply Obj. 1. The existence of God and other like truths about God, which can be known by natural reason, are not articles of faith, but are preambles to the articles, for faith presupposes natural knowledge, even as grace presupposes nature and perfection the perfectible. Nevertheless, there is nothing to prevent a man, who cannot grasp a proof, from accepting, as a matter of faith, something which in itself is capable of being scientifically known and demonstrated.

Question 2, Article 2.

Reply Obj. 2. When the existence of a cause is demonstrated from an effect, this effect takes the place of the definition of the cause in proving the cause's existence. This is especially the case in regard to God, because, in order to prove the existence of anything, it is necessary to accept as a middle term the meaning of the name, and not its essence, for the question of its essence follows on the question of its existence. Now the names given to God are derived from His effects, as will be later shown. Consequently, in demonstrating the existence of God from His effects, we may take for the middle term the meaning of the name *God.*

Reply Obj. 3. From effects not proportioned to the cause no perfect knowledge of that cause can be obtained. Yet from every effect the existence of the cause can be clearly demonstrated, and so we can demonstrate the existence of God from His effects; though from them we cannot know God perfectly as He is in His essence.

WHETHER GOD EXISTS

On the contrary, It is said in the person of God: *I am Who am* (*Exod.* iii. 14).

I answer that, The existence of God can be proved in five ways.

The first and more manifest way is the argument from motion. It is certain, and evident to our senses, that in the world some things are in motion. Now whatever is moved is moved by another, for nothing can be moved except it is in potentiality to that towards which it is moved whereas a thing moves inasmuch as it is in act. For motion is nothing else than the reduction of something from potentiality to actuality. But nothing can be reduced from potentiality to actuality, except by something in a state of actuality. Thus that which is actually hot, as fire, makes wood, which is potentially hot, to be actually hot, and thereby moves and changes it. Now it is not possible that the same thing should be at once in actuality and potentiality in the same respect, but only in different respects. For what is actually hot cannot simultaneously be potentially hot; but it is simultaneously potentially cold. It is therefore impossible that in the same respect and in the same way a thing should be both mover and moved, i. e., that it should move itself. Therefore, whatever is moved must be moved by another. If that by which it is moved be itself moved, then this also must needs be moved by another, and that by another again. But this cannot go on to infinity, because

Question 2, Article 3.

then there would be no first mover, and, consequently, no other mover, seeing that subsequent movers move only inasmuch as they are moved by the first mover, as the staff moves only because it is moved by the hand. Therefore, it is necessary to arrive at a first mover, moved by no other; and this everyone understands to be God.*

The second way is from the nature of efficient cause. In the world of sensible things we find there is an order of efficient causes. There is no case known (neither is it, indeed, possible) in which a thing is found to be the efficient cause of itself; for so it would be prior to itself, which is impossible. Now in efficient causes it is not possible to go on to infinity, because in all efficient causes following in order, the first is the cause of the intermediate cause, and the intermediate is the cause of the ultimate cause, whether the intermediate cause be several, or one only. Now to take away the cause is to take away the effect. Therefore, if there be no first cause among efficient causes, there will be no ultimate, nor any intermediate, cause. But if in efficient causes it is possible to go on to infinity, there will be no first efficient cause, neither will there be an ultimate effect, nor any intermediate efficient causes; all of which is plainly false. Therefore it is necessary to admit a first efficient cause, to which everyone gives the name of God.†

The third way is taken from possibility and necessity, and runs thus. We find in nature things that are possible to be and not to be, since they are found to be generated, and to be corrupted, and consequently, it is possible for them to be and not to be. But it is impossible for these always to exist, for that which can not-be at some time is not. Therefore, if everything can not-be,. then at one time there was nothing in exist-

* Note here the following remarks of St. Thomas from the *Summa Contra Gentiles* (Chap. 13, 30):

"Now two things would seem to weaken the above arguments. The first of these is that they proceed from the supposition of the eternity of movement, and among Catholics this is supposed to be false. To this we reply that the most effective way to prove God's existence is from the supposition of the eternity of the world, which being supposed, it seems less manifest that God exists. For if the world and movement had a beginning, it is clear that we must suppose some cause to have produced the world and movement, because whatever becomes anew must take its origin from some cause of its becoming, since nothing evolves itself from potentiality to act, or from non-being to being.

"The *second,* is that the aforesaid arguments suppose that the first moved thing, namely the heavenly body, has its motive principle in itself, whence it follows that it is animated: and by many this is not granted.

"To this we reply that if the first mover is not supposed to have its motive principle in itself, it follows that it is immediately moved by something altogether immovable. Hence also Aristotle draws this conclusion with an alternative, namely that either we must come at once to a first mover immovable and separate, or to a self-mover from which again we come to a first mover immovable and separate."

† In connection with this argument the following statement from the *Summa Theologica* should be studied: "In efficient causes it is impossible to proceed to infinity

ence. Now if this were true, even now there would be nothing in existence, because that which does not exist begins to exist only through something already existing. Therefore, if at one time nothing was in existence, it would have been impossible for anything to have begun to exist; and thus even now nothing would be in existence— which is absurd. Therefore, not all beings are merely possible, but there must exist something the existence of which is necessary. But every necessary thing either has its necessity caused by another, or not. Now it is impossible to go on to infinity in necessary things which have their necessity caused by another, as has been already proved in regard to efficient causes. Therefore we cannot but admit the existence of some being having of itself its own necessity, and not receiving it from another, but rather causing in others their necessity. This all men speak of as God.

The fourth way is taken from the gradation to be found in things. Among beings there are some more and some less good, true, noble, and the like. But *more* and *less* are predicated of different things according as they resemble in their different ways something which is the maximum, as a thing is said to be hotter according as it more nearly resembles that which is hottest; so that there is something which is truest, something best, something noblest, and, consequently, something which is most being, for those things that are greatest in truth are greatest in being, as it is written in *Metaph.* II (*Metaph.* Ia, 1 993b30). Now the maximum in any genus is the cause of all in that genus, as fire, which is the maximum of heat, is the cause of all hot things, as is said in the same book (993b25). Therefore there must also be something which is to all beings the cause of their being, goodness, and every other perfection; and this we call God.

The fifth way is taken from the governance of the world. We see that things which lack knowledge, such as natural bodies, act for an

---

por 30. Thus, there cannot be an infinite number of causes that are *per se* required for a certain effect; for instance, that a stone be moved by a stick, the stick by the hand, and so on to infinity. But it is not impossible to proceed to infinity *accidentally* as regards efficient causes; for instance, if all the causes thus infinitely multiplied should have the order of only one cause, while their multiplication is accidental: e. g., as an artificer acts by means of many hammers accidentally, because one after the other is broken. It is accidental, therefore, that one particular hammer should act after the action of another, and it is likewise accidental to this particular man as generator to be generated by another man; for he generates as a man, and not as the son of another man. For all men generating hold one grade in the order of efficient causes— viz., the grade of a particular generator. Hence it is not impossible for man to be generated by man to infinity; but such a thing would be impossible if the generation of this man depended upon this man, and on an elementary body, and on the sun, and so on to infinity." (Question 46, Article 2, Reply to Objection 7.)

end, and this is evident from their acting always, or nearly always in the same way, so as to obtain the best result. Hence it is plain that they achieve their end, not fortuitously, but designedly. Now whatever lacks knowledge cannot move towards an end, unless it be directed by some being endowed with knowledge and intelligence; as the arrow is directed by the archer. Therefore some intelligent being exists by whom all natural things are directed to their end; and this being we call God.

STUDY QUESTIONS

1. According to Aquinas, what are the two ways or methods of demonstration? How does his demonstration of God's existence differ from Anselm's?
2. Since it is an article of faith that God exists, and since faith is not a matter of demonstration, why does it follow (or not) that the existence of God cannot be demonstrated?
3. If we accept the existence of God upon faith, why should we be concerned to demonstrate his existence?
4. What features do all the five ways have in common?
5. How does Aquinas explain the nature of change? Why does he say that a thing cannot be in actuality and potentiality at the same time and in the same respect? Give some examples in addition to the one used in the argument?
6. On what grounds does Aquinas deny the possibility of an infinite regress of moved and movers, causes and effects, etc.? Do you think his position is justified? Compare your conclusion with the remarks in the note to the second way.
7. Why does Aquinas assume the eternity of the universe in the first way? Do the notions of time and eternity cause any difficulty in your understanding of the five ways? Comment.
8. Which one of the five ways do you find the most persuasive? The least persuasive? Why?

Meister Eckhart

RELIGION AS DETACHMENT

Biographical Note.   MEISTER ECKHART (1260?–1328?), the great German mystic of the Middle Ages, was a nobleman by birth. He entered the Dominican order at an early age and underwent a rigorous program of scholastic studies, which—after interruption by services to the order— ended in Paris in 1302 with his graduation as master of theology. The highest administrative and teaching positions within the order were now open to him, and he distinguished himself in both fields. He also became a most popular preacher, which latter activity toward the end of his life led to charges of heresy being raised against him. His trial, which began in 1326, was concluded by a papal Bull, issued after his death, which condemned a number of his pronouncements as heretical.

Eckhart's works can be divided into two groups: his sermons and tractates, written in medieval German, to which the following selection belongs, and his Latin writings, most of them being parts of his *Opus Tripartitum,* a comprehensive theological work of which only a small portion has come down to us.

* * *

Introductory Note.   Religion, generally speaking, concerns man's con- frontation with the Absolute, the Infinite; and the story of religion is the

From Meister Eckhart, *Selected Treatises and Sermons,* translated by James M. Clark and John V. Skinner, London, Faber & Faber, Ltd., 1958, pp. 160–171. Used by permission of Faber & Faber, Ltd.

story of man's comprehension of his relatedness to a realm of the Infinite, finite though he is. Accordingly the functions of the great world religions have always been at least twofold: (1) to make man aware of an existing inter-penetration of these two realms and of its impact upon the individual and society; (2) to promote a way of human life that would assure the most complete harmonization of the realm of the finite with that of the Infinite.

Reaching for this goal of a voluntary and conscious attunement of man and the world of man to—as Western religion expresses it—God and His order has at the same time been recognized as finite man's most difficult task. Yet universal as human shortcomings and limitations are, they have not been considered as necessarily interfering with such conformity. Under certain conditions attunement could be brought about; "uniformity," even "union" with God could actually be achieved. This would require a definite mental and spiritual orientation and discipline which, however hard to prepare for and to practice, was thought in no way to be beyond the reach of even the simplest person.

Religious thinkers who demonstrated through their lives and teachings ways leading toward such spiritual fulfillment are called mystics, and to them we owe a formulation and expression of what constitutes the very core of religion. Such a mystic was Meister Eckhart, the Christian theologian who in his teaching more than anything else tried to clarify what can and must be done "to bring about a certain similarity between God and man."

The following essay exemplifies this approach to religion. Meister Eckhart introduces "detachment" as man's highest virtue, higher than love, humility, or mercy. It enables man to use all the powers of the soul to benefit the "inward man" and accounts for a "detached heart," from which everything is removed that could interfere with God's working upon it. Prayer then ceases to be meaningful in any specific sense and so does even rightful joy over matters of passing comfort. But striving to be ready for what Eckhart calls "the Divine inflowing" will not lose anything for man; on the contrary, the more he strives "the happier he is, and whoever can place himself in the highest readiness for it also dwells in the highest happiness."

DETACHMENT: THE HIGHEST VIRTUE

I have read many writings of both heathen masters and prophets, and of the Old and the New Testament, and have sought earnestly and with utmost diligence to find out what is the best and highest virtue, with the aid of which man could be most closely united with God, by which man could become by grace what God is by nature, and by which man would be most like the image of what he was when he was in God, when there was no difference between him and God, before God had created the world.

And when I search these writings thoroughly, as far as my reason can fathom and know, I just find that pure detachment stands above all things; for all virtues pay some regard to the creatures, yet detachment is free from all creatures. Hence it was that our Lord said to Martha: "One thing is needful" (Lk. 10:42), that is to say, he who wishes to be untroubled and pure must have one thing, namely detachment.

The masters praise love most highly, as St. Paul does when he says: "In whatever tribulation I may find myself, if I have not love, I am nothing" (I Cor. 13:2, 3). But I praise detachment more than all love. First, because the best thing about love is that it forces me to love God. On the other hand, detachment forces God to love me. Now it is much nobler that I should force God to myself than that I should force myself to God. And the reason is that God can join Himself to me more closely and unite Himself with me better than I could unite myself with God. That detachment forces God to me I can prove by the fact that everything likes to be in its own natural place. Now God's own and natural place is unity and purity, and they come from detachment. Hence God must of necessity give Himself to a detached heart.

Secondly, I praise detachment more than love because love forces me to suffer all things for the sake of God, but detachment makes me receptive of nothing but God. Now it is far nobler to be receptive of nothing but God than to suffer all things for the sake of God. For in suffering man pays some attention to the creatures from whom his sufferin comes. On the other hand, detachment is completely free from all creatures. That detachment is receptive of nothing but God I prove by the fact that whatever is to be received must be received in something or other. Now detachment is so near nothingness that nothing is so delicate that it could remain in detachment except God alone. He is so simple and delicate that He can be quite well contained in the detached heart. Therefore detachment is receptive of nothing but God.

The masters also praise humility above many other virtues. But I praise detachment above all humility, and for this reason: humility can exist without detachment, but perfect detachment cannot subsist without perfect humility. For perfect humility aims at annihilation of self; but detachment borders so closely on nothing that between perfect detachment and nothingness there can be nothing. Therefore perfect detachment cannot exist without humility. Now two virtues are always better than one.

The second reason why I praise detachment more than humility is that perfect humility bows down beneath all creatures, and in this bending down man goes out of himself and into the creatures. But detachment remains within itself. Now no going out can ever be so noble as the indwelling is in itself. Therefore the prophet said: "The king's daughter has all her glory from her inwardness" (Ps. 45:13). Perfect detachment is not in the least inclined to bow down beneath any creature or above any creature. It wishes to be neither below nor above; it wishes to stand by itself, neither giving joy nor sorrow to anyone, and wishing to have neither equality nor inequality with any creature, desiring neither this nor that. It does not wish for anything but to exist. To be either this or that is not its wish. For if anyone wishes to be this or that, he wants to be something, but detachment wishes to be nothing. For this reason it is not a burden to anything. . . .

I also praise detachment more than all mercy, for mercy simply means that man, going out of himself, turns to the failings of his fellowmen and for this reason his heart is troubled. Detachment is free from this; it remains in itself and does not allow itself to be troubled by anything, because, as long as anything can trouble a man, it is not well with him. In short, if I consider all virtues I find that none is so completely without defects and so applicable to God as is detachment.

There is a master named Avicenna,* who says: "The nobility of the soul that is detached is so great that whatever it looks upon is true, and whatever it asks for is granted, and whatever it orders must be obeyed." And you should know as a fact that whenever the free spirit is to be found in true detachment, it forces God to its being. If it could exist in a formless state and without any contingency, then it would receive God's properties in itself. But God cannot give that to anyone but Himself; hence God cannot do anything more for the detached spirit than to give Himself to it. And the man who thus stands in complete detachment is rapt into eternity in such a way that no transient thing can move him and he feels nothing at all that is physical. He is said to be dead to the world, for nothing that is worldly tastes good to him. This is what St. Paul had in mind when he said: "I live and yet not I, Christ lives in me" (Gal. 2:20).

IMMOVABILITY OF DETACHMENT

Now you might ask, what is detachment, since it is so noble in itself? Here you should know that true detachment is nothing other than this: the spirit stands as immovable in all the assaults of joy or sorrow, honor, disgrace or shame, as a mountain of lead stands im-

* Arabian scientist and philosopher around 1000 A.D.

movable against a small wind. This immovable detachment brings about in man the greatest similarity with God. For if God is God, He has it from His immovable detachment, and from this detachment He has His purity, His simplicity and His unchangeableness. And therefore, if man is to become like God, as far as a creature can possess similarity to God, it must be by means of detachment. It is this that leads man to purity and from purity to simplicity and from simplicity to unchangeableness. And these things bring about a certain similarity between God and man. But this similarity must take place through grace, for grace draws man away from all temporal things and purifies him from all transient things.

It is right that you should know that to be empty of all creatures is to be full of God, and to be full of creatures is to be empty of God. You should also know that in this immovable detachment God has dwelt eternally and He still dwells in it. And you should know that when God created heaven and earth and all creatures, that affected his immovable detachment as little as if the creatures had never been created. Indeed, I will say more: all the prayers and all the good works which man can perform in the world have as little effect on God's detachment as if neither prayers nor good works had ever been carried out. On that account God will not be any milder or more favorably inclined to man because he engaged in prayers or good works. Indeed, I will go further: when the Son in the Deity wished to become man, and did so, and suffered His Passion, that affected the immovable detachment of God as little as if He had never become man.

Now you might say: "That means that all prayers and all good works are lost, because God does not accept them so as to be moved by anyone by these means. Yet it is said that God wishes to be asked for everything." Here you should pay careful attention and rightly understand, if you can, that God in His first eternal vision, if we could assume that there was a first, considered all things to see how they were to take place, and saw in this vision when and how He was to create the creatures and when the Son was to become man and suffer. He also saw the smallest prayer and good work that anyone should perform, and He considered what prayer and devotion He would or should answer. He saw that you will urgently call upon Him tomorrow and earnestly pray, and this call and prayer God will not answer tomorrow, for He has already answered it in His eternity before you ever became man. But if your prayer is not wholehearted and is not sincere, God will not refuse you now, for He has refused you already in His eternity.

Thus, in His first eternal vision God has considered all things, and

God performs nothing anew, since it has all been affected beforehand. And so God dwells always in His immovable detachment; and yet for this reason the prayers and good works of people are not lost. For, if anyone does well he will be well rewarded, and he who does evil will also be rewarded accordingly. St. Augustine says the same thing in the fifth book of *On Trinity,* in the last chapter: "God forbid that anyone should say that God loved anyone in time, for with Him nothing has passed away and also nothing is future, and He loved all the Saints before the world was made, as He foresaw. When it happens that He makes manifest in time what He foresaw in eternity, people think that God has turned to them with a new love. And in the same way, when He is angry or does a kind action, it is we who are changed, whereas He remains unchangeable, just as the sun's rays hurt weak eyes and do good to healthy ones, although the sun's rays remain unchangeable in themselves." Similarly, Augustine says in the twelfth book of *On Trinity,* in the fourth chapter, "God does not see in a temporal manner and no new sight arises in Him."

In this sense also Isidore* speaks in his book, *Of the Highest Good,* as follows: "Many people ask what God was doing before he created heaven and earth, or from whence came the new intention in God to make the creatures? And I answer thus: No new intention ever arose in God, for although the creature did not exist in itself as it is now, it was from eternity in God and in His reason." God did not create heaven and earth as we think of it in our worldly fashion when we have Him say, "Let there be . . . ;" for all creatures were spoken together in the eternal Word. Moreover, we can also quote the words which the Lord spoke to Moses when Moses said to the Lord: "Lord, if Pharaoh asks me who you are, how am I to answer him?" Then the Lord said: "Then say: He-Who-Is has sent me" (Ex. 3:13, 14). That means He who is unchangeable in Himself, He has sent me.

Now one might say: Had Christ also this immovable detachment when he said: "My soul is sorrowful even unto death" (Mt. 26:38), and Mary when she stood beneath the Cross? And yet much has been said about her grief. How can all this be reconciled with immovable detachment? In this connection you should know that the masters tell us that in every man there are two kinds of men. The first is called the outward man, that is, sensitivity. This man is served by the five senses and yet the outer man operates by the power of the soul. The second man is called the inward man: that is the inmost part of the man. Now you should know that a spiritual man who loves God uses the powers

* Spanish bishop, theologian, and philosopher around 600 A.D.

of the soul in the outward man no further than what the five senses require as a matter of necessity. And the inward man does not heed the five senses, except in so far as he is their guide and leader. He takes care that they are not used in animal fashion as some people do who live according to the lusts of the flesh, like animals which are without reason. Such people are more properly called beasts than men.

Whatever powers the soul has left over from what she gives to the five senses, the soul gives these powers entirely to the inward man, and when he has any high and noble object in view, the soul draws to herself all the powers which she has lent to the five senses. This man is then called 'out of his senses' and enraptured, for his object is an intellectual image or something transcending reason without an image. Know then that God expects every spiritual man to love Him with all the powers of his soul. Hence He said: "Love thy God with all thy heart" (Deut. 6:5, Mt. 23:37). Now there are some men who completely dissipate the powers of the soul in the outward man. These are the people who direct all their senses and reason towards transient possessions, and who know nothing of the inward man.

Now you should know that the outward man may be undergoing trials, although the inward man is quite free from them and immovable. Even in Christ there were an outward man and an inward man, and also in our Lady. Whatever Christ and our Lady ever said of outward things was spoken by the outer man, and the inner man dwelt in immovable detachment. It was thus that Christ said: "My heart is sorrowful even unto death." And however much our Lady grieved and whatever she said, she was always in her inmost heart in immovable detachment. Let us take an analogy of this. A door opens and shuts on a hinge. Now if I compare the outer boards of the door with the outward man, I can compare the hinge with the inward man. When the door opens or closes the outer boards move to and fro, but the hinge remains immovable in one place and it is not changed at all as a result. So it is also here, if you only know how to act rightly.

OBJECT AND FRUIT OF DETACHMENT

Now I ask: what is the object of pure detachment? I answer that neither this nor that is the object of pure detachment. It rests on a mere nothing and I will tell you why: pure detachment rests on what is highest of all in which God can work entirely according to His will. But God cannot work in all hearts absolutely according to His will. For, in spite of the fact that God is almighty, He cannot work unless He finds readiness or effects it. And I say "or effects it," because of St. Paul, since He found no readiness in him, but He prepared him by means of the inpouring of grace. It is for this reason that I say that God works according as He finds readiness in us. His operation is different in men and in stones. We find a parable of this in nature. If one heats an oven and puts in it a piece of dough made of oats and one of barley and one of rye and one of wheat, there is only one heat in the oven and yet it does not work equally in all the pieces of dough. For one of them turns into a fine loaf, the second is rougher, and the third is rougher still. The heat is not to blame for this, but the material, which is unequal. In the same way, God does not work alike in all hearts, but according as He finds readiness and receptivity. If in some heart there is this or that, there may be something in the 'this' or 'that' as a result of which God cannot work unhampered.

Hence, if the heart is to be prepared for what is highest of all, it must rest on a pure nothing and in this there is the greatest possibility that can exist. For when the detached heart has the highest readiness, it must stand on the nothing, because in this there is the greatest receptivity. Take a parable from nature: if I want to write on a wax tablet, then no matter how noble the thing is that is written on the tablet, it will confuse me to such an extent that I cannot write on the tablet. If I really want to write, I must delete everything that is written on the tablet, and the tablet is never so suitable for writing as when absolutely nothing is written on it. In the same way, when God wishes to write on my heart in the most sublime manner, everything must come out of my heart that can be called 'this' or 'that'; thus it is with the detached heart. Then God can work in the sublimest manner and according to His highest will. Hence the object of the detached heart is neither this nor that.

But now I ask: what is the prayer of the detached heart? I answer that detachment and purity cannot pray. For if anyone prays he asks God that something may be given to him, or asks that God may take something away from him. But the detached heart does not ask for anything at all, nor has it anything at all that it would like to be rid of. Therefore it is free from all prayer and its prayer is nothing else than to be uniform with God. On this alone the prayer of detachment rests.

In this sense we may understand what was said by St. Dionysius* on the words of St. Paul: "There are many who all run for the crown,

---

* A Christian of the fifth century who wrote on mystical theology under the pseudonym of Dionysius and who was falsely identified with a saint of the same name.

and yet only one can win it" (I Cor. 9:24). All of the powers of the soul run towards the crown and yet it only falls to innermost being. Dionysius says in this connection: "The race is nothing but a turning away from all creatures and unification with uncreatedness." When the soul comes to this she loses her name and God draws her into Himself, so that she becomes annihilated in herself, as the sun draws the dawn into itself, so that it becomes annihilated. Nothing brings man to this but pure detachment. Here we may cite the words of Augustine: "The soul has a secret entrance into the Divine nature in which all things become annihilated for her." On earth this entrance is simply pure detachment. When the detachment reaches its highest perfection, it becomes unknowing through knowledge, loveless through love and dark through light.

Hence we may also quote the words of a master: "The poor in spirit are those who have surrendered all things to God, as He had them when we did not exist." No one can do this but a pure detached heart. That God prefers to be in a detached heart rather than in any other, is clear, for if you ask me: What does God seek in all things? I should answer in the words of the Book of Wisdom, where He says: "In all things I seek rest" (Ecclesiasticus 24:11). There is nowhere complete rest except in the detached heart alone. For this reason God would rather be there than in any other things or virtues.

You should also know that the more man strives to be receptive of the Divine inflowing, the happier he is, and whoever can place himself in the highest preparedness for it also dwells in the highest happiness. Now no man can make himself receptive of the Divine inflowing except by uniformity with God. For according as every man is uniform with God, he is to that extent receptive of the Divine inflowing. Now uniformity comes from the submission of man to God; in the same measure as man submits himself to the creatures, the less he is uniform with God. Now the pure detached heart is free from all creatures, hence it is entirely subject to God and stands in the greatest possible uniformity with God and it is also most receptive of the Divine inflowing. This is the meaning of St. Paul's words: "Put on Jesus Christ" (Ro. 13:14), and he meant: through uniformity with Christ; for the putting on can only take place through uniformity with Christ.

You must know that when Christ became man, He did not become an individual man, but He adopted human nature. Therefore empty yourself of all things in such a way that there only remains what Christ adopted, and in this way you will have put on Christ. If anyone wishes to recognize the nobility and value of perfect detachment, let him take notice of the words of Christ, speaking of His humanity to His disciples: "It is to your advantage that I go away from you, for if I go not away, the Holy Spirit cannot come to you" (John 16:7). It was just as if he had said: "You have taken too much joy in My physical presence, hence the perfect joy of the Holy Spirit cannot be imparted to you." Therefore strip yourselves of the images and unite yourselves with formless Being, for God's spiritual consolation is tender. Therefore He will only offer Himself to those who spurn bodily joy.

Now all thoughtful people should take note. No one is more confident than the one who lives in the greatest detachment. There can never be any physical or fleshly comfort without spiritual loss, for the flesh contends against the spirit and the spirit against the flesh. Therefore, if anyone sows in the flesh improper love, he reaps eternal death, and if anyone sows in the spirit proper love, he will reap from the spirit eternal life. Hence, the more quickly man flees from the creatures, the more quickly the Creator hastens towards him. All thoughtful people should take note of this: if the joy that we might have in the physical presence of Christ is an obstacle to us in the reception of the Holy Spirit, how much more detrimental in our search for God will be the rightful joy which we take in transient comfort. Therefore, detachment is the very best thing. It purifies the soul, cleanses the conscience, inflames the heart, arouses the spirit, quickens desire and makes God known. It separates off the creatures and unites the soul with God.

Now take note, all thoughtful men! The swiftest animal that bears you to perfection is suffering, for no one will enjoy more eternal sweetness than those who stand with Christ in the greatest bitterness. Suffering is bitter as gall, but to have suffered is honey-sweet. Nothing disfigures the body before men so much as suffering, and yet nothing beautifies the soul before God so much as to have suffered. The securest foundation on which this perfection can rest is humility. For while the natural man crawls here in the deepest lowliness, his spirit flies up into the heights of Divinity, for love brings sorrow and sorrow brings love. If anyone wishes to attain perfect detachment, let him strive for perfect humility, then he will come closest to Divinity. May the highest detachment, that is, God Himself, assist us to achieve this.

STUDY QUESTIONS

1. Why is detachment considered the highest virtue, even higher than love?
2. What does immovability of detachment mean?

3. Why can God never be moved by anyone's prayers or good works?
4. How can Christ and Mary be said to have demonstrated immovable detachment?
5. In what way are the "outward man" and the "inward man" related to each other?
6. What is the object of pure detachment?
7. What must man do on his part to be acted upon by God?
8. How can man dwell "in the highest happiness"?
9. Why must man flee from physical (even rightful) comfort as well as from other men?
10. How are suffering and humility related to man's perfection?

Ludwig Feuerbach

RELIGION AS ILLUSION

Biographical Note.   LUDWIG FEUERBACH (1804–1872) was born at Landshut in Bavaria, the son of an eminent jurist. He studied theology at Heidelberg and natural science and philosophy at Berlin. In Berlin he spent two years studying under Hegel, and it was because of the latter's influence that he turned to the study of philosophy and received his degree in that subject. It was his attack on religion and especially Christianity that won for him the admiration of the Marxists. Although he had strong sympathies with the Socialistic movement of the time, he never became an active part of it. He remained fundamentally the scholar rather than the revolutionary. He has often been termed the spiritual father of Marxism, and certainly Marx's teachings on religion reveal the influence of Feuerbach. On the reception of his principal work, *The Essence of Christianity,* Engels declared: "There was widespread enthusiasm . . . we all straightway became Feuerbachians."

* * *

Introductory Note.   Atheism in philosophy has usually been expressed in the negative manner of simply denying the existence of God or the validity of any knowledge concerning such a being. Few philosophers have attempted to set up a more positive form of Atheism as a philosophy, and perhaps none has attempted this more effectively than Feuerbach. Following

From the *Essence of Christianity,* translated by Marian Evans, London, Kegan Paul, Trench, Trubner and Co., 1893, pp. viii–xv, 12–30, and 283.

the death of Hegel, Feuerbach became the leader of what might be termed left-wing Hegelianism, a movement that tended to accept Hegel's method of dialectic, but abandoned his notion of God and his conception of reality as spirit or idea. Feuerbach's *Critique of the Hegelian Philosophy* held that the metaphysics of Hegel was merely a kind of rational theology. For such a metaphysics, Feuerbach substituted a materialistic philosophy that attempted to destroy both metaphysics and religion. In place of the Hegelian theology, Feuerbach would substitute a naturalistic religion based upon the love of humanity. In a word, for Feuerbach the only true God is man, the God of man is man himself, *Homo homini deus est.* "Gods," he says, "are men's wishes in a corporeal form." The notion of God is a myth that expresses the aspirations and dreams of man. The effect of Feuerbach's teaching was most significant, particularly for the Marxist movement. In fact, Marx's famous dictum that religion is the opium of the masses had its origin in Feuerbach's contention that religion expresses the dreams of man.

In the material that follows, we find Feuerbach first stating the principles of his naturalistic philosophy and his rejection of Hegelianism (Speculation). He declares that atheism is the true religion because it alone believes in the divinity of human nature. God is merely an illusory projection of man's own nature, religion is the dream of the human mind, and the knowledge of God is only self-knowledge. On such bases he analyzes the historical development of religion and concludes that the "object and contents of the Christian religion are altogether human." Agnosticism is rejected as merely a disguised form of atheism. And the possibility of an analogy between the human and the divine attributes is rejected, since he contends that God is nothing more than the attributes of man. The true atheist, he says, is one who denies both God as the subject of attributes and as the attributes. For any attributes that we may predicate as God's are, he insists, merely our own human attributes, and once we become aware of this, then God is no more than man himself, *Homo homini deus est.*

PRINCIPLES AND PURPOSE

. . . I am nothing but a *natural philosopher in the domain of mind;* and the natural philosopher can do nothing without instruments, without material means. In this character I have written the present work, which consequently contains nothing else than the principle of a new philosophy verified practically, i. e. *in concreto,* in application to a special object, but an object which has a universal significance: namely, to religion, in which this principle is exhibited, developed, and thoroughly carried out. This philosophy is essentially distinguished from the systems hitherto prevalent, in that it corresponds to the real complete nature of man; but for that very reason it is antagonistic to minds perverted and crippled by a superhuman, i. e., anti-human, anti-natural religion and speculation . . .

This philosophy has for its principle, not the Substance of Spinoza, not the *ego* of Kant and Fichte, not the Absolute Identity of Schelling, not the Absolute Mind of Hegel, in short, no abstract, merely conceptional being, but a *real* being, the true *Ens realissimum*—man; its principle, therefore, is in the highest degree positive and real. It generates thought from the *opposite* of thought, from Matter, from existence, from the senses; it has relation to its object first through the senses, i. e. passively, before defining it in thought. Hence my work, as a specimen of this philosophy, so far from being a production to be placed in the category of Speculation,—although in another point of view it is the true, the incarnate result of prior philosophical systems,— is the direct opposite of speculation, nay, puts an end to it by explaining it. Speculation makes religion say only what it has itself thought, and expressed far better than religion; it assigns a meaning to religion without any reference to the *actual* meaning of religion; it does not look beyond itself. I, on the contrary, let religion itself speak; I constitute myself only its listener and interpreter, not its prompter. Not to invent, but to discover, "to unveil existence," has been my sole object; to *see* correctly, my sole endeavor. It is not I, but religion that worships man, although religion, or rather theology, denies this; it is not I, an insignificant individual, but religion itself that says: God is man, man is God; it is not I, but religion that denies the God who is *not* man, but only an *ens rationis,*—since it makes God become man, and then constitutes this God, not distinguished from man, having a human form, human feelings, and human thoughts, the object of its worship and veneration. I have only found the key to the cipher of the Christian religion, only extricated its true meaning from the web of contradictions and delusions called theology;—but in doing so I have certainly committed a sacrilege. If therefore my work is negative, irreligious, atheistic, let it be remembered that atheism—at least in the sense of this work—is the secret of religion itself; that religion itself, not indeed on the surface, but fundamentally, not in intention or according to its own supposition, but in its heart, in its essence, believes in nothing else than the truth and divinity of human nature. . . .

Religion is the dream of the human mind. But even in dreams we do not find ourselves in emptiness or in heaven, but on earth, in the realm of reality; we only see real things in the entrancing splendour of imagination and caprice, instead of in the simple daylight of reality and necessity. Hence I do nothing more to religion—and to speculative philosophy and theology also—than to open its eyes, or rather to turn its gaze from the internal towards the external, i. e., I change the object as it is in the imagination into the object as it is in reality.

But certainly for the present age, which prefers the sign to the thing signified, the copy to the original, fancy to reality, the appearance to the essence, this change, inasmuch as it does away with illusion, is an absolute annihilation, or at least a reckless profanation; for in these days *illusion* only is *sacred, truth profane.* . . .

My principal theme is Christianity, is Religion, as it is the *immediate object,* the *immediate nature,* of man. Erudition and philosophy are to me only the means by which I bring to light the treasure hid in man.

THE ESSENCE OF RELIGION

In the perceptions of the senses consciousness of the object is distinguishable from consciousness of self; but in religion, consciousness of the object and self-consciousness coincide. The object of the senses is out of man, the religious object is within him, and therefore as little forsakes him as his self-consciousness or his conscience; it is the intimate, the closest object. "God," says Augustine, for example, "is nearer, more related to us, and therefore more easily known by us, than sensible corporeal things". The object of the senses is in itself indifferent—independent of the disposition or of the judgment; but the object of religion is a selected object; the most excellent, the first, the supreme being; it essentially presupposes a critical judgment, a discrimination between the divine and the non-divine, between that which is worthy of adoration and that which is not worthy. And here may be applied, without any limitation, the proposition: the object of any subject is nothing else than the subject's own nature taken objectively. Such as are a man's thoughts and dispositions, such is his God; so much worth as a man has, so much and no more has his God. Consciousness of God is self-consciousness, knowledge of God is self-knowledge. By his God thou knowest the man, and by the man, his God; the two are identical. Whatever is God to a man, that is his heart and soul; and conversely, God is the more manifested inward nature, the expressed self of a man, —religion the solemn unveiling of a man's hidden treasures, the revelation of his intimate thoughts, the open confession of his love secrets.

But when religion—consciousness of God—is designated as the self-consciousness of man, this is not to be understood as affirming that the religious man is directly aware of this identity; for, on the contrary, ignorance of it is fundamental to the peculiar nature of religion. To preclude this misconception, it is better to say, religion is man's earliest and also indirect form of self-knowledge. Hence, religion everywhere precedes philosophy, as in the history of the race, so also in that of the individual. Man first of all sees his nature as if *out of* himself, before he finds it in himself. His own nature is in the first instance contemplated by him as that of another being. Religion is the childlike condition of humanity; but the child sees his nature—man—out of himself; in childhood a man is an object to himself, under the form of another man. Hence the historical progress of religion consists in this; that what by an earlier religion was regarded as objective, is now recognized as subjective; that is, what was formerly contemplated and worshipped as God is now perceived to be something *human*. What was at first religion becomes at a later period idolatry; man is seen to have adored his own nature. Man has given objectivity to himself, but has not recognized the object as his own nature: a later religion takes this forward step; every advance in religion is therefore a deeper self-knowledge. But every particular religion, while it pronounces its predecessors idolatrous, excepts itself—and necessarily so, otherwise it would no longer be religion—from the fate, the common nature of all religions: it imputes only to other religions what is the fault, if fault it be, of religion in general. Because it has a different object, a different tenor, because it has transcended the ideas of preceding religions, it erroneously supposes itself exalted above the necessary eternal laws which constitute the essence of religion—it fancies its objects, its ideas, to be superhuman. But the essence of religion, thus hidden from the religious, is evident to the thinker, by whom the religion is viewed objectively, which it cannot be by its votaries. And it is our task to show that the antithesis of divine and human is altogether illusory, that it is nothing else than the antithesis between the human nature in general and the human individual; that, consequently, the object and contents of the Christian religion are altogether human.

THE DIVINE ATTRIBUTES

. . . The divine being is nothing else than the human being, or, rather, the human nature, purified, freed from the limits of the individual man, made objective—i. e., contemplated and revered as another, a distinct being. All the attributes of the divine nature are, therefore, attributes of the human nature.

In relation to the attributes, the predicates of the Divine Being, this is admitted without hesitation, but by no means in relation to the subject of these predicates. The negation of the subject is held to be irreligion, nay, atheism; though not so the negation of the predicates. But that which has no predicates or qualities, has no effect upon me; that which has no effect upon me has no existence for me. To deny all the qualities of a being is equivalent to denying the being himself. A being without qualities is one which cannot become an object to the mind, and such a being is virtually non-existent. Where man deprives God of all qualities, God is no longer anything more to him than a negative being. To the truly religious man, God is not a being without qualities, because to him he is a positive, real being. The theory that God cannot be defined, and consequently cannot be known by man, is therefore the offspring of recent times, a product of modern unbelief. . . . On the ground that God is unknowable, man excuses himself to what is yet remaining of his religious conscience for his forgetfulness of God, his absorption in the world: he denies God practically by his conduct,—the world has possession of all his thoughts and inclinations,—but he does not deny him theoretically, he does not attack his existence; he lets that rest. But this existence does not affect or incommode him; it is merely negative existence, an existence without existence, a self-contradictory existence,—a state of being which, as to its effects, is not distinguishable from non-being. The denial of determinate, positive predicates concerning the divine nature is nothing else than a denial of religion, with, however, an appearance of religion in its favor, so that it is not recognized as a denial; it is simply a subtle, disguised atheism. The alleged religious horror of limiting God by positive predicates is only the irreligious wish to know nothing more of God, to banish God from the mind. Dread of limitation is dread of existence. . . .

There is, however, a still milder way of denying the divine predicates than the direct one just described. It is admitted that the predicates of the divine nature are finite, and more particularly, human qualities, but their rejection is rejected; they are even taken under protection, because it is necessary to man to have a definite conception of God, and since he is man he can form no other than a human conception of him. In relation to God, it is said, these predicates are certainly without any objective validity; but to me, if he is to exist for me, he cannot appear otherwise than as he does appear to me, namely, as a being with attributes analogous to the human. But this distinction between what God is in himself, and what he is for me destroys the peace of religion, and is besides in itself an unfounded and untenable distinction. I cannot know whether God is something else in himself or for himself than he is for me; what he is to me is to me all that he is. . . . In the distinction above stated, man takes a point of view above himself, i. e., above his nature, the absolute measure of his being; but this transcendentalism is only an illusion; for I can make the distinction between the object as it is in itself, and the object as it is for me, only where an object can really appear otherwise to me, not where it appears to me such as the absolute measure of my nature determines it to appear—such as it must appear to me. . . .

Scepticism is the arch-enemy of religion; but the distinction between object and conception—between God as he is in himself, and God as he is for me—is a sceptical distinction, and therefore an irreligious one. . . .

Wherever, therefore, this idea, that the religious predicates are only anthropomorphisms, has taken possession of a man, there has doubt, has unbelief, obtained the mastery of faith. And it is only the inconsequence of faint-heartedness and intellectual imbecility which does not proceed from this idea to the formal negation of the predicates, and from thence to the negation of the subject to which they relate. If thou doubtest the objective truth of the predicates, thou must also doubt the objective truth of the subject whose predicates they are. . . .

Thou believest in love as a divine attribute because thou thyself lovest; thou believest that God is a wise, benevolent being because thou knowest nothing better in thyself than benevolence and wisdom; and thou believest that God exists, that therefore he is a subject—whatever exists is a subject, whether it be defined as substance, person, essence, or otherwise—because thou thyself existest, art thyself a subject. . . . God is an existence, a subject to thee, for the same reason that he is to thee a wise, a blessed, a personal being. The distinction between the divine predicates and the divine subject is only this, that to thee the subject, the existence, does not appear an anthropomorphism, because the conception of it is necessarily involved in thy own existence as a subject, whereas the predicates do appear anthropomorphisms, because their necessity—the necessity that God should be conscious, wise, good, etc., —is not an immediate necessity, identical with the being of man, but is evolved by his self-consciousness, by the activity of his thought. I am a subject, I exist, whether I be wise or unwise, good or bad. To exist is to man the first datum; it constitutes the very idea of the subject; it is presupposed by the predicates. Hence man relinquishes the predicates, but the existence of God is to him a settled, irrefragable, absolutely certain, objective truth. But, nevertheless, this distinction is merely an apparent one. The necessity of the subject lies only in the necessity of the predicate. . . . Subject and predicate are distinguished only as existence and essence. The negation of the predicates is therefore the negation of the subject. What remains of the human subject when abstracted from the human attributes? Even in the language of common life the divine predicates—Providence, Omniscience, Omnipotence—are put for the divine subject. . . .

Religion is that conception of the nature of the world and of man which is essential to, i. e., identical with, a man's nature. . . . How then can I doubt of God, who is my being? To doubt of God is to doubt of myself. Only when God is thought of abstractly, when his predicates are the result of philosophic abstraction, arises the distinction or separation between subject and predicate, existence and nature—arises the fiction that the existence of the subject is something else than the predicate, something immediate, indubitable, in distinction from the predicate, which is held to be doubtful. But this is only a fiction. A God who has abstract predicates has also an abstract existence. . . .

Thus what theology and philosophy have held to be God, the Absolute, the Infinite, is not God; but that which they have held not to be God is God: namely, the attribute, the quality, whatever has reality. Hence he alone is the true atheist to whom the predicates of the Divine Being,—for example, love, wisdom, justice,—are nothing; not he to whom merely the subject of these predicates is nothing. And in no wise is the negation of the subject necessarily also a negation of the predicates considered in themselves. These have an intrinsic, independent reality; they force their recognition upon man by their very nature; they are self-evident truths to him; they prove, they attest themselves. It does not follow that goodness, justice, wisdom, are chimeras because the existence of God is a chimera, nor truths because this is a truth. The idea of God is dependent on the idea of justice, of benevolence; a God who is not benevolent, not just, not wise, is no God; but the converse does not hold. The fact is not that a quality is divine because God has it, but that God has it because it is in itself divine; because without it God would be a defective being. . . .

Now, when it is shown that what the subject is lies entirely in the attributes of the subject; that is, that the predicate is the true subject; it is also proved that if the divine predicates are attributes of the human nature, the subject of those predicates is also of the human nature. . . .

CONCLUSION

Man has his highest being, his God, in himself; not in himself as an individual, but in his essential nature, his species. No individual is an adequate representation of his species, but only the human individual is conscious of the distinction between the species and the individual; in the sense of this distinction lies the root of religion. The yearning of man after something above himself is nothing else than the longing after the perfect type of his nature, the yearning to be free from himself, i. e., from the limits and defects of his individuality. Individuality is the self-conditionating, the self-limitation of the species. Thus man has cognizance of nothing above himself, of nothing beyond the nature of humanity; but to the individual man this nature presents itself under the form of an individual man. Thus, for example, the child sees the nature of man *above itself* in the form of its parents, the pupil in the form of his tutor. But all feelings which man experiences toward a superior man, nay, in general, all moral feelings which man has towards man, are of a religious nature. *Man feels nothing towards God which he does not also feel toward man. Homo homini deus est.* . . . Thus even in religion man bows before the nature of man under the form of a personal human being; religion itself expressly declares—and all anthropomorphisms declare this in opposition to Pantheism,—*quod supra nos nihil ad nos;* that is, a God who inspires us with no human emotions, who does not reflect our own emotions, in a word, who is not a man,—such a God is nothing to us, has no interest for us, does not concern us.

STUDY QUESTIONS

1. Discuss the meaning and the implications of the phrase "Homo homini deus est."
2. What is agnosticisim? On what grounds does Feuerbach reject it?
3. Comment on the significance of Feuerbach's statement "I am nothing but a natural philosopher in the domain of mind" for his atheistic philosophy.
4. How can atheism be a religion for Feuerbach? What does he mean by *true* atheism?
5. Comment on the statement that "every advance in religion is therefore a deeper self-knowledge."
6. What distinction does Feuerbach draw between the divine predicates and the divine subject? Why would he rule out any doctrine of analogy regarding the divine predicates?
7. To what extent is religious scepticism possible on the basis of Feuerbach's principles?

Alfred N. Whitehead

🙵🙵🙵🙵🙵🙵🙵🙵🙵🙵🙵🙵🙵🙵🙵🙵🙵🙵🙵🙵🙵🙵🙵🙵🙵🙵🙵🙵🙵🙵🙵🙵🙵🙵🙵🙵🙵

RELIGION AND SCIENCE

🙵🙵🙵

Biographical Note. ALFRED NORTH WHITEHEAD (1861–1947) was born in a rural district of southern England, not far from Canterbury. His father was head of a private school and later became a minister of the Anglican Church. Whitehead received his university education at Cambridge, where he resided for thirty years, first as a Scholar and then as a Fellow and Senior Lecturer in mathematics. Continuing as university teacher of mathematics in London and Kensington from 1911 to 1924, he then accepted, at the age of sixty-three, a call to join the faculty of Harvard University as Professor of Philosophy. He remained in this position until his retirement in 1937.

His major research was distributed over three different fields, to each of which he rendered outstanding contributions. He began in mathematical logic, terminating this activity with the three volume *Principia Mathematica,* published jointly with Bertrand Russell (1910-1913). During the following ten years he wrote mainly on the philosophy of science, until at Harvard he turned to metaphysics, gaining here his greatest distinction. The first work of this final period was *Science and the Modern World* (1925), from which the following selection is taken, and its culmination was reached with *Process and Reality* (1929), the definitive formulation of his philosophy. Widely read later publications were *Adventures of Ideas* (1933) and *Modes of Thought* (1938).

* * *

Introductory Note. In his essay *Religion and Science*, Whitehead desires not merely to compare these two fields of human aspiration, but by way of this comparison to throw new light upon the nature of religion itself and upon the cause of what to him was an incontestable fact: the "gradual decay of religious influence in European civilization." Western religion is conceived by Whitehead as suffering from a disease-like loss of power, and he casts himself in the role of a doctor trying to diagnose the source of the trouble and to instigate its proper treatment.

Religion is introduced as an equal of science, both of them constituting "the two strongest forces which influence man—the force of our religious intuitions and the force of our impulse to accurate observation and logical deduction." Their areas of active pursuit are thus entirely different: "Science is concerned with the general conditions which are observed to regulate physical phenomena; whereas religion is wholly wrapped up in the contemplation of moral and aesthetic values." Religion then stands for an equally permanent engagement of man, an engagement, as he formulates it, in "a vision of something that gives meaning to all that passes, and yet eludes apprehension; something whose possession is the final good and yet is beyond reach." That this vision as an element in human experience has persistently shown "an upward trend," and that the history of this vision has been one "of persistent expansion," is named as "our one ground for optimism."

If so much is right with religion, if apart from it human life appears as nothing better than "a bagatelle of transient experience," what then is wrong with it today, what is the cause of its ever-waning influence? It is here that Whitehead uses the comparison with science to light up a basic characteristic that religion shares with science.

"Both religion and science have always been in a state of continual development." The principles of religion, Whitehead declares, "may be eternal, but the expression of those principles requires continual development." The evolution of religion is the ongoing quest for an ever-increasing purity and depth in the expression of its ideas, for its ever-new disengagement from "the adventitious notions which have crept into it by reason of the expression of its own ideas in terms of the imaginative picture of the world entertained in previous ages." In other words, religion, through a necessary imagery that it employs, is always bound to a respective imperfect stage of science, which is at the base of such imagery, and religion must modify its thought to keep up with advancing science.

Unfortunately, such adjustment of religious thought to an evolving world imagery as directed by science has not occurred in the history of Western civilization. Science has not been regarded and has not been used as the

natural friend, the natural helpmate of religion in its own continuous upward development, but rather as an enemy to be fought. Theologians in
general have "shirked the task of disengaging their spiritual message from
the association of a particular imagery."

If such has been the major cause of trouble in the historical movement
of religion, the prescription of its effective remedy can be in no doubt:
"Religion will not regain its old power until it can face change in the same
spirit as does science."

CONFLICT AND THE EVOLUTION OF KNOWLEDGE

The difficulty in approaching the question of the relations between
Religion and Science is, that its elucidation requires that we have in
our minds some clear idea of what we mean by either of the terms,
'religion' and 'science.' Also I wish to speak in the most general way
possible, and to keep in the background any comparison of particular
creeds, scientific or religious. We have got to understand the type of
connection which exists between the two spheres, and then to draw
some definite conclusions respecting the existing situation which at
present confronts the world.

The *conflict* between religion and science is what naturally occurs
to our minds when we think of this subject. It seems as though, during
the last half-century, the results of science and the beliefs of religion
had come into a position of frank disagreement, from which there can
be no escape, except by abandoning either the clear teaching of science,
or the clear teaching of religion. This conclusion has been urged by
controversialists on either side. Not by all controversialists, of course, but
by those trenchant intellects which every controversy calls out into
the open.

The distress of sensitive minds, and the zeal for truth, and the sense
of the importance of the issues, must command our sincerest sympathy.
When we consider what religion is for mankind, and what science is, it
is no exaggeration to say that the future course of history depends
upon the decision of this generation as to the relations between them.
We have here the two strongest general forces (apart from the mere
impulse of the various senses) which influence men, and they seem
to be set one against the other—the force of our religious intuitions,
and the force of our impulse to accurate observation and logical
deduction.

A great English statesman once advised his countrymen to use large-
scale maps, as a preservative against alarms, panics, and general mis-

understanding of the true relations between nations. In the same way in dealing with the clash between permanent elements of human nature, it is well to map our history on a large scale, and to disengage ourselves from our immediate absorption in the present conflicts. When we do this, we immediately discover two great facts. In the first place, there has always been a conflict between religion and science; and in the second place, both religion and science have always been in a state of continual development. In the early days of Christianity, there was a general belief among Christians that the world was coming to an end in the life time of people then living. We can make only indirect inferences as to how far this belief was authoritatively proclaimed; but it is certain that it was widely held, and that it formed an impressive part of the popular religious doctrine. The belief proved itself to be mistaken, and Christian doctrine adjusted itself to the change. Again in the early Church individual theologians very confidently deduced from the Bible opinions concerning the nature of the physical universe. In the year A.D. 535 a monk named Cosmas wrote a book which he entitled, *Christian Topography*. He was a travelled man who had visited India and Ethiopia; and finally he lived in a monastery at Alexandria, which was then a great centre of culture. In this book, basing himself upon the direct meaning of Biblical texts as construed by him in a literal fashion, he denied the existence of the antipodes, and asserted that the world is a flat parallelogram whose length is double its breadth.

In the seventeenth century the doctrine of the motion of the earth was condemned by a Catholic tribunal. A hundred years ago the extension of time demanded by geological science distressed religious people, Protestant and Catholic. And today the doctrine of evolution is an equal stumbling-block.* These are only a few instances illustrating a general fact.

But all our ideas will be in a wrong perspective if we think that this recurring perplexity was confined to contradictions between religion and science; and that in these controversies religion was always wrong, and science was always right. The true facts of the case are very much more complex, and refuse to be summarized in these simple terms.

Theology itself exhibits exactly the same character of gradual development, arising from an aspect of conflict between its own proper ideas. This fact is a commonplace to theologians, but is often obscured in the stress of controversy. I do not wish to overstate my case; so I will confine myself to Roman-Catholic writers. In the seventeenth century a learned

---

* The reader is reminded that Whitehead wrote this in 1925.

Jesuit, Father Petavius, showed that the theologians of the first three centuries of Christianity made use of phrases and statements which since the fifth century would be condemned as heretical. Also Cardinal Newman devoted a treatise to the discussion of the development of doctrine. He wrote it before he became a great Catholic ecclesiastic; but throughout his life, it was never retracted and continually reissued.

Science is even more changeable than theology. No man of science could subscribe without qualification to Galileo's beliefs, or to Newton's beliefs, or to all his own scientific beliefs of ten years ago.

In both regions of thought, additions, distinctions, and modifications have been introduced. So that now, even when the same assertion is made today as was made a thousand, or even fifteen hundred years ago, it is made subject to limitations or expansions of meaning, which were not contemplated at the earlier epoch. We are told by logicians that a proposition must be either true or false, and that there is no middle term. But in practice, we may know that a proposition expresses an important truth, but that it is subject to limitations and qualifications which at present remain undiscovered. It is a general feature of our knowledge, that we are insistently aware of important truths; and yet that the only formulations of these truths which we are able to make presuppose a general standpoint of conceptions which may have to be modified. I will give you two illustrations, both from science: Galileo said that the earth moves and that the sun is fixed; the Inquisition said that the earth is fixed and the sun moves; and Newtonian astronomers, adopting an absolute theory of space, said that both the sun and the earth move. But now we say that any one of these three statements is equally true, provided that you have fixed your sense of 'rest' and 'motion' in the way required by the statement adopted. At the date of Galileo's controversy with the Inquisition, Galileo's way of stating the facts was, beyond question, the fruitful procedure for the sake of scientific research. But in itself it was not more true than the formulation of the Inquisition. But at that time the modern concepts of relative motion were in nobody's mind; so that the statements were made in ignorance of the qualifications required for their more perfect truth. Yet this question of the motions of the earth and the sun expresses a real fact in the universe; and all sides had got hold of important truths concerning it. But with the knowledge of those times, the truths appeared to be inconsistent.

Again I will give you another example taken from the state of modern physical science. Since the time of Newton and Huyghens in the seventeenth century there have been two theories as to the physical nature of light. Newton's theory was that a beam of light consists of a stream of very minute particles, or corpuscles, and that we have the sensation of light when these corpuscles strike the retinas of our eyes. Huyghens' theory was that light consists of very minute waves of trembling in an all-pervading ether, and that these waves are travelling along a beam of light. The two theories are contradictory. In the eighteenth century Newton's theory was believed, in the nineteenth century Huyghens' theory was believed. Today there is one large group of phenomena which can be explained only on the wave theory, and another large group which can be explained only on the corpuscular theory. Scientists have to leave it at that, and wait for the future, in the hope of attaining some wider vision which reconciles both.

We should apply these same principles to the questions in which there is a variance between science and religion. We would believe nothing in either sphere of thought which does not appear to us to be certified by solid reasons based upon the critical research either of ourselves or of competent authorities. But granting that we have honestly taken this precaution, a clash between the two on points of detail where they overlap should not lead us hastily to abandon doctrines for which we have solid evidence. It may be that we are more interested in one set of doctrines than in the other. But, if we have any sense of perspective and of the history of thought, we shall wait and refrain from mutual anathemas.

We should wait: but we should not wait passively, or in despair. The clash is a sign that there are wider truths and finer perspectives within which a reconciliation of a deeper religion and a more subtle science will be found.

In one sense, therefore, the conflict between science and religion is a slight matter which has been unduly emphasized. A mere logical contradiction cannot in itself point to more than the necessity of some readjustments, possibly of a very minor character on both sides. Remember the widely different aspects of events which are dealt with in science and in religion respectively. Science is concerned with the general conditions which are observed to regulate physical phenomena; whereas religion is wholly wrapped up in the contemplation of moral and aesthetic values. On the one side there is the law of gravitation, and on the other the contemplation of the beauty of holiness. What one side sees, the other misses; and vice versa. . . .

It would, however, be missing the point to think that we need not trouble ourselves about the conflict between science and religion. In an intellectual age there can be no active interest which puts aside all hope of a vision of the harmony of truth. To acquiesce in discrepancy is destructive of candour, and of moral cleanliness. It belongs to the self-respect of intellect to pursue every tangle of thought to its final unravelment. If you check that impulse, you will get no religion and no science from an awakened thoughtfulness. The important question is, In what spirit are we going to face the issue? There we come to something absolutely vital.

A clash of doctrines is not a disaster—it is an opportunity. . . . In formal logic, a contradiction is the signal of a defeat: but in the evolution of real knowledge it marks the first step in progress towards a victory. This is one great reason for the utmost toleration of variety of opinion. Once and forever, this duty of toleration has been summed up in the words, "Let both grow together until the harvest" (Mt. 13:30). The failure of Christians to act up to this precept, of the highest authority, is one of the curiosities of religious history. But we have not yet exhausted the discussion of the moral temper required for the pursuit of truth. There are short cuts leading merely to an illusory success. It is easy enough to find a theory, logically harmonious and with important applications in the region of fact, provided that you are content to disregard half your evidence. Every age produces people with clear logical intellects, and with the most praiseworthy grasp of the importance of some sphere of human experience, who have elaborated, or inherited, a scheme of thought which exactly fits those experiences which claim their interest. Such people are apt resolutely to ignore, or to explain away, all evidence which confuses their scheme with contradictory instances. What they cannot fit in is for them nonsense. An unflinching determination to take the whole evidence into account is the only method of preservation against the fluctuating extremes of fashionable opinion. This advice seems so easy, and is in fact so difficult to follow.

One reason for this difficulty is that we cannot think first and act afterwards. From the moment of birth we are immersed in action, and can only fitfully guide it by taking thought. We have, therefore, in various spheres of experience to adopt those ideas which seem to work within those spheres. It is absolutely necessary to trust to ideas which are generally adequate, even though we know that there are subtleties and distinctions beyond our ken. Also apart from the necessities of action, we cannot even keep before our minds the whole evidence except under the guise of doctrines which are incompletely harmonised. We cannot think in terms of an indefinite multiplicity of detail; our evidence can acquire its proper importance only if it comes before us marshalled by general ideas. These ideas we inherit—they form the tradition of our civilization. Such traditional ideas are never static. They are either fading into meaningless formulae, or are gaining power by the new lights thrown by a more delicate apprehension. They are transformed by the urge of critical reason, by the vivid evidence of emotional experience, and by the cold certainties of scientific perception. One fact is certain, you cannot keep them still. No generation can merely reproduce its ancestors. You may preserve the life in a flux of form, or preserve the form amid an ebb of life. But you cannot permanently enclose the same life in the same mould.

THE NEED FOR CHANGE IN RELIGION

The present state of religion among the European races illustrates the statements which I have been making. The phenomena are mixed. There have been reactions and revivals. But on the whole, during many generations, there has been a gradual decay of religious influence in European civilisation. Each revival touches a lower peak than its predecessor, and each period of slackness a lower depth. The average curve marks a steady fall in religious tone. In some countries the interest in religion is higher than in others. But in those countries where the interest is relatively high, it still falls as the generations pass. Religion is tending to degenerate into a decent formula wherewith to embellish a comfortable life. A great historical movement on this scale results from the convergence of many causes. I wish to suggest two of them which lie within the scope of this chapter for consideration.

In the first place for over two centuries religion has been on the defensive, and on a weak defensive. The period has been one of unprecedented intellectual progress. In this way a series of novel situations have been produced for thought. Each such occasion has found the religious thinkers unprepared. Something, which has been proclaimed to be vital, has finally, after struggle, distress, and anathema, been modified and otherwise interpreted. The next generation of religious apologists then congratulates the religious world on the deeper insight which has been gained. The result of the continued repetition of this undignified retreat, during many generations, has at last almost entirely destroyed the intellectual authority of religious thinkers. Consider this contrast: when Darwin or Einstein proclaim theories which modify our ideas, it is a triumph for science. We do not go about saying that there is another defeat for science, because its old ideas have been abandoned. We know that another step of scientific insight has been gained.

Religion will not regain its old power until it can face change in the same spirit as does science. Its principles may be eternal, but the expression of those principles requires continual development. This evolution of religion is in the main a disengagement of its own proper ideas from the adventitious notions which have crept into it by reason of the expression of its own ideas in terms of the imaginative picture of the world entertained in previous ages. Such a release of religion from the bonds of imperfect science is all to the good. It stresses its own genuine message. The great point to be kept in mind is that normally an advance in science will show that statements of various religious beliefs require some sort of modification. It may be that they have to be expanded or explained, or indeed entirely restated. If the religion is a sound expression of truth, this modification will only exhibit more adequately the exact point which is of importance. This process is a gain. In so far, therefore, as any religion has any contact with physical facts, it is to be expected that the point of view of those facts must be continually modified as scientific knowledge advances. In this way, the exact relevance of these facts for religious thought will grow more and more clear. The progress of science must result in the unceasing modification of religious thought, to the great advantage of religion.

The religious controversies of the sixteenth and seventeenth centuries put theologians into a most unfortunate state of mind. They were always attacking and defending. They pictured themselves as the garrison of a fort surrounded by hostile forces. All such pictures express half-truths. That is why they are so popular. But they are dangerous. This particular picture fostered a pugnacious party spirit which really expresses an ultimate lack of faith. They dared not modify, because they shirked the task of disengaging their spiritual message from the associations of a particular imagery.

Let me explain myself by an example. In the early medieval times, Heaven was in the sky, and Hell was underground; volcanoes were the jaws of Hell. I do not assert that these beliefs entered into the official formulations; but they did enter into the popular understanding of the general doctrines of Heaven and Hell. These notions were what everyone thought to be implied by the doctrine of the future state. They entered into the explanations of the most influential exponents of Christian belief. For example, they occur in the *Dialogues* of Pope Gregory, the Great, a man whose high official position is surpassed only by the magnitude of his services to humanity. I am not saying what we ought to believe about the future state. But whatever be the right doctrine, in this instance the clash between religion and science, which has relegated the earth to the position of a second-rate planet attached to a second-rate sun, has been greatly to the benefit of the spirituality of religion by dispersing these medieval fancies.

Another way of looking at this question of the evolution of religious thought is to note that any verbal form of statement which has been before the world for some time discloses ambiguities; and that often such ambiguities strike at the very heart of the meaning. The effective sense in which a doctrine has been held in the past cannot be determined by the mere logical analysis of verbal statements, made in ignorance of the logical trap. You have to take into account the whole reaction of human nature to the scheme of thought. This reaction is of a mixed character, including elements of emotion derived from our lower natures. It is here that the impersonal criticism of science and of philosophy comes to the aid of religious evolution. Example after example can be given of this motive force in development. For example, the logical difficulties inherent in the doctrine of the moral cleansing of human nature by the power of religion rent Christianity in the days of Pelagius and Augustine—that is to say, at the beginning of the fifth century. Echoes of that controversy still linger in theology.

So far, my point has been this: that religion is the expression of one type of fundamental experiences of mankind: that religious thought develops into an increasing accuracy of expression, disengaged from adventitious imagery: that the interaction between religion and science is one great factor in promoting this development.

I now come to my second reason for the modern fading of interest in religion. This involves the ultimate question which I stated in my opening sentences. We have to know what we mean by religion. The churches, in their presentation of their answers to this query, have put forward aspects of religion which are expressed in terms either suited to the emotional reactions of bygone times or directed to excite modern emotional interests of a nonreligious character. What I mean under the first heading is that religious appeal is directed partly to excite that instinctive fear of the wrath of a tyrant which was inbred in the unhappy populations of the arbitrary empires of the ancient world, and in particular to excite that fear of an all-powerful arbitrary tyrant behind the unknown forces of nature. This appeal to ready instinct of brute fear is losing its force. It lacks any directness of response, because modern science and modern conditions of life have taught us to meet occasions of apprehension by a critical analysis of their causes and conditions. Religion is the reaction of human nature to its search for God. The presentation of God under the aspect of power awakens every modern instinct of critical reaction. This is fatal; for religion collapses unless its main positions command immediacy of assent. In this respect the old phraseology is at variance with the psychology of modern civilisations. This change in psychology is largely due to science, and is one of the chief ways in which the advance of science has weakened the hold of the old religious forms of expression. The nonreligious motive which has entered into modern religious thought is the desire for a comfortable organisation of modern society. Religion has been presented as valuable for the ordering of life. Its claims have been rested upon its function as a sanction to right conduct. Also the purpose of right conduct quickly degenerates into the formation of pleasing social relations. We have here a subtle degradation of religious ideas, following upon their gradual purification under the influence of keener ethical intuitions. Conduct is a by-product of religion—an inevitable by-product, but not the main point. Every great religious teacher has revolted against the presentation of religion as a mere sanction of rules of conduct. St. Paul denounced the Law, and Puritan divines spoke of the filthy rags of righteousness. The insistence upon rules of conduct marks the ebb of religious fervor. Above and beyond all things, the religious life is not a research after comfort. I must now state, in all diffidence, what I conceive to be the essential character of the religious spirit.

Religion is the vision of something which stands beyond, behind, and within, the passing flux of immediate things; something which is real, and yet waiting to be realized; something which is a remote possibility, and yet the greatest of present facts; something that gives meaning to all that passes, and yet eludes apprehension; something whose possession is the final good, and yet is beyond reach; something which is the ultimate ideal, and the hopeless quest.

The immediate reaction of human nature to the religious vision is worship. Religion has emerged into human experience mixed with the crudest fancies of barbaric imagination. Gradually, slowly, steadily the vision recurs in history under nobler form and with clearer expression. It is the one element in human experience which persistently shows an upward trend. It fades and then recurs. But when it renews its force, it recurs with an added richness and purity of content. The fact of the religious vision, and its history of persistent expansion, is our one ground for optimism. Apart from it, human life is a flash of occasional enjoyments lighting up a mass of pain and misery, a bagatelle of transient experience.

The vision claims nothing but worship; and worship is a surrender to the claim for assimilation, urged with the motive force of mutual love. The vision never overrules. It is always there, and it has the power of love presenting the one purpose whose fulfilment is eternal harmony. Such order as we find in nature is never force—it presents itself as the one harmonious adjustment of complex detail. Evil is the brute motive force of fragmentary purpose, disregarding the eternal vision. Evil is overruling, retarding, hurting. The power of God is the worship He inspires. That religion is strong which in its ritual and its modes of thought evokes an apprehension of the commanding vision. The worship of God is not a rule of safety—it is an adventure of the spirit, a flight after the unattainable. The death of religion comes with the repression of the high hope of adventure.

STUDY QUESTIONS

1. Explain and illustrate in what sense both religion and science have always been in a state of continual development.
2. How is it shown that the progress of science or religion does not necessarily invalidate important truth formerly held, but rather qualifies it?
3. What example can be given from science to demonstrate that even contradictory theories are allowed to exist side by side?
4. How should and how should not a clash of theories be looked upon?
5. Why must the progress of science result in the unceasing modification of religious thought?
6. What is the consequence of theologians consistently "shirking the task" of disengaging the spiritual message of their religion from the imagery of an outdated science?
7. In what way are science and philosophy meant to help rather than to hinder religion?
8. What does religious vision stand for and how does it compare with other elements of human experience throughout their histories?

Martin Buber

▨▨

RELIGION AND PHILOSOPHY

▨▨

Biographical Note. MARTIN BUBER (1878–   ), one of the leading religious philosophers of our age, was born in Poland into a Jewish community and raised by his grandfather, a banker and scholarly editor of classic
rabbinic texts. He studied philosophy at the Universities of Vienna and
Berlin, writing his doctoral dissertation on Christian mystics of the Renaissance and Reformation. He became active in the Zionist cause at the turn
of the century and for more than fifty years has helped to shape its policy.
From 1904 on, he engaged for a number of years in an intensive study of
Hasidism, a movement of Jewish mysticism, originating in 18th century
Eastern Europe and continuing to the present. A considerable portion of
Buber's written work is devoted to the publication and interpretation of the
traditions and teachings of this religious sect.

For seven years prior to 1923, he worked as editor of a German Jewish
journal. He then accepted an appointment to the newly created chair of
Jewish philosophy, later extended to include the history of religions, at the
University of Frankfurt, which he held until his dismissal by the National-
Socialist regime in 1933. Five years later he departed for Palestine to become professor of social philosophy at the Hebrew University in Jerusalem,
in which position he remained until his retirement in 1951.

The work that laid the foundation for his religious philosophy is *I and*

Thou, first published in 1923. Important philosophic essays are found in *Between Man and Man* (1947), *Good and Evil* (1953), *Eclipse of God* (1953), from which a selection follows, and *Pointing the Way* (1957).

* * *

Introductory Note.   Blaise Pascal, the French mathematician and religious thinker of the seventeenth century, recorded as his greatest moment in life a divine encounter which he described in part as follows: "God of Abraham, God of Isaac, God of Jacob, not of the philosophers and the learned!" In this exclamation a problem is contained which has troubled Western thinkers ever since the time of the ancient Greeks: the problem of the essential difference between philosophy and religion. Both these fields of human endeavor concern themselves with God, they face up to his existence, they arrive at decisions or conclusions regarding him, but where does the difference lie? Does one of them perhaps constitute a superior, more mature form of treating the problem of God, and is the other one immature, inferior, to be left behind in the future evolution of mankind? The words of Pascal merely testify to the fact that the God of religion, the God of Abraham, of Isaac, of Jacob, is not the God of the philosophers. They do in no way indicate the nature of the distinction.

The life work of Buber as a religious thinker, a "religious existentialist," as he is also called, addresses itself to this question. In his pioneering work, *I and Thou,* he developed first the categories by way of which the dimension of the problem as he saw it can be grasped. His later works were dedicated to an ever-renewed, ever-deepened, ever-amplified application of these categories.

As the following selection indicates, religion—and that means for Buber the "religious relationship," the relationship between God and man—invariably implies an involvement of the whole person such as only happens where an *I* meets a *Thou.* But the religious relationship is distinguished from every other I–Thou relationship as one "in which unlimited Being becomes, as absolute person, my partner." In contrast to this, "philosophy is founded on the duality of subject and object," its characterizing relationship is not I–Thou, but *I–It.* The philosophic attitude splits apart a possible togetherness "into two entirely distinct modes of existence, one which is able to do nothing but observe and reflect and one which is able to do nothing but be observed and reflected upon."

These two relationships are shown to belong to the structure of human existence itself: they are complementary. Religion and philosophy therefore, representing their highest respective manifestations in human experience, are equally interdependent: they require each other for their ever-evolving movement. But Buber leaves no doubt either that ultimately religion stands for a fulfillment which philosophy cannot but serve, since only in the former is man involved with his whole existence. It is religion, not philosophy, which demonstrates to man its supreme existential relevance.

DUALITY IN RELIGION AND PHILOSOPHY

The difficulty of making a radical distinction between the spheres of philosophy and religion, and, at the same time, the correct way of overcoming this difficulty, appear most clearly to us when we contrast two figures who are representative of the two spheres—Epicurus and Buddha.

Not only does Epicurus teach that there are gods, that is to say, immortal and perfect beings who live in the spaces between the worlds and yet are without power over the world or interest in it, but he also holds that one should worship these gods through pious representations of them and through the traditional rites, especially devout and fitting sacrifices. He says that he himself worships and sacrifices, but then cites the words of a character from a comedy: "I have sacrificed to gods who take no notice of me." Here is a kind of dogma and also a cultic practice, and yet clearly a philosophical rather than a religious attitude.

Buddha treats the gods of popular belief, so far as he deigns to mention them at all, with calm and considered good-will, not unmixed with irony. These gods are, to be sure, powerful, and, unlike the gods of Epicurus, concerned with the human world. But they are bound like men by the chain of desire, heavenly figures entangled, even as men, in the "wheel of births." One may worship them, but the legends consistently picture them as paying homage to him, the Buddha, the "Awakened One," freed and freeing from the wheel of births. On the other hand, Buddha knows a genuinely divine, an "Unborn, Unoriginated, Uncreated." He knows it only in this wholly negative designation, and he refuses to make any assertions about it. Yet he stands related to it with his whole being. Here is neither proclamation nor worship of a deity, yet unmistakable religious reality.

Thus the personal manifestation of the divine is not decisive for the genuineness of religion. What is decisive is that I relate myself to the divine as to Being which is over against me, though *not* over against me *alone*. Complete inclusion of the divine in the sphere of the human self abolishes its divinity. It is not necessary to know something about God in order really to believe in Him: many true believers know how to talk *to* God, but not *about* Him. If one dares to turn toward the unknown God, to go to meet Him, to call to Him, Reality is present: He who refuses to limit God to the transcendent has a fuller conception of Him than he who does so limit Him. But he who confines God within the immanent means something other than Him. . . .

All great religiousness shows us that reality of faith means living in relationship to Being "believed in," that is, unconditionally affirmed, absolute Being. All great philosophy, on the other hand, shows us that cogitative truth means making the absolute into an object from which all other objects must be derived. Even if the believer has in mind an unlimited and nameless absolute which cannot be conceived in a personal form, if he really thinks of it as existing Being which stands over against him, his belief has existential reality. Conversely even if he thinks of the absolute as limited within personal form, if he reflects on it as on an object, he is philosophizing. Even when the "Unoriginated" is not addressed with voice or soul, religion is still founded on the duality of I and Thou. Even when the philosophical act culminates in a vision of unity, philosophy is founded on the duality of subject and object. The duality of I and Thou finds its fulfilment in the religious relationship; the duality of subject and object sustains philosophy while it is carried on. The first arises out of the original situation of the individual, his living before the face of Being, turned toward him as he is turned toward it. The second springs from the splitting apart of this togetherness into two entirely distinct modes of existence, one which is able to do nothing but observe and reflect and one which is able to do nothing but be observed and reflected upon. I and Thou exist in and by means of lived concreteness; subject and object, products of abstraction, last only as long as that power is at work. The religious relationship, no matter what different forms and constellations it takes, is in its essence nothing other than the unfolding of the existence that is lent to us. The philosophical attitude is the product of a consciousness which conceives of itself as autonomous and strives to become so. In philosophy the spirit of man gathers itself by virtue of the spiritual work. Indeed, one might say that here, on the peak of consummated thought, spirituality, which has been disseminated throughout the person, first becomes spiritual substance. But in religion, when this is nothing other than unfolded simple existence standing as a whole over against eternal Being, spirituality too becomes a part of personal wholeness.

Philosophy errs in thinking of religion as founded in an intellectual act, even if an inadequate one, and in therefore regarding the essence of religion as the knowledge of an object which is indifferent to being known. As a result, philosophy understands faith as an affirmation of truth lying somewhere between clear knowledge and confused opinion. Religion, on the other hand, insofar as it speaks of knowledge at all, does not understand it as a mental relation of a thinking subject to a neutral object of thought, but rather as a mutual contact, as the genuinely reciprocal meeting in the fullness of life between one active existence and another. Similarly, it understands faith as the entrance into this reciprocity, as binding oneself in relationship with an undemonstrable and unprovable, yet even so, in relationship, knowable Being, from whom all meaning comes. . . .

THE LIFE-CHARACTER OF RELIGION

The more real religion is, so much the more it means its own overcoming. It wills to cease to be the special domain "Religion" and wills to become life. It is concerned in the end not with specific religious acts, but with redemption from all that is specific. Historically and biographically, it strives toward the pure Everyday. Religion is in the religious view the exile of man; his homeland is unarbitrary life "in the face of God." It goes against the most real will of religion to describe it in terms of the special characteristics that it has developed rather than in terms of its life-character. Religion must, of course, be described in such a way that its special characteristics do not evaporate into universality but are instead seen as grounded in the fundamental relation of religion to the whole of life.

When we look at the history of a historical religion, we see the reoccurrence in different periods and phases of an inner battle which remains essentially the same. It is the struggle of the religious element against the non-religious elements which invade it from all sides—metaphysics, gnosis, magic, politics, etc. This medley seeks to take the place of the flowing life of faith which is renewed in the flux. It finds helpers in myth and cult, both of which originally served only as expression of the religious relationship. In order to preserve its purity the religious element must combat the tendency of this conglomerate to become autonomous and to make itself independent of the religious life of the person. This battle is consummated in prophetic protest, heretical revolt, reformational retrenchment, and a new founding which arises through the desire to return to the original religious element. It is a struggle for the protection of lived concreteness as the meeting-place between the human and the divine. The actually lived concrete is the "moment" in its unforeseeableness and its irrecoverableness, in its undivertible character of happening but once, in its decisiveness, in its secret dialogue between that which happens and that which is willed, between fate and action, address and answer. This lived concreteness is threatened by the invasion of the extra-religious elements, and it is protected on all fronts by the religious in its unavoidable aloneness.

The religious essence in every religion can be found in its highest certainty. That is the certainty that the meaning of existence is open and accessible in the actual lived concrete, not above the struggle with reality but in it.

That meaning is open and accessible in the actual lived concrete does not mean it is to be won and possessed through any type of analytical or synthetic investigation or through any type of reflection upon the lived concrete. Meaning is to be experienced in living action and suffering itself, in the unreduced immediacy of the moment. Of course, he who aims at the experiencing of experience will necessarily miss the meaning, for he destroys the spontaneity of the mystery. Only he reaches the meaning who stands firm, without holding back or reservation, before the whole might of reality and answers it in a living way. He is ready to confirm with his life the meaning which he has attained.

Every religious utterance is a vain attempt to do justice to the meaning which has been attained. All religious expression is only an intimation of its attainment. The reply of the people of Israel on Sinai, "All that the Lord has spoken we will do" (Ex. 19:8), expresses the decisive with naïve and unsurpassable pregnancy. The meaning is found through the engagement of one's own person; it only reveals itself as one takes part in its revelation.

All religious reality begins with what Biblical religion calls the "fear of God." It comes when our existence between birth and death becomes incomprehensible and uncanny, when all security is shattered through the mystery. This is not the relative mystery of that which is inaccessible only to the present state of human knowledge and is hence in principle discoverable. It is the essential mystery, the inscrutableness of which belongs to its very nature; it is the unknowable. Through this dark gate (which is only a gate and not, as some theologians believe, a dwelling) the believing man steps forth into the everyday which is henceforth hallowed as the place in which he has to live with the mystery. He steps forth directed and assigned to the concrete, contextual situations of his existence. That he henceforth accepts the situation as given him by the Giver is what Biblical religion calls the "fear of God."

An important philosopher of our day, Whitehead, asks how the Old Testament saying that the fear of God is the beginning of wisdom is to be reconciled with the New Testament saying that God is love. Whitehead has not fully grasped the meaning of the word "beginning." He who begins with the love of God without having previously experienced the fear of God, loves an idol which he himself has made, a god whom it is easy enough to love. He does not love the real God who is, to begin with, dreadful and incomprehensible. Consequently, if he then perceives, as Job and Ivan Karamazov perceive, that God is dreadful and incomprehensible, he is terrified. He despairs of God and the world if God does not take pity on him, as He did on Job, and bring him to love Him Himself. This is presumably what Whitehead meant when he said that religion is the passage from God the void to God the enemy and from Him to God the companion. That the believing man who goes through the gate of dread is directed to the concrete contextual situations of his existence means just this: that he endures in the face of God the reality of lived life, dreadful and incomprehensible though it be. He loves it in the love of God, whom he has learned to love.

For this reason, every genuine religious expression has a personal character (whether it is open or hidden), for it is spoken out of a concrete situation in which the person takes part as a person. This is true also in those instances where, out of a noble modesty, the word "I" is in principle avoided. Confucius, who spoke of himself almost as unwillingly as of God, once said: "I do not murmur against God, and I bear no ill will toward men. I search here below, but I penetrate above. He who knows me is God." Religious expression is bound to the concrete situation.

That one accepts the concrete situation as given does not, in any way, mean that he must be ready to accept that which meets him as "God-given" in its pure factuality. He may, rather, declare the extremest enmity toward this happening and treat its "givenness" as only intended to draw forth his own opposing force. But he will not remove himself from the concrete situation as it actually is; he will, instead, enter into it, even if in the form of fighting against it. Whether field of work or field of battle, he accepts the place in which he is placed. He knows no floating of the spirit above concrete reality; to him even the sublimest spirituality is an illusion if it is not bound to the situation. Only the spirit which is bound to the situation is prized by him as bound to the Pneuma, the spirit of God. . . .

INTERDEPENDENCE OF RELIGION AND PHILOSOPHY

Religion, however, is not allowed to remain blind to philosophy's great engagement. To this engagement necessarily belongs the actual, ever-recurring renunciation of the original relational bond, of the reality which takes place between I and Thou, of the spontaneity of the moment. Religion must know knowledge not only as a need but also as a duty of man. It must know that history moves along the way of this need and duty, that, Biblically speaking, the eating of the tree of knowledge leads out of Paradise but into the world.

The world, the world as objective and self-contained connection of all being, natural and spiritual, would not exist for us if our thinking, which develops in philosophizing, did not melt together the world-concreta which are presented to us. It would not exist if our thinking did not merge these world-concreta with one another and with all that man has ever experienced and has ever comprehended as experienceable. And spirit all the more would not genuinely exist for us as objective connection if thought did not objectify it, if spirit itself as philosophy did not objectify and unite itself. Only through the fact that philosophy radically abandoned the relation with the concrete did that amazing construction of an objective thought-continuum become possible, with a static system of concepts and a dynamic one of problems. Every man who can "think" may enter this continuum through the simple use of this ability, through a thinking comprehension of thought. Only through this is there an "objective" mutual understanding, that is, one which does not, like the religious, entail two men's each recognizing the other by the personal involvement in life which he has achieved. Instead, both fulfil a function of thought which demands no involvement in life and bear in fruitful dialectic the tension between the reciprocal ideas and problems.

The religious communication of a content of being takes place in paradox. It is not a demonstrable assertion (theology which pretends to be this is rather a questionable type of philosophy), but a pointing toward the hidden realm of existence of the hearing man himself and that which is to be experienced there and there alone. . . . A content of being is objectively communicable and translatable only in and through philosophy, consequently only through the objectifying elaboration of the situation.

A sceptical verdict about the ability of philosophy to lead to and contain truth is in no way here implied. The possibility of cogitative truth does not, indeed, mean a cogitative possession of being, but a cogitative real relation to being. Systems of thought are manifestations of genuine thought-relations to being made possible through abstraction. They are not mere "aspects," but rather valid documents of these cogitative voyages of discovery.

A similarity and a difference between the ways in which religion and philosophy affect the person remain to be mentioned.

In religious reality the person has concentrated himself into a whole, for it is only as a unified being that he is able to live religiously. In this wholeness thought is naturally also included as an autonomous province but one which no longer strives to absolutize its autonomy. A totalization also takes place in genuine philosophers but no unification. Instead, thinking overruns and overwhelms all the faculties and provinces of the person. In a great act of philosophizing even the finger-tips think—but they no longer feel.

For man whatever exists is either face-to-face being or passive object. The essence of man arises from this twofold relation to what exists. These are not two external phenomena but the two basic modes of being related to what exists. The child that calls to his mother and the child that watches his mother—or to give a more exact example, the child that silently speaks to his mother through nothing other than looking into her eyes and the same child that looks at something on the mother as at any other object—show the twofoldness in which man stands and remains standing. Something of the sort is sometimes even to be noticed in those near death. What is here apparent is the double structure of human existence itself: the two basic modes of our existence in general—I–Thou and I–It. I–Thou finds its highest intensity and transfiguration in religious reality, in which unlimited Being becomes, as absolute person, my partner. I–It finds its highest concentration and illumination in philosophical knowledge. In this knowledge the extraction of the subject from the I of the immediate lived togetherness of I and It and the transformation of the It into the object detached in its essence produces the exact thinking of contemplated existing beings, yes, of contemplated Being itself.

Divine truth, according to a saying of Franz Rosenzweig,* wishes to be implored "with both hands," that of philosophy and that of theology. "He who prays with the double prayer of the believer and the unbeliever," he continues, "to him it will not deny itself." But what is the prayer of the unbeliever? Rosenzweig means by this Goethe's prayer to his own destiny, a prayer whose Thou is no Thou. But there is another prayer of the philosophers still farther from the Thou, and yet, it seems to me, more important.

The religious reality of the meeting with the Meeter who shines through all forms and is Himself formless, knows no image of Him, nothing comprehensible as object. It knows only the presence of the Present One. Symbols of Him, whether images or ideas, always exist first when and insofar as Thou becomes He, and that means It. But

---

* German philosopher and theologian; a late friend of Buber's.

the ground of human existence in which it gathers and becomes whole is also the deep abyss out of which images arise. Symbols of God come into being, some of which allow themselves to be fixed in lasting visibility even in earthly material and some of which tolerate no other sanctuary than that of the soul. Symbols supplement one another, they merge, they are set before the community of believers in plastic or theological forms. And God, so we may surmise, does not despise all these similarly and necessarily untrue images, but rather suffers that one look at Him through them. Yet they always quickly desire to be more than they are, more than signs and pointers toward Him. It finally happens ever again that they swell themselves up and obstruct the way to Him, and He removes Himself from them. Then comes round the hour of the philosopher, who rejects both the image and the God which it symbolizes and opposes to it the pure idea, which he even at times understands as the negation of all metaphysical ideas. This critical "atheism" (*Atheoi* is the name which the Greeks gave to those who denied the traditional gods) is the prayer which is spoken in the third person in the form of speech about an idea. It is the prayer of the philosopher to the again unknown God. It is well suited to arouse religious men and to impel them to set forth right across the God-deprived reality to a new meeting. On their way they destroy the images which manifestly no longer do justice to God. The spirit moves them which moved the philosopher.

STUDY QUESTIONS

1. How can the examples of Epicurus and Buddha be used to distinguish between the spheres of philosophy and religion?
2. How does all great "religiousness" differ from all great philosophy?
3. What types of duality are religion and philosophy based upon respectively?
4. Why is religion in the religious view the "exile of man"?
5. Why can no religious utterance do justice to the meaning of what it is to convey?
6. In what way does love of God presuppose fear of God?
7. What indispensable service does philosophy render to religion?
8. What two basic modes of man's existential relationships determine his essence?
9. How can it be explained that symbols of God in an ever-renewing process first come into existence and then go out of it again?

VI

Social and
Political Philosophy

St. Thomas Aquinas

❧❧❧

THE NATURAL LAW

❧❧❧

Introductory Note. The medieval conception of Natural Law had its inception in the ancient Stoic doctrine, and more particularly in the very influential expression of this doctrine in the *Republic* of Cicero. Cicero's doctrine that there is a universal law of nature based upon the providence of God and the social nature of man made his ideas most favorable to the Christian philosophy and theology. Given such a doctrine, plus his own conception of God as the creator and the efficient and final cause of the universe, it was not difficult for Aquinas to arrive at a Christian conception of natural law.

Defining law as "nothing else than an ordinance of reason for the common good, promulgated by him who has the care of the community," Aquinas proceeds to his famous fourfold division of law into the Eternal Law, the Divine Law, the Natural Law, and the Human Law. The Eternal Law is simply God's reason ordering the universe to its proper ends. It can be known only in part by man, just as man has but an imperfect knowledge of the Divine Nature. The Divine Law represents that portion of the Eternal Law that has been revealed by God to man. It is the more positive expression of the Eternal Law that man possesses through divine revelation. Thus the

* For biographical information see the note included with the selection from Aquinas in the Philosophy of Religion, (page 331).

From St. Thomas Aquinas, *Summa Theologica*, I-II., Qq. 90, 91, 93, 94. Reprinted with the permission of Random House, New York, 1954, and Burns & Oates Ltd., London.

Mosaic Law would be a revelation and exemplification of the Divine Law. The Divine Law was revealed through faith because of the difficulty that men would otherwise have in ascertaining the divine purposes through the Natural Law. The Natural Law—or the natural moral law, to distinguish it from mere physical laws—would be that aspect of the eternal law that man can grasp through reason. Such a law is a reflection of the divine reason and the means by which man can realize his rational and social nature. Finally, the Human Law parallels the Divine Law, in that it is or ought to be the positive expression of the principles of the Natural Law. It is called human law because it is the creation of man and is designed by man to meet the more particular requirements of his social and political needs. It may be illustrated by the civil and criminal statutes of a state. It is neces-, sary because not all men can attain an understanding of the principles of the natural law, and hence men require this more positive expression of such a law for their guidance.

ON THE ESSENCE OF LAW

WHETHER LAW IS SOMETHING PERTAINING TO REASON?

. . . *Obj. 3.* Further, the law moves those who are subject to it to act rightly. But it belongs to the will to move to act, as is evident from what has been said above.[1] Therefore law pertains, not to the reason, but to the will, according to the words of the Jurist: *Whatsoever pleaseth the sovereign has the force of law.* [Dig. I, iv., 1 (I, 35a)].

On the contrary, it belongs to the law to command and to forbid. But it belongs to reason to command, as was stated above. (Q. 17, a. 1.) Therefore law is something pertaining to reason.

I answer that, Law is a rule and measure of acts, whereby man is induced to act or is restrained from acting; for *lex* [law] is derived from *ligare* [to bind], because it binds one to act. Now the rule and measure of human acts is the reason, which is the first principle of human acts, as is evident from what has been stated above. (Q. 1, a. 1, *ad* 3). For it belongs to the reason to direct to the end, which is the first principle in all matters of action, according to the Philosopher. [Phys. II]. Now that which is the principle in any genus is the rule and measure of that genus: for instance, unity in the genus of numbers, and the first move-ment in the genus of movements. Consequently, it follows that law is something pertaining to reason. . . .

Reply Obj. 3. Reason has its power of moving from the will, as was stated above; (Q. 17, a. 1) for it is due to the fact that one wills the end, that the reason issues its commands as regards things ordained to

[1] Q. 9., a. 1.

the end. But in order that the volition of what is commanded may have the nature of law, it needs to be in accord with some rule of reason. And in this sense is to be understood the saying that the will of the sovereign has the force of law; or otherwise the sovereign's will would savor of lawlessness rather than of law.

WHETHER LAW IS ALWAYS DIRECTED TO THE COMMON GOOD?

. . . *I answer that,* As we have stated above, law belongs to that which is a principle of human acts, because it is their rule and measure. Now as reason is a principle of human acts, so in reason itself there is something which is the principle in respect of all the rest. Hence to this principle chiefly and mainly law must needs be referred. Now the first principle in practical matters, which are the object of the practical reason, is the last end: and the last end of human life is happiness or beatitude, as we have stated above. [Q. 2, a. 7; q. 3, a. 1; Q. 69, a. 1] Consequently, law must needs concern itself mainly with the order that is in beatitude. Moreover, since every part is ordained to the whole as the imperfect to the perfect, and since one man is a part of the perfect community, law must needs concern itself properly with the order directed to universal happiness. Therefore the Philosopher, in the above definition of legal matters, mentions both happiness and the body politic, since he says that we call those legal matters *just which are adapted to produce and preserve happiness and its parts for the body politic.* [Eth., V, 1, 1129b 17.] For the state is a perfect community, as he says in Politics i. [Polit., I., 1 (1252a 5)].

Now, in every genus, that which belongs to it chiefly is the principle of the others, and the others belong to that genus according to some order towards that thing. Thus fire, which is chief among hot things, is the cause of heat in mixed bodies, and these are said to be hot in so far as they have a share of fire. Consequently, since law is chiefly ordained to the common good, any other precept in regard to some individual work must needs be devoid of the nature of a law, save in so far as it regards the common good. Therefore every law is ordained to the common good.

WHETHER PROMULGATION IS ESSENTIAL TO LAW?

We proceed thus to the Fourth Article:-

Objection 1. It would seem that promulgation is not essential to law. For the natural law, above all, has the character of law. But the natural law needs no promulgation. Therefore it is not essential to law that it be promulgated. . . .

I answer that, As was stated above, a law is imposed on others as a rule and measure. Now a rule or measure is imposed by being applied to those who are to be ruled and measured by it. Therefore, in order that a law obtain the binding force which is proper to a law, it must needs be applied to the men who have to be ruled by it. But such application is made by its being made known to them by promulgation. Therefore promulgation is necessary for law to obtain its force.

Thus, from the four preceding articles, the definition of law may be gathered. Law is nothing else than an ordinance of reason for the common good, promulgated by him who has the care of the community.

Reply Obj. 1. The natural law is promulgated by the very fact that God instilled it into man's mind so as to be known by him naturally.

ON THE VARIOUS KINDS OF LAW

WHETHER THERE IS AN ETERNAL LAW?

. . . *I answer that,* As we have stated above, law is nothing else but a dictate of practical reason emanating from the ruler who governs a perfect community. (Q. 90, a. 1, a. 3 and 4.) Now it is evident, granted that the world is ruled by divine providence, as was stated in the First Part, [Q. 22, a. 1, ad 2.] that the whole community of the universe is governed by the divine reason. Therefore the notion of the government of things in God, the ruler of the universe, has the nature of a law. And since the divine reason's conception of things is not subject to time, but is eternal, according to *Prov.* viii. 23, therefore it is that this kind of law must be called eternal.

WHETHER THERE IS IN US A NATURAL LAW?

We proceed thus to the Second Article:-

Objection 1. It would seem that there is no natural law in us. For man is governed sufficiently by the eternal law, since Augustine says that *the eternal law is that by which it is right that all things should be most orderly.* (De Lib. Arb., I. 6) But nature does not abound in superfluities as neither does she fail in necessaries. Therefore man has no natural law.

Obj. 2. Further, by the law man is directed, in his acts to the end, as was stated above. (Q. 90, a. 2) But the directing of human acts to their end is not a function of nature, as is the case in irrational creatures, which act for an end solely by their natural appetite; whereas man acts for an end by his reason and will. Therefore man has no natural law. . . .

I answer that, As we have stated above, (Q. 90, a. 1, ad 1.) law, being a rule and measure, can be in a person in two ways: in one way, as in him that rules and measures; in another way, as in that which is ruled and measured, since a thing is ruled and measured in so far as it partakes of the rule or measure. Therefore, since all things subject to divine providence are ruled and measured by the eternal law, as was stated above, it is evident that all things partake in some way in the eternal law, in so far as, namely, from its being imprinted on them, they derive their respective inclinations to their proper acts and ends. Now among all others, the rational creature is subject to divine providence in a more excellent way, in so far as it itself partakes of a share of providence, by being provident both for itself and for others. Therefore it has a share of the eternal reason, whereby it has a natural inclination to its proper act and end; and this participation of the eternal law in the rational creature is called the natural law. Hence the Psalmist, after saying (Ps. iv. 6): *Offer up the sacrifice of justice,* as though someone asked what the works of justice are, adds: *Many say, Who showeth us good things?* in answer to which question he says: *The light of Thy countenance, O Lord, is signed upon us.* He thus implies that the light of natural reason, whereby we discern what is good and what is evil, which is the function of the natural law, is nothing else than an imprint on us of the divine light. It is therefore evident that the natural law is nothing else than the rational creature's participation of the eternal law.

Reply Obj. 1. This argument would hold if the natural law were something different from the eternal law; whereas it is nothing but a participation thereof, as we have stated above.

Reply Obj. 2. Every act of reason and will in us is based on that which is according to nature, as was stated above. (Q. 10, a. 1) For every act of reasoning is based on principles that are known naturally, and every act of appetite in respect of the means is derived from the natural appetite in respect of the last end. Accordingly, the first direction of our acts to their end must needs be through the natural law.

WHETHER THERE IS A HUMAN LAW?

. . . *I answer that,* As we have stated above, a law is a dictate of the practical reason (Q. 90, a. 1, *ad.* 2) Now it is to be observed that the same procedure takes place in the practical and in the speculative reason, for each proceeds from principles to conclusions, as was stated above. (*Ibid.*) Accordingly, we conclude that, just as in the speculative reason from naturally known indemonstrable principles we draw the conclusions of the various sciences, the knowledge of which is not imparted to us by nature, but acquired by the efforts of reason, so too it is that from the precepts of the natural law, as from common and indemonstrable principles, the human reason needs to proceed to the more particular determination of certain matters. These particular determinations, devised by human reason, are called human laws, provided that the other essential conditions of law be observed, as was stated above. (Q. 90) . . .

WHETHER THERE WAS ANY NEED FOR A DIVINE LAW?

. . . *I answer that,* Besides the natural and human law it was necessary for the directing of human conduct to have a divine law. And this for four reasons. First, because it is by law that man is directed how to perform his proper acts in view of his last end. Now if man were ordained to no other end than that which is proportionate to his natural ability, there would be no need for man to have any further direction, on the part of his reason, in addition to the natural law and humanly devised law which is derived from it. But since man is ordained to an end of eternal happiness which exceeds man's natural ability, as we have stated above, (Q. 5, a. 5.) therefore it was necessary that, in addition to the natural and the human law, man should be directed to his end by a law given by God.

Secondly, because, by reason of the uncertainty of human judgment, especially on contingent and particular matters, different people form different judgments on human acts; whence also different and contrary laws result. In order, therefore, that man may know without any doubt what he ought to do and what he ought to avoid, it was necessary for man to be directed in his proper acts by a law given by God, for it is certain that such a law cannot err.

Thirdly, because man can make laws in those matters of which he is competent to judge. But man is not competent to judge of interior movements, that are hidden, but only of exterior acts which are observable; and yet for the perfection of virtue it is necessary for man to conduct himself rightly in both kinds of acts. Consequently, human law could not sufficiently curb and direct interior acts, and it was necessary for this purpose that a divine law should supervene.

Fourthly, because, as Augustine says, [*De Lib. Arb.,* I, 5] human law cannot punish or forbid all evil deeds, since, while aiming at doing away with all evils, it would do away with many good things, and would hinder the advance of the common good, which is necessary for human living. In order, therefore, that no evil might remain unforbidden and unpunished, it was necessary for the divine law to supervene, whereby all sins are forbidden.

THE NATURAL LAW

WHETHER THE NATURAL LAW CONTAINS SEVERAL PRECEPTS OR ONLY ONE?

We proceed thus to the Second Article:-

Objection 1. It would seem that the natural law contains not several precepts, but only one. For law is a kind of precept, as was stated above. (Q. 92, a. 2) If therefore there were many precepts of the natural law, it would follow that there are also many natural laws. . . .

On the contrary, The precepts of the natural law in man stand in relation to operable matters as first principles do to matters of demonstration. But there are several first indemonstrable principles. Therefore there are also several precepts of the natural law.

I answer that, As was stated, above, the precepts of the natural law are to the practical reason what the first principles of demonstration are to the speculative reason, because both are self-evident principles. (Q. 91, a. 3) Now a thing is said to be self-evident in two ways: first, in itself; secondly, in relation to us. Any proposition is said to be self-evident in itself, if its predicate is contained in the notion of the subject; even though it may happen that to one who does not know the definition of the subject, such a proposition is not self-evident. For instance, this proposition, *Man is a rational being,* is, in its very nature, self-evident, since he who says *man,* says *a rational being;* and yet to one who does not know what a man is, this proposition is not self-evident. Hence it is that, as Boethius says, (*De Hebdom.*) certain axioms or propositions are universally self-evident to all; and such are the propositions whose terms are known to all, as, *Every whole is greater than its part,* and, *Things equal to one and the same thing are equal to one another.* But some propositions are self-evident only to the wise, who understand the meaning of the terms of such propositions. Thus to one who understands that an angel is not a body, it is self-evident that an angel is not circumscriptively in a place. But this is not evident to the unlearned, for they cannot grasp it.

Now a certain order is to be found in those things that are apprehended by men. For that which first falls under apprehension is *being,* the understanding of which is included in all things whatsoever a man apprehends. Therefore the first indemonstrable principle is that *the same thing cannot be affirmed and denied at the same time,* which is based on the notion of *being* and *not-being:* and on this principle all others are based, as is stated in *Metaph.* iv. (Aristotle, Metaph., III, 3 1005b 29) Now as *being* is the first thing that falls under the apprehension absolutely, so *good* is the first thing that falls under the apprehension of the practical reason, which is directed to action (since every agent acts for an end, which has the nature of good). Consequently, the first principle in the practical reason is one founded on the nature of good, viz., that *good is that which all things seek after.* Hence this is the first precept of law, that *good is to be done and promoted, and evil is to be avoided.* All other precepts of the natural law are based upon this; so that all the things which the practical reason naturally apprehends as man's good belong to the precepts of the natural law under the form of things to be done or avoided.

Since, however, good has the nature of an end, and evil, the nature of the contrary, hence it is that all those things to which man has a natural inclination are naturally apprehended by reason as being good, and consequently as objects of pursuit, and their contraries as evil, and objects of avoidance. Therefore, the order of the precepts of the natural law is according to the order of natural inclinations. For there is in man, first of all, an inclination to good in accordance with the nature which he has in common with all substances, inasmuch, namely, as every substance seeks the preservation of its own being, according to its nature; and by reason of this inclination, whatever is a means of preserving human life, and of warding off its obstacles, belongs to the natural law. Secondly, there is in man an inclination to things that pertain to him more specially, according to that nature which he has in common with other animals; and in virtue of this inclination, those things are said to belong to the natural law *which nature has taught to all animals,* (Dig., I., i) such as sexual intercourse, the education of offspring and so forth. Thirdly, there is in man an inclination to good according to the nature of his reason, which nature is proper to him. Thus man has a natural inclination to know the truth about God, and to live in society; and in this respect, whatever pertains to this inclination belongs to the natural law: *e. g.,* to shun ignorance, to avoid offending those among whom one has to live, and other such things regarding the above inclination.

Reply Obj. 1. All these precepts of the law of nature have the character of one natural law, inasmuch as they flow from one first precept.

WHETHER THE NATURAL LAW IS THE SAME IN ALL MEN?

. . . I answer that, As we have stated above, to the natural law belong those things to which a man is inclined naturally; and among these it is proper to man to be inclined to act according to reason. Now it belongs to the reason to proceed from what is common to what is proper, as is stated in Physics i. [Aristotle, Phys., I, i 184a 16] The speculative reason, how-

ever, is differently situated, in this matter, from the practical reason. For, since the speculative reason is concerned chiefly with necessary things, which cannot be otherwise than they are, its proper conclusions, like the universal principles, contain the truth without fail. The practical reason, on the other hand, is concerned with contingent matters, which is the domain of human actions; and, consequently, although there is necessity in the common principles, the more we descend towards the particular, the more frequently we encounter defects. Accordingly, then, in speculative matters truth is the same in all men, both as to principles and as to conclusions; although the truth is not known to all as regards the conclusions, but only as regards the principles which are called *common notions.* (Boethius, *De Hebdom.*) But in matters of action, truth or practical rectitude is not the same for all as to what is particular, but only as to the common principles; and where there is the same rectitude in relation to particulars, it is not equally known to all.

It is therefore evident that, as regards the common principles whether of speculative or of practical reason, truth or rectitude is the same for all, and is equally known by all. But as to the proper conclusions of the speculative reason, the truth is the same for all, but it is not equally known to all. Thus, it is true for all that the three angles of a triangle are together equal to two right angles, although it is not known to all. But as to the proper conclusions of the practical reason, neither is the truth or rectitude the same for all, nor, where it is the same, is it equally known by all. Thus, it is right and true for all to act according to reason, and from this principle it follows, as a proper conclusion, that goods entrusted to another should be restored to their owner. Now this is true for the majority of cases. But it may happen in a particular case that it would be injurious, and therefore unreasonable, to restore goods held in trust; for instance, if they are claimed for the purpose of fighting against one's country. And this principle will be found to fail the more, according as we descend further towards the particular, *e. g.,* if one were to say that goods held in trust should be restored with such and such a guarantee, or in such and such a way; because the greater the number of conditions added, the greater the number of ways in which the principle may fail, so that it be not right to restore or not to restore.

Consequently, we must say that the natural law, as to the first common principles, is the same for all, both as to rectitude and as to knowledge. But as to certain more particular aspects, which are conclusions, as it were, of those common principles, it is the same for all in the majority of cases, both as to rectitude and as to knowledge; and yet in some few cases it may fail, both as to rectitude, by reason of certain obstacles (just as natures subject to generation and corruption fail in some few cases because of some obstacle), and as to knowledge, since in some the reason is perverted by passion, or evil habit, or an evil disposition of nature. Thus at one time theft, although it is expressly contrary to the natural law, was not considered wrong among the Germans, as Julius Caesar relates. [Caesar, *De Bello Gallico*, VI, 23]

STUDY QUESTIONS

1. What relation exists between law and reason? Between law and the will?
2. Why does Aquinas say that every law is directed to the common good? Do you think there could be an exception here?
3. Why is promulgation essential to the nature of law? What is Aquinas' final definition of law?
4. State and give examples of each of the different kinds of law.
5. What is the place and the function of human law? What need was there for the divine law?
6. In what sense is the natural law in us? What is meant by the natural light of reason and what is its function?
7. Explain fully Aquinas' statement that "the precepts of the natural law are to the practical reason what the first principles of demonstration are to the speculative reason" . . .
8. What is the first precept of the natural law? State some of the other precepts of the natural law and show how they are related to it.
9. Are the following violations of the natural law: (a) divorce, (b) infanticide, (c) duelling, (d) cheating at cards, (e) shoplifting, (f) birth control, (g) smoking? Discuss and prove where possible.

Thomas Hobbes

🮲🮲🮲🮲🮲🮲🮲🮲🮲🮲🮲🮲🮲🮲🮲🮲🮲🮲🮲🮲🮲🮲🮲🮲🮲🮲🮲🮲🮲🮲🮲🮲🮲🮲🮲🮲🮲🮲🮲

THE ORIGIN AND NATURE
OF THE STATE

🮲🮲🮲🮲🮲🮲🮲🮲🮲🮲🮲🮲🮲🮲🮲🮲🮲🮲🮲🮲🮲🮲🮲🮲🮲🮲🮲🮲🮲🮲🮲🮲🮲🮲🮲🮲🮲🮲🮲

Biographical Note. THOMAS HOBBES (1588–1679) was born at Malmesbury, England. He entered Oxford University at the age of fifteen, and shortly after receiving a degree of bachelor of arts he became a tutor for William Cavendish, afterwards the second Earl of Devonshire. At the age of forty, Hobbes chanced upon a copy of Euclid's *Elements,* and from this moment on became fascinated with the study of mathematics. In 1631 he became tutor to the third Earl of Devonshire, and this gave him the opportunity for profitable travel on the Continent. It was at this time that he met Galileo, Mersenne, and many other famous scientists. Toward the end of the decade, his interests turned to politics. In 1651 he published his great classic on political philosophy, *Leviathan.* Despite the fact that he presented the king with a manuscript copy, both the political philosophy and the theology expressed in *Leviathan* were to bring Hobbes into difficulty with the royal family. Eventually, however, his wit, charm, and good disposition brought him once more into favor with the Court after the Restoration. Although occasionally in difficulty on charges of atheism, he led a comfortable and scholarly existence (he translated the *Iliad* and *Odyssey* of Homer at the age of 86) until his death—shortly after he reached ninety. His philosophy might be best described as a rationalistic materialism.

* * *

The following material is taken from Chapters 13–15 and 17–18 of the *Leviathan,* J. M. Dent (Everyman) London, no date.

Introductory Note.   Thomas Hobbes is one of the few British thinkers to develop a systematic philosophy and one of the few philosophers in history to develop a consistent and systematic materialism. His materialism is constructed on the scientific principles of the sixteenth century and on his conviction that all nature can be reduced to matter in motion in space. Nature, including man, is a mechanical and deterministic system capable of explanation in physicalistic terms and with mathematical precision. And political philosophy, Hobbes believed, is an integral part of such a materialistic system, for human behavior is merely another aspect of matter in motion in space. By endeavoring to reduce all human behavior to scientific laws—psychological and physical laws. Hobbes was impelled to break with the traditional theory of natural law and the Aristotelian conception of man. One consequence of this was the interpretation of natural law in terms of physical causes and psychological motives rather than ethical values or theological ends. For Hobbes the end of human existence is self-preservation and man is basically an egoist. On these assumptions he endeavors to explain the origin of societies and the structure of the state. Actually, society is not real but artificial, it arises out of the need of man to preserve himself, it is a means and not an end. Thus Hobbes' political philosophy emerges as completely individualistic and utilitarian.

The material from *Leviathan* illustrates these several points. The condition of man in a state of nature is described as a state of war, for the relative equality of men in such a state and their desire for gain, security, and reputation cause them to war upon one another. In such a state there is no justice and no moral law; hence men are impelled by their desire for self-preservation to seek for peace. The articles of such a peace are what Hobbes refers to as the Laws of Nature.

To attain peace, men contract or covenant with one another and transfer those rights which they enjoyed in a state of nature to a third party who agrees that the power or right which he has received in this way shall be used to preserve the peace and secure the lives and property of individuals. For Hobbes, the sovereign, or monarch, is not a party to the contract and therefore has no moral or legal obligation to the individuals in society. The civil power has no moral or theological basis. Kings have no divine right, only a regal might. It was this aspect of Hobbes' political theory that made it suspect to both the royalists (who wished to establish their sovereignty on moral or theological grounds) and the parliamentarians (who based the power of the sovereign on the consent of the governed). For Hobbes it is power and not any abstract principle of natural law that determines the rights of the sovereign. In fact the sovereign is the source of all civil laws and rights.

OF THE NATURAL CONDITION OF MANKIND

Nature hath made men so equal, in the faculties of the body and the mind, that though there be found one man sometimes manifestly stronger in body, or of quicker mind than another; yet when all is reckoned together, the difference between man, and man, is not so considerable, as that one man can thereupon claim to himself any benefit, to which another may not pretend, as well as he. For as to the strength of body, the weakest has strength enough to kill the strongest, either by secret machination, or by confederacy with others, that are in the same danger with himself.

And as to the faculties of the mind, setting aside the arts grounded upon words, and especially that skill of proceeding upon general, and infallible rules, called science; which very few have, and but in few things; as being not a native faculty, born with us; nor attained, as prudence, while we look after somewhat else, I find yet a greater equality amongst men, than that of strength. For prudence, is but experience; which equal time, equally bestows on all men, in those things they equally apply themselves unto. That which may perhaps make such equality incredible, is but a vain conceit of one's wisdom, which almost all men think they have in a greater degree, than the vulgar; that is, than all men but themselves, and a few others, whom by fame, or for concurring with themselves, they approve. For such is the nature of man, that howsoever they may acknowledge many others to be more witty, or more eloquent, or more learned, yet they will hardly believe there be many so wise as themselves; for they see their own wit at hand, and other men's at a distance. But this proveth rather that men are in that point equal, than unequal. For there is not ordinarily a greater sign of the equal distribution of any thing, than that every man is contented with his share.

From this equality of ability, ariseth equality of hope in the attaining of our ends. And therefore if any two men desire the same thing, which nevertheless they cannot both enjoy, they become enemies; and in the way to their end, which is principally their own conservation, and sometimes their delectation only, endeavor to destroy, or subdue one another. And from hence it comes to pass, that where an invader hath no more to fear, than another man's single power; if one plant, sow, build, or possess a convenient seat, others may probably be expected to come prepared with forces united, to dispossess, and deprive him, not only of the fruit of his labor, but also of his life, or liberty. And the invader again is in the like danger of another.

And from this diffidence of one another, there is no way for any man to secure himself, so reasonable, as anticipation; that is, by force, or wiles, to master the persons of all men he can, so long, till he see no other power great enough to endanger him: and this is no more than his own conservation requireth, and is generally allowed. Also because there be some, that taking pleasure in contemplating their own power in the acts of conquest, which they pursue farther than their security requires; if others, that otherwise would be glad to be at ease within modest bounds, should not by invasion increase their power, they would not be able, long time, by standing only on their defence, to subsist. And by consequence, such augmentation of dominion over men being necessary to a man's conservation, it ought to be allowed him.

Again, men have no pleasure, but on the contrary a great deal of grief, in keeping company, where there is no power able to over-awe them all. For every man looketh that his companion should value him, at the same rate he sets upon himself: and upon all signs of contempt, or undervaluing, naturally endeavors, as far as he dares (which amongst them that have no common power to keep them in quiet, is far enough to make them destroy each other), to extort a greater value from his contemners, by damage; and from others, by the example.

So that in the nature of man, we find three principal causes of quarrel. First, competition; secondly, diffidence; thirdly, glory.

The first maketh men invade for gain; the second, for safety; and the third, for reputation. The first use violence, to make themselves masters of other men's persons, wives, children, and cattle; the second, to defend them; the third, for trifles, as a word, a smile, a different opinion, and any other sign of undervalue, either direct in their persons, or by reflection in their kindred, their friends, their nation, their profession, or their name.

Hereby it is manifest, that during the time men live without a common power to keep them all in awe, they are in that condition which is called war; and such a war, as is of every man, against every man. For WAR, consisteth not in battle only, or the act of fighting; but in a tract of time, wherein the will to contend by battle is sufficiently known: and therefore the notion of *Time,* is to be considered in the nature of war; as it is in the nature of weather. For as the nature of foul weather, lieth not in a shower or two of rain, but in an inclination thereto of many days together: so that nature of war, consisteth not in actual fighting, but in the known disposition thereto, during all the time, there is no assurance to the contrary. All other time is PEACE.

Whatsoever therefore is consequent to a time of war, where every man is enemy to every man; the same is consequent to the time, wherein men live without other security, than what their own strength, and their own invention shall furnish them withal. In such condition, there is no place for industry; because the fruit thereof is uncertain: and consequently no culture of the earth; no navigation, nor use of the commodities that may be imported by sea; no commodious building; no instruments of moving, and removing, such things as require much force; no knowledge of the face of the earth; no account of time; no arts; no letters; no society; and which is worst of all, continual fear, and danger of violent death; and the life of man, solitary, poor, nasty, brutish, and short.

It may seem strange to some man, that has not well weighed these things, that nature should thus dissociate, and render men apt to invade, and destroy one another: and he may therefore, not trusting to this inference, made from the passions, desire perhaps to have the same confirmed by experience. Let him therefore consider with himself, when taking a journey, he arms himself, and seeks to go well accompanied; when going to sleep, he locks his doors; when even in his house he locks his chests; and this when he knows there be laws, and public officers, armed, to revenge all injuries shall be done him; what opinion he has of his fellow-subjects, when he rides armed; of his fellow-citizens, when he locks his doors; and of his children, and servants, when he locks his chests. Does he not there as much accuse mankind by his actions, as I do by my words? But neither of us accuse man's nature in it. The desires, and other passions of man, are in themselves no sin. No more are the actions, that proceed from those passions, till they know a law that forbids them: which till laws be made they cannot know: nor can any law be made, till they have agreed upon the person that shall make it.

It may peradventure be thought, there was never such a time, nor condition of war as this: and I believe it was never generally so, over all the world: but there are many places where they live so now. For the savage people in many places of America, except the government of small families, the concord whereof dependeth on natural lust, have no government at all; and live at this day in that brutish manner, as I have said before. Howsoever, it may be perceived what manner of life there would be, where there were no common power to fear, by the manner of life, which men that have formerly lived under a peaceful government, use to degenerate into, in a civil war.

But though there had never been any time, wherein particular men were in a condition of war one against another; yet in all times, kings, and persons of sovereign authority, because of their independency, are in continual jealousies, and in the state and posture of gladiators; having their weapons pointing, and their eyes fixed on one another; that is, their forts, garrisons, and guns upon the frontiers of their kingdoms; and continual spies upon their neighbors; which is a posture of war. But because they uphold thereby, the industry of their subjects; there does not follow from it, that misery, which accompanies the liberty of particular men.

To this war of every man, against every man, this also is consequent; that nothing can be unjust. The notions of right and wrong, justice and injustice have there no place. Where there is no common power, there is no law: where no law, no injustice. Force and fraud are in war the two cardinal virtues. Justice and injustice are none of the faculties neither of the body, nor of the mind. If they were, they might be in a man that were alone in the world, as well as his senses, and passions. They are qualities, that relate to men in society, not in solitude. It is consequent also to the same condition, that there be no propriety, no dominion, no *mine* and *thine* distinct; but only that to be every man's, that he can get; and for so long, as he can keep it. And thus much for the ill condition which man by mere nature is actually placed in; though with a possibility to come out of it, consisting partly in the passions, partly in his reason.

The passions that incline men to peace, are fear of death; desire of such things as are necessary to commodious living; and a hope by their industry to obtain them. And reason suggesteth convenient articles of peace, upon which men may be drawn to agreement. These articles, are they, which otherwise are called the Laws of Nature: whereof I shall speak more particularly in the two following chapters.

OF THE FIRST AND SECOND NATURAL LAWS, AND OF CONTRACTS

The RIGHT OF NATURE, which writers commonly call *jus naturale*, is the liberty each man hath, to use his own power, as he will himself, for the preservation of his own nature; that is to say, of his own life; and consequently, of doing any thing, which in his own judgment, and reason, he shall conceive to be the aptest means thereunto.

By LIBERTY, is understood, according to the proper signification of the word, the absence of external impediments: which impediments, may oft take away part of a man's power to do what he would; but cannot hinder him from using the power left him, according as his judgment, and reason shall dictate to him.

A LAW OF NATURE, *lex naturalis*, is a precept or general rule, found out by reason, by which a man is forbidden to do that, which is destructive of his life, or taketh away the means of preserving the same; and to omit that, by which he thinketh it may be best preserved. For though they that speak of this subject, use to confound *jus* and *lex*, *right* and *law*: yet they ought to be distinguished; because RIGHT, consisteth in liberty to do, or to forbear; whereas LAW, determineth, and bindeth to one of them: so that law, and right, differ as much, as obligation, and liberty; which in one and the same matter are inconsistent.

And because the conditions of man, as hath been declared in the precedent chapter, is a condition of war of everyone against every one: in which case every one is governed by his own reason; and there is nothing he can make use of, that may not be a help unto him, in preserving his life against his enemies: it followeth, that in such a condition, every man has a right to every thing; even to one another's body. And therefore, as long as this natural right of every man to every thing endureth, there can be no security to any man, how strong or wise soever he be, of living out the time, which nature ordinarily alloweth men to live. And consequently it is a precept, or general rule of reason, *that every man, ought to endeavor peace, as far as he has hope of obtaining it; and when he cannot obtain it, that he may seek, and use, all helps, and advantages of war.* The first branch of which rule, containeth the first and fundamental law of nature; which is, *to seek peace and follow it.* The second, the sum of the right of nature; which is, *by all means we can, to defend ourselves.*

From this fundamental law of nature, by which men are commanded to endeavor peace, is derived this second law; *that a man be willing, when others are so too, as far-forth, as for peace, and defence of himself he shall think it necessary, to lay down this right to all things; and be contented with so much liberty against other men, as he would allow other men against himself.* For as long as every man holdeth this right of doing any thing he liketh, so long are all men in the condition of war. But if other men will not lay down their right, as well as he, then there is no reason for any one, to divest himself of his: for that were to expose himself to prey, which no man is bound to, rather than to dispose himself to peace. This is that law of the Gospel; *whatsoever you require that others should do to you, that do ye to them.* . . .

To *lay down* a man's *right* to any thing, is to *divest* himself of the *liberty,* of hindering another of the benefit of his own right to the same.

For he that renounceth, or passeth away his right, giveth not to any other man a right which he had not before; because there is nothing to which every man had not right by nature: but only standeth out of his way, that he may enjoy his own original right, without hindrance from him; not without hindrance from another. So that the effect which redoundeth to one man, by another man's defect of right, is but so much diminution of impediments to the use of his own right original.

Right is laid aside, either by simply renouncing it; or by transferring it to another. By *simply* RENOUNCING; when he cares not to whom the benefit thereof redoundeth. By TRANSFERRING; when he intendeth the benefit thereof to some certain person, or persons. And when a man hath in either manner abandoned, or granted away his right, then is he said to be OBLIGED, or BOUND, not to hinder those, to whom such right is granted, or abandoned, from the benefit of it: and that he *ought*, and it is his DUTY, not to make void that voluntary act of his own: and that such hindrance is INJUSTICE, and INJURY, as being *sine jure;* the right being before renounced, or transferred. So that *injury,* or *injustice,* in the controversies of the world, is somewhat like to that, which in the disputations of scholars is called *absurdity*. For as it is there called an absurdity, to contradict what one maintained in the beginning: so in the world, it is called injustice, and injury, voluntarily to undo that, which from the beginning he had voluntarily done. The way by which a man either simply renounceth, or transferreth his right, is a declaration, or signification, by some voluntary and sufficient sign, or signs, that he doth so renounce, or transfer; or hath so renounced, or transferred the same, to him that accepteth it. And these signs are either words only, or actions only; or, as it happeneth most often both words, and actions. And the same are the BONDS, by which men are bound, and obliged: bonds, that have their strength, not from their own nature, for nothing is more easily broken than a man's word, but from fear of some evil consequence upon the rupture.

Whensoever a man transferreth his right, or renounceth it; it is either in consideration of some right reciprocally transferred to himself; or for some other good he hopeth for thereby. For it is a voluntary act: and of the voluntary acts of every man, the object is some *good to himself.* And therefore there be some rights, which no man can be understood by any words, or other signs, to have abandoned, or transferred. As first a man cannot lay down the right of resisting them, that assault him by force, to take away his life; because he cannot be understood to aim thereby, at any good to himself. The same may be said of wounds, and chains, and imprisonment; both because there is no benefit consequent to such patience; as there is to the patience of suffering another to be wounded, or imprisoned: as also because a man cannot tell, when he seeth men proceed against him by violence, whether they intend his death or not. And lastly the motive, and end for which this renouncing, and transferring of right is introduced, is nothing else but the security of a man's person, in his life, and in the means of so preserving life, as not to be weary of it. And therefore if a man by words, or other signs, seem to despoil himself of the end, for which those signs were intended, he is not to be understood as if he meant it, or that it was his will; but that he was ignorant of how such words and actions were to be interpreted.

The mutual transferring of right, is that which men call CONTRACT. . . .

Again, one of the contractors, may deliver the thing contracted for on his part, and leave the other to perform his part at some determinate time after, and in the mean time be trusted; and then the contract on his part, is called PACT, or COVENANT: or both parts may contract now, to perform hereafter: in which cases, he that is to perform in time to come, being trusted, his performance is called *keeping of promise,* or faith; and the failing of performance, if it be voluntary, *violation of faith.*

When the transferring of right, is not mutual; but one of the parties transferreth, in hope to gain thereby friendship, or service from another, or from his friends; or in hope to gain the reputation of charity, or magnanimity; or to deliver his mind from the pain of compassion; or in hope of reward in heaven; this is not contract, but GIFT, FREE GIFT, GRACE: which words signify one and the same thing. . . .

If a covenant be made, wherein neither of the parties perform presently, but trust one another; in the condition of mere nature, which is a condition of war of every man against every man, upon any reasonable suspicion, it is void: but if there be a common power set over them both, with right and force sufficient to compel performance, it is not void. For he that performeth first, has no assurance the other will perform after; because the bonds of words are too weak to bridle men's ambition, avarice, anger, and other passions without the fear of some coercive power; which in the condition of mere nature where all men are equal, and judges of the justness of their own fears, cannot possibly be supposed. And therefore he which performeth first, does but betray himself to his enemy; contrary to the right, he can never abandon, of defending his life, and means of living.

But in a civil estate, where there is a power set up to constrain those that would otherwise violate their faith, that fear is no more reasonable; and for that cause, he which by the covenant is to perform first, is obliged so to do. . . .

OF OTHER LAWS OF NATURE

From that law of nature by which we are obliged to transfer to another such rights, as being retained, hinder the peace of mankind, there followeth a third, which is this, *that men perform their covenants made:* without which, covenants are in vain, and but empty words; and the right of all men to all things remaining, we are still in the condition of war.

And in this law of nature consisteth the fountain and original of JUSTICE. For where no covenant hath preceded, there hath no right been transferred, and every man has right to every thing; and consequently, no action can be unjust. But when a covenant is made, then to break it is *unjust:* and the definition of INJUSTICE is no other than the *not performance of covenant.* And whatsoever is not unjust is *just.*

But because covenants of mutual trust, where there is a fear of not performance on either part, as hath been said in the former chapter, are invalid; though the original of justice be the making of covenants; yet injustice actually there can be none, till the cause of such fear be taken away; which, while men are in the natural condition of war, cannot be done. Therefore before the names of just and unjust can have place, there must be some coercive power, to compel men equally to the performance of their covenants, by the terror of some punishment greater than the benefit they expect by the breach of their covenant; and to make good that propriety, which by mutual contract men acquire, in recompense of the universal right they abandon: and such power there is none before the erection of a commonwealth. And this is also to be gathered out of the ordinary definition of justice in the Schools; for they say, that *justice is the constant will of giving to every man his own.* And therefore where there is no *own,* that is, no propriety, there is no injustice; and where there is no coercive power erected, that is, where there is no commonwealth, there is no propriety; all men having right to all things: therefore where there is no commonwealth, there nothing is unjust. So that the nature of justice consisteth in keeping of valid covenants: but the validity of covenants begins not but with the constitution of a civil power, sufficient to compel men to keep them: and then it is also that propriety begins. . . .

OF THE CAUSES, GENERATION, AND
DEFINITION OF A COMMON-WEALTH

The final cause, end, or design of men, who naturally love liberty, and dominion over others, in the introduction of that restraint upon themselves, in which we see them live in commonwealths, is the foresight of their own preservation, and of a more contented life thereby; that is to say, of getting themselves out from that miserable condition of war, which is necessarily consequent, as hath been shown previously, to the natural passions of men, when there is no visible power to keep them in awe, and tie them by fear of punishment to the performance of their covenants, and observation of those laws of nature set down in the fourteenth and fifteenth chapters [pp. 398–399 in this text].

For the laws of nature, as *justice, equity, modesty, mercy* and, in sum, *doing to others, as we would be done to,* of themselves, without the terror of some power, to cause them to be observed, are contrary to our natural passions, that carry us to partiality, pride, revenge, and the like. And covenants, without the sword, are but words, and of no strength to secure a man at all. Therefore nothwithstanding the laws of nature, which every man hath then kept, when he has the will to keep them, when he can do it safely, if there be no power erected, or not great enough for our security; every man will, and may lawfully rely on his own strength and art, for caution against all other men. And in all places, where men have lived by small families, to rob and spoil one another, has been a trade, and so far from being reputed against the law of nature, that the greater spoils they gained, the greater was their honor; and men observed no other laws therein, but the laws of honor; that is, to abstain from cruelty, leaving to men their lives, and instruments of husbandry. And as small families did then; so now do cities and kingdoms, which are but greater families, for their own security, enlarge their dominions, upon all pretences of danger, and fear of invasion, or assistance that may be given to invaders, and endeavor as much as they can, to subdue or weaken their neighbors, by open force, and secret arts, for want of other caution, justly; and are remembered for it in after ages with honor.

Nor is it the joining together of a small number of men, that gives them this security; because in small numbers, small additions on the one side or the other, make the advantage of strength so great, as is sufficient to carry the victory; and therefore gives encouragement to an invasion. The multitude sufficient to confide in for our security, is not determined by any certain number, but by comparison with the enemy we fear; and is then sufficient, when the odds of the enemy is not of so visible and conspicuous moment, to determine the event of war, as to move him to attempt.

And be there never so great a multitude; yet if their actions be directed according to their particular judgments, and particular appetites, they can expect thereby no defence, nor protection, neither against a common enemy, nor against the injuries of one another. For being distracted in opinions concerning the best use and application of their strength, they do not help but hinder one another; and reduce their strength by mutual opposition to nothing: whereby they are easily, not only subdued by a very few that agree together; but also when there is no common enemy, they make war upon each other, for their particular interests. For if we could suppose a great multitude of men to consent in the observation of justice, and other laws of nature, without a common power to keep them all in awe; we might as well suppose all mankind to do the same; and then there neither would be, nor need to be any civil government, or commonwealth at all; because there would be peace without subjection.

Nor is it enough for the security which men desire should last all the time of their life, that they be governed, and directed by one judgment, for a limited time; as in one battle, or one war. For though they obtain a victory by their unanimous endeavor against a foreign enemy; yet afterwards, when either they have no common enemy, or he that by one part is held for an enemy, is by another part held for a friend, they must needs by the difference of their interests dissolve, and fall again into a war amongst themselves.

It is true, that certain living creatures, as bees, and ants, live socially one with another, which are therefore by Aristotle numbered amongst political creatures; and yet have no other direction, than their particular judgments and appetites; nor speech, whereby one of them can signify to another, what he thinks expedient for the common benefit: and therefore some man may perhaps desire to know, why mankind cannot do the same. To which I answer,

First, that men are continually in competition for honor and dignity, which these creatures are not; and consequently amongst men there ariseth on that ground envy and hatred, and finally war; but amongst these not so.

Secondly, that amongst these creatures, the common good differeth not from the private; and being by nature inclined to their private, they procure thereby the common benefit. But man, whose joy consisteth in comparing himself with other men, can relish nothing but what is eminent.

Thirdly, that these creatures, having not, as man, the use of reason, do not see, nor think they see any fault in the administration of their common business; whereas amongst men, there are very many, that think themselves wiser, and abler to govern the public, better than the rest; and these strive to reform and innovate, one this way, another that way; and thereby bring it into distraction and civil war.

Fourthly, that these creatures, though they have some use of voice, in making known to one another their desires, and other affections; yet they want that art of words, by which some men can represent to others, that which is good, in the likeness of evil; and evil, in the likeness of good; and augment, or diminish the apparent greatness of good and evil; discontenting men, and troubling their peace at their pleasure.

Fifthly, irrational creatures cannot distinguish between *injury* and *damage;* and therefore as long as they be at ease, they are not offended with their fellows: whereas man is then most troublesome, when he is most at ease: for then it is that he loves to show his wisdom, and control the actions of them that govern the commonwealth.

Lastly, the agreement of these creatures is natural; that of men, is by covenant only, which is artificial: and therefore it is no wonder if there be somewhat else required, besides covenant, to make their agreement constant and lasting; which is a common power, to keep them in awe, and to direct their actions to the common benefit.

The only way to erect such a common power, as may be able to defend them from the invasion of foreigners, and the injuries of one another, and thereby to secure them in such sort, as that by their own industry, and by the fruits of the earth, they may nourish themselves and live contentedly; is, to confer all their power and strength upon one man, or upon one assembly of men, that may reduce all their wills, by plurality of voices, unto one will: which is as much as to say, to appoint one man, or assembly of men, to bear their person; and every one to own, and acknowledge himself to be author of whatsoever he that so beareth their person, shall act, or cause to be acted, in those things which concern the common peace and safety; and therein to submit their wills, every one to his will, and their judgments, to his judgment. This is more than consent, or concord; it is a real unity of them all, in one and the same person, made by covenant of every man with every man, in such manner, as if every man should say to every man, *I authorize and give up my right of governing myself, to this man, or to this assembly of men, on this condition, that thou give up thy right to him, and authorize all his actions in like manner.* This done, the multitude so united in one person, is called a COMMONWEALTH, in Latin CIVITAS. This is the generation of that great LEVIATHAN, or rather, to speak more reverently, of that *mortal god,* to which we owe under the *immortal God,* our peace and defence. For by this authority, given him by every particular man in the commonwealth, he hath the use of so much power and strength conferred on him, that by terror thereof, he is enabled to perform the wills of them all, to peace at home, and mutual aid against their enemies abroad. And in him consisteth the essence of the commonwealth; which, to define it, is *one person, of whose acts a great multitude, by mutual covenants one with another, have made themselves every one the author, to the end he may use the strength and means of them all, as he shall think expedient, for their peace and common defence.*

And he that carrieth this person, is called SOVEREIGN, and said to have *sovereign power;* and everyone besides, his SUBJECT.

The attaining to this sovereign power, is by two ways. One, by natural force; as when a man maketh his children, to submit themselves, and their children to his government, as being able to destroy them if they refuse; or by war subdueth his enemies to his will, giving them their lives on that condition. The other, is when men agree amongst themselves, to submit to some man, or assembly of men, voluntarily, on confidence to be protected by him against all others. This latter, may be called a political commonwealth, or commonwealth by *institution;* and the former, a commonwealth by *acquisition.* And first, I shall speak of a commonwealth by institution.

OF THE RIGHTS OF SOVEREIGNS BY INSTITUTION

A *commonwealth* is said to be *instituted,* when a *multitude* of men do agree, and *covenant, every one, with every one,* that to whatsoever *man,* or *assembly of men,* shall be given by the major part, the *right* to present the person of them all, that is to say, to be their representative; every one, as well he that *voted* for it, as he that *voted against it,* shall *authorize* all the actions and judgments, of that man, or assembly of men, in the same manner, as if they were his own, to the end, to live peaceably amongst themselves, and be protected against other men.

From this institution of a commonwealth are derived all the *rights,* and *faculties* of him, or them, on whom sovereign power is conferred by the consent of the people assembled.

First, because they covenant, it is to be understood, they are not obliged by former covenant to anything repugnant hereunto. And consequently they that have already instituted a commonwealth, being thereby bound by covenant, to own the actions, and judgments of one, cannot lawfully make a new covenant, amongst themselves, to be obedient to any other, in any thing whatsoever, without his permission. And therefore, they that are subject to a monarch, cannot without his leave cast off monarchy, and return to the confusion of a disunited multitude; nor transfer their person from him that beareth it to another man, or other assembly of men: for they are bound, every man to every man, to own, and be reputed author of all, that he that already is their sovereign, shall do, and judge fit to be done: so that any one man dissenting, all the rest should break their covenant made to that man, which is injustice: and they have also every man given the sovereignty to him that beareth their person; and therefore if they depose him, they take from him that which is his own, and so again it is injustice. Besides, if he that attempteth to depose his sovereign, be killed, or punished by him for such attempt, he is author of his own punishment, as being by the institution, author of all his sovereign shall do: and because it is injustice for a man to do anything, for which he may be punished by his own authority, he is also upon that title, unjust. And whereas some men have pretended for their disobedience to their sovereign, a new covenant, made, not with men, but with God; this also is unjust: for there is no covenant with God, but by mediation of somebody that representeth God's person; which none doth but God's lieutenant, who hath the sovereignty under God. But this pretence of covenant with God, is so evident a lie, even in the pretenders' own consciences, that it is not only an act of an unjust, but also of a vile, and unmanly disposition.

Secondly, because the right of bearing the person of them all, is given to him they make sovereign, by covenant only of one to another, and not of him to any of them; there can happen no breach of covenant on the part of the sovereign; and consequently none of his subjects, by any pretence of forfeiture, can be freed from his subjection. That he which is made sovereign maketh no covenant with his subjects beforehand, is manifest; because either he must make it with the whole multitude, as one party to the covenant; or he must make a several covenant with every man. With the whole, as one party, it is impossible; because as yet they are not one person: and if he make so many several covenants as there be men, those covenants after he hath the sovereignty are void; because what act soever can be pretended by any one of them for breach thereof, is the act both of himself, and of all the rest, because done in the person, and by the right of every one of them in particular. Besides, if any one, or more of them, pretend a breach of the covenant made by the sovereign at his institution; and others, or one other of his subjects, or himself alone, pretend there was no such breach, there is in this case, no judge to decide the controversy; it returns therefore to the sword again; and every man recovereth the right of protecting himself by his own strength, contrary to the design they had in the institution. It is therefore in vain to grant sovereignty by way of proceding covenant. The opinion that any monarch receiveth his power by covenant, that is to say, on condition, proceedeth from want of understanding this easy truth, that covenants being but words and breath, have no force to oblige, contain, constrain, or protect any man, what it has from the public sword; that is, from the untied hands of that man, or assembly of men that hath the sovereignty, and whose actions are avouched by them all, and performed by the strength of them all, in him united. But when an assembly of men is made sovereign; then no man imagineth any such covenant to have passed in the institution; for no man is so dull as to say, for example, the people of Rome made a covenant with the Romans, to hold the sovereignty on such or such conditions; which not performed, the Romans might lawfully depose the Roman people. That men see not the reason to be alike in a monarchy, and in a popular government, proceedeth from the ambition of some, that are kinder to the government of an assembly, whereof they may hope to participate, than of monarchy, which they despair to enjoy.

Thirdly, because the major part hath by consenting voices declared a sovereign; he that dissented must now consent with the rest; that is, be contented to avow all the actions he shall do, or else justly be destroyed by the rest. For if he voluntarily entered into the congregation of them that were assembled, he sufficiently declared thereby his will, and therefore tacitly covenanted, to stand to what the major part should ordain: and therefore if he refuse to stand thereto, or make protestation against any of their decrees, he does contrary to his covenant, and therefore unjustly. And whether he be of the congregation or not; and whether his consent be asked, or not, he must either submit to their decrees, or be left in the condition of war he was in before; wherein he might without injustice be destroyed by any man whatsoever. . . .

STUDY QUESTIONS

1. In what ways does Hobbes consider men to be equal in a state of nature? What consequences does this equality have for man in a state of nature?

2. What are the three principal causes for conflict in a state of nature? Comment on each.

3. (a) Discuss at some length—showing your agreement or disagreement —Hobbes' famous statement that in a state of nature the "life of man is solitary, poor, nasty, brutish and short."

   (b) What arguments does Hobbes use to show that the state of nature is one of war?

4. Would you agree with Hobbes that in such a state of nature there is neither right nor wrong, nor justice nor injustice? Do you think there ever was such a state of nature?

5. Following his description of the state of nature, Hobbes notes that "reason suggesteth convenient articles of peace," which he calls the Laws of Nature. But if men are so ruled by their passions in a state of nature, how can any *rational* agreement be possible?

6. Discuss more fully Hobbes' conception of a law of nature, noting the distinction between *right* and *law*. What does he consider to be the fundamental law of nature?

7. What is Hobbes' conception of "contract"? What is necessary to make a contract among men effective? What is the relation of such a social contract to the notions of justice and right?

8. Show specifically and concretely how and why according to Hobbes a commonwealth comes into being. Why is the commonwealth termed a *Leviathan?*

9. With respect to the origin of the state (or commonwealth), Hobbes maintains that the sovereign is not a party to the contract whereby the state comes into being. Would you agree or disagree?

10. Comment on the rights of the sovereign in Hobbes' state. Is such a sovereign absolute? Is he subject to the law? To God? Does the citizen of such a state have any rights against his sovereign? Can he justly dissent or rebel?

John Locke

THE NATURAL RIGHTS OF MAN

Biographical Note.   JOHN LOCKE (1632–1704) was born in Somerset, England. His father was a lawyer and later a member of the Parliamentary army. At fourteen, Locke was sent to Westminster School, and upon graduation he went to Oxford University. His formal training in philosophy was the traditional medieval Aristotelianism, but his real interests in philosophy developed more from his reading of Descartes. After graduation from Oxford he became a lecturer in Greek. For a time he was tempted to take holy orders, but in 1667 he met Sydenham, one of the great medical scholars of the time. Through his influence he turned to medicine, and in 1674 he received his medical degree. In the meantime he had become a friend of Lord Ashley, later the first Earl of Shaftesbury. He served Shaftesbury as doctor and secretary, and through him became actively interested in politics. For a brief period Locke visited France, where he met the leading exponents of Cartesianism and became acquainted with the work of the scientist Gassendi. Returning to England in 1679, he again became active in politics, but soon found the political situation dangerous, and the failure of Shaftesbury's intrigues against the future James II forced Locke to flee to Holland. Here he lived for a time under the alias of Dr. Van der Linden, but after the "Glorious Revolution" of 1688 he returned to England and

From the *Second Treatise of Civil Government,* chapters II, III, V, VIII, and XIX, in John Locke, *Two Treatises of Government,* 1690.

took up permanent residence in Essex. Here he remained, writing and visiting with family and friends until his death.

* * *

Introductory Note. Locke's philosophy has a twofold significance: epistemological and political. His epistemology launched the modern British empirical movement and was the direct inspiration of both Berkeley and Hume. In his empiricism, Locke vigorously rejects any doctrine of innate ideas and insists that all our knowledge is ultimately derived from the ideas of sense experience. Politically, the philosophy of Locke is significant because it crystallizes the principles of two revolutions—The British "Glorious Revolution" of 1688 and the American revolution of 1776. In his political philosophy Locke is not always consistent. He accepts the principles of natural rights as self-evident and inalienable, but nowhere offers any empirical proof of them. Apparently they are innate to man. In addition Locke attempted an unsuccessful synthesis of the medieval doctrine of natural law, which he knew from Hooker, and the individualism and utilitarianism of Thomas Hobbes.

Thus Locke attacks the Hobbesian conception of a state of nature, for it would deny the intrinsic nature of morality and make law and the power of law the determinant of morality. Locke was convinced that prior to the state and its laws there existed the natural moral law and that the state of nature was "one of peace, good will, mutual assistance and preservation." Locke himself does little to develop this particular aspect of natural law doctrine. His own conception of such a law and the natural rights based on it is summed up entirely in his analysis of the right of property and by property he means not merely physical possessions but life and liberty as well.

Like Hobbes he resorts to the fiction of a social contract to explain the origin of political society, which he ascribes to the need of man for security and the protection of his natural rights. Unlike Hobbes he declares that the contract is one between the people and the future ruler and binding upon both. Thus government comes into being, as resting upon the consent of the governed. He assumes that the consent of all individuals to such an arrangement is a unanimous consent and that the majority will always arrive at just and reasonable decisions.

The actual form of government will depend upon the will of the people. Locke's own preference was the parliamentary form, a form which not only would assure the supremacy of a Parliament but in which the Parliament would for the most part represent the interests of the middle classes. Should such a government attempt to nullify the purposes for which a political society was created, then the ultimate right of revolution could be exercised by the people.

OF THE STATE OF NATURE

To understand political power right, and derive it from its original, we must consider what state all men are naturally in, and that is a state of perfect freedom to order their actions and dispose of their possessions and persons as they think fit, within the bounds of the law of nature, without asking leave or depending upon the will of any other man.

A state also of equality, wherein all the power and jurisdiction is reciprocal, no one having more than another; there being nothing more evident than that creatures of the same species and rank, promiscuously born to all the same advantages of nature and the use of the same faculties, should also be equal one amongst another without subordination or subjection; unless the lord and master of them all should, by any manifest declaration of his will, set one above another, and confer on him by an evident and clear appointment an undoubted right to dominion and sovereignty. . . .

But though this be a state of liberty, yet it is not a state of licence; though man in that state have an uncontrollable liberty to dispose of his persons or possessions, yet he has not liberty to destroy himself, or so much as any creature in his possession, but where some nobler use than its bare preservation calls for it. The state of nature has a law of nature to govern it which obliges every one; and reason, which is that law, teaches all mankind who will but consult it that, being all equal and independent, no one ought to harm another in his life, health, liberty, or possessions; for men being all the workmanship of one omnipotent and infinitely wise Maker—all the servants of one sovereign master, sent into the world by his order, and about his business—they are his property whose workmanship they are, made to last during his, not one another's pleasure; and being furnished with like faculties, sharing all in one community of nature, there cannot be supposed any such subordination among us that may authorize us to destroy one another, as if we were made for one another's uses as the inferior ranks of creatures are for ours. Every one as he is bound to preserve himself and not to quit his station willfully, so by the like reason, when his own preservation comes not in competition, ought he, as much as he can, to preserve the rest of mankind, and may not, unless it be to do justice to an offender, take away or impair the life, or what tends to the preservation of life: the liberty, health, limb, or goods of another.

And that all men may be restrained from invading others' rights and from doing hurt to one another, and the law of nature be observed which willeth the peace and preservation of all mankind, the execution of the law of nature is, in that state, put into every man's hands, whereby everyone has a right to punish the transgressors of that law to such a degree as may hinder its violation; for the law of nature would, as all other laws that concern men in this world, be in vain, if there were nobody that in the state of nature had a power to execute that law and thereby preserve the innocent and restrain offenders. And if any one in the state of nature may punish another for any evil he has done, every one may do so; for in that state of perfect equality where naturally there is no superiority or jurisdiction of one over another, what any may do in prosecution of that law, everyone must needs have a right to do. . . .

And here we have the plain difference between the state of nature and the state of war which, however, some men have confounded, are as far distant as a state of peace, good-will, mutual assistance, and preservation, and a state of enmity, malice, violence, and mutual destruction are one from another. Men living together and according to reason, without a common superior on earth with authority to judge between them, is properly the state of nature. But force, or a declared design of force, upon the person of another, where there is no common superior on earth to appeal to for relief, is the state of war; and it is the want of such an appeal gives a man the right of war even against an aggressor, though he be in society and a fellow subject. Thus a thief, whom I cannot harm but by an appeal to the law for having stolen all that I am worth, I may kill when he sets on me to rob me but of my horse or coat; because the law, which was made for my preservation, where it cannot interpose to secure my life from present force, which, if lost, is capable of no reparation, permits me my own defence and the right of war, a liberty to kill the aggressor, because the aggressor allows not time to appeal to our common judge, nor the decision of the law, for remedy in a case where the mischief may be irreparable. Want of a common judge with authority puts all men in a state of nature; force without right upon a man's person makes a state of war both where there is, and is not, a common judge. . . .

To avoid this state of war—wherein there is no appeal but to heaven, and wherein every the least difference is apt to end in war, where there is no authority to decide between the contenders—is one great reason of men's putting themselves into society and quitting the state of nature; for where there is an authority, a power on earth from which relief can be had by appeal, there the continuance of the state of war is excluded, and the controversy is decided by that power. . . .

OF PROPERTY

God, who hath given the world to men in common, hath also given them reason to make use of it to the best advantage of life and convenience. The earth and all that is therein is given to men for the support and comfort of their being. And though all the fruits it naturally produces and beasts it feeds belong to mankind in common, as they are produced by the spontaneous hand of nature; and nobody has originally a private dominion exclusive of the rest of mankind in any of them, as they are thus in their natural state; yet, being given for the use of men, there must of necessity be a means to appropriate them some way or other before they can be of any use or at all beneficial to any particular man. The fruit or venison which nourishes the wild Indian, must be his, and so his, *i. e.*, a part of him, that another can no longer have any right to it before it can do him any good for the support of his life.

Though the earth and all inferior creatures be common to all men, yet every man has a property in his own person; this nobody has any right to but himself. The labor of his body and the work of his hands, we may say, are properly his. Whatsoever then he removes out of the state that nature hath provided and left it in, he hath mixed his labor with, and joined to it something that is his own, and thereby makes it his property. It being by him removed from the common state nature hath placed it in, it hath by this labor something annexed to it that excludes the common right of other men. For this labor being the unquestionable property of the laborer, no man but he can have a right to what that is once joined to, at least where there is enough and as good left in common for others.

He that is nourished by the acorns he picked up under an oak, or the apples he gathered from the trees in the wood, has certainly appropriated them to himself. Nobody can deny but the nourishment is his. I ask, then, when did they begin to be his? When he digested? or when he ate? or when he boiled? or when he brought them home? or when he picked them up? And it is plain, if the first gathering made them not his, nothing else could. That labor put a distinction between them and common; that added something to them more than nature, the common mother of all, had done; and so they became his private right. . . .

It will perhaps be objected to this that "if gathering the acorns, or other fruits of the earth, etc., makes a right to them, then any one may engross as much as he will." To which I answer: not so. The same law of nature that does by this means give us property does also bound that property too. "God has given us all things richly" (1 Tim. vi. 17), is the voice of reason confirmed by inspiration. But how far has he given it to us? To enjoy. As much as any one can make use of to any advantage of life before it spoils, so much he may by his labor fix a property in; whatever is beyond this is more than his share, and belongs to others. Nothing was made by God for man to spoil or destroy. And thus, considering the plenty of natural provisions there was a long time in the world, and the few spenders, and to how small a part of that provision the industry of one man could extend itself and engross it to the prejudice of others, especially keeping within the bounds set by reason of what might serve for his use, there could be then little room for quarrels or contentions about property so established. . . .

God gave the world to men in common; but since he gave it them for their benefit and the greatest conveniences of life they were capable to draw from it, it cannot be supposed he meant it should always remain common and uncultivated. He gave it to the use of the industrious and rational—and labor was to be his title to it—not to the fancy or covetousness of the quarrelsome and contentious. He that had as good left for his improvement as was already taken up needed not complain, ought not to meddle with what was already improved by another's labor; if he did, it is plain he desired the benefit of another's pains which he had no right to, and not the ground which God had given him in common with others to labor on, and whereof there was as good left as that already possessed, and more than he knew what to do with, or his industry could reach to.

OF THE BEGINNING OF POLITICAL SOCIETIES

Men being, as has been said, by nature all free, equal and independent, no one can be put out of this estate and subjected to the political power of another without his own consent. The only way whereby any one divests himself of his natural liberty, and puts on the bonds of civil society, is by agreeing with other men to join and unite into a community for their comfortable, safe, and peaceable living one amongst another, in a secure enjoyment of their properties and a greater security against any that are not of it. This any number of men may do, because it injures not the freedom of the rest; they are left as they were in the liberty of the state of nature. When any number of men have so consented to make one community or government, they are thereby presently incorporated and make one body politic wherein the majority have a right to act and conclude the rest.

For when any number of men have, by the consent of every individual, made a community, they have thereby made that community one body, with a power to act as one body, which is only by the will and determination of the majority; for that which acts any community, being only the consent of the individuals of it, and it being necessary to that which is one body to move one way, it is necessary the body should move that way whither the greater force carries it, which is the consent of the majority; or else it is impossible it should act or continue one body, one community, which the consent of every individual that united into it agreed that it should; and so every one is bound by that consent to be concluded by the majority. And therefore we see that in assemblies impowered to act by positive laws, where no number is set by that positive law which impowers them, the act of the majority passes for the act of the whole, and, of course, determines, as having by the law of nature and reason the power of the whole.

And thus every man by consenting with others to make one body politic under one government, puts himself under an obligation to every one of that society to submit to the determination of the majority, and to be concluded by it; or else this original compact, whereby he with others incorporates into one society, would signify nothing, and be no compact, if he be left free and under no other ties than he was in before in the state of nature. For what appearance would there be of any compact? What new engagement if he were no farther tied by any decrees of the society than he himself thought fit and did actually consent to? This would be still as great a liberty as he himself had before his compact, or any one else in the state of nature hath who may submit himself and consent to any acts of it if he thinks fit.

For if the consent of the majority shall not in reason be received as the act of the whole and conclude every individual, nothing but the consent of every individual can make anything to be the act of the whole; but such a consent is next to impossible ever to be had if we consider the infirmities of health and avocations of business which in a number though much less than that of a commonwealth, will necessarily keep many away from the public assembly. To which, if we add the variety of opinions and contrariety of interests which unavoidably happen in all collections of men, the coming into society upon such terms would be only like Cato's coming into the theatre only to go out again.[1] Such a constitution as this would make the mighty leviathan of a shorter duration than the feeblest creatures, and not let it outlast the day it was born in; which cannot be supposed till we can think that

[1] Cato (239–149 B.C.) was a moralist who disapproved of the theatre.

rational creatures should desire and constitute societies only to be dissolved; for where the majority cannot conclude the rest, there they cannot act as one body, and consequently will be immediately dissolved again.

Whosoever, therefore, out of a state of nature unite into a community must be understood to give up all the power necessary to the ends for which they unite into society to the majority of the community, unless they expressly agreed in any number greater than the majority. And this is done by barely agreeing to unite into one political society, which is all the compact that is, or needs be, between the individuals that enter into or make up a commonwealth. And thus that which begins and actually constitutes any political society is nothing but the consent of any number of freemen capable of a majority to unite and incorporate into such a society. And this is that, and that only, which did or could give beginning to any lawful government in the world.

OF THE ENDS OF POLITICAL SOCIETY AND GOVERNMENT

If man in the state of nature be so free, as has been said, if he be absolute lord of his own person and possessions, equal to the greatest, and subject to nobody, why will he part with his freedom, why will he give up his empire and subject himself to the dominion and control of any other power? To which it is obvious to answer that though in the state of nature he hath such a right, yet the enjoyment of it is very uncertain and constantly exposed to the invasion of others; for all being kings as much as he, every man his equal, and the greater part no strict observers of equity and justice, the enjoyment of the property he has in this state is very unsafe, very insecure. This makes him willing to quit a condition which, however free, is full of fears and continual dangers; and it is not without reason that he seeks out and is willing to join in society with others who are already united, or have a mind to unite, for the mutual preservation of their liberties, lives, and estates, which I call by the general name "property."

The great and chief end, therefore of men's uniting into commonwealths and putting themselves under government is the preservation of their property. To which in the state of nature there are many things wanting:

First, There wants an established, settled, known law, received and allowed by common consent to be the standard of right and wrong and the common measure to decide all controversies between them; for though the law of nature be plain and intelligible to all rational creatures, yet men, being biased by their interest as well as ignorant for want of studying it, are not apt to allow of it as a law binding to them in the application of it to their particular cases.

Secondly, In the state of nature there wants a known and indifferent judge with authority to determine all differences according to the established law; for everyone in that state being both judge and executioner of the law of nature, men being partial to themselves, passion and revenge is very apt to carry them too far and with too much heat in their own cases, as well as negligence and unconcernedness to make them too remiss in other men's.

Thirdly, In the state of nature, there often wants power to back and support the sentence when right, and to give it due execution. They who by any injustice offend will seldom fail, where they are able, by force, to make good their injustice; such resistance many times makes the punishment dangerous and frequently destructive to those who attempt it.

Thus mankind, notwithstanding all the privileges of the state of nature, being but in an ill condition while they remain in it, are quickly driven into society. Hence it comes to pass that we seldom find any number of men live any time together in this state. The inconveniences that they are therein exposed to by the irregular and uncertain excercise of the power every man has of punishing the transgressions of others make them take sanctuary under the established laws of government and therein seek the preservation of their property. It is this makes them so willingly give up every one his single power of punishing, to be exercised by such alone as shall be appointed to it amongst them; and by such rules as the community, or those authorized by them to that purpose, shall agree on. And in this we have the original right of both the legislative and executive power, as well as of the governments and societies themselves.

For in the state of nature, to omit the liberty he has of innocent delights, a man has two powers:

The first is to do whatsoever he thinks fit for the preservation of himself and others within the permission of the law of nature, by which law, common to them all, he and all the rest of mankind are one community, make up one society, distinct from all other creatures. And, were it not for the corruption and viciousness of degenerate men, there would be no need of any other, no necessity that men should separate from this great and natural community and by positive agreements combine into smaller and divided associations.

The other power a man has in the state of nature is the power to punish the crimes committed against that law. Both these he gives up when he joins in a private, if I may so call it, or particular political society and incorporates into any commonwealth separate from the rest of mankind.

The *first* power, *viz.,* of doing whatsoever he thought fit for the preservation of himself and the rest of mankind, he gives up to be regulated by laws made by the society, so far forth as the preservation of himself and the rest of that society shall require; which laws of the society in many things confine the liberty he had by the law of nature.

Secondly, The power of punishing he wholly gives up, and engages his natural force—which he might before employ in the execution of the law of nature by his own single authority, as he thought fit—to assist the executive power of the society, as the law thereof shall require; for being now in a new state, wherein he is to enjoy many conveniences from the labor, assistance, and society of others in the same community as well as protection from its whole strength, he is to part also with as much of his natural liberty, in providing for himself, as the good, prosperity, and safety of the society shall require, which is not only necessary, but just, since the other members of the society do the like.

But though men when they enter into society give up the equality, liberty, and executive power they had in the state of nature into the hands of the society, to be so far disposed of by the legislative as the good of the society shall require, yet it being only with an intention in every one the better to preserve himself, his liberty and property—for no rational creature can be supposed to change his condition with an intention to be worse—the power of the society, or legislative constituted by them, can never be supposed to extend farther than the common good, but is obliged to secure every one's property by providing against those three defects above-mentioned that made the state of nature so unsafe and uneasy. And so whoever has the legislative or supreme power of any commonwealth is bound to govern by established standing laws, promulgated and known to the people, and not by extemporary decrees; by indifferent and upright judges who are to decide controversies by those laws; and to employ the force of the community at home only in the execution of such laws, or abroad to prevent or redress foreign injuries, and secure the community from inroads and invasion. And all this to be directed to no other end but the safety, peace, and public good of the people.

OF THE DISSOLUTION OF GOVERNMENT

The reason why men enter into society is the preservation of their property; and the end why they choose and authorize a legislative is that there may be laws made and rules set as guards and fences to the properties of all the members of the society, to limit the power and moderate the dominion of every part and member of the society; for since it can never be supposed to be the will of the society that the legislative should have a power to destroy that which every one designs to secure by entering into society, and for which the people submitted themselves to legislators of their own making. Whenever the legislators endeavor to take away and destroy the property of the people, or to reduce them to slavery under arbitrary power, they put themselves into a state of war with the people who are thereupon absolved from any further obedience, and are left to the common refuge which God hath provided for all men against force and violence. Whensoever, therefore, the legislative shall transgress this fundamental rule of society, and either by ambition, fear, folly, or corruption, endeavor to grasp themselves, or put into the hands of any other, an absolute power over the lives, liberties, and estates of the people, by this breach of trust they forfeit the power the people had put into their hands for quite contrary ends, and it devolves to the people who have a right to resume their original liberty, and by the establishment of a new legislative, such as they shall think fit, provide for their own safety and security, which is the end for which they are in society. What I have said here concerning the legislative in general holds true also concerning the supreme executor, who having a double trust put in him—both to have a part in the legislative and the supreme execution of the law—acts against both when he goes about to set up his own arbitrary will as the law of the society. . . .

Here, it is likely, the common question will be made: "Who shall be judge whether the prince or legislative act contrary to their trust?" This, perhaps, ill-affected and factious men may spread amongst the people, when the prince only makes use of his due prerogative. To this I reply: The people shall be judge; for who shall be judge whether his trustee or deputy acts well and according to the trust reposed in him but he who deputes him and must, by having deputed him, have still a power to discard him when he fails in his trust? If this be reasonable in particular cases of private men, why should it be otherwise in that of the greatest moment where the welfare of millions is concerned, and also where the evil, if not prevented, is greater and the redress very difficult, dear, and dangerous?

But further, this question, "Who shall be judge?" cannot mean that there is no judge at all; for where there is no judicature on earth to decide controversies amongst men, God in heaven is Judge. He alone, it is true, is Judge of the right. But every man is judge for himself, as in all other cases, so in this, whether another hath put himself into a state of war with him, and whether he should appeal to the Supreme Judge . . .

If a controversy arise betwixt a prince and some of the people in a matter where the law is silent or doubtful, and the thing be of great consequence, I should think the proper umpire in such a case should be the body of the people; for in cases where the prince hath a trust reposed in him and is dispensed from the common ordinary rules of the law, there, if any men find themselves aggrieved and think the prince acts contrary to or beyond that trust, who so proper to judge as the body of the people—who, at first, lodged that trust in him—how far they meant it should extend? But if the prince, or whoever they be in the administration, decline that way of determination, the appeal then lies nowhere but to heaven; force between either persons who have no known superior on earth, or which permits no appeal to a judge on earth, being properly a state of war wherein the appeal lies only to heaven; and in that state the injured party must judge for himself when he will think fit to make use of that appeal and put himself upon it.

To conclude, the power that every individual gave the society when he entered into it can never revert to the individuals again as long as the society lasts, but will always remain in the community, because without this there can be no community, no commonwealth, which is contrary to the original agreement; so also when the society hath placed the legislative in any assembly of men, to continue in them and their successors with direction and authority for providing such successors, the legislative can never revert to the people whilst that government lasts, because having provided a legislative with power to continue for ever, they have given up their political power to the legislative and cannot resume it. But if they have set limits to the duration of their legislative and made this supreme power in any person or assembly only temporary, or else when by the miscarriages of those in authority it is forfeited, upon the forfeiture, or at the determination of the time set, it reverts to the society, and the people have a right to act as supreme and continue the legislative in themselves, or erect a new form, or under the old form place it in new hands, as they think good.

STUDY QUESTIONS

1. What is Locke's conception of the state of nature? (Compare his conception to Hobbes' if you read the selection from Hobbes.) How correct do you think is Locke's description.
2. According to Locke, does man have any rights in a state of nature? To what extent are such rights based on a law of nature?
3. Describe the essential differences between the state of nature and the state of war. How can man best avoid the state of war?
4. What does Locke mean by property? Describe in detail how he justifies the right of property.
5. Describe Locke's version of the origin of a political society. What role does the majority play in Locke's analysis? Do you think he is justified in the extent to which he would subject the individual to the consent and the power of the majority?
6. In his consideration of the chief end of a political society, do you think Locke is exaggerating the importance of property? What similarities, if any, do you find in his views here and those of our own constitution?
7. What specific disadvantages exist for the individual in a state of nature? Does such a state have any real existence, or do you think Locke regards it merely as a convenient fiction to explain the origins of a political society?
8. What is Locke's answer to the question: "Who shall be judge whether the prince or legislative act contrary to their trust?" Does this mean that any individual or group of individuals has the right of revolution? By what process would a new form of government replace an existing form of government?

James Madison

THE PROBLEM OF FACTIONALISM

Biographical Note. JAMES MADISON (1751–1836) was raised on his father's plantation in Virginia and tutored at home. He went to the College of New Jersey, now Princeton, at the age of eighteen, and received his B.A. degree two years later. In 1775 he entered politics and remained in it for forty-two years.

Beginning his political career at the Virginia House of Delegates, he went from there to the Continental Congress and then to the Constitutional Convention of 1787. The outline of a new system of government that became the basis of the convention's deliberations was drawn up by him. He served in the U. S. House of Representatives during the crucial first eight years of Congress, continued as Secretary of State in Jefferson's Cabinet, and followed Jefferson as President for two successive terms. He then retired from politics.

Madison's writings pertain mostly to political and social thought. Best known are a series of essays entitled "The Federalist," to which he contributed and which were published in the winter of 1787–1788 to meet objections brought against the proposed constitution. The following selection is the tenth paper in the series.

* * *

From *The Federalist,* A Collection of Essays by Alexander Hamilton, John Jay, and James Madison. Philadelphia, J. B. Lippincott & Co., 1866, Number X.

Introductory Note.   James Madison, like all the other great law-givers of the past from Solon on, wanted to found a government that would administer the affairs of the state "with sole regard to justice and the public good." The specific kind of government which he helped to set up is called "popular government," in which the highest authority rests with the people.

The operation of a popular government, so Madison demonstrates in the essay, is inevitably beset by a problem that threatens the exercise of justice to which the government is dedicated: the problem of factionalism. Since popular government always proceeds by majority rule, the danger is ever present that a "faction" of citizens constituting a majority might use its power to enact what is "adverse to the rights of other citizens, or to the permanent and aggregate interests of the community;" that it might allow "some common impulse of passion, or of interest" to override the demands of justice. This is all the more a distinct possibility as the latent causes of the problem are "sown in the nature of man" itself. They derive from a diversity of opinion as well as of faculties of men such as necessarily leads to a "division of society into different interests and parties." And as "the most common and durable source of faction," Madison describes "the various and unequal distribution of property." This perhaps more than anything else divides people "into different classes, actuated by different sentiments and views."

Quite obviously it is "the principal task of modern legislation" to regulate and mediate between these various and interfering interests and to do it with the "most exact impartiality," rendering them "subservient to the public good." Yet ordinarily "no man is allowed to be a judge in his own cause," whereas in an act of legislation "the parties are and must be themselves the judges." What then could prevent a predominant party from yielding to the temptation of majority power "to trample on the rule of justice"?

In a brilliant analysis, Madison shows how a solution to the problem can best be approached and why it is bound up with the establishment of a union of states.

THE MISCHIEFS OF FACTION

Among the numerous advantages promised by a well constructed union, none deserves to be more accurately developed than its tendency to break and control the violence of faction. The friend of popular governments, never finds himself so much alarmed for their character and fate, as when he contemplates their propensity to this dangerous vice. He will not fail therefore to set a due value on any plan which, without violating the principles to which he is attached, provides a proper cure for it. The instability, injustice and confusion introduced into the public councils, have in truth been the mortal diseases under which popular governments have everywhere perished; as they continue to be the favorite and fruitful topics from which the adversaries to liberty derive their most specious declamations. The valuable improvements made by the American constitutions on the popular models, both ancient and modern, cannot certainly be too much admired; but it would be an unwarrantable partiality, to contend that they have as effectually obviated the danger on this side as was wished and expected. Complaints are everywhere heard from our most considerate and virtuous citizens, equally the friends of public and private faith, and of public and personal liberty; that our governments are too unstable; that the public good is disregarded in the conflicts of rival parties; and that measures are too often decided, not according to the rules of justice, and the rights of the minor party; but by the superior force of an interested and over-bearing majority. However anxiously we may wish that these complaints had no foundation, the evidence of known facts will not permit us to deny that they are in some degree true. It will be found indeed, on a candid review of our situation, that some of the distresses under which we labor, have been erroneously charged on the operation of our governments; but it will be found, at the same time, that other causes will not alone account for many of our heaviest misfortunes; and particularly, for that prevailing and increasing distrust of public engagements, and alarm for private rights, which are echoed from one end of the continent to the other. These must be chiefly, if not wholly, effects of the unsteadiness and injustice, with which a factious spirit has tainted our public administrations.

By a faction I understand a number of citizens, whether amounting to a majority or minority of the whole, who are united and actuated by some common impulse of passion, or of interest, adverse to the rights of other citizens, or to the permanent and aggregate interests of the community.

There are two methods of curing the mischiefs of faction: the one, by removing its causes; the other, by controlling its effects.

REMOVING THE CAUSES OF FACTION

There are again two methods of removing the causes of faction: the one by destroying the liberty which is essential to its existence; the other, by giving to every citizen the same opinions, the same passions, and the same interests.

It could never be more truly said than of the first remedy, that it is worse than the disease. Liberty is to faction, what air is to fire, an aliment without which it instantly expires. But it could not be a less folly to abolish liberty, which is essential to political life, because it nourishes faction, than it would be to wish the annihilation of air, which is essential to animal life, because it imparts to fire its destructive agency.

The second expedient is as impracticable, as the first would be unwise. As long as the reason of man continues fallible, and he is at liberty to exercise it, different opinions will be formed. As long as the connection subsists between his reason and his self-love, his opinions and his passions will have a reciprocal influence on each other; and the former will be objects to which the latter will attach themselves. The diversity in the faculties of men from which the rights of property originate, is not less an insuperable obstacle to a uniformity of interests. The protection of these faculties is the first object of government. From the protection of different and unequal faculties of acquiring property, the possession of different degrees and kinds of property immediately results; and from the influence of these on the sentiments and views of the respective proprietors, ensues a division of the society into different interests and parties.

The latent causes of faction are thus sown in the nature of man; and we see them everywhere brought into different degrees of activity, according to the different circumstances of civil society. A zeal for different opinions concerning religion, concerning government and many other points, as well of speculation as of practice; an attachment to different leaders ambitiously contending for pre-eminence and power; or to persons of other descriptions whose fortunes have been interesting to the human passions, have in turn divided mankind into parties, inflamed them with mutual animosity, and rendered them much more disposed to vex and oppress each other, than to cooperate for their common good. So strong is this propensity of mankind to fall into mutual animosities that where no substantial occasion presents itself, the most frivolous and fanciful distinctions have been sufficient to kindle their unfriendly passions, and excite their most violent conflicts. But the most common and durable source of factions, has been the various and unequal distribution of property. Those who hold, and those who are without property, have ever formed distinct interests in society. Those who are creditors, and those who are debtors, fall under a like discrimination. A landed interest, a manufacturing interest, a mercantile interest, a moneyed interest, with many lesser interests, grow up of necessity in civilized nations, and divide them into different classes, actuated by different sentiments and views. The regulation of these various and interfering interests forms the principal task of modern legislation, and involves the spirit of party and faction in the necessary and ordinary operations of Government.

No man is allowed to be a judge in his own cause; because his interest would certainly bias his judgment, and, not improbably, corrupt his integrity. With equal, nay with greater reason, a body of men, are unfit to be both judges and parties, at the same time; yet, what are many of the most important acts of legislation, but so many judicial determinations, not indeed concerning the rights of single persons, but concerning the rights of large bodies of citizens; and what are the different classes of legislators, but advocates and parties to the causes which they determine? Is a law proposed concerning private debts? It is a question to which the creditors are parties on one side, and the debtors on the other. Justice ought to hold the balance between them. Yet the parties are and must be themselves the judges; and the most numerous party, or, in other words, the most powerful faction must be expected to prevail. Shall domestic manufactures be encouraged, and in what degree, by restrictions on foreign manufactures? [these] are questions which would be differently decided by the landed and the manufacturing classes; and probably by neither with a sole regard to justice and the public good. The apportionment of taxes on the various descriptions of property, is an act which seems to require the most exact impartiality; yet, there is perhaps no legislative act in which greater opportunity and temptation are given to a predominant party, to trample on the rules of justice. Every shilling with which they over-burden the inferior number, is a shilling saved to their own pockets.

It is in vain to say, that enlightened statesmen will be able to adjust these clashing interests, and render them all subservient to the public good. Enlightened statesmen will not always be at the helm: Nor, in many cases, can such an adjustment be made at all, without taking into view indirect and remote considerations, which will rarely prevail over the immediate interest which one party may find in disregarding the rights of another, or the good of the whole.

The inference to which we are brought, is, that the *causes* of faction cannot be removed; and that relief is only to be sought in the means of controlling its *effects*.

CONTROLLING THE EFFECTS OF FACTION

If a faction consists of less than a majority, relief is supplied by the republican principle, which enables the majority to defeat its sinister views by regular vote. It may clog the administration, it may convulse the society; but it will be unable to execute and mask its violence under the forms of the constitution. When a majority is included in a faction, the form of popular government on the other hand enables it to sacrifice to its ruling passion or interest, both the public good and the rights of other citizens. To secure the public good, and private rights, against the danger of such a faction, and at the same time to preserve the spirit and the form of popular government, is then the great object to which our enquiries are directed. Let me add that it is the great desideratum, by which alone this form of government can be rescued from the opprobrium under which it has so long labored, and be recommended to the esteem and adoption of mankind.

By what means is this object attainable? Evidently by one of two only. Either the existence of the same passion or interest in a majority at the same time must be prevented; or the majority, having such co-existent passion or interest, must be rendered, by their number and local situation, unable to concert and carry into effect schemes of oppression. If the impulse and the opportunity be suffered to coincide, we well know that neither moral nor religious motives can be relied on as an adequate control. They are not found to be such on the injustice and violence of individuals, and lose their efficacy in proportion to the number combined together; that is, in proportion as their efficacy becomes needful.

From this view of the subject, it may be concluded, that a pure democracy, by which I mean, a society, consisting of a small number of citizens, who assemble and administer the government in person, can admit of no cure from the mischiefs of faction. A common passion or interest will, in almost every case, be felt by a majority of the whole; a communication and concert results from the form of government itself; and there is nothing to check the inducements to sacrifice the weaker party, or an obnoxious individual. Hence it is, that such democracies have ever been spectacles of turbulence and contention; have ever been found incompatible with personal security, or the rights of property; and have in general been as short in their lives, as they have been violent in their deaths. Theoretic politicians, who have patronized this species of government, have erroneously supposed, that by reducing mankind to a perfect equality in their political rights, they would, at the same time, be perfectly equalized and assimilated in their possessions, their opinions, and their passions.

A republic, by which I mean a government in which the scheme of representation takes place, opens a different prospect, and promises the cure for which we are seeking. Let us examine the points in which it varies from pure democracy, and we shall comprehend both the nature of the cure, and the efficacy which it must derive from the union.

The two great points of difference between a democracy and a republic are, first, the delegation of the government, in the latter, to a small number of citizens elected by the rest: secondly, the greater number of citizens, and greater sphere of country, over which the latter may be extended.

The effect of the first difference is, on the one hand to refine and enlarge the public views, by passing them through the medium of a chosen body of citizens, whose wisdom may best discern the true interest of their country, and whose patriotism and love of justice, will be least likely to sacrifice it to temporary or partial considerations. Under such a regulation, it may well happen that the public voice pronounced by the representatives of the people, will be more consonant to the public good, than if pronounced by the people themselves convened for the purpose. On the other hand, the effect may be inverted. Men of factious tempers, of local prejudices, or of sinister designs, may by intrigue, by corruption or by other means, first obtain the suffrages, and then betray the interests of the people. The question resulting is, whether small or extensive republics are most favorable to the election of proper guardians of the public weal; and it is clearly decided in favor of the latter by two obvious considerations.

In the first place it is to be remarked that however small the republic may be, the representatives must be raised to a certain number, in order to guard against the cabals of a few; and that however large it may be, they must be limited to a certain number, in order to guard against the confusion of a multitude. Hence the number of representatives in the two cases, not being in proportion to that of the constituents, and being proportionally greatest in the small republic, it follows, that if the proportion of fit characters, be not less, in the large than in the small republic, the former, will present a greater option, and consequently a greater probability of a fit choice.

In the next place, as each representative will be chosen by a greater number of citizens in the large than in the small republic, it will be more difficult for unworthy candidates to practice with success the vicious arts, by which elections are too often carried; and the suffrages of the people being more free, will be more likely to centre on men who possess the most attractive merit, and the most diffusive and established characters.

It must be confessed, that in this, as in most other cases, there is a mean, on both sides of which inconveniences will be found to lie. By enlarging too much the number of electors, you render the representative too little acquainted with all their local circumstances and lesser interests; as by reducing it too much, you render him unduly attached to these, and too little fit to comprehend and pursue great and national objects. The federal constitution forms a happy combination in this respect; the great and aggregate interests being referred to the national, the local and particular, to the state legislatures.

The other point of difference is, the greater number of citizens and extent of territory which may be brought within the compass of republican, than of democratic government; and it is this circumstance principally which renders factious combinations less to be dreaded in the former, than in the latter. The smaller the society, the fewer probably will be the distinct parties and interests composing it; the fewer the distinct parties and interest, the more frequently will a majority be found of the same party; and the smaller the number of individuals composing a majority, and the smaller the compass within which they are placed, the more easily will they concert and execute their plans of oppression. Extend the sphere, and you take in a greater variety of parties and interests; you make it less probable that a majority of the whole will have a common motive to invade the rights of other citizens; or if such a common motive exists, it will be more difficult for all who feel it to discover their own strength, and to act in unison with each other. Besides other impediments, it may be remarked, that where there is a consciousness of unjust or dishonorable purposes, communication is always checked by distrust, in proportion to the number whose concurrence is necessary.

UNION: THE REPUBLICAN REMEDY

Hence it clearly appears, that the same advantage, which a republic has over a democracy, in controlling the effects of faction, is enjoyed by a large over a small republic—is enjoyed by the union over the states composing it. Does this advantage consist in the substitution of representatives, whose enlightened views and virtuous sentiments render them superior to local prejudices, and to schemes of injustice? It will not be denied, that the representation of the union will be most likely to possess these requisite endowments. Does it consist in the greater security afforded by a greater variety of parties, against the event of any one party being able to outnumber and oppress the rest? In an equal degree does the increased variety of parties, comprised within the union, increase this security. Does it, in fine, consist in the greater obstacles opposed to the concert and accomplishment of the secret wishes of an unjust and interested majority? Here, again, the extent of the union gives it the most palpable advantage.

The influence of factious leaders may kindle a flame within their particular states, but will be unable to spread a general conflagration through the other states: a religious sect, may degenerate into a political faction in a part of the confederacy; but the variety of sects dispersed over the entire face of it, must secure the national councils against any danger from that source: a rage for paper money, for an abolition of debts, for an equal division of property, or for any other improper or wicked project, will be less apt to pervade the whole body of the union, than a particular member of it; in the same proportion as such a malady is more likely to taint a particular county or district, than an entire state.

In the extent and proper structure of the union, therefore, we behold a republican remedy for the diseases most incident to republican government. And according to the degree of pleasure and pride, we feel in being republicans, ought to be our zeal in cherishing the spirit, and supporting the character of federalists.

STUDY QUESTIONS

1. What are "mortal diseases" of popular governments?
2. In what sense is the formation of "factions" an ever-present danger to popular governments?
3. Why can this danger not be removed by way of the causes?
4. How are the latent causes of faction connected with the very nature of man?
5. Why can the principle that no man is allowed to be a judge in his own cause not be applied to the acts of legislation of popular governments?
6. By what means can the effects of faction be controlled?
7. Why does "pure Democracy" admit of no cure for the mischiefs of faction?
8. Why are extensive Republics rather than small ones most favorable to controlling the effects of faction?
9. What is the advantage of a Union over the States composing it?

G. W. F. Hegel

🔲🔲🔲🔲🔲🔲🔲🔲🔲🔲🔲🔲🔲🔲🔲🔲🔲🔲🔲🔲🔲🔲🔲🔲🔲🔲🔲🔲🔲🔲🔲🔲🔲

THE STATE AND THE
DESTINY OF THE WORLD

🔲🔲🔲🔲🔲🔲🔲🔲🔲🔲🔲🔲🔲🔲🔲🔲🔲🔲🔲🔲🔲🔲🔲🔲🔲🔲🔲🔲🔲🔲🔲🔲🔲

Biographical Note. GEORG WILHELM FRIEDRICH HEGEL
(1770–1831) was born in Southern Germany, the son of a jurist. He attended the University of Tübingen, where he completed the curriculum in
theology. Seven years of service as a private tutor followed, until 1801,
when he began his teaching career at the University of Jena. He left Jena
in the wake of its occupation by the Napoleonic Army in 1806, despite his
great admiration for Napoleon himself. On the occasion of seeing him riding
through the streets of Jena he wrote: "It is indeed marvellous to see such an
individual, a mere human on horseback, who extends his influence over the
whole world and controls it   such advances are only possible to this extraordinary man whom you cannot but admire."

An interlude as high school principal ended in 1816 with his appointment as professor of philosophy at the University of Heidelberg, from
which he accepted a call to Berlin two years later. Here he continued as
university teacher until his death, while his philosophy mainly because of its
socio-political implications became increasingly identified with that of the
Prussian State of his time.

Hegel's most important works are *Phenomenology of Spirit* (1806), *Sci-*

From Georg Wilhelm Friedrich Hegel, *Lectures on the Philosophy of History,*
translated by John Sibree, London, G. Bell & Sons, 1902. From the Introduction,
with minor alterations.

ence of Logic (1812), and *Encyclopedia of the Philosophical Sciences* (1817). To this must be added a number of his lecture courses which were published from his manuscripts and his students' notebooks after his death. Among these were *Lectures on the Philosophy of History,* from which the selection here is taken.

* * *

Introductory Note. It has been an unquestioned assumption of philosophers like Hobbes or Locke that political and social organizations owe their existence to inherent basic needs of man (such as are implied in the phrase "pursuit of happiness") whose adequate satisfaction can never be sought apart from a framework of law and order that is apart from the establishment of the institutions of a state. And their political philosophy was primarily motivated by the question: "What form of state, what type of government would best answer these needs?"

Such dependence of the fulfillment of man's "needs, passions and interests" upon the authority of a state as its only possible guarantor would not be denied by Hegel. Yet he would consider this an extremely superficial and narrow account that in no way touches upon the root of things as philosophy endeavors to do. Specifically he would claim three major deficiencies apparent in a political philosophy that takes its cue from nothing higher than the interests of individuals.

First of all, he would maintain, whatever happens in a political world that consists of nation-states is most intimately related to the cultural whole of which it forms an integral part, to what constitutes the whole life of a people—its "art, law, morals, religion, science." And this life has a definite purpose: it "brings a certain fruit to maturity."

Secondly, every nation-state "is only one individual in the course of world history." It represents a certain stage in a "restless succession" of "infinitely manifold forms" of peoples, states, and individuals. But these successive forms do not merely produce the same life afresh. They "come forth ever more exalted, transfigured." They are oriented toward a destiny, "the destiny of the world at which the progress of history has been continually aiming."

Thirdly, this destiny or ultimate purpose of world history presiding over the history of individuals and of the peoples to which they belong can finally not be understood from itself, but must be referred to a Providence or Sovereign of the world—to God as the ultimately controlling power. The world and its history are rooted in "the plan of Divine Providence," which is a plan of Reason for the comprehension of which "the time has finally come."

Thus for Hegel political philosophy turns into a philosophy of history as the framework for its proper pursuit, opening up in fact a new field for philosophic inquiry. And in his *Lectures on the Philosophy of History,* he indeed deals with the question of the highest form of political organization (which for him is Monarchy as embodied in the Prussian State of his time), but seen entirely as part of a developing process through which "God's purpose with the world" will be fulfilled.

The selection is concerned with the two interrelated problems of what the destiny of the world consists in and what part individuals and nation-states necessarily play to bring it about. "World-Spirit" is the name used by Hegel for Divine Providence in so far as it acts upon world history. This Spirit, whose sole truth is said to be *freedom,* manifests itself concretely in nation-states, which are therefore called "world-historical national Spirits," and also in every man, especially in the "heroes," the "great historical men whose particular aims involve the large issues which are the will of World-Spirit." Stated in Hegel's terminology, the problem he presents us with is the understanding of history as a movement that progressively unfolds and realizes the aim of World-Spirit—which is freedom—through a chain of progression of national Spirits, while the heroes in every epoch serve as the special agents of World-Spirit, bringing to light "the very truth for their age, for their world; the species next in order, so to speak, which was already formed in the womb of time."

PHILOSOPHY OF HISTORY AND RELIGION

The most general definition that can be given is that the Philosophy of History means nothing but the thoughtful consideration of it. . . . The only thought which philosophy brings with it to the contemplation of history, is the simple conception of Reason; that Reason is the Sovereign of the world; that the history of the world, therefore, presents us with a rational process. . . .

We have next to notice the rise of this idea—that Reason governs the world—in connection with a further application of it, well known to us, in the form, viz. of the religious truth, that the world is not abandoned to chance and external contingent causes, but that a Providence controls it. . . . The truth, then, that a Providence (that of God) presides over the events of the world corresponds to the proposition in question; for Divine Providence is Wisdom, endowed with an infinite power, which realizes its aims, viz. the absolute rational destiny of the world. Reason is thought freely determining itself.

But a difference—rather an opposition—will manifest itself between this belief and our principle. . . . For that belief is indefinite; it is what is called a belief in a general Providence, and is not followed out into definite application, into its bearing on the grand total—the entire course of human history. . . . But in the history of the world, the individuals we have to do with are peoples; totalities that are States. We cannot, therefore be satisfied with what we may call a trifling view of Providence; nor with the merely abstract, undefined belief in a Providence leaving its definite acts undetermined. On the contrary, our earnest endeavor must be directed to the recognition of the ways of Providence, the means it uses, and the historical phenomena in which it manifests itself; and we must show their connection with the general principle above mentioned.

But in noticing the recognition of the plan of Divine Providence generally, I have implicitly touched upon a prominent question of the day; viz. that of the possibility of knowing God: or rather—since public opinion has ceased to allow it to be a matter of question—the doctrine which has now become a prejudice that it is impossible to know God. In direct contravention of what is commanded in Holy Scripture as the highest duty—that we should not merely love, but know God—the prevalent dogma involves the denial of what is there said; viz. that it is the Spirit that leads into truth, knows all things, penetrates even the depths of Divinity. . . .

It was for a while the fashion to profess admiration for the wisdom of God, as displayed in animals, plants, and isolated occurrences. But, if it be allowed that Providence manifests itself in such objects and forms of existence, why not also in world history? This is deemed too great a matter to be thus regarded. But Divine Wisdom, *i.e.* Reason, is one and the same in the great as in the little; and we must not imagine God to be too weak to exercise his wisdom on a grand scale. Our intellectual striving aims at recognizing that what eternal wisdom intended is actually accomplished in the domain of existent, active Spirit, as well as in that of mere nature.

Our mode of treating the subject is, in this aspect, a theodicy—a justification of the ways of God—which Leibniz attempted metaphysically, in his method, *i.e.* in indefinite abstract categories, so that the evil that is found in the world may be comprehended, and the thinking Spirit be reconciled with it. Indeed, nowhere is such a harmonizing view more pressingly demanded than in world history; and it can be attained only through the recognition of the positive elements in which that negative element disappears as something subordinate and vanquished. On the one hand, the destiny of the world must be perceived; and, on the other hand, the fact that this destiny has been actually realized in it, and that evil has not been able permanently to assert a competing position. But this conviction involves much more than the mere belief in a superintending Reason or in Providence. Reason, whose sovereignty over the world has been maintained, is as indefinite a term as Providence, supposing the term to be used by those who are unable to characterize it distinctly, to show wherein it consists, so as to enable us to decide whether something is rational or irrational. What we need is an adequate definition of Reason. Without such a definition we get no farther than mere words.

THE SPIRIT IN HISTORY

The question of how Reason is *determined* in itself—as far as it is considered in reference to the world—is identical with the question, what is the *destiny of the world?* And the expression implies that that destiny is to be actualized and realized.

It must be observed at the outset, that the phenomenon we investigate, *world history,* belongs to the realm of Spirit. The term "world," includes both physical and psychical nature. Physical nature also plays its part in world history. But Spirit, and the course of its development, is our substantial object. Our task does not require us to contemplate nature as a rational system in itself—though in its own proper domain it proves itself such—but simply in its relation to *Spirit.* On the stage on which we are observing it—world history—Spirit displays itself in its most concrete reality. Notwithstanding this (or rather for the very purpose of comprehending the general idea of this concrete existence of Spirit) we must premise some abstract characteristics of the *nature of Spirit.* . . .

The nature of Spirit may be understood by a glance at its direct opposite—matter. As the essence of matter is gravity, so, on the other hand, we may affirm that the substance, the essence, of Spirit is freedom. It is immediately plausible to everyone that Spirit, among other properties, is also endowed with freedom; but philosophy teaches that all the qualities of Spirit exist only through freedom; that all are but means for attaining freedom; that all seek and produce this and this alone. It is a result of speculative philosophy that freedom is the sole truth of Spirit. . . .

Following this abstract definition it may be said of world history that it is the exhibition of Spirit in the process of working out the knowledge of that which it is potentially. And as the germ bears in itself the whole nature of the tree, and the taste and form of its fruits, so do the first traces of Spirit virtually contain the whole of that history.

The Orientals do not yet know that Spirit—man as such—is free; and because they do not know this they are not free. They only know that *one* is free. But on this very account, the freedom of that one is only caprice, ferocity, brutal recklessness, or passion, or a mildness and tameness of the desires, which is itself only an accident of nature, mere caprice. This one is therefore only a despot; not a free man.

The consciousness of freedom first arose among the Greeks, and therefore they were free; but they, and the Romans likewise, knew only that *some* are free, not man as such. Even Plato and Aristotle did not know this. The Greeks, therefore, had slaves; and their whole life and the maintenance of their splendid liberty, was implicated with the institution of slavery: a fact moreover, which made that liberty on the one hand only an accidental, transient and limited growth, on the other hand, a rigorous servitude of the human.

The Germanic nations, under the influence of Christianity, were the first to attain the consciousness, that man, as man, is free: that it is the freedom of Spirit which constitutes its essence. This consciousness arose first in religion, the inmost region of Spirit. But to introduce the principle into the various relations of the actual world, involves a more extensive problem than its simple implantation; a problem whose solution and application require a severe and lengthened process of culture. In proof of this, we may note that slavery did not cease immediately on the reception of Christianity. Still less did liberty predominate in states; or governments and constitutions adopt a rational organization, or recognize freedom as their basis. The application of this principle to the condition of the world through molding and interpenetrating it is precisely the long process of history. . . .

World history is the progress of the consciousness of freedom; a progress whose development according to the necessity of its nature, it is our business to investigate. The general statement given above, of the various grades in the consciousness of freedom—and which we applied in the first instance to the fact that the Eastern nations knew only that *one* is free; the Greek and Roman world only that *some* are free; while *we* know that all men absolutely, that is, as men, are free—supplies us with the natural division of world history and with the manner in which we will treat it.

The destiny of the world of Spirit, and—since this is the substantial world, while the physical remains subordinate to it, or, in the language of speculation, has no truth as against the first—the *destiny of the world* has been said to be the Spirit's consciousness of its own freedom and thereby the actualization of this freedom. . . . This ultimate purpose it is, at which the process of world history has been continually aiming; and to which the sacrifices that have ever and anon been laid on the vast altar of the earth, through the long lapse of ages, have been offered. This is the only aim that sees itself realized and fulfilled; the only pole of repose amid the ceaseless change of events and conditions, and the sole efficient principle that pervades them. This final aim is God's purpose with the world; but God is the absolutely perfect Being, and can, therefore, will nothing other than himself—his own Will. The nature of His Will—that is, His Nature itself—is what we here call the Idea of freedom; translating the language of religion into that of thought. The question, then, which we may next put, is: What means does this principle of freedom use for its realization?

MEANS OF REALIZATION

The question of the *means* by which freedom develops itself to a world, conducts us to the phenomenon of history itself. Although freedom is, primarily, an undeveloped idea, the means it uses are external and phenomenal; presenting themselves in history directly before our eyes. The first glance at history convinces us that the actions of men proceed from their needs, their passions, their characters and talents; and impresses us with the belief that such needs, passions and interests are the sole springs of action—the efficient main agents in this scene of activity. Among these may, perhaps, be found purposes of a liberal or universal kind—benevolence it may be, or noble patriotism; but such virtues and general views are but insignificant as compared with the world and its doings. We may perhaps see the ideal of Reason actualized in those who adopt such aims, and within the sphere of their influence; but they bear only a trifling proportion to the mass of the human race; and the extent of that influence is limited accordingly. Passions, private aims, and the satisfaction of selfish desires, are on the other hand, most effective springs of action. Their power lies in the fact that they respect none of the limitations which justice and morality would impose on them; and that these natural impulses have a more direct influence over man than the artificial and tedious discipline that tends to order and self-restraint, to law and morality. . . .

We assert then that nothing has been accomplished without interest on the part of those who brought it about; and—if interest be called passion, inasmuch as the whole individuality, to the neglect of all other actual or possible interests and claims, is devoted to an object with every fibre of volition, concentrating all its desires and powers upon it—we may affirm absolutely that *nothing great in the world* has been accomplished without passion. Two elements therefore enter into our investigation: first, the Idea, secondly, the complex of human passions; the one the warp, the other the woof of the vast tapestry of world history. . . .

I will endeavor to make what has been said more vivid and clear by examples.

The building of a house is, in the first instance, a subjective aim and design. On the other hand we have, as means, the several substances required for the work—iron, wood, stones. The elements are made use of in working up this material: fire to melt the iron, wind to blow the fire, water to set wheels in motion in order to cut the wood, etc. The result is, that the wind, which has helped to build the house, is shut out by the house; so also are the violence of rains and floods and the destructive powers of fire, so far as the house is made fireproof. The stones and beams obey the law of gravity, press downwards, and so high walls are carried up. Thus the elements are made use of in accordance with their nature and they cooperate for a product by which they are restricted. In a similar way the passions of men are gratified; they develop themselves and their aims in accordance with their natural tendencies, and build up the edifice of human society; thus they fortify a structure for law and order *against* themselves. . . .

Caesar was contending for the maintenance of his position, honor, and safety; and, since the power of his opponents included the sovereignty over the provinces of the Roman Empire, his victory secured for him the conquest of that entire Empire; and he thus became—though leaving the form of the constitution—the sole ruler of the state. That which secured for him the execution of his originally negative purpose, domination over Rome, was at the same time an independently necessary feature in the history of Rome and of the world. It was not, then, his private gain merely, but an unconscious impulse that occasioned the accomplishment of that for which the time was ripe.

Such are all great historical men whose own particular aims involve those large issues which are the will of the World-Spirit. They may be called *Heroes,* inasmuch as they have derived their purposes and their vocation, not from the calm, regular course of things, sanctioned by the existing order; but from a concealed fount—one which has not attained to phenomenal, present existence—from that inner Spirit, still hidden beneath the surface, which, impinging on the outer world as on a shell, bursts it in pieces, because it is another kernel than that which belonged to the shell. They are men, therefore, who appear to draw the impulse of their life from themselves; and whose deeds have produced a condition of things and a complex of historical relations which appear to be only *their* interest, and *their* work.

Such individuals had no consciousness of the general Idea they were unfolding, while prosecuting those aims of theirs; on the contrary, they were practical, political men. But at the same time they were thinking men, who had an insight into the requirements of the time, what was needed and *timely*. This was the very truth for their age, for their world; the species next in order, so to speak, which was already formed in the womb of time. It was theirs to know this nascent principle; the necessary, directly sequent step in progress, which their world was to take; to make this their aim, and to expend their energy in promoting it. World-historical men—the Heroes of an epoch—must, therefore, be recognized as its seers; their deeds, their words are the best of that time. . . .

If we go on to cast a look at the fate of these world-historical persons, whose vocation it was to be the agents of the World-Spirit, we shall find it to have been no happy one. They attained no calm enjoyment; their whole life was labor and trouble; their whole being was in their passion. When their object is attained they fall off like empty hulls from the kernel. They die early, like Alexander; they are murdered like Caesar; transported to St. Helena, like Napoleon. . . .

A world-historical individual is not so unwise as to indulge a variety of wishes to divide his regards. He is devoted to the one aim, regardless of all else. It is even possible that such men may treat other great, even sacred interests, inconsiderately; a conduct which indeed subjects them to moral reprehension. But so mighty a figure must trample down many an innocent flower, crush to pieces many an object in its path.

The special interest of passion is thus inseparable from the active development of a general principle: for it is from the particular and determinate and from its negation, that the universal results. It is the particular which exhausts itself in the struggle and part of which is destroyed. It is not the general idea that is implicated in opposition and combat, and that is exposed to danger. It remains in the background, untouched and uninjured. This may be called the *cunning of reason*, that it sets the passions to work for itself, allowing that which establishes its existence through such impulsion to pay the penalty and to suffer the loss. For it is *phenomenal* being that is so treated, which in part is of no value, in part positive. The particular is for the most part of too trifling value as compared with the general: individuals are sacrificed and abandoned. The Idea pays the tribute of existence and transience not from itself, but from the passions of individuals. . . .

THE STATE AS EMBODIMENT OF SPIRIT

What is the object to be realized by these means; *i.e.* what is the form it assumes in the realm of reality? We have spoken of means; but in the carrying out of a subjective, limited aim, we have also to take into consideration the element of a *material,* either already present or which has to be procured. Thus the question would arise: What is the material in which the ideal of Reason is wrought out? It is first of all the subjective agent itself, human desires, subjectivity in general. In human knowledge and volition, as its material element, Reason attains positive existence. We have considered subjective volition where it has a purpose which is the truth and essence of a reality, viz. where it constitutes a great world-historical passion. As a subjective will, occupied with limited passions, it is dependent, and can fulfill its purposes only within the limits of this dependence. But the subjective will has also a substantial life, a reality, in which it moves in the region of essential being and has the essential itself as the object of its existence. This essential being is the union of the subjective with the rational will: it is the moral whole, the *State,* which is that form of reality in which the individual has and enjoys his freedom; but only as knowing, believing, and willing the universal. . . .

Subjective volition, passion, is that which sets men in activity, that which actualizes and realizes. The Idea is the interior; the State is the actually existing, genuinely moral life. For it is the unity of the universal, essential will, with that of the individual; and this is morality. The individual living in this unity has a moral life; possesses worth that consists in this substantiality alone. Sophocles' Antigone says, "The divine commands are not of yesterday, nor of today; no, they have an infinite existence, and no one could say whence they came." The laws of morality are not accidental, but are rationality itself. It is the very object of the State to make what is essential prevail and maintain itself in the actual doings of men and in their dispositions. It is the absolute interest of Reason that this moral whole should exist; and herein lies the justification and merit of heroes who have founded states, however crude these may have been.

In the history of the world, only those people can come under our notice which form a State. For it must be understood that this latter is the realization of freedom, *i.e.* of absolute destiny, and that it exists for its own sake. It must further be understood that all the worth which the human being possesses, all spiritual reality, he possesses only through the State. For his spiritual reality consists in this, that his own essence—Reason—is objectively present to him, that it possesses objective immediate existence for him. Thus only is he fully conscious; thus only is he a partaker of morality, of a just and moral life of the State. For the true is the unity of the universal and subjective will; and the universal is to be found in the State, in its laws, its universal and rational provisions. The State is the Divine Idea as it exists on earth. Thus the State is the definite object of world history proper; that in which freedom obtains objectivity, and lives in the enjoyment of this objectivity. . . .

It is only by a constitution that the abstract entity of the State attains life and reality; but this involves the distinction between those who command and those who obey. . . . The primary consideration is, then, the distinction between the governing and the governed, and constitutions have rightly been classified into monarchy, aristocracy, and democracy; which gives occasion, however, to the remark that monarchy itself must further be divided into despotism and monarchy proper; that in all the divisions to which the leading idea gives rise, only the generic character is to be emphasized, it being not intended thereby that the particular category under review should be exhausted as a type or species in its concrete realization. But above all it must be observed that those divisions admit of a multitude of particular modifications, not only such as lie within the limits of those classes themselves, but also such as are mixtures of several essentially distinct classes, and which are consequently misshapen, unstable and inconsistent forms. . . .

We have established as the two points of our discussion, first, the idea of freedom as absolute destiny, and secondly, the means for realizing it, *i.e.* the subjective side of knowledge and will, with its life, movement, and activity. We then recognized the State as the moral whole and the reality of freedom, and consequently as the objective unity of these two elements. . . . The State is therefore the basis and center of the other concrete aspects of the life of a people, of art, law, morals, religion, science. All the activity of Spirit has only this object: to become conscious of this union, *i.c.* of its own freedom.

Among the forms of this conscious union *religion* is foremost. In it the Spirit existing in the world becomes conscious of absolute Spirit and in this consciousness of the Absolute the will of man renounces its particular interest; it lays this aside in devotion in which he is not concerned anymore with particulars. By sacrifice man expresses his renunciation of his property, his will, his individual feelings. The religious concentration of the soul appears as emotion, but also passes into reflection: public worship is an expression of reflection.

The second form of the union of the objective and the subjective in the human spirit is *art*. This advances farther into the realm of the actual and sensible than religion. In its noblest endeavor it is occupied with representing, not indeed, the Spirit of God, but certainly the Form of God; and then that which is divine and spiritual generally. Its office is to render visible the Divine; presenting it to the imaginative and intuitive faculties.

But the true is the object not only of conceiving and feeling, as in religion, and of concrete perception, as in art, but also of the thinking Spirit; and this gives us the third form of union in question—*philosophy*. It is in this respect the highest, freest, and wisest form. . . .

Summing up what has been said of the State, we find that we have been led to call its vital principle, as actuating the individuals who compose it, morality. The State, its laws, its institutions, are the rights of its members. Its natural features, its mountains, air and waters, are their country, their fatherland, their outward material property; the history of this State, their deeds, and what their ancestors have produced, belongs to them and lives in their memory. All is their possession, just as they are possessed by it; for it constitutes their existence, their being. Their minds are full of it and their wills are their willing of these laws and of this fatherland. . . .

Furthermore, the particular national Spirit is only one individual in the course of world history. For that history is the exhibition of the divine, absolute development of Spirit in its highest forms—that gradual progress by which it attains its truth and self-consciousness. The forms which these stages assume are the world-historical national Spirits, the definiteness of their moral life, of their government, their art, religion, and science. To realize these stages is the boundless impulse of the World-Spirit—the goal of its irresistible urging; for this differentiation and its realization is its Idea. World history only shows how Spirit gradually attains the consciousness of and the will to truth; dawn rises in the Spirit, it discovers focal points, and at last it arrives at full consciousness. . . .

THE COURSE OF WORLD HISTORY

World history, as already indicated, shows the development of the consciousness of freedom on the part of Spirit, and of the consequent realization of that freedom. This development implies a gradation, a series of further expressions or manifestations of freedom which result from its idea. The logical, and, even more, the *dialectical* nature of the idea in general, viz. that it is self-determined, that it assumes successive forms which it successively transcends; and by this very process of transcending its earlier stages, gains an affirmative, and, in fact, a richer and more concrete shape;—this necessity of its nature, and the necessary series of pure abstract forms which the idea successively assumes, is exhibited in the department of Logic. Here we need adopt only one of its results, viz. that every step in the process, as differing from any other, has its determinate peculiar principle. In history this principle is concreteness of Spirit—particular national Spirit. . . .

If we cast a glance at world history in general, we see a vast picture of transformations and actions; of infinitely manifold forms of peoples, states, individuals, in restless succession. Everything that can enter into and interest the soul of man, every sentiment of goodness, beauty, greatness is called into play. Everywhere aims are adopted and pursued, which we recognize, whose accomplishment we desire, for which we hope and fear. In all these occurrences we behold human acting and being acted upon predominant; everywhere something akin to ourselves, and therefore everywhere something that excites our interest for or against. Sometimes it attracts us by beauty, freedom, and richness; sometimes by energy such as enables even vice to make itself interesting. Sometimes we see the more comprehensive mass of some general interest advancing with comparative slowness, and subsequently sacrificed to an infinite complexity of trifling circumstances, and pulverized. Then, again, with a vast expenditure of power a trivial result is produced; while from what appears unimportant a tremendous issue proceeds. Everywhere there is the motliest throng of events drawing us within the circle of its interest, and when one combination vanishes another immediately appears in its place.

The general thought, the category which first presents itself in this restless succession of individuals and peoples, existing for a time and then vanishing, is that of *change* in general. To comprehend this change from its negative side, all we have to do is to look at the ruins of past splendor. What traveller among the ruins of Carthage, of Palmyra, Persepolis, or Rome has not been moved to think of the transiency of kingdoms and men, to mourn the passing of a vigorous and rich life—a mourning which does not expend itself on personal losses and the transitoriness of one's own undertakings, but is a disinterested sorrow at the fall of splendid and highly developed human life.

But the next consideration which allies itself with that of change, is that change while it imports dissolution, involves at the same time the rise of a new life, that while death is the issue of life, life is also the issue of death. This is a grand conception; one which the Orientals comprehended, and which is perhaps the highest in their metaphysics. In the idea of migration of souls we find it contained in its relation to individual existence. But a myth more generally known is that of the *Phoenix* as the life of nature, eternally preparing for its own funeral pyre, and consuming itself upon it; but so that from its ashes is produced the new, renovated, fresh life. But this image is only Asiatic; oriental not occidental. Spirit consuming the outward form of its existence does not merely pass into another form, not only rises rejuvenated from the ashes of its previous form; it comes forth exalted, transfigured, a purer spirit. It certainly makes war upon itself, consumes its own existence; but in this very destruction it works upon it, and what was form becomes in its turn a material working on which Spirit exalts itself to a new form.

If we consider Spirit in this aspect—regarding its changes not merely as rejuvenated transitions, *i.e.* returns to the same form, but rather elaborations upon itself by which it multiplies the material for future endeavors—we see it exerting itself in a variety of modes and directions; developing its powers and gratifying its desires in a variety which is inexhaustible; because every one of its creations, in which it has already found gratification, meets it anew as material, and is a new stimulus for further elaboration. . . .

It is of the highest importance in apprehending and comprehending history to have and to understand the thought involved in this transition. The individual traverses as a unity various grades of development, and remains the same individual; in like manner also does a people, up to the stage which is the universal stage of its Spirit. In this point lies the fundamental, the conceptual necessity of transition. This is the soul, the distinctive characteristic of the philosophical comprehension of history.

Spirit is essentially the result of its own activity; its activity is the transcending of immediate, simple, unreflected existence, the negation of that existence, and the returning into itself. We may compare it with the seed; for with this the plant begins, yet it is also the result of the plant's entire life. But the weak side of life is exhibited in the fact that the beginning and the result are disjoined from each other. Thus also is it in the life of individuals and peoples. The life of a people brings a certain fruit to maturity; its activity aims at the complete manifestation of the principle which it embodies. But the fruit does not fall back into the womb of the people that produced and matured it. On the contrary, it turns into a bitter drink for this people. The people cannot abandon it, for it has an insatiable thirst for it: the taste of the draught is its annihilation, though at the same time the rise of a new principle.

We have already discussed the final purpose of this progression. The principles of the successive stages of Spirit that animate the nations are themselves only steps in the development of the one universal Spirit, which through them in history elevates and completes itself to a self-comprehending *totality*.

STUDY QUESTIONS

1. What fault does Hegel find with a belief in a general Providence or with what he calls "a trifling view of Providence"?
2. In what sense does he claim that his philosophy of history is concerned with a theodicy?
3. What is the nature of Spirit in terms of some abstract characteristics?
4. What three stages in the historical development of man's consciousness of freedom can be distinguished?
5. What means does Spirit use in world history to realize its Idea?
6. How are the world-historical persons related to the working of the World-Spirit?
7. In what sense is the state said to exist for its own sake?
8. How do religion, art, and philosophy arise through the activity of Spirit within the life of a people?
9. Why is the myth of the Phoenix insufficient to characterize the process of continuous transitions occurring in history?
10. What limited role do individuals and peoples (nations) play in the development of the one universal Spirit?

Joseph Stalin

DIALECTICAL MATERIALISM

Biographical Note.   JOSEPH V. STALIN (1879–1953) was born in the Caucasus, the son of freed serfs. He attended an orthodox parochial school, and proving himself a brilliant student was awarded a scholarship at the theological seminary in Tiflis at the age of fifteen. Four years later he was expelled because of his subversive political views. Many years of underground revolutionary activities followed, interspersed with terms served in prison and in Siberian exile. In 1912, Lenin appointed him to the Bolshevik Central Committee; after this, Stalin founded the newspaper *Pravda*. At the beginning of the Revolution, Stalin belonged to the Party leadership; he was made Secretary General in 1922. During these early Soviet years he drafted the first U.S.S.R. Constitution, which was adopted in 1924. Upon Lenin's death the same year he became ruler of the Soviet Union by virtue of his power as Secretary General, and he remained in this position for almost thirty years—until his death.

Among his most important books are *Problems of Leninism* (1934), *Foundation of Leninism* (1939), and *History of the Communist Party of the Soviet Union* (1939), the last of which he was co-author and from which the selection here was chosen.

* * *

From Joseph Stalin, *Dialectical and Historical Materialism*, New York, International Publishers Co., Inc., copyright 1940. Used by permission of International Publishers Co., Inc. This is a reprint of part of Chapt. 4 of the *History of the Communist Party of the Soviet Union* (New York, 1939).

4 4 7

Introductory Note.   Karl Marx and Friedrich Engels, the German 19th century political thinkers, are the originators of what is called "dialectical materialism," which is the philosophy that constitutes the basis—"the world outlook"—of present-day communism. The selection that follows summarizes this philosophy and its application to the life and history of society.

For their peculiar "dialectical" method, Marx and Engels are indebted to Hegel, whose "dialectics of history"—that is, the description of the fundamental structure of the dynamics of history—they entirely took over. They agreed with Hegel that the process of historic development should be understood "not as a movement in a circle, but as an onward and upward movement, a development from the simple to the complex, from the lower to the higher." And with Hegel they conceived of this development "as a disclosure of the contradictions inherent in things and phenomena, as a 'struggle' of opposite tendencies which operate on the basis of these contradictions."

They disagreed, however, with Hegel's interpretation of the forces which keep the world in continuous motion as an embodiment of "Spirit," tracing them rather to "different forms of matter in motion," to the laws of "the development of moving matter" which stand "in no need of a universal Spirit." In other words, Marx and Engels held that matter and material life is primary while spiritual life—that is, life dependent on the human mind and will, is secondary, derivative, a mere reflection of the former. And from here their basic presupposition regarding human culture immediately follows: "Whatever are the conditions of material life of a society such are the ideas, theories, political views and political institutions of that society."

History then, in its dialectical movement, becomes the development of the conditions of the material life of society from lower to higher forms. And what is the specific force governing such a development? The answer to this question provides the basic perspective of the Marxian political and social philosophy: "This force, historical materialism holds, is the method of procuring the means of life necessary for human existence, the mode of production of material values." Five such modes are distinguished: primitive communal, slave, feudal, capitalist, and socialist. Each of these systems, compared with its predecessor, provides for improvements, for an extensive growth of the respective productive forces of society, requiring new organizational structures and new social relations for those who are the agents of this production.

The struggle by way of which the transition from one mode of production to the other occurs is called "class struggle," and it constitutes the most dynamic type of contradictions reflected in the dialectical movement of history. The transition itself is said to start out invariably as an evolutionary process, but "only up to a certain moment." When the new and developing productive forces have sufficiently matured, the old mode of production as represented by the ruling classes becomes "that 'insuperable' obstacle which can only be removed by the conscious action of the new classes, by revolution."

The conclusion is finally reached that capitalism stands for a method of production which has outgrown its usefulness and must give way to socialism, following the law of history that the more efficient mode of production must prevail over the less efficient one. For capitalism, which has given rise to new "productive forces to a tremendous extent, has become enmeshed in contradictions"; its private ownership of the means of production has shown itself incapable of handling the social character of the process of production as demonstrated in the periodical economic crises to which it inevitably falls victim. The old system of production must yield to the establishment of the new system.

THE MARXIST DIALECTICAL METHOD

Dialectical Materialism is the world outlook of the Marxist-Leninist party. It is called dialectical materialism because its approach to the phenomena of nature, its method of studying and apprehending them, is *dialectical*, while its interpretation of the phenomena of nature, its conception of these phenomena, its theory, is *materialistic*.

Historical materialism is the extension of the principles of dialectical materialism to the study of social life, an application of the principles of dialectical materialism to the phenomena of the life of society, to the study of society and its history. . . .

Dialectics comes from the Greek *dialego,* to discourse, to debate. In ancient times dialectics was the art of arriving at the truth by disclosing the contradictions in the argument of an opponent and overcoming these contradictions. There were philosophers in ancient times who believed that the disclosure of contradictions in thought and the clash of opposite opinions was the best method of arriving at the truth. This dialectical method of thought, later extended to the phenomena of nature, developed into the dialectical method of apprehending nature, which regards the phenomena of nature as being in constant movement and undergoing constant change, and the development of nature as the result of the development of the contradictions in nature, as the result of the interaction of opposed forces in nature.

The principal features of the Marxist *dialectical method* are as follows:

a. . . . Dialectics does not regard nature as an accidental agglomeration of things, of phenomena, unconnected with, isolated from, and independent of, each other, but as a connected and integral whole, in which things, phenomena, are organically connected with, dependent on, and determined by, each other.

The dialectical method therefore holds that no phenomenon in nature can be understood if taken by itself, isolated from surrounding phenomena, inasmuch as any phenomenon in any realm of nature may become meaningless to us if it is not considered in connection with the surrounding conditions, but divorced from them; and that, vice versa, any phenomenon can be understood and explained if considered in its inseparable connection with surrounding phenomena, as one conditioned by surrounding phenomena.

b. . . . Dialectics holds that nature is not a state of rest and immobility, stagnation and immutability, but a state of continuous movement and change, of continuous renewal and development, where something is always arising and developing, and something always disintegrating and dying away.

The dialectical method therefore requires that phenomena should be considered not only from the standpoint of their interconnection and interdependence, but also from the standpoint of their movement, their change, their development, their coming into being and going out of being.

The dialectical method regards as important primarily not that which at the given moment seems to be durable and yet is already beginning to die away, but that which is arising and developing, even though at the given moment it may appear to be not durable, for the dialectical method considers invincible only that which is arising and developing. . . .

Dialectics, Engels says, "takes things and their perceptual images essentially in their interconnection, in their concatenation, in their movement, in their rise and disappearance."

c. . . . Dialectics does not regard the process of development as a simple process of growth, where quantitative changes do not lead to qualitative changes, but as a development which passes from insignificant and imperceptible quantitative changes to open fundamental changes, to qualitative changes; a development in which the qualitative changes occur not gradually, but rapidly and abruptly, taking the form of a leap from one state to another; they occur not accidentally but as the natural result of an accumulation of imperceptible and gradual quantitative changes.

The dialectical method therefore holds that the process of development should be understood not as a movement in a circle, not as a simple repetition of what has already occurred, but as an onward and upward movement, as a transition from an old qualitative state to a new qualitative state, as a development from the simple to the complex, from the lower to the higher. . . .

d. . . . Dialectics holds that internal contradictions are inherent in all things and phenomena of nature, for they all have their negative and positive sides, a past and a future, something dying away and something developing; and that the struggle between these opposites, the struggle between the old and the new, between that which is dying away and that which is being born, between that which is disappearing and that which is developing, constitutes the internal content of the process of development, the internal content of the transformation of quantitative changes into qualitative changes.

The dialectical method therefore holds that the process of development from the lower to the higher takes place not as a harmonious unfolding of phenomena, but as a disclosure of the contradictions inherent in things and phenomena, as a "struggle" of opposite tendencies which operate on the basis of these contradictions.

"In its proper meaning," Lenin says, "dialectics is the study of the contradiction *within the very essence of things.*" . . .

SOCIAL APPLICATION: SOCIAL SYSTEMS AND MOVEMENTS

It is easy to understand how immensely important is the extension of the principles of the dialectical method to the study of social life and the history of society, and how immensely important is the application of these principles to the history of society and to the practical activities of the party of the proletariat.

If there are no isolated phenomena in the world, if all phenomena are interconnected and interdependent, then it is clear that every social system and every social movement in history must be evaluated not from the standpoint of "eternal justice" or some other preconceived idea, as is not infrequently done by historians, but from the standpoint of the conditions which gave rise to that system or that social movement and with which they are connected.

The slave system would be senseless, stupid and unnatural under modern conditions. But under the conditions of a disintegrating primitive communal system, the slave system is a quite understandable and natural phenomenon, since it represents an advance on the primitive communal system.

The demand for a bourgeois-democratic republic when tsardom and bourgeois society existed, as, let us say, in Russia in 1905, was a quite understandable, proper and revolutionary demand, for at that time a bourgeois republic would have meant a step forward. But now, under the conditions of the U.S.S.R., the demand for a bourgeois-democratic republic would be a meaningless and counter-revolutionary demand, for a bourgeois republic would be a retrograde step compared with the Soviet republic.

Everything depends on the conditions, time and place.

It is clear that without such a *historical* approach to social phenomena, the existence and development of the science of history is impossible, for only such an approach saves the science of history from becoming a jumble of accidents and an agglomeration of most absurd mistakes.

Further, if the world is in a state of constant movement and development, if the dying away of the old and the upgrowth of the new is a law of development, then it is clear that there can be no "immutable" social systems, no "eternal principles" of private property and exploitation, no "eternal ideas" of the subjugation of the peasant to the landlord, of the worker to the capitalist.

Hence the capitalist system can be replaced by the socialist system, just as at one time the feudal system was replaced by the capitalist system.

Hence we must not base our orientation on the strata of society which are no longer developing, even though they at present constitute the predominant force, but on those strata which are developing and have a future before them, even though they at present do not constitute the predominant force. . . .

MARXIST PHILOSOPHICAL MATERIALISM

The principal features of Marxist philosophical *materialism* are as follows:

a. Contrary to idealism, which regards the world as the embodiment of an "absolute idea," a "universal spirit," "consciousness," Marx's philosophical materialism holds that the world is by its very nature *material,* that the multifold phenomena of the world constitute different forms of matter in motion, that interconnection and interdependence of phenomena, as established by the dialectical method, are a law of the development of moving matter, and that the world develops in accordance with the laws of movement of matter and stands in no need of a "universal spirit." "The materialist world outlook," says Engels, "is simply the conception of nature as it is, without any reservations."

Speaking of the materialist views of the ancient philosopher, Heraclitus, who held that "the world, the all in one, was not created by any god or any man, but was, is and ever will be a living flame, systematically flaring up and systematically dying down," Lenin comments: "A very good exposition of the rudiments of dialectical materialism."

b. Contrary to idealism, which asserts that only our mind really exists, and that the material world, being, nature, exists only in our mind, in our sensations, ideas and perceptions, the Marxist materialist philosophy holds that matter, nature, being, is an objective reality existing outside and independent of our mind; that matter is primary, since it is the source of sensations, ideas, mind, and that mind is secondary, derivative, since it is a reflection of matter, a reflection of being; that thought is a product of matter which in its development has reached a high degree of perfection, namely, of the brain, and the brain is the organ of thought; and that therefore one cannot separate thought from matter without committing a grave error. . . .

Describing the Marxist philosophy of materialism, Lenin says:

> Materialism in general recognizes objectively real being (matter) as independent of consciousness, sensation, experience. . . . Consciousness is only the reflection of being, at best, an approximately true (adequate, ideally exact) reflection of it.

c. Contrary to idealism, which denies the possibility of knowing the world and its laws, which does not believe in the authenticity of our knowledge, does not recognize objective truth, and holds that the world is full of "things-in-themselves" that can never be known to science, Marxist philosophical materialism holds that the world and its laws are fully knowable, that our knowledge of the laws of nature, tested by experiment and practice, is authentic knowledge having the validity of objective truth, and that there are no things in the world which are unknowable, but only things which are still not known, but which will be disclosed and made known by the efforts of science and practice. . . .

SOCIAL APPLICATION: MATERIAL AND SPIRITUAL LIFE OF SOCIETY

It is easy to understand how immensely important is the extension of the principles of philosophical materialism to the study of social life, of the history of society, and how immensely important is the application of these principles to the history of society and to the practical activities of the party of the proletariat.

If the connection between the phenomena of nature and their inter-dependence are laws of the development of nature, it follows, too, that the connection and interdependence of the phenomena of social life are laws of the development of society, and not something accidental. . . .

Further, if nature, being, the material world, is primary, and mind, thought, is secondary, derivative; if the material world represents objective reality existing independently of the mind of men, while the mind is a reflection of this objective reality, it follows that the material life of society, its being, is also primary, and its spiritual life secondary, derivative, and that the material life of society is an objective reality existing independently of the will of men, while the spiritual life of society is a reflection of this objective reality, a reflection of being.

Hence the source of formation of the spiritual life of society, the origin of social ideas, social theories, political views and political institutions, should not be sought for in the ideas, theories, views and political institutions themselves, but in the conditions of the material life of society, in social being, of which these ideas, theories, views, etc., are the reflection.

Hence, if in different periods of the history of society different social ideas, theories, views and political institutions are to be observed; if under the, slave system we encounter certain ideas, theories, views and political institutions, under feudalism others, and under capitalism others still, this is not to be explained by the "nature," the "properties" of the ideas, theories, views and political institutions themselves but by the different conditions of the material life of society at different periods of social development.

Whatever is the being of a society, whatever are the conditions of material life of a society, such are the ideas, theories, political views and political institutions of that society.

In this connection, Marx says:

> It is not the consciousness of men that determines their being, but, on the contrary, their social being that determines their consciousness.

It does not follow from Marx's words, however, that social ideas, theories, political views and political institutions are of no significance in the life of society, that they do not reciprocally affect social being, the development of the material conditions of the life of society. We have been speaking so far of the *origin* of social ideas, theories, views and political institutions, of *the way they arise*, of the fact that the spiritual life of society is a reflection of the conditions of its material life. As regards the *significance* of social ideas, theories, views and political institutions, as regards their *role* in history, historical materialism, far from denying them, stresses the role and importance of these factors in the life of society, in its history.

There are different kinds of social ideas and theories. There are old ideas and theories which have outlived their day and which serve the interests of the moribund forces of society. Their significance lies in the fact that they hamper the development, the progress of society. Then there are new and advanced ideas and theories which serve the interests of the advanced forces of society. Their significance lies in the fact that they facilitate the development, the progress of society; and their significance is the greater the more accurately they reflect the needs of development of the material life of society. . . .

New social ideas and theories arise precisely because they are necessary to society, because it is *impossible* to carry out the urgent tasks of development of the material life of society without their organizing, mobilizing and transforming action. Arising out of the new tasks set by the development of the material life of society, the new social ideas and theories force their way through, become the possession of the masses, mobilize and organize them against the moribund forces of society, and thus facilitate the overthrow of these forces which hamper the development of the material life of society. . . .

In this connection, Marx says: "Theory becomes a material force as soon as it has gripped the masses."

That is the answer historical materialism gives to the question of the relation between social being and social consciousness, between the conditions of development of material life and the development of the spiritual life of society. . . .

SOCIETY AND THE MODE OF PRODUCTION

What, then, is the chief force in the complex of conditions of material life of society which determines the physiognomy of society, the character of the social system, the development of society from one system to another?

This force, historical materialism holds, is the *method of procuring the means of life* necessary for human existence, the *mode of production of material values*—food, clothing, footwear, houses, fuel, instruments of production, etc.—which are indispensable for the life and development of society.

Aspects and Features of Production

In order to live, people must have food, clothing, footwear, shelter, fuel, etc.; in order to have these material values, people must produce them; and in order to produce them, people must have the instruments of production with which food, clothing, footwear, shelter, fuel, etc., are produced; they must be able to produce these instruments and to use them.

The *instruments of production* wherewith material values are produced, the *people* who operate the instruments of production and carry on the production of material values thanks to a certain *production experience* and *labor skill*—all these elements jointly constitute the *production forces* of society.

But the productive forces are only one aspect of production, only one aspect of the mode of production, an aspect that expresses the relation of men to the objects and forces of nature which they make use of for the production of material values. Another aspect of production, another aspect of the mode of production, is the relation of men to each other in the process of production, men's *relations of production*. Men carry on a struggle against nature and utilize nature for the production of material values not in isolation from each other, not as separate individuals, but in common, in groups, in societies. Production, therefore, is at all times and under all conditions *social* production. In the production of material values men enter into mutual relations of one kind or another within production, into relations of production of one kind or another. These may be relations of co-operation and mutual help between people who are free from exploitation; they may be relations of domination and subordination; and, lastly, they may be transitional from one form of relations of production to another. . . .

Consequently, production, the mode of production, embraces both the productive forces of society and men's relations of production, and is thus the embodiment of their unity in the process of production of material values.

One of the features of production is that it never stays at one point for a long time and is always in a state of change and development, and that, furthermore, changes in the mode of production inevitably call forth changes in the whole social system, social ideas, political views and political institutions—they call forth a reconstruction of the whole social and political order. At different stages of development people make use of different modes of production, or, to put it more crudely, lead different manners of life. In the primitive commune there is one mode of production, under slavery there is another mode of production, under feudalism a third mode of production, and so on. And, correspondingly, men's social system, the spiritual life of men, their views and political institutions also vary.

Whatever is the mode of production of a society, such in the main is the society itself, its ideas and theories, its political views and institutions.

Or, to put it more crudely, whatever is man's manner of life, such is his manner of thought. . . .

Hence the clue to the study of the laws of history of society must not be sought in men's minds, in the views and ideas of society, but in the mode of production practiced by society in any given historical period; it must be sought in the economic life of society. . . .

A *second feature of production* is that its changes and development always begin with changes and development of the productive forces, and, in the first place, with changes and development of the instruments of production. Productive forces are therefore the most mobile and revolutionary element of production. First the productive forces of society change and develop, and then, *depending* on these changes and *in conformity with them,* men's relations of production, their economic relations, change. This, however, does not mean that the relations of production do not influence the development of the productive forces and that the latter are not dependent on the former. While their development is dependent on the development of the productive forces, the relations of production in their turn react upon the development of the productive forces, accelerating or retarding it. In this connection it should be noted that the relations of production cannot for too long a time lag behind and be in a state of contradiction to the growth of the productive forces, inasmuch as the productive forces can develop in full measure only when the relations of production correspond to the character, the state of the productive forces and allow full scope for their development. . . .

An instance in which the relations of production do not correspond to the character of the productive forces, conflict with them, is the economic crises in capitalist countries, where private capitalist ownership of the means of production is in glaring incongruity with the social character of the process of production, with the character of the productive forces. This results in economic crises, which lead to the destruction of productive forces. Furthermore, this incongruity itself constitutes the economic basis of social revolution, the purpose of which is to destroy the existing relations of production and to create new relations of production corresponding to the character of the productive forces. . . .

TYPES OF RELATIONS OF PRODUCTION

In conformity with the change and development of the productive forces of society in the course of history, men's relations of production, their economic relations also changed and developed.

Five *main* types of relations of production are known to history: primitive communal, slave, feudal, capitalist and socialist.

The basis of the relations of production under the primitive communal system is that the means of production are socially owned. This in the main corresponds to the character of the productive forces of that period. Stone tools, and later, the bow and arrow, precluded the possibility of men individually combating the forces of nature and beasts of prey. In order to gather the fruits of the forest, to catch fish, to build some sort of habitation, men were obliged to work in common if they did not want to die of starvation, or fall victim to beasts of prey or to neighboring societies. Labor in common led to the common ownership of the means of production, as well as of the fruits of production. Here the conception of private ownership of the means of production did not exist, except for the personal ownership of certain implements of production which were at the same time means of defense against beasts of prey. Here there was no exploitation, no classes.

The basis of the relations of production under the slave system is that the slave owner owns the means of production; he also owns the worker in production—the slave, whom he can sell, purchase, or kill as though he were an animal. Such relations of production in the main correspond to the state of the productive forces of that period. Instead of stone tools, men now have metal tools at their command; instead of the wretched and primitive husbandry of the hunter, who knew neither pasturage, nor tillage, there now appear pasturage, tillage, handicrafts, and a division of labor between these branches of production. There appears the possibility of the exchange of products between individuals and between societies, of the accumulation of wealth in the hands of a few, the actual accumulation of the means of production in the hands of a minority, and the possibility of subjugation of the majority by a minority and their conversion into slaves. . . .

The basis of the relations under the feudal system is that the feudal lord owns the means of production and does not fully own the worker in production—the serf, whom the feudal lord can no longer kill, but whom he can buy and sell. Alongside of feudal ownership there exists individual ownership by the peasant and the handicraftsman of his implements of production and his private enterprise based on his personal labor. Such relations of production in the main correspond to the state of the productive forces of that period. Further improvements in the smelting and working of iron; the spread of the iron plough and the loom; the further development of agriculture, horticulture, viniculture and dairying; the appearance of manufactories alongside of the handicraft workshops—such are the characteristic features of the state of the productive forces.

The new productive forces demand that the laborer shall display some kind of initiative in production and an inclination for work, an interest in work. The feudal lord therefore discards the slave, as a laborer who has no interest in work and is entirely without initiative, and prefers to deal with the serf, who has his own husbandry, implements of production, and a certain interest in work essential for the cultivation of the land and for the payment in kind of a part of his harvest to the feudal lord.

Here private ownership is further developed. Exploitation is nearly as severe as it was under slavery—it is only slightly mitigated. A class struggle between exploiters and exploited is the principal feature of the feudal system.

The basis of the relations of production under the capitalist system is that the capitalist owns the means of production, but not the workers in production—the wage laborers, whom the capitalist can neither kill nor sell because they are personally free, but who are deprived of means of production and, in order not to die of hunger, are obliged to sell their labor power to the capitalist and to bear the yoke of exploitation. Alongside of capitalist property in the means of production, we find, at first on a wide scale, private property of the peasants and handicraftsmen in the means of production, these peasants and handicraftsmen no longer being serfs, and their private property being based on personal labor. In place of the handicraft workshops and manufactories there appear huge mills and factories equipped with machinery. In place of the manorial estates tilled by the primitive implements of production of the peasant, there now appear large capitalist farms run on scientific lines and supplied with agricultural machinery.

The new productive forces require that the workers in production shall be better educated and more intelligent than the downtrodden and ignorant serfs, that they be able to understand machinery and operate it properly. Therefore, the capitalists prefer to deal with wage workers who are free from the bonds of serfdom and who are educated enough to be able properly to operate machinery.

But having developed productive forces to a tremendous extent, capitalism has become enmeshed in contradictions which it is unable to solve. By producing larger and larger quantities of commodities, and reducing their prices, capitalism intensifies competition, ruins the mass of small and medium private owners, converts them into proletarians and reduces their purchasing power, with the result that it becomes impossible to dispose of the commodities produced. On the other hand, by expanding production and concentrating millions of workers in huge mills and factories, capitalism lends the process of production a social character and thus undermines its own foundation, inasmuch as the social character of the process of production demands the social ownership of the means of production; yet the means of production remain private capitalist property, which is incompatible with the social character of the process of production.

These irreconcilable contradictions between the character of the productive forces and the relations of production make themselves felt in periodical crises of overproduction, when the capitalists, finding no effective demand for their goods owing to the ruin of the mass of the population which they themselves have brought about, are compelled to burn products, destroy manufactured goods, suspend production, and destroy productive forces at a time when millions of people are forced to suffer unemployment and starvation, not because there are not enough goods, but because there is an over-production of goods.

This means that the capitalist relations of production have ceased to correspond to the state of productive forces of society and have come into irreconcilable contradiction with them.

This means that capitalism is pregnant with revolution, whose mission it is to replace the existing capitalist ownership of the means of production with socialist ownership. . . .

CHANGES IN SYSTEMS OF PRODUCTION

The rise of new productive forces and of the relations of production corresponding to them does not take place separately from the old system, after the disappearance of the old system, but within the old system; it takes place not as a result of the deliberate and conscious activity of man, but spontaneously, unconsciously, independently of the will of man. It takes place spontaneously and independently of the will of man for two reasons.

First, because men are not free to choose one mode of production or another, because as every new generation enters life it finds productive forces and relations of production already existing as the result of the work of former generations, owing to which it is obliged at first to accept and adapt itself to everything it finds ready made in the sphere of production in order to be able to produce material values.

Secondly, because, when improving one instrument of production or another, one element of the productive forces or another, men do not realize, do not understand or stop to reflect what *social* results these improvements will lead to, but only think of their everyday interests, of lightening their labor and of securing some direct and tangible advantage for themselves. . . .

When the Russian capitalists, in conjunction with foreign capitalists, energetically implanted modern large-scale machine industry in Russia, while leaving tsardom intact and turning the peasants over to the tender mercies of the landlords, they, of course, did not know and did not stop to reflect what *social* consequences this extensive growth of productive forces would lead to, they did not realize or understand that this big leap in the realm of productive forces of society would lead to a re-grouping of social forces that would enable the proletariat to effect a union with the peasantry and to bring about a victorious socialist revolution. They simply wanted to expand industrial production to the limit, to gain control of the huge home market, to become monopolists, and to squeeze as much profit as possible out of the national economy. Their conscious activity did not extend beyond their commonplace, strictly practical interests. . . .

This, however, does not mean that changes in the relations of production, and the transition from old relations of production to new relations of production proceed smoothly, without conflicts, without upheavals. On the contrary, such a transition usually takes place by means of the revolutionary overthrow of the old relations of production and the establishment of new relations of production. Up to a certain period the development of the productive forces and the changes in the realm of the relations of production proceed spontaneously, independently of the will of men. But that is so only up to a certain moment, until the new and developing productive forces have reached a proper state of maturity. After the new productive forces have matured, the existing relations of production and their upholders—the ruling classes—become that "insuperable" obstacle which can only be removed by the conscious action of the new classes, by revolution. Here there stands out in bold relief the *tremendous role* of new social ideas, of new political institutions, of a new political power, whose mission it is to abolish by force the old relations of production. Out of the conflict between the new productive forces and the old relations of production, out of the new economic demands of society there arise new social ideas; the new ideas organize and mobilize the masses; the masses become welded into a new political army, create a new revolutionary power, and make use of it to abolish by force the old system of relations of production, and firmly to establish the new system. The spontaneous process of development yields place to the conscious actions of men, peaceful development to violent upheaval, evolution to revolution. . . .

"Force is the midwife of every old society pregnant with a new one." (Karl Marx, *Capital.*). . . .

Such is Marxist materialism as applied to social life, to the history of society.

Such are the principal features of dialectical and historical materialism.

STUDY QUESTIONS

1. What do the terms "dialectical materialism" and "historical materialism" mean?
2. What are some of the principal features of the Marxist dialectical method?
3. Why is struggle considered necessary for the process of development from the lower to the higher in nature?
4. What are some of the principal features of Marxist philosophical materialism?
5. How is the spiritual life of society related to its material life?
6. What is the significance of social and political ideas for the life of society?
7. What are the constituent factors in the mode of production of material values?
8. What does it mean to say: "Whatever is man's manner of life, such is his manner of thought"?
9. How do the different types of relations of production develop out of one another?
10. Why do changes from old relations of production to new relations usually take place by way of revolution rather than evolution?

VII

Philosophy of Art

Aristotle

THE ART FORM OF TRAGEDY

Introductory Note.   Aristotle's discussion of the poetic arts, to which his analysis of tragedy belongs, illustrates one of the vital functions of all philosophy. When concerned with a special area of human endeavor and achievement such as art, philosophy aims at bringing to light the essential contribution that is made there to human life and culture, and its aim is to safeguard and even to perfect such contribution. In Aristotle's time, the art form of tragedy had been securely established in Athens for well over a century and a half, and it had been accepted as an indispensable element of its culture. What are those basic features with which it could play its peculiar role most effectively and which had to be preserved so it might continue to do so in the future?

Tragedy is first of all described as an imitation of human action—noble action, that is, not ignoble—as performed by personages who are above the level of goodness of the ordinary man. The people portrayed are invariably, as Aristotle expresses it, men and women of worth standing out from among their fellowmen by an inherent nobility of bearing.

The actions represented are further combined into a unified whole of incidents by what is called the story or plot, the most important part of a

From Aristotle, *De Arte Poetica,* translated by Ingram Bywater, London, Oxford University Press, 1911. Used by permission of the Clarendon Press. Omissions are not indicated in the text.
For biographical information, see the note included with the selection on Ethics (pages 35-36).

tragedy. Having human life as its theme, the story deals with man's happiness and misery, to one of which human activity inevitably leads. More specifically, the story of a tragedy is meant to show how the hero's fortunes change from a state of happiness to that of misery.

The cause of misfortune is also specified as necessarily contained in a tragic situation. The hero is said to bring his misery upon himself "not by vice and depravity but by some fault." In other words, in a tragedy the misfortunes which befall the hero appear in no way as deserved through his prior actions, but rather as undeserved, although they are occasioned by a certain fault of his; yet a fault the measure of which is represented as standing in no proportion to the immensity of the ensuing misery.

So far Aristotle's characterization of Greek tragedy has not been difficult to follow. But there is at least one pronouncement within his detailed description whose meaning has become a serious problem. It indicates what is "the distinctive function of this kind of imitation." Aristotle's definition of a tragedy reads in part as follows: "A Tragedy, then, is the imitation of an action . . . with incidents *arousing pity and fear, wherewith to accomplish its catharsis of such emotions.*" The words of the final clause are clear enough. Their significance within the context in which they appear, however, is far from evident. And there is reason to believe that some further explanation of that point of the analysis was contained in the same work's second part, which has been lost.* The proper evaluation of this Aristotelian requirement of a cathartic or purging effect of tragedy through aroused emotions of fear and pity has therefore remained a matter for interpretation and a continuing challenge to scholarship.

THE POETIC ARTS AND THEIR ORIGIN

Epic poetry and Tragedy, as also Comedy, Dithyrambic poetry, and most flute-playing and lyre-playing, are all, viewed as a whole, modes of imitation. But at the same time they differ from one another in three ways, either by a difference of kind in their means, or by differences in the objects, or in the manner of their imitations.

I. Just as color and form are used as means by some, who (whether by art or constant practice) imitate and portray many things by their aid, and the voice is used by others; so also in the above mentioned group of arts, the means with them as a whole are rhythm, language, and music—used, however, either singly or in certain combinations. A combination of music and rhythm alone is the means in flute-playing and lyre-playing, and in any other art which has a similar function, e.g. pipe-playing. Rhythm alone, without music, is the means in the dancers'

* Cf. Aristotle, *Politics,* Book VIII, Ch. 7 (1341 b 38/40).

imitations; for even they, by the rhythms of their postures, may represent men's characters, as well as what they do and suffer.

There are, lastly, certain other arts, which combine all the means enumerated, rhythm, melody, and verse, *e.g.* Dithyrambic and Nomic poetry,* Tragedy and Comedy; with this difference, however, that the three kinds of means are in some of them all employed together, and in others brought in separately, one after the other. These elements of difference in the above arts I term the means of their imitation.

II. The objects the imitator represents are actions, with agents who are necessarily either good men or bad—the diversities of human character being nearly always derivative from this primary distinction, since the line between virtue and vice is one dividing the whole of mankind. It follows, therefore, that the agents represented must be either above our own level of goodness, or beneath it, or just such as we are. It is clear that each of the above-mentioned arts will admit of these differences, and that it will become a separate art by representing objects with this point of difference. Even in dancing, flute-playing, and lyre-playing such diversities are possible.

This difference it is that distinguishes Tragedy and Comedy also; the one would represent personages as worse, and the other as better, than the men of the present day.

III. A third difference in these arts is in the manner in which each kind of object is represented. Given both the same means and the same kind of object for imitation, one may either (1) speak at one moment in narrative and at another in an assumed character, as Homer does; or (2) one may remain the same throughout, without any such change; or (3) actors may represent the whole story dramatically, as though they were actually doing the things described.

As we said at the beginning, therefore, the differences in the imitation of these arts come under three heads, their means, their objects, and their manner.

It is clear that the general origin of poetry was due to two causes, each of them part of human nature. Imitation is natural to man from childhood, one of his advantages over the other animals being this, that he is the most imitative creature in the world, and learns at first by imitation. And it is also natural for all to delight in works of imitation. The truth of this second point is shown by experience: though the objects themselves may be painful to see, we delight to view the most realistic representations of them in art, figures for example of loathsome animals

* Two forms of lyric sung in honor of Dionysus and Apollo to flute and lyre accompaniment.

and of dead bodies. The explanation is to be found in a further fact: to be learning something is the greatest of pleasures not only to the philosopher but also to the rest of mankind, however small their capacity for it; the reason of the delight in seeing the picture is that one is at the same time learning—gathering the meaning of things, *e.g.* that the man there is so-and-so; for if one has not seen the thing before, one's pleasure will not be in the picture as an imitation of it, but will be due to the execution or coloring or some similar cause. Imitation, then, being natural to men—as also are music and rhythm, the meters being obviously species of rhythm—it was from spontaneous beginnings, and by a series of improvements for the most part gradual on their first efforts, that they created poetry out of their improvizations.

Poetry, however, soon broke up into two kinds according to the differences of character in the individual poets; for the more serious among them would represent noble actions, and those of noble personages, and the meaner sort the actions of the ignoble. The latter class produced satires at first, just as others did hymns and eulogies. Homer's position is peculiar: just as he was in the serious style the poet of poets, standing alone not only through literary excellence, but also through the dramatic character of his imitations, so too he was the first to outline for us the general forms of Comedy by producing not a dramatic satire, but a dramatic picture of the Ridiculous. As soon, however, as Tragedy and Comedy appeared in the field, those naturally drawn to the one line of poetry became writers of comedies, and those naturally drawn to the other, writers of tragedies, because these new modes of art were grander and of more esteem than the old.

Tragedy certainly began in improvizations—as did also Comedy; the one originating with the authors of the Dithyramb, the others with those of the phallic songs, which still survive as institutions in many of our cities. And its advance after that was little by little, through their improving on whatever they had before them at each stage. It was in fact only after a long series of changes that the movement of Tragedy stopped on its attaining to its natural form. (1) The number of actors was first increased to two by Aeschylus, who curtailed the business of the Chorus, and made the dialogue, or spoken portion, take the leading part in the play. (2) A third actor and scenery were due to Sophocles. (3) Tragedy acquired also its magnitude. Descarding short stories and a ludicrous diction, through its passing out of its satiric stage, it assumed, though only at a late point in its progress, a tone of dignity; and its metre changed then from trochaic to iambic. The reason for their original use of the trochaic tetrameter was that their poetry was satiric and more connected with dancing than it now is. As soon, however, as a spoken part came in, nature herself found the appropriate metre. The iambic, we know, is the most speakable of metres, as is shown by the fact that we very often fall into it in conversation, whereas we rarely talk hexameters, and only when we depart from the speaking tone of voice. (4) Another change was a plurality of episodes or acts.

As for Comedy, it is (as has been observed) an imitation of men worse than the average; worse, however, not as regards the full range of badness, but only as regards one particular kind, the Ridiculous, which is a species of the Ugly. The Ridiculous may be defined as a mistake or deformity not productive of pain or harm to others; the comic mask for instance, that excites laughter, is something ugly and distorted without causing pain.

Epic poetry has been seen to agree with Tragedy to this extent, that of being an imitation of serious subjects in a grand kind of verse. It differs from it, however, (1) in that it has a single metre and is narrative; and (2) in its length—which is due to its action having no fixed limit of time, whereas Tragedy endeavors to keep as far as possible within a single circuit of the sun, or something near that. This, I say, is another point of difference between them, though at first the practice in this respect was just the same in tragedies as in epic poems. They differ also (3) in their constituent parts, some being common to both and others peculiar to Tragedy—hence a judge of good and bad in Tragedy is a judge of that in epic poetry also. All the parts of an epic are included in Tragedy; but those of Tragedy are not all of them to be found in the Epic.

DEFINITION OF TRAGEDY AND ITS ELEMENTS

A Tragedy, then, is the imitation of an action that is serious and also, as having magnitude complete in itself; in language with pleasurable accessories, each kind brought in separately in the parts of the work; in a dramatic, not in a narrative form; with incidents arousing pity and fear, wherewith to accomplish its catharsis of such emotions. Here by 'language with pleasurable accessories' I mean that which has rhythm and melody; and by 'the kinds separately' I mean that some portions are worked out with verse only, and others in turn with song.

Since the imitation is achieved through action, it follows that in the first place the stage-appearance of the actors must be some part of the whole; and in the second Melody and Diction, these two being the means of the imitation. Here by 'Diction' I mean merely this, the composition of the verses; and by 'Melody,' what is too completely understood to require explanation. But further: what is represented also is an action; and the action involves agents, who must necessarily have their distinctive qualities both of character and thought, since it is from these that we ascribe certain qualities to their actions. For thought and character are two natural causes of action, and it is because of these that all men fail or succeed. Now the action (that which was done) is represented in the play by the Fable or Plot. The Fable, in our present sense of the term, is simply this, the combination of the incidents, or things done in the story; whereas Character is what makes us ascribe certain moral qualities to the agents; and Thought is shown in all they say when proving a particular point or, it may be, enunciating a general truth.

There are six parts consequently of every tragedy, which give it its quality. These are (1) Fable or Plot, (2) Character, (3) Diction, (4) Thought, (5) Spectacle or Stage-appearance, and (6) Melody; two of them (3, 6) arising from the means, one (5) from the manner, and three (1, 2, 4) from the objects of the dramatic imitation; and there is nothing else besides these six. Of these elements, then, not a few of the dramatists have made due use, as every play, one may say, admits of Spectacle (Stage-appearance), Character, Fable, Diction, Melody, and Thought.

The most important of the six is the combination of the incidents of the story. Tragedy is essentially an imitation not of persons but of action and life, of happiness and misery. All human happiness or misery takes the form of action; the end for which we live is a certain kind of activity, not a quality. Character gives us qualities, but it is in our actions—what we do—that we are happy or the reverse. In a play accordingly they do not act in order to portray the Characters; they include the Characters for the sake of the action. So that it is the action in it, *i.e.* its Fable or Plot, that is the end and purpose of the tragedy; and the end is everywhere the chief thing. Besides this, a tragedy is impossible without action, but there may be one without Character.

We maintain, therefore, that the first essential, the life and soul, so to speak, of Tragedy is the Plot; and that Character comes second. Third comes the element of Thought, *i.e.* the power of saying what can be said, or what is appropriate to the occasion. Fourth among the literary elements is the Diction of the personages, *i.e.*, as before explained, the expression of their thoughts in words, which is practically the same thing with verse as with prose. As for the two remaining parts, the Melody is the greatest of the pleasurable accessories of Tragedy. The

Spectacle or Stage-appearance, though an attraction, is the least artistic of all the parts, and has least to do with the art of poetry. The tragic effect is quite possible without a public performance and actors; and besides, arranging the Stage-appearance is more a matter for the costumier than the poet.

CONSTRUCTION OF THE STORY OR PLOT

After these definitions let us now consider the proper construction of the Fable or Plot, as that is at once the first and the most important thing in Tragedy. We have laid it down that a Tragedy is an imitation of an action that is complete in itself, as a whole of some magnitude; for a whole may be of no magnitude to speak of. Now a whole is that which has beginning, middle, and end. A beginning is that which does not necessarily follow anything else, while something by nature follows or results from it; an end is that which naturally follows something else, either as its necessary or usual consequent, but nothing follows it; and a middle, that which by nature follows and is followed by something. A well-constructed Plot, therefore, cannot either begin or end at random; beginning and end in it must be of the forms just described.

Furthermore, everything beautiful, whether it be a living creature or any whole made up of parts, must not only present a certain order in its arrangement of parts, but also be of a certain definite magnitude. Beauty is a matter of size and order, and therefore impossible either (1) in a very minute creature, or (2) in a creature of vast size since, in that case, instead of the object being seen all at once, the unity and wholeness of it is lost to the beholder. Just in the same way, then, as a beautiful whole made up of parts, or a beautiful living creature, must be of some size, but a size to be taken in by the eye, so a story or Plot must be of some length, but of a length to be taken in by the memory.

The Unity of a Plot does not consist, as some suppose, in its having one man as its single hero. An infinity of things happen to one man, some of which it is impossible to reduce to unity; and in like manner there are many actions of one man which cannot be made to form one action. The truth is that, just as in the other imitative arts one imitation is always of one thing, so in poetry the story, as an imitation of action, must represent one action, a complete whole, with its several incidents so closely connected that the transposal or withdrawal of any one of them will disjoin and dislocate the whole. For that which makes no perceptible difference by its presence or absence is no real part of the whole.

From what we have said it will be seen that the poet's function is to describe, not the thing that has happened, but a kind of thing that might happen, *i.e.* what is possible according to probability or necessity. The distinction between historian and poet is not in the one writing prose and the other verse—you might put the work of Herodotus into verse, and it would still be a species of history; it consists really in this, that the one describes the thing that has been, and the other a kind of thing that might be. Hence poetry is something more philosophic and of graver import than history, because it tends to give general truths, whereas history gives particular facts. By a "general truth" I mean what such or such a kind of man will probably or necessarily say or do— which is the aim of poetry, though it affixes proper names to the characters.

It is evident from the above that the poet must be a maker of stories rather than of verses, inasmuch as he is a poet by virtue of the imitative element of his work, and it is actions that he imitates. And if he should come to take a subject from actual history, he is none the less a poet for that; since some historic occurrences may very well be in the probable and possible order of things; and it is in that aspect of them that he is their poet.

Tragedy, however, is an imitation not only of a complete action, but also of incidents arousing pity and fear. Such incidents have the very greatest effect on the mind when they occur unexpectedly and at the same time in consequence of one another; there is more of the marvellous in them than if they happened of themselves or by mere chance. Even matters of chance seem most marvellous if there is an appearance of design as it were in them. A Plot, therefore, of this sort is necessarily finer than others.

The next points after what we have said above will be these: (1) What is the poet to aim at, and what is he to avoid, in constructing his Plots? and (2) What are the conditions on which the tragic effect depends?

We assume that, for the finest form of Tragedy, the Plot must imitate actions arousing fear and pity, since that is the distinctive function of this kind of imitation. It follows, therefore, that there are three forms of Plot to be avoided. (1) A good man must not be seen passing from happiness to misery, or (2) a bad man from misery to happiness. The first situation is not fear-inspiring or piteous, but simply odious to us. The second is the most untragic that can be; it has none of the requisites of Tragedy; it does not appeal either to the human feeling in us, or to our pity, or to our fears. Nor, on the other hand, should

(3) an extremely bad man be seen falling from happiness into misery. Such a story may arouse the human feeling in us, but it will not move us to either pity or fear; pity is occasioned by undeserved misfortune, and fear by misfortune of one like ourselves; so that there will be nothing either piteous or fear-inspiring in the situation.

There remains, then, the intermediate kind of personage, a man not pre-eminently virtuous and just, whose misfortune, however, is brought upon him not by vice and depravity but by some fault; a man of great reputation and prosperity, like Oedipus, Thyestes, and the men of note of similar families. The perfect Plot, accordingly, must have a single, and not (as some tell us) a double issue; the change in the hero's fortunes must be not from misery to happiness, but on the contrary from happiness to misery; and the cause of it must lie not in any depravity, but in some great fault on his part; the man himself being either such as we have described, or better, not worse, than that.

The tragic fear and pity may be aroused by the Stage-appearance or Spectacle; but they may also be aroused by the very structure and incidents of the play—which is the better way and shows the better poet. The Plot in fact should be so framed that, even without seeing the things take place, he who simply hears the account of them shall be filled with horror and pity at the incidents; which is just the effect that the mere recital of the story in *Oedipus* would have on one. To produce this same effect by means of the Stage-appearance is less artistic, and requires extraneous aid. Those, however, who make use of the Stage-appearance to put before us that which is merely monstrous and not productive of fear, are wholly out of touch with Tragedy; not every kind of pleasure should be required of a tragedy, but only its own proper pleasure.

The tragic pleasure is that of pity and fear, and the poet has to produce it by a work of imitation; it is clear, therefore, that this quality should be included in the incidents of his story. Let us see, then, what kinds of incident strike one as horrible, or rather as piteous. In a deed of this description the parties must necessarily be either friends, or enemies, or indifferent to one another. Now when enemy does it to enemy, there is nothing to move us to pity either in his doing or in his meditating the deed, except so far as the actual pain of the sufferer is concerned; and the same is true when the parties are indifferent to one another. Whenever the tragic deed, however, is done within the family —when murder or the like is done or meditated by brother on brother, by son on father, by mother on son, or son on mother—these are the situations the poet should seek after. The traditional stories, accordingly, must be kept as they are, *e.g.* the murder of Clytemnestra by Orestes.

On the construction of the Plot, and the kind of Plot required for Tragedy, enough has now been said.

CHARACTER, THOUGHT AND DICTION

Concerning "Character" there are four points to aim at. First and foremost, that the character should be worthy. There will be an element of character in the play, if (as has been observed) what a person says or does reveals a certain moral purpose; and there will be a worthy element of character, if the purpose so revealed is worthy. This is possible in every type of personage, even in a woman or a slave, though the one is perhaps an inferior, and the other wholly insignificant. The second point is to make the characters appropriate. The Character before us may be, say, manly; but it is not appropriate in a female Character to be manly, or clever. The third is to make them lifelike, which is not the same as their being worthy and appropriate, in our sense of the term. The fourth is to make them consistent and the same throughout; even if inconsistency be part of the man portrayed as presenting that form of character, he should still be consistently inconsistent.

As Tragedy is an imitation of personages better than the ordinary man, we in our way should follow the example of good portrait-painters, who reproduce the distinctive features of a man, and at the same time, without losing the likeness, make him handsomer than he is. The poet in like manner, in portraying men quick or slow to anger, or with similar infirmities of character, must know how to represent them as such, and at the same time as men of worth, as Agathon and Homer have represented Achilles.

The Plot and Characters having been discussed, it remains to consider the Diction and Thought. As for the Thought, we may assume what is said of it in our Art of Rhetoric, as it belongs more properly to that department of inquiry. The Thought of the personages is shown in everything to be effected by their language—in every effort to prove or disprove, to arouse emotion (pity, fear, anger, and the like), or to maximize or minimize things.

As regards the Diction, one subject for inquiry under this head is the various modes of speech; *e.g.* the difference between command and prayer, simple statement and threat, question and answer, and so forth. The theory of such matters, however, belongs to Elocution and the professors of that art. Whether the poet knows these things or not, his art as a poet is never seriously criticized on that account. So we may leave this topic as appertaining to another art, and not to that of poetry.

Let this, then, suffice as an account of Tragedy, the art imitating by means of action on the stage.

STUDY QUESTIONS

1. Explain and illustrate the three ways in which the poetic arts differ from one another.
2. What was the general origin of poetry?
3. What was the origin and the development of tragedy?
4. How is tragedy defined?
5. What are the six parts or elements of a tragedy, and why are some of them more important than others?
6. What does it mean to speak of a tragedy "as a whole of some magnitude"?
7. How does the poet's function differ from the historian's?
8. What is the poet to aim at, and what is he to avoid in constructing the plot of a tragedy?
9. What are the conditions on which the tragic effect depends?
10. What must the poet keep in mind when portraying the characters of his personages and why is this necessary?

David Hume

OF THE STANDARD OF TASTE

Introductory Note. For Hume, beauty cannot be defined; it is discerned, he says, "only by taste or sensation." Beauty is constituted by the
pleasure it gives the beholder, it has its source in the sentiments or feelings of
the individual. The problem for Hume is to determine the grounds and the
justification of any standards of taste based on the sentiments of the individual. He recognizes the fact of the diversity of tastes, but has a real concern to show that there is some measure of uniformity in our standards of
taste. He believes that although we cannot attain certitude in the sciences
and philosophy, aesthetic judgments based on feelings may yield more immediate certainties. Feeling and not reason is the criterion for our judgments
in aesthetics. Instead of arguing for some *a priori* rules of artistic form, Hume
emphasizes the claims of feeling and imagination. Furthermore, aesthetics—
being structured on the feelings of the individual is less immune to the
sceptical attack on reason and our knowledge of matters of fact. For beauty
is always something that resides within the individual, and Hume will argue
that a standard of beauty is more attainable for the individual than is a
standard of intellectual judgment. All sentiment, he will say, is right, but
not all determinations of the understanding are right. That all sentiment is
right has some empirical verification in the measure of uniformity in tastes

From David Hume, *Essays Moral, Political and Literary*, London, Green and
Grose, 1898.
For biographical information, see the note included with the selection on
Epistemology (pages 162-163).

that can be achieved. Man's nature being what it is, we may count upon certain standards or norms despite the variations of judgment that arise. After all, men do agree on certain norms of beauty; the classics endure, but the opinions and beliefs of science do not. "Aristotle and Plato," he says, "may yield to each other, but Terence and Virgil maintain an universal undisputed empire over the minds of men." Thus, despite all diversity, there are certain general principles of taste. This leads Hume to explain why differences arise in our aesthetic judgments. On the one hand, he declares that our failure to appreciate a work of beauty may result merely from our own insensitivity to beauty—to a certain lack of delicacy. The fault lies within us rather than within the principles of aesthetic judgment. On the other hand, the perception of beauty can be perfected. Through the practice of art and the "frequent survey or contemplation of a particular species of beauty," we may achieve such a perfection of taste—provided we check the influence of prejudice, which is destructive of sound judgment. This does not mean that a universality of good judgment and taste can be achieved. Few men, Hume declares, are qualified to give judgment on any work of art or to establish their own sentiments as the standard of beauty. His analysis is concluded by noting how the differences among men and the differences of time, place, and manners explain many of the variations that occur in our aesthetic judgments.

THE DIVERSITY OF TASTE

The great variety of Taste, as well as of opinion, which prevails in the world, is too obvious not to have fallen under every one's observation. . . . We are apt to call *barbarous* whatever departs widely from our own taste and apprehension: But soon find the epithet of reproach retorted on us. And the highest arrogance and self-conceit is at last startled, on observing an equal assurance on all sides, and scruples, amidst such a contest of sentiment, to pronounce positively in its own favor.

As this variety of taste is obvious to the most careless enquirer; so will it be found, on examination, to be still greater in reality than in appearance. The sentiments of men often differ with regard to beauty and deformity of all kinds, even while their general discourse is the same. There are certain terms in every language, which import blame, and others praise; and all men, who use the same tongue, must agree in their application of them. Every voice is united in applauding elegance, propriety, simplicity, spirit in writing; and in blaming fustian, affectation, coldness, and a false brilliancy: But when critics come to particulars, this seeming unanimity vanishes: and it is found, that they had affixed a very different meaning to their expressions. In all matters of opinion and science, the case is opposite: The difference among men is there oftener found to lie in generals than in particulars; and to be less in reality than in appearance. An explanation of the terms commonly ends the controversy; and the disputants are surprised to find, that they had been quarrelling, while at bottom they agreed in their judgment. . . .

JUDGMENT AND SENTIMENT

It is natural for us to seek a *Standard of Taste;* a rule by which the various sentiments of men may be reconciled; at least a decision afforded, confirming one sentiment, and condemning another.

There is a species of philosophy, which cuts off all hopes of success in such an attempt, and represents the impossibility of ever attaining any standard of taste. The difference, it is said, is very wide between judgment and sentiment. All sentiment is right; because sentiment has a reference to nothing beyond itself, and is always real, wherever a man is conscious of it. But all determinations of the understanding are not right; because they have a reference to something beyond themselves, to wit, real matter of fact; and are not always conformable to that standard. Among a thousand different opinions which different men may entertain of the same subject, there is one, and but one, that is just and true; and the only difficulty is to fix and ascertain it. On the contrary, a thousand different sentiments, excited by the same object, are all right: Because no sentiment represents what is really in the object. It only marks a certain conformity or relation between the object and the organs or faculties of the mind; and if that conformity did not really exist, the sentiment could never possibly have being. Beauty is no quality in things themselves: It exists merely in the mind which contemplates them; and each mind perceives a different beauty. One person may even perceive deformity, where another is sensible of beauty; and every individual ought to acquiesce in his own sentiment, without pretending to regulate those of others. To seek the real beauty, or real deformity, is as fruitless an enquiry, as to pretend to ascertain the real sweet or the real bitter. According to the disposition of the organs, the same object may be both sweet and bitter; and the proverb has justly determined it to be fruitless to dispute concerning tastes. It is very natural, and even quite necessary, to extend this axiom to mental, as well as bodily taste; and thus common sense, which is so often at variance with philosophy, especially with the sceptical kind, is found, in one instance at least to agree in pronouncing the same decision. . . .

EXPERIENCE AND THE RULES OF ART

It is evident that none of the rules of composition are fixed by reasonings *a priori,* or can be esteemed abstract conclusions of the understanding, from comparing those habitudes and relations of ideas, which are eternal and immutable. Their foundation is the same with that of all the practical sciences, experience; nor are they any thing but general observations, concerning what has been universally found to please in all countries and in all ages. Many of the beauties of poetry and even of eloquence are founded on falsehood and fiction, on hyperboles, metaphors, and an abuse or perversion of terms from their natural meaning. To check the sallies of the imagination, and to reduce every expression to geometrical truth and exactness, would be the most contrary to the laws of criticism; because it would produce a work, which, by universal experience, has been found the most insipid and disagreeable. But though poetry can never submit to exact truth, it must be confined by rules of art, discovered to the author either by genius or observation. If some negligent or irregular writers have pleased, they have not pleased by their transgressions of rule or order, but in spite of these transgressions: They have possessed other beauties, which were comformable to just criticism; and the force of these beauties has been able to overpower censure, and give the mind a satisfaction superior to the disgust arising from the blemishes. . . .

But though all the general rules of art are founded only on experience and on the observation of the common sentiments of human nature, we must not imagine, that, on every occasion, the feelings of men will be conformable to these rules. Those finer emotions of the mind are of a very tender and delicate nature, and require the concurrence of many favorable circumstances to make them play with facility and exactness, according to their general and established principles . . . A perfect serenity of mind, a recollection of thought, a due attention to the object; if any of these circumstances be wanting, our experiment will be fallacious, and we shall be unable to judge of the catholic and universal beauty. The relation, which nature has placed between the form and the sentiment, will at least be more obscure; and it will require greater accuracy to trace and discern it. We shall be able to ascertain its influence not so much from the operation of each particular beauty, as from the durable admiration, which attends those works, that have survived all the caprices of mode and fashion, all the mistakes of ignorance and envy.

The same HOMER, who pleased at Athens and Rome two thousand years ago, is still admired at Paris and London. All the changes of climate, government, religion, and language, have not been able to obscure his glory. Authority or prejudice may give a temporary vogue to a bad poet or orator; but his reputation will never be durable or general. When his compositions are examined by posterity or by foreigners, the enchantment is dissipated, and his faults appear in their true colors. On the contrary, a real genius, the longer his works endure, and the more wide they are spread, the more sincere is the admiration which he meets with . . .

SENTIMENT AND BEAUTY

It appears then, that, amidst all the variety and caprice of taste, there are certain general principles of approbation or blame, whose influence a careful eye may trace in all operations of the mind. Some particular forms or qualities, from the original structure of the internal fabric, are calculated to please, and others to displease; and if they fail of their effect in any particular instance, it is from some apparent defect or imperfection in the organ. A man in a fever would not insist on his palate as able to decide concerning flavors; nor would one, affected with the jaundice, pretend to give a verdict with regard to colors. In each creature, there is a sound and a defective state; and the former alone can be supposed to afford us a true standard of taste and sentiment. If, in the sound state of the organ, there be an entire or a considerable uniformity of sentiment among men, we may thence derive an idea of the perfect beauty; in like manner as the appearance of objects in daylight, to the eye of a man in health, is denominated their true and real color, even while color is allowed to be merely a phantasm of the senses. . . .

One obvious cause, why many feel not the proper sentiment of beauty, is the want of that *delicacy* of imagination, which is requisite to convey a sensibility of those finer emotions. This delicacy every one pretends to: Every one talks of it; and would reduce every kind of taste or sentiment to its standard. But as our intention in this essay is to mingle some light of the understanding with the feelings of sentiment, it will be proper to give a more accurate definition of delicacy, than has hitherto been attempted. And not to draw our philosophy from too profound a source, we shall have recourse to a noted story in DON QUIXOTE.

It is with good reason, says SANCHO to the squire with the great nose, that I pretend to have a judgment in wine: This is a quality hereditary in our family. Two of my kinsmen were once called to give their opinion of a hogshead, which was supposed to be excellent, being old and of a good vintage. One of them tastes it; considers it; and after mature reflection pronounces the wine to be good, were it not for a small taste of leather, which he perceived in it. The other, after using the same precautions, gives also his verdict in favor of the wine; but with the reserve of a taste of iron, which he could easily distinguish. You cannot imagine how much they were both ridiculed for their judgment. But who laughed in the end? On emptying the hogshead, there was found at the bottom, an old key with a leathern thong tied to it. . . .

The great resemblance between mental and bodily taste will easily teach us to apply this story. Though it be certain, that beauty and deformity, more than sweet and bitter, are not qualities in objects, but belong entirely to the sentiment, internal or external; it must be allowed, that there are certain qualities in objects, which are fitted by nature to produce those particular feelings. Now as these qualities may be found in a small degree, or may be mixed and confounded with each other, it often happens, that the taste is not affected with such minute qualities, or is not able to distinguish all the particular flavors amidst the disorder, in which they are presented. Where the organs are so fine, as to allow nothing to escape them; and at the same time so exact, as to perceive every ingredient in the composition: This we call delicacy of taste, whether we employ these terms in the literal or metaphorical sense. Here then the general rules of beauty are of use; being drawn from established models, and from the observation of what pleases or displeases, when presented singly and in a high degree: And if the same qualities, in a continued composition and in a smaller degree, affect not the organs with a sensible delight or uneasiness, we exclude the person from all pretentions to this delicacy. To produce these general rules or avowed patterns of composition is like finding the key with the leathern thong; which justified the verdict of SANCHO's kinsmen, and confounded those pretended judges who had condemned them. Though the hogshead had never been emptied, the taste of the one was still equally delicate, and that of the other equally dull and languid. But it would have been more difficult to have proved the superiority of the former, to the conviction of every bystander. In like manner, though the beauties of writing had never been methodized, or reduced to general principles; though no excellent models had ever been acknowledged; the different degrees of taste would still have subsisted, and the judgment of one man been preferable to that of another; but it would not have been so easy to silence the bad critic, who might always insist upon his particular sentiment, and refuse to submit to his antagonist. But when we show him an avowed principle of art; when we prove, that the same principle may be applied to the present case, where he did not perceive or feel its influence: He must conclude, upon the whole that the fault lies in himself, and that he wants the delicacy, which is requisite to make him sensible of every beauty and every blemish, in any composition or discourse.

THE PERFECTION OF TASTE

It is acknowledged to be the perfection of every sense or faculty, to perceive with exactness its most minute objects, and allow nothing to escape its notice and observation. The smaller the objects are, which become sensible to the eye, the finer is that organ, and the more elaborate its make and composition. A good palate is not tried by strong flavors; but by a mixture of small ingredients, where we are still sensible of each part, notwithstanding its minuteness and its confusion with the rest. In like manner, a quick and acute perception of beauty and deformity must be the perfection of our mental taste; nor can a man be satisfied with himself while he suspects, that any excellence or blemish in a discourse has passed him unobserved. In this case, the perfection of the man, and the perfection of the sense or feeling, are found to be united. A very delicate palate, on many occasions, may be a great inconvenience both to a man himself and to his friends: But a delicate taste of wit or beauty must always be a desirable quality; because it is the source of all the finest and most innocent enjoyments, of which human nature is susceptible. In this decision the sentiments of all mankind are agreed. Wherever you can ascertain a delicacy of taste, it is sure to meet with approbation; and the best way of ascertaining it is to appeal to those models and principles, which have been established by the uniform consent and experience of nations and ages.

But though there be naturally a wide difference in point of delicacy between one person and another, nothing tends further to increase and improve this talent, than *practice* in a particular art, and the frequent survey or contemplation of a particular species of beauty. . . .

So advantageous is practice to the discernment of beauty, that, before we can give judgment on any work of importance, it will be requisite, that that very individual performance be more than once perused by us, and be surveyed in different lights with attention and deliberation. There is a flutter or hurry of thought which attends the first perusal of any piece, and which confounds the genuine sentiment of beauty. The relation of the parts is not discerned: The true characters of style are little distinguished: The several perfections and defects seem wrapped up in a species of confusion, and present themselves indistinctly to the imagination. Not to mention, that there is a species of beauty, which, as it is florid and superficial, pleases at first; but being found incompatible with a just expression either of reason or passion, soon palls upon the taste, and is then rejected with disdain, at least rated at a much lower value.

It is impossible to continue in the practice of contemplating any order of beauty, without being frequently obliged to form *comparisons* between the several species and degrees of excellence, and estimating their proportion to each other. A man, who has had no opportunity of comparing the different kinds of beauty, is indeed totally unqualified to pronounce an opinion with regard to any object presented to him. . . . One accustomed to see, and examine, and weigh the several performances, admired in different ages and nations, can alone rate the merits of a work exhibited to his view, and assign its proper rank among the productions of genius.

But to enable a critic more fully to execute this undertaking, he must preserve his mind free from all prejudice, and allow nothing to enter into his consideration, but the very object which is submitted to his examination. We may observe, that every work of art, in order to produce its due effect on the mind, must be surveyed in a certain point of view, and cannot be fully relished by persons, whose situation, real or imaginary, is not conformable to that which is required by the performance. . . .

It is well known, that in all questions, submitted to the understanding, prejudice is destructive of sound judgment, and perverts all operations of the intellectual faculties: It is no less contrary to good taste; nor has it less influence to corrupt our sentiment of beauty. It belongs to *good sense* to check its influence in both cases; and in this respect, as well as in many others, reason, if not an essential part of taste, is at least requisite to the operations of this latter faculty. In all the nobler productions of genius, there is a mutual relation and correspondence of parts; nor can either the beauties or blemishes be perceived by him, whose thought is not capacious enough to comprehend all those parts, and compare them with each other, in order to perceive the consistence and uniformity of the whole. Every work of art has also a certain end or purpose, for which it is calculated; and is to be deemed more or less perfect, as it is more or less fitted to attain this end. The object of eloquence is to persuade, of history to instruct, of poetry to please by means of the passions and the imagination. These ends we must carry constantly in our view, when we peruse any performance; and we must be able to judge how far the means employed are adapted to their respective purposes. Besides, every kind of composition, even the most poetical, is nothing but a chain of propositions and reasonings; not always, indeed, the justest and most exact, but still plausible and specious, however disguised by the coloring of the imagination. The persons introduced in tragedy and epic poetry, must be represented as reasoning, and thinking, and concluding, and acting, suitably to their character and circumstances; and without judgment, as well as taste and invention, a poet can never hope to succeed in so delicate an undertaking. Not to mention, that the same excellence of faculties which contributes to the improvement of reason, the same clearness of conception, the same exactness of distinction, the same vivacity of apprehension, are essential to the operations of true taste, and are its infallible concomitants. It seldom, or never happens, that a man of sense, who has experience in any art, cannot judge of its beauty; and it is no less rare to meet with a man who has a just taste without a sound understanding.

Thus, though the principles of taste be universal, and nearly if not entirely the same in all men; yet few are qualified to give judgment on any work of art, or establish their own sentiments as the standard of beauty. The organs of internal sensation are seldom so perfect as to allow the general principles their full play, and produce a feeling correspondent to those principles. They either labor under some defect, or are vitiated by some disorder; and by that means, excite a sentiment, which may be pronounced erroneous. When the critic has no delicacy, he judges without any distinction, and is only affected by the grosser and more palpable qualities of the object: The finer touches pass unnoticed and disregarded. Where he is not aided by practice, his verdict is attended with confusion and hesitation. Where no comparison has been employed, the most frivolous beauties, such as rather merit the name of defects, are the object of his admiration. Where he lies under the influence of prejudice, all his natural sentiments are perverted. Where good sense is wanting, he is not qualified to discern the beauties of design and reasoning, which are the highest and most excellent. Under some or other of these imperfections, the generality of men labor; and hence a true judge in the finer arts is observed, even during the most polished ages, to be so rare a character: Strong sense, united to delicate sentiment, improved by practice, perfected by comparison, and cleared of all prejudice, can alone entitle critics to this valuable character; and the joint verdict of such, wherever they are to be found, is the true standard of taste and beauty.

TRUE CRITICS AND TRUE STANDARDS OF TASTE

But where are such critics to be found? By what marks are they to be known? How distinguish them from pretenders? These questions are embarrassing; and seem to throw us back into the same uncertainty, from which, during the course of this essay, we have endeavored to extricate ourselves.

But if we consider the matter aright, these are questions of fact, not of sentiment. Whether any particular person be endowed with good sense and a delicate imagination, free from prejudice, may often be the subject of dispute, and be liable to great discussion and enquiry: But that such a character is valuable and estimable will be agreed in by all mankind. . . .

But in reality the difficulty of finding, even in particulars, the standard of taste, is not so great as it is represented. Though in speculation, we may readily avow a certain criterion in science and deny it in sentiment, the matter is found in practice to be much more hard to ascertain in the former case than in the latter. Theories of abstract philosophy, systems of profound theology, have prevailed during one age: In a successive period, these have been universally exploded: Their absurdity has been detected: Other theories and systems have supplied their place, which again give place to their successors: And nothing has been experienced more liable to the revolutions of chance and fashion than these pretended decisions of science. The case is not the same with the beauties of eloquence and poetry. Just expressions of passion and nature are sure, after a little time, to gain public applause, which they maintain for ever. ARISTOTLE, and PLATO, and EPICURUS, and DESCARTES, may successively yield to each other: But TERENCE and VIRGIL maintain an universal, undisputed empire over the minds of men. The abstract philosophy of CICERO has lost its credit: The vehemence of his oratory is still the object of our admiration.

Though men of delicate taste be rare, they are easily to be distinguished in society, by the soundness of their understanding and the superiority of their faculties above the rest of mankind. The ascendant, which they acquire, gives a prevalence to that lively approbation, with which they receive any productions of genius, and renders it generally predominant. Many men, when left to themselves, have but a faint and dubious perception of beauty, who yet are capable of relishing any fine stroke, which is pointed out to them. Every convert to the admiration of the real poet or orator is the cause of some new conversion. And though prejudices may prevail for a time, they never unite in celebrating any

rival to the genius, but yield at last to the force of nature and just sentiment. Thus, though a civilized nation may easily be mistaken in the
choice of their admired philosopher, they never have been found long
to err, in their affection for a favorite epic or tragic author.

SOURCES OF DIVERSITY

But not withstanding all our endeavors to fix a standard of taste, and
reconcile the discordant apprehensions of men, there still remain two
sources of variation, which are not sufficient indeed to confound all the
boundaries of beauty and deformity, but will often serve to produce a
difference in the degrees of our approbation or blame. The one is the
different humors of particular men; the other, the particular manners
and opinions of our age and country. The general principles of taste are
uniform in human nature: Where men vary in their judgments, some
defect or perversion in the faculties may commonly be remarked; proceeding either from prejudice, from want of practice, or want of delicacy;
and there is just reason for approving one taste, and condemning another. But where there is such a diversity in the internal frame or external situation as is entirely blameless on both sides, and leaves no room
to give one the preference above the other; in that case a certain degree
of diversity in judgment is unavoidable, and we seek in vain for a standard, by which we can reconcile the contrary sentiments.

A young man, whose passions are warm, will be more sensibly touched
with amorous and tender images, than a man more advanced in years,
who takes pleasure in wise, philosophical reflections concerning the conduct of life and moderation of the passions. At twenty, OVID may be
the favorite author; HORACE at forty; and perhaps TACITUS at fifty.
Vainly would we, in such cases, endeavor to enter into the sentiments of
others, and divest ourselves of those propensities, which are natural to
us. We choose our favorite author as we do our friend, from a conformity of humor and disposition. Mirth or passion, sentiment or reflection,
whichever of these most predominates in our temper, it gives us a peculiar sympathy with the writer who resembles us.

One person is more pleased with the sublime; another with the tender;
a third with raillery. One has a strong sensibility to blemishes, and is extremely studious of correctness: Another has a more lively feeling of
beauties, and pardons twenty absurdities and defects for one elevated or
pathetic stroke. The ear of this man is entirely turned towards concise-
ness and energy; that man is delighted with a copious, rich, and har-

monious expression. Simplicity is affected by one; ornament by another. Comedy, tragedy, satire, odes, have each its partizans; who prefer that particular species of writing to all others. It is plainly an error in a critic, to confine his approbation to one species or style of writing, and condemn all the rest. But it is almost impossible not to feel a predilection for that which suits our particular turn and disposition. Such preferences are innocent and unavoidable, and can never reasonably be the object of dispute, because there is no standard, by which they can be decided.

For a like reason, we are more pleased, in the course of our reading, with pictures and characters, that resemble objects which are found in our own age or country, than with those which describe a different set of customs. . . . For this reason, comedy is not easily transferred from one age or nation to another. A Frenchman or Englishman is not pleased with the ANDRIA of TERENCE, or CLITIA of MACHIAVEL; where the fine lady, upon whom all the play turns, never once appears to the spectators, but is always kept behind the scenes, suitably to the reserved humor of the ancient Greeks and modern Italians. A man of learning and reflection can make allowance for these peculiarities of manners; but a common audience can never divest themselves so far of their usual ideas and sentiments, as to relish pictures which no wise resemble them.

But here occurs a reflection which may, perhaps, be useful in examining the celebrated controversy concerning ancient and modern learning; where we often find the one side excusing any seeming absurdity in the ancients from the manners of the age, and the other refusing to admit this excuse. . . . In my opinion, the proper boundaries in this subject have seldom been fixed between the contending parties. Where any innocent peculiarities of manners are represented, such as those above mentioned, they ought certainly to be admitted; and a man, who is shocked with them, gives an evident proof of false delicacy and refinement. The poet's *monument more durable than brass,* must fall to the ground like common brick or clay, were men to make no allowance for the continual revolutions of manners and customs, and would admit of nothing but what was suitable to the prevailing fashion. Must we throw aside the pictures of our ancestors, because of their ruffs and fardingales? But where the ideas of morality and decency alter from one age to another, and where vicious manners are described, without being marked with the proper characters of blame and disapprobation: this must be allowed to disfigure the poem, and to be a real deformity. I cannot, nor is it proper I should, enter into such sentiments; and however I may excuse the poet, on account of the manners of his age, I never can relish the composition. The want of humanity and decency, so conspicuous in the characters drawn by several of the ancient poets, even sometimes by HOMER and the Greek tragedians, diminishes considerably the merit of their noble performances, and gives modern authors an advantage over them. We are not interested in the fortunes and sentiments of such rough heroes: We are displeased to find the limits of vice and virtue so much confounded: And whatever indulgence we may give to the writer on account of his prejudices, we cannot prevail on ourselves to enter into his sentiments, or bear an affection to characters, which we plainly discover to be blameable.

The case is not the same with moral principles, as with speculative opinions of any kind. These are in continual flux and revolution. The son embraces a different system from the father. Nay, there is scarcely any man, who can boast of great constancy and uniformity in this particular. Whatever speculative errors may be found in the polite writings of any age or country, they detract but little from the value of those compositions. There needs but a certain turn of thought or imagination to make us enter into all the opinions, which then prevailed, and relish the sentiments or conclusions derived from them. But a very violent effort is requisite to change our judgment of manners, and excite sentiments of approbation or blame, love or hatred, different from those to which the mind from long custom has been familiarized. And where a man is confident of the rectitude of that moral standard, by which he judges, he is justly jealous of it, and will not pervert the sentiments of his heart for a moment, in complaisance to any writer whatsoever.

Of all speculative errors, those which regard religion are the most excusable in compositions of genius; nor is it ever permitted to judge of the civility or wisdom of any people, or even of single persons, by the grossness or refinement of their theological principles. The same good sense, that directs men in the ordinary occurrences of life, is not hearkened to in religious matters, which are supposed to be placed altogether above the cognizance of human reason. On this account, all the absurdities of the pagan system of theology must be overlooked by every critic, who would pretend to form a just notion of ancient poetry; and our posterity, in their turn, must have the same indulgence to their forefathers. No religious principles can ever be imputed as a fault to any poet, while they remain merely principles, and take not such strong possession of his heart, as to lay him under the imputation of *bigotry* or *superstition*. Where that happens, they confound the sentiments of morality, and alter the natural boundaries of vice and virtue. They are therefore eternal blemishes, according to the principle above mentioned; nor are the prejudices and false opinions of the age sufficient to justify them.

STUDY QUESTIONS

1. With respect to writing, how would you define the following terms that Hume uses: elegance, propriety, simplicity, spirit, fustian, affectation, coldness, and false brilliancy? Can you think of any examples to which these terms might be applicable?

2. What does Hume mean by a *Standard of Taste*? What militates against the success of achieving such a standard? Why is it said that "all sentiment is right"? Comment on the phrase "Beauty is no quality in things themselves."

3. What is the role of experience with respect to the rules of art? Are there any *a priori* rules of art? Does Hume believe that all men will feel the same about these rules of art? Do you think the Mona Lisa is more admired today than it was a century ago? Why?

4. Comment on Hume's analysis of the relation of beauty and sentiment? Exactly what does he mean by the "delicacy of the imagination"?

5. What are the essential elements in the perfection of taste? Comment more fully on one of them.

6. What are the marks of the true critic and how are they to be found? Is this a question of fact or sentiment? Explain.

7. Explain in some detail what Hume considers to be the two sources of variation that render it difficult to fix a standard of taste.

8. What ethical implications respecting standards of taste does Hume note? What judgment do you think he might make of the contemporary novel?

Leo Tolstoy

▩▩▩

ON THE NATURE OF ART

▩▩▩

Biographical Note.   LEO (LYEV) NIKOLAYEVICH TOLSTOY, COUNT (1828–1910) was born of Russian gentry in the province of Tula. His family had been ennobled by Peter the Great in the sixteenth century. Tolstoy's parents died early and he was brought up by relatives; he received his early education from French tutors and his higher education at the Kazan University from 1844–1847. He then resided in Moscow for a few years, and later enlisted in the army and served in the Caucacus. In 1854 he was commissioned in the army and saw service at the siege of Sevastopol. Following a brief residence in St. Petersburg, where he met and quarreled with Turgenev, he retired from the army and traveled abroad until his marriage in 1862. His marriage was a happy one and also coincided with his most productive literary period. It was during this time that he produced his two literary masterpieces, *War and Peace* (1864–1869) and *Anna Karenina* (1873–1879). In 1876 he underwent a serious religious conversion, in which he developed an interpretation of Christianity that was to dominate his life from this time on. He regarded Christianity as a wholly ethical and anthropocentric religion. His later literary works, *Death of Ivan Ilyich* and *Kreutzer Sonata* (1899), reflect his religious beliefs. His famous *What is Art* contains a synthesis of his religious ideas as well as a philosophy of art.

* * *

From Leo Tolstoy, *What is Art?* translated by Aylmer Maude, London, Oxford University Press, 1930, selected material from Chapters 5, 15, and 16. Reprinted with the permission of the publishers.

Introductory Note. Tolstoy's philosophy of art is expressed principally in his book *What is Art,* a work that was the result of some fifteen years of reflection. Tolstoy first points out the sacrifices that have been made to art and questions whether they can be justified. Rejecting the notion that the criterion of art can be defined in terms of the beautiful, he is led to consider and summarize various theories of aesthetics from Baumgarten (1714–1762), the founder of aesthetics, down to the end of the nineteenth century. All the proposed definitions of beauty lead, he says, to two fundamental conceptions: that beauty is objective and that it is a kind of pleasure. The first conception can be reduced to the second, for he argues that no objective definition of beauty can be attained. On the other hand, he declares that beauty cannot serve as a definition of art. To avoid these confusions in the definition of art, we must find a more authentic and comprehensible definition of art, apart from the conception of beauty. Tolstoy then introduces his own definition of art as a human activity in which we communicate our feelings and emotions to others. Such an activity of art is infectious and a means of uniting men in the same experience. From this preliminary analysis, Tolstoy proceeds to distinguish between true and false art. He holds that art that exists for the sake of pleasure is false art. Such a conception of art was common, he maintains, during the Renaissance, at which time the upper classes detached themselves from the religious point of view and considered the function of art to be enjoyment. Modern art has been affected by a similar perversion and is characterized by: (1) an impoverished subject matter (2) affectation and obscurantism (3) insincerity and artificiality. Furthermore, he says, modern art is not merely an irreligious art but a counterfeit art.

In the more constructive aspects of his theory of aesthetics, Tolstoy develops the nature of true art and its criteria. The nature of true art lies in the religious consciousness, and it is only through the religious consciousness that art can achieve a universality and unite men in common feelings. The basic criterion of true art, a criterion that is intuitively known and that does not err, is the infectiousness of art. The degrees of such an infectiousness depend upon: (1) the greater or lesser originality of the feeling transmitted (2) the clarity with which the feeling is transmitted, and (3) the sincerity of the artist. Of these the most important is sincerity, which actually includes the others. Any art that does not possess these conditions is counterfeit art. The religious consciousness of the age reveals the true criterion of art, and Tolstoy finds this represented among his predecessors by Victor Hugo (*Les Miserables*), George Eliot (*Adam Bede*), Dostoevski (*The House of the Dead*), and others. He rejects Beethoven's *Ninth Symphony* as bad art, but accepts Millet's *Angelus* as good art. The end of art for Tolstoy is clear. It is to introduce into the human consciousness those truths that proceed from the religious conception of the age. Its task is to unite men in brotherhood and to cause violence to be set aside.

DEFINITIONS OF ART

What is art if we put aside the conception of beauty which confuses the whole matter? The latest and most comprehensible definitions of art, apart from the conception of beauty, are the following: (1) *a*, Art is an activity arising even in the animal kingdom, and springing from sexual desire and the propensity to play (Schiller, Darwin, Spencer), and *b*, accompanied by a pleasurable excitement of the nervous system (Grant Allen). This is the physiological-evolutionary definition. (2) Art is the external manifestation, by means of lines, colors, movements, sounds, or words, of emotions felt by man (Véron). This is the experimental definition. According to the very latest definition (Sully), (3) Art is 'the production of some permanent object or passing action which is fitted not only to supply an active enjoyment to the producer, but to convey a pleasurable impression to a number of spectators or listeners, quite apart from any personal advantage to be derived from it.'

Notwithstanding the superiority of these definitions to the metaphysical definitions which depended on the conception of beauty, they are yet far from exact. The first, the physiological-evolutionary definition (1) *a*, is inexact, because instead of speaking about the artistic activity itself, which is the real matter in hand, it treats of the derivation of art. The modification of it, *b*, based on the physiological effects on the human organism, is inexact because within the limits of such definition many other human activities can be included, as has occurred in the neo-aesthetic theories which reckon art as the preparation of handsome clothes, pleasant scents, and even of victuals.

The experimental definition, (2), which makes art consist in the expression of emotions, is inexact because a man may express his emotions by means of lines, colors, sounds, or words and yet may not act on others by such expression—and then the manifestation of his emotions is not art.

The third definition (that of Sully) is inexact because in the production of objects or actions affording pleasure to the producer and a pleasant emotion to the spectators or hearers apart from personal advantage, may be included the showing of conjuring tricks or gymnastic exercises, and other activities which are not art. And further, many things the production of which does not afford pleasure to the producer and the sensation received from which is unpleasant, such as gloomy, heart-rending scenes in a poetic description or a play, may nevertheless be undoubted works of art.

The inaccuracy of all these definitions arises from the fact that in them all (as also in the metaphysical definitions) the object considered is the pleasure art may give, and not the purpose it may serve in the life of man and of humanity.

In order to define art correctly it is necessary first of all to cease to consider it as a means to pleasure, and to consider it as one of the conditions of human life. Viewing it in this way we cannot fail to observe that art is one of the means of intercourse between man and man.

Every work of art causes the receiver to enter into a certain kind of relationship both with him who produced or is producing the art, and with all those who, simultaneously, previously, or subsequently, receive the same artistic impression.

Speech transmitting the thoughts and experiences of men serves as a means of union among them, and art serves a similar purpose. The peculiarity of this latter means of intercourse, distinguishing it from intercourse by means of words, consists in this, that whereas by words a man transmits his thoughts to another, by art he transmits his feelings.

·The activity of art is based on the fact that a man receiving through his sense of hearing or sight another man's expression of feeling, is capable of experiencing the emotion which moved the man who expressed it. To take the simplest example: one man laughs, and another who hears becomes merry, or a man weeps and another who hears feels sorrow. A man is excited or irritated, and another man seeing him is brought to a similar state of mind. By his movements or by the sounds of his voice a man expresses courage and determination or sadness and calmness, and this state of mind passes on to others. A man suffers, manifesting his sufferings by groans and spasms, and this suffering transmits itself to other people; a man expresses his feelings of admiration, devotion, fear, respect, or love, to certain objects, persons, or phenomena, and others are infected by the same feelings of admiration, devotion, fear, respect, or love, to the same objects, persons or phenomena.

And it is on this capacity of man to receive another man's expression of feeling and to experience those feelings himself, that the activity of art is based.

If a man infects another or others directly, immediately, by his appearance or by the sounds he gives vent to at the very time he experiences the feeling; if he causes another man to yawn when he himself cannot help yawning, or to laugh or cry when he himself is obliged to laugh or cry, or to suffer when he himself is suffering—that does not amount to art.

TOLSTOY'S DEFINITION

Art begins when one person with the object of joining another or others to himself in one and the same feeling, expresses that feeling by certain external indications. To take the simplest example: a boy having experienced, let us say, fear on encountering a wolf, relates that encounter, and in order to evoke in others the feeling he has experienced, describes himself, his condition before the encounter, the surroundings, the wood, his own lightheartedness, and then the wolf's appearance, its movements, the distance between himself and the wolf, and so forth. All this, if only the boy when telling the story again experiences the feelings he had lived through, and infects the hearers and compels them to feel what he had experienced—is art. Even if the boy had not seen a wolf but had frequently been afraid of one, and if wishing to evoke in others the fear he had felt, he invented an encounter with a wolf and recounted it so as to make his hearers share the feelings he experienced when he feared the wolf, that also would be art. And just in the same way it is art if a man, having experienced either the fear of suffering or the attraction of enjoyment (whether in reality or in imagination), expresses these feelings on canvas or in marble so that others are infected by them. And it is also art if a man feels, or imagines to himself, feelings of delight, gladness, sorrow, despair, courage, or despondency, and the transition from one to another of these feelings, and expresses them by sounds so that the hearers are infected by them and experience them as they were experienced by the composer.

The feelings with which the artist infects others may be most various—very strong or very weak, very important or very insignificant, very bad or very good: feelings of love of one's country, self-devotion and submission to fate or to God expressed in a drama, raptures of lovers described in a novel, feelings of voluptuousness expressed in a picture, courage expressed in a triumphal march, merriment evoked by a dance, humor evoked by a funny story, the feeling of quietness transmitted by an evening landscape or by a lullaby, or the feeling of admiration evoked by a beautiful arabesque—it is all art.

If only the spectators or auditors are infected by the feelings which the author has felt, it is art.

To evoke in oneself a feeling one has once experienced and having evoked it in oneself then by means of movements, lines, colors, sounds, or forms expressed in words, so to transmit that feeling that others experience the same feeling—this is the activity of art.

Art is a human activity consisting in this, that one man consciously by means of certain external signs, hands on to others feelings he has lived through, and that others are infected by these feelings and also experience them.

Art is not, as the metaphysicians say, the manifestation of some mysterious Idea of beauty or God; it is not, as the aesthetic physiologists say, a game in which man lets off his excess of stored-up energy; it is not the expression of man's emotions by external signs; it is not the production of pleasing objects; and, above all, it is not pleasure; but it is a means of union among men joining them together in the same feelings, and indispensable for the life and progress towards well-being of individuals and of humanity.

EXTENT AND NECESSITY OF ART

As every man, thanks to man's capacity to express thoughts by words, may know all that has been done for him in the realms of thought by all humanity before his day, and can in the present, thanks to this capacity to understand the thoughts of others, become a sharer in their activity and also himself hand on to his contemporaries and descendants the thoughts he has assimilated from others as well as those that have arisen in himself; so, thanks to man's capacity to be infected with the feelings of others by means of art, all that is being lived through by his contemporaries is accessible to him, as well as the feelings experienced by men thousands of years ago, and he has also the possibility of transmitting his own feelings to others.

If people lacked the capacity to receive the thoughts conceived by men who preceded them and to pass on to others their own thoughts, men would be like wild beasts, or like Kasper Hauser.[1]

And if men lacked this other capacity of being infected by art, people might be almost more savage still, and above all more separated from, and more hostile to, one another.

And therefore the activity of art is a most important one, as important as the activity of speech in itself and as generally diffused.

As speech does not act on us only in sermons, orations, or books, but in all those remarks by which we interchange thoughts and experiences with one another, so also art in the wide sense of the word permeates our

---

[1] 'The foundling of Nuremberg,' found in the market-place of that town on 23rd May 1828, apparently some sixteen years old. He spoke little and was almost totally ignorant even of common objects. He subsequently explained that he had been brought up in confinement underground and visited by only one man, whom he saw but seldom.

whole life, but it is only to some of its manifestations that we apply the term in the limited sense of the word.

We are accustomed to understand art to be only what we hear and see in theatres, concerts, and exhibitions; together with buildings, statues, poems, and novels. . . . But all this is but the smallest part of the art by which we communicate with one another in life. All human life is filled with works of art of every kind—from cradle-song, jest, mimicry, the ornamentation of houses, dress, and utensils, to church services, buildings, monuments, and triumphal processions. It is all artistic activity. So that by art, in the limited sense of the word, we do not mean all human activity transmitting feelings but only that part which we for some reason select from it and to which we attach special importance.

TRUE ART

There is one indubitable sign distinguishing real art from its counterfeit—namely, the infectiousness of art. If a man without exercising effort and without altering his standpoint, on reading, hearing, or seeing another man's work experiences a mental condition which unites him with that man and with others who are also affected by that work, then the object evoking that condition is a work of art. . . .

And not only is infection a sure sign of art, but the degree of infectiousness is also the sole measure of excellence in art.

The stronger the infection the better is the art, as art, speaking of it now apart from its subject-matter—that is, not considering the value of the feelings it transmits.

And the degree of the infectiousness of art depends on three conditions:

(1) On the greater or less individuality of the feeling transmitted; (2) on the greater or lesser clearness with which the feeling is transmitted; (3) on the sincerity of the artist, that is, on the greater or lesser force with which the artist himself feels the emotion he transmits.

ART AND RELIGION

Art like speech is a means of communication and therefore of progress, that is, of the movement of humanity forward towards perfection. Speech renders accessible to men of the latest generations all the knowledge discovered by the experience and reflection both of preceding generations and of the best and foremost men of their own times;

art renders accessible to men of the latest generations all the feelings experienced by their predecessors and also those felt by their best and foremost contemporaries. And as the evolution of knowledge proceeds by truer and more necessary knowledge dislodging and replacing what was mistaken and unnecessary, so the evolution of feeling proceeds by means of art—feelings less kind and less necessary for the well-being of mankind being replaced by others kinder and more needful for that end. That is the purpose of art. And speaking now of the feelings which are its subject-matter, the more art fulfils that purpose the better the art, and the less it fulfils it the worse the art.

The appraisement of feelings (that is, the recognition of one or other set of feelings as more or less good, more or less necessary for the well-being of mankind) is effected by the religious perception of the age. . . .

The religious perception of our time in its widest and most practical application is the consciousness that our well-being, both material and spiritual, individual and collective, temporal and eternal, lies in the growth of brotherhood among men—in their loving harmony with one another. This perception is not only expressed by Christ and all the best men of past ages, it is not only repeated in most varied forms and from most diverse sides by the best men of our times, but it already serves as a clue to all the complex labor of humanity, consisting as this labor does on the one hand in the destruction of physical and moral obstacles to the union of men, and on the other hand in establishing principles common to all men which can and should unite them in one universal brotherhood. And it is on the basis of this perception that we should appraise all the phenomena of our life and among the rest of our art also: choosing from all its realms and highly prizing and encouraging whatever transmits feelings flowing from this religious perception, rejecting whatever is contrary to it, and not attributing to the rest of art an importance that does not properly belong to it. . . .

The essence of the Christian perception consists in the recognition by every man of his sonship to God and of the consequent union of men with God and with one another, as is said in the Gospel (John xvii.21). Therefore the subject-matter of Christian art is of a kind that feeling can unite men with God and with one another.

The expression *unite men with God and with one another* may seem obscure to people accustomed to the misuse of these words that is so customary, but the words have a perfectly clear meaning nevertheless. They indicate that the Christian union of man (in contradiction to the partial, exclusive, union of only certain men) is that which unites all without exception.

Art, all art, has this characteristic, that it unites people. Every art causes those to whom the artist's feeling is transmitted to unite in soul with the artist and also with all who receive the same impression. But non-Christian art while uniting some people, makes that very union a cause of separation between these united people and others; so that union of this kind is often a source not merely of division but even of enmity towards others. Such is all patriotic art, with its anthems, poems, and monuments; such is all Church art, that is, the art of certain cults, with their images, statues, processions, and other local ceremonies. Such art is belated and non-Christian, uniting the people of one cult only to separate them yet more sharply from the members of other cults, and even to place them in relations of hostility to one another. Christian art is such only as tends to unite all without exception, either by evoking in them the perception that each man and all men stand in a like relation towards God and towards their neighbor, or by evoking in them identical feelings, which may even be the very simplest, provided that they are not repugnant to Christianity and are natural to every one without exception. . . .

Christian art either evokes in men feelings which through love of God and of one's neighbor draw them to closer and ever closer union and make them ready for, and capable of, such union; or evokes in them feelings which show them that they are already united in the joys and sorrows of life. And therefore the Christian art of our time can be and is of two kinds: first, art transmitting feelings flowing from a religious perception of man's position in the world in relation to God and to his neighbor—religious art in the limited meaning of the term; and secondly, art transmitting the simplest feelings of common life, but such always as are accessible to all men in the whole world—the art of common life—the art of the people—universal art. Only these two kinds of art can be considered good art in our time. . . .

Whatever the work may be and however it may have been extolled, we have first to ask whether this work is one of real art, or a counterfeit. Having acknowledged, on the basis of the indication of its infectiousness even to a small class of people, that a certain production belongs to the realm of art, it is necessary on this basis to decide the next question, Does this work belong to the category of bad exclusive art opposed to religious perception, or of Christian art uniting people? And having acknowledged a work to belong to real Christian art, we must then, according to whether it transmits feelings flowing from love of God and man, or merely the simple feelings uniting all men, assign it a place in the ranks of religious art, or in those of universal art.

Only on the basis of such verification shall we find it possible to select from the whole mass of what in our society claims to be art, those works which form real, important, necessary, spiritual food, and to separate them from all the harmful and useless art and from the counterfeits of art which surround us. Only on the basis of such verification shall we be able to rid ourselves of the pernicious results of harmful art and avail ourselves of that beneficent action which is the purpose of true and good art, and which is indispensable for the spiritual life of man and of humanity.

STUDY QUESTIONS

1. State the three definitions of art that Tolstoy lists. What difficulties does he find in each?
2. What are the prerequisites for an accurate definition of art according to Tolstoy? Would you agree with his rejection of art as a means to pleasure? Why or why not?
3. How does the activity of art differ from that of speech? What is the basis for the activity of art?
4. Describe in some detail and evaluate Tolstoy's definition of art.
5. According to Tolstoy, how important and how extensive is the activity of art?
6. Comment on Tolstoy's criterion of 'infectiousness' for distinguishing true art from counterfeit art. Would you agree with him that the "degree of infectiousness is also the sole measure of excellence in art"? Discuss.
7. What distinctive function does religion play in the fulfilment of the purpose of art? What is the nature of the religious perception?
8. What is the essence of the Christian perception and what is the subject matter of Christian art? Explain the differences (as Tolstoy sees them) between Christian and non-Christian art.

George Santayana

╔═══╗

THE NATURE OF BEAUTY

╔═══╗

Biographical Note.   GEORGE SANTAYANA (1863–1952) was born
in Madrid, Spain; he came to America at the age of nine. His family settled
in Boston, and Santayana later attended Harvard University and obtained
a doctor's degree in 1887. For the next two years he studied in Berlin, after
which he returned to Harvard and taught there alongside his old masters,
Royce and James. He retired from Harvard in 1912, traveled extensively, and
then settled in Italy, where he spent the last thirty years of his life writing.
He was not only one of the most eminent philosophers of his time, but also a
noted poet, novelist, and literary critic. His principal publications are *The
Life of Reason* (1905–1906), a work somewhat resembling the *Phenomenology of Hegel; Scepticism and Animal Faith* (1923), *Realms of Being* (appearing as the successive *Realm of Essence, Realm of Matter, Realm of
Truth,* and *Realm of Spirit,* between 1927 and 1940); *The Last Puritan*
(1963), a novel; and *Dominations and Powers* (1951).

* * *

Introductory Note.   In contrast to the concern of nineteenth century
philosophy with history and contemporary philosophy with logic, Santayana's
interests lie primarily in moral philosophy in the broad sense of the ideals of
the good, the true, and the beautiful. Such values, he believes, are inherent
in nature and open to man's attainment through poetry and science. The

From George Santayana, *Sense of Beauty,* New York, Charles Scribner's Sons,
1896, Chapter one (omitting Sections 6 and 7).

emphasis on poetic insight and the supremacy of a life of values based upon the nature of things has contributed to the characterization of Santayana as a poetic naturalist. The source of his naturalism is to be found in Greek philosophy. His conviction that by reflecting upon nature, by living the life of reason, man can attain the ultimate values, is derived from Spinoza. Quite unlike Dewey, he considered the point of view of philosophy to be a detached one. He preferred to be the "spectator of all time and existence" rather than a participant in the struggles of humanity.

His principal early work was *Life of Reason,* which came to be regarded as the "Bible of naturalism." His more mature and major work, the *Realms of Being,* at times gives the impression of diverging from his basic naturalistic beliefs. However, he remained fundamentally a naturalist. "Naturalism," he declared, "is something to which I am so thoroughly wedded that I like to call it materialism, so as to prevent all confusion from *romantic* naturalism like Goethe's, for instance, or that of Bergson. Mine is the hard, non-humanistic naturalism of the Ionian philosophies of Democritus, Lucretius, and Spinoza . . . My naturalism is fundamental and includes man and all his works . . ."

The selection to follow is taken from Santayana's first philosophical book and was originally embodied in lectures given at Harvard in 1892–1895. The book is essentially a theoretical inquiry devoted to four principal topics: (1) *The Nature of Beauty,* (2) *The Materials of Beauty,* (3) *The Form of Beauty,* and (4) *The Expression of Beauty.* In *The Nature of Beauty,* Santayana is concerned to show first what is meant by a philosophy of beauty and how beauty springs from the irrational part of our nature. This is followed by developing and contrasting the nature of moral and aesthetic values and the distinction between work and play. Taking aesthetic pleasure as the highest value, Santayana next considers certain possible differentiae of pleasure and beauty. He rejects the differentiae of disinterestedness and universality, and maintains that the real differentia of aesthetic pleasure lies in its objectification and the definition that "beauty is pleasure regarded as the quality of a thing."

THE PHILOSOPHY OF BEAUTY IS A THEORY OF VALUES

It would be easy to find a definition of beauty that should give in a few words a telling paraphrase of the word. We know on excellent authority that beauty is truth, that it is the expression of the ideal, the symbol of divine perfection, and the sensible manifestation of the good. A litany of these titles of honor might easily be compiled, and repeated in praise of our divinity. Such phrases stimulate thought and give us momentary pleasure, but they hardly bring any permanent enlightenment. A definition that should really define must be nothing less than the exposition of the origin, place, and elements of beauty as an object of human experience. We must learn from it, as far as possible, why, when, and how beauty appears, what conditions an object must fulfill to be beautiful, what elements of our nature make us sensible of beauty, and what the relation is between the constitution of the object and the excitement of our susceptibility. Nothing less will really define beauty or make us understand what aesthetic appreciation is. . . .

The historical titles of our subject may give us a hint towards the beginning of such a definition. Many writers of the last century called the philosophy of beauty *Criticism,* and the word is still retained as the title for the reasoned appreciation of works of art. We could hardly speak, however, of delight in nature as criticism. A sunset is not criticized; it is felt and enjoyed. The word "criticism," used on such an occasion, would emphasize too much the element of deliberate judgment and of comparison with standards. Beauty, although often so described, is seldom so perceived, and all the greatest excellences of nature and art are so far from being approved of by a rule that they themselves furnish the standard and ideal by which critics measure inferior effects.

This age of science and of nomenclature has accordingly adopted a more learned word, *Aesthetics,* that is, the theory of perception or of susceptibility. If criticism is too narrow a word, pointing exclusively to our more artificial judgments, aesthetics seems to be too broad and to include within its sphere all pleasures and pains, if not all perceptions whatsoever. Kant used it, as we know, for his theory of time and space as forms of all perception; and it has at times been narrowed into an equivalent for the philosophy of art.

If we combine, however, the etymological meaning of criticism with that of aesthetics, we shall unite two essential qualities of the theory of beauty. Criticism implies judgment, and aesthetics perception. To get the common ground, that of perceptions which are critical, or judgments which are perceptions, we must widen our notion of deliberate criticism so as to include those judgments of value which are instinctive and immediate, that is, to include pleasures and pains; and at the same time we must narrow our notion of aesthetics so as to exclude all perceptions which are not appreciations, which do not find a value in their objects. We thus reach the sphere of critical or appreciative perception, which is, roughly speaking, what we mean to deal with. And retaining the word "aesthetics," which is now current, we may therefore say that aesthetics is concerned with the perception of values. The meaning and conditions of value is, then, what we must first consider.

Since the days of Descartes it has been a conception familiar to philosophers that every visible event in nature might be explained by previous visible events, and that all the motions, for instance, of the tongue in speech, or of the hand in painting, might have merely physical causes. If consciousness is thus accessory to life and not essential to it, the race of man might have existed upon the earth and acquired all the arts necessary for its subsistence without possessing a single sensation, idea, or emotion. Natural selection might have secured the survival of those automata which made useful reactions upon their environment. An instinct of self-preservation would have been developed, dangers would have been shunned without being feared, and injuries revenged without being felt.

In such a world there might have come to be the most perfect organization. There would have been what we should call the expression of the deepest interests and the apparent pursuit of conceived goods. For there would have been spontaneous and ingrained tendencies to avoid certain contingencies and to produce others; all the dumb show and evidence of thinking would have been patent to the observer. Yet there would surely have been no thinking, no expectation, and no conscious achievement in the whole process.

The onlooker might have feigned ends and objects of forethought, as we do in the case of the water that seeks its own level, or in that of the vacuum which nature abhors. But the particles of matter would have remained unconscious of their collocation, and all nature would have been insensible of their changing arrangement. We only, the possible spectators of that process, by virtue of our own interests and habits, could see any progress or culmination in it. We should see culmination where the result attained satisfied our practical or aesthetic demands, and progress wherever such a satisfaction was approached. But apart from ourselves, and our human bias, we can see in such a mechanical world no element of value whatever. In removing consciousness, we have removed the possibility of worth.

But it is not only in the absence of all consciousness that value would be removed from the world; by a less violent abstraction from the totality of human experience, we might conceive beings of a purely intellectual cast, minds in which the transformations of nature were mirrored without any emotion. Every event would then be noted, its relations would be observed, its recurrence might even be expected; but all this would happen without a shadow of desire, of pleasure, or of regret. No event would be repulsive, no situation terrible. We might, in a word, have a world of idea without a world of will. In this case, as completely as if consciousness were absent altogether, all value and excellence would be gone. So that for the existence of good in any form it is not merely consciousness but emotional consciousness that is needed. Observation will not do, appreciation is required.

PREFERENCE IS ULTIMATELY IRRATIONAL

We may therefore at once assert this axiom, important for all moral philosophy and fatal to certain stubborn incoherences of thought, that there is no value apart from some appreciation of it, and no good apart from some preference of it before its absence or its opposite. In appreciation, in preference, lies the root and essence of all excellence. Or, as Spinoza clearly expresses it, we desire nothing because it is good, but it is good only because we desire it. . . .

Values spring from the immediate and inexplicable reaction of vital impulse, and from the irrational part of our nature. The rational part is by its essence relative; it leads us from data to conclusions, or from parts to wholes; it never furnishes the data with which it works. . . .

It is evident that beauty is a species of value, and what we have said of value in general applies to this particular kind. A first approach to a definition of beauty has therefore been made by the exclusion of all intellectual judgments, all judgments of matter of fact or of relation. To substitute judgments of fact for judgments of value, is a sign of a pedantic and borrowed criticism. If we approach a work of art or nature scientifically, for the sake of its historical connexions or proper classification, we do not approach it aesthetically. . . .

In an opposite direction the same substitution of facts for values makes its appearance, whenever the reproduction of fact is made the sole standard of artistic excellence. Many half-trained observers condemn the work of some naive or fanciful masters with a sneer, because, as they truly say, it is out of drawing. The implication is that to be correctly copied from a model is the prerequisite of all beauty. Correctness is, indeed, an element of effect and one which, in respect to familiar objects, is almost indispensable, because its absence would cause a disappointment and dissatisfaction incompatible with enjoyment. We learn to value truth more and more as our love and knowledge of nature increase. But fidelity is a merit only because it is in this way a factor in our pleasure. It stands on a level with all other ingredients of effect. When a man raises it to a solitary pre-eminence and becomes incapable of appreciating anything else, he betrays the decay of aesthetic capacity. The scientific habit in him inhibits the artistic.

That facts have a value of their own, at once complicates and explains this question. We are naturally pleased by every perception, and recognition and surprise are particularly acute sensations. When we see a striking truth in any imitation, we are therefore delighted, and this kind of pleasure is very legitimate, and enters into the best effects of all the representative arts. Truth and realism are therefore aesthetically good, but they are not all-sufficient, since the representation of everything is not equally pleasing and effective. The fact that resemblance is a source of satisfaction, justifies the critic in demanding it, while the aesthetic insufficiency of such veracity shows the different value of truth in science and in art. Science is the response to the demand for information, and in it we ask for the whole truth and nothing but the truth. Art is the response to the demand for entertainment, for the stimulation of our senses and imagination, and truth enters into it only as it subserves these ends.

Even the scientific value of truth is not, however, ultimate or absolute. It rests partly on practical, partly on aesthetic interests. As our ideas are gradually brought into conformity with the facts by the painful process of selection,—for intuition runs equally into truth and into error, and can settle nothing if not controlled by experience,—we gain vastly in our command over our environment. This is the fundamental value of natural science, and the fruit it is yielding in our day. We have no better vision of nature and life than some of our predecessors, but we have greater material resources. To know the truth about the composition and history of things is good for this reason. It is also good because of the enlarged horizon it gives us, because the spectacle of nature is a marvellous and fascinating one, full of a serious sadness and large peace, which gives us back our birthright as children of the planet and naturalizes us upon the earth. This is the poetic value of the scientific *Weltanschauung*. From these two benefits, the practical and the imaginative, all the value of truth is derived.

Aesthetic and moral judgments are accordingly to be classed together in contrast to judgments intellectual; they are both judgments of value, while intellectual judgments are judgments of fact. If the latter have any value, it is only derivative, and our whole intellectual life has its only justification in its connexion with our pleasures and pains.

CONTRAST BETWEEN MORAL AND AESTHETIC VALUES

The relation between aesthetic and moral judgments, between the spheres of the beautiful and the good, is close, but the distinction between them is important. One factor of this distinction is that while aesthetic judgments are mainly positive, that is perceptions of good, moral judgments are mainly and fundamentally negative, or perceptions of evil. Another factor of the distinction is that whereas, in the perception of beauty, our judgment is necessarily intrinsic and based on the character of the immediate experience, and never consciously on the idea of an eventual utility in the object, judgments about moral worth, on the contrary, are always based, when they are positive, upon the consciousness of benefits probably involved. Both these distinctions need some elucidation.

Hedonistic ethics have always had to struggle against the moral sense of mankind. Earnest minds, that feel the weight and dignity of life, rebel against the assertion that the aim of right conduct is enjoyment. Pleasure usually appears to them as a temptation, and they sometimes go so far as to make avoidance of it a virtue. The truth is that morality is not mainly concerned with the attainment of pleasure; it is rather concerned, in all its deeper and more authoritative maxims, with the prevention of suffering. There is something artificial in the deliberate pursuit of pleasure; there is something absurd in the obligation to enjoy oneself. We feel no duty in that direction; we take to enjoyment naturally enough after the work of life is done, and the freedom and spontaneity of our pleasures is what is most essential to them.

The sad business of life is rather to escape certain dreadful evils to which our nature exposes us,—death, hunger, disease, weariness, isolation, and contempt. By the awful authority of these things, which stand like spectres behind every moral injunction, conscience in reality speaks, and a mind which they have duly impressed cannot but feel, by contrast, the hopeless triviality of the search for pleasure. It cannot but feel that a life abandoned to amusement and to changing impulse must run unawares into fatal dangers. The moment, however, that society emerges from the early pressure of the environment and is tolerably secure against primary evils, morality grows lax. The forms that life will further assume are not to be imposed by moral authority, but are determined by the genius of the race, the opportunities of the moment, and the tastes and resources of individual minds. The reign of duty gives place to the reign of freedom, and the law and the covenant to the dispensation of grace.

The appreciation of beauty and its embodiment in the arts are activities which belong to our holiday life, when we are redeemed for the moment from the shadow of evil and the slavery to fear, and are following the bent of our nature where it chooses to lead us. The values, then, with which we here deal are positive; they were negative in the sphere of morality. The ugly is hardly an exception, because it is not the cause of any real pain. In itself it is rather a source of amusement. If its suggestions are vitally repulsive, its presence becomes a real evil towards which we assume a practical and moral attitude. And, correspondingly, the pleasant is never, as we have seen, the object of a truly moral injunction.

WORK AND PLAY

We have here, then, an important element of the distinction between aesthetic and moral values. It is the same that has been pointed to in the famous contrast between work and play. These terms may be used in different senses and their importance in moral classification differs with the meaning attached to them. We may call everything play which is useless activity, exercise that springs from the physiological impulse to discharge the energy which the exigencies of life have not called out. Work will then be all action that is necessary or useful for life. Evidently if work and play are thus objectively distinguished as useful and useless action, work is a eulogistic term and play a disparaging one. It would be better for us that all our energy should be turned to account, that none of it should be wasted in aimless motion. Play, in this sense, is a sign of imperfect adaptation. It is proper to childhood, when the body and mind are not yet fit to cope with the environment, but it is unseemly in manhood and pitiable in old age, because it marks an atrophy of human nature, and a failure to take hold of the opportunities of life. . . .

At the same time there is an undeniable propriety in calling all the liberal and imaginative activities of man play, because they are spontaneous, and not carried on under pressure of external necessity or danger. Their utility for self-preservation may be very indirect and accidental, but they are not worthless for that reason. On the contrary, we may measure the degree of happiness and civilization which any race has attained by the proportion of its energy which is devoted to free and generous pursuits, to the adornment of life and the culture of the imagination. For it is in the spontaneous play of his faculties that man finds himself and his happiness. Slavery is the most degrading condition of which he is capable, and he is as often a slave to the niggardness of the earth and the inclemency of heaven, as to a master or an institution. He is a slave when all his energy is spent in avoiding suffering and death, when all his action is imposed from without, and no breath or strength is left him for free enjoyment.

Work and play here take on a different meaning, and become equivalent to servitude and freedom. The change consists in the subjective point of view from which the distinction is now made. We no longer mean by work all that is done usefully, but only what is done unwillingly and by the spur of necessity. By play we are designating, no longer what is done fruitlessly, but whatever is done spontaneously and for its own sake, whether it have or not an ulterior utility. Play, in this sense, may be our most useful occupation. So far would a gradual adaptation to the environment be from making this play obsolete, that it would tend to abolish work, and to make play universal. For with the elimination of all the conflicts and errors of instinct, the race would do spontaneously whatever conduced to its welfare and we should live safely and prosperously without external stimulus or restraint.

ALL VALUES ARE IN ONE SENSE AESTHETIC

In this second and subjective sense, then, work is the disparaging term and play the eulogistic one. All who feel the dignity and importance of the things of the imagination, need not hesitate to adopt the classification which designates them as play. We point out thereby, not that they have no value, but that their value is intrinsic, that in them is one of the sources of all worth. Evidently all values must be ultimately intrinsic. The useful is good because of the excellence of its consequences; but these must somewhere cease to be merely useful in their turn, or only excellent as means; somewhere we must reach the good that is good in itself and for its own sake, else the whole process is futile, and the utility of our first object illusory. We here reach the second factor in our distinction between aesthetic and moral values, which regards their immediacy.

If we attempt to remove from life all its evils, as the popular imagination has done at times, we shall find little but aesthetic pleasures remaining to constitute unalloyed happiness. The satisfaction of the passions and the appetites, in which we chiefly place earthly happiness, themselves take on an aesthetic tinge when we remove ideally the possibility of loss or variation. What could the Olympians honor in one another or the seraphim worship in God except the embodiment of eternal attributes, of essences which, like beauty, make us happy only in contemplation? The glory of heaven could not be otherwise symbolized than by light and music. Even the knowledge of truth which the most sober theologians made the essence of the beatific vision, is an aesthetic delight; for when the truth has no further practical utility, it becomes a landscape. The delight of it is imaginative and the value of it aesthetic.

This reduction of all values to immediate appreciations, to sensuous or vital activities, is so inevitable that it has struck even the minds most courageously rationalistic. Only for them, instead of leading to the liberation of aesthetic goods from practical entanglements and their establishment as the only pure and positive values in life, this analysis has led rather to the denial of all pure and positive goods altogether. Such thinkers naturally assume that moral values are intrinsic and supreme; and since these moral values would not arise but for the existence or imminence of physical evils, they embrace the paradox that without good no evil whatever is conceivable.

The harsh requirements of apologetics have no doubt helped them to this position, from which one breath of spring or the sight of one well-begotten creature should be enough to dislodge them. Their ethical temper and the fetters of their imagination forbid them to reconsider their original assumption and to conceive that morality is a means and not an end; that it is the price of human non-adaptation, and the consequence of the original sin of unfitness. It is the compression of human conduct within the narrow limits of the safe and possible. Remove danger, remove pain, remove the occasion of pity, and the need of morality is gone. To say "thou shalt not" would then be an impertinence.

But this elimination of precept would not be a cessation of life. The senses would still be open, the instincts would still operate, and lead all creatures to the haunts and occupations that befitted them. The variety of nature and the infinity of art, with the companionship of our fellows, would fill the leisure of that ideal existence. These are the elements of our positive happiness, the things which, amid a thousand vexations and vanities, make the clear profit of living.

THE DIFFERENTIA OF AESTHETIC PLEASURE NOT ITS DISINTERESTEDNESS

The distinction between pleasure and the sense of beauty has sometimes been said to consist in the unselfishness of aesthetic satisfaction. In other pleasures, it is said, we gratify our senses and passions; in th contemplation of beauty we are raised above ourselves, the passions are silenced and we are happy in the recognition of a good that we do not seek to possess. The painter does not look at a spring of water with the eyes of a thirsty man, nor at a beautiful woman with those of a satyr. The difference lies, it is urged, in the impersonality of the enjoyment. But this distinction is one of intensity and delicacy, not of nature, and it seems satisfactory only to the least aesthetic minds.

In the second place, the supposed disinterestedness of aesthetic delights is not very fundamental. Appreciation of a picture is not identical with the desire to buy it, but it is, or ought to be, closely related and preliminary to that desire. The beauties of nature and of the plastic arts are not consumed by being enjoyed; they retain all the efficacy to impress a second beholder. But this circumstance is accidental, and those aesthetic objects which depend upon change and are exhausted in time, as are all performances, are things the enjoyment of which is an object of rivalry and is coveted as much as any other pleasure. . . .

The truth which the theory is trying to state seems rather to be that when we seek aesthetic pleasures we have no further pleasure in mind; that we do not mix up the satisfactions of vanity and proprietorship with the delight of contemplation. This is true, but it is true at bottom of all pursuits and enjoyments. Every real pleasure is in one sense disinterested. It is not sought with ulterior motives, and what fills the mind is no calculation, but the image of an object or event, suffused with emotion. . . .

THE DIFFERENTIA OF AESTHETIC PLEASURE NOT ITS UNIVERSALITY

The supposed disinterestedness of our love of beauty passes into another characteristic of it often regarded as essential,—its universality. The pleasures of the senses have, it is said, no dogmatism in them; that anything gives me pleasure involves no assertion about its capacity to give pleasure to another. But when I judge a thing to be beautiful, my judgment means that the thing is beautiful in itself, or (what is the ‹ ‹ ‹ more critically expressed) that it should seem so to every‹ ‹niversality is, according to this doctrine, the essence ‹t makes the perception of beauty a judgment rather

of universality is such a natural inaccuracy will not There is notoriously no great agreement upon aesthetic matters; and such agreement as there is, is based upon similarity of origin, nature, and circumstance among men, a similarity which, where it exists, tends to bring about identity in all judgments and feelings. It is unmeaning to say that what is beautiful to one man *ought* to be beautiful to another. If their senses are the same, their associations and dispositions similar, then the same thing will certainly be beautiful to both. . . . Evidently this obligation of recognizing the same qualities is conditioned by the possession of the same faculties. But no two men have exactly the same faculties, nor can things have for any two exactly the same values. . . .

The great actual unity of human taste within the range of conventional history helps the pretension. But in principle it is untenable. Nothing has less to do with the real merit of a work of imagination than the capacity of all men to appreciate it; the true test is the degree and kinds of satisfaction it can give to him who appreciates it most. The symphony would lose nothing if half mankind had always been deaf, as nine-tenths of them actually are to the intricacies of its harmonies; but it would have lost much if no Beethoven had existed. And more: incapacity to appreciate certain types of beauty may be the condition *sine qua non* for the appreciation of another kind; the greatest capacity both for enjoyment and creation is highly specialized and exclusive, and hence the greatest ages of art have often been strangely intolerant. . . .

THE DIFFERENTIA OF AESTHETIC PLEASURE: ITS OBJECTIFICATION

There is, however, something more in the claim to universality in aesthetic judgments than the desire to generalize our own opinions. There is the expression of a curious but well-known psychological phenomenon, viz. the transformation of an element of sensation into the quality of a thing. If we say that other men should see the beauties we see, it is because we think those beauties *are in the object*, like its color, proportion, or size. Our judgment appears to us merely the perception and discovery of an external existence, of the real excellence that is without. But this notion is radically absurd and contradictory. Beauty, as we have seen, is a value; it cannot be conceived as an independent existence which affects our senses and which we consequently perceive. It exists in perception, and cannot exist otherwise. A beauty not perceived is a pleasure not felt, and a contradiction. . . .

. . . Beauty is an emotional element, a pleasure of ours, which nevertheless we regard as a quality of things. But we are now prepared to understand the nature of this exception. It is the survival of a tendency originally universal to make every effect of a thing upon us a constituent of its conceived nature. The scientific idea of a thing is a great abstraction from the mass of perceptions and reactions which that thing produces; the aesthetic idea is less abstract, since it retains the emotional reaction, the pleasure of the perception, as an integral part of the conceived thing.

Nor is it hard to find the ground of this survival in the sense of beauty of an objectification of feeling elsewhere extinct. Most of the pleasures which objects cause are easily distinguished and separated from the perception of the object: the object has to be applied to a particular organ, like the palate, or swallowed like wine, or used and operated upon in some way before the pleasure arises. The cohesion is therefore slight between the pleasure and the other associated elements of sense; the pleasure is separated in time from the perception, or it is localized in a different organ, and consequently is at once recognized as an effect and not as a quality of the object. But when the process of perception itself is pleasant, as it may easily be, when the intellectual operation, by which the elements of sense are associated and projected, and the concept of the form and substance of the thing produced, is naturally delightful, then we have a pleasure intimately bound up in the thing, inseparable from its character and constitution, the seat of which in us is the same as the seat of the perception. We naturally fail, under these circumstances, to separate the pleasure from the other objectified feelings. It becomes, like them, a quality of the object, which we distinguish from pleasures not so incorporated in the perception of things, by giving it the name of beauty.

THE DEFINITION OF BEAUTY

We have now reached our definition of beauty, which, in the terms of our successive analysis and narrowing of the conception, is value positive, intrinsic, and objectified. Or, in less technical language, Beauty is pleasure regarded as the quality of a thing.

This definition is intended to sum up a variety of distinctions and identifications which should perhaps be here more explicitly set down. Beauty is a value, that is, it is not a perception of a matter of fact or of a relation: it is an emotion, an affection of our volitional and appreciative nature. An object cannot be beautiful if it can give pleasure to nobody: a beauty to which all men were forever indifferent is a contradiction in terms.

In the second place, this value is positive, it is the sense of the presence of something good, or (in the case of ugliness) of its absence. It is never the perception of a positive evil, it is never a negative value. That we are endowed with the sense of beauty is a pure gain which brings no evil with it. When the ugly ceases to be amusing or merely uninteresting and becomes disgusting, it becomes indeed a positive evil: but a moral and practical, not an aesthetic one. In aesthetics that saying is true—often so disingenuous in ethics—that evil is nothing but the absence of good: for even the tedium and vulgarity of an existence without beauty is not itself ugly so much as lamentable and degrading. The absence of aesthetic goods is a moral evil: the aesthetic evil is merely relative, and means less of aesthetic good than was expected at the place and time. No form in itself gives pain, although some forms give pain by causing a shock of surprise even when they are really beautiful: as if a mother found a fine bull pup in her child's cradle, when her pain would not be aesthetic in its nature.

Further, this pleasure must not be in the consequence of the utility of the object or event, but in its immediate perception; in other words, beauty is an ultimate good, something that gives satisfaction to a natural function, to some fundamental need or capacity of our minds. Beauty is therefore a positive value that is intrinsic; it is a pleasure. These two circumstances sufficiently separate the sphere of aesthetics from that of ethics. Moral values are generally negative, and always remote. Morality has to do with the avoidance of evil and the pursuit of good: aesthetics only with enjoyment.

Finally, the pleasures of sense are distinguished from the perception of beauty, as sensation in general is distinguished from perception; by the objectification of the elements and their appearance as qualities rather of things than of consciousness. The passage from sensation to perception is gradual, and the path may be sometimes retraced: so it is with beauty and the pleasures of sensation. There is no sharp line between them, but it depends upon the degree of objectivity my feeling has attained at the moment whether I say "It pleases me," or "It is beautiful." If I am self-conscious and critical, I shall probably use one phrase; if I am impulsive and susceptible, the other. The more remote, interwoven, and inextricable the pleasure is, the more objective it will appear; and the union of two pleasures often makes one beauty. In Shakespeare's LIVth sonnet are these words:

Oh how much more doth beauty beauteous seem
By that sweet ornament which truth doth give!
The rose looks fair, but fairer we it deem
For that sweet odor which doth in it live.
The canker-blooms have full as deep a dye
As the perfumèd tincture of the roses,
Hang on such thorns, and play as wantonly
When summer's breath their maskèd buds discloses.
But, for their beauty only is their show,
They live unwooed and unrespected fade;
Die to themselves. Sweet roses do not so:
Of their sweet deaths are sweetest odors made.

One added ornament, we see, turns the deep dye, which was but show and mere sensation before, into an element of beauty and reality; and as truth is here the cooperation of perceptions, so beauty is the cooperation of pleasures. If color, form, and motion are hardly beautiful without the sweetness of the odor, how much more necessary would they be for the sweetness itself to become a beauty! If we had the perfume in a flask, no one would think of calling it beautiful: it would give us too detached and controllable a sensation. There would be no object in which it could be easily incorporated. But let it float from the garden, and it will add another sensuous charm to objects simultaneously recognized, and help to make them beautiful. Thus beauty is constituted by the objectification of pleasure. It is pleasure objectified.

STUDY QUESTIONS

1. State the requirements that Santayana lays down for an adequate definition of beauty. What meaning does he attach to "criticism"?
2. According to Santayana, in what respects do "criticism" and "aesthetics" supply the essential qualities for a theory of beauty?
3. State the basis for Santayana's contention that "there is no value apart from some appreciation of it."
4. On the basis of your reading of Santayana (and others), discuss each of the following questions: (a) Does a work of art have value because it is correct and representative? (b) Because it is true? (c) Are aesthetic judgments in any sense judgments of fact? (d) Are intellectual judgments in any sense judgments of value?
5. Describe the relationship of moral and aesthetic values as developed by Santayana. What important distinction is drawn between them?
6. In what sense are the values of aesthetics positive rather than negative?

Why does Santayana refuse to consider the "ugly" as an exception to this rule.

7. Regarding the relation between work and play, discuss the basis for Santayana's contentions:

    (a) That "work" is a eulogistic term and "play" a disparaging one.

    (b) That "play" is a eulogistic term and "work" a disparaging one.

8. Why does Santayana say that all values must be ultimately intrinsic? What does he mean by the immediacy of all values? Does he consider that moral values are intrinsic and supreme? What conclusions would you draw from this whole discussion of the distinction between aesthetic and moral values?

9. Why does Santayana say that the distinction between pleasure and the sense of beauty does not consist in the unselfishness of aesthetic satisfaction? That the differentia of aesthetic pleasure is not its universality?

10. What is Santayana's final definition of beauty? State the various elements that make up his definition of beauty. Would you agree that beauty is "pleasure objectified"? Why or why not?

VIII

Philosophy
of Science

Charles Peirce

▱▱

METHODS OF KNOWING

▱▱

Biographical Note. CHARLES SANDERS PEIRCE (1839–1914) was born at Cambridge, Massachusetts, the son of Benjamin Peirce, a professor of mathematics. Peirce was considerably influenced by his father, as his interests in mathematics and logic reveal. He studied at Harvard, but apparently did not have the temperament suited for an academic career. The greater part of his life was spent in the service of the U. S. Coastal Survey. At one time he lectured briefly at Harvard, and for five years was a lecturer at Johns Hopkins. He retired in 1891, but his later life was not a happy one, and he was frequently in financial difficulty. He had a close relationship with William James, who contributed to his financial support. The difficulties of his personality are summed up well by James: "As for Charles Peirce, it is the most curious instance of talents not making a career. He dished himself at Harvard by inspiring dislike in Eliot . . . He is now so mature in character with rather fixed half-bohemian habits, and no habit of teaching, that it would be risky to appoint him. I yield to no one in admiration of his genius, but he is paradoxical and unsociable of intellect, and hates to make connection with anyone he is with."

Peirce wrote a great deal, but the bulk of his writings remained forgotten until his genius was recognized by Dewey in *The Pragmatism of Peirce* and by C. I. Lewis in his *Survey of Symbolic Logic.* This led to the publication

From Charles Peirce, "The Fixation of Belief," *Popular Science Monthly,* November, 1877.

of many excerpts from his works in Cohen's *Chance, Love and Logic*. His *Collected Papers* were not published until 1931. Since then he has been recognized by many as America's greatest philosopher.

* * *

Introductory Note. Pragmatism has generally been associated primarily with William James, and it is undoubtedly true that he did far more to popularize certain conceptions of this philosophy than any other man. However, the real founder of American pragmatism was Charles Peirce, who first formulated its meaning in the maxim: "Consider what effects, that might conceivably have practical bearings we conceive the object of conception to have. Then, our conception of these effects is the whole of our conception of the object." The unfortunate obscurity of this statement led to varying interpretations and particularly the interpretation of James that all thinking must be practical in nature. But whereas James is essentially anti-intellectual in his outlook, Peirce's greater breadth of vision led him to regard pragmatism as essentially logical and scientific in character. Like James he distrusted traditional metaphysics, but rejected it not on practical or emotional grounds, but insofar as it failed to conform to his conception of the notion of truth as an ideal of scientific method.

In logic, Peirce anticipated many of the later developments in symbolic logic. His theory of knowledge he termed a "Critical Commonsensism." Unlike Descartes, he denies that we must begin with doubt. "Let us not pretend to doubt in philosophy," he says, "what we do not doubt in our hearts." A Cartesian scepticism, he feels, can lead only to an excessive individualism in philosophy. But the ultimate aim of philosophy is not the satisfaction of the doubts of an individual. Truth is a scientific ideal to be achieved in the community of science; truth is public.

The "Fixation of Belief" contains the epitome of many of Peirce's essential teachings on the true method of inquiry. He begins by clarifying various notions of belief, doubt, thought, knowledge, and experience. Belief is a habit, a rule of action. It is effective until we encounter a perplexity, a doubt, a felt difficulty. What Peirce terms *inquiry* is the attempt to remove these difficulties, the irritations of doubt, and to refix belief. "Thought in action," he says, "has for its only possible motive the attainment of Thought at rest."

Next he observes the various methods by which belief as a habit may be fixed. These are the Method of Tenacity, a sheerly irrational rejection of any other alternative to the held belief; the Method of Authority, in which the tenacity of the individual is substituted by that of the group, belief being fixed by the community; the Method of Agreeableness to Reason, which is that found in traditional metaphysics and by which we would persuade others to believe as we do; and finally, the Method of Science, which is the only true Method of Inquiry. This method holds that there is *one* discoverable answer to all inquiries, that which is attained in scientific research. Hence, although all our beliefs in a certain fashion seek the truth and claim the truth, only the scientific thinker knows how to attain the truth which he claims conforms to the objective opinions of the community of science itself.

OF DOUBT AND BELIEF

. . . We generally know when we wish to ask a question and when we wish to pronounce a judgment, for there is a dissimilarity between the sensation of doubting and that of believing.

But this is not all which distinguishes doubt from belief. There is a practical difference. Our beliefs guide our desires and shape our actions. The Assassins, or followers of the Old Man of the Mountain, used to rush into death at his least command, because they believed that obedience to him would insure everlasting felicity. Had they doubted this, they would not have acted as they did. So it is with every belief, according to its degree. The feeling of believing is a more or less sure indication of there being established in our nature some habit which will determine our actions. Doubt never has such an effect.

Nor must we overlook a third point of difference. Doubt is an uneasy and dissatisfied state from which we struggle to free ourselves and pass into the state of belief; while the latter is a calm and satisfactory state which we do not wish to avoid, or to change to a belief in anything else. On the contrary, we cling tenaciously, not merely to believing, but to believing just what we do believe.

Thus, both doubt and belief have positive effects upon us, though very different ones. Belief does not make us act at once, but puts us into such a condition that we shall behave in a certain way, when the occasion arises. Doubt has not the least effect of this sort, but stimulates us to action until it is destroyed. This reminds us of the irritation of a nerve and the reflex action produced thereby; while for the analogue of belief, in the nervous system, we must look to what are called nervous associations—for example, to that habit of the nerves in consequence of which the smell of a peach will make the mouth water.

The irritation of doubt causes a struggle to attain a state of belief. I shall term this struggle *inquiry,* though it must be admitted that this is sometimes not a very apt designation.

The irritation of doubt is the only immediate motive for the struggle to attain belief. It is certainly best for us that our beliefs should be such as may truly guide our actions so as to satisfy our desires; and this reflection will make us reject any belief which does not seem to have been so formed as to insure this result. But it will only do so by creating a doubt in the place of that belief. With the doubt, therefore, the struggle begins, and with the cessation of doubt it ends. Hence, the sole object of inquiry is the settlement of opinion. We may fancy that this is not enough for us, and that we seek not merely an opinion, but a true opinion. But put this fancy to the test, and it proves groundless; for as soon as a firm belief is reached we are entirely satisfied, whether the belief be false or true. And it is clear that nothing out of the sphere of our knowledge can be our object, for nothing which does not affect the mind can be a motive for a mental effort. The most that can be maintained is, that we seek for a belief that we shall *think* to be true. But we think each one of our beliefs to be true, and, indeed, it is mere tautology to say so.

That the settlement of opinion is the sole end of inquiry is a very important proposition. It sweeps away, at once, various vague and erroneous conceptions of proof. A few of these may be noticed here.

1. Some philosophers have imagined that to start an inquiry it was only necessary to utter a question or set it down on paper, and have even recommended to us to begin our studies with questioning everything! But the mere putting of a proposition into the interrogative form does not stimulate the mind to any struggle after belief. There must be a real and living doubt, and without this all discussion is idle.

2. It is a very common idea that a demonstration must rest on some ultimate and absolutely indubitable propositions. These, according to one school, are first principles of a general nature; according to another, are first sensations. But, in point of fact, an inquiry, to have that completely satisfactory result called demonstration, has only to start with propositions perfectly free from all actual doubt. If the premises are not in fact doubted at all, they cannot be more satisfactory than they are.

3. Some people seem to love to argue a point after all the world is fully convinced of it. But no further advance can be made. When doubt ceases, mental action on the subject comes to an end; and, if it did go on, it would be without a purpose.

METHOD OF TENACITY

If the settlement of opinion is the sole object of inquiry, and if belief is of the nature of a habit, why should we not attain the desired end, by taking any answer to a question, which we may fancy, and constantly reiterating it to ourselves, dwelling on all which may conduce to that belief, and learning to turn with contempt and hatred from anything which might disturb it? This simple and direct method is really pursued by many men. I remember once being entreated not to read a certain newspaper lest it might change my opinion upon free-trade. "Lest I might be entrapped by its fallacies and misstatements," was the form of the expression. "You are not," my friend said, "a special student of political economy. You might, therefore, easily be deceived by fallacious arguments upon the subject. You might, then, if you read this paper, be led to believe in protection. But you admit that free-trade is the true doctrine; and you do not wish to believe what is not true." I have often known this system to be deliberately adopted. Still oftener, the instinctive dislike of an undecided state of mind, exaggerated into a vague dread of doubt, makes men cling spasmodically to the views they already take. The man feels that, if he only holds to his belief without wavering, it will be entirely satisfactory. Nor can it be denied that a steady and immovable faith yields great peace of mind. It may, indeed, give rise to inconveniences, as if a man should resolutely continue to believe that fire would not burn him, or that he would be eternally damned if he received his *ingesta* otherwise than through a stomach pump. But then the man who adopts this method will not allow that its inconveniences are greater than its advantages. He will say, "I hold steadfastly to the truth and the truth is always wholesome." And in many cases it may very well be that the pleasure he derives from his calm faith overbalances any inconveniences resulting from its deceptive character. Thus, if it be true that death is annihilation, then the man who believes that he will certainly go straight to heaven when he dies, provided he have fulfilled certain simple observances in this life, has a cheap pleasure which will not be followed by the least disappointment. A similar consideration seems to have weight with many persons in religious topics, for we frequently hear it said, "Oh, I could not believe so-and-so, because I should be wretched if I did." When an ostrich buries its head in the sand as danger approaches, it very likely takes the happiest course. It hides the danger, and then calmly says there is no danger; and, if it feels perfectly sure there is none, why should it raise its head to see? A man may go through life, systematically keeping out of view all that might cause a change in his opinions, and if he only succeeds—basing his method, as he does, on two fundamental psychological laws—I do not see what can be said against his doing so. It would be an egotistical impertinence to object that his procedure is irrational, for that only amounts to saying that his method of settling belief is not ours. He does not propose to himself to be rational, and indeed, will often talk with scorn of man's weak and illusive reason. So let him think as he pleases.

But this method of fixing belief, which may be called the method of tenacity, will be unable to hold its ground in practice. The social impulse is against it. The man who adopts it will find that other men think differently from him, and it will be apt to occur to him in some saner moment that their opinions are quite as good as his own, and this will shake his confidence in his belief. This conception, that another man's thought or sentiment may be equivalent to one's own, is a distinctly new step, and a highly important one. It arises from an impulse too strong in man to be suppressed, without danger of destroying the human species. Unless we make ourselves hermits, we shall necessarily influence each other's opinions; so that the problem becomes how to fix belief, not in the individual merely, but in the community.

METHOD OF AUTHORITY

Let the will of the state act, then, instead of that of the individual. Let an institution be created which shall have for its object to keep correct doctrines before the attention of the people, to reiterate them perpetually, and to teach them to the young; having at the same time power to prevent contrary doctrines from being taught, advocated, or expressed. Let all possible causes of a change of mind be removed from men's apprehensions. Let them be kept ignorant, lest they should learn of some reason to think otherwise than they do. Let their passions be enlisted, so that they may regard private and unusual opinions with hatred and horror. Then, let all men who reject the established belief be terrified into silence. Let the people turn out and tar-and-feather such men, or let inquisitions be made into the manner of thinking of suspected persons, and, when they are found guilty of forbidden beliefs, let them be subjected to some signal punishment. When complete agree ment could not otherwise be reached, a general massacre of all who have not thought in a certain way has proved a very effective means of settling opinion in a country. If the power to do this be wanting, let a list of opinions be drawn up, to which no man of the least independence of thought can assent, and let the faithful be required to accept all these propositions, in order to segregate them as radically as possible from the influence of the rest of the world.

This method has, from the earliest times, been one of the chief means of upholding correct theological and political doctrines, and of preserving their universal or catholic character. In Rome, especially, it has been practiced from the days of Numa Pompilius to those of Pius Nonus. This is the most perfect example in history; but .wherever there is a priesthood—and no religion has been without one—this method has been more or less made use of. Wherever there is aristocracy, or a guild, or any association of a class of men whose interests depend or are supposed to depend on certain propositions, there will be inevitably found some traces of this natural product of social feeling. Cruelties always accompany this system: and when it is consistently carried out, they become atrocities of the most horrible kind in the eyes of any rational man. Nor should this occasion surprise, for the officer of a society does not feel justified in surrendering the interests of that society for the sake of mercy, as he might his own private interests. It is natural, therefore, that sympathy and fellowship should thus produce a most ruthless power.

In judging this method of fixing belief, which may be called the method of authority, we must in the first place, allow its immeasurable mental and moral superiority to the method of tenacity. Its success is proportionally greater, and in fact it has over and over again worked the most majestic results. The mere structures of stone which it has caused to be put together—in Siam, for example, in Egypt, and in Europe— have many of them a sublimity hardly more than rivaled by the greatest works of Nature. And, except the geological epochs, there are no periods of time so vast as those which are measured by some of these organized faiths. If we scrutinize the matter closely, we shall find that there has not been one of their creeds which has remained always the same; yet the change is so slow as to be imperceptible during one person's life, so that individual belief remains sensibly fixed. For the mass of mankind, then, there is perhaps no better method than this. If it is their highest impulse to be intellectual slaves, then slaves they ought to remain.

But no institution can undertake to regulate opinions upon every subject. Only the most important ones can be attended to, and on the rest men's minds must be left to the action of natural causes. This imperfection will be no source of weakness so long as men are in such a state of culture that one opinion does not influence another—that is, so long as they cannot put two and two together. But in the most priestridden states some individuals will be found who are raised above that condition. These men possess a wider sort of social feeling; they see that men in other countries and in other ages have held to very different doctrines from those which they themselves have been brought up to believe; and they cannot help seeing that it is the mere accident of their having been taught as they have, and of their having been surrounded with the manners and associations they have, that has caused them to believe as they do and not far differently. And their candor cannot resist the reflection that there is no reason to rate their own views at a higher value than those of other nations and other centuries; and this gives rise to doubts in their minds.

They will further perceive that such doubts as these must exist in their minds with reference to every belief which seems to be determined by the caprice either of themselves or of those who originated the popular opinions. The willful adherence to a belief, and the arbitrary forcing of it upon others, must, therefore, both be given up and a new method of settling opinions must be adopted, which shall not only produce an impulse to believe, but shall also decide what proposition it is which is to be believed.

A PRIORI METHOD

Let the action of natural preferences be unimpeded, then, and under the influence let men conversing together and regarding matters in different lights, gradually develop beliefs in harmony with natural causes. This method resembles that by which conceptions of art have been brought to maturity. The most perfect example of it is to be found in the history of metaphysical philosophy. Systems of this sort have not usually rested upon observed facts, at least not in any great degree. They have been chiefly adopted because their fundamental propositions seemed "agreeable to reason." This is an apt expression; it does not mean that which agrees with experience, but that which we find ourselves inclined to believe. Plato, for example, finds it agreeable to reason that the distances of the celestial spheres from one another should be proportional to the different lengths of strings which produce harmonious chords. Many philosophers have been led to their main conclusions by considerations like this; but this is the lowest and least developed form which the method takes, for it is clear that another man might find Kepler's (earlier) theory, that the celestial spheres are proportional to the inscribed and circumscribed spheres of the different regular solids, more agreeable to *his* reason. But the shock of opinions will soon lead men to rest on preferences of a far more universal nature. Take, for example, the doctrine that man only acts selfishly—that is, from the consideration that acting in one way will afford him more pleasure than acting in another. This rests on no fact in the world, but it has had a wide acceptance as being the only reasonable theory.

This method is far more intellectual and respectable from the point of view of reason than either of the others which we have noticed. But its failure has been the most manifest. It makes of inquiry something similar to the development of taste, but taste, unfortunately, is always more or less a matter of fashion, and accordingly, metaphysicians have never come to any fixed agreement, but the pendulum has swung backward and forward between a more material and a more spiritual philosophy, from the earliest times to the latest. And so from this, which has been called the *a priori* method, we are driven, in Lord Bacon's phrase, to a true induction. We have examined into this *a priori* method as something which promised to deliver our opinions from their accidental and capricious element. But development, while it is a process which eliminates the effect of some casual circumstances, only magnifies that of others. This method, therefore, does not differ in a very essential way from that of authority. The government may not have lifted its finger to influence my convictions; I may have been left outwardly quite free to choose, we will say, between monogamy and polygamy, and appealing to my conscience only, I may have concluded that the latter practice is in itself licentious. But when I come to see that the chief obstacle to the spread of Christianity among a people of as high culture as the Hindoos has been a conviction of the immorality of our way of treating women, I cannot help seeing that, although governments do not interfere, sentiments in their development will be very greatly determined by accidental causes. Now, there are some people, among whom I must suppose that my reader is to be found, who, when they see that any belief of theirs is determined by any circumstance extraneous to the facts, will from that moment not merely admit in words that that belief is doubtful, but will experience a real doubt of it, so that it ceases to be a belief.

METHOD OF SCIENCE

To satisfy our doubts, therefore, it is necessary that a method should be found by which our beliefs may be caused by nothing human, but by some external permanency—by something upon which our thinking has no effect. Some mystics imagine that they have such a method in a private inspiration from on high. But that is only a form of the method of tenacity, in which the conception of truth as something public is not yet developed. Our external permanency would not be external, in our sense, if it was restricted in its influence to one individual. It must be something which affects, or might affect every man. And, although these affections are necessarily as various as are individual conditions, yet the method must be such that the ultimate conclusion of every man shall be the same. Such is the method of science. Its fundamental hypothesis, restated in more familiar language, is this. There are real things, whose characters are entirely independent of our opinions about them; those realities affect our senses according to regular laws, and, though our sensations are as different as our relations to the objects, yet, by taking advantage of the laws of perception, we can ascertain by reasoning how things really are, and any man, if he have sufficient experience and reason enough about it, will be led to the one true conclusion. The new conception here involved is that of reality. It may be asked how I know that there are any realities. If this hypothesis is the sole support of my method of inquiry, my method of inquiry must not be used to support my hypothesis. The reply is this: (1) If investigation cannot be re- garded as proving that there are real things, it at least does not lead to a contrary conclusion; but the method and the conception on which it is based remain ever in harmony. No doubts of the method, therefore, necessarily arise from its practice, as in the case with all the others. (2) The feeling which gives rise to any method of fixing belief is a dis- satisfaction at two repugnant propositions. But here already is a vague concession that there is some *one* thing to which a proposition should conform. Nobody, therefore, can really doubt that there are realities, or if he did, doubt would not be a source of dissatisfaction. The hypothesis, therefore, is one which every mind admits. So that the social impulse does not cause me to doubt it. (3) Everybody uses the scientific method about a great many things, and only ceases to use it when he does not know how to apply it. (4) Experience of the method has not led me to doubt it, but, on the contrary, scientific investigation has had the most wonderful triumphs in the way of settling opinion. These afford the explanation of my not doubting the method or the hypothesis which it supposes; and not having any doubt, nor believing that anybody else whom I could influence has, it would be the merest babble for me to say more about it. If there be anybody with a living doubt upon the sub- ject, let him consider it.

To describe the method of scientific investigation is the object of this series of papers. At present I have only room to notice some points of contrast between it and the other methods of fixing belief.

This is the only one of the four methods which presents any distinction of a right and a wrong way. If I adopt the method of tenacity and shut myself out from all influences, whatever I think necessary to doing this is necessary according to that method. So with the method of authority: the state may try to put down heresy by means which, from a scientific point of view, seems very ill-calculated to accomplish its purposes; but the only test *on that method* is what the state thinks, so that it cannot pursue the method wrongly. So with the *a priori* method. The very essence of it is to think as one is inclined to think . . . But with the scientific method the case is different. I may start with known and observed facts to proceed to the unknown, and yet the rules which I follow in doing so may not be such as investigation would approve. The test of whether I am truly following the method is not an immediate appeal to my feelings and purposes, but, on the contrary, itself involves the application of the method. Hence it is that bad reasoning as well as good reasoning is possible, and this fact is the foundation of the practical side of logic.

CONCLUSION

It is not to be supposed that the first three methods of settling opinion present no advantage whatever over the scientific method. On the contrary, each has some peculiar convenience of its own. The *a priori* method is distinguished for its comfortable conclusions. It is the nature of the process to adopt whatever belief we are inclined to, and there are certain flatteries to one's vanities which we all believe by nature, until we are awakened from our pleasing dream by rough facts. The method of authority will always govern the mass of mankind; and those who wield the various forms of organized force in the state will never be convinced that dangerous reasoning ought not to be suppressed in some way. If liberty of speech is to be untrammeled from the grosser forms of constraint, then uniformity of opinion will be secured by a moral terrorism to which the respectability of society will give its thorough approval. Following the method of authority is the path of peace. Certain non-conformities are permitted, certain others (considered unsafe) are forbidden. These are different in different countries and in different ages; but, wherever you are, let it be known that you seriously hold a tabooed belief, and you may be perfectly sure of being treated with a cruelty no less brutal but more refined than hunting you like a wolf. Thus, the greatest intellectual benefactors of mankind have never dared, and dare not now, to utter the whole of their thought, and thus a shade of *prima facie* doubt is cast upon every proposition which is considered essential to the security of society. Singularly enough, the persecution does not all come from without; but a man torments himself and is oftentimes most distressed at finding himself believing propositions which he has been brought up to regard with aversion. The peaceful and sympathetic man will, therefore, find it hard to resist the temptation to submit his opinions to authority. But most of all I admire the method of tenacity for its strength, simplicity, and directness. Men who pursue it are distinguished for their decision of character, which becomes very easy with such a mental rule. They do not waste time in trying to make up their minds to what they want, but, fastening like lightning upon whatever alternative comes first, they hold to it to the end, whatever happens, without an instant's irresolution. This is one of the splendid qualities which generally accompany brilliant, unlasting success. It is impossible not to envy the man who can dismiss reason, although we know how it must turn out at last.

Such are the advantages which the other methods of settling opinions have over scientific investigation. A man should consider well of them; and then he should consider that, after all, he wishes his opinions to coincide with the fact, and that there is no reason why the results of these three methods should do so. To bring about this effect is the prerogative of the method of science. Upon such considerations he has to make his choice—a choice which is far more than the adoption of any intellectual opinion, which is one of the ruling decisions of his life, to which when once made he is bound to adhere. The force of habit will sometimes cause a man to hold on to old beliefs, after he is in a condition to see that they have no sound basis. But reflection upon the state of the case will overcome these habits, and he ought to allow reflection full weight. People sometimes shrink from doing this, having an idea that beliefs are wholesome which they cannot help feeling rest on nothing. But let such persons suppose an analogous though different case from their own. Let them ask themselves what they would say to a reformed Mussulman who should hesitate to give up his old notions in regard to the relations of the sexes, or to a reformed Catholic who should still shrink from the Bible. Would they not say that these persons ought to consider the matter fully, and clearly understand the new doctrine, and then ought to embrace it in its entirety? But, above all, let it be considered that what is more wholesome than any particular belief, is integrity of belief, and that to avoid looking into the support of any belief from a fear that it may turn out rotten is quite as immoral as it is disadvantageous. The person who confesses that there is such a thing as truth, which is distinguished from falsehood simply by this, that if acted on it will carry us to the point we aim at and not astray, and then though convinced of this, dares not know the truth and seeks to avoid it, is in a sorry state of mind, indeed.

Yes, the other methods do have their merits: a clear logical conscience does cost something—just as any virtue, just as all that we cherish, costs us dear. But, we should not desire it to be otherwise. The genius of a man's logical method should be loved and reverenced as his bride, whom he has chosen from all the world. He need not condemn the others; on the contrary, he may honor them deeply, and in doing so he only honors her the more. But she is the one that he has chosen, and he knows that he was right in making that choice. And having made it, he will work and fight for her, and will not complain that there are blows to take, hoping that there may be as many and as hard to give, and will strive to be the worthy knight and champion of her from the blaze of whose splendors he draws his inspiration and his courage.

STUDY QUESTIONS

1. State the principal differences between doubt and belief as Peirce sees them. Would you agree?
2. What conceptions of proof does Peirce describe as vague and erroneous?
3. How does Peirce define inquiry? What is the end of inquiry?
4. Describe and give an example of the method of tenacity. Why does Peirce say that the social impulse is against it?
5. Comment on the method of authority. To what extent is it superior to the method of tenacity? Can you conceive of any instance in which the method of authority might be justified? Explain.
6. Comment on the *a priori* method, noting some reasons for its adoption. Why does Peirce say that this method does not differ essentially from the method of authority?
7. What does Peirce mean by the external permanency of belief? State his conception of the fundamental hypothesis of the method of science. What reasons does he give for not doubting such a method?
8. What are the principal differences between the scientific method and the other three? Do these other methods have any advantages or conveniences that the method of science does not have? Enumerate in some detail.

James B. Conant

⌘⌘

SCIENTIFIC METHOD AND THE
ADVANCE OF SCIENCE

⌘⌘

Biographical Note. JAMES BRYANT CONANT (1893–) received his education at Harvard. He then served there for sixteen years as teacher of chemistry, winning recognition as a brilliant organic chemist, and he continued as Harvard's president for another twenty years. He represented the United States in West-Germany from 1953 to 1957, first as High Commissioner and then as Ambassador to the newly founded Federal Republic. Returning from Europe, he took up an earlier interest in public education and has made a name for himself as a leader of the movement promoting a reappraisal of American public education. He has been the recipient of forty nine honorary degrees from colleges and universities all over the world.

Apart from his publications in the field of chemistry, he wrote in the areas of general science, philosophy of science, and education. *On Understanding Science* (1947), *Modern Science and Modern Man* (1952), from which a selection follows, and *The American High School Today* (1959) exemplify the range of his contributions.

* * *

Introductory Note. Conant raises the question of the reasons for the enormous progress of science since the beginning of the 17th century. In

From James B. Conant, *Modern Science and Modern Man,* New York and London, Columbia University Press, 1952, pp. 18–30. Used by permission of the Columbia University Press.

particular, he tries to prove unjustified a widely held belief that there is a so-called scientific method that can be credited with past achievements and that will guarantee still greater ones in the future.

In fact, he says, "what the scientist does in his laboratory," using a scientific method, is much more modest than it has been popularly attributed to be. It "is simply to carry over, into another frame of reference, habits that go back to the caveman." Even in the most "systematized and well-ordered empirical inquiries," the scientist may still engage in mere "trial and error experimentations," which can effect advances in "the practical arts" but not in the theoretical sciences themselves. Their progress, although never independent of the use of a scientific method, requires the inclusion of an entirely different element: the evolution of "new ideas of broad significance." It is the interplay between such theoretical elements newly introduced and the "experimentation of the artisan" that can alone account for the spectacular development of the sciences.

Thus Conant rejects most definitely the notion that efficient training of vast numbers of scientists will by itself bring about progress in science. It can do this no more than, let us say, the training of large numbers of artists can produce a flowering of the arts. For its real achievements, for its real advances, science depends on the genius in whose mind new concepts, new conceptual schemes are formed "that serve as working hypotheses on a grand scale." Mere observation or systematization of facts progresses to the "principles which explain them and which give the mind an intelligent mastery over them."

THE SCIENTIFIC METHOD IN THE POPULAR VIEW

I should like to examine a little more closely the procedures employed by the scientists today in physics, in chemistry, in biology, and in the application of science for practical ends in the whole area of the natural sciences. If in so doing, I appear to be underlining the obvious, I hope I shall be forgiven; for although a discussion of the so-called scientific method is almost a standard topic in a university, what I have to say is so antithetical to much of the current doctrine that I venture to present it in some detail here.

It would be my thesis that those historians of science, and I might add philosophers as well, who emphasize that there is no such thing as *the* scientific method are doing a public service. To my mind, some of the oversimplified accounts of science and its workings to be found in the elementary texts in high schools, for example, are based on a fallacious reading of the history of physics, chemistry, and biology. I will not attempt to trace back the sources of what seems to some of us a set of erroneous conclusions. Let me rather present my own analysis of the nature of science, if I may.

In order to produce a straw man that I may knock down, let me quote a definition of the scientific method written some years ago in an elementary text of chemistry of which I am a joint author: "The scientific way of thinking requires the habit of facing reality quite unprejudiced by any earlier conceptions. Accurate observation and dependence upon experiments are the guiding principles. The watchword is not 'what does the book say about this or that, but let's try to find out for ourselves.'" Then follows an account of the steps in the process of finding out. Such accounts in many textbooks, including the one I helped to write, usually run as follows: "Scientists collect their facts by carefully observing what is happening. They group them and try to interpret them in the light of other facts that are already known. Then a scientist sets up a theory or picture that will explain the newly discovered facts, and finally he tests out his theory by getting more data of a similar kind and comparing them with the facts he got through the earlier experiments. When his theory does not quite fit the facts, he must modify it and at the same time verify the facts by getting more data."

Another and more sophisticated account by a biologist is entitled "Steps in the Scientific Method." Note the use of the word "the" rather than the plural "scientific methods." Here the steps are listed: "Recognize that an indeterminate situation exists. This is a conflicting or obscure situation demanding inquiry. Two, state the problem in specific terms. Three, formulate a working hypothesis. Four, devise a controlled method of investigation by observation . . . or by experimentation or both. Five, gather and record the testimony or 'raw data.' Six, transform these raw data into a statement having meaning and significance. Seven, arrive at an assertion which appears to be warranted. If the assertion is correct, predictions may be made from it. Eight, unify the warranted assertion, if it proves to be new knowledge in science, with the body of knowledge already established."

TWO STREAMS OF ACTIVITY
AND THE DEGREE OF EMPIRICISM

The simplified account from my own elementary textbook and the more sophisticated version of the biologist, I have become convinced, serve only to confuse a layman. The basic fault is a failure to distinguish between two closely related activities which together have made fabric, the story of the development of various electronic devices, including the new solid material as a substitute for a vacuum tube—all these would illustrate the same point.

THE ADVANCE OF SCIENCE

In emphasizing the distinction between developments in which new theories have played an important part and those based on essentially empirical procedures, I have perhaps done less than justice to one change which has been going on during the whole period of the growth of modern science. We have learned that there are ways in which empirical procedures can be improved without the introduction of theory. We have, as it were, empirically improved empiricism. The inventor in the last century working in his attic might more or less erratically try first this procedure and then that in order to get a better way of carrying out a step in his process, for there was no one to criticise him; if his methods were far from being effective, that was no one's business but his own. But when invention was replaced by the work of scientists in laboratories, then self-criticism was replaced by group criticism. People learned that if a specific problem is to be solved as rapidly as possible, accurate observations of each experiment should be kept; furthermore, even in trial-and-error procedures there is a difference between well-ordered and disordered empiricism. Take the simple homely example of finding out what is wrong with the electric light; we can all imagine procedures which systematically test one limited working hypothesis and then another or helter-skelter methods of operating where the same trial is repeated several times to no purpose.

What is often defined as the scientific method is nothing more or less than an approximate description of a well-ordered, systematized empirical inquiry. Now, systematized or well-ordered empirical inquiries are one element in the advance of science; the other element is the use of new concepts, new conceptual schemes that serve as working hypotheses on a grand scale. Only by the introduction of a theoretical element can the degree of empiricism be reduced. Only by the use of new ideas of broad significance has science advanced—such ideas as those embodied in Newton's laws, as the notion that the earth is surrounded by a sea of air which exerts pressure, that light is a vibratory motion in an all-pervading ether, that matter is composed of atoms that unite in definite proportions to form compounds. The essential element in the advance of modern science has been the curious interplay between such theoretical notions and the experimentation of the artisan; through such an interplay scientists have built up a fabric of interconnected concepts and conceptual schemes.

Without unduly laboring the obvious, let me repeat: by well-ordered empirical procedures it has been possible to make great progress in the practical arts. Such procedures are still being used in almost all branches of applied science. In metallurgy and organic chemistry, for example, the degree of empiricism is still high, but the development of new concepts and wide conceptual schemes was essential to the progress of physics, chemistry, and biology in the last three hundred and fifty years. As these sciences became equipped with more and more satisfactory theories, the degree of empiricism in the arts related to these sciences diminished. As a consequence, in these practical endeavors it became more and more possible to attain the accuracy of prediction of such undertakings as those of the surveyor. The practical significance of the advance in theoretical science lies right here. The history of the last hundred and fifty years in particular shows what occurs when advances are made in pure science. New principles evolve which can be related to empirical observations; at that point it becomes possible to control with far greater accuracy than before what one is doing in the practical arts and to predict the outcome of a large-scale operation directed towards making a commercial product.

No better illustration of this can be found than in applied biology, the very field that John Tyndall was discussing. I referred to Tyndall's words which were concerned with the practical art of brewing. Explaining why the brewer could not proceed as long as his art was founded entirely upon empirical observations, he said, "But he had to contend and still has to contend against unexplained perplexities. Over and over again his care has been rendered nugatory; his beer has fallen into acidity or rottenness and disastrous losses have been sustained of which he has been unable to assign the cause. It is the hidden enemies against which the physician and the brewer have hitherto contended that recent researches are dragging into the light of day, thus preparing the way for their final extermination." These researches had been instituted by Louis Pasteur in his study of fermentation. He had shown that living microorganisms were the "hidden enemies" with which the brewer had contended without knowing it. This knowledge was the consequence of a bold working hypothesis on a grand scale by Pasteur, namely, that fermentation and putrefaction were the consequences of the growth of microorganisms. Armed with this theory, Pasteur reduced the degree of empiricism in the whole range of fermentation industries. We accept the working hypothesis of Pasteur today as an established principle; we base all our procedures for handling food on the assumption of its correctness. Furthermore, this theory or principle is basic to medicine and public health. One need elaborate no further on this example of what theory can do to practice.

Let me give a reverse case where the failure to have any satisfactory theory has led to surprising consequences. I refer to the question of the action of chemicals on living organisms. In spite of an enormous amount of experimentation by chemists in making new substances and pharmacologists in testing them on animals and on men, one can say that it is almost impossible to predict the action of a chemical substance of a given structure on a human being or on a microorganism. An adequate theory would enable one to write down the molecular architecture of a substance and from this structure predict the effect of the compound on a living organism. Such predictions are possible today only within very narrow limits and with very special classes of substances. And even here the correlation is essentially empirical—we have no broad, overall theory of drug action. Only within the last half a dozen years has some glimmering of hope appeared that chemotherapy can become a science.

To recapitulate, the inventor was largely an empiricist; he continued the tradition of the ingenious artisan. His place today has largely been taken by teams of scientists and engineers. To a considerable degree they likewise operate empirically; but their procedures are well ordered and systematized; they are disciplined by experience. In almost every field into which theory has been introduced, the degree of empiricism has been lessened. The teams of scientists in industry and in medicine are engaged both in reducing further the degree of empiricism and in applying the theories of science as they now stand. All this has become an organized social undertaking. As a sociological phenomenon modern science deserves careful study. Agriculture, medicine, public health, and the production of raw materials and their processing in industry are all interpenetrated heavily by well trained empiricists using modern instruments to assist their trial and error experimentations. For the most part their success in advancing science, that is to say, developing new theories and testing these theories by experiment, are publicly recorded. Scientific societies and scientific journals make this intercommunication possible. Destroy the social nature of scientific research in the sense of destroying the intercommunication of scientists, and the advance of science would almost cease. . . .

The history of science demonstrates beyond a doubt that the really revolutionary and significant advances come not from empiricism but from new theories.

STUDY QUESTIONS

1. How does the popular view conceive of scientific method?
2. Why is it wrong to speak of "the" scentific method?
3. Under what conditions do experimental procedures result in no more than "cookbook information"?
4. In what way is the "degree of empiricism" in a branch of science indicative of its stage of development?
5. What distinguishes the inventor of the last century from scientists working in laboratories today?
6. What are the two elements in the advance of science?
7. How would you illustrate the interplay of these elements?
8. What part does the social nature of scientific research play in the progress of science?

Karl Popper

SCIENTIFIC THEORY
AND FALSIFIABILITY

Biographical Note.　　KARL R. POPPER (1902–) was born in Austria, the son of a barrister. He was educated at the University of Vienna and received his doctor's degree from that institution. For several years he was Lecturer in Philosophy at Canterbury University College of the University of New Zealand, and he held the post of Reader in Logic at the University of London from 1945 to 1948. He was appointed William James Lecturer at Harvard in 1950, and within the next several years he served as visiting lecturer at Yale, Princeton, the University of Chicago, and Emory University. In 1956 he was appointed a Fellow at the Center for Advanced Study in Behavioral Sciences at Stanford University. He has also served as visiting professor at the University of California (Berkeley) and the Minnesota Center for the Philosophy Science. His most important publications are *Logic of Discovery* (1935), *The Open Society and Its Enemies* (1945), and *Poverty of Historicism* (1957). At present he is Professor of Logic and Scientific Method at the London School of Economics and Politics.

* * *

Introductory Note.　　In the field of philosophy of science, Karl Popper is one of the most outstanding methodologists. His classic work in this field

From Karl Popper, *Conjectures and Refutations*, New York, Basic Books, 1963, pp. 33-39. Reprinted by permission of the publisher.

is the *Logik der Forschung* (1935), recently translated into English. This work has been overshadowed somewhat by his *The Open Society and Its Enemies,* a somewhat less technical work and one that aroused considerable comment because of its attack on Plato. As a methodologist, Popper has been particularly concerned with the social sciences, and this interest is reflected in his *The Poverty of Historicism.* His major contributions to methodology have consisted in: (1) His attack on the pseudo-sciences and the formulation of principles for distinguishing genuinely empirical sciences from false ones. his most important principle here is that of refutability or falsifiability, which Carnap held was merely a different version of the verifiability principle. (2) His rejection of the traditional account of scientific method as inductive generalization from observations to the formulation of hypotheses. For Popper, the important aspect of method is not generalization but criticism—the testing of our generalizations. Induction, he holds, is not really a problem, because the function of scientific method is the criticism of hypotheses and not an explanation of how they are formed. Scientific theories are not simply instruments, nor do they endeavor to offer ultimate explanations of the essences of things. Basically, their function is informative, and their distinguishing characteristic is the possibility of their refutation or falsifiability.

The "Personal Report" selection is concerned predominantly with the principle of falsifiability and how it can be used to resolve what Popper calls the "demarcation problem," the distinction between true and false science. The traditional inductive method is inadequate to explain the distinction and he notes that certain pseudo-sciences, e. g. astrology, may rely heavily on observations of an empirical nature and the generalizations drawn from such observations. The problem is then illustrated by his analysis of three specific scientific theories that became prominent after the first world war: Marx's theory of history, Freud's psychoanaylsis, and Adler's individual psychology. Popper develops the shortcomings of each of these theories and contrasts them with the more truly scientific theory of Einstein on gravitation. The analysis of these pseudo-sciences leads him to an account of the meaning of confirmation of scientific theory. The difficulties of confirming or verifying such theories are then summarized, and the conclusion is drawn that only falsifiability, not verification or confirmation, is the criterion of the scientific status of a theory. He concludes that falsifiability as a criterion cannot be adequately met by the theories of Marx, Freud, and Adler, and that therefore their theories may contain truths but that they are not genuinely scientific.

SCIENTIFIC THEORY AND FALSIFIABILITY

I

When I received the list of participants in this course and realized that I had been asked to speak to philosophical colleagues, I came to the conclusion, after some hesitation and consultation, that you would prob-ably prefer me to speak about those problems which interest me most, and about those developments with which I am most intimately ac-quainted. I therefore decided to do what I have never done before: to give you a report about my own work in the field of the philosophy of science, since the autumn of 1919 when I first began to grapple with the problem, *'When should a theory be ranked as scientific?'* or, *'Is there a criterion of the scientific character or status of a theory?'*

The problem which troubled me at the time was neither, When is a theory true? nor, When is a theory acceptable? My problem was dif-ferent. *I wished to distinguish between science and pseudo-science;* knowing very well that science often errs, and that pseudo-science may happen to stumble upon the truth.

I knew, of course, what was the most widely accepted answer to my problem: that science is distinguished from pseudo-science—or from 'metaphysics'—by its *empirical method;* that it is essentially inductive, proceeding from observation and experiment. But this did not satisfy me. On the contrary, I often formulated my problem as one of dis-tinguishing between a genuinely empirical method and a non-empirical or even a pseudo-empirical one; i. e. a method which does in fact appeal to observation and experiment but does not come up to scientific stand-ards. Astrology, with its stupendous mass of empirical evidence based on observed horoscopes and biographies, is a case in point.

But this was not the example which led me to my problem; and it may perhaps interest you if I briefly describe the atmosphere in which my problem arose. Following the collapse of the Austrian Empire, there had been a revolution in Austria; the air was full of revolutionary slogans, ideas, and new and often wild theories. Among the theories which interested me, Einstein's theory of relativity was no doubt by far the most important. Three others were Marx's theory of history, Freud's psycho-analysis, and Alfred Adler's so-called 'individual psy-chology'.

There was a lot of popular nonsense talked about these theories, and especially about relativity (as still happens even today) but I was for-tunate in those who introduced me to the study of this theory. We all —the little circle of students to which I belonged—were thrilled with the result of the eclipse observation which in 1919 brought the first important confirmation of Einstein's theory of gravitation. It was a great experience for us—one which had a lasting influence on my intellectual development.

The three other theories I have mentioned were also widely discussed among students at that time. I myself happened to come into personal contact with Alfred Adler, and even to co-operate with him in his social work among the children and young people in the working-class districts of Vienna where he had established social guidance clinics.

It was during the summer of 1919 that I began to feel more and more dissatisfied with these three theories—the Marxist theory of history, psycho-analysis, and individual psychology—and dubious about their claims to scientific status. One might say that my problem first took the form, 'What is wrong with Marxism, psycho-analysis, and individual psychology? Why are they so different from mathematical physics and especially from the theory of relativity?'

In order to appreciate this contrast, I might mention that few of us at the time would have said that they believed in the *truth* of Einstein's theory of gravitation. This shows that it was not any doubt of the *truth* of these other three theories which bothered me: it was a different thing. Yet neither was it that I merely felt mathematical physics to be more exact than the sociological or psychological type of theory. Thus what worried me was neither the problem of truth, at that stage at least, nor the problem of exactness or of measurability. It was rather that I felt that these other three theories posed as sciences while in fact they were of the character of primitive myths rather than of science; that they resembled astrology rather than astronomy.

I found that those of my friends who were admirers of Marx, Freud, and Adler, were strongly impressed by a number of points shared by these theories, and especially by their apparent *explanatory power*. These theories appeared to be able to explain practically everything that happened, within the fields to which they referred. Their study had the effect of an intellectual conversion or revelation—of opening your eyes to the truth hidden from those not yet initiated. Once your eyes were thus opened, you saw confirming instances everywhere: the world was full of *verifications* of the theory. Whatever happened always confirmed it. Thus its truth appeared obvious; and unbelievers were, clearly, people who did not want to see the truth—either because it was against their class interest, or because of their repressions which were still 'unanalysed', and crying aloud for treatment.

The most characteristic element in the situation seemed to me the incessant stream of confirmations, of observations which 'verified' the theories in question; and this was the point constantly emphasized by their adherents. A Marxist could not open a newspaper without finding on every page confirming evidence for his interpretation of history—not only in the news, but also in the way it was presented (revealing the class bias of the paper), and especially, of course, in what the paper did *not* say. The Freudian analysts emphasized that their theories were daily, nay, hourly, verified by their 'clinical observations'. And as to Adler, I was much impressed by a personal experience. Once, in 1919, I reported to him a case which to me did not seem particularly Adlerian, but which he found no difficulty whatever in analysing in terms of his theory of inferiority feelings, although he had not even seen the child. Slightly shocked, I asked him how he could be so sure about all this. 'Because of my thousandfold experience', he replied; where upon I could not help saying: 'And with this new case, I suppose, your experience is now even thousand-and-one fold.'

What I had in mind was that his previous observations may not have been much sounder than this new one; that each had been interpreted in the light of 'previous experience', and, at the same time, counted as additional confirmation. What, I asked myself, did it confirm? No more than the possibility of interpreting a case in the light of the theory. But this meant very little, I reflected, since every conceivable case could be interpreted in the light of Adler's theory, or equally of Freud's. To illustrate this, take two very different cases of human behavior—one, let us say, of a man who pushes a child into the water with the intention of drowning it; and another, of a man who sacrifices his life in an attempt to save the child. Each of these two cases can be explained with equal ease in Freudian as well as in Adlerian terms. According to Freud, the first man suffered from repression (say, of some component of his Oedipus complex), while the second had achieved sublimation. According to Adler, the first man suffered from feelings of inferiority (producing, perhaps, the need to prove to himself that he dared to commit a crime, etc.), and so did the second man (whose need was to prove to himself that he dared to rescue the child). I could not think of any conceivable instance of human behavior which could not be interpreted in terms of either theory. It was precisely this fact—that they always fitted, that they were always confirmed—which, in the eyes of their admirers, constituted the strongest arguments in favor of these theories. It began to dawn on me that this apparent strength was in fact their greatest weakness.

With Einstein's theory, the situation was strikingly different. Take one typical instance—Einstein's prediction, just then confirmed by the findings of Eddington's expedition. Einstein's gravitational theory had led to the result that light was attracted by heavy bodies (such as the sun) very much as material bodies were attracted. It could be calculated that, as a consequence, light from a distant fixed star whose apparent position was close to the sun would reach the earth from such a direction that the star would seem to be slightly shifted away from the sun; or in other words, that stars close to the sun would look as if they had moved a little away from the sun, and from one another. This is a thing which cannot normally be observed since normally such stars are invisible, owing to the sun's overwhelming brightness; but during an eclipse, it is possible to take photographs showing such stars. If the same constellation is photographed without the sun, one can measure the distances on the two photographs, and check the predicted effect.

Now the impressive thing about this case is the *risk* involved in a prediction of this kind. If observation shows that the predicted effect is definitely absent, then the theory is simply refuted. The theory is *incompatible with certain possible results of observation*—in fact, with results which, before Einstein, everybody would have expected. This is a vastly different situation from the one I have previously described when it turned out that the theories in question were compatible with the most divergent human behavior so that is was practically impossible to describe human behavior which could not be interpreted as being in agreement with these theories.

These considerations led me, in the winter of 1919-20, to conclusions which I may now reformulate as follows.

(1) It is easy to obtain confirmations, or verifications, for nearly every theory—if we look for confirmations.

(2) Confirmations should count only if they are the result of *risky predictions*; that is to say, if, unenlightened by the theory in question, we should have expected an event which was incompatible with the theory—an event which, had it happened, would have refuted the theory.

(3) Every 'good' scientific theory is one which forbids certain things to happen; the more a theory forbids, the better it is.

(4) A theory which is not refutable by any conceivable event is non-scientific. Irrefutability is not a virtue of a theory (as people often think) but a vice.

(5) Every genuine test of a theory is an attempt to falsify it, or to refute it. Testability is falsifiability; but there are degrees of testability: some theories are more testable, more exposed to refutation, than others; they take, as it were, greater risks.

(6) Confirming evidence does not count except *when it is the result of a genuine test of the theory*; and this means that it can be presented as an unsuccessful but serious attempt to falsify the theory.

(7) Some genuinely testable theories, when found to be false, are still upheld by their admirers—for example, by introducing *ad hoc* some

auxiliary assumption, or by re-intepreting the theory *ad hoc* in such a way that it escapes refutation. Such a procedure is always possible, but it rescues the theory from refutation only at the price of destroying or at least lowering its scientific status. (I later described such a rescuing operation as a *'conventionalist twist'*, or as a *'conventionalist stratagem'*).

One can sum up all this by saying that *falsifiability or refutability, is a criterion of the scientific status of a theory.*

II

I may perhaps exemplify this with the help of the various theories so far mentioned. Einstein's theory of gravitation clearly satisfies the criterion of falsifiability. Even if our measuring instruments at the time did not allow us to pronounce the result of the test with complete as-surance, there was clearly a possibility of refuting the theory.

Astrology did not pass the test. Clearly, astrologers were impressed, and misled, by what they believed to be confirming evidence—so much so that they were quite unimpressed by an unfavorable evidence. More-over, by making their interpretations and prophecies sufficiently vague, they were able to explain away anything that might have been a refuta-tion of the theory, had the theory and the prophecies been more pre-cise. In order to escape falsification, they destroyed the testability of their theory. It is a typical soothsayer's trick to predict things so vaguely that the predictions can hardly fail; that they become irrefutable.

The Marxist theory of history, in spite of the serious efforts of some of its founders and followers, ultimately adopted this soothsaying prac-tice. In some of its earlier formulations (for example in Marx's analysis of the character of the 'coming social revolution'), their predictions were testable, but in fact falsified. Yet instead of recognizing this, the followers of Marx re-interpreted both the theory and the evidence to make them agree. In this way they rescued the theory from refutation; but they did so at the price of adopting a device which made it irre-futable. They thus gave a 'conventionalist twist' to the theory; and by this stratagem, they destroyed its much advertised claim to scientific status.

The two psycho-analytic theories were in a different class. They were simply non-testable, irrefutable. There was no conceivable human be-havior which could contradict them. This does not mean that Freud and Adler were not seeing certain things correctly; I personally do not doubt that much of what they say is of considerable importance, and may well play its part one day in a psychological science which is test-able. But it does mean that the 'clinical observations' which analysts naively believe to confirm their theory[1] cannot do this any more than the daily confirmations which astrologers find in their practice. And as for Freud's epic of the Egos, the Super Egos, and the Ids, no substantially stronger claim to scientific status can be made for it than for Homer's collected stories from the Olympus. These theories describe some facts, but in the manner of myths. They contain most interesting psychological suggestions, but not in a testable form.

At the same time, I realized that such myths may be developed, and become testable; that, historically speaking, all (or nearly all) scientific theories originate from myths, and that a myth may contain important anticipations of scientific theories. Examples are Empedocles' theory of evolution by trial and error, or Parmenides' myth of the unchanging block universe in which nothing ever happens and which, if we add another dimension, becomes Einstein's block universe (in which too, nothing ever happens, since everything is, four-dimensionally speaking, determined and laid down from the beginning). I thus felt that, if a theory is found to be non-scientific, or 'metaphysical' (as we might say), it is not thereby found to be unimportant, or insignificant, or 'meaningless', or 'nonsensical.'[2] But it cannot claim to be backed by empirical evidence in the scientific sense—although it may easily be, in some genetic sense, the 'result of observation'.

(There were a great many other theories of this pre-scientific or pseudo-scientific character, some of them, unfortunately, as influential as the Marxist interpretation of history; for example, the racialist interpretation of history—another of those impressive and all-explanatory theories which act like revelations upon weak minds.)

---

[1] 'Clinical observations', like all other observations, are *interpretations in the light of theories* . . . ; and for this reason alone, they are apt to seem to support those theories in the light of which they were interpreted. But real support can be obtained only by observations undertaken as tests (by 'attempted refutations'); and for this purpose, *criteria of refutation* have to be laid down beforehand: it must be agreed which observable situations, if actually observed, mean that the theory is refuted. But what kind of clinical responses would refute, to the satisfaction of the analyst, not merely a particular analytic diagnosis but psycho-analysis itself? And have such criteria ever been discussed, or agreed upon by analysts? Is there not, on the contrary, a whole family of analytic concepts, such as 'ambivalence' (I do not suggest that there is no such thing as ambivalence), which would make it difficult, if not impossible, to agree upon such criteria? Moreover, how much headway has been made in investigating the question of the extent to which the (conscious or unconscious) expectations and theories held by the analyst influence the 'clinical responses' of the patient? (I say nothing about the conscious attempts to influence the patient by proposing interpretations to him, etc.) Years ago, I introduced the term '*Oedipus effect*' to describe the influence of a theory, or expectation, or prediction, *upon the event which it predicts* or describes: it will be remembered that the causal chain leading to Oedipus' parricide was started by the oracle's prediction of this event. This is a characteristic and recurrent theme of such myths, but one which seems to have failed to attract the interest of the analysts; perhaps not quite accidentally.

[2] The case of astrology, nowadays a typical pseudo-science, may illustrate this point. It

Thus the problem which I tried to solve by proposing the criterion of falsifiability was neither a problem of meaningfulness or significance, nor a problem of truth or acceptability. It was the problem of drawing a line (as well as this can be done) between the statements, or systems of statements, of the empirical sciences, and all other statements—whether they are of a religious or of a metaphysical character, or simply pseudo-scientific. Years later—it must have been in 1928 or 1929—I called this first problem of mine the *'problem of demarcation'*. The criterion of falsifiability is a solution of this problem of demarcation, for it says that, in order to be ranked as scientific, statements or systems of statements must be capable of conflicting with possible, or conceivable, observations.

STUDY QUESTIONS

1. What distinction does Popper note between science and pseudo-science? To what did this distinction lead him?
2. With respect to Popper's analysis of the Marxist theory of history, psychoanalysis, and individual psychology, show in detail what his doubts were regarding the scientific status of these theories. Would you agree that these theories resemble more astrology than astronomy?
3. What contrast does he draw between the theories mentioned in the preceding question and Einstein's theory of gravitation. Why does he maintain the superiority of the Einstein theory over the others.
4. According to Popper, what are the criteria of a good scientific theory? What restrictions does he place upon the confirmation or verification of a scientific theory?
5. Comment at some length upon his summary conclusion that "falsifiability or refutability, is a criterion of the scientific status of a theory." How does Einstein's theory satisfy this criterion?
6. Show in what respects the Marxist theory and astrology fail to meet the test of falsifiability.
7. Why does Popper say that the two psychoanalytic theories were irrefutable? What fault does he find with the "clinical observations" of the analysts? Does he find anything of value in the work of the psychoanalysts?
8. What does Popper mean by the "problem of demarcation" and why does he say that the principle of falsifiability is a solution of this problem?

was attacked by Aristotelians and other rationalists, down to Newton's day, for the wrong reason—for its now accepted assertion that the planets had an 'influence' upon terrestrial ('sublunar') events. In fact, Newton's theory of gravity, and especially the lunar theory of the tides, was an offspring of astrological lore, and it thus comes from the same stable as, for example, the theory that 'influenza' epidemics are due to an astral 'influence'.

John Hospers

⌯⌯

ON SCIENTIFIC EXPLANATION

⌯⌯

Biographical Note. JOHN HOSPERS (1918–) was born at Pella, Iowa. He received his B. A. degree at Central College and his M. A. at the State University of Iowa. In 1946 he received his doctor's degree from Columbia University. For a few years he served as an instructor in philosophy at Columbia, and in 1948 he received an appointment to the University of Minnesota. He served there as an assistant professor and associate professor of philosophy until 1956, when he accepted an appointment as professor of philosophy at Brooklyn College—a position he still holds. He was appointed a Fulbright research scholar at the University of London in 1954-1955, and visiting professor of philosophy at the University of California (Los Angeles) in 1960-1961. In addition to numerous journal articles, primarily in aesthetics, he has published the following major works: *Meaning and Truth in the Arts* (1946); with W. Sellars, *Readings in Ethical Theory* (1952); *Introduction to Philosophical Analysis* (1953); and *Human Conduct* (1961).

* * *

Introductory Note. It might be said that before the impact of philosophical analysis and logical positivism upon the philosophy of science, the primary concern of the philosophy of science was with the broader aspects of the problem of scientific method, with attempts to state the nature of the

From John Hospers, "What is Explanation?" *The Journal of Philosophy*, June, 1946. Reprinted by permission of the publishers.

scientific method, and to show how it led to the phenomenal growth of scientific knowledge. Now, however, the philosophy of science has turned more to analysis of some of the basic concepts of science and their *meanings* for both science and philosophy.

It is to the fundamental question of scientific explanation that Professor Hospers addresses himself. Noting the need for clarity in the concept of explanation, he first shows that one of the simplest "explanations" of an event is in terms of its purpose. This kind of explanation, he maintains, is primitive and no longer an essential part of the meaning of explanation. Another suggestion offered is that explanation may be analyzed in terms of the reduction to that which is more familiar in our experience. Despite the fact that this view has support from such philosophers of science as Norman Campbell and Percy Bridgman, the author thinks such an interpretation, although possessing some merit, is basically mistaken. It is the contention of Professor Hospers that to explain an event is to bring it under a law, that explanation must be in terms of laws, with the term "law" being used in the broad sense of any uniformity of nature. He then proceeds to elaborate upon the role of deduction in explanation, raising such issues as whether an event can have more than one explanation, and in particular the problem of whether a deductive requirement is a necessary condition for explanation. He claims that such a condition is not sufficient, and that a true explanation must have not only predictive value but a capability of disproof by empirical observations. In this way, certain nonnaturalistic hypotheses can be avoided. He claims that all of this is implicit in the requirement that an explanation must be in terms of law or laws. Turning next to purposive explanation, he shows that an analysis of the nature of purpose limits such an explanation entirely to human laws validly established. Explanation in terms of divine purposes cannot be used, for they have not been established as laws. He then comments briefly upon the extent of explanation and concludes his essay with some interesting distinctions between *description, explanation,* and *explaining away*.

THE NATURE OF EXPLANATION

We are sometimes presented with a statement describing some observed fact, and when we ask 'Why?' we are presented with another statement which is said to constitute an explanation of the first. What is the relation between these two statements? What is it that makes the second statement an 'explanation' of the first? By virtue of what does it explain. Though everyone is constantly uttering statements which are supposed in one way or another to explain, few persons are at all clear about what it is that makes such statements explanations. Nor is the situation clarified when it is declared on the one hand that science explains everything and on the other hand that science never explains at all but only describes. . . .

What, then, is it to explain why an event occurs? (1) It has sometimes been said that we have explained it if we have stated its *purpose*. 'Why did you walk through the snow for ten miles when you could have taken the bus?' 'Because I wanted to win a wager.' 'Why does that dog scratch at the door?' 'He's cold and he wants to get in.' When such answers are given we are inclined to feel that our question has been answered and that the event has been satisfactorily explained; and it has been explained with reference to a purpose which some sentient being(s) had in attaining a certain end. This is the most primitive conception of explanation. People like to feel that there is a purposive explanation for everything: if not in terms of human or animal purposes, then of divine ones, or mysterious forces and powers. We tend to extend what holds true of some events to all events whatever; we know what conscious motivation is like from our own experience, and so we 'feel at home' with this kind of explanation.

We shall examine the scope and legitimacy of purposive explanation later in this paper. It is enough to remark here that if explanation must always be in terms of purpose, then the physical sciences do not explain anything. The properties of uranium, the rise of aeroplanes, the phenomena of magnetism are not explained in terms of any purposes at all; biologists even avoid talking about animal events such as the hen sitting on eggs in terms of purpose. However animistically the nature of explanation may at one time have been conceived, purposiveness is certainly no essential part of its meaning now. The stone is no longer held to fall because it wants to get to the centre of the earth.

(2) Another account of the nature of explanation is that an event has been explained when it has been shown to be an instance of some class of events which is already familiar to us. For example, when a person's behavior seems strange to us, we are satisfied when it is 'explained' to us as being really impelled by the same sort of motives and desires as occur in us, and are therefore familiar to us. . . . When we observe that a balloon ascends rather than descends, unlike most objects, and it is made clear to us that air has weight and that the gas inside the balloon weighs less than would an equal volume of air, we are satisfied; the phenomenon has been 'reduced' to something already familiar to us in every day experience, such as a dense object sinking in water while a hollow one floats. The event is no longer unusual, strange, or unique; it has been shown to illustrate a principle with which we

were already acquainted. When we want to know why gases diffuse when released into a chamber from which the air has been pumped out, the explanation offered by the kinetic theory of gases is satisfactory to us because it asserts that molecules behave *like* particles with which we are already acquainted in our everyday experience.

. . . "by tracing a relation between the unfamiliar changes which gases undergo when their temperature or volume is altered, and the extremely familiar changes which accompany the motions and mutual reactions of solid bodies, we are rendering the former more intelligible; we are explaining them." (Norman Campbell, *What is Science?*, Dover, N. Y., p. 84.)

Professor Bridgman holds that all explanation is of this kind. . . . And yet I am sure that such a view as this must be mistaken. In the *first* place, we may seek explanations for the most familiar events as well as those unfamiliar to us. We may ask why stones fall as well as why aeroplanes rise, and be curious for an answer equally in both cases. . . . In the *second* place, the explanation may not be familiar at all: it may be far less familiar than the event to be explained. The discoloration of a painted kitchen wall when gas heat is used may be a familiar phenomenon to the housewife—surely more familiar than its explanation in terms of the chemical combination of sulphur in the gas fumes with elements in the paint, producing a compound that is dark in color. Yet this is the true explanation. If the explanation is not familiar, one is tempted to say, it ought to be, as long as it is true. Surely its familiarity is irrelevant to its validity as an explanation. Familiarity is, in any case, a subjective matter—what is familiar to you may not be familiar to me; and yet the explanation, if true, is as true for me as for you.

The only grain of truth in the view that explaining is rendering familiar seems to be this: the law that does the explaining may not be familiar, *but* the fact that the phenomenon in question, such as the flight of an aeroplane, *can* be subsumed under a law—the fact that the behavior *is* lawlike and hence predictable—tends to make it less mysterious, less like a miracle, and thus in a sense more familiar. To show that the behavior of something is lawlike is to show it to be a part of the order of nature, and in that sense familiar, although the particular law or laws stating the uniformity may be quite unfamiliar.

In what, then, *does* the explanation consist? The answer, I think, is quite simple: (3) to explain an event is simply to bring it under a law; and to explain a law is to bring it under another law. It does not matter whether the law is one about purposes or not, or whether it is familiar or not; what matters is that if the explanation is to be *true* (and we surely seek true explanations, not false ones), the law invoked must be true: indeed, this is already implied in the use of the word 'law', which refers to a true, i. e. a really existing, uniformity of nature; if the uniformity turned out to be only imaginary, or having exceptions, we would no longer call it a law.

In saying that explanation is in terms of laws, I use the word 'law' in a wider sense than is sometimes employed: in the sense I mean, any uniformity of nature is a law. Thus it is a law that iron rusts, and it is a law that iron is magnetic—although both of these are usually listed in textbooks as 'properties of iron' rather than as laws. In this sense, it seems to me that explaining why something occurs always involves a law. If we ask 'Why don't the two liquids in the flask mix?' and someone answers, 'Don't you see, the one is transparent and the other is red? this does not strike us as an explanation (i.e. as a true explanation) of the phenomenon, because we know of no law according to which red liquids will not mix with transparent ones. But when we are told that the red liquid is colored water and that the transparent liquid is gasoline, we consider the phenomenon to be explained, for we hold it to be a law of nature that water and gasoline do not mix. In the sense in which I am using the word 'law', the non-mixture of water and gasoline is a law; and *only* if a law is brought in do we have an explanation of the phenomenon.

One further qualification: We have said that we explain particular events in terms of laws, and laws in terms of wider laws. But sometimes we give at least tentative explanations of them in terms not of law but of general *hypotheses:* if a law is a well-established statement of how nature works, a statement about nature's workings that is not well established, or perhaps not even probable but only possible, cannot be a law. And yet we use it to explain a law. But to whatever degree the hypothesis is uncertain, to that degree the explanation is jeopardized. An explanation cannot be known to be true if it involves a hypothesis which (by the definition of 'hypothesis') is not known to be true. Whether the explanation is a true explanation, then, depends on the fate of the hypothesis. . . .

EXPLANATION AND DEDUCTION

Thus far we have been content to answer the question 'Why does A do B?' by saying 'Because all A's do B'. But there are those who say that such an answer is no explanation at all. 'To say that all gases expand when heated', says Norman Campbell (*What Is Science*, p. 80), 'is not to explain why hydrogen expands when heated; it merely leads us to ask immediately why all gases expand. An explanation which leads immediately to another question of the same kind is no explanation at all.'

I want to insist that the answer given is an explanation of the occurrence in question; to say 'Hydrogen is a gas, and all gases expand when heated' is a perfectly satisfactory answer to the question why hydrogen expands when heated. But it is *not*, of course, an answer to *another* question—Why do all gases expand when heated?—and this is probably the question which the person meant to ask in the first place. These questions must not be confused with each other; I believe Campbell's position is the result of this confusion. It is fatally easy to telescope (unconsciously) two questions into one, and then be dissatisfied with the answer. Distinguishing them, we get:

> Question 1. Why does this gas expand when heated?
> Explanation. It is hydrogen, and hydrogen expands when heated.
> Question 2. Why does hydrogen expand when heated?
> Explanation. Hydrogen is a gas, and all gases expand when heated.
> Question 3. Why do all gases expand when heated?

Here we attempt to give an explanation in terms of the kinetic theory of gases. To criticize Answer 1 because it is not an answer to Question 2, or Answer 2 because it is not an answer to Question 3, is surely a confusion. I want to say that Answer 1 is a perfectly satisfactory explanation for the phenomenon referred to in Question 1, though of course not for those referred to in Questions 2 and 3. But there is a frequent tendency to telescope these questions and demand to Question 1 the answer to Question 3. . . .

Can an event have two explanations? Why not? Let us suppose that we want to explain an event E and that we have a law saying that every time conditions A are fulfilled, E happens, and another law saying that every time conditions B are fulfilled, E happens. A will then be a complete explanation for the occurrence of E, and B will also be a complete explanation. Whether any such state of affairs actually occurs in the world is, of course, another question. Most of the suggested double explanations of events are in fact parts of a single explanation. Thus, for example, if we are asked to explain why the burglar committed the robbery last night, the detective may explain it in terms of his expertness at picking locks, the butler may explain it in terms of the family being out of the room, the maid may say it was because the bedroom window was open, the policeman may say it was because the night was foggy and visibility at a minimum, the sociologist may explain it in terms of the criminal's background of slum conditions, and the psychologist may explain it in terms of pseudo-aggressive impulses dating from a child-hood period marked by intense family quarrels. All these explanations are probably correct enough as far as they go. It may well be that in the absence of any one of these factors the burglary would not have oc-curred. But these are, it would surely seem, parts and aspects of *one* complete explanation—and in explaining human actions the whole ex-planation may be inconceivably complex. Still, the possibility remains that in some cases there may be two separate and complete explanations for an occurrence; at least it cannot be ruled out *a priori*.

Must there be a *deductive* relation between the thing to be explained and the explanation, such that one can deduce the statement of the phenomenon to be explained from the explanation?

> All copper conducts electricity
> This wire is made of copper
> ∴. This wire conducts electricity

Here the explanation yields the desired conclusion easily, and it is quite clear that what we have here is a genuine explanation. The question is, must all explanation conform to this model? Have we failed to give an explanation if we have failed to deduce the explanandum from the explanation?

Let us first note that in many cases, if this is required, the explanation would be bewilderingly complex, and the premises in the deduction ex-tremely numerous. Consider the burglary example just cited. From the fact that the weather was foggy and that the man had tendencies to steal and that he had a poor background . . . etc., we cannot deduce the fact that he committed the theft. We cannot deduce it, indeed, from any set of premises known to be true. What we need for deducing it is a law, to the effect that if such-and-such conditions are fulfilled an act of this kind will always occur, and then a minor premise to the effect that these conditions were in fact fulfilled. The conditions would indeed have to be extremely numerous, and the statement of the law immensely complicated. Yet such a law is required if the desired con-clusion is to be deduced. . . .

Thus far in enquiring about the need for a deductive relationship, we have considered only the explanation of particular events: we have deduced them from two premises, one stating a law and the other stating a particular condition: 'All copper conducts electricity; this is copper, therefore this conducts electricity.' 'All water freezes at 32°F., the water in the pond went below 32° last night; therefore the water in the pond froze.' And so on. But, as we saw earlier, we not only explain particular events; we also explain *laws*. And the same question could be repeated here: is the deductive requirement necessary? There is no doubt that in the 'neat, tidy' cases it is fulfilled: for example, Kepler's laws of planetary motion can be deduced from Newton's laws of motion together with the law of gravitation; and thus the latter clearly explain the former. But is this strictly a requirement for *all* explanation of laws? Again, some would say that it is—that anything short of this is not a full explanation. Others would say that it is not—that the deductive case is only the ideal one but that explanation does not require it. For example, a law can be explained in terms of a very general theory, from which the law cannot be strictly deduced, but which will nevertheless entitle the theory to be called an explanation. (The deductivist will reply that it is not *known* to be an explanation until the acid test, i. e. the deduction is performed.)

In any case, whether deducibility is a necessary condition of explanation or not, it is not a sufficient condition. One can deduce that this watch will not work from the premises that watches will not work if gremlins get into them and that gremlins are in fact in this watch. Yet no one would accept this as an explanation for the misbehavior of the watch. Similarly, one might deduce it from the premises that whatever God wills happens and that God has willed the misbehavior of this watch. One can deduce anything if one selects one's premises carefully.

One might remark at this point that it is also necessary that the premises be *true*, and that this is the required addition. I would unhesitatingly agree that the premises must indeed be true—false statements cannot form parts of true explanations (indeed, if explanation is in terms of law, and a law is a true statement of a uniformity, i. e., one that actually occurs, then this proviso has already been implicit in our account of explanation). But suppose we make this proviso explicit —is it enough? I do not believe so. It might be true that God wills everything that happens, but as long as we have no means of knowing this, we cannot use it as a premise in our explanation. That is, we cannot use it as an explanation unless the proposition is not only true, but is *known to be so*.

Suppose, then, that we accept this last revision—will it do the trick?

I hardly think so; it still misses the main point. Let us imagine a deeply religious scientist who holds that everything that happens is the result of divine will; he may yet reject the theological explanation as an account of *why* things happen as they do. The reason is surely fairly obvious: what the scientist wishes to discover is why this happened *rather than that,* and the theological explanation will not enable him to make this discrimination: whatever happens, one can deduce it from the premises that God willed it to happen and that whatever He wills happens.

What condition, then, remains to be supplied? The condition seems to be a rather simple one, yet one which it is difficult to state precisely. What we have in mind is this: we want to eliminate the indiscriminate 'explanatory' power of the gremlin-hypothesis and the God-hypothesis, even though they slip through the deductive net, because they do not enable us to explain why this happens *rather than that.* 'What explains everything explains nothing.'

This *can* be put by saying that the explanation must have *predictive* value, but this is a bit misleading. For one thing, it places undue emphasis upon the future, whereas explanation of past is just as important as explanation of future; we would have, then, to use a tenseless sense of 'predict'. For another thing, there are many explanations which seem to be true but whose predictive power is minimal or at any rate difficult to see: many biological phenomena can be explained in terms of laws of mutations, for example, but it is not clear what these laws enable us to *predict*—certainly not where or when a mutation will occur or what kind it will be when it does arise.

Perhaps what we want to say can be best expressed by the simple proviso that the explanation must explain *other* phenomena than those it is invoked to explain, and yet, unlike the God-hypothesis, not just everything indiscriminately: in other words, it should explain other events (whether past, present or future makes no difference), but it should all the same be capable of disproof by empirical observations; whether or not any actual empirical observations ever disprove it, it must be capable of testing. Without this condition it would not be considered an explanation in any science.

In fact all this is implicit in our requirement that an explanation be in terms of law or laws. A law is a universal proposition about all events or processes in a certain class, and if it holds for A, a member of the class (a present event), it also holds for members B, C, and D (future events); thus by the very nature of a law, laws explain more than a single event. The testability of explanations is also implicit in the concept of law, for a law is an empirical statement of a uniformity of nature, and, being contingent, it is always subject to disconfirmation by obervation. Still, it is well to make the implicit explicit to show why the deductive requirement is not enough and what is required of an explanation.

EXPLANATION AND PURPOSE

No mention has thus far been made of explanation in terms of *purpose*. And yet this is the oldest concept of explanation and still the one most frequently employed by primitive peoples. And there are contexts in which we still employ the concept of purpose in giving explanations—for example, when we say that my purpose in going to the store was to do some Christmas shopping, and that this is *why* I went.

The word 'purpose' is of course, ambiguous. (*a*) Most frequently in ordinary usage a purpose is something of which I am conscious—a conscious intent to do something. The conscious intent is not the whole of the purpose: part of the criterion of whether it is my purpose to do X is whether I am disposed towards doing X, whether I take steps towards X and do X if I have the chance. (*b*) Some tendencies to act are not accompanied by any state of awareness; and here psychologists speak of unconscious purposes. . . . (*c*) We speak of inanimate objects as having purposes—for example, the purpose of a hammer is to drive nails. This of course is not a purpose consciously envisaged by the hammer. All we mean here is that the mechanical object *reflects* the conscious purposes of its makers. We had a conscious purpose in making the hammer, and thus we speak elliptically of the hammer as having that purpose. Strictly speaking, of course, the purpose is ours and not the hammer's.

In all of these cases a purpose implies a purposer, or someone to have the purpose. We do sometimes use the word 'purpose' in another sense which carries no such implication, (*d*) when we say, 'What is the purpose of the heart?' 'To pump blood through the body.' Here purpose simply means function—*i. e.* what does it *do*? what part does it play in the bodily economy? If the word 'purpose' is used here I would view it as a 'degenerate' usage—a misleading locution in which another word, 'function', would serve much better. . . .

Having disentangled these senses of 'purposes', let us ask about the legitimacy of purposive explanations. Briefly I think it comes to this:

explanations require laws, and if there are laws *about* purposes, there is no reason why they cannot figure in some explanations just as laws about falling bodies figure in other explanations. To the extent that laws about purposes have been established, they can be used as explanations like any other laws. Unfortunately the only laws (if any) that we are in a position to make about purposes are about human ones.

Explanations in terms of divine purposes cannot be employed because no laws about divine purposes have ever been established. Even explanations of biological events in terms of animal purposes is frowned upon; we do not count it an explanation if it is said that the hen sits on her eggs *in order* to hatch chicks, because we have no indication that the hen does so with this purpose in mind; even if this is true, we do not know it, and therefore we cannot use it as a law in our explanation. . . .

The chief mistake which people are in the habit of making with regard to purposive explanation is probably that of wanting an answer to a why-question in terms of purpose when the conditions under which a purpose-answer is legitimate are not fulfilled. People extend their questioning unthinkingly from areas in which purposive explanation is in order into areas in which it is not. Thus: 'Why did he go to New York?' 'Well, in response to impulses from certain centres in his brain, some muscles in his arms and legs started moving towards the airport . . .' 'No, that's not what I mean. I mean, why did he go? what did he go for? what purpose did he have in view?' 'He went in order to see some operas.' Contrast this with the following: 'Why did he die?' 'well, a bullet entered his lung, puncturing some blood vessels, and the blood filled his lung so that he couldn't breathe any more, and . . .' 'No, that's not what I mean. I mean, *why* did he die?' But here we can no longer give an answer in terms of purpose—unless that is, our talk is rooted in a theological context and we are willing to say that, just as the first person went to New York because he wanted to see operas, so the second person died because God had some purpose (intent) in seeing to it that he was murdered. If this is what is meant, one could try to answer the question in the theistic context of divine purposes; but if this context is rejected, the why-question demanding an answer in terms of purpose is meaningless, because an answer is being demanded when the only conditions under which the question is meaningful are not fulfilled.

EXTENT OF EXPLANATION

This leads us directly into an important question. How far can ex planation go? We may explain an event in terms of a law, and this law in terms of other laws, and so on, but must we not finally come to a stop? . . . Are there ultimate laws, laws which explain but even in principle cannot be explained.

In practice we come rather quickly to laws which cannot be explained further. Laws about atomic structure are typical of such laws. Laws of psycho-physical correlation are another example. *Why* do I have a certain color sensation which I call red, indescribable but qualitatively different from all others, when light within a certain range of wavelength impinges upon my retina, and another indescribably different sensation which I call yellow when rays of another wave-length strike the retina? That this wave-length is correlated with this visual experience seems to be sheer brute fact—a law which cannot be explained in terms of anything more ultimate than itself.

At the same time, we should be careful in dismissing any uniformity we cannot explain as a 'brute fact' or 'basic law'. Many things, such as why this element has this melting point and these spectral lines, were once considered basic and unexplainable properties of the element, but have since been explained in terms of the intra-molecular structure of the element. No matter how much at a loss we may be for an explanation, we can always ask and speculate. If it had been accepted as a basic law that water starts to expand when it gets below 39°F., we would never have gone on to discover anything about the structure of the water-molecule. Fruitful scientific procedure depends on assuming that no given law is basic; if scientists did not continue always to ask the question 'Why?' the process of scientific inquiry would stop dead in its tracks.

Thus, if there are basic laws, it seems that we cannot know of any given law that it is one. We can know that it is *not,* by explaining it in terms of other laws; but how could we know that it *is?* Discovering basic laws is epistemologically similar to discovering uncaused events: if there are uncaused events, we can never know that there are, for all we can safely say is that we have not yet found causes for them.

DESCRIPTION, EXPLANATION, AND EXPLAINING AWAY

One sometimes encounters the complaint that science does not really explain but only describes. 'Science doesn't tell us *why* things happen,' it is said, 'it only tells us *how* things happen.' Now it does often happen that the exact intention of the user of a why-question is not very clear —as we have already seen. But in the way in which the term 'why' is most commonly used, science does explain why; for example, the bursting of pipes, the formation of ice at the top of ponds rather than at the bottom, and many other phenomena, are explained by reference to the law that water expands when it freezes. . . .

'But is not explanation after all merely description?' It is all very well to say that when we explain something we actually describe—e. g. stating laws of nature is describing how nature works. But this does not preclude the fact that we *are* explaining. When the question is asked why pressing the button turns on the light, we explain by describing just what goes on—currents, open and closed circuits, conduction of electricity by wires, dynamos in the power plant, and so on. But have we not in so doing explained the phenomenon about which we were asking? We have explained by describing, if you will; but certainly we have explained. To say that because we are describing we cannot be explaining would be like saying that because an object is red it cannot also be colored.

A similar complaint is sometimes voiced against scientific explanation that it 'explains things *away*'. Explaining something is interpreted as equivalent to explaining it away. Now the precise meaning of the phrase 'explaining away' is one which I have never been able to discover. What is one supposed to be doing when he explains something away? Surely not to declare that it does not exist! Explanation deprives us of no facts we had before. To 'explain color' in terms of light-waves is not, of course (as should have been obvious), to take away the fact of color-experiences. 'Thinking is nothing but the occurrence of certain neural impulses' should be changed into 'When thinking takes place (and that it does is just as incontrovertible a fact as the neurons are), there are neural impulses.'

In the special context of beliefs, perhaps 'explaining away' may mean impugning the truth of one's conclusions. If so, there are again no grounds for fear. To 'explain away' someone's politically reactionary tendencies by saying, 'He's old, and people always get conservative when they get old', does not for a moment take away whatever truth the person's opinions may have; at most, it only exposes part of the causal genesis of his having them. And if the views of this person were 'explained away' by these biographical observations, the views of his opponent would be equally vulnerable: 'You needn't pay any attention to that young upstart, they're all hot communists when they're young.' Reference to biography may, together with laws of human nature (if any are known in this area), explain why a person held a certain belief at a certain time, but the truth or falsity of the belief is quite unaffected by this and, of course, is tested on different grounds entirely. The idea that reference to a person's mental or physical condition could explain away the truth of a belief is one of the most flagrant blunders of the materialistically minded laity of our day.

STUDY QUESTIONS

1. Would you be satisfied with an explanation of all events in terms of *purpose?* Why or why not? Why does Hospers regard this as the most primitive conception of explanation?
2. State and illustrate the meaning of explanation as the reduction of the unfamiliar to the familiar.
3. What objections does Hospers have to the views of Campbell and Bridgman that explanation is the reduction of the unfamiliar to the familiar? Does he find any virtue at all in this method of explanation?
4. Comment on Hospers' view that explanation is in terms of laws. What does he mean by law?
5. What exception does Hospers take to Campbell's account of explanation in terms of deduction? Comment on the distinction he brings out in the two examples on the behavior of hydrogen.
6. What conclusions does Hospers arrive at on the possibility of an event having two explanations?
7. "Must there be a deductive relation between the thing to be explained and the explanation?" Indicate the author's conclusions on this question.
8. Explain the author's statement that "whether deducibility is a necessary condition of explanation or not, it is not a sufficient condition." Why is it necessary that the premises in a deductive explanation be true?
9. What importance does · predictive value have for explanation? What limitations does Hospers note here? Comment on the significance of testability for scientific explanation. How is testability implicit in the concept of law?

INDEX